Structured
Methods

Other McGraw-Hill Books of Interest

To order or receive additional information on these or any other McGraw-Hill titles, please call 1-800-822-8158 in the United States. In other countries, contact your local McGraw-Hill representative.

MH93

Structured Methods

Merging Models, Techniques, and CASE

Andrew Topper

Daniel Ouellette

Paul Jorgensen

McGraw-Hill, Inc.

New York   San Francisco   Washington, D.C.   Auckland   Bogotá
Caracas   Lisbon   London   Madrid   Mexico City   Milan
Montreal   New Delhi   San Juan   Singapore
Sydney   Tokyo   Toronto

Library of Congress Cataloging-in-Publication Data

Topper, Andrew G.
    Structured methods : models, techniques, and CASE / Andrew G.
Topper, Daniel J. Ouellette, Paul C. Jorgensen.—
        p.   cm.
    Includes bibliographical references and index.
    ISBN 0-07-064884-0
    1. Electronic data processing—Structered techniques. 2.
Software engineering. I. Ouellette, Daniel J. II. Jorgensen, Paul C.
III. Title.
    QA76.9.S84T66   1993
    005.1'13—dc20   93-11220
                                                            CIP

1 2 3 4 5 6 7 8 9 0   DOC/DOC   9 8 7 6 5 4 3

ISBN 0-07-064884-0

The sponsoring editor for this book was Jeanne Glasser.

Printed and bound by R. R. Donnelley and Sons Company.

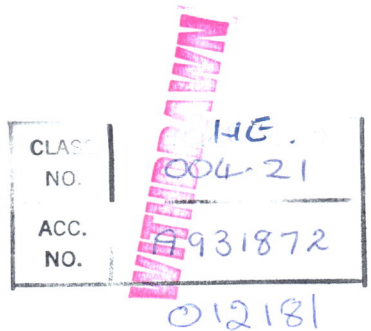

Contents

Part 3 Advanced Development Techniques

Preface

The process of writing a book is not unlike the process of building software. In our case, we worked as a team, each member with different expectations and experiences, and in some cases, very different points of view. As with a software development effort, we had to rely on one another to deliver representations of the book so that they could be formally reviewed prior to delivery of the finished manuscript. As with other development projects, we found our book needed late synthesis and awkward manpower loading to be completed.

The result is this book, which took many hours of creative thought, discipline, and hard work. When we began writing the book, we had a few overall goals:

1. Deliver a book that covers a wide range of software engineering topics, with enough depth of information to be useful to anyone considering using software development techniques and tools.

2. Introduce and show examples of the major software development techniques, hopefully allowing organizations to make comparisons among the various methods, notations, and tools.

3. Clarify the role development techniques and tools have in the overall software development environment and the impact they can have on improving software quality.

4. Describe our opinions on various issues related to software development, drawing on our collective experience and the successes and failures we have been involved with in prior circumstances.

5. Provide a serious and objective discussion of the basic characteristics of software and development methods.

Only you, the reader, will know if we indeed achieved our goals. Future versions of this book will include additional insight, based on our future experiences, and any comments and criticisms from members of the software engineering community. Like a software product, this book represents an evolutionary thing that will need to be modified as circumstances dictate.

Two administrative notes as you read this book. With some of our diagrams, you may notice diagram symbols that have three circles in line underneath, with the middle circle filled in or solid (O●O). We used System Architect from Popkin Software and Systems as our CASE tool of choice, principally because it was available under Windows and supported the widest variety of diagram types, and the three circles represent peculiar characteristics of that product. In this case, the middle circle filled in indicates that there is a lower-level diagram that is linked to the symbol in question.

For the prototype of the Library system described in Chapter 9, we used DataFlex from Data Access Corp., a PC-based fourth-generation language, and the screens and reports were all created on the PC under DOS.

This book draws on the experience of many talented software engineering professionals who provided ideas and practical observations on the process of developing software. All of these professionals deserve credit for their contributions, not only to this work, but in helping to shape the collective experience of software development as an engineering discipline. We specifically want to thank Joan Colwell, Jerry Huchzermeier, and Kim Addington for their assistance in researching the material for this book.

We certainly could not have written this book without the help and support of our families, whom we love very much, and to them we owe a debt of gratitude. To Carol, Katia, and Kirsten Jorgensen, Susan, Claire, and Emily Ouellette, and Amy, Samantha, and Steven Topper, we say "Thank You."

Structured
Methods

PART 1

Software Engineering Concepts

Chapter 1
The Software Engineering Triad

The number 3 occurs widely and with much significance: physicists study the three body problem of collisions, Christianity has a triune God, yogis examine three views of Self, and mystics have an endless preoccupation with the number. You are reading the third reorganization of this book, and it was written by three practitioners. As we tried to coalesce and present our ideas, the first two outlines just didn't work out. We finally realized we were dealing with a three-part whole, and our organizing problems came from trying to decide which part should come first. We call this three-part whole the *software engineering triad*; its elements are software process, techniques, and CASE technology.

We will examine each of these briefly in this chapter to set the stage for the remainder of the book. Even within this chapter, the ordering is problematic — CASE first? Last? Our best view is that the elements of the software engineering triad drive and supplement one another. Maybe you should read this chapter three times, starting with a different element each time. If you did this, you would move quickly to our view of the flow, harmony, and inseparable nature of software process, techniques, and CASE technology.

This chapter ends with a discussion of where the software engineering triad fits into the larger picture of an overall framework for software production. The final section lays the groundwork for all subsequent chapters, and offers alternative ways of incorporating development techniques and tools into an organization.

1.1 Software Process

Notice, we didn't title this section "the software process" — there's no such thing. Freshman philosophy students inevitably endure a discussion of "chair" when they first study epistemology. Philosophy instructors will assert that The Chair can never exist, yet we all can recognize chairs, and we can do a fair job at defining "chairness." (Convicts on Death Row know exactly what The Chair is — an interesting point where philosophy meets reality.)

"Software process" refers to the way software is developed. There are as many software processes as there are software developers and organizations that develop software. Software process can refer to an individual or a group activity. In fact, much of the complexity of software process comes from the communication and organizational problems endemic to group activities. The process/product dichotomy helps: The end product of the software process is software. We like the following distinction: A program is written in some source language, software is a program plus several representations at higher levels. A quality process yields a quality product. This is no mystery to most industries — think about automobiles, Detroit, and Japan.

The product/process pairing has some limitations. Does a good process always yield a good product? Can an inferior process ever result in a good product? Is a process repeatable? Is it reasonable to judge a process by its products? Eventually we'd like answers to questions such as these. For now, we ask them to bring you closer to our mindset. Sharing a viewpoint fosters communication — remember, all the Death Row convicts know exactly what The Chair is.

1.1.1 Working Definition

To help focus this discussion, we offer a characterization of software process:

A group activity, conducted with limited resources, that yields an intangible product (software).

Before going on, let's parse this characterization. Because software process is a group activity, communication is an essential element. Participants in a process must hold a shared view of the process, in which individual roles are understood and expectations are clear. Because it is conducted with limited resources (time, effort, talent, support tools), software process must always have a management component. One thing becomes immediately clear: Insufficient resources, especially time, often impair software process. To fully understand our characterization, we need to know more about the "intangible product" part.

A NASA project manager, so the story goes, was asked by a technician responsible for calculating payload weight how much his software weighed. When he replied that it didn't weigh anything, he was rebuffed: "If it's on my list, I need to know its weight." Rather than try to explain the reality of software to the technician, the project manager bought some time by asking what units of measure he should use. While waiting for an official response (about two weeks), the project manager found an old card punch machine and had an object deck punched. When the technician returned, he pointed to the object deck and proudly said, "The software is in the box." The technician was upset by the delay — "Why didn't you give me this in the first place?" "You don't understand," explained the project manager. "The software is the holes, and they are in exactly the right places."

The intangible nature of software raises the last major issue in our working definition — how software is represented. As a software process is conducted, the participants (should) create a series of representations: a requirements definition, a specification of constraints, possibly several designs that assign functionality to hardware or software components, a source language description, object code, and maybe a user's manual. Each of these representations can also be considered a deliverable resulting from a software process and can generally be measured.

These representations raise ancillary issues: Which representations? How are they written down? Are they written, or are they in some repository? How are they managed so that they are all consistent? What if they overlap? Worse, what if something is missing? Do we represent what a system *is*, or what it *does*? Or both? Ultimately, faults in software are the result of flaws in (at least) one of the representations.

Because representations are at least more tangible, it is easy to equate a software process with the series of representations produced during the process. Doing so is an oversimplification that leads to an obsession with The Software Development Life Cycle (another misnomer, like The Chair).

Having raised the issues concerning software process, we present our working definition of software process:

A social activity, highly creative in nature, that is conducted in an environment of limited resources and produces a series of representations (or deliverables) of an intangible product, software.

1.1.2 Software Process Models

Models of software development life cycles (SDLCs) have been used to describe the (sic) software process. Any model is a compromise with reality that is used to convey information about the greater reality. In the next chapter, we'll discuss the traditional model of software development, the waterfall model, and several alternative paradigms that arose in response to deficiencies in the waterfall model.

"Any form of life cycle is a project management structure imposed on system development. To contend that any life cycle scheme, even with variations, can be applied to all system development is either to fly in the face of reality or to assume a life cycle so rudimentary as to be vacuous."
D. McCracken [MCC81].

Despite McCracken and Jackson, if we understand process models, we have better insights into a software process itself. The various life cycle models are all based on the series of representations produced as a software process is conducted. In the waterfall model, for example, we speak of a series of phases; one good set of names for these phases is shown in Figure 1.1.

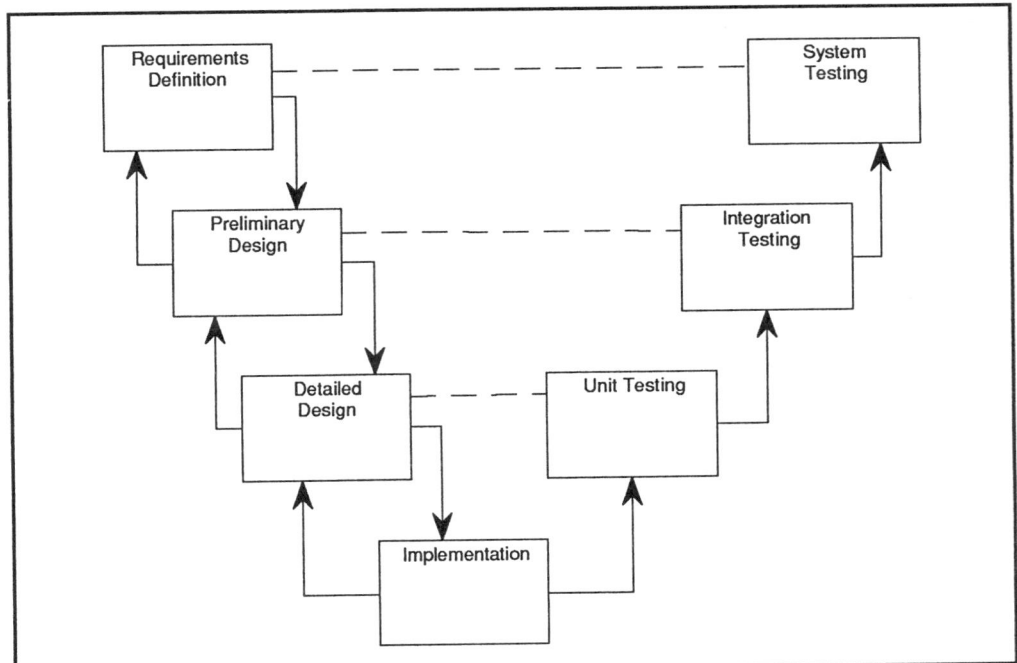

Figure 1.1
The Waterfall software development life cycle model.

Notice that the development phases are echoed by corresponding levels of testing and abstraction. Each development phase produces a representation, and the levels in Figure 1.1 correspond to levels of abstraction of these representations. When the representations are complete, good practice (good process!) dictates a review that leads to some form of management or technical approval. The little cycles shown between successive phases are "what/how" feedback cycles: The end product or deliverable of one phase defines what must be done in the next phase, and the work product of the next phase describes how the predicated functionality will be accomplished.

A model such as this is comfortable: A reasonable flow of activities is defined, feedback and control points are established, and progress can be measured. One of the major criticisms of the waterfall model is that it is essentially artificial and when rigorously applied, stifles creativity. Studies show that, when experts develop software, they flit across levels of abstraction in seemingly haphazard ways. This is the essence of McCracken's and Jackson's objection: Rigid adherence to any such model can easily degenerate to counterproductive management. For more on the Waterfall and other life cycles, see Chapter 2.

Another view or model of software process is that various pieces of information are being created by different developers, often in parallel. If we posit some database model of this information, we can view software development as the gradual population of a gigantic database. Some of the characteristics of this view are listed in Figure 1.2.

Software Development	Database Theory
1. Information content is structured (document contents, coding standards,etc.)	1. Data content is structured
2. Phased information creation	2. Phased DBMS population
3. Information dependencies	3. Data dependencies (e.g., weak relations)
4. Many sources of information	4. Many sources of data
5. Change control is needed to keep consistency among representations	5. Database integrity
6. Elimination (reduction) of redundant information	6. Elimination (reduction) of redundant data
7. Project management	7. Database management
8. Information used by many project participants	8. Data used by many possible queries
9. Erroneous information is problematic	9. Garbage In Garbage Out (GIGO)

Figure 1.2
Analogies between software development and a database management system.

The creation of information during a systems development project has a protracted analogy with the definition, population, and management of a large database. In both of these, information is derived from many sources, its integrity must be maintained to support consistent, unforeseen uses, and the information acquisition process must be carefully managed. It is useful, then, to view the system development process as the gradual population of a large database. With this view, the database becomes the infrastructure of the project. Entities in the database are developed in response to steps postulated by the system development process. Very often, dependencies exist among these entities, hence the population of the database is correctly viewed as concurrent, with the existence of one piece of information stimulating the creation of "contiguous" pieces.

The key element in the database view of systems development is that development documents may be viewed as being generated by (macro) queries of the database. This view is particularly useful in terms of consistent (and nonredundant) information, which is normally the domain of software quality assurance and configuration management. The database view can also serve as the basis for project management metrics; for example, milestone completeness is the extent to which various relations are populated. Quality may be considered as the extent to which database integrity is maintained.

Entities in the database are produced by designers at various stages of the development process. Attributes of the entities are defined by the software process. Relationships among the entities indicate the ways in which the entities are (or should be) used by various project participants. Figure 1.3 shows a fragment of a database infrastructure of a software process.

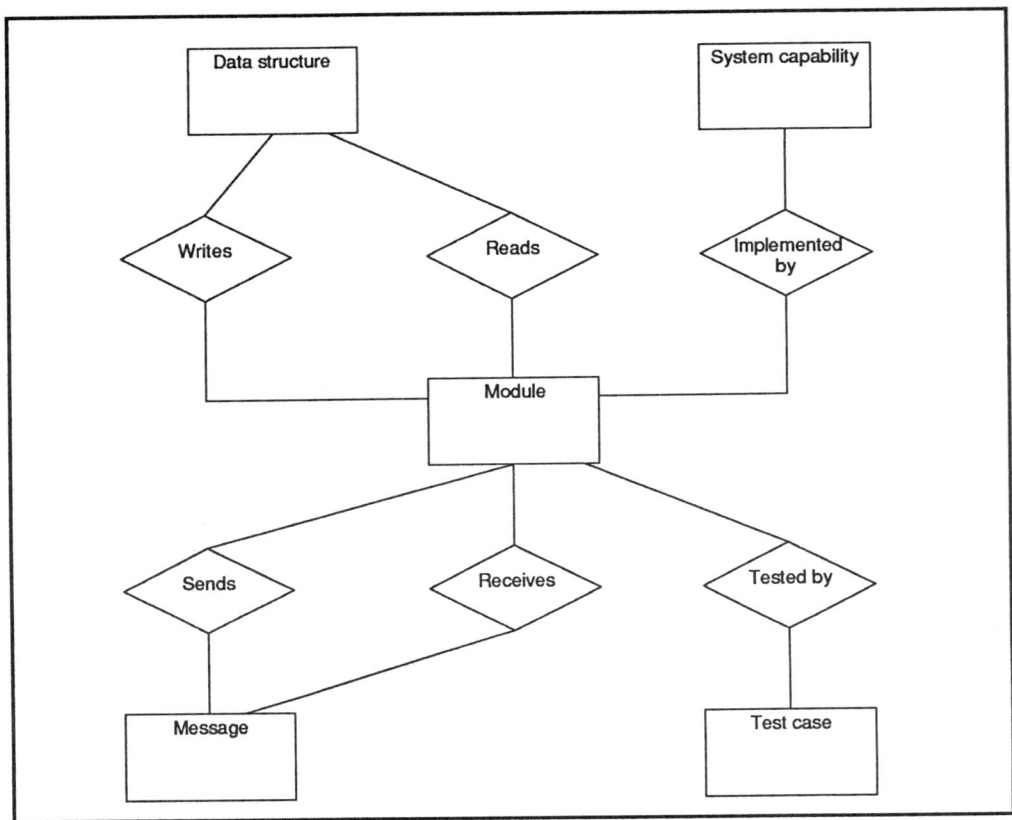

Figure 1.3
Partial data model
of a software
development
database
infrastructure.

One observation of the development database view is that the various roles (or disciplines) all create portions of the eventual information, or artifacts, and this can be a highly concurrent process. Problems arise when there are sequential dependencies among pieces of concurrently produced information, or when there is disagreement among the stakeholders as to which information should be collected and by whom.

System dynamics is another view of software process; it uses feedback loops to model control systems, especially where the item being controlled is a social activity. Still other models of software process focus on organizational maturity, quality improvement, and goal-oriented development.

One of the interesting aspects of these models is that they use techniques (representations) that are used in the software process to model the process itself. Thus software process can be correctly viewed as a real-time system. Software process models have themselves evolved, and their evolutionary trend is to capture the dynamic, social interactions that are an inherent part of software process.

1.1.3 Software Process Sophistication or Maturity

"If builders built buildings the way programmers develop software, a wood-pecker could destroy civilization."
Gerald Weinberg (paraphrased).

Weinberg suggests that software processes, whatever they are, are pretty shaky. Yet we know that some organizations are good at software development, while others are not. We'll revisit this in greater detail in Chapter 9. For now we'll look at several models of individual and group sophistication.

Meilir Page-Jones and his associates at the Wayland Systems Institute have identified seven levels of individual software engineering sophistication [PAG91] (see Chapter 13). This model is often used to assess organizational readiness for CASE technology, our third triad element. The underlying premise is that any software process depends to some extent on the talent and education of its participants.

Perhaps the most widely-known model of software process is the Software Engineering Institute's Software Process Maturity Model (SPMM), described in Figure 1.4. Ed Yourdon proclaims the paper that first described this model to be "the most significant Software Engineering paper of the 1980s."

The SEI SPMM describes a growth path that results from actions recommended for organizations at each level. The model views software process as something that is repeatable, defined and understood, measured, and eventually optimized. Looking at these, the model clearly has a management focus. No mention of techniques or supporting technologies is even made.

1. Initial	No defined process, no use of project planning or estimation models. "Ad hoc" or "seat of the pants"
2. Repeatable	Ad hoc process, used and backed by management. "Know the ropes"
3. Defined	Formally defined process is understood and accepted by all participants. The process is used for its own merits and is qualified but not quantified.
4. Managed	Software process is measured, and data are used to modify the process. Process related to quality.
5. Optimizing	Software process is under measured control. Weak spots are identified and modified.

Figure 1.4
Software process maturity model from SEI.

Various groups have polled software development organizations to see where they fit in the SEI model. The consensus is that most organizations are at one of the two lowest levels, and that only a few even have a defined process. It is worth noting that several major corporations seeking the Baldridge Quality Award use the defined level as their near-term (three-year) goal.

As defined by SEI, software process growth can take years (see Figure 1.5). Process growth requires fundamental and extensive changes to a corporate culture, and change takes time. It is tempting to assert that larger corporations will grow more slowly than smaller ones. It is possible that an organization's growth rate is determined more by how hard it tries, and trying entails significant personal and budgetary commitment. One of the basic tenets of this book is that process growth is accelerated by the adoption of improved techniques and intelligent use of CASE technology.

Since the SEI Software Process Maturity Model has become so widely known, it tends to be accepted almost by default, because of the dearth of competing models. As we said earlier, any model is a compromise with reality [BOL91]. In this section, we outline some of the shortcomings of the SEI Software Process Maturity Model.

1. *Questionable Basis*: Process maturity is assessed by responses to 110 questions, and only 85 of these are actually used. Many major issues are completely ignored in this list.

2. *Single Growth Path*: The model asserts that there is only one growth path, and this is primarily in the management direction. Many organizations find that they respond "correctly" to questions pertaining to higher levels of maturity, yet they are categorized into lower levels by deficiencies in other areas.

3. *Homogeneity*: The model presumes that organizations are homogeneous; in larger organizations, some groups are far superior to others. No "credit" is given for this disparity.

4. *Monotonicity*: The model presumes that process growth is a monotonic process. There are several circumstances which can reverse process growth, including rapid staff growth, acquisitions, and drastic changes in management personnel.

We will investigate software process maturity and improvement in more detail in Chapter 12.

Figure 1.5
Rate of process maturity growth.

From initial to repeatable:	1 -- 2 years
From repeatable to defined:	2 -- 4 years
From defined to managed:	2 -- 4 years
From managed to optimized:	1 -- 3 years

1.2 Techniques

After watching a beginning cross-country skier, who happened to be an engineer, change the wax on his skis three times in the first mile, Sven Wiik, the former U.S. Nordic Team coach, observed: "Cross-country skiing is only 10 percent wax and 90 percent technique." We tend to emphasize the paraphernalia, hoping that better equipment will somehow compensate for inferior technique. Notice that most of this book is dedicated to technique. Part of the reason for this is that we can buy equipment, but technique is harder to acquire.

Techniques are the "how" of software process. Recall that our working definition describes software as a series of representations. How are these representations expressed? In some notation. How did we get this information? Technique. We prefer the term "technique" to its more popular rivals: software development methodology, software development methods, structured methods, etc. Part of our preference for "technique" is that it carries some of the connotations of craftsmanship. In the medieval craft guilds, apprentices learned techniques from those who had mastered the craft. Some of this nomenclature is embedded in the Wayland Systems Institute model.

Prior to proceeding, we need to delineate techniques, notations, and representations.

A _representation_ is the expression of the results of applying a process to an application. The process is based on a notation, and technique refers to how the notation is used to describe the problem. Representations (should) have levels of abstraction, and there's a good argument that there should be some continuity of thought that flows across a series of representations. Examples of representations might be models of data, process, and control for a system under study or the source and executable code for a system in production. Each of these acts as a representation of the system during or after development. Representations are sometimes called deliverables.

Techniques are specific ways of doing something, in this case developing software, that have proven to be successful in the past. In many cases, techniques employ common practices or schools of thought. Structured Analysis, for example, is a technique for analyzing a system that uses functional decomposition of requirements. Technique refers to knowing how to use a notation (and which one to use) in software development.

Notations are simply practical ways of expressing representations in a given technique. To borrow from Webster, a notation is a system of figures, signs, and symbols which conveys information.

Representations employ notations, and there are dozens of notations: natural language, decision tables, program description languages (PDLs), finite state machines, data flow diagrams, entity-relationship models, Petri nets, predicate calculus, and your favorite notation. A quick way to assess process sophistication is to observe how a notation is used on an application. Neophyte practitioners are confined by the dictates of a notation, while advanced practitioners know its limitations, and know when to break the rules.

Some notations are so powerful, that they become the basis of a technique. Decision tables, for example, can be used as the skeleton of an interview between an analyst and a customer. As the analyst goes through the mechanics of a complete decision table, the interview forces consideration of obscure combinations of circumstances that otherwise would probably not be recognized.

"Knowing the ropes" is a sailing term. On a square-rigged sailboat, each sail has a halyard (to raise the sail) and two sheets (to control the sail). Sails are named by the mast they are on, and their position on the mast. Thus a square-rigger with 14 sails would have 42 ropes, each with its own name and function. To sail such a boat, especially in an emergency, each sailor has to know the name, place, and function of each rope (another instance of the value of a shared view). Technique also refers to knowing the ropes — to knowing how things are (or should be) done.

When there is no shared view of how software is developed in an organization, a "chaotic" or "ad hoc" approach takes hold. In these organizations, the process of developing software is rarely managed or controlled. In many cases, software development proceeds in a haphazard fashion, with the software delivered requiring massive changes and rewrites before it is implemented.

Software has evolved from early monolithic, amorphous programs through structured programs to collections of objects. During this evolution, various techniques and notations have been used and found to be useful.

Techniques can be used to capture a view of an application. We describe six techniques in this book, based on six different viewpoints or orientations: function, data, information, control, object, and prototype. Two of these have evolved into highly-prominent software processes: Structured Analysis and Structured Design (SA/SD) and Information Engineering (IE). The majority of front-end CASE products support one of these two techniques. While IE and SA/SD have received the majority of success, object orientation seems to be garnering a lot of interest and may eventually surpass other techniques.

1.2.1 Working Definition

Prior to introducing our working definition of technique, we should discuss some of the issues related to techniques. Some practitioners have found advocates of a specific technique similar in personality to religious fanatics. These zealots argue, adamantly, about the strength of their approach and the failures of all other approaches. While specific techniques may work better than others in certain development environments, we believe that any technique, if correctly applied, can help an organization develop software more efficiently.

All techniques were originally created by individuals or groups of individuals, and many techniques are often identified by the people that created them. The Yourdon Structured Method (YSM), for example, was created and popularized by Ed Yourdon, who later sold his name to Yourdon Inc. Ward/Mellor is a popular real-time technique, and one of the architects of this approach has gone on to develop an object-oriented approach with Sally Shlaer (Shlaer/Mellor).

One characteristic of techniques is that they usually evolve, just like the people that use them. YSM has moved progressively through three different versions since its introduction over 15 years ago. The original version of the Yourdon technique was based on functional decomposition. This was followed by event partitioning, and the Yourdon technique was modified to include state-transition diagrams. The current version includes object-oriented analysis as part of the YSM technique. In this sense, techniques move through a series of versions or revisions and can change significantly through their useful life (just like software).

Prior to proceeding, we need to present our working definition of *technique*:

> *The use of an engineering, disciplined approach to developing software which typically can be characterized by five criteria: it (the technique) is written down, repeatable, teachable, measurable, and automatable. Techniques can make use of notations and diagraming tools for modeling, specifying, and designing software, and these diagrams or specifications become the representations of the software.*

Techniques that are used but not taught, that are not written down or measured, or that are practiced by only a certain individual in an organization cannot be considered "techniques" as we have defined them and cannot be automated with a set of popular tools.

1.2.2 Justification for Techniques

Why should today's organization use techniques? As we have said, when there is no shared view of how software is developed in an organization, a "chaotic" or "ad hoc" approach takes hold and software development proceeds in a haphazard fashion. In addition, post-implementation maintenance is far more difficult in the ad hoc environment because the representations normally resulting from a technique are nonexistent.

Unfortunately, most organizations today take this ad hoc approach to developing and maintaining software. Within the same organization, one group may take one development approach and another group may take another approach. Moreover, within the same development group, the approach may change from project to project. Rarely do these approaches resemble the techniques described in this book. There is a growing movement toward technique usage, however, as organizations scramble to apply dwindling resources to aging software. Organizations envision a number of benefits through adoption and application of a technique; these are described in more detail in Chapter 11.

We will describe only one of these potential benefits in this chapter.

Standardized Approach

A technique represents a consistent approach to software development within an organization. This has several advantages over ad hoc methods:

Standardized Deliverables. Regardless of the project, developers clearly know what deliverables are to be produced. Users can track the progress of the development effort better and can track the requirements for the system throughout the life cycle of the software.

Project Measurement. Measurement of a project is practical with techniques since the same approach is used from project to project. Measurements from one project can be used to estimate subsequent projects.

Project Management. Projects are easier to manage, since the tasks completed and pending are already known. As metrics are collected, estimates for new projects become easier and more reliable.

Tool Support. A consistent approach means that CASE tools can now be brought in to support the approach. This contrasts with multiple "ad hoc" approaches for which there may be no CASE support possible.

Training. A standardized approach is something that can be taught to developers so they can all share the common view for the organization.

Technique Improvement. A standardized approach also means that improvements can be made and those improvements can be tracked and monitored. This can lead to improvement of the development process.

1.2.3 Use of Techniques

Various techniques have gained widespread use throughout the world. Figure 1.6 shows use of techniques in the United States, and Figure 1.7 shows their use in Europe and Japan. One interesting observation is the general lack of acceptance of techniques by software developers. Most estimates indicate that less than 20% of software developers are currently using some form of technique as we have defined it. Some have hypothesized that techniques have not been widely accepted because of the amount of work and rigor required to use them. Others have indicated that using techniques stifles their "creativity." For whatever reason, techniques have failed to gain widespread use in the United States and one reason for this trend is lack of adequate automated support for techniques in CASE tools.

With the current set of CASE tools on the market, using a technique is now practical for medium- to large-scale projects. A CASE tool, for example, makes changing specifications, models, and designs much easier than it would be for a person with only a pencil and eraser. CASE tools also can perform sophisticated verification checking of models and designs, track requirements, share information among developers, and generate code, test cases, and documentation. These and other capabilities make using techniques more appealing to organizations. We will look more closely at CASE tools in the next section.

1.2.4 Comparison of Techniques

There is no evidence suggesting that one technique produces "better" software than another. Development techniques have emerged and evolved for nearly two decades, and, thus far, no one technique has dominated. What is becoming increasingly clear, however, is that organizations should take a more consistent approach to their software development. This means adopting *some* technique, and there are general guidelines for doing so.

When evaluating or comparing popular techniques used to develop software, we should consider many factors. The type of applications or systems under development, the type of organization, the existing experience of the development staff, and the current development environment are all issues to consider when evaluating techniques.

For example, some techniques are better suited for real-time or embedded software development, while others are more oriented towards business software development. Likewise, some organizations may already be using techniques or methods that can be incorporated into their development process. In other cases, techniques may not fit in with the established way of developing software and may have to be tailored or enhanced to gain widespread use in the organization.

Also, techniques are not in themselves perfect. One of the criticisms of the venerable Structured Analysis Structured Design approach is the awkward transition from analysis to design. The object-oriented techniques show promise because of their consistency of representation and their superior ability to model the real world. Information-oriented techniques focus on strategic planning and organization-wide data and process modeling. These techniques are applied to all levels of an organization -- from top management down to the most junior developer -- and as such can require the most significant cultural change.

Figure 1.6
Use of develop-
ment techniques
in the United
States.

Use of formal development methods in the United States and worldwide

By the end of 1990, it was estimated that only 10 to 17 percent of all software engineers in the United States were using CASE tools.

By 1995, it is estimated that 50 percent of software engineers in the United States will be using CASE tools.

In the United States, of those organizations using structured techniques, the methods most widely used are:

	1989	1990	Planned
Yourdon structured design	29.1%	24.9%	13%
Gane & Sarson structured analysis	13.8%	11.2%	15%
DeMarco structured analysis	12.3%	9.5%	10%
Warnier/Orr structured design	7.2%	7.1%	8%
Jackson structured design	2.4%	3.6%	
Information engineering		11.2%	5%
Other			13%
Inhouse methods	35.2%	32.5%	36%

Worldwide, the percentage of organizations using structured methods :*

United Kingdon	33%
France	28%
United States	17%
Germany	16%

In Japan, formal methods in current use include:

Yourdon, Gane/Sarson & DeMarco	50%
Jackson structured design	25%
Object-oriented methods	10%
Other	15%

* From an Ovum survey of 400 DP sites in four countries in 1989.

Figure 1.7
Use of develop-
ment techniques
worldwide.

We will discuss the process of selecting development techniques further in Chapter 10.

1.2.5 Orientation of Techniques

Data processing systems are so-called because they have two primary ingredients: a data component and a processing component. A data processing system for a library stores data about books, authors, borrowers, etc. The system also performs operations on the data, such as adding book information, marking a book as "checked out," and many other library functions. Some data processing systems, called real-time systems, have a third ingredient called a control component. A good way to discuss techniques is to examine what part of a system they emphasize. For example, some techniques stress the processing component of a system. These are called function-oriented techniques. As mentioned, we will examine six technique orientations in this text:

Function-oriented techniques stress the processing or functionality of a system. Typically, in these techniques, processing is defined first and data follow process.

Data-oriented techniques accent the data component of a system. In one data-oriented technique, output data are defined first, then input data needed to support that output are determined, and, finally, the processing needed to move from inputs to outputs is defined.

Control-oriented techniques are extensions of the function-oriented techniques that focus on the control behavior of a system.

Information-oriented techniques examine software in the context of an organization. They emphasize high-level data and process models, and the integration of applications via these models.

Object-oriented techniques feature the integration of data and the valid processing (encapsulation) of that data into a construct called an object. These are the newest approaches and attempt to address some of the inadequacies of earlier techniques.

Prototype-oriented techniques underscore the use of system simulations prior to building and maintaining systems.

As we study the various techniques, we will provide a common set of representations by applying each technique to the Library system or the Simple Simon automated tellor machine (ATM) system. The Library system represents the data processing required by a typical university library; it was selected because libraries are familiar to readers and the Library system itself has a richness of features. The

Simple Simon ATM (SSATM) was selected because it represents more complex functional and control behavior than the Library system and is also very familiar to most readers.

1.2.6 Adopting Techniques

Putting a technique to use in an organization invariably involves more than simply choosing one. The techniques described in this book do not jump out of shrink-wrapped boxes and become operational in an organization. They have to be integrated into the existing development environment, and this requires change in that environment. This primarily involves (1) studying the development environment to see what approaches are working now and (2) determining which popular technique(s) will best incorporate those successes.

More often than not, once a popular technique has been selected, an organization will tailor it so that it fits in with the way the organization already develops software. For example, the DeMarco Structured Analysis technique calls for four system models to be created in sequence: a current physical, a current logical, a proposed logical, and finally a proposed physical. An organization may decide that only a current physical and a proposed physical model are necessary in the analysis of a system. Current logical and proposed logical modeling would be skipped, and the organization would determine its own transition from current physical to proposed physical modeling. This adoption/adaption relationship will be discussed further in Part 4.

1.3 CASE Technology

The third element in our software engineering triad, CASE technology, raises an immediate question. Does the acronym abbreviate Computer-Aided Software Engineering? Computer-Aided System Engineering? Or, as some CASE industry watchers quip, Concerted Attempt to Snow Everyone? The system engineering alternative is used less often, so we capitulate to the more popular choice, software engineering.

The broadest definition of CASE technology includes any programs that automate some portion of the (sic) software development process. Since this definition includes compilers and editors, we need a little more refinement. The next most common definition swings too far the other way: any program that automates an activity associated with some phase of (the) software development life cycle. The unstated assumption here is the intent to use the waterfall model to help define CASE.

Defining the boundaries of CASE technology is a little like defining The Chair. Part of the reason for this is a bandwagon phenomenon: When CASE technology became popular in the late 1980s, there was a rush of companies claiming that their products were CASE tools all along. Whatever the boundaries, it is clear that CASE technology is here to stay. The CASE tool industry reached sales of $1 billion in 1990 and is continuing to grow.

The growth rate, and the bandwagon effect, prompted Ken Orr's comment: "More has been written about CASE than is known."

The most useful view of CASE may be as an enabling technology. Both Ed Yourdon and Larry Constantine (authors of the SA/SD technique) maintain that CASE makes their technique feasible for industrial-strength applications. Since many of the techniques entail graphical notations, one characteristic of CASE tools is that the drafting problems are resolved. A second characteristic of many techniques is that there is usually some textual supplement to a graphical notation. CASE tools strengthen this connection by providing a repository for such information and mechanisms to ensure that both the textual and the graphical views are compatible.

1.3.1 Working Definition

For purposes of this book, we define *Computer-Aided Software Engineering* (CASE) to be:

The automation of techniques, notations, and methods for the development of software. CASE often includes diagraming tools for models and specifications, verification checking, a common repository, and generation capabilities for documentation, code, and test cases.

At a very basic level, CASE tools automate a specific technique. The Information Engineering Facility (IEF) from Texas Instruments, for example, automates the Information Engineering (IE) methodology (Chapter 7). Built into the IEF product are the rules for developing software using the IE method and the tool supports the appropriate notations and diagrams required by the method. Ideally, the CASE tool should not hinder but enhance the use of techniques and provide verification checking and automated support for the routine, mundane aspects of applying the technique to a large project.

With over 300 CASE products currently available, it is becoming increasingly difficult to determine which tools actually match the definition we use and which do not. Future CASE products will provide support for object-oriented techniques, and with the movement towards tool integration, selecting CASE products should be easier. Chapter 11 covers CASE tools in more detail.

1.3.2 Components of CASE Products

When looking at CASE tools, it is often helpful to consider products based on a common set of functions or components. Most (if not all) of the CASE tools currently available support a common set of functions, including the following:

A *central repository* or dictionary is used to store, report and control access to the information collected in the development of the software. This repository is used to collect information on the system in all phases of system development, to control access to the objects contained within it, and to provide reporting and verification of the various deliverables in the development life cycle.

Some CASE tools refer to the central repository as a data dictionary, while others refer to it as an encyclopedia. Most sophisticated CASE tools have a repository and many provide multiuser access to it via a mainframe, minicomputer, or local area network configuration. Generally included with a repository is configuration management for any objects stored and requirements traceability. Change control, version control, and associating objects with functional requirements to indicate they have been satisfied are all typical repository functions.

Diagraming tools support structured diagrams and create pictures of the system and its components. These tools help to describe and define the pieces of a system and also help to model the system so that it can be better understood. A by-product of these tools is a better form of communication between development team members and the end-user community. The tools should automate drawing the diagrams and provide syntax checking for the diagrams to ensure that they are not drawn incorrectly.

Prototyping or simulation tools simulate the functionality of the system for developers and end users. Through the use of these tools, the developers can verify that their models are correct and accurate. Sometimes tests can be run on a system before the design and coding have been completed. These tools help developers of embedded systems determine if the systems they are modeling and designing can be implemented under the constraints imposed.

Specification/diagram checking tools automatically detect incomplete, incorrect, and/or inconsistent specifications and drawings. These tools allow the developer to verify that the models and designs conform to the rules and constraints of the technique being used. When discrepancies are found, they can be identified and corrected prior to the coding of programs. Examples of verification checking include cross-diagram checking, completeness and consistency checking, and functional decomposition checking.

An *Export/import capability* provides a means of exporting and importing the various objects created in the development process so that they may be used by other tools or systems. Since no one CASE tool provides all the capabilities to support all phases of the development life cycle, there is a need to use the deliverables from one CASE tool as input to another. This capability is especially useful when PC-based system analysis and design tools are used with a mainframe code generator, since there must be a way to migrate the design components to the code generator.

1.3.3 CASE Tool Integration

Most users of component CASE tools find that the analysis and design tools on the market can be linked to a few of the code generators, but that these interfaces or links leave a lot to be desired. The information that can be carried from a front-end CASE tool into a back-end product is generally very limited. This often results in redundant entry of data. In short, CASE customers using bridges or links between different products find these links to be extremely limited.

CASE tool vendors can enhance their tool sets by accessing information in a repository, thus enhancing integration between tools. In fact, most of the major CASE tool vendors have announced their plans to support import/export from/to the repositories from IBM, HP and DEC.

With the announcement of IBM's AD/Cycle and DEC's Cohesion, the CASE marketplace has recently solidified to a larger extent. HP and Unisys have also made competitive announcements, and the issue of integration between CASE tools may be resolved in the next few years.

IBM originally announced that its Repository Manager (RM) product would be available only on a mainframe or minicomputer. After learning that its customers require support for a repository on workstations and servers, IBM decided to support its RM on these platforms. DEC has plans to support a distributed repository, CDD/Repository, under its Cohesion environment. Organizations must decide how RM and CDD/Repository will meet their needs and where they will store and control the software development information.

Potential buyers of CASE products should consider the short-term benefits derived from AD/Cycle or Cohesion products and their competitors. But until the fruits of AD/Cycle and Cohesion have ripened, the question of how these announcements affect a CASE tool decision may be moot, since no one knows how these strategies will actually work. Since most CASE tool vendors have announced support for AD/Cycle and Cohesion, in the near term the products now on the market have lost nothing in terms of market appeal over the IBM and DEC business partner products.

It is too early to determine to what extent products that are tightly incorporated into AD/Cycle and Cohesion will differ from products that do not support these architectures. Since much of the groundwork for the RM from IBM and the CDD/ Repository from DEC remains to be completed, any products that are sold as part of AD/Cycle or Cohesion will have few (if any) benefits over competitive products. Figure 1.8 describes major CASE tool integration standards efforts that are underway and indicates major areas of discussion and emphasis for each. We will discuss CASE tools and issues related to the current CASE products in more detail in Chapter 11.

1.3.4 Comparing CASE Tools

Organizations that are interested in using CASE tools will find over 300 different products on the marketplace and may have difficulty determining which products might be best for their needs.

One CASE tool evaluation process that many organizations have successfully used is based on a three-phase method for comparing and selecting products [TOP91a]. The phases involved are:

Phase I - *initial evaluation*: a process to help reduce the number of potential CASE products and eliminate from the evaluation process those tools that will not support the least common set of criteria required by a potential buyer.

Phase II - *detailed evaluation*: an in-depth evaluation of a few CASE products (hopefully between two and five) performed in-house to objectively measure the strengths and weaknesses of the tools in any given development environment.

Phase III - *follow-up evaluation*: an ongoing evaluation of the tools and techniques used to support a quality control mechanism for the software development process.

Assuming that it is not reasonable (or even possible) to perform a detailed evaluation of the more than 300 CASE products currently available, potential buyers need some way of reducing this number to a handful of products that they can then evaluate in more depth. One method for performing an initial evaluation is to establish some basic requirements for a CASE tool and then review the marketplace for possible "best in class" products.

Once this has been done, selected tools can be further evaluated using an extension to these criteria and a weighting system to compare the products and determine their relative strengths and weaknesses. Other methods for comparing CASE tools can be by the phases of the development life cycle the tool supports or by the specific structured methodologies the product supports. While there are problems with these approaches, if used correctly they can offer potential buyers a

Standard efforts	Data Repository Services	Interconnect Services	(Tool to Tool) Semantic Interconnection	Task Management Services	Message Server Network	User Interface
CALS/Industry Steering Group/ Software Products	E	E	E	-	-	-
EIA/CDIF-CASE Data Interchange Format	-	S	E	-	-	-
CIS-CASE Integration Services	E	E	E	E	E	-
ECMA TC33 PCTE	E	E	-	E	S	-
IEEE-CS P1175	S	S	E	-	S	-
ANSI/IRDS X3H4	E	S	E	S	-	E
ISO JTC1/SC-7	S	S	S	S	-	S
ISO JTC1/SWG-AP	S	E	-	E	E	E
PDES	E	E	E	-	-	-
ECMA TC35 User-System Interface	S	S	-	S	S	E
Object Management Group	S	E	S	S	E	S
E = Emphasis, S = Some Discussion, - = No Discussion or Not Applicable						

Figure 1.8
Major CASE standards efforts.

sound basis for comparing different products. Several alternative methods for comparing CASE products are shown in Figure 1.9. We will discuss the process of selecting and implementing development methods and CASE tools in more detail in Chapter 13.

1.4 Interrelationships in the Triad

In the preceding sections, discussing a particular triad element without mentioning at least one of the others has been awkward. Here we'll look at some of the prominent relationships among elements of the software engineering triad. Figure 1.10 shows the relationships in this triad.

1.4.1 Software Process and Techniques

If we were making an entity-relationship diagram with software process and technique as entities, we would assert a many-to-many relationship between them. It is clear that a given technique can be used in several software processes. The converse, that a software process employs several techniques, is a little controversial. There are organizations (and CASE vendors) that have a fervent, missionarylike zeal about "the one, true way" of software development.

Barry Boehm once said, "If your only tool is a hammer, pretty soon all your problems begin to look like nails." Software process is enriched by the variety of techniques it incorporates. The real driver is the application being developed by a software process. Given an application, a good software process will first consider which techniques are most appropriate, and then use them. If an organization always deals with a homogeneous set of applications, there is a chance that one technique will suffice.

It is more likely, however, that organizations will face a mixture of application types, and this mixture may demand a combination of techniques. This leads to the second major relationship: changes in techniques will force changes in the associated software processes. We have all had occasion to do some fairly repetitive but unfamiliar task. Painting a picket fence is a good example. Even if you have a clumsy start, by the time you're done, you've got it down to a system. The only trouble is, by the time you need to paint the fence again, you have forgotten your system. Look how the fence painting process improves as your technique improves. You learn how much paint the brush will hold, then you learn to paint from the top down, and so on. By analogy, the same thing happens when improved techniques are used in a software process: The process itself is improved. This is why we have such an emphasis on techniques in our book.

A short, software-related example is in order. When practitioners tried to apply SA/SD techniques to real-time applications, they soon found that the control aspects inherent in real-time systems are difficult to represent in the SA/SD notation.

Figure 1.9
Methods of
comparing
CASE tools.

By functionality
By life cycle phases supported
By DBMS/programming languages supported
By repository support
By method/technique support

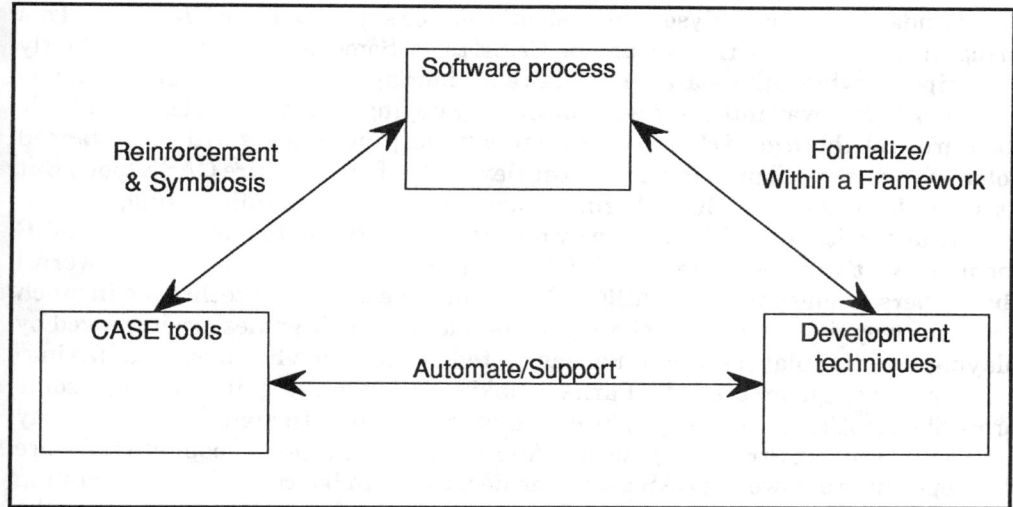

Figure 1.10
Relationships in
the Software
Engineering Triad.

Various real-time extensions to SA/SD were developed; the techniques changed to meet the needs of the applications. The new techniques, in turn, changed the software process for developing real-time systems. The use of executable requirements specifications could lead to another significant change in the real-time software (or systems) development processes.

1.4.2 Techniques and CASE

At the early CASE conferences, one of the recurring themes was the chicken/egg question: CASE first or methodology first? The popular answer was "methodology," and we agree, only we prefer the term "technique." We might paraphrase Sven Wiik: Software development is 90 percent technique, and only 10 percent CASE. There is even financial evidence for this. In studies of companies that have made successful use of CASE technology, the training budgets far exceed the CASE prices.

The economic reality of CASE product development is such that CASE tools are technique-specific. Vendors typically decide that it is better to support one technique well than to support parts of many techniques. We should clarify what it means for a CASE tool to support a technique. Just supporting the notation, typically drawings, is not enough. Most techniques have supplemental information and standard types of analyses; these should also be supported by a CASE tool. This brings us to another distinction among CASE tools. Some are Teutonic or explicitly prescriptive, while others are laissez-faire in their approach. If an organization is trying to buy its way into a software process by buying CASE technology, Teutonic tools are probably a good choice. On the other hand, practitioners with an advanced software process will probably prefer the flexibility of laissez-faire CASE tools. But at a very basic level, CASE tools simply help to automate specific techniques.

Thus far, it sounds like a one-way relationship between techniques and CASE technology; it's really bidirectional. Clearly, some CASE tools are more powerful than others. Using powerful CASE tools can improve a person's technique in much the same way that tennis and chess players find that their games are improved by playing superior players. David Parnas hinted at this when he advocated "faking" a rational design process. To Parnas, "faking it" involves going through some prescribed motions. Doing so produces useful results, even though the motions may not be understood. Stretching this to CASE technology, when a neophyte software developer uses a powerful CASE tool, the neophyte can be "carried along," gaining mental momentum from the tool. Of course, there is always the danger that the neophyte will be overwhelmed. The Wayland Systems Institute's answer to this is to always have some journeymen or masters available to lower-level personnel.

1.4.3 CASE and Software Process

In part of the discussion of their Software Process Maturity Model, SEI asserts that organizations should be at the defined level before trying to introduce CASE technology. This is certainly bad news for the 95 percent of companies that are not there yet, and even worse news for the CASE vendors.

In our industrial experience, we have observed a symbiosis, or mutual reinforcement, between tools and process. This shouldn't be too surprising — many non-software processes are improved by better tools, and in turn, organizations with mature processes seek even further tool improvements. The linkage that makes this possible is technique. An example of this type of reinforcement might help explain the relationship.

In 1968, a software development organization was required by contract to provide flowchart documentation of all delivered software. Flowcharts were manually done by the drafting department, and there was always a six-week backlog of flowcharts in the drafting department. Software developers soon learned that they could "save a place in line" by submitting an incomplete (or even wrong) flowchart. Milestone deadlines appeared to be met, yet the developers had six weeks of slack time to revise their flowcharts and simply exchange them for the "placeholders" (placebo is probably more accurate).

In that software process, flowcharts had an ex post facto role: They served only as after-the-fact documentation. They were never reviewed or used as communication tools. Along came a flowchart drawing tool which accepted a textual description that entry-level technicians could produce from hand-drawn flowcharts, and produced a high-quality drawing on a plotter. Within a month, the six-week backlog shrunk to two days, which in turn caused problems for designers, because now their six weeks of slack time was gone. After about four months, process participants caught on and actually started using their flowcharts. Even better, since changes were easy to make, the flowcharts stayed consistent with changes to the source code. This experience shows that tools can clearly improve a process, but there is a catch: The developers had to learn how to use flowcharts as a design and communication tool, not just a documentation device.

What about the converse — can an improved process result in better tools? Again the answer is an emphatic *yes*, and again the linkage is via technique.

In the same organization where the automatic flowcharter was built, the support software group was responsible for developing what we would now call CASE tools. It was an enthusiastic group — they were happy to build tools for their own sake, even if these tools were never used. The management soon noticed this, and issued a policy that no tool could be developed until the technique it implemented had been used on a "live" project. This accomplished several things. First, if the technique did not work out, there was no wasted effort building a tool that would not be used. Second, using a technique helped to sharpen the tool requirements, very much like prototyping. Finally, if effort statistics were kept on the manual version of the technique, the tool development cost was easier to justify.

The relationship between CASE technology and software process is so strong that CASE technology, if used intelligently, can be used to accelerate software process growth [JOR90]. As a scenario, suppose an SEI level 1 company decides to improve its software process. One approach is to start with a simple, inexpensive front-end CASE tool, invest in some technique training, and use the tool on a couple of projects. There will be a repetition of the automatic flowcharter pattern, and soon the staff will actually use the tool-produced drawings. Management will expect them as deliverables, and soon this part of the software process will be institutionalized. The tool has improved the process.

What usually happens next is that the tool users become annoyed by the limitations of the tool, and start looking for something better, typically with more flexibility, greater analytic features, and more report-generating capabilities. Once such a tool is purchased (along with training), the staff sees what the analytic features can do for them, and management comes to expect tailored reports. Again the tool improves the process, and the process becomes institutionalized. At this point, a choice must be made: front-end CASE, back-end CASE or integrated CASE?

Now for the big question: Why not skip all these iterations of new tool and improved process, and just put in *the final* CASE tool in the first place? We alluded to this earlier when we noted that we have a tendency to buy technology as a cure-all. Once again, the answer is technique. By way of analogy, would you prefer to learn to fly in a Boeing 767 or a Cessna? Software process is complex; part of the complexity is technical, but part is also social. An organization must "grow into" a software process.

1.5 A Software Production Framework

Many organizations have tried and failed to implement formal software development methods and automated tools. We include some practical experiences in Chapter 15 of this book; these experiences are provided as an experiential report from organizations that have attempted to adopt techniques and CASE tools.

In our experience, problems occur most often in organizations that bring in techniques or tools or try to force a rigid, formal development process without considering the cultural and organizational impact of this adoption on their staff and clients. Many companies have sought a partial solution to their perceived "software problem" without attempting to see the bigger picture related to overall software production. While we do not believe we have all the answers to the problems facing development organizations today, we can offer some insight into the experiences we have had related to helping organizations move towards a software engineering environment.

We recommend that organizations take a holistic view of software development, and we offer the term software production framework (SPF) to define all the organizational, technical, and cultural aspects of software development and maintenance. In our view, the SPF includes all the components commonly described or written about, including the software engineering triad, software development life cycles and notations, as well as the interrelationships of these components within the organization.

We further offer our view of the organizational levels in the SPF, and the discussion that follows suggests some perspectives to keep in mind when reading the remaining chapters of this book. Figure 1.11 describes the SPF along with its components and the affected organizational levels, from top to bottom.

Software development life cycles (SDLCs) define a series of tasks and stages for software production, and the sequence and dependencies between these stages and tasks. Generally included are stages for planning, analysis, design, programming, testing, and maintenance. SDLCs focus on the highest organizational level, deal with the role of development in the organization, and provide a schedule for software development and maintenance. Some SDLCs are linear, while others are iterative or evolutionary, allowing for cycles of activities or tasks with feedback loops built in. SDLCs deal with organizational and high-level management issues. SDLCs are discussed further in Chapter 2.

   A software process defines the roles, responsibilities, staff dynamics, and management tools and techniques for software development and maintenance. Software processes focus at the development organization or group level, but may include other stakeholders in the development process, such as clients, quality assurance staff, and auditors. Software processes deal with interaction and staff control issues, and provide the *who, what,* and *when* of a development process. *Who* does *what, when* in software production is addressed by the software process.

   Software process models help organizations understand and potentially improve the process they use to develop software by allowing them to quantify, study, and analyze their process using standard symbols and notations. Several types of software process models are available, including the SEI Software Process Maturity Model (SPMM) [KEL89], the TAME Goal Oriented Approach [OIV92], system dynamic models [ABD91], and quality improvement models [CLA91]. These and other models and a generic software process improvement approach are described in more detail in Chapter 12.

   Development techniques provide specific tasks, methods, and representations (or deliverables) for the creation of software product artifacts throughout the development process. Techniques focus at the project team level and describe group-related activities that require communication, standard methods and procedures, and a shared view of the development process and the products created. Automated tools, including CASE tools, can support techniques and the representations they require. Techniques support specific tasks within the SDLC and software process

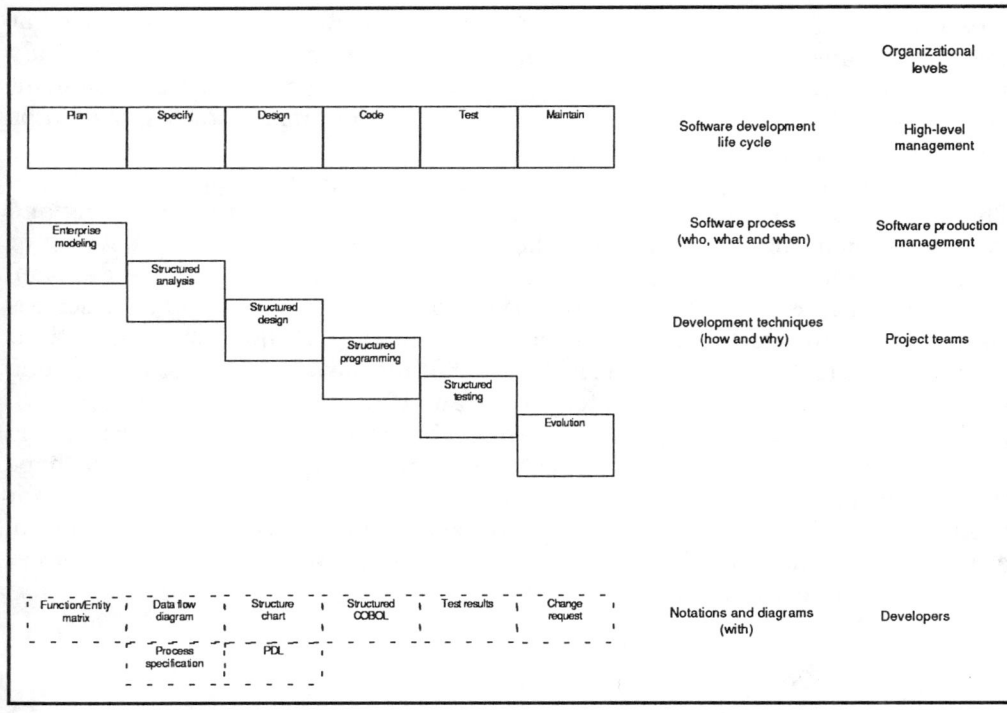

Figure 1.11
Components and organizational levels of a software production framework.

and provide the *how* and *why* of the process, where *how* a task is accomplished and *why* it is necessary are defined by the technique. Development techniques are a major focus of this book, and issues related to comparing techniques are discussed in Chapter 10, automation issues are discussed in Chapter 11, and adoption issues are discussed in Chapter 13.

Notations and diagraming tools define the actual content of the representations used in the techniques and provide standard symbols and notations for each deliverable or artifact. Notations are aimed at the lowest level within the organization, individual developers, and provide guidelines for describing the artifacts called for in the development technique. Notations describe the *with* for the technique's *how*. In other words, the development techniques describe *how* a task is accomplished, but the notation describes *with* what specific tool the representation is created.

Another term that is commonly used in reference to software production is methodology, which actually means the study of methods. The generally accepted use of this term maps methodology to a specific SDLC, a software process, and some particular techniques and notations. Commercially available methodologies usually include specific stages, tasks, roles and responsibilities, development techniques, and supporting notations and diagrams. Methodology issues are discussed in more depth in Chapter 14.

A holistic view of software production should include all of these perspectives, and should consider the development staff and the different levels. For instance, software process, and by implication software process improvement, is focused at the middle management level of an organization, and any attempt to define or study an existing process should begin at this level. Likewise, adopting new development techniques will affect development staff and project organization, and should be considered from this vantage point first.

Some organizations may choose to adopt a software process improvement view. These organizations can use Chapter 12 of this book for advice on modeling and improving their software process. Other organizations may wish to develop or acquire a methodology to address all the aspects of the SPF in a single decision. While we don't recommend this approach to all organizations, Chapter 14 describes issues related to selecting and adopting a methodology. Still other organizations may choose to focus directly on the adoption of formal development techniques and automated tools, and can use Chapters 10, 11, and 13 as guidelines for this approach. In this book, we have tried to offer as many different perspectives on selecting and adopting software development methods and technology as possible, with the hope that organizations can pick and choose the approach that is most appropriate for their situation. By focusing on the organizational levels most affected by adoption, as described by our SPF, we feel organizations can improve their chances of success in adopting these new methods and tools.

1.6 Summary

Developing software is a social process that involves three related components: a process, techniques, and automated tools (CASE). A software process defines the tasks, deliverables, and resources that are used to produce software, or the *who, what,* and *when.* Techniques are the *how* and *why* of software process, and there is a wide variety of popular development methods or techniques. CASE tools make using techniques practical for medium- to large-sized projects, and define *with* what notations development staff will communicate. Organizations that develop software without fully understanding or considering each of those components, or the overall framework of software production, cannot realize the promise of improved software quality and developer productivity. By realizing that software development is a group activity, involving people with differing views and backgrounds, organizations can begin to focus on the critical issues of software production.

In the following chapters, we will introduce the concept of a software development life cycle, describe the various popular techniques for software development, discuss technique and CASE tool selection and implementation issues, and look at case studies of organizations that have attempted to implement these tools and techniques. Hopefully, the information in these chapters will help to clarify and explain the complexities of software engineering, and will provide insight into the transition to a formal, development environment.

1.7 References

[ABD91]   Abdel-Hamid, T. and S.E. Madnick, *Software Project Dynamics - An Integrated Approach*, Prentice-Hall, 1991.

[BOL91]   Bollinger, T. and C. McGowan, "A Critical Look at Software Capability Evaluations," *IEEE Software*, July 1991, pp. 25-41.

[CLA91]   Clay, A. W., Grzybowski, G., Webber, S., and Yourdon, E., "Quality Metrics at AG Communication Systems," *American Programmer*, vol. 4, no. 9, September 1991.

[HAT91]   Hatley, D.J., "The Case for Parallel Development," *Embedded Systems Programming*, vol. 4, no. 1, Jan. 1991, pp. 20 - 33.

[HUM88]   Humphrey, W.S., "Characterizing the Software Process: A maturity Framework," *IEEE Software*, March 1988, pp. 73-79.

[JOR70]   Jorgensen, P.C., "AELFlow: An Automatic Drafting System," *Automatic Electric Laboratories Technical Journal*, vol. 12, no. 4, October 1970.

[JOR70]   Jorgensen, P.C., "AELFlow: An Automatic Drafting System,"
           Automatic Electric Laboratories Technical Journal, vol. 12, no.
           4, October 1970.

[JOR90]   Jorgensen, P.C., "Accelerating Process Maturity with CASE," *American
           Programmer*, vol. 3, no. 9, September 1990, pp. 10-15.

[KEL89]   Kellner, M. I., "Representation Formalisms for Software Process
           Modeling," *Proceedings of the 4th International Software Process
           Workshop: Representing and Enacting the Software Process*; also in
           ACM Software Engineering Notes, vol. 14, no. 4, June 1989.

[MCC81]   McCracken, D.D. and M.A. Jackson, "A Minority Dissenting Position" in
           Systems Analysis and Design - A Foundation for the 1980's, Elsevier
           Science Publishing Co., 1981.

[OIV92]   Oivo, M., and V.R. Basili, "Representing Software Engineering Models:
           The TAME Goal Oriented Approach," *IEEE Trans. on Soft. Eng.*, vol. 18,
           no. 10, pp. 886-898.

[OUE91]   Ouellette, D., "Managing CASE Implementation - A User's Perspective,"
           Proceedings of CASE World Fall 1991, Boston, MA, August, 1991.

[PAG91]   Page-Jones, M., Keynote Address, *Proceedings of the Structured
           Development Forum XII*, Portland, OR, July, 1991.

[SHA90]   Sharon, D. and P. Radding, "The CASE of the Missing Links: The
           Current State of CASE Standards Efforts," *American Programmer*, vol.
           3, no. 9, September 1990, pp. 16-28.

[TOP91a]   Topper, A., "Evaluating CASE Tools: Guidelines for Comparison,"
           American Programmer, vol. 4, no. 7, July 1991, pp. 12-20.

[TOP91b]   Topper, A., "Evaluating CASE Tools," *Embedded Systems
           Programming*, vol. 4, no. 9, Sept. 1991, pp. 24 - 32.

Chapter 2
Software Development Life Cycles

No software development technique can be used in isolation. Regardless of the orientation or view used to develop the requirements for a system or the mapping used to design a solution, any software development effort must be placed within a framework under which deliverables can be managed, roles and responsibilities are spelled out, and management control can be applied to real-world projects.

Software development life cycles (SDLCs) have been around for many years, with the original waterfall model, the spiral model and various other versions of the development process described and used over the past 30 years. One way of looking at the software development process is by applying the notations, techniques, and representations used to develop software to the development process itself. The results of studies of development models have proven enlightening and are discussed in this chapter. Chapters 12 and 13 discuss software process improvement and adopting tools and techniques in more depth and are companion chapters to this one.

Software life cycle models are used to model the high-level stages and tasks in software production and include sequence, iteration, and dependencies between stages. We have chosen to call these models life cycle models because they are often viewed in terms of the life cycle of software and focus on the organizational aspects of software. SDLCs are often studied by management, which is concerned with the discrete stages and tasks involved and with estimating the resources and time required to deliver the final product. This level of management is also concerned with tracking whether or not a project is on schedule.

In the previous chapter we defined our view of the software engineering triad and the three components: software process, development techniques, and CASE tools. In this chapter we will look at the overall development process with a focus on high-level aspects of software development. The models we describe help organizations view software development as a series of stages and tasks, that are performed by people — some individually, some in groups — and produce both intermediate and finished products.

We begin this chapter with a discussion of various models of software development life cycles so that organizations can begin thinking about software development as a formal process. These models are to software engineering what set theory is to mathematics: You can't talk about one without talking about the other. By definition, anyone who develops software anywhere follows some development

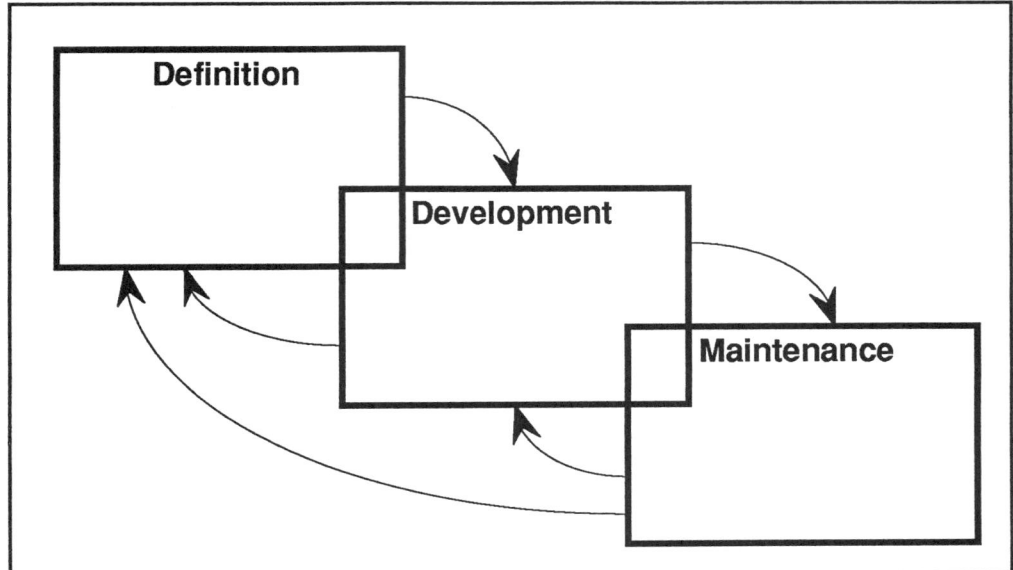

Figure 2.1
Simplified
development
life cycle.

process, and that process can be broken into stages, so software life cycles are inevitable. Our goal here is to discuss some of the mainline life cycle models, and some of the directions we see emerging, to provide a context for the rest of the book. Along the way, we'll pass on our own insights and observations, many of which we haven't seen elsewhere.

As you read and think about these life cycle models, we suggest you keep in mind three background considerations. The first is the difference between analysis and synthesis; the second is two rival strategies, decomposition and composition; and the third is known behavior of talented software developers. We find that these three considerations shed a lot of light on the selection of appropriate life cycle models. In a sense, this discussion also serves as a foundation for our later discussion of software process improvement in Chapter 12.

2.1 Introduction

One simplistic view of software development phases is shown in Figure 2.1. This view, offered by Pressman [PRE88], divides the development life cycle for software into three basic overlapping phases or stages:

Definition, which defines what a system will do
Development of a solution, which defines how the system will be
  implemented based on the environment

Maintenance (or evolution), which represents change to the
software product over its useful life

One benefit of this view is that it clearly delineates the phases and also shows
the inherent overlap between them. Definition describes in detail what a system will
do without implementation considerations. Development takes the definition of
what the system will do and, considering the implementation characteristics of the
system, creates a proposed solution that includes automated components. Maintenance includes both definition and development, but for changes to the system once
it becomes operational. These phases are intertwined, and developers often move
between them as a project progresses.

Definition, for example, may overlap development and include aspects of a
system that describe how the system will be implemented. Specified requirements
may cause additional questions to be asked that pertain to implementation issues,
which may result in changes to the requirements. Likewise, solutions recommended
in development may cause reevaluation of requirements based on the cost and time
to deliver the solution.

Software development is not a linear process, and must be considered from an
iterative or evolutionary perspective. Organizations that differentiate between the
activities of definition and development find exceptions that must be considered for
successful development of quality systems. In the discussion on development life
cycle models that follows, keep these factors in mind.

2.1.1 Analysis and Synthesis

Analysis: separation of a whole into its component parts; an examination of a
complex, its elements, and their relations.

Synthesis: the composition or combination of parts or elements so as to form a
whole; deductive reasoning. [Webster]

Analysis and synthesis are closely related to decomposition and composition,
respectively, which are discussed below. Analysis is most often seen as breaking
down a problem into lower-level problems, and further breaking down these, until
"manageable" problems are reached. This process is the cornerstone of the concept
of "systems analysis," adopted by the U.S. Army in the 1930s and widely used since
then.

Synthesis is exactly the reverse process: When we synthesize, we put pieces
together to make a larger whole. All engineering disciplines, especially software
engineering, prosper when there is a sequence of alternating cycles of analysis and
synthesis. It will be instructive to see where analysis and synthesis occur in the
various life cycle models.

One view that helps people better understand the differences and similarities of these concepts is to consider analysis as a discovery process which has as its goal a complete understanding of the problem. Synthesis is a development process that builds something from what is already understood. If developers have a poor or incomplete understanding of what is required, the chances that they can build something new that will satisfy the requirements are slim.

2.1.2 Composition and Decomposition

Compose: to form by putting together; to form the substance of.

Decompose: to separate into constituent parts or elements or into simpler compounds. [Webster]

Analysis typically proceeds by decomposing a problem into smaller problems, thus reducing complexity. One of the best questions to ask when using decomposition is what are the criteria by which a problem is decomposed? As we will see in Chapter 4, there are several guidelines for decomposing system functions. A corollary question is, if there are several decomposition criteria, how do we choose which to use? Decomposition and analysis have dominated software development thinking and practice, but both have their limitations. Performing a good decomposition, for example, requires that the people doing the decomposition have very complete knowledge of the problem being decomposed. Anything less than complete understanding will probably result in an imperfect decomposition.

Composition occurs when we build something with known components. There is a nice analogy with sculpture: One approach is to start with a large block of marble and remove all unwanted regions until what remains is the desired form. Mathematicians joke about how easy it was for Michelangelo to sculpt _David_: start with a piece of marble, and simply remove all non-_David_. There is a museum outside Florence, Italy that contains a room full of Michelangelo's abandoned starts.

Even Michelangelo knew the main problem with decomposition: One mistake, and the project is ruined. The alternative approach to sculpture is to use a plastic medium such as wax. The wax sculptor composes with wax, adding and removing until the desired form is reached. Later, a plaster cast of the wax original is made, the wax is melted out, and the plaster serves as a mold for molten bronze. The antiquity of this process (the lost wax process) testifies to how long the basic idea of composition has been used in our culture.

2.1.3 Developer Behavior

One way to consider the process of developing software is to evaluate the way the good software developers work to produce quality software. In a now famous study of designer behavior [GUI89], researchers made a videotape of designers as they worked on a problem. Rather than following a strictly top-down approach — or a strictly bottom-up one, for that matter — the researchers found designers jumped all over what turned out to be levels of abstraction in the resulting design. Their "thinking behavior" is suggested by the graph in Figure 2.2. What we see, and what the researchers concluded, is that good designers follow a pattern of analysis followed by synthesis, alternating cycles of decomposition and composition.

As we shall see in Section 2.2.4, one of the main criticisms of the waterfall model of software development is that it forces developers into a mode of analysis and decomposition. In Chapter 4 we will see other criticisms of top-down development methods that force developers to begin at the top of a system and work down in a restricted fashion. These approaches fail to consider the way developers normally work and thus may be doomed to failure if applied rigorously in an organization.

2.2 The Waterfall Life Cycle

In 1970, W. W. Royce presented a paper [ROY70] describing what we now know as the waterfall model of software development. The name comes from the popular way of drawing the phases of the model as cascading downward, as shown in Figure

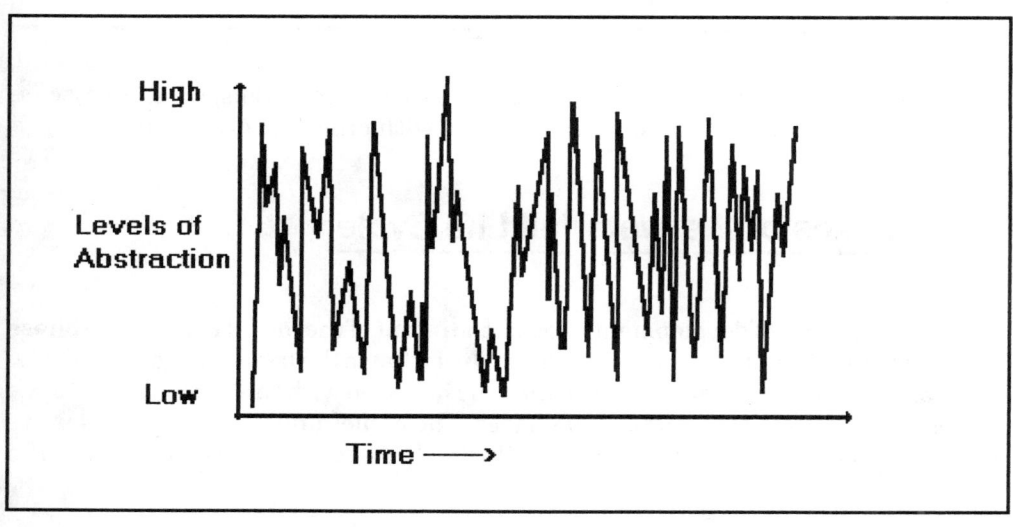

Figure 2.2
Developer thinking behavior — levels of abstraction.

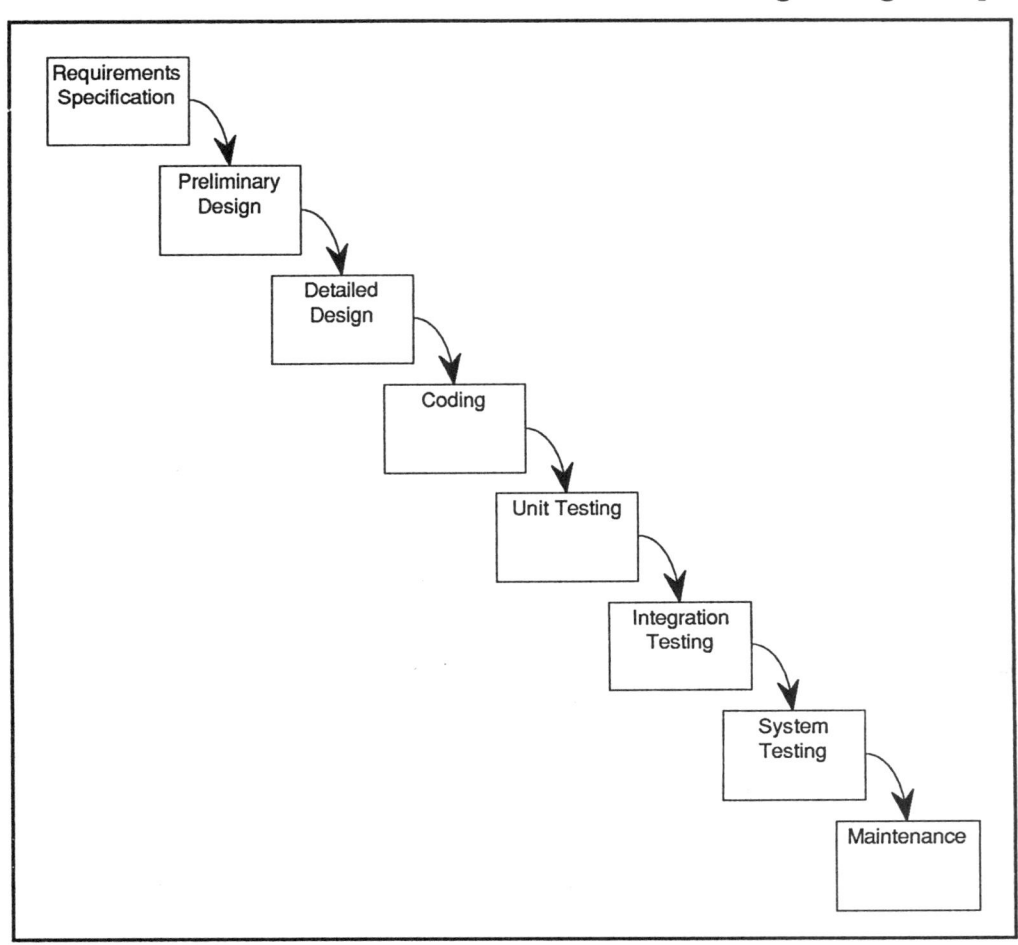

Figure 2.3
Waterfall model
life cycle.

2.3. Since this model is the basis for most of the successor models, we shall discuss it in detail, and use it as a basis of comparison with other life cycle models.

2.2.1 Phases of the Waterfall Life Cycle

We see a series of development phases; the intent of the model is that each phase culminates in a document (or other work product) that is the basis for the next phase. There are several variations at this point: One has to do with the names given to the phases, the other with the number of phases. The names and number of phases are secondary (one paper proposed a "generic" life cycle model with thirteen phases); the important point is that once the basics of the waterfall model are understood, these trivial variations are immediately clear.

2.2.1.1 Requirements Specification

The first phase of the Waterfall life cycle is the subject of most of the debate and study. We have already begged one question by the name we chose. Some variations have a requirements definition phase followed by a specification phase. This difference is worth noting, because it hinges on the relationship between the user (or customer) of the system being developed and the producer (or developer) of the system. The real issue in this phase (or phases) is the communication between the user and the producer. Very often the user doesn't know the capabilities of the producer, and conversely, the producer doesn't know what the user really wants.

Now the relationship: Are the user and the producer adversaries, or do they cooperate? If there is an adversarial relationship, it is most useful to have a requirements definition phase, in which the user states the system requirements, followed by a specification phase, in which the producer specifies how the requirements will be met. The requirements document then usually serves as the basis of a contract between the user and the producer.

The other choice is for the user and the producer to jointly produce one document, which we call the requirements specification. Such a cooperative effort reduces the adversarial relationship and this typically leads to better-quality systems. The choice between these two relationships is project-dependent; for our discussion we chose the cooperative scenario.

During the requirements specification phase, the user and the producer must work together to arrive at a description of the system to be developed. The audience for this description is broader than that for any of the other documents produced in the waterfall model phases; it includes the user and various producer functions: the developer, the system tester, project management, the maintainer, and a host of secondary users, including installation, training, quality assurance, configuration management, marketing, and (hopefully not) the legal department. Each of these roles or functions has its own information needs thus the user and the producer have a tremendous burden to create the appropriate information. Studies show that over half (some say as high as 60 percent) of all system problems are due to an inadequate requirements specification.

There are several standards that attempt to define what information should appear in a requirements specification. The most comprehensive is DoD 2167A, the Department of Defense standard, which occupies two notebooks. The IEEE professional society has produced a requirements specification standard (IEEE Std. 830), which is being revised as we go to press. Commercial CASE products define a de facto standard by the capabilities they support. We think the best standard is project-dependent. One approach would be to assemble all the users (among those listed

above), ask what information they need (and will use) in a requirements specification, and use this to guide both the requirements specification process and the eventual review of the product.

2.2.1.2 Preliminary Design

Given a description of system requirements, the task of preliminary design is to start transforming the what into a viable how. The traditional distinction between requirements specification and preliminary design is that the former focuses on what, while the latter describes how. This distinction sounds nice, but in practice, it's hard to apply. We like to think of design as the process of allocating resources to functionality or, conversely, assigning functionality to resources. Resources can be hardware components, software components, data structures, program modules, interfaces, and so on.

The goal of preliminary design is to devise an architecture of software and hardware components such that, when executed, the required functionality is implemented. If the issue in requirements specification is communication, then the issue in design is creativity. Design is by far the most creative phase of the waterfall model and, because of this, the phase least amenable to measurement and assessment (and teaching, for that matter). The best advice we have is to propose trial architectures and play mainline scenarios of behavior (derived from the requirements specification) against the trial architectures. One useful consideration in this "playing" is that performance requirements come into play here (sorry for the pun). One architecture may be better than another with respect to some performance criterion. This is the phase at which to look for such differences.

The end product of preliminary design is a document, sometimes called the "preliminary design" or "high level design" specification, which describes the major software and hardware components and the interfaces among them. In addition, the major data structures are identified as part of this phase. In practice, we have found these interfaces to be one of the most important parts of this phase, and because our view of design centers on the allocation of functionality of components, we strongly recommend some form of matrix representation of this assignment, in which rows correspond to functions and columns correspond to components. An "X" in a row/column position signifies that the function is partially implemented by the component. It turns out that such a function/component matrix is surprisingly useful, especially during the maintenance phase.

2.2.1.3 Detailed Design

The detailed design phase is a point of "fan-out" in a project. The components identified in the preliminary design phase are fleshed out at a more detailed level. Here we make algorithmic choices, implement project naming conventions, attempt to find reusable components, and so on. The alert reader might ask why we didn't look for reusable components during preliminary design. The short answer is that to do so lets the tail wag the dog: It's better to postulate what you really need and then see if you have something that will work. The U. S. Navy calls this "beat to fit, paint to match."

One of the main goals of detailed design is to see that the interfaces identified during preliminary design "will work." It's easy to imagine a data structure, for example, that seemed sufficient early on and is used by several modules. At detailed design time, we know more about the project, and we might find out that one of the client modules has information needs that are not met by the data structure.

The outcome of this phase is a detailed design specification that includes the low-level logic of the modules and definitions of the data structures used and the interfaces between the modules.

2.2.1.4 Coding

Coding used to be the primary activity of software development; we have all seen the cartoon in which the project leader says to a team of programmers in a sea of desks: "You guys start coding, I'll go and find out what they want." The point of the early waterfall model phases is to eliminate the recoding and testing that has proved to be so expensive and time-consuming. Given a good detailed design, coding should represent no more than 15 percent of the total project development effort.

Coding takes the design specifications created in the previous steps and translates them into implementation-specific language and file constructs. Some form of programming language may be used in this phase to manually create a system that supports the functionality defined in the first phase, or an automated tool may generate the code from the design specifications.

2.2.1.5 Unit Testing

Unit testing is the first of three levels of testing; one consequence of the waterfall model is that bottom-up testing is the most natural approach. Individual components are tested, as units, to see if they support their postulated functions within their given interfaces. If they do, the assumption is that their contribution to overall system function is correct and that they can be depended upon by others. Here is one point where the function/component matrix comes in handy. Unit testing can be performed by an independent (from the coder) tester; we have found in practice, however, that it is more efficient to have one person do the detailed design, coding, and unit testing of a module.

2.2.1.6 Integration Testing

Integration testing is the first opportunity for synthesis in the waterfall model. This is the point at which separately tested units are tested together, the objective being to verify the interfaces. There are several approaches to this integration: bottom-up, top-down, and "big bang." We find the bottom-up approach to be the most natural, particularly because some form of integration testing can begin as soon as enough modules have been unit tested. Top-down testing requires that the uppermost modules be unit tested first; these are then integrated with the next level, and so on down the decomposition tree. For completeness, the "big bang" approach lets you wait until everything has been unit tested; then you put it all together and listen for the big bang. The essential problem here is that when (not if!) something goes wrong, finding the problem is very difficult.

2.2.1.7 System Testing

The highest level of developer testing is system testing. This is also the level at which the user might do customer acceptance testing. In fact, there is an economy if the user and producer jointly develop the requirements specification and then jointly perform system testing. One good question is to find where integration testing stops and system testing starts. The V-shaped drawing of the waterfall model phases in Figure 2.4 helps clarify this. We like to think that system-level testing is conducted only with system-level inputs and outputs that are available to the user. Integration testing, on the other hand, usually involves stub or driver modules, and utilities that let the tester capture memory contents.

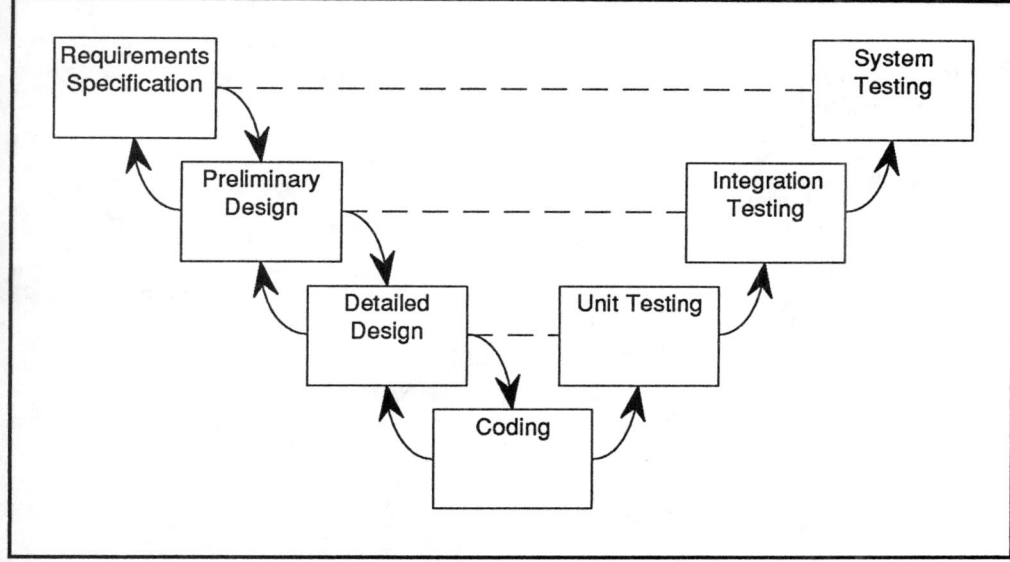

Figure 2.4
Levels of
abstraction in
the waterfall
model.

2.2.1.8 Maintenance

Once a software product has been developed, it must be delivered to the user community and supported throughout its useful life. The maintenance of the software produce may extend for 20 years or even longer, depending on the organization. Maintenance includes all the previous stages combined into a single stage, and includes all, or at least most, of the deliverables created.

Maintenance is chiefly concerned with the evolution of a system, based on changing client needs. Software products cannot stay static, but must evolve to include more functionality, meet different requirements, and adopt to new technologies. Most estimates place maintenance at over 60 percent of the overall cost of a system, indicating that the most potential savings in the SDLC can be realized in this phase. Recently, some automated tools have begun to address the needs of software maintenance, specifically reverse engineering products. These products are described in more depth in Chapter 11.

2.2.2 Symmetries and Feedback

It is important to understand the symmetries and feedback cycles within the waterfall model. The symmetries help us understand the dividing lines between pairs of phases and how the levels of abstraction are mapped between development

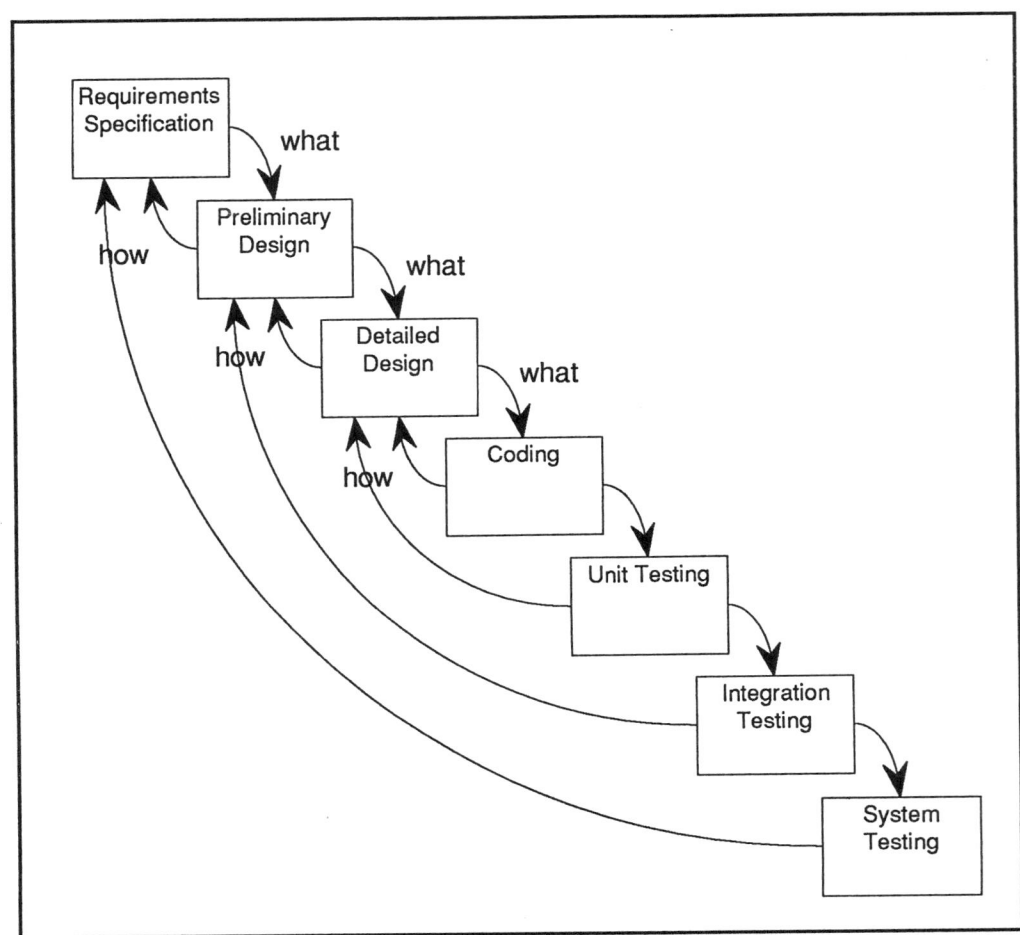

Figure 2.5
Primary feedback
cycles in the
waterfall model.

and testing. In Figure 2.5, there are short feedback cycles between adjacent early phases; these are labeled _what_ and _how_. The preliminary design answers how the requirements specification is implemented, the detailed design answers how the preliminary design is implemented, and the coding answers how the detailed design is implemented. Each of these short feedback cycles is often best accomplished with a formal software review.

The longer feedback cycles are between levels of testing and the early phases. We can picture an "axis of symmetry" running through the coding phase. If people were infallible developers, we would run through the waterfall model phases just once, and the longer feedback cycles would demonstrate that the corresponding early phases were correct. We will soon see that this is one of the major weaknesses of the waterfall model.

2.2.3 Advantages

Of all the life cycle models in use, the Waterfall model is the most widely accepted and practiced. It has been in explicit use since the Garmisch-Partenkirken conference in 1968, and it was obviously in use in a limited way before that. One of the reasons for this longevity is that it works — it serves the needs of organizations. For one thing, it is a very comfortable framework: The phases of the model correspond exactly to levels of abstraction, to organization hierarchy charts, and to packaging levels available in most programming languages.

These levels were borrowed from hardware designers, who think in terms of systems, subsystems, frames, racks, cards, chips, and gates. These compatible treelike structures provide for "natural" management points. Each phase has a defined work product that can be reviewed and approved.

The concept of functional decomposition (see Chapter 4) maps easily into a work breakdown structure for project management purposes, and the fan-out at the early stages maps to personnel allocation, so that many modules can be developed in parallel, thereby reducing the overall development interval. Within this framework, all participants can easily see how they fit in, and where the whole project is going. Project management has the control points it needs to get progress reports and early warning of possible project slips.

2.2.4 Disadvantages

Given all this, what more could we ask? One inherent problem with the waterfall model is its dependence on a linear sequential development process, where one phase must be completed before another phase can begin. This is impractical on most projects, as work continues on the requirements specification phase while the preliminary or detailed design is underway. This view also prohibits an evolutionary perspective from being used in software development, something we have found essential to delivering quality software products.

Perhaps the best reference on the limitations of the waterfall life cycle is by Bill Agresti [AGR86], who makes the following observations.

2.2.4.1 Perfect Foresight

Because the waterfall model is intertwined so closely with functional decomposition, it is vulnerable to the basis on which decomposition is made. If the developers

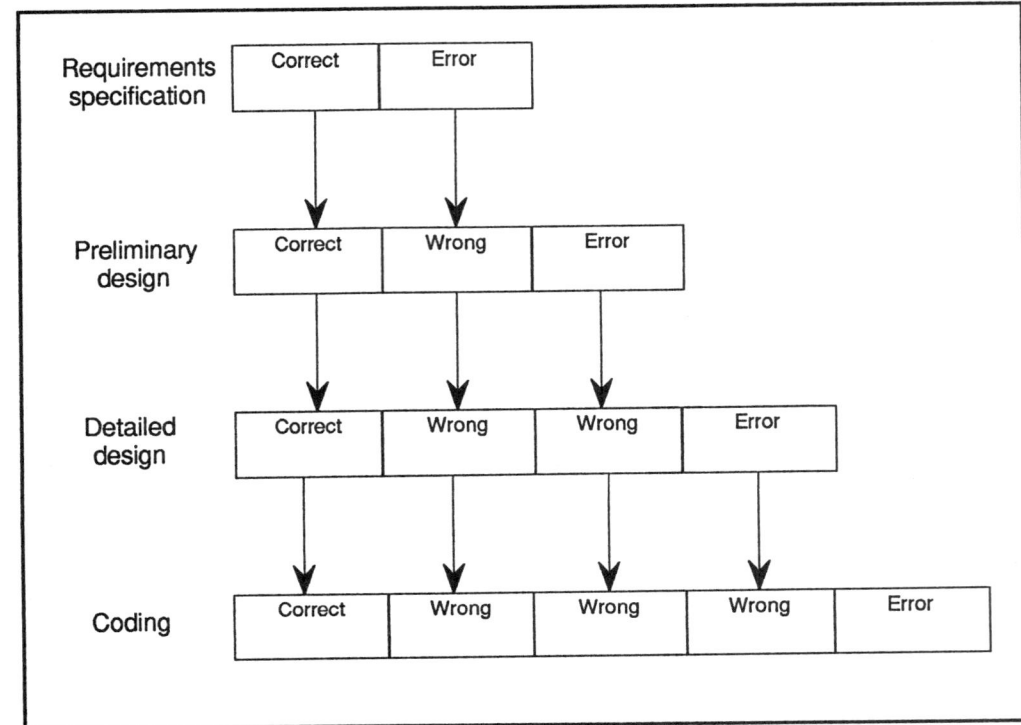

Figure 2.6
Error propagation
in the waterfall
model.

had what Agresti calls "perfect foresight," they could anticipate all the consequences of their early decisions. Obviously no one has this gift, and what typically happens is that decisions made early in a project end up being changed because of information gathered later in the project. This often leads to projects that run late and require additional staffing to be competed on time.

Closely tied to this is the need for complete understanding. If mistakes are made and not caught, they propagate, and we get the error waterfall shown in Figure 2.6.

2.2.4.2 Long Feedback Cycles

We discussed the feedback cycles in the preceding section. The consequence of these is that if mistakes are found during system testing, a lot of time has elapsed since the customer last saw the project at the requirements specification review. This means that any errors not found until system testing will require very expensive fixes. Some studies estimate that the repair cost of such errors is 100 times the cost to fix the same error at the requirements specification review. Figure 2.5

displays an idealistic view of waterfall development, in which the developers make few mistakes. A better view is shown in Figure 2.7, which shows that when an error is found, the scope of the error indicates that possibly several phases need to be repeated.

The real significance of Figure 2.7 is that each of the additional feedback cycles shown represents actual work that must be done, yet this effort is rarely ever planned for initially, so the idealistic work breakdown structures simply do not include all the feedback effort shown. Small wonder deadlines are missed!

2.2.4.3 Artificial View for Management

Recall the study of developer behavior mentioned earlier in this chapter. This behavior simply doesn't fit the waterfall model, with its sequential linear view of development. Given this conflict, which view should prevail — the developer's view or the management view? Designers usually find it unnatural to be told they cannot look ahead into the next phase to see the consequences of decisions they must make. Likewise, project managers cannot tolerate developers that jump around, starting some tasks for which the prerequisite tasks are still unfinished. Some authors maintain that "any form of life cycle model exists solely for the convenience of management" [MCC81]. To the extent that a life cycle is artificial, they suggest, it is clearly detrimental to any project.

2.2.4.4 Late Synthesis

We mentioned earlier that the first opportunity for synthesis in the waterfall model occurs at integration testing time. The waterfall model fosters analysis to the near exclusion of synthesis, allowing synthesis only in the middle stage of testing. By this time, making changes is far more difficult because of all the dependencies that have been created. Late synthesis is also closely related to the long feedback cycle problem.

What is required is recognition that synthesis provides substantial benefits in earlier stages of the life cycle, including preliminary and detailed design, and that alternative cycles of analysis and synthesis may deliver the best result. Synthesis allows for the formulation of potential solutions in the design that can be tested for acceptability in the finished product, but analysis is required to verify if the proposed solution has other, prohibitive implications.

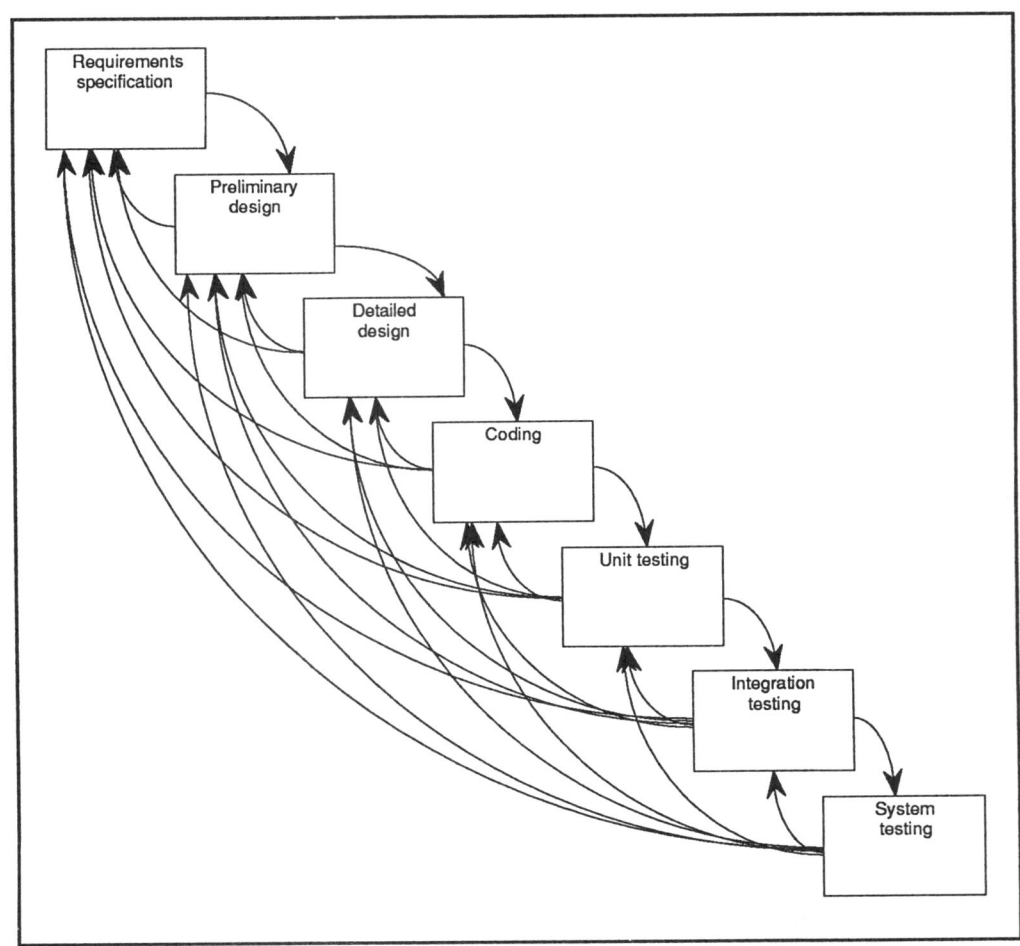

Figure 2.7
Latent feedback
cycles in the
waterfall model.

2.2.4.5 Awkward Manpower Loading

We apparently contradict ourselves here, because earlier we said that an advantage of the waterfall model is that it allows for manpower fan-out in the early stages. While this is a nice concept, not many organizations have vast manpower pools from which these resources can be drawn. This is compounded by the reality of the "latent" feedback cycles shown in Figure 2.7.

Our experience suggests that most projects have less staff available in later stages, not more, and often these staff are overworked and made to take shortcuts to meet the deadline. This leads to poor-quality software delivered to users and substantial modifications required when the system is in production.

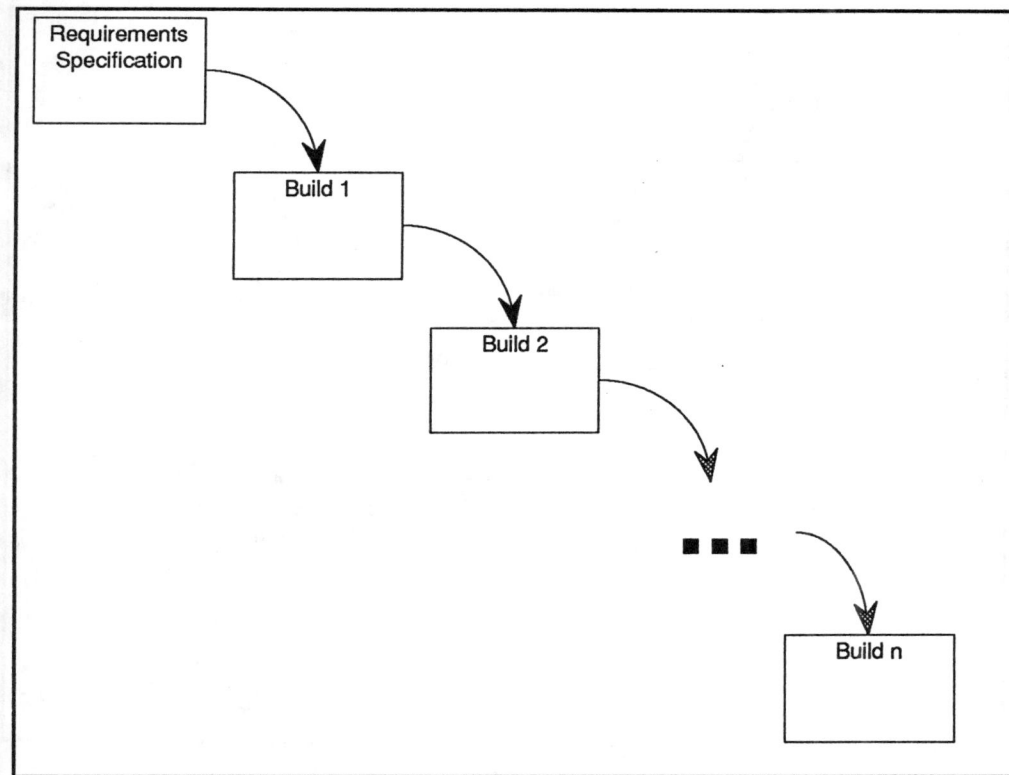

Figure 2.8
Incremental life
cycle.

2.3 Waterfall Variations

After a decade of use, organizations discovered Agresti's objections for themselves. Their responses to these problems were manifested in two variations of the
original waterfall model.

2.3.1 Incremental Development

The difficulty of meeting the manpower loading problem led to the simplest
variation of the waterfall model — incremental development. As shown in Figures
2.8 and 2.9, software development in this model consists of the original requirements specification followed by a series of builds (increments, loads), where each
build spans the original waterfall model phases from detailed design through
system testing, plus a new phase, regression testing. Incremental development

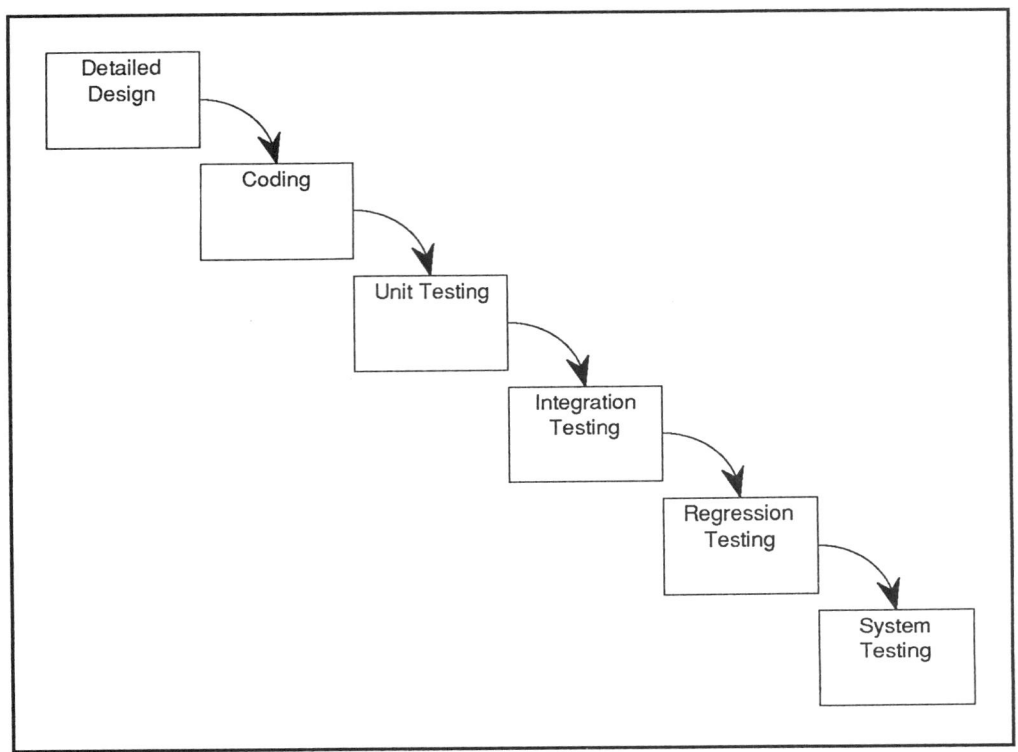

Figure 2.9
Incremental life
cycle — build
contents.

moves incrementally, as its name implies, adding detail in increments as the project proceeds.

With incremental development, the task of preliminary design is somewhat expanded: It is now necessary to identify the build sequence and describe, in detail, the contents of each build. The function/component matrix discussed earlier becomes very useful at this point. Several questions must be resolved: How many builds shall there be? What are the relative sizes of the builds? What is their relative difficulty? How much of the original waterfall shall a build span? The answer to most of these is a consequence of the new phase — regression testing.

Every build after the first can be seen as a superset of the previous build. As such, new builds must be integrated with the software in the previous build. Everyone who has ever made a change to an existing system knows that changes frequently have unexpected side effects, and that things that used to work no longer work. Hence the need for regression testing. It might be better to change system testing to progression testing. We need to know that the contents of build 2 don't disrupt portions of build 1 that were successfully progression tested, and similarly for the remaining builds.

In addition to regression testing, builds also contain the rework that is shown in Figure 2.7, the latent feedback cycles. Recall that these all represent tasks that are necessitated when errors are found at some level of testing. Because incremental development forces consideration of all this rework, we might expect that the corresponding work breakdown structures would be more accurate. In our experience, they are. Thus when we do build 2, we make corrections to the build 1 version of the preliminary design, the build 1 version of the detailed design, and portions of build 1 code. We do unit testing on build 2 modules, and then integrate them, both among themselves (hard) and together with build 1 software (more natural). The next step is regression testing, which may be as simple as a repetition of build 1 progression testing. This turns out to be a poor choice, especially when a project is divided into a large number of builds. Build 1 regression tests are executed $n - 1$ times!

At the end of regression testing, a choice must be made: If regression testing is deemed successful, build 2 progression testing can begin. Sometimes it happens that regression testing is a total disaster, and there is no point in progression testing.

The repeated execution of regression testing suggests that the build sequence should be relatively small, say less than six. This is pretty arbitrary, but we once worked on a project that was divided into nine builds, and the retesting became very significant.

What about the size of builds? If each build is about the same size, the carry-over of rework to the next build gets larger and larger (there's probably an analogy with the national debt here). If manpower loading is a problem, one strategy is to make build 1 the largest, and make the remaining builds successively smaller. The resulting effort per build is more uniform.

This strategy works against one of the advantages of incremental development: early synthesis. Recall that synthesis first occurs in integration testing. Since we develop only one build at a time, at least some synthesis occurs earlier. Theoretically, the user could see the results of build 1 progression testing when it is complete, thereby significantly reducing one of the long feedback cycles that is a disadvantage of the waterfall model. All of this argues for a small first build. Similar comments apply to relative difficulty. It's probably better to make the first build the most difficult, and let the others get progressively easier. In practice, however, we tend to make the early builds smaller and easier.

The remaining question is the most interesting: How much of the original waterfall is spanned by a build? We are adamant about preserving preliminary design as a single step, not spreading it out over the series of builds. This is also a point that differentiates incremental development from evolutionary development. The two reasons for this are, first, that if the preliminary design is phased, how are the build contents identified? Second, a phased preliminary design is very likely to contain some early design decisions that turn out to be poor choices for the later builds. We should state, for the record, that we learned this the hard way on the project that had nine builds.

2.3.2 Evolutionary Development

As just noted, evolutionary development is very similar to incremental development. Both models view software as being developed in a sequence of builds, and both involve regression testing. The biggest difference is that the build sequence is not known "up front" in evolutionary development as it is in incremental development. Rather, the contents of a build are determined at the completion of the previous build. The user sees the previous build and, based on it, helps determine the contents of the next build. This forces preliminary design to become part of a build, and we know what that means! The system evolves, in response to directions from the user. In this sense, the feedback problem of waterfall development is even further resolved. The main problem is that, in the evolution of a system, some generations (or builds) may be less well developed than earlier generations.

2.4 Rapid Prototyping

Rapid prototyping is another response to the deficiencies of the waterfall model. Earlier, we noted that one major problem of the requirements specification phase is communication between the user and the producer. The user understands the application, but frequently doesn't know what the producer can develop. At the same time, the producer knows his or her capabilities, but doesn't know what the user really wants. This communication gap is complicated by the computing jargon that producers use and by terms that have special meanings in the user's application. To make matters worse, a producer might do an excellent job of capturing the users requirements in a medium such as data flow diagrams, then find that the customer doesn't know how to read them. With waterfall development, any difference between the user's and the producer's views will go unnoticed until the system is delivered. Once the delivered system is in use, the user can easily find points of dissatisfaction.

Barry Boehm jokes about the user's Lament: "I don't know what I want, but I'll recognize it when I see it" [BOE88]. There's an important truth hidden in that line; it's the difference between a structural view, which describes what a system is, and an operational view, which describes what a system does. producers tend to be more comfortable with the structural view, while users perceive a system in terms of what it does.

Rapid prototyping answers both the long feedback problem and the user/producer communication problem by improving communication at the onset of a project. Looking at Figure 2.10, we see that the requirements specification phase is replaced by a three-element cycle. In order to elicit a better requirements definition, the producer develops a prototype of the system, and then the customer "plays with" the prototype to see if that is what is really wanted. Note that the customer gets a

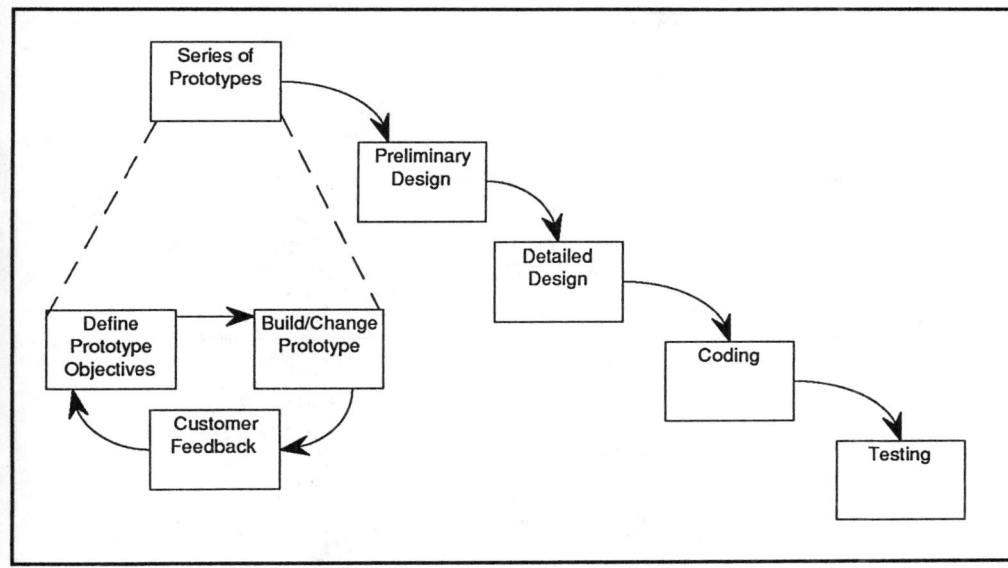

Figure 2.10
Rapid prototyping
life cycle.

chance to see the system "in use" very early, so rapid prototyping also accomplishes early synthesis. Based on prototype usage, the customer can more clearly state the parts that are acceptable and those that are either deficient or missing. It may be necessary to build a second, and even a third prototype. Once the user is satisfied that the prototype represents the requirements, the prototype is the requirements specification. From that point on, development proceeds through the remaining traditional waterfall phases. We will cover prototyping in more detail in Chapter 9.

Rapid prototyping is highly effective, especially in applications where the user interface is the main issue. Getting an early, accurate, and complete definition of the user's expectations provides the "perfect foresight" that the remaining waterfall part of the development requires. Note also that the error part of the error waterfall is Figure 2.6 is greatly reduced. Several studies attest to the fact that the time needed to develop a series of prototypes is more than offset by the reduction in error correction after testing cycles. We can offer one anecdotal experience. An undergraduate software engineering class was asked to develop the Library problem (see Chapter 3) during a one-semester course. There were five teams, each with four or five members. One team chose to use rapid prototyping; the other four followed the waterfall model. In a thirteen week development interval (in one semester), the rapid prototyping team delivered their system two weeks early!

On the negative side, rapid prototyping can make project managers very nervous. How many prototyping cycles will be needed? In general, we cannot say. This makes scheduling impossible until the requirements specification phase is done. Another problem is that a prototype, if kept, is an unusual artifact to maintain

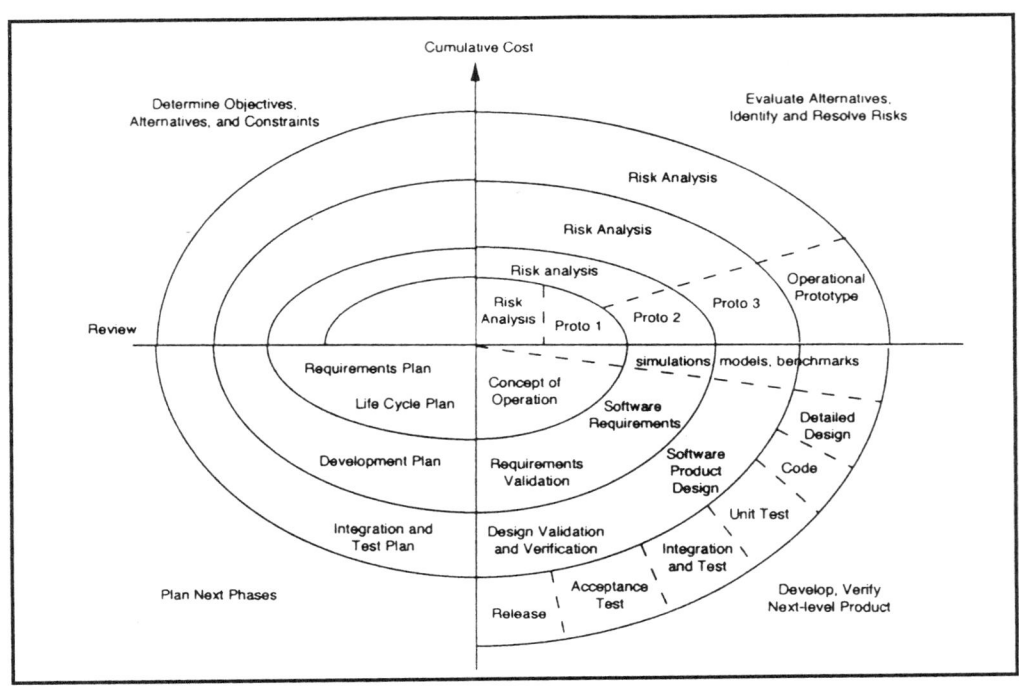

Figure 2.11
Spiral life cycle
model.

under configuration management. Finally, it will always be tempting, especially when schedules get tight, to "borrow" components from a prototype, with the intention of "doing them right" later. Rapid prototyping is a requirements specification technique; it does nothing for the remaining waterfall model phases except provide a very good starting point.

2.5 The Spiral Life Cycle

The spiral model developed by Barry Boehm [BOE88] is a blend of evolutionary development and rapid prototyping. The main contribution of the spiral model is that before any work is done, a risk analysis and a cost/benefit analysis are performed. As seen in Figure 2.11, the spiral model shows development activities proceeding through four quadrants. In the first quadrant, the focus is on determining the objectives of a project, determining what alternatives might be available, such as build or buy, and identifying the primary constraints, such as time, budget, available talent, market pressure, etc. In the second quadrant, the focus shifts to evaluating the alternatives and identifying risks. Alternatives are chosen to reduce the risk of the project. Next, the focus is on developing and verifying the next level of the project; and in the fourth quadrant, the next phases are planned.

Each spiral circuit around the four quadrants is called a "round," and any round culminates in a review followed by either commitment to the next round or rework of portions of the round just completed. Round 0 is concerned only with project feasibility. During this round, the high-level risks and mainline alternatives and constraints lead to a go/no-go decision on a project. Round 0 represents only a small effort, of the order of two or three person-months. If the review at the end of round 1 results in a "go," the commitment for the next round is to develop a concept of operations. This is to ensure that all parties share a common view of the project, and to identify further, more specific, risks.

Round 1 usually requires four to six times the effort of round 0. Again, once the round 1 activities are complete, there is a formal review which may or may not result in commitment to the next round. From this point on, the spiral model echoes the phases of the waterfall model. Round 2 is dedicated to high-level requirements, and round 3 covers preliminary design. The succeeding rounds may be used to produce a build sequence.

Notice that the spiral model makes extensive use of rapid prototyping and emphasizes the identification of risks and alternatives. The framework is flexible enough to permit the incorporation of desirable features of many of the life cycle models we have discussed.

2.6 Future Life Cycles

There are four other life cycle models that are on the practitioner's horizon. Some of these have been used successfully on realistic applications; others are "laboratory curiosities." We include them here because they capture the direction of the trend in software development life cycle models.

2.6.1 Operational Specification

An operational specification was first proposed by Pamela Zave at Bell Labs in 1982 [ZAV82]. In her view of operational specification, the developer uses a high-level, functional, applicative language to specify a system. Zave developed a language she named PAISLey, which is a significant extension of LISP, that facilitates the description of highly concurrent tasks. A PAISLey specification can be interpretively executed, thereby providing many of the benefits of rapid prototyping. In Zave's view, the operational specification is the implementation.

The operational specification life cycle model is based on the executable specification aspect of Zave's work. As seen in Figure 2.12, the difference between traditional waterfall model development and the operational specification paradigm is that the requirements specification phase is replaced by a three-element

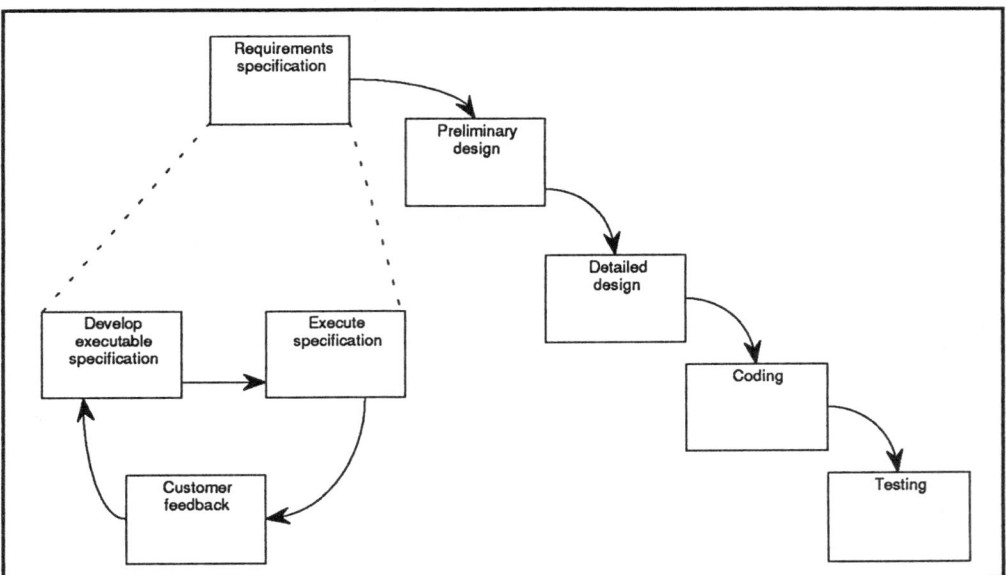

Figure 2.12
Operational
specification
life cycle.

cycle (very similar to rapid prototyping), in which the producer develops an executable specification which is executed by the user. user feedback is gathered, and a new operational specification is developed. This cycle is repeated until the user is satisfied with the specified behavior of the system. Then development proceeds in the remaining traditional waterfall phases.

2.6.1.1 Prototyping vs. Operational Specification

Rapid prototyping and operational specification seem so similar that we need to identify how they are different. Both are used to obtain user feedback. Rapid prototyping is successful in applications where the user interface is a major issue, while operational specification is better used in real-time applications. Unlike rapid prototyping, there is no keep or pitch decision for operational specification, because it only simulates system behavior. Rapid prototyping can use a variety of tools, while operational specification depends on a very formal specification language. Finally, an operational specification is not as rapid as a rapid prototype; more effort is spent in developing the executable requirements specification.

2.6.1.2 Advantages and Disadvantages

Operational specification brings to real-time applications all the advantages that rapid prototyping brings to interface-intensive MIS applications. One advantage of operational specification is that the process is nearly always based on composition. We identify scenarios of system behavior, and express these in the formal specification language; thus the analysis-intensive defect of waterfall development is overcome. One interesting advantage is that with most operational specification languages, system test scenarios can be nearly automatically derived. This accomplishes a very strong view of requirements tracing, and the additional effort of developing a specification is offset by the reduced effort of system test plan development.

The main disadvantage of operational specification is that a powerful specification language must be learned and used. This, in turn, is compounded by there being very few tools that support operational specification. We know of only a few commercially available CASE tools that support operational specification: the StateMate system from i-Logix, Design/CPN from Meta Software, and ASA/Geode/Logiscope from Verilog USA.

2.6.2 Transformational Implementation

Transformational implementation is a "lab curiosity" life cycle model and is shown in Figure 2.13. The entire waterfall life cycle is replaced by a very formal specification which is transformed into a working system that is executed and tested by the user. Any problems are to be resolved by changing the specification. Notice that all the remaining waterfall model phases are eliminated: no more design and coding, no testing, and no more maintenance. Sounds great until we hear the success stories. Transformational implementation has been successfully applied to such systems as finding the greatest common divisor of two integers, inserting an element into a sorted list, and finding the average of a list of numbers.

The main advantage of transformational implementation is that it demonstrates the feasibility of a major breakthrough. We suspect there is a fair analogy between the present state of transformational implementation and the Wright Brothers' first aircraft at Kitty Hawk. Today there are lots of disadvantages: The formal language required is much more difficult than that required for operational specification, the series of transformations is hardly understood, and it is very difficult to scale up to realistic applications. Perhaps the most significant disadvan-

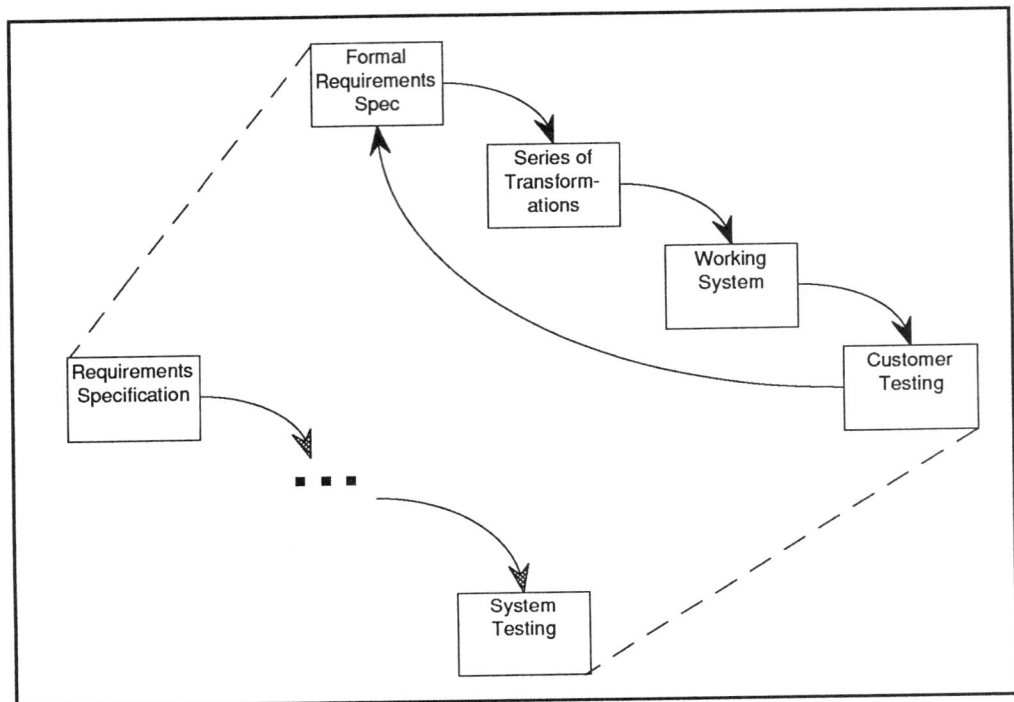

Figure 2.13
Transformational
life cycle.

tage will be the notion of moving maintenance back to the specification phase. Given an undesired behavior, how will the specifier know what changes to make to the formal specification, especially if the series of transformations is not well understood? (Some 800 transformations were needed by the greatest common divisor application.) To capture this difficulty, think about the difficulty of backing up a car with an attached boat trailer. Your steering is just the opposite of that of a car with no trailer. Now imagine backing with five or six boat trailers chained together. It would be very hard for the driver to know what changes are needed to make the chain of boat trailers go where they want.

2.6.3 Software Synthesis

Software synthesis refers to a set of tools that provide automatic code generation from models and specifications of a system. This has been a Holy Grail for software engineering since the 1960s. The quick view is that all of the intelligence needed in the waterfall development process must somehow be put into the program that automatically generates code. This is quite an order, but there are some potential answers. One answer is to compromise on how much code is generated. Some code generators will produce a skeleton consisting of procedure names and pairs of Begin, End statements; others will produce 90 percent of the eventual working COBOL code. Another approach has been to follow the lead of fourth generation languages and produce application-specific code generators. Still another answer is to accept that certain types of software applications are not suited to software synthesis and remove them from the discussion. While this may involve large portions of the software required, it also simplifies the technology required to implement software synthesis. For instance, embedded or hard real-time systems may be outside the scope of the capabilities of code generation products.

The main difference between software synthesis and transformational implementation is that software synthesis begins with a more familiar starting point, typically data flow diagrams (see Chapter 4). Some concepts of software synthesis can also be found in tools that generate code and include an object perspective. One such tool, Netron/CAP, generates or assembles working code from existing objects (frames) that provide generic or specialized facilities.

2.6.4 Repository-Centered Software Development

The last of our futuristic life cycle models is very attractive. Most of the other life cycle models view software development in terms of producing a series of documents or representations which become successively more specific to the point of being executable. Repository-centered software development takes a completely orthogonal view: Suppose we developed a database that contains the information normally produced during software development (see Chapter 1). The database would contain information about inputs, outputs, components, test cases, and so on. Developers would view their work not as the production of documents, but rather as the population of the database. Since the database must be carefully designed, it acquires a new name: repository. Once populated, documents are derived from the repository as very large queries.

Repository-centered software development maximizes the opportunity for parallel development by a large number of developers, and many of the expected project management problems are resolved by existing distributed database management system technology. This paradigm also maximizes composition, and the repository becomes a vehicle for synthesis. Perhaps the most attractive feature is that once any change is made, all "documents" are instantly updated and are, by definition, consistent with one another — quite a boon to configuration management. This advantage is also a weakness: Repository-centered software development will always be very vulnerable to corrupt "data" contents. To make it worse, we know how to review documents, but how will we review a database?

One major drawback to realizing this repository-centered view of software development is in deciding what the underlying repository constructs will be and how they will function. To a large extent, the definitions of these constructs will vary by application. Some in the industry have suggested that there must be some basic, inherent repository components that can be effectively mapped to any software development process. Interestingly, those vendors that have attempted to provide an all-encompassing repository, most notably IBM and DEC, have had problems delivering working products that satisfy even a few of their clients.

Some promising research has been undertaken in this area, including the work of the Amdahl Australian Intelligent Tools Program [CYB92]. In this study, hypertext was used as the integration mechanism for development information collected in a repository. Another study that shows promise is the TAME approach to representing development models [OIV92]. TAME provides a framework for integrating development models, methods, tools, and metrics with an experience factory that provides the recording and analysis or development experience. TAME includes two types of software development knowledge: descriptive, which defines how a process or method is used, and procedural, which is used to set goals, answer questions, and collect data. For more on these two approaches, see Chapter 11.

2.7 References

[AGR86]   Agresti, W.W., *New Paradigms for Software Development*, IEEE Computer Society Press, Washington, D.C., 1986.

[BOE88]   Boehm, B.W.,"A Spiral Model of Software Development and Enhancement," *IEEE Computer*, vol. 21, no. 5, IEEE Computer Society Press, Washington, D.C., May 1988, pp. 61 - 72.

[CYB92]   Cybulski, J.L. and K. Reed, "A Hypertext Based Software-Engineering Environment," *IEEE Software*, March 1992, pp. 62-68.

[GUI89]   Guindon, R., "Knowledge Exploited by Experts during software systems design," *MCC Tech. Rpt. STP-032-90*, October 4, 1989.

[IEEE84]   Software Engineering Technical Committee of the IEEE Computer Society, *IEEE Guide to Software Requirements Specification*, ANSI/IEEE Std. 830-1984.

[MCC81]   McCracken, D. D. and Jackson, M. A. "A Minority Dissenting Position," *Systems Analysis and Design — A Foundation for the 1980's*, W. W. Cotterman et al.,editors, Elsevier Publishing Co., Inc., 1981.

[OIV92]   Oivo, M., and V.R. Basili, "Representing Software Engineering Models: The TAME Goal Oriented Approach," *IEEE Trans. on Soft. Eng.*, vol. 18, no. 10, pp. 886-898.

[PRE88]   Pressman, R., *Software Engineering:A Beginner's Guide*, McGraw-Hill, 1988.

[ROY70]   Royce, W. W., "Managing the Development of Large Software Systems: Concepts and Techniques," *Proceedings of WESCON*, August 1970.

[ZAV82]   Zave, P., "An operational approach to requirement specifications for embedded sysstems," *IEEE Trans. on Soft. Eng.*, vol. SE-8, no. 3, pp. 250-269, May 1982.

Chapter 3
The Application Domain

Prior to describing the six popular software development techniques in Chapters 4 through 9, we supplement our discussion on development life cycles (from the previous chapter) with some background on software application domains.

In this chapter, we will introduce the concept of application types or domains, along with the two example problems which are used in subsequent chapters to explain and describe the different development techniques. We also review possible taxonomies for characterizing applications and introduce our own taxonomy for applications. Our three-dimensional taxonomy is based on the primary views or aspects of all software systems, function, data, and control, and these three views map directly to the techniques described in Chapters 4, 5 and 6. We have found the three-dimensional taxonomy to be helpful in discussing development methods. In providing a basis for comparing and selecting appropriate methods and tools, and in this chapter we also suggest possible values for the three axes of our workspace.

We have found this taxonomy to be helpful in our own work, and comparable to taxonomies suggested by other authors. The process provides a framework within which the reader can make intelligent choices among the many possibilities for specifying and designing an application.

3.1 Introduction

Domain: a sphere of influence or activity; the set of elements to which a mathematical or logical variable is limited; the set on which a function is defined.

Taxonomy: the study of the general principles of scientific classification; orderly classification of plants and animals according to their presumed natural relationships. [Webster]

One of the main contributions of object-oriented thinking is a renewed awareness of the application domain. The early object-oriented writers [BOO83] asked us to consider an application in two spaces: the problem domain and the solution domain. Choice of appropriate objects reduces the "conceptual distance" between the problem and the solution space, thus the solution has higher fidelity to the real-world problem. More recently, object-oriented thinkers have asked us to focus on "domain analysis."

Compare this emphasis on problem domain considerations to the methodology heyday of the 1970s, when purveyors of new methodologies typically claimed that their notation, technique, or representation was universally applicable. Practical experience suggests that no individual method or technique is equally applicable to all possible software applications.

In this text, we define the problem domain to be that area of interest or study specific to the known problem. We further define the solution domain to be that area of technical and cultural focus for a solution to the problem defined in the problem domain. While there may be multiple solutions to a problem, they will all theoretically fall within the solution domain. Later in the chapter we will investigate possible application domains and application types.

When looking at the types of software systems commonly developed, we find it is helpful to characterize or categorize these applications into discrete, albeit arbitrary, software system types. Others in the industry have suggested possible application types, including Pressman [PRE88] [PRE87] and Yourdon [YOU89].

In this chapter, we present two applications that will be used throughout the book to illustrate the six viewpoints discussed in Chapters 4 through 9. We chose these examples for several reasons: They are very familiar, so "conceptual distance" is reduced, they are very typical of the kinds of applications that confront practitioners, they are small enough to be treated fairly completely, and they illustrate many of the issues that the various viewpoints try to address. One last reason: They are strong enough to show some of the limitations of the six viewpoints.

3.2 The Library Problem

The library problem is very popular in software engineering literature. It has been a conference problem at several major national and international conferences [WIN88], the Software Engineering Institute uses it in selected curriculum modules, and, more recently, various CASE vendors use it as a demonstration problem. The Jackson design advocates claim it is the "best example" for their method [CAM86], and a very formal specification is given in [KEM85]. The usual problem statement follows.

3.2.1 Problem Statement

Consider a small university library system with the following transactions or functions:

1. Add a copy of a book to the library.
2. Remove a copy of a book from the library.
3. Check out a copy of a book from the library.
4. Return a copy of a book to the library.
5. Get the list of books in the library written by a particular author.
6. Get the list of books currently checked out by a particular borrower.
7. Find out what borrower most recently checked out a particular copy of a book.

Within the library system, there are two types of users: library staff and ordinary borrowers. Transactions 1, 2, 3, 4, 5, 6, and 7 are restricted to library staff, while ordinary borrowers can use transaction 6 to find out the list of books they currently have checked out.

Finally, there are three additional constraints on the library system:

1. All copies of books in the library must be either available for checkout or checked out (no reserve books).
2. No copy of a book can be both available for checkout and checked out at the same time.
3. An ordinary borrower may not have more than a predefined number of books checked out at one time (there is a set borrowing limit).

3.2.2 Discussion

In a software development project for the library problem, a first step would be to express the given requirements with some notation using an associated technique. In the process of reexpressing the stated requirements, it is likely that some flaws or unspecified issues in the original narrative requirements description will be discovered. Some examples of outstanding issues for the library problem include:

1. How does the library system differentiate between staff users and ordinary borrowers?
2. What is the "predefined maximum borrowing limit" for a user? How is this information entered?
3. Regarding transaction 5, what does "in the library" mean? The possibilities are "available for checkout" (i.e., physically in the library) or "either available for checkout or checked out" (owned by the library).
4. Transactions 6 and 7 suggest data structures which, with prolonged system use, will grow very large. How will these structures be managed by the library system? (See point 6 below)
5. Where do library books come from? Where do they go when they are removed?

Additional requirements for the library system might include the following:

6. Modify the library system to archive the lists of books checked out to a specific user and the list of users that have checked out a book when these lists have 100 entries.
7. Modify the library system to implement a two-week loan period and to apply a late fee of $ 0.50 per day for books returned after the due date. Also create a list of users who have overdue books and a list of all overdue books checked out to a specific user.

In addition, when designing possible solutions to the library problem, there are a number of details that should be addressed, including:

1. How will the library system be implemented? As a mainframe-based, screen-oriented system? As a PC-based system?
2. What type of file or database support is available for implementing the library system? Will a database be used?
3. What programming environment will the library system be developed in? A 3GL? A 4GL?

In Chapters 4 through 9, we will see how the use of notations, representations, and techniques, including data and process modeling, help raise and hopefully resolve some or all of these questions.

3.3 Simple Simon Automatic Teller Machine System

Automatic teller machines (ATM) are common and are good examples of interactive systems. One essential characteristic of interactive systems is that they are event-driven, and the events can occur in many orders. An ATM system has a very strong control component, exhibiting context-dependent behavior, and only minimal process and data components. As such, it is a nice complement to the more traditional Library problem.

3.3.1 Problem Statement

The Simple Simon ATM system communicates with bank customers via the 16 screens shown in Figures 3.2 and 3.3. Using a terminal with the features shown in Figure 3.1, Simple Simon ATM customers can select any of three transaction types, deposits, withdrawals, and balance inquiries, and these can be done on two types of accounts, checking and savings.

When a bank customer arrives at a Simple Simon ATM station, screen S1 is displayed. The bank customer accesses the Simple Simon ATM System with a plastic card encoded with a personal account number (PAN), which is a key to an internal customer account file containing, among other things, the customer's name and account information. If the customer's PAN matches the information in the customer account file, the system presents screen S2 to the customer. If the customer's PAN is not found, screen S4 is displayed, and the card is kept.

At screen S2, the customer is prompted to enter his personal identification number (PIN). If the PIN is correct (i.e., matches the information in the customer account file), the system displays screen S5; otherwise, screen S3 is displayed. The customer has three chances to get the PIN correct; after three failures, screen S4 is displayed, and the card is kept.

On entry to screen S5, the system adds two pieces of information to the customer's account file: the current date and an increment to the number of ATM sessions. The customer selects the desired transaction from the options shown on screen S5; then the system immediately displays screen S6, where the customer chooses the account to which the selected transaction will be applied.

If a balance is requested, the system checks the local ATM file for any unposted transactions, and reconciles these with the beginning balance for that day from the customer account file. Screen S14 is then displayed. If a sensor detects that the transaction receipt tape is gone, the system displays screen S16 and updates a field in the Terminal Control file.

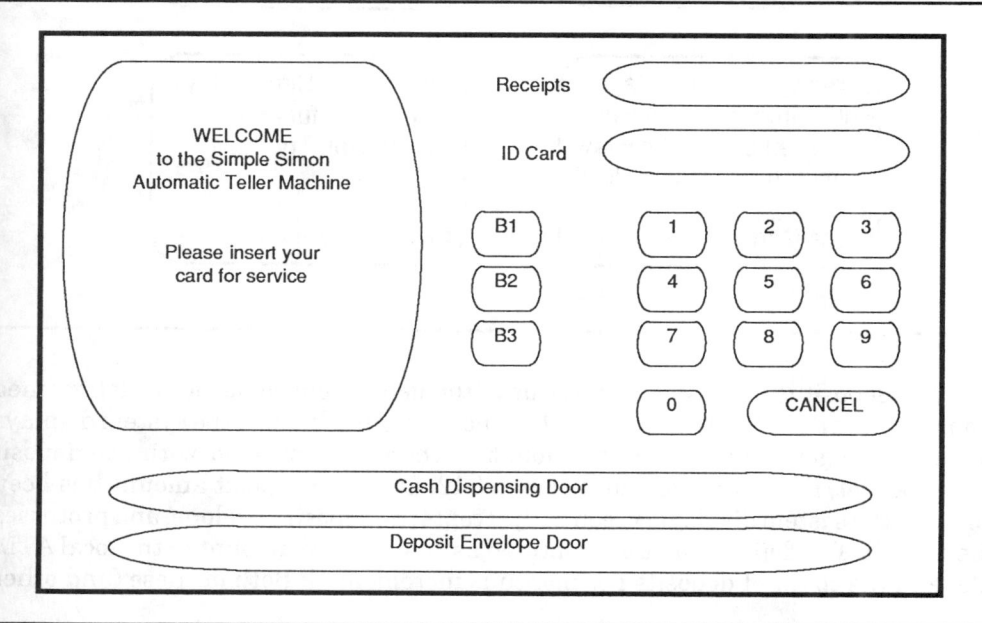

Figure 3.1
Simple Simon ATM user interface.

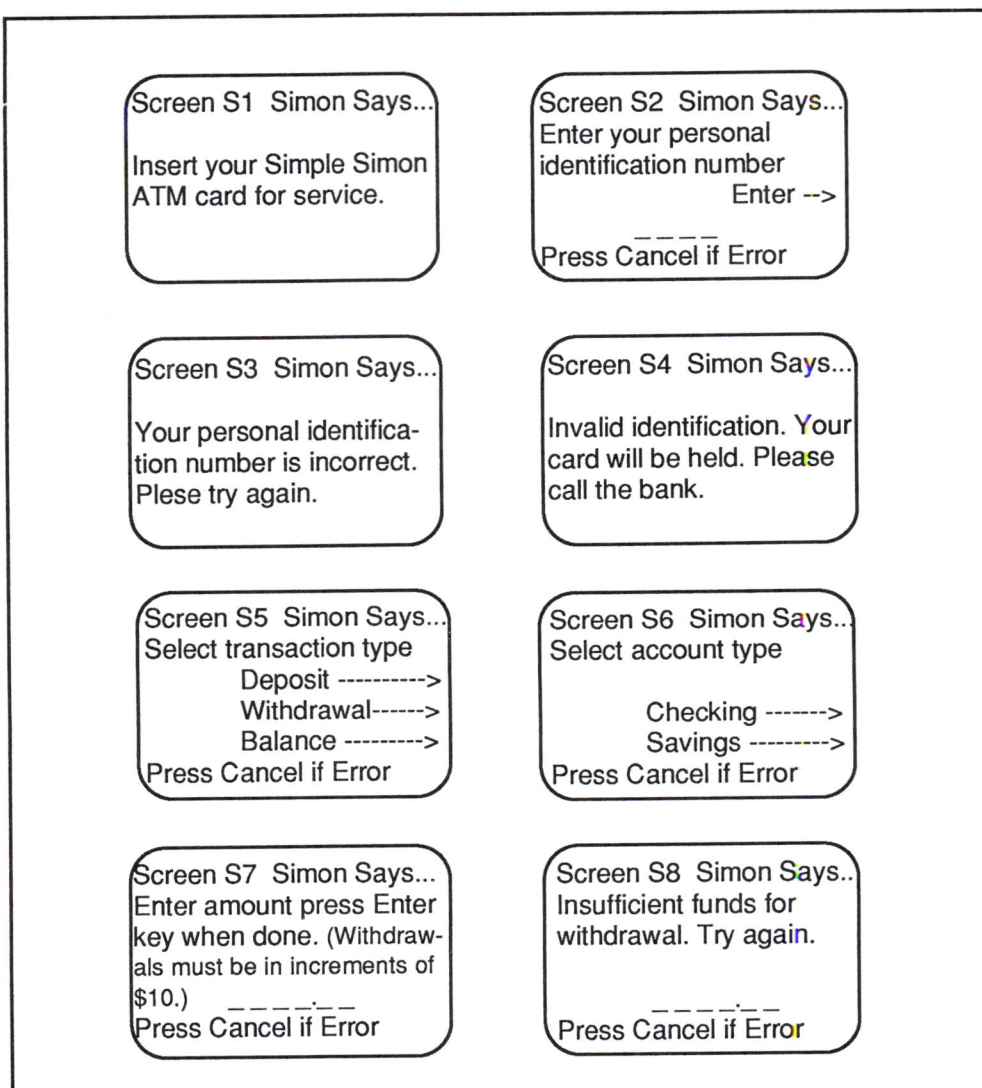

Figure 3.2
SSATM screens.

If a deposit is requested, the status of the deposit envelope slot is determined from a field in the Terminal Control file. If no problem is known, the system displays screen S7 to get the transaction amount. If there is a problem with the deposit envelope slot, the system displays screen S12. Once the deposit amount has been entered, the system displays screen S13, accepts the deposit envelope, and processes the deposit. The deposit amount is entered as an unposted amount in the local ATM file, and the count of deposits per month is incremented. Both of these (and other

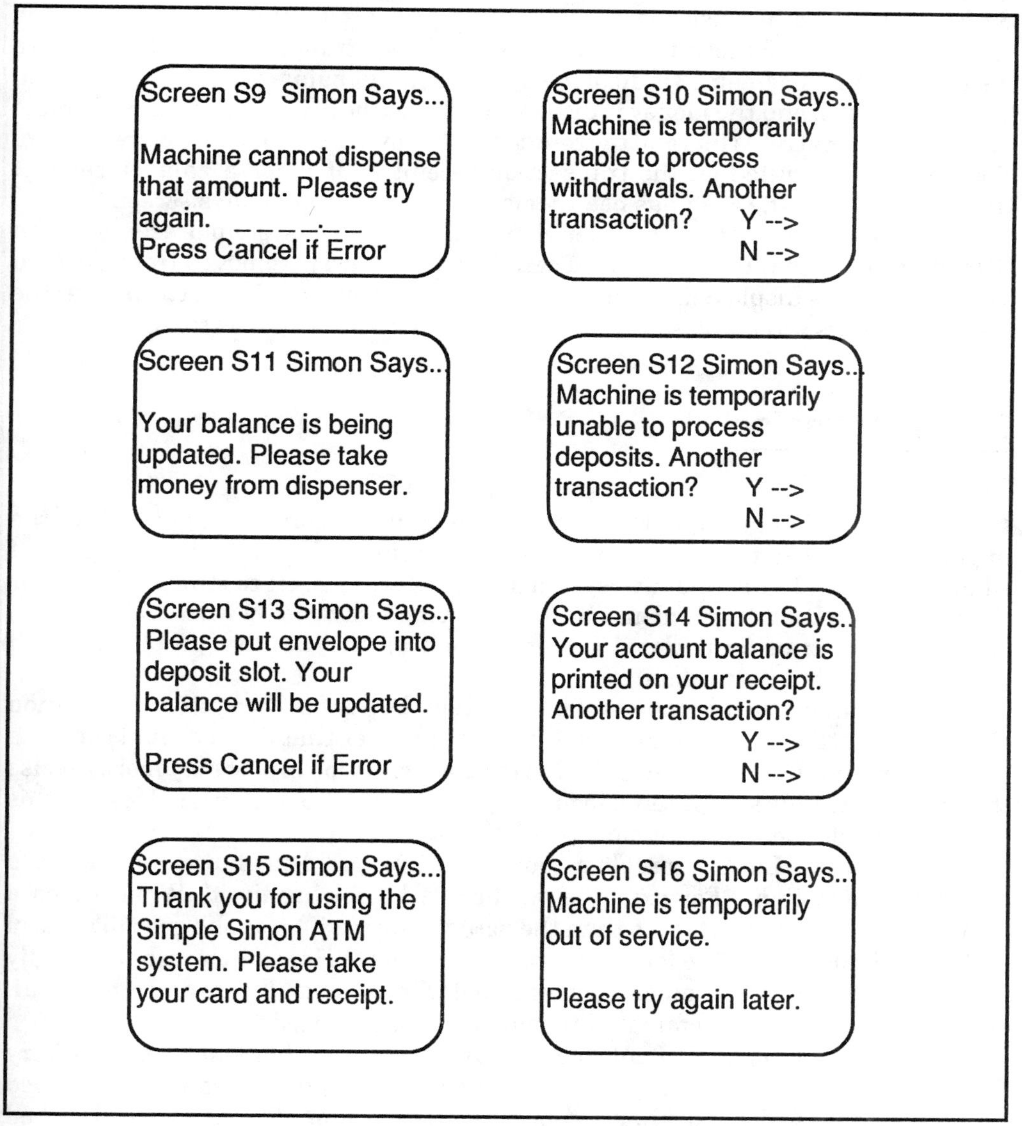

Screen S9 Simon Says...

Machine cannot dispense that amount. Please try again. _ _ _ _._ _
Press Cancel if Error

Screen S10 Simon Says...
Machine is temporarily unable to process withdrawals. Another transaction?   Y -->
                                       N -->

Screen S11 Simon Says...

Your balance is being updated. Please take money from dispenser.

Screen S12 Simon Says...
Machine is temporarily unable to process deposits. Another transaction?   Y -->
                                       N -->

Screen S13 Simon Says...
Please put envelope into deposit slot. Your balance will be updated.

Press Cancel if Error

Screen S14 Simon Says...
Your account balance is printed on your receipt. Another transaction?
                            Y -->
                            N -->

Screen S15 Simon Says...
Thank you for using the Simple Simon ATM system. Please take your card and receipt.

Screen S16 Simon Says...
Machine is temporarily out of service.

Please try again later.

Figure 3.3
SSATM screens (continued).

information) are processed by the master ATM (centralized) system once per day. The system then displays screen S14.

If a withdrawal is requested, the system checks the status (jammed or free) of the withdrawal chute in the Terminal Control file. If it is jammed, screen S10 is displayed; otherwise, screen S7 is displayed so that the customer can enter the withdrawal amount. Once the withdrawal amount is entered, the system checks the Terminal Status file to see if it has enough money to dispense. If it does not, screen

S9 is displayed; otherwise the withdrawal is processed. The system checks the customer's balance (as described in the balance request transaction), and if there are insufficient funds, screen S8 is displayed. If the account balance is sufficient, screen S11 is displayed, and the money is dispensed. The withdrawal amount is written to the unposted local ATM file, and the count of withdrawals per month is incremented. The balance is printed on the transaction receipt as it is for a balance request transaction. After the cash has been removed, the system displays screen S14.

When an "N" is entered in screen S10, S12, or S14, the system presents screen S15 and returns the customer's ATM card. Once the card is removed from the card slot, screen S1 is displayed. When a "Y" is entered in screen S10, S12, or S14, the system presents screen S5 so the customer can select additional transactions.

3.3.2 Discussion

We added this example to permit a strong discussion (in Chapter 6) of the importance of the dynamic behavior of an application. ATM systems are typical of what David Harel calls "reactive systems" because they react to stimuli that occur at their system boundary and maintain an ongoing relationship with their context, as opposed to transformational systems, such as the Library problem, which transform inputs into outputs.

There is a surprising amount of information "buried" in the system description above. For instance, if you read it closely, you can infer that the terminal contains only ten-dollar bills (see screen S7). This textual definition is probably more precise than what is usually encountered in practice. We have deliberately tried to keep this example simple (hence the name).

As with the Library problem, our narrative problem statement raises a plethora of questions. For example, is there a borrowing limit? What keeps a customer from taking out more than the actual balance if he or she goes to several ATM terminals? There are lots of "start-up" questions: How much cash is initially in the machine? How are new customers added to the system? These and other "real-world" refinements are eliminated to maintain simplicity.

One of the problems of interactive systems is that "completeness" is very difficult to attain. For example, is it sufficient to capture just the prescribed behavior, things which must happen, or must the specifier also describe proscribed behavior, things that cannot or should not happen? If we do attempt to describe proscribed behavior, how far do we go? In practice, it is not feasible to anticipate all the unusual possibilities. One analyst at the bank which provided this example related that one day, someone tried to deposit a fish sandwich in the deposit door.

As with the Library example, the SSATM problem does not provide all the information one might want in designing and implementing a solution for the bank. Some issues that are unresolved pertaining to the SSATM system include:

1. What bank functions are available to the ATM system? Does the ATM have a file of all bank accounts, or must it request verification of a valid account from an external bank system?
2. Where does the current account balance come from? Is it updated by the ATM system? By an external system?
3. What time constraints are in place for the ATM system? For instance, if a person is in the middle of a transaction and then does not respond to a prompt from the ATM within 3 minutes, how should the SSATM respond? Should it keep the card? Allow more transactions?
4. How are the ATM statuses set to determine if the various hardware components are working? For instance, how is the withdrawal chute status set to Jammed? How is it reset?

<u>Acknowledgment</u>

Mr. Jeff Smith, a graduate student at Grand Valley State University and an analyst at Old Kent Bank, developed the Simple Simon ATM system as a class example.

The sample problems serve a dual purpose in this text: They provide a vehicle for examining the different development techniques, notations, and representations, and they also serve as examples of the types of software applications common in most development shops. Both of the example problems are representative of common software applications and have the same characteristics of systems developed, including nontrivial data structures, functional complexity, context-dependent behavior, and ambiguous requirements. While these examples have common attributes of other systems, it is also helpful to consider generic types of applications and the unique characteristics they require when considering software development techniques and tools.

3.4 Taxonomies of the Application Domain

There have been several proposed taxonomies of the application domain, many of which are simple dichotomies: traditional EDP vs. real-time, small vs. large, transformational vs. reactive, and centralized vs. distributed. The thread common to these pairings is that the distinctions were usually made to support advantages claimed for a particular method or technique. Our view is that no one technique will be sufficient for all applications; therefore the inherent nature of the application dictates which approach(es) should be used.

3.4.1 Application Types

Roger Pressman [PRE87] [PRE88] and others in the industry [YOU89] have suggested possible classification schemes for software applications that can help characterize and differentiate types of software systems. Pressman identifies seven generic types of applications including:

System software: operating systems, DBMS, utilities, telecommunications systems, etc., that process complex information and are driven by events that are usually deterministic.

Real-time (reactive) software: data collection, data monitoring, and data analysis systems that must deal with events that occur in real time. We differentiate between time-dependent systems and context-dependent systems as follows: Time-dependent systems fail in their operation if they are unable to respond to events within a predefined time frame; context-dependent systems must respond differently based on the context in which they operate when they receive events.

MIS or business software: systems such as payroll, accounts payable, insurance, order entry, etc., that are discrete and process large amounts of transactions against a fixed data structure.

Engineering and Scientific software: systems for astronomy, space shuttle orbital dynamics, simulations, molecular biology, etc., that often have complex logical algorithms with little or no substantive data.

Embedded software: hardware control, industrial and manufacturing equipment control, automated warehouse equipment, etc., that must be placed in small, constrained computer systems with special-purpose operating systems that often manage small amounts of data but perform in a time-dependent environment.

Personal computer software: spreadsheets, word processing software, graphics, etc., that have extensive man-machine interfaces (graphical user interfaces) and complex data and functional requirements.

Artificial intelligence (knowledge-based) software: pattern recognition, theorem proving, game playing, role playing, etc., that uses expert systems or rule-based processing to solve complex problems.

These application types, while not universal, help to place the possible application domains into perspective and offer some categories for considering appropriate development techniques and tools.

3.4.2 Identifying the Three Dimensions of an Application

We have found a three-dimensional view to be particularly useful when considering software application types. Imagine an application vector space, in which a particular application has three components: data, function, and control (see Figure 3.4).

The data dimension refers to the extent to which an application is data-driven or data-oriented. Data structures may be complex, requiring database management systems (DBMS), or simple, supported by sequential file systems. When an application makes only minor computational changes to a very rich set of data structures, it is clearly a data-intensive application. We could look at the Library problem as an example of a data-intensive application. If we did, we could focus on major data structures, probably for library users and for books, and the various transactions given in the requirements definition could be mapped into database updates and integrity rules.

The second dimension refers to the functional or processing perspective. Functionality may be complex, involving sophisticated numerical algorithms, or simple, such as transactions applied against data structures. Function-intensive applications are characterized by complex computations or high levels of functionality. In systems that are strongly functional, the actual data inputs and outputs may be minimal, separated by very complex transformations. Scientific and engi-

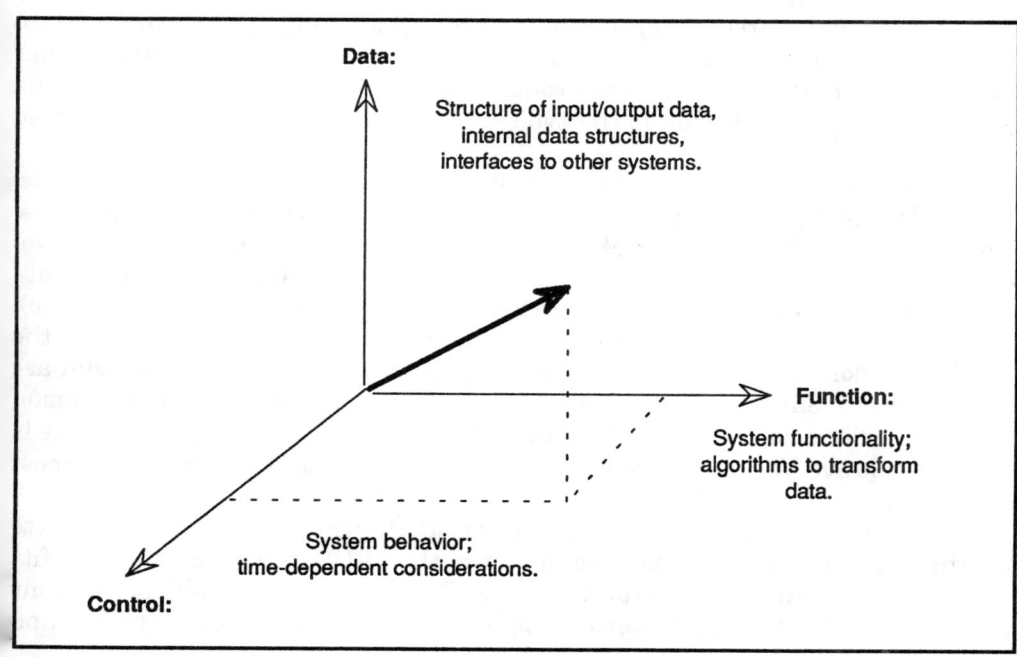

Figure 3.4
Three-dimensional vector space.

neering problems are good examples of process-intensive applications. Consider the problem of determining the launch window for the space shuttle: A colleague once likened this to being on a golf course, and hitting a golf ball so well that it passes through an open window on a passing train; the problem is that the golfer is in California and the train is in Florida.

The third perspective is the dynamic or control view. Dynamic behavior and time-dependent conditions may exist in software applications that require response times in the milliseconds for systems to function properly. In control-intensive applications, the focus shifts from structure to behavior, or from what a system is to what it does. Control-intensive applications are frequently interactive, and may involve deep concurrency. Real-time systems are control intensive, and the Simple Simon ATM system was chosen as an example so that we could address the control dimension in this book.

3.4.3 The Three-Dimensional Taxonomy and Application Types

What becomes interesting and helpful is to consider how the different application types, or application domains, map to the three-dimensional taxonomy described above. We have found that some applications have only one strong or dominant component, perhaps the function or data perspective, while others may have two or even three strong views. An order-processing system might be an example of an application that has only one strong view, in this case data. Other systems might have a pronounced control perspective with minimal data and processing components; this is the typical pattern for real-time and embedded systems.

Other systems might have two dominant or distinct dimensions — for example, strong data and processing components with only minimal control components, which is typical for traditional MIS applications. Other examples of strong two-dimensional applications include insurance applications (data and function), data collection systems (data and control), and embedded systems (function and control).

In our experience, most often two of the three components will dominate the application domain: It's difficult (but not impossible) to find applications that are strictly one-dimensional, and three-dimensional applications, while more common than single-dimension applications, are still not the norm. The important issue is that the relative size of each component is an indicator of which views are most appropriate.

There are some general guidelines for considering techniques when it comes to the three-dimensional taxonomy. For instance, the CRUD view of functionality fits nicely into a strong data perspective. The CRUD acronym stands for the four processes needed for data-intensive applications: create, retrieve, update, and delete (see Chapter 5). We will investigate these considerations and others in more depth in Chapter 10.

3.4.4 Mapping the Sample Problems to the Three-Dimensional Taxonomy

As we have already seen, if your only tool is a hammer, pretty soon all your problems begin to look like nails. Using this approach, we could take either of our sample problems and view it exclusively along one axis of our taxonomy. The data axis is the likely choice for the Library problem, and the control axis is the likely choice for the Simple Simon ATM system. If we did this, and did a conscientious job, the result would be serviceable.

One of the points we wish to make is that the three views supplement one another. It is typically difficult to express data structures in control-oriented techniques, and vice versa, and neither of these does particularly well with function. Why then would anyone choose to be limited by just one view?

We've done the Library problem several different ways on at least a dozen different CASE tools, and when we look at these exercises, the data and processing views tend to dominate the control view. As an exercise, we tried to start with a control-based approach, but we found that while there are some control aspects to the Library problem (for instance, books must be acquired before they can be loaned, they must be returned before they can be retired, the borrowing limit can redirect

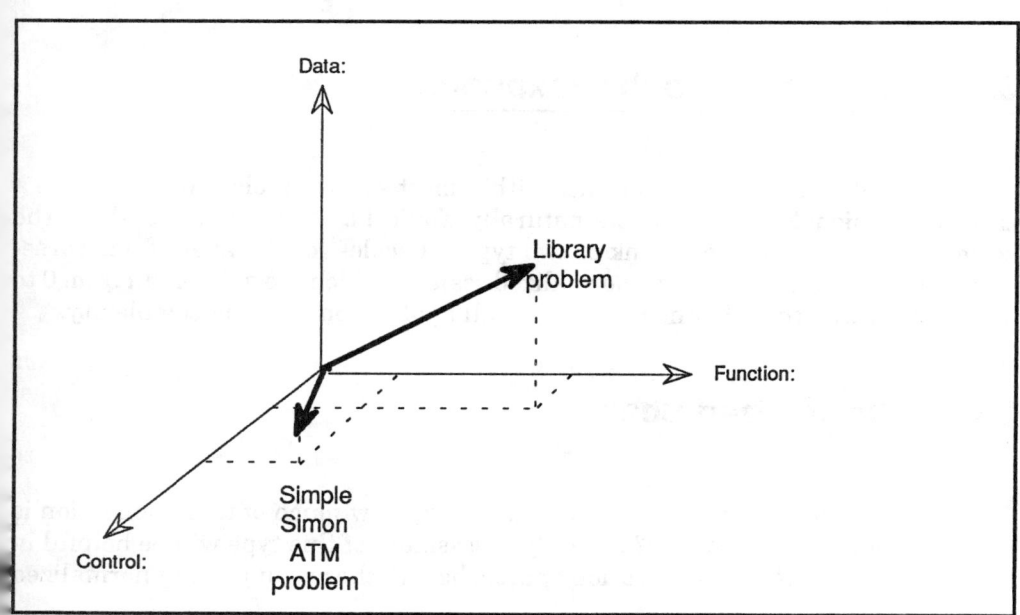

Figure 3.5
Example problems in the three-dimensional vector space.

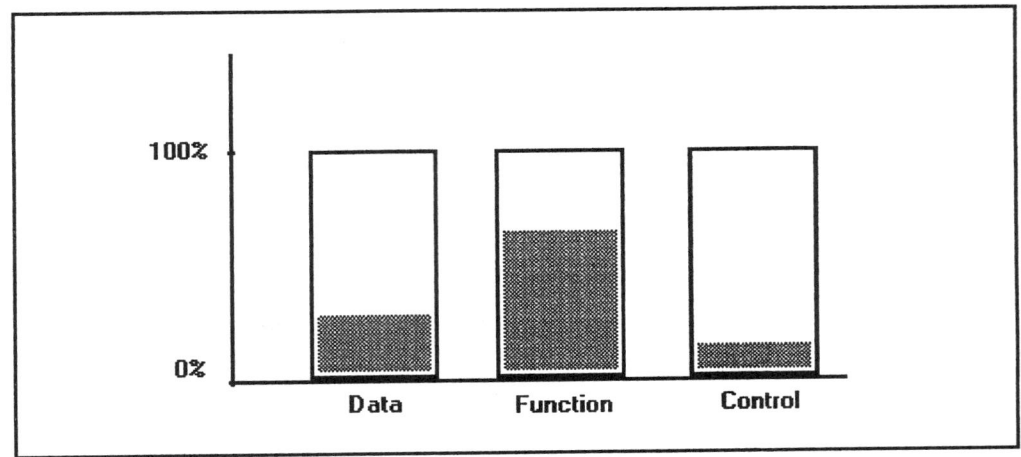

Figure 3.6
Bar chart of the
Library problem
using normalized
scales.

a loan transaction, and so on), the control view isn't nearly as interesting as the data and processing views.

The Simple Simon ATM system makes up for the control deficiency of the Library problem, and the fact that it is interactive makes the control view the natural starting point for this example. We found that the processing view is less important than the data view, and in fact, the processing view is pretty boring: change balances for deposits and withdrawals, and count types of transactions. The Library problem and the Simple Simon ATM problem are shown in Figure 3.5 as we view them in the three-dimensional taxonomy vector space described in Section 3.4.2.

3.4.5 Refinements to the Taxonomy

A kernel of a mathematician lies within most software folks. When we see a three-dimensional description, we naturally would like to know more about the scales on the axes. We can think of two types of scales for the axes of our three-dimensional taxonomy; one is a normalized scale, in which the values run from 0 to 100 percent, and the other deals with overall application size and complexity.

3.4.5.1 Normalized Scales

When we look at an example, we might ask, How much of this application is data, and how much is control? An early assessment of this type will be helpful in selecting requirements specification approaches. Rather than putting normalized

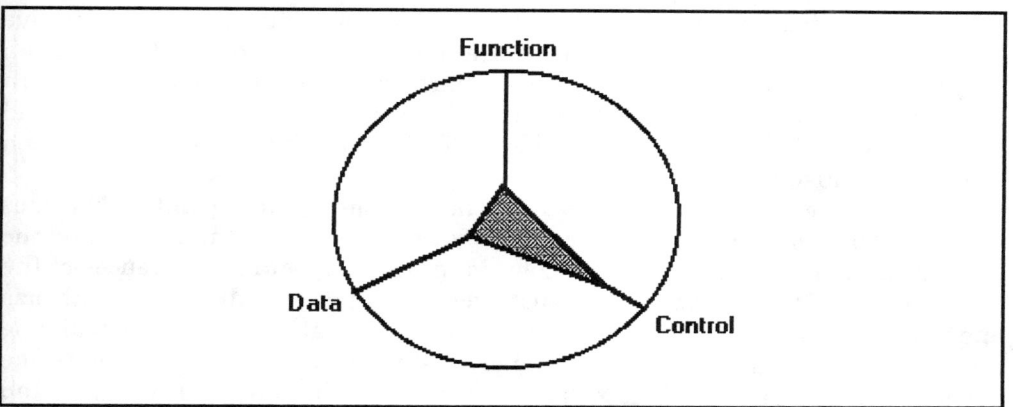

Figure 3.7
Kiviat chart of the SSATM problem using normalized scales.

scales on our two-dimensional drawing of our three-dimensional space, we prefer one of the alternatives given in Figures 3.6 and 3.7. The bar chart approach is easier to draw; if you use this view, make sure your percentages total 100 percent. Figure 3.6 shows how the Library problem would be represented with values for the three views.

The Kiviat chart shown in Figure 3.7 represents the same information from a different point of view. When drawing a Kiviat chart, one spoke is used for each independent variable of the three dimensions in our taxonomy, and each scale is arranged from small to large. To simplify this approach, we used a range from 0 to 100 percent, then marked a value on each spoke and connected these marks to form a polygon.

Keep in mind that these assessments are very primitive, and serve only to help select which approaches will be used for an application. Chapter 10 discusses these and other issues involved in comparing and selecting appropriate techniques for application domains.

3.4.5.2 Quantized Axes

While the normalized scales are simple and convenient, we may wish to use more quantitative values to help define the axes. For instance, if we had quantities associated with each axis, this information would be helpful for project management purposes. The two quantities that are most obvious are size and complexity. Along the processing axis, we could represent size as either lines of code (LOC) or function points (FP) [DRE89]. Function points are generally preferred because they can be estimated earlier and are not subject to all the problems of lines of code — for instance, How do you count them? Is more better than less? Relative difficulty?

A function point is a measurable, external aspect of a software system. The five basic types of function points measured are inputs to a program, outputs from a program, user inquiries to a program, file or database updates, and interfaces with other programs or systems. Function points could be used for both the process and the data axes, but may not be available until after the requirements have been formally specified in analysis.

The Halstead metrics offer yet another possibility for quantitative axes [HAL77]. These metrics count the number of distinct operators (functions) and the number of distinct operands (data), then count the number of occurrences of the operators and of the operands. The Halstead metrics give an indication of both size and complexity, but they too are based on information that generally isn't available until later in the development process, perhaps not until coding is complete. One advantage of using Halstead metrics is that we can develop one set of operators and operands for the processing axis and another set for the data axis.

We can see two possibilities for the control axis: One is to use McCabe's Cyclomatic Complexity metric and the other is to slightly refine the control taxonomy [MCC76]. McCabe's Cyclomatic Complexity metric is derived from topological properties of source code. It ends up being computed from the number of decisions in the source code. McCabe's Cyclomatic Complexity does not deal with size, and this has been one of the historical criticisms of the metric. In our three-dimensional view, this is not a problem, because size is more properly dealt with along the data and processing axes. We could, for example, develop a notion of McCabe's Complexity for each of the three control notations discussed in Chapter 6 (decision tables, finite state machines, and Petri nets), so that this information could be available after a requirements specification is complete. We could also analyze our existing systems to determine where our typical applications fit into the complexity view.

In our experience, a four-way refinement of the control axis is very useful. We need to make two distinctions: whether an application is static or dynamic, and whether it is implemented sequentially or concurrently. We have already hinted at the static/dynamic choice when we referred to Harel's reactive systems. Reactive systems are dynamic; transformational systems are static. An easy way to see the difference is to consider the set of inputs that determines an execution-time trace of a system. If all of these inputs are available before the system executes (as they are in traditional data processing applications), we say the application is static. If any of this path selecting information first becomes available once the system is executing, we say the system is dynamic. Concurrency introduces a whole set of control considerations (see Chapter 6). Thus we distinguish between sequential and concurrent implementations. Using these together, we can speak of four types of control situations: static sequential, dynamic sequential, dynamic concurrent, and static concurrent. (We left static concurrent at the end because this is relatively obscure.)

The other three are listed in order of increasing control complexity, although they are definitely not a linear scale. (The jump from static sequential to dynamic sequential is not nearly as great as the jump from dynamic sequential to dynamic concurrent.)

3.4.6 Mapping Application Domains to the Three-Dimensional Taxonomy

Using the application types described in Section 3.4.1, we have categorized each type of software system based on where we believe it fits into the three-dimensional taxonomy. Figure 3.8 describes examples of each of the application types, along with checkmarks to indicate which of the three dimensions are dominant or strong for each type. While these should not be viewed as absolute values for each application type, they can be helpful in considering other application domains and how they fit into the three-dimensional taxonomy. We will consider mapping the values in the three-dimensional taxonomy to possible development techniques in Chapter 10.

3.5 Perspectives on Techniques

We should start with recognition of Larry Constantine's abhorrence of the word "methodology," which actually means the study of methods. As used, methodology refers to the systematic way in which an organization or an individual approaches a software development task. We prefer the term _technique_, which we use throughout this text, but we provide insight into a methodology perspective in Chapter 14.

In the next six chapters, we will explore as many approaches to describing an application. We will generally start with the mainline notation for an approach, and then emphasize techniques based on the notation. In our experience, representations become almost technique-dependent, and within a technique, a representation becomes a goal or deliverable of the technique, so techniques are clearly affected by representations. The converse is also true: Techniques result in a representation, but the difference is that techniques may be common to several representations. Also, notations that are nearly equivalent map to the same set of techniques. In Chapter 10, we compare the techniques described in Chapters 4 through 9.

	Application types, examples and their dominant views	Function	Data	Control
Operating system	Operating Systems	✔		✔
	Centralized DBMS	✔	✔	
	Distributed DBMS	✔	✔	✔
Real-time system	Data collection/analysis system			✔
M.I.S.	Accounts Payable system	✔	✔	
	Insurance system (excluding policy rating)		✔	
	Order Processing system		✔	
Engineer-ing/ scientific system	Space Shuttle system	✔	✔	✔
	Simulation system	✔		✔
Embedded system	Hardware control system	✔		✔
PC-based software	Word processor (GUI)	✔	✔	✔
	Spreadsheet (non-GUI)	✔	✔	
	Graphics tool (GUI)	✔		✔
Expert system	Pattern Recognition system		✔	✔

Figure 3.8
Example applications and types in the three-dimenstional taxonomy.

3.6 Appropriate Choices

Recall the goal of this chapter: the ability to make an appropriate choice of approach, notation, technique, and representation for a given application. Recall also the limited soul who has only a hammer to work with. When confronted with an application, how do you start? We recommend looking at it in terms of the three axes of our taxonomy. Once you are familiar with the subject matter of Chapters 4, 5, and 6 you will be able to "imagine" the system from each of these viewpoints. Usually one, or maybe two, of the viewpoints will appear to be the most promising when considering development techniques.

Try it as a start, and we think you'll soon find that you want to jump to another viewpoint. If two seem equally promising, use the one you like better. Great, use it, and get new insights from the process. Eventually, you will move happily around among the three views. This will eventually create another problem: What if you are inconsistent across views? This may happen, for example, if a term is used in one sense in the processing view and in another sense in the control view. If you are working in a CASE environment, the repository may resolve such problems.

3.7 Resource List

For references on the domains and application types, see [BOO83], [ISC88], [SHE87], and [YOU89]. See [CAM86], [HUR91], [KEM85], and [WIN88] for information on the Library problem. Many excellent books and articles are available on software metrics, including [CUR79], [DRE89], [FEL89], [GRA87], [GRE76], [HAL77], [MCC76], and [WAG87].

3.8 References

[ARA89]   Arango, G., "Domain Analysis: From Art Form to Engineering Discipline," *SIGSOFT Engineering Notes*, vol. 14, no. 3, May 1989.

[BRE88]   Brereton, P. (ed), *Software Engineering Environments*, Wiley, 1988.

[BOO83]   Booch, G., *Software Engineering with Ada*, Benjamin Cummings, 1983.

[CAM86]   Cameron, J.R., "An Overview of JSD," *IEEE Trans. on Soft. Eng.*, vol. SE-12 (2): 222 - 240, 1986.

[CUR79]   Curtis, W., et al., "Measuring the Psychological Complexity of Software Maintenance Tasks with the Halstead and McCabe Metrics," *IEEE Trans. on Soft. Eng.*, vol. 5 (2), 1979, pp. 96-104.

[DRE89]   Dreger, B., *Function Point Analysis*, Prentice-Hall, 1989.

[FEL89] Felican, L., and G. Zalateu, "Validating Halstead's Theory for Pascal Programs," *IEEE Trans. on Soft. Eng.*, vol. 15, no. 12, December, 1989, pp. 1630-1632.

[GRA87] Grady, R.B., and D.L. Caswell, *Software Metrics: Establishing a Company-Wide Program*, Prentice-Hall, 1987.

[GRE76] Green, T.F., et al., "Program Structures, Complexity and Error Characteristics," in *Computer Software Engineering*, (J. Fox, ed.) Polytechnic Press, New York, 1976, pp. 139-154.

[HAL77] Halstead, M., *Elements of Software Science*, North Holland, 1977.

[HUR91] Hurwitcz, M., "Health Food for Programmers," *LAN Magazine*, May 1991, pp. 138-152.

[ISC88] Iscoe, N., *Domain Models for Program Specification and Generation*, University of Texas, 1988.

[KEM85] Kemmerer, R.A., "Testing Formal Specifications to Detect Design Errors," *IEEE Trans. on Soft. Eng.*, vol. SE-1, no. 1, Jan. 1985, IEEE Computer Society Press, Washington, D.C., pp. 32 - 42.

[MCC76] McCabe, T., "A Complexity Measure," *IEEE Trans. on Soft. Eng.*, December 1976, pp. 308-320.

[PRE87] Pressman, R., *Software Engineering: A Practitioner's Approach*, Second Edition, McGraw-Hill, 1987.

[PRE88] Pressman, R., *Software Engineering: A Beginner's Guide*, McGraw-Hill, 1988.

[SHE87] Shemer, I., "Systems Analysis: A Systemic Analysis of a Conceptual Model," *CACM*, vol. 30, no. 6, June 1987.

[WAG87] Waguespack, L.J., and S. Badlani, "Software Complexity Assessment: An Introduction and Annotated Bibliography," *ACM Software Engineering Notes*, vol. 12, no. 4, October 1987, pp. 52-71.

[WIN88] Wing, J.M., "A Study of 12 Specifications of the Library Problem," *IEEE Software*, July 1988, pp 66 - 76, IEEE Computer Society Press, Washington, D.C.

[YOU89] Yourdon, E., *Modern Structured Analysis*, Yourdon Press, 1989.

PART 2

Basic Development Techniques

Chapter 4
Function-Oriented Techniques

Of the six basic types of techniques described in this text, the function-oriented techniques are the best known and most widely used. As their name implies, these techniques focus on program or system functions — i.e., what a system does. Synonyms for function might include process, activity, transformation, computation, procedure, method, action, etc. The common basis for all of these views is that the function-oriented techniques are action-oriented — i.e., functions do things, preferably to data. Functions, or any of the other synonyms, consume inputs and produce outputs, and all of the notations for describing functionality provide mechanisms to express these facilities.

If we recall the historical growth of software engineering techniques, the early focus was on programming, especially in procedural languages such as COBOL and FORTRAN. These languages emphasize function, and the thought patterns are reflected in notations such as HIPO (hierarchy plus input, processing, and output) charts, flowcharts, and most importantly, data flow diagrams. The sidebar beginning on page 116 describes the history of the evolution of function-oriented techniques.

Throughout this book, we illustrate the various techniques with two widely used problems, the Library problem and a simplified automatic teller machine system. The Library problem is widely used in the literature for several reasons: It is a familiar application, so there are no difficult conceptual barriers; it typifies many of the problems of business information systems, so the points illustrated can be applied directly to many business applications; and it is sufficiently complex to highlight many of the issues we wish to discuss both in this chapter and in the other five technique chapters. The ATM problem exhibits reactive behavior and is also fairly well understood.

In this chapter, we will apply the function-oriented techniques to the Library problem and examine the notations, representations, and techniques commonly used in these methods to analyze, design, and program a solution based on the functionality of a system.

4.1 Introduction

Data processing, the term used throughout the 1960s and 1970s to describe software development, includes a data view and a process view. Within the function-oriented techniques, the original focus was on the processing and not on the data.

Data structures were included in the original view, but only in relationship to memory-resident data stores. From a historical standpoint, permanent data stores were added to the function-oriented techniques after the fact.

The original function-oriented techniques included structured analysis, structured design, and structured programming and were defined in the mid 1970s. Together, these techniques became known as the structured revolution, and they popularized a functional view of software development. Structured programming brought concepts of modularity, top-down partitioning, and stepwise refinement to the process of programming a solution to a problem using a procedural, third-generation language. But structured programming required that a program be defined as a hierarchy of modules, and this led to the definition of the structure chart and structured design. Prior to partitioning a design into a hierarchy, the functional requirements for a system needed to be specified and mapped into the solution. This led to the development of structured analysis and the use of bubble charts or data flow diagrams to specify the functions and the transformations in the problem domain. The processes used to create data flow diagrams for a system underwent significant changes through the 1980s as structured analysis matured. Structured design has stayed basically the same throughout its lifetime, and structured programming has been relegated to less significant status with the increased use of code generators.

4.1.1 Definitions

Prior to looking in depth at the function-oriented techniques, we should define some terms used in these methods.

Function: the action for which a person or thing is specially fitted or used or for which a thing exists; to serve. [Webster]

Module: the smallest unit of code in a system, which includes a collection of statements of four basic types — input/output, function, mechanics, and local data.

Cohesion: one measure of the strength of functional association of processing activities, usually within a single module.

Coupling: the degree of dependence of one module on another; specifically, a measure of the chance that a defect in one module will appear as a defect in the other, or the chance that a change to one module will necessitate a change to the other [PAG88].

Essential model: an idealized requirements model with its details restricted to those required by a hypothetical perfect implementation technology. The processes within this model are responses to events (stimuli) arising in the system's environment, and the data stores are representations of system-related entities. [WAR92].

The following briefly describe each phase of the structured life cycle most often used within the function-oriented techniques.

Structured analysis refers to the use of structured tools (data flow diagrams, data dictionary, process specifications, decision tables, decision trees, etc.) and functional decomposition to build a structured or functional requirements specification. Specifically, structured analysis uses tools to help partition a requirements document (data flow diagrams) based on system functionality, a means of tracking and evaluating interfaces between parts of the system (a data dictionary), and tools to describe the logic and policy of the system (structured English, miniature specifications, decision trees, decision tables, etc.).

Structured design refers to a technique that uses functional partitioning and hierarchical organization in a top-down fashion, with special emphasis on reduced coupling and strong cohesion. Structured design seeks to design a system based on black boxes that are placed together in a hierarchy of control with minimized interfaces between the modules.

Structured programming is a programming technique that uses a top-down, stepwise refinement strategy to produce code built from a small set of logical constructs. Some of the ideas associated with this approach include top-entry, bottom-exit; single entry/exit, small, singular functionality modules; and black-box subroutines or functions.

4.1.2 History

The concepts of structured programming were defined in the 1960s, and structured design followed from the use of these concepts in the early 1970s. Structured analysis was defined in the late 1970s but didn't gain widespread use until the 1980s, when Yourdon, Inc. emerged as a prominent consulting and training firm for software development. The sidebar beginning on page 116 describes the history of the structured methods in more detail.

From a historical perspective, the original structured analysis method required modeling the current physical, current logical, new logical, and new physical aspects of a system. Many who used this original method of structured analysis found it to be an unnecessarily tiresome process.

In the early 1980s, modern structured analysis (MSA) was born, and with it a movement away from modeling existing systems to building an essential model of a system and an implementation model. Experience showed that developers found it difficult to differentiate between the logical and physical models, and this led to the identification of a model that represented the essence of a system, or what a system must do in order to satisfy the user requirements, with as little as possible specified about how the system was to be implemented.

As the structured methods were used, they evolved to meet the needs of those using them. For instance, early users of structured analysis had trouble mapping from the representations to those used in structured design. Other phases of the development life cycle, most notably planning, were often overlooked in the function-oriented techniques and the focus remained on analysis, design, and programming.

Subsequent to widespread use of MSA, the method was further extended to include support for control modeling (see Chapter 6). At about the same time, the base method was modified to include better support for data modeling and integration of data and process. The widespread use of database management systems (DBMS) led to the acceptance, however grudging, of data modeling and data structure design within the structured camp (see Chapter 5). MSA evolved to build an essential model of the system and substituted a technique known as "event partitioning" for functional decomposition.

When the concepts of structured design were identified, the majority of systems developed were batch or on-line, transaction-based applications. In the 1990s, applications often have a strong data orientation and use DBMS for data management.

Recently, the structured methods have been extended to support object-oriented development (see Chapter 8). More than any others, the function-oriented techniques have evolved over the years to meet the changing needs of the software development industry.

4.2 Philosophy

All the function-oriented techniques have as their focus the definition of what a system does. In analysis, the functional requirements for a system are defined using a process or functional model, most typically a set of data flow diagrams and process specifications. While some of the function-oriented techniques include data structure notations in analysis (entity-relationship diagram), these were often added as an afterthought and to map only indirectly to the functional view.

In design, the function model is partitioned into a hierarchy of control based on modules as the singular units of work in a program. The chief representation of structured design is the structure chart and program logic representation for the individual modules. The structure chart is then used in programming to specify the architecture of a program and the flow of data and control along the hierarchy of modules.

In structured programming, a system is organized around its functionality, and black boxes are defined for each functional piece in a program or system. Structured programs are composed of discrete modules that have intrinsic characteristics: Each module is called within a hierarchy of control, each module has a single point of entry and exit, and each module should fit onto a single printed page.

Key issues in the function-oriented techniques are how the requirements model maps to the design, how the architecture and logic for a system are represented using structure charts and module specifications, respectively, and how data structures are integrated into these specifications. We will be looking at each of these items in subsequent sections.

4.3 Characteristics

Originally, structured analysis (SA) was driven by functional decomposition. This process took a high-level view of a system, typically described beginning with a context diagram. From this view, using a top-down process, SA describes more and more detail about the functionality of the system, using data flow diagrams (DFD) at the higher levels and process specifications at the lowest levels. As each higher-level process or function is defined, it is exploded into more detail at the next lower-level and maps to another DFD at that level. Thus a hierarchy of functions is created, with the context or system view at the top and primitive or lower-level functions at the bottom.

Unfortunately, the fact that the resulting representation was a top-down hierarchy of processes led developers to think that the only way to build this hierarchy was to start at the top and work down. This led to confusion about how structured analysis should be practiced. The techniques of structured analysis do not mandate the use of a top-down method of requirements definition, even though the resulting models will reflect a top-down hierarchy.

Structured design (SD) takes a similar view in designing a solution by creating a hierarchy of control beginning with a top-level module that controls all subsequent modules. A structure chart is used to depict the hierarchy, with each node representing a module that is in turn defined in more detail using other charts or notations. Eventually, when a module cannot be further decomposed, it is described using some form of Program Design Language (PDL) or other descriptive language. This view fits very easily with the procedural languages prominent in the 1960s and 1970s when SD was conceived, but has less applicability with the declarative languages of the 1990s.

Also defined in the structure chart are data elements and structures passed between the various levels within the chart. These data structures, called couples, can be of two forms, data or flags, and are shared between the modules as they would be in a common data area within a 3GL program. Underlying each module in the structure chart is a description of the logic required to carry out the functionality. Different design methods use different notations, which include pseudocode, structured English, action diagrams, flowcharts, Jackson structure diagrams, decision tables/trees, Warnier-Orr diagrams, and Nassi-Schneiderman diagrams.

4.3.1 Notation

While notations for some aspects of function-oriented techniques may vary, there are generic notations commonly used in all methods. For example, each function-oriented technique includes data flow diagrams, process specifications, and a data dictionary for the requirements specification, and structure charts and some module descriptive language for the design specification. Some function-oriented techniques include data modeling notations, prototyping, and extensions to support the dynamic behavior of systems, which are described in more detail in the appropriate chapters.

4.3.1.1 Data Flow Diagrams

"The data flow diagram is one of the most commonly used systems-modeling tools, particularly for operational systems in which the functions of the system are of paramount importance and more complex than the data that the system manipulates. DFDs were first used in the software engineering field as a notation for studying systems design issues." E. Yourdon [YOU89].

The most widely used notation for describing the functional view of requirements is the data flow diagram (DFD), developed originally by Larry Constantine and Ed Yourdon and extended by many others. DFDs, which form the basis for structured analysis, are now probably the most widely used requirements specification tool. The term "structured analysis" has evolved over two decades of usage to mean different things to different people, but it originally referred to the use of data flow diagrams for the specification of functional requirements.

Figure 4.1 shows the basic symbols used in the data flow diagram notation: Rectangular or square boxes represent external entities, circles or rounded rectangles represent transformations (functions or processes), pairs of parallel lines or open-ended boxes represent data stores, and labeled arrows represent data or information flows between symbols.

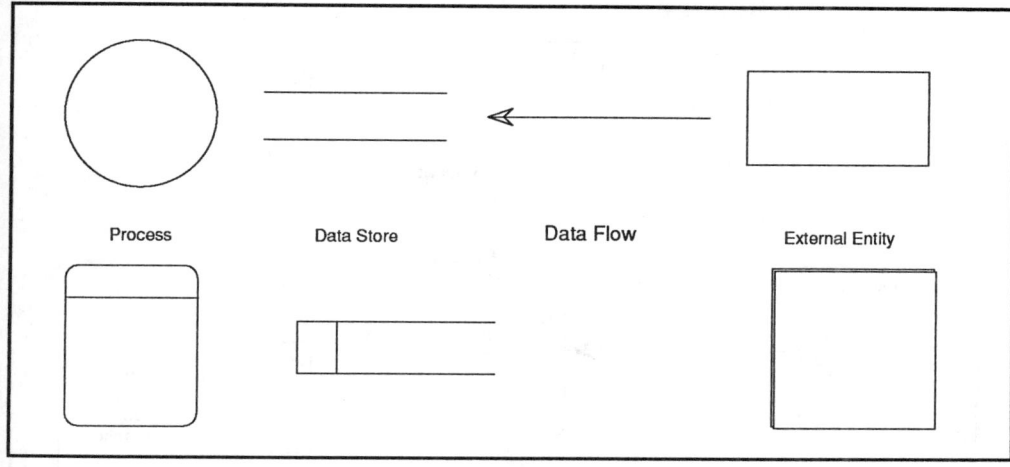

Figure 4.1
Basic data flow
diagram symbols.

The original DFD had only three components: transformations, data flows, and terminators, but data stores were added later to support the concept of data permanence. DFDs model the functional requirements for a system, and originally data stores represented the data structure definitions for a system. This proved to be cumbersome for systems that included complex data structures or database systems, and the function-oriented techniques were often criticized for their general lack of support for the data view.

Processes within DFDs represent the transformation of data and should be named and numbered, with the name assigned as a verb. Processes decompose to form other, lower-level DFDs or process specifications.

Data flows represent the movement of data (data in motion) between processes and, eventually, between data stores and processes. Data flows are data elements, data structures, or data models and are named to represent the meaning of a packet of data that moves along the flow. When unnamed, the flow is assumed to be the entire contents of the data store. Data flows show the direction of data moving in a system, can be consolidated, and may converge and diverge into or out of a process.

Data stores represent data at rest, a necessary time-delayed storage area, but may represent either a computer-based data store (i.e., DBMS) or a manual store (i.e., a physical file cabinet). Data stores are passive, so data do not travel along the flow unless a process explicitly asks for the data. Data stores should also be named and numbered, and typically are assigned a noun as their name. Data stores can also be considered as internal entities within the DFD.

External entities, also called terminators, are sources and sinks for data, and represent entities which are outside the boundary of the system but with which the system must communicate. External entities are outside the system, and their contents or the way they work cannot be changed by the system. Flows between terminators are not shown in the DFD. In addition, terminators appear in the context-level DFD and occasionally in the next lowest level, but not in any other

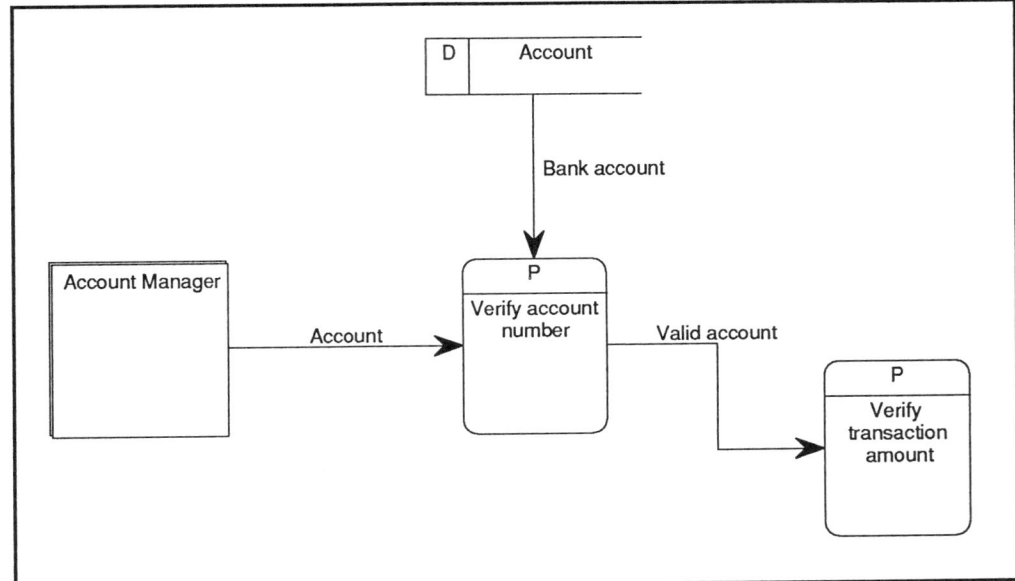

Figure 4.2
Example of a
Gane/Sarson
DFD.

level. Figure 4.2 shows part of a Gane/Sarson DFD for a bank account verification process.

This graphical vocabulary allows developers to focus on the sources and destinations of system information, i.e., the external entities, the flows of information "inside" the system, and the various transforms applied to the information flows. This view considers functions or processes as simply consumers and producers of data. Without dwelling on the specifics, this notation is simply a tool to describe or explain the functional representation of requirements. Once explained, DFDs are intuitively obvious and understood, fit easily onto a page, and can be easily automated with tools.

Through widespread usage, some common rules about "well-formed" data flow diagrams have emerged. These include:

1. Flows should not occur directly between a pair of external entities.
2. Process bubbles should have at least one input flow and one output flow.
3. Flows should not occur directly between a pair of data stores.

In addition to these basic notions, there are several lesser conventions:

1. Data flows may converge or diverge.
2. External entities and data stores may be replicated to reduce crossing flow lines.
3. It's nice, but not required, if information flows generally from left to right.

Developers should avoid overly complex DFDs, i.e., DFDs with too many flows, processes, stores, or terminators. DeMarco suggests that a DFD should have not more than seven bubbles, plus or minus two, based on studies done on human cognition. DFDs model the data transformations within a system with levels of detail, where a top level is defined (context diagram), and subsequent levels are defined using functional decomposition. A leveled set of DFDs represents all the functional characteristics of a system.

4.3.1.2 Context Diagrams

When a system is described with a set of data flow diagrams, a single bubble is drawn to represent the entire system in a context diagram. Sources and destinations of system-level inputs and outputs appear as external entities, with flow lines to and from the system bubble. External entities model people, organizations, or systems outside the application with which it must interact or exchange information.

Some notations allow data stores at the context level. If data is a "natural occurrence" at the context level, there's no harm done in representing it as a data store. A rather arbitrary way to resolve questions such as this is to follow whatever the chosen CASE tool permits. (See Section 4.8.1 for more on this topic.) Conversely, organizations holding strong feelings about questions such as this should include these in any CASE tool selection criteria. Naming conventions for context diagrams indicate that the system bubble should be named for the entire system or based on an agreed-upon acronym for the system.

4.3.1.3 Process Specifications

Process specifications, primitive specifications, or mini-specs represent a description of the transformation process for a single bubble in a DFD. Process specs define what the process does, but not how. When a system has been fully decomposed, the lowest-level or most detailed functions are described using process specifications. Process specifications define what occurs within the processes to transform inputs into outputs.

The most common form of process specification is a PDL, pseudocode or structured English. This textual description defines what the bottom-level components "do" with their inputs to produce their outputs.

One caution when using PDLs is that they often use structures that are very similar to the target programming language to express the sequence, selection, and repetition of what must be performed by the item being described, and this can lead to performing design while still in analysis. These control structures are applied to natural language phrases rather than to program variables. The main advantage of a PDL is that it forces the designer to think in an organized way about what the item must do. Also, since PDLs look a lot like the eventual code, the effort in the coding stage can be reduced when they are used.

4.3.1.4 Data Dictionary

A data dictionary is a textual supplement to the set of data flow diagrams and contains information about data items and processing components. Data dictionaries can be maintained manually; however, one of the advantages of most CASE products is that they enforce a rigorous data dictionary. In practice, we find that the data dictionary becomes one of the most used deliverables, especially during software maintenance activities.

A data dictionary contains all definitions of the symbols on any diagram and includes their meaning, composition, values, or components and any relationships between components. Early data dictionaries were nothing more than textual definitions, but they later evolved to include expressions and relationships between components. Simple expressions often used in a data dictionary are of the form Higher_Level_Component=Lower_Level_Component+Other_Components. Within some CASE tools, data dictionaries have evolved to become repositories for all development information.

4.3.1.5 Structure Charts

A structure chart is a hierarchy of modules represented as rectangles, each with a name inside that is a statement of its function or what it does. The modules are connected by lines that indicate the flow of control or the calling relationship. In addition, short arrows along the lines represent essential data couples (hollow circles) and control couples, or flags (filled circles). Data couples are data structures passed between or shared by modules, while flags are conditional data elements or indicators of conditions (end-of-file, etc.). Figure 4.3 offers an example of a structure chart for the bank example described in the DFD in Figure 4.2.

Structure charts also include symbols for code that is physically contained within other modules (hats), iterative activation of selected modules, and concurrent activation of modules. Structure charts don't define the sequence in which the modules are called (i.e., there is no implied left-to-right execution), but only show the hierarchy of control in the program or module.

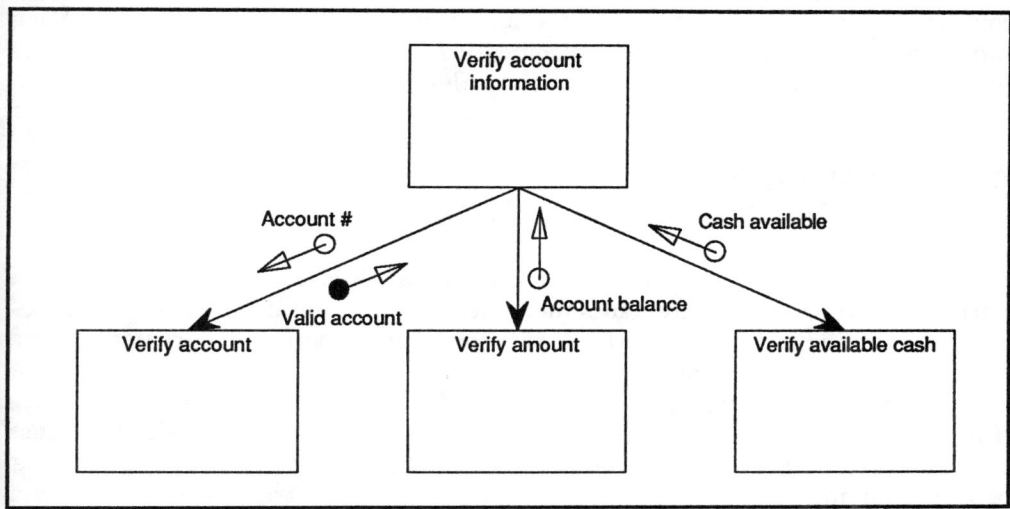

Figure 4.3
Example of a
structure chart.

Some design notations [PAR71] include information clusters, which allow a set of modules to be represented to access data that has a complex structure, has sensitive security, or has device dependence (i.e., a DBMS). Access to shared data areas or data structures can be managed using information clusters.

Guidelines for drawing structure charts have been developed over the years. Modules may be split or combined to include/exclude functionality (factoring) based on guidelines including module size. Each module should be approximately one-half page of program listing in any high-level language. Each function should be placed in a module of its own to clarify a system. Work should be separated out for simplified management and control.

4.3.1.6 Module Specifications

Module specifications describe the logic of each module defined in the structure charts. Some techniques require module specifications for every module, while others require specifications only for the primitive or lowest-level modules. These specifications differ from the process specifications defined above in that they describe how the outputs are created from the inputs and they closely follow the sequence, structure, and format of programming languages.

Many alternative notations can be used to describe the logic of a module, including structured English, PDL, action diagrams, flowcharts, Jackson structure diagrams, decision tables/trees, Warnier-Orr diagrams, and Nassi-Schneiderman diagrams. Some organizations have had success using third- and fourth-generation language statements as module specifications. Some CASE tools support the generation of programming code from these design specifications.

4.3.2 Technique

The prominent function-oriented techniques are functional decomposition and partitioning function requirements into a design representation. Several alternative partitioning schemes have been proposed, including event partitioning and most recently, object-oriented analysis.

Functional decomposition is the process of splitting up higher-level processes (functions) into lower-level, more detailed processes. This decomposition process continues until only low-level processes, those that can be described in a page of text or less, remain. Functions are decomposed based on the transformation of data within each process, and data stores are used to represent data structures external to a process.

One problem that results from the top-down nature of a requirements document is that developers feel they have to apply a top-down technique to arrive at the process model. Creating a functional decomposition can be undertaken from any number of views, including a middle-out or even a bottom-up approach. The key is that the resulting representation will be a functional hierarchy, but the process used to achieve the result does not have to be top-down.

Early users of functional decomposition found that the requirement that a context diagram be created first hindered their understanding of the system requirements. Often developers do not have a clear view of the overall system boundaries but have a list of requirements or external events. This led to the use of event partitioning as a tool for beginning the process by listing the events in a system and a middle-out approach to analysis.

Structured design controls complexity by partitioning a system in such a way that each box solves one well-defined piece of the problem, the function of each black box is easy to understand, any connection between black boxes is introduced only because of a connection between pieces of the problem, the connections between the black boxes are as simple as possible, and the boxes are as independent as possible.

"Structured design uses a definition of the problem to guide the definition of the solution, conquers complexity by partitioning a system into black boxes and organizing them into a hierarchy." M. Page-Jones [PAG88].

Several strategies for moving from analysis to design have been proposed, including transform- and transaction-centered methods. A transform-centered

1. Trace each input data stream from its external source through the data flow diagram until it disappears.
2. Back through each output stream from its external data sink until it disappears.
3. Identify the "central transform" which marks the split between input and output.
4. Place the central transform at the top of a new structure chart.
5. Build the structure chart in such a way that processes along the input streams become modules on the left side of the chart and processes along the output streams become modules on the right side.
6. Continue to refine the modules until only primitive modules exist.

Figure 4.4
One path from DFDs to SCs.

view identifies a core process where a transition occurs within the system and external data is mapped into internal formats. A transaction-centered view holds that data moves along an incoming path based on a transaction center that determines which outgoing path will be taken. Figure 4.4 briefly describes the transform-centered approach.

Each of these is a function-oriented mapping of processes in DFDs to modules in structure charts. The question is how the functions defined in the DFDs map to an architectural design for the system so that cohesion for single-function modules is increased and coupling is decreased for better maintenance and testing.

The problem arises when higher level processes must be mapped to higher-level modules, and control and communication must be coordinated between modules. How should modules be split or combined to best meet the needs of the implementation environment? In addition, any design decisions made for implementing data structures that are shared by multiple modules might cause any one-to-one mapping between DFD processes and SC modules to be discarded or reworked.

Structured design picks up where structured programming leaves off and applies to medium- and large-sized systems. SD works exclusively with modules in a top-down organization (hierarchy) and is a logical but major extension to modular programming and top-down design. In SD, developers are concerned almost entirely with the outside view of a module, i.e., with what a module does, not how it does it.

The transition from structured design to structured programming is fairly easy, since the modules and the architecture are clearly defined within the structure chart. Data and control couples in the structure chart represent data structures shared by modules in a program. Given the procedural view of the structure chart, programming from these diagrams in a 3GL is a straightforward process.

4.3.3 Representation

Structured analysis builds a functional specification, also called a structured specification, which consists of a leveled set of DFDs, a data dictionary, process specs, and optionally, a data model and a prototype. While the representations created are fairly well understood, the process used to achieve the result is less uniformly applied and has changed significantly over the last 20 years.

The primary deliverable from all function-oriented techniques is a set of data flow diagrams. This set of diagrams emphasizes the functionality, and represents it in terms of levels of abstraction, or hierarchy. Part of the technique is evident here: The final representation may have been constructed using functional decomposition, but it also could have been created using a process of functional composition. Most likely, there was some combination of these two strategies.

The assumption made with function-oriented techniques is that they include a top-down process, functional decomposition, and that they begin with the definition of a context diagram that specifies the system boundaries and high-level inputs and outputs. This assumption is largely impractical, since in practice many developers have found that a middle-out approach, where specific functions are defined at the second or third level in the decomposition and then combined into a single bubble or set of bubbles, also works quite well.

The original view of structured analysis called for the creation of several distinct models of the requirements of a system, which included logical and physical, as well as current and future perspectives. This led to much confusion regarding where the logical view ended and the physical view began, and much management concern about modeling both the existing and the future implementation of an application.

McMenamin and Palmer [MCM84] originally described a process whereby events would drive the analysis process, which became known as event partitioning. Either approach can deliver the finished product: a leveled set of data flow diagrams, process specifications, and data dictionary. The latter approach has led to the belief that a structured analysis model is actually a network of responses and not a hierarchy of functions; this substantially changed the representation for MSA.

Key to the use of MSA is the concept of defining and modeling the essential aspects of a system without any implementation-specific details or considerations. Once the essential model has been created, only then can practical implementation considerations be brought into the picture.

Structured design builds an implementation specification or a functional hierarchy which includes structure charts, module specifications, and some data structure definitions. The functional specification created in analysis is used to

A data flow, data store, or terminator must be defined in the
      data dictionary.
A process must be defined in a lower-level DFD or a process
      specification.
Any reference to a data flow, data store, process, or terminator
      must map to a single definition in the data dictionary.
Inputs must match outputs along vertical levels of decomposition
      (law of conservation of data).
Every data store in a DFD must map to an entity, relationship, or
      combination of these in a data model (if used).
Entity names must match data store names (if used).

Figure 4.5
Structured
analysis model
balancing rules.

begin the design process by evaluating lower-level processes for implementation as modules in the design specification. While the structure chart represents the hierarchy of modules, the module specification describes the logic and interfaces for each module in the structure chart. The data structure definition is required for complex or permanent data stores and may map to a DBMS or file access method.

4.3.3.1 Leveled Diagrams

As the decomposition unfolds, lower-level information flows, which are invisible at higher levels, are added to represent information used and produced by lower-level functions. The overall functional decomposition is therefore represented by a tree, in which nodes of the tree are processes. Viewing the decomposition as a tree leads to the dominant referential scheme, where levels of the tree correspond to levels of data flow diagrams. The context diagram is level 0, its decomposition is level 1, and so on. If there are n processes in the first-level decomposition, they are numbered 1.1, 1.2, 1.n. Any of these may be further decomposed, adding another decimal position to the numbering scheme.

Thus process 1.3 might be decomposed into 1.3.1, 1.3.2, and 1.3.3. The end result is called a *leveled set* of data flow diagrams. Some of the early writers went a step further, and described a *fully flattened diagram,* which consists only of processes that are the leaves of the decomposition tree [PAG88] [PRE88]. While this is an interesting concept, it is difficult to draw by hand, and we know of no CASE tool that supports fully flattened diagrams. As already seen, there are specific rules that apply when diagrams are exploded into more detail; these are summarized in Figure 4.5.

In the process of producing a leveled set of data flow diagrams, developers must be careful to preserve what might be called "data flow integrity." All inputs and outputs to a process at some level are inherited by the decomposition of that process at the next lower level. A physicist might refer to this as the Law of Conservation of Data; in structured analysis circles, this notion is more simply known as "vertical balancing." A leveled set of data flow diagrams is vertically balanced if, at each process decomposition, the inputs and outputs are preserved, that is, inputs and outputs are neither gained nor lost. Most CASE tools will check for vertical balancing.

Why spend so much time on vertical balancing? It seems natural enough, but in practice, it turns out to be an extremely useful concept. As already seen, the reason is that developers typically don't follow a strict top-down, leveled thinking process. They are more inclined to flit across several levels of decomposition and coalesce these thoughts on paper later. This is compounded when several people produce one definition. The end result is that, when various data flow diagrams are first merged, they are usually far from balanced.

While balancing is important, it can only assure a minimum level of information integrity. For example, a DFD might show a higher-level flow which diverges in the lower-level diagram. For more on this limitation, see [TAO90].

4.4 Stages and Tasks

When Tom DeMarco originally defined the process of structured analysis [DEM78], he envisioned two views of any system: logical and physical. For the existing system, both a logical and a physical representation are created, along with similar representations for the new or proposed system. The original structured life cycle is shown in Figure 4.6.

Later, others in the Yourdon camp offered a different approach which began by defining the essence of a system. This essential view led to what became modern structured analysis and has since been widely used in industry. MSA tasks include the following:

1. Develop an environmental model, or a set of diagrams that describe how the system interacts with its environment (external view).
2. Build a behavioral model, or a set of diagrams that describe the behavior of the system (internal view). Together, these models form the essential model of a system.

Structured design has stayed largely the same over the years and involves the following tasks:

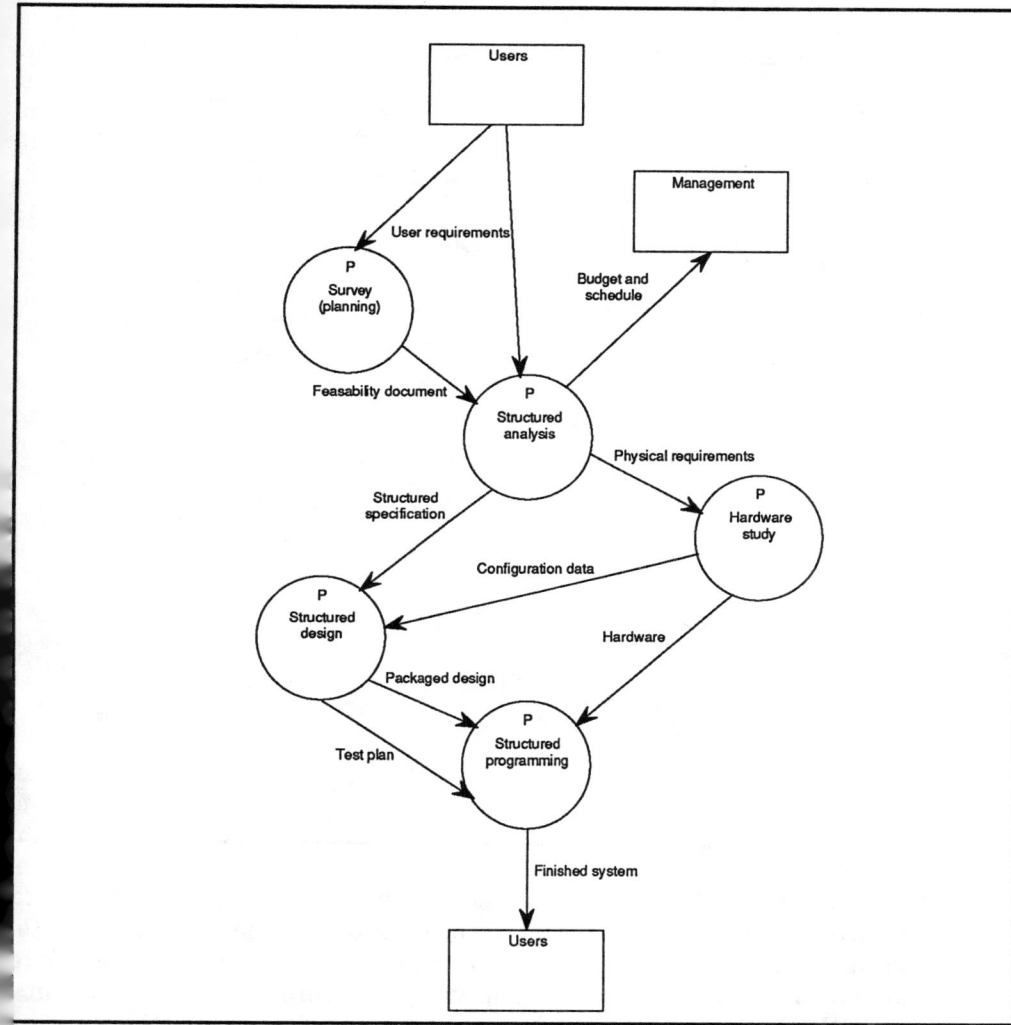

Figure 4.6
Original structured
life cycle
(DeMarco).

1. Allocate specifications to processors.
2. Allocate specifications to tasks.
3. Derive structure charts from data flow diagrams.
4. Evaluate and refine structure charts.
5. Design low-level modules.
6. Design the database.
7. Package and deliver the design.

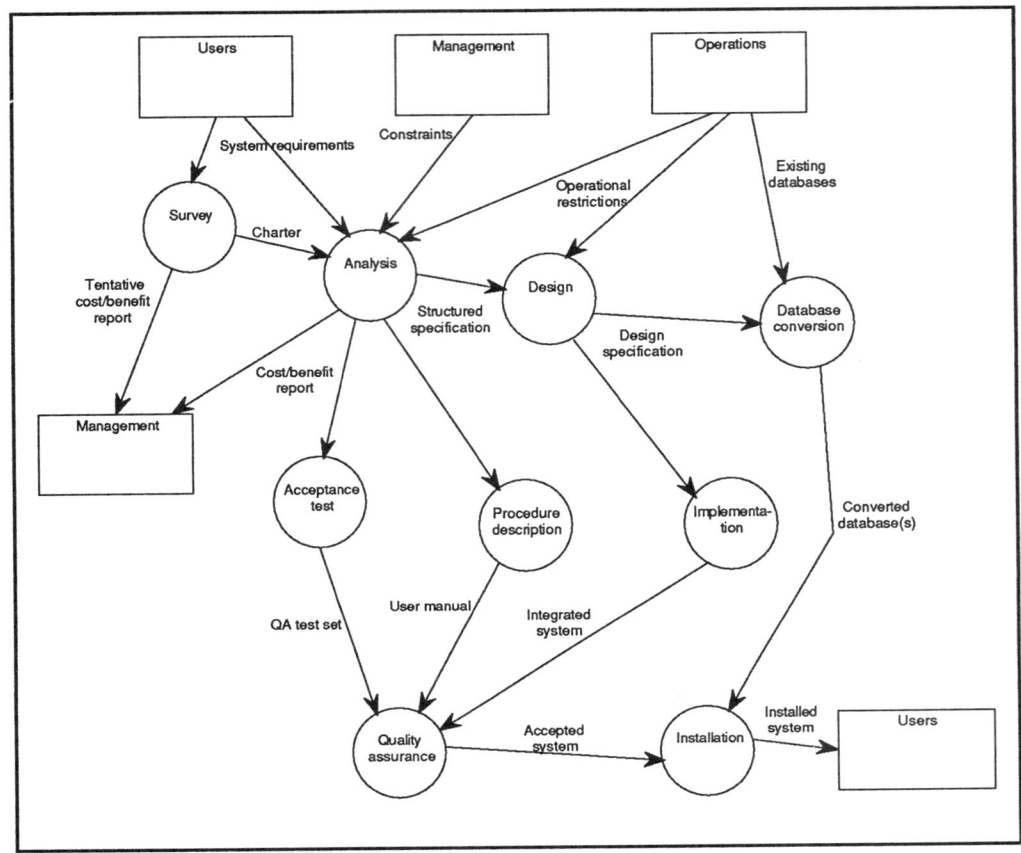

Figure 4.7
Modern
structured life
cycle
(Yourdon).

A major subtask within structured design is mapping the process model to
physical structures and logic to best meet the needs of the functional requirements.
This can be accomplished by converting the data flow diagrams to structure charts
or by looking at the data structures and deriving structure charts from the data
structures used by the processes. Two techniques defined by Yourdon and Constantine
for this process are transform analysis and transaction analysis, which were
described in Section 4.3.2. The modern structured life cycle is shown in Figure 4.7.

4.5 Deliverables

The primary deliverable from structured analysis is the functional specification, which consists of a set of leveled data flow diagrams, process specifications, and
data dictionary. These models, often called process models, form the basic deliverable from the function-oriented techniques. MSA builds essential models of the

system, while traditional structured analysis builds logical and physical models of the current and future systems.

The deliverables from the design phase include a set of structure charts and module specifications. Together, these form the procedural design document which describes the system architecture, intermodule communication, and the low-level logic for each module.

The deliverables from the structured programming phase are the structured programs, documentation, and any test information. A whole school of thinking has arisen from the view of testing systems based on their structure.

Some of the function-oriented techniques now include data and control models, but questions remain about how these models integrate with the process models which are the heart of the function-oriented techniques. Some recent implementations of the function-oriented techniques include prototyping and database design specifications, but as with the data and control modeling extensions described above, these components may not fully integrate with the design specification.

4.6 Suitable Applications

While any application that includes a functional view is a candidate for the function-oriented techniques, there are also some general guidelines for using them.

When structured programming constructs are required for easier maintenance of systems, the function-oriented techniques all deliver structured design documents that map directly to structured programming constructs. There is some question how the function-oriented techniques can integrate with CASE tools that generate systems, since many of these products do not generate structured code.

When a complex functional view is present in a system, the function-oriented techniques include tools that can adequately represent this complexity, and functional decomposition or event partitioning may offer the best technique for dealing with it. The function-oriented techniques work well when the functional view of a system is more complex than the data or control view.

Systems that support a strong data view may be inadequately supported with the function-oriented techniques, unless data modeling and database design are included as part of these methods. Organizations planning to use a function-oriented technique with a DBMS should evaluate how well and at what level the data model maps to the process model, and what types of database design support are provided in the representations and techniques.

Reactive or real-time systems that include a strong functional view may be supported with the extensions to the function-oriented techniques described in Chapter 6. Also, prototyping can be included as part of the function-oriented techniques; this is further described in Chapter 9.

4.7 Benefits and Drawbacks

The most obvious benefit to using the function-oriented techniques is the fact that they are the most widely used methods available. Since they have been in widespread use for almost 25 years, they also represent the most studied methods. Given their widespread use, they are also the most widely supported techniques, with more automated tools, training, and consulting available than for any other method.

As previously stated, the function-oriented techniques have been extended to support data- and control-intensive applications and may represent the best alternative for systems that must include two or all three of the dimensions discussed in Chapter 2. (See Chapter 10 for more on this subject.)

Drawbacks to using the function-oriented techniques include the migration from analysis models to design specifications. SA was developed to model large, complex systems, while SD was developed (initially) to design individual programs running on a single CPU. These divergent views must be brought together if the function-oriented techniques are to be used for the newer distributed or GUI applications prominent in the 1990s.

The migration from SA to SD is still complex and difficult, and not all systems exhibit transform- or transaction-centered behavior. For those systems that do not, there are few documented methods for moving from the process model to the design specification.

Perhaps the biggest drawback to using the function-oriented techniques is their lack of full support for data modeling and database design. Even though some of the methods include these tasks, they are not well integrated with the representations. For instance, mapping data stores and data flows to entities, attributes, and relationships is clumsy and difficult to verify automatically.

Finally, the generation of code from the design specifications (structure charts and module specifications) is difficult, since both views are required to generate functional systems. The structure is needed to create the architecture of a system, while the module specifications are used to represent the low-level logic of the programming language. In addition, some form of data structure definition is also required and may not be included with the function-oriented technique.

4.8 The Library Example

We chose to use the Library example to represent the function-oriented techniques because the functional requirements map very easily to the notation and techniques used. As we developed the Library system, we made assumptions about the system. These assumptions include:

1. More than one copy of a book may be available in the library.
2. An implementation-specific security system will be available during the design phase to address the issue of restricting access to library transactions by user type.
3. The Library system will be implemented using a data structure which supports keyed access to data.
4. The archive process can be handled by batch (off-line) components of the library system.

4.8.1 Context Diagram

Identifying a system bubble for the Library problem is fairly easy, since it is simply the Library system. Deciding on the external entities for the system is more difficult. Figure 4.8 shows three possible context diagrams for the Library system: 1) the system might include a single external entity, User; 2) the system might also include two external entities, a Staff User and a Ordinary User; or 3) the system might include five external entities, an Acquisition Desk, a Staff Desk, a Loan Desk, a User Terminal, and something called Member Services. Whichever diagram is chosen will determine the decomposition for the Library system. We don't have the space in this chapter to follow each view, but it might be a nice exercise for the "interested reader." For this section, we chose the single-entity version, because it gave us the most flexibility in how we could do our functional decomposition (see Figure 4.9).

If you look closely at the information flows in the candidate context diagram, you will see that there are decompositions already present:

<User Request>   =   <Staff Requests> | <Borrower Requests>
<Staff Requests>   =   <Add Book> | <Delete Book> |
                          <Request Staff Report> | <Add User>
                          | <Delete User> | <Borrow Book>
                          | <Return Book>
<System Response> =   <Staff Responses> | <Borrower Responses>
<Staff Responses>   = <Confirmation> | <Staff Report>

Had we chosen the rich context diagrams, the blanket flows User Request and System Response would have been the more specific ones shown above. We see, then, that our choice to postpone decomposition from the context diagram shifted the burden to the data dictionary. This is important: The work doesn't "go away," so our choice was more one of where to do the work.

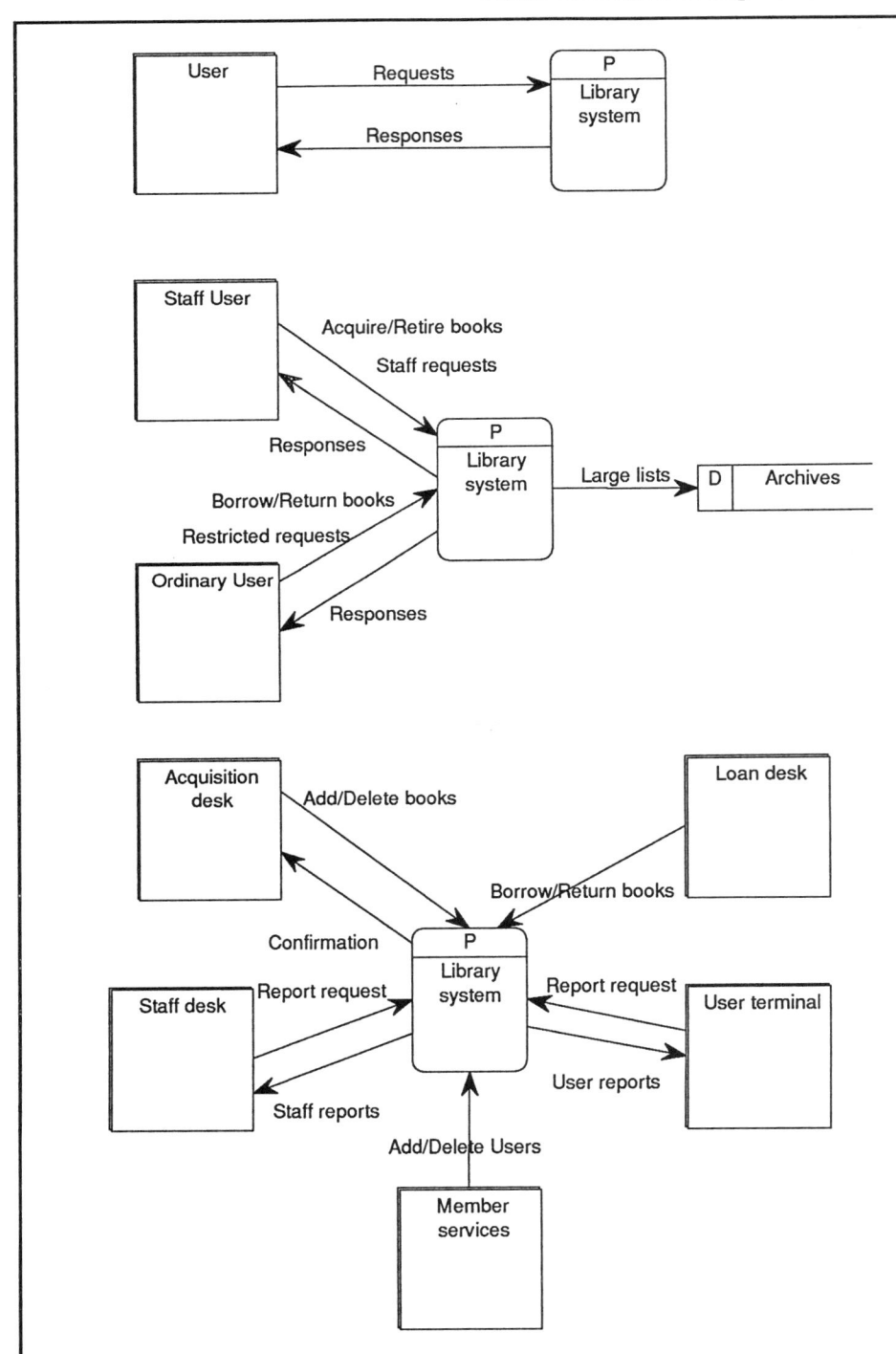

Figure 4.8
Three possible
Library context
diagrams.

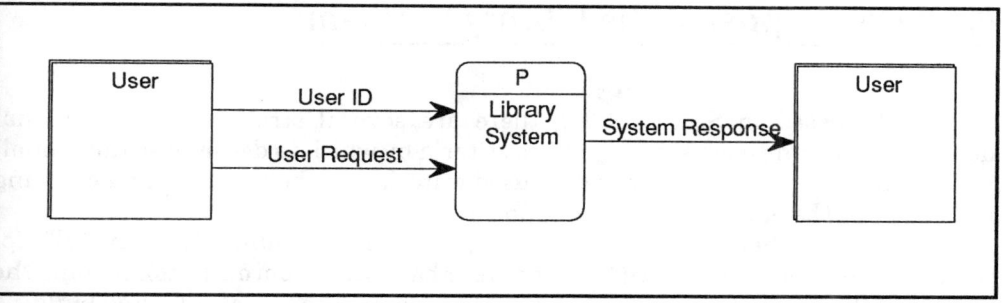

Figure 4.9
Final Library
context
diagram.

We have already come to a major element of technique, one that is ignored by many writers and is, in fact, suppressed by the waterfall model. When we are doing requirements specification, we are also doing design. The waterfall model suggests that requirements specification and preliminary design are separate activities, and that the end result of requirements specification is the starting point for preliminary design. But where does specification end and design begin? Here are some possible answers:

1. Requirements specification is concerned with what design addresses how.
2. When a requirements specification is complete, it should neither predispose nor preclude any design choices.
3. Design involves allocation of resources to functionality; specification does not.
4. System test plans should be derivable from the requirements specification, and integration test plans should be derivable from the preliminary design.

Now, if we only knew how to differentiate system test cases from integration test cases, we would have a guideline. One possibility might be to consider system testing as having access only to system-level primitive actions, specifically, information flows to and from external entities.

5. Requirements specifiers need to "look ahead" into design, to be sure that the specified requirements will be feasible.
6. Requirements specification and design are deeply interrelated; it is counter-productive to try to separate them.

We have found that the fifth and sixth alternatives listed above seem to be true most often. For an interesting paper on this, see [SWA82]. In fact, you don't really have to read the paper, the title says it all: "On the Inevitable Intertwining between Specification and Implementation." Viewing design as an allocating process also turns out to be a helpful device in later sections.

4.8.2 Decomposing the Library Problem

As discussed in Section 4.3.2, there are several strategies for functional decomposition, and each strategy offers criteria by which to decompose functionality. The best known and most widely used criteria are the cohesion and coupling notions from the early work of Larry Constantine.

There are other strategies, including information hiding, "directional" approaches (i.e., working forward from inputs or backward from outputs), echoing the structure of the data (see Jackson system development in Chapter 5), and building with existing components (reuse).

We stopped our decomposing of the Library system because of space limitations, clearly a very artificial stopping criterion. When to stop decomposing is a very interesting question, however. Our preference for coupling and cohesion leads us to prefer these as stopping criteria: Stop decomposing when you reach "single-purpose" or functionally cohesive processes. One popular guideline is that the specification of a bottom-level process should fit on one page. This probably has its origins in pre-terminal days, and a companion guideline advises that the source code for a bottom level process should fit on one page.

Reuse is another good criterion, and it turns out to be related to cohesion. We may wish to decompose down to modules that have a high potential for reuse. Superficially, size seems to be an indicator of potential for reuse: It's hard to reuse large programs, and easier to reuse smaller ones. There's a limit, though: Individual modules are highly reusable, but they have little "content." When we look at successful examples of reuse (the best example is libraries of mathematical functions), we find that single-purpose, highly cohesive modules are easiest to reuse. What we have, then, is a convergence: The ideas of cohesion, reuse, and effort (size) all argue for small, single-purpose modules.

Figure 4.10 shows the lowest-level DFD for one of the processes in the functional hierarchy, Check Out Book. We can see from the DFD that inputs to the process include the user, book, and copy information. Outputs from the process include the number of books checked out to the user (updated), updated book and copy information reflecting the user has checked out the book. We can also see from the diagram that Assign Copy is dependent on other processes in the DFD.

4.8.3 Library Process Specifications

Process specifications offer a micro-level view of the functionality described in data flow diagrams. In Chapter 5, we will see that data dictionaries offer a similar micro-level view of the macro-level definition of entity-relationship diagrams. In practice, process specifications are done as the last step of requirements specification; they might even be considered as part of the detailed design phase.

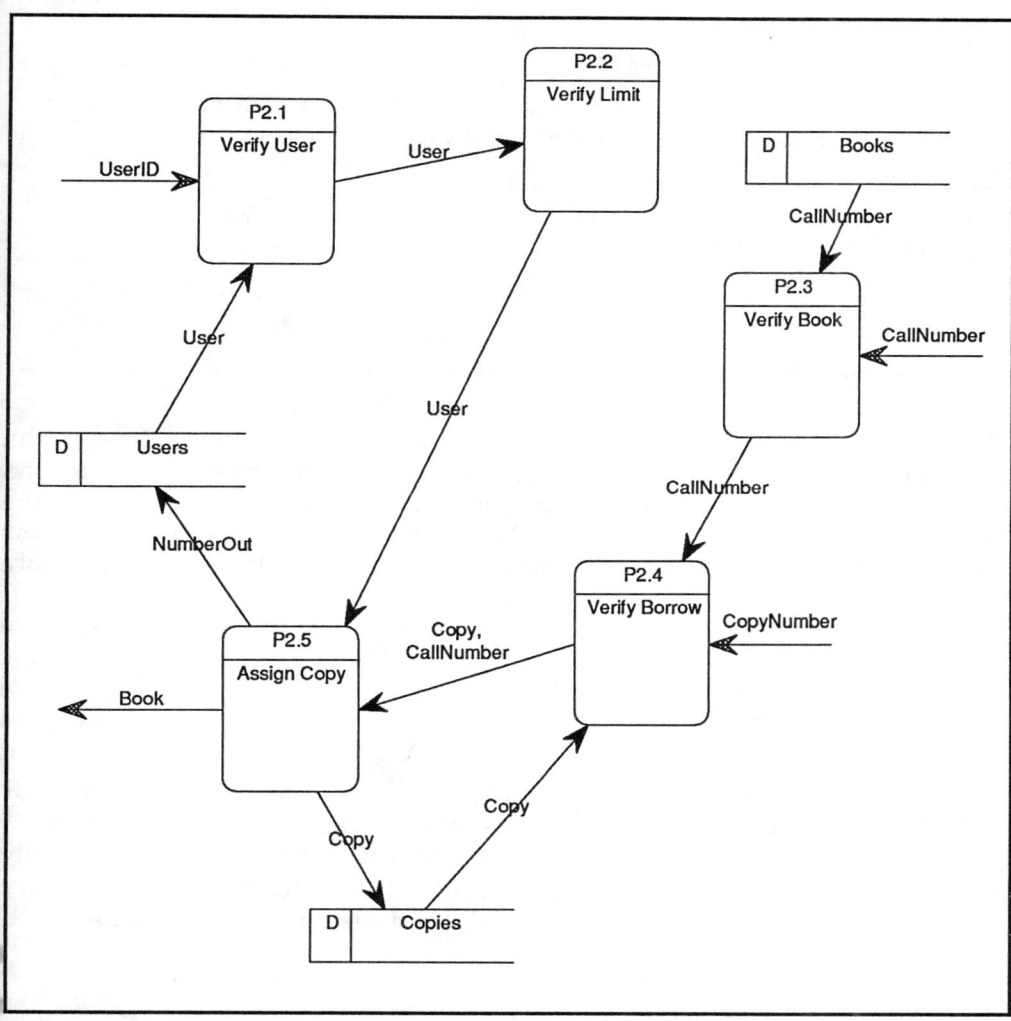

Figure 4.10
Low-level DFD
for Check Out
Book.

Get today's date from the system and add 14 days to it for the due date. Update the copy information with these dates and link it to the user. Update the number of books checked out by this user.

Figure 4.11
Process
specification for
Assign Copy.

Name	Object	Type
Add Author	Symbol	Process
Add Author	Definition	Process
Add Author	Definition	Module
Add Author	Symbol	Module
Add Book	Symbol	Module
Add Book	Diagram	Structure Chart
Add Book	Symbol	Module

Figure 4.12
Excerpts from the Library data dictionary.

Figure 4.11 shows the PDL associated with process 2.5, Assign Copy, in the DFD in Figure 4.10. This process calculates the due date for the book, updates the copy information to indicate that the copy is checked out to this user, and updates the user borrow count. We chose to use PDL or structured English in our process specification mainly because most people are familiar with it and it is easily translated to module specifications in design.

4.8.4 Library Data Dictionary

The library example represents a significant amount of information in analysis in the form of the data dictionary. While it is not possible to show the entire contents of this dictionary, we offer the definitions in Figure 4.12 as examples. This is actually a report from the Library data dictionary that describes each object in the dictionary and its type. For more on data structures and data models in the data dictionary, see Chapter 5.

4.8.5 Library Structure Charts

When designing a solution to the Library problem, there are many assumptions that must be made regarding the implementation environment. For example, questions about which programming language will be used for the system, which hardware and software environment the system will run on, which database or file access methods will be available, etc. must all be answered before we can fully design a solution.

The assumptions we made when designing the Library system are described in Chapter 3. Some of these assumptions served to keep the example problem simple, while others were made to keep the example realistic. The resulting system was considered to be an on-line application with menus that provided access to the

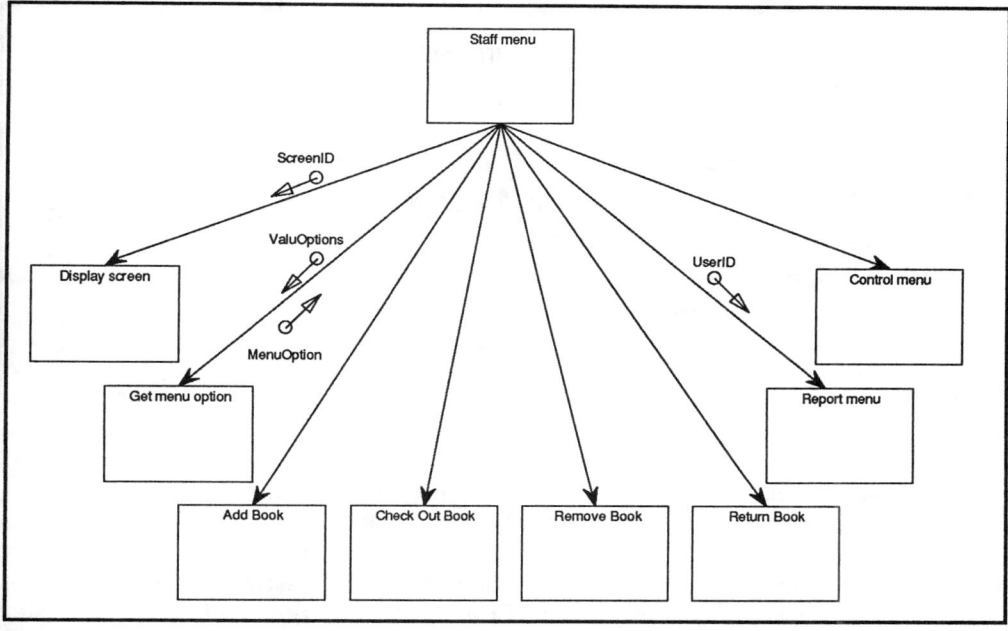

Figure 4.13
Top-level
structure chart
for the Library
system.

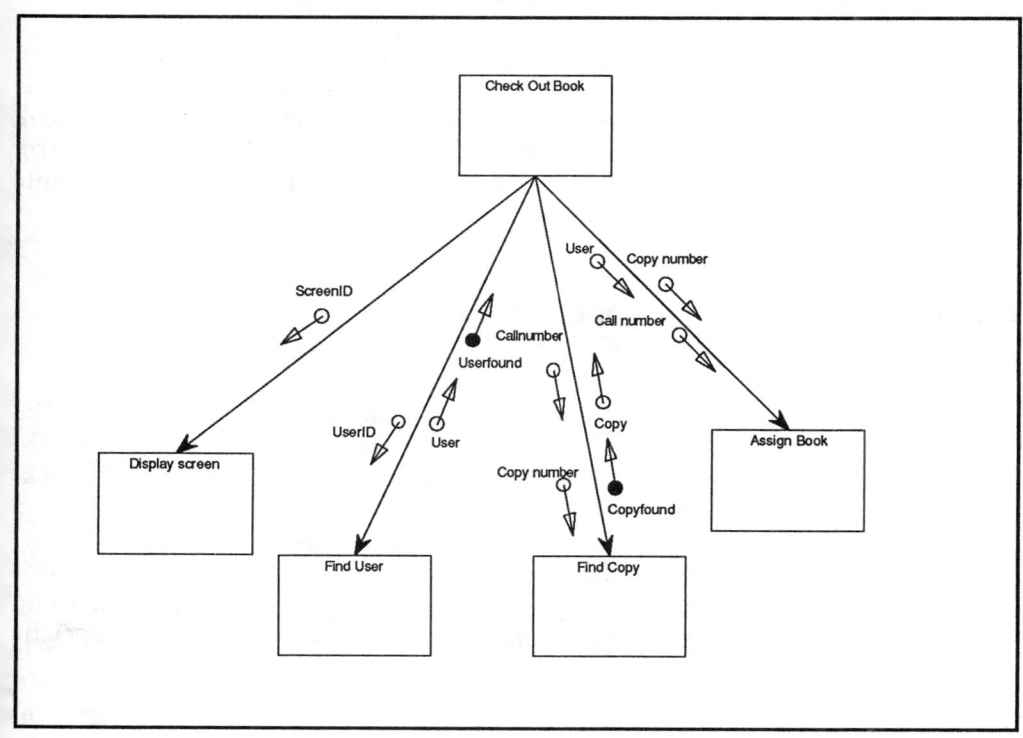

Figure 4.14
Structure chart for
the Check Out
Book module.

```
Inputs: User, CallNumber, CopyNumber
Outputs: (none)

Set DateOut to today's date
Set DateDue to today's date plus 14 days
Write updated copy record in copies file
Link user record to copy record using UserID
Increment NumberCheckedOut
Write updated user record in users file
Return
```

various system functions or transactions. This followed our view in analysis that the Library system is a transaction-centered application.

In the Library system, an initial sign-on screen requires that a user enter a name and password, and the resulting security system restricts access to the rest of the system based on the type of user. Library staff would be allowed to transfer to a staff menu screen, while regular library users would be transferred to a user menu that allowed them access to only appropriate programs or reports.

Based on these assumptions, we created the top-level structure chart shown in Figure 4.14. As is shown in the chart, the library system is organized by functions. Following the Check Out Book module down the hierarchy, we decomposed the module into the structure chart shown in Figure 4.14. This chart shows how a book is checked out to a user, and the high-level module (Check Out Book) passes control and data to four lower-level modules. Further decomposing the Assign Copy module leads us to the module specification shown in Figure 4.15.

4.8.6 Library Module Specifications

The module specification shown in Figure 4.15 describes the logic within the module that assigns a copy of a book to a user. The module receives the data userID, book (call number) and copy number from the higher-level module (Check Out Book) and updates the user and copy data structures to reflect the book's being checked out to the user. The module returns no data elements or structures to the higher-level module but does update the files that contain the book, copy, and user information. The individual module logic commands, Write, Link, etc., could represent third- or fourth-generation language commands that map to a specific DML command.

4.9 Resource List

While there are a variety of good resources available on the function-oriented techniques, we recommend the Yourdon book [YOU89] for modern structured analysis and the Page-Jones book [PAG88] for a description of the concepts of structured design.

Other good sources for function-oriented techniques include the Blank [BLA83], Meyers [MEY78], Mittra [MIT88], Pressman [PRE88] and Weinberg [WEI78][WEI79] books. For information on the original methods, see the books of DeMarco [DEM78], Gane/Sarson [GAN78], and Yourdon/Constantine [YOU78]. For information on the essential view, see the McMenamin and Palmer [MCM84] book.

The November 1991 issue of *American Programmer* is dedicated to structured techniques and includes several excellent articles on the function-oriented techniques. Parnas has written several papers on functional decomposition, including [PAR71] and [PAR72].

For a comparison of structured techniques, see the Marshall book [MAR86]. For information on structured programming, see the papers of Dijkstra [DIJ65][DIJ76] and Emery [EME62] and the books of Friedman [FRI77], McCracken [MCC76], and Wells [WEL86a] and [WEL86b].

For books on structured testing, see Meyers [MEY79] and Perry [PER83].

4.10 References

[BLA83]   Blank, J., and M.J. Krijger, *Software Engineering: Methods and Techniques*, Wiley-Interscience, 1983.

[DEM78]   DeMarco, T., *Structured Analysis and Systems Specification*, Yourdon Press, 1978.

[DIJ65]   Dijkstra, E., "Programming Considered as a Human Activity," in *Proc. 1965 IFIP Congress*, North-Holland Publishing Co., 1965.

[DIJ76]   Dijkstra, E., "Structured Programming," in *Software Engineering, Concepts and Techniques*, J. Buxton et al., eds., Van Nostrand Reinhold, 1976.

[EME62]   Emery, J.C., "Modular Data Processing Systems in COBOL," *CACM*, vol. 5, no. 5 (May 1962), pp. 263-268.

[FRI77]   Friedman, F.L., and E.B. Koffman, *Problem Solving and Structured Programming in FORTRAN*, Addison-Wesley, 1977.

[GAN78]   Gane, C., and T. Sarson, *Structured Systems Analysis: Tools and Techniques*, Prentice-Hall, 1978.

[GAN89]   Gane, C., *Rapid System Development: Using Structured Techniques and Relational Technology*, Prentice-Hall, 1989.

[HAT88]   Hatley, D.J., and I.A. Pirbhai, *Strategies for Real-Time System Specification*, Dorsett House, 1988.

[KEU91]   Keuffel, W., "The House of Structure," *Unix Review*, February 1991, pp. 28 ff.

[MAR86]   Marshall, G. R., *Systems Analysis and Design: Alternative Structured Approaches*, Prentice-Hall, 1986.

[MAR67]   Martin, D., and G. Estrin, "Models of Computations and Systems - Evaluations of Vertext Probabilities in Graphical Models of Computations," *Journal of the ACM*, vol. 14, no. 2, April 1967, pp. 281-299.

[MCC76]   McCracken, D.D., *A Simplified Guide to Structured COBOL Programming*, Wiley & Sons, 1986.

[MCM84]   McMenamin, S., and J. Palmer, *Essential Systems Analysis*, Yourdon Press, 1984.

[MEY78]   Meyers, G., *Composite / Structured Design*, Van Nostrand Reinhold, 1978.

[MEY79]   Meyers, G., *The Art of Software Testing*, Wiley, 1979.

[MIT88]   Mittra, S., *Structured Techniques of Systems Analysis, Design, and Implementation*, Wiley-Interscience, 1988.

[NAS73]   Nassi, I., and B. Schneiderman, "Flowchart Techniques for Structured Programming," *SIGPLAN Notices*, ACM, August 1973.

[PAG88]   Page-Jones, M., *Practical Guide to Structured Systems Design*, Yourdon Press, 1988.

[PAR71]   Parnas, D., "Information Distributing Aspects of Design Methodology," *Proceedings of the 1971 IFIP Congress*, Booklet TA-3, North-Holland, 1972.

[PAR72]   Parnas, D.L., "On the Criteria to be Used in Decomposing Systems," *CACM*, vol. 15, no. 5, 1972, pp. 1053-1058.

[PER83]   Perry, W.E., *A Structured Approach to Systems Testing*, Prentice-Hall, 1983.

[PRE88]   Pressman, R., *Software Engineering: A Beginner's Guide*, McGraw-Hill, 1988.

[STE91]   Stevens, W., "Structured Design, Structured Analysis, and Structured Programming," *American Programmer*, vol. 4, no. 11, pp. 23-30.

[STE74]   Stevens, W., G. Myers, and L. Constantine, "Structured Design," *IBM Systems Journal*, vol. 13, no. 2 (1974), pp. 115-139.

[SWA82]   Swartout, W., and R. Balzer, "On the Inevitable Intertwining of Specification and Implementation," *CACM*, vol. 25, no. 7, July 1982, pp. 438-440.

[TAO90]   Tao, Y., "Toward a Formal Basis for Flow Diagram-Based Requirements Analysis Techniques," Ph.D. Thesis, Computer Sciences Dept., University of Iowa, December 1990.

[WAR92] Ward, P.T., "The Evolution of Structured Analysis: Part III," *American Programmer*, November 1992, pp. 41-53.

[WAR86] Ward, P.T., and S. Mellor, *Structured Development of Real-Time Systems*, Volumes 1-3, Yourdon Press, 1986.

[WEA87] Weaver, M., *Using the Structured Techniques - A CASE Study*, Prentice-Hall, 1987.

[WEI76] Weinberg, G., *An Introduction to General System Thinking*, Wiley-Interscience, 1976.

[WEI78] Weinberg, V., *Structured Analysis*, Yourdon Press, 1978.

[WEI79] Weingerg, G., *On the Design of Stable Systems*, Wiley-Interscience, 1979.

[WEL86a] Wells, T., *Structured Systems Development in COBOL*, Yourdon, 1986.

[WEL86b] Wells, T., *Structured Systems Development in Pascal*, Yourdon, 1986.

[YOU89] Yourdon, E., *Modern Structured Analysis*, Yourdon Press, 1989.

[YOU78] Yourdon, E., and L. Constantine, *Structured Design*, Yourdon Press, 1978.

A Historical Perspective on the Structured Revolution

The concepts of *structured programming* were defined by Dijkstra and others and became popular in the early 1960s. Structured programming delivers programs and systems that are easier to debug, understand, and maintain, and this leads to reduced maintenance costs for the system. While it was generally believed that structured programs are easier to follow and understand, the process of creating structured programs was originally driven by a process of breaking a system down into its functional parts (functional decomposition) and creating programs or modules for each component part.

One guiding principle behind structured programming is that a program or system can be decomposed into small, discrete pieces (modules) that each have a basic function and only one entry and one exit. Another basic premise is that each module should be compact enough to fit onto a single printed page, so as to make following the flow of control easier.

Structured programming recognizes that any program can be composed of basic building blocks or constructs (black boxes) using three types of instructions: sequence, selection, and iteration. Through a process of stepwise refinement, structured programming helps developers create a program or system composed of modules within a hierarchy of control.

Structured design is a design approach based on partitioning programs and modules through functional decomposition. The seminal paper for this technique was "Structured Design," which Larry Constantine wrote with Wayne Stevens and Glen Myers in 1974. Constantine also wrote *Structured Design* with Ed Yourdon, which was published in 1978.

The notation for structure charts was born in the late 1960s, and with it the concepts of coupling, cohesion, modularity, transform analysis, and transaction analysis. While the structure chart contains a subset of the symbols commonly used in a traditional flowchart, the two diagrams are substantially different in their representation. A structure chart shows the flow of control through a system, with the lines connecting modules used to indicate an exchange of control, while a flowchart shows only the transfer of control. A structure chart describes both the flow of control in a program or module and the flow of data passed up and down the hierarchy of control.

The concept of a structure chart was created to help developers deliver specifications for programming that addressed the goals of structured programming, namely that a program or system would be designed in small pieces which could be easily related to the whole system and which would be relatively independent of one another. By partitioning the modules within a system, a hierarchy of modules can be created, with each module considered a black box.

Structure charts are a model of the module hierarchy and the data and control flow of a program or system. As such, they are a representation of the software at a point in time, following the design phase. Interestingly, structure charts do not show any of the low-level details of the individual modules. To complete the design specification, developers must include PDL, pseudocode or some other detailed design representation that describes the content of the individual modules in a structure chart.

History tells us that Constantine was teaching a class in structured design in 1967 when he found that his students were having trouble building structure charts using functional decomposition. The story goes that he happened to have a copy of the ACM paper by Martin and Estrin describing a program graph (see below) and suggested his students build a program graph to describe the system, then convert the program graph to a structure chart by adding the flow of control. This original use of bubble charts, later called data flow diagrams, became the basis for *structured analysis*.

While data flow diagrams were not widely used until the mid 1970s, the idea was put into practice by the consultants and instructors at Yourdon, Inc. based on the original work of Larry Constantine. In 1975, the original data flow diagram was expanded to include data stores (files) and external entities (terminators). Both Tom DeMarco and Chris Gane and Trish Sarson published books describing how to use data flow diagrams in analysis, and these formed the basis for all the structured analysis work that followed.

Data flow diagrams, data flow graphs or program graphs, were based on the work of David Martin and Gerald Estrin in their paper written in 1967. In their book, Constantine and Yourdon focused on the transformation of data by processes, and this became the basis of structured analysis.

Data flow diagrams allow developers to model and study the flow of data through a system. As Constantine and Yourdon stated in their book *Structured Design*, "Hence, we need a method of restating the problem itself (i.e., 'functional requirements' or 'systems specification') in a manner that emphasizes the data flow and de-emphasizes (in fact, almost ignores) the procedural aspects of the problem."

Following the original work of DeMarco and Gane/Sarson, John Palmer and Steve McMenamin published their book, *Essential Systems Analysis*, which describes a slightly different approach to structured analysis. The McMenamin/Palmer approach uses event partitioning instead of functional decomposition to guide the analysis process and others followed this approach in their own work (see Ward/Mellor and Hatley/Pirbhai).

Under the original structured analysis technique, analysts would build a number of different models to describe the system under study. These included a current physical, current logical, future logical, and future physical model, of a system. Needless to say building all of these models took time and many organizations became frustrated with all the model building. Some instructors and consultants began suggesting that developers build only a single model, the future physical, to describe the finished system. This also led to discussion about how to derive the correct model of a system, which became known as the essential model.

Data flow diagrams are models of the processing of data through a system and as such do not describe all aspects of a system under investigation. Traditional data flow diagrams cannot show time-dependent behavior, lower-level process descriptions, or data structure definitions. To model the data in a system, a data model is needed to supplement the data flow diagrams, along with a data dictionary to contain the descriptions of flows, data stores, and processes. For real-time systems, the control behavior of the system must also be modeled, and subsequent notations defined a control view to be added to the data flow models.

Chapter 5
Data-Oriented Techniques

In the previous chapter, we examined a set of techniques that centers around the definition of the functions performed by a system. The function-oriented techniques guide the design of an application so that the definition of data follows the definition of function. The resulting application is thus structured around the functions it performs.

In this chapter, we will examine a set of techniques that takes the opposite approach. That is, they first focus on the data structures needed by an application, and then determine the functions required to support those data structures. We call these techniques the data-oriented techniques.

The very terms historically used to describe software development, such as data processing and management information systems, include a data perspective balancing a process or function perspective. Indeed, it seems impossible to separate the two views, data and process, from any computer software undertaking.

As we will see, the data-oriented techniques described in this chapter focus on the data structures an application stores and maintains and place less emphasis on the processing or functionality required of the application. As the function-oriented techniques described in the last chapter consider data as an afterthought, the data-oriented techniques in this chapter view functions as simply actions applied against the data.

5.1 Introduction

For purposes of our discussion, we will differentiate between two different types of data-oriented techniques: those that operate at a system level, and those that operate at an enterprise level (i.e., multiple systems) within an organization. The two different approaches have much in common, but also take a slightly different perspective on how software products are developed.

Like many of the techniques discussed in this text, the system-level data-oriented techniques focus on and help design individual software applications. In comparison, the enterprise-level data-oriented techniques can be used to develop systems and data structures which support multiple applications. The enterprise-level data-oriented techniques are often used in developing integrated database applications where the cost of redundant data is very high. These methods form the basis for the information-oriented techniques described in Chapter 7.

5.1.1 Definitions

Before beginning a discussion of these techniques, some basic terms should be defined along with the context in which they are used. Figure 5.1 displays the connections among the items defined below.

Data, the plural form of *datum*, is defined by Webster's Seventh New Collegiate Dictionary as "factual material used as a basis especially for discussion or decision." In a computerized data processing system, data can be input from several sources, stored in an electronic medium, and delivered in various forms, including screens and reports. Data typically represents a logical collection of related information acted on by a software system.

A *data element* is the smallest addressable unit of information normally stored by a system. Synonyms for data elements include attributes, characteristics, record fields, and table columns. For example, in a payroll record, data elements may include *Employee-Number*, *Pay-Rate,* and *Social-Security-Number*.

A *data structure*, in its simplest form, is a collection of data elements. Synonyms for data structures include records and tables. Using the payroll system as an example, an *Employee-Information* data structure may be composed of the data elements *Employee-Number*, *Employee-Name*, *Social-Security-Number*, and *Pay-Rate*. In a more complex form, a data structure could be a collection of other data structures. For example, an *Organization* data structure may be composed of the department-level data structures *Employee, Marketing, Sales, Warehouse, Accounts Payable, Accounts Receivable*, and *Administration*. Physical data structures may be implemented in different forms, including files, records, arrays, queues or stacks.

Figure 5.1
Sample data,
data elements,
and data
structures.

	Employee Information		
Data Structure -->			
Data Elements -->	Employee Number	Employee Name	Social Security Number	Pay Rate
Data -->	40170	Mahanti, Robert	205-45-0128	8.75
	42063	Treadwell, Doug	629-81-2943	8.50
	50109	Brooks, Phillip	720-11-5794	10.25
	...	....	...	...

A *data model* is a set of concepts used to describe the structure of and operations on a database or file system. Data models typically include attributes, relationships, and constraints for the data structures.

A *database schema* is a description of a database structure, usually in the form of language constructs for a DBMS.

5.1.2 History

The concepts underlying the system-level data-oriented techniques were created and developed by three research groups, headed, respectively, by Jean-Dominique Warnier in France, Michael Jackson in England, and Ken Orr in the United States [HIG83].

In the late 1960s, Warnier and his team in Paris, France developed the concepts underlying the earliest data-structured technique, logical construction of programs (LCP). Warnier recognized that the best-designed programs were those whose structures matched the data being processed. LCP may be the most widely used program design approach outside the United States. Warnier followed LCP with a more comprehensive technique called logical construction of systems (LCS).

In the 1970s, Jackson developed the principles of program design based on data structures. Jackson system development (JSD) became the broader term for development using the Jackson approach. A JSD specification consists of a distributed network of sequential processes, each with its own local data structures.

Also during the 1970s, Orr adapted the work of Warnier and Jackson to create a technique called structured program design (SPD). He later expanded it into a more comprehensive approach called data structured systems development (DSSD). In addition to Warnier and Jackson, Orr drew on the work of Edsger Dijkstra of Holland, one of the creators of structured programming [ORR77]. Techniques from Warnier, Jackson, and Orr are used to design single applications.

More recently, with the advent of DBMSs and the need for integration of data across organizations, enterprise-level data-oriented techniques from Peter Chen and others have been developed and are used to design data structures supporting multiple applications. These methods tend to view applications as transactions applied against an integrated database and include techniques for reducing the errors common in sharing data across an organization.

The need for development techniques that support integrated database (IDB) systems and the acceptance of relational database management systems (RDBMS) have also contributed to the evolution of the enterprise-level data-oriented techniques into the information-oriented techniques described in Chapter 7.

As organizations required more complex data structures, the need arose for database management systems (DBMS) to support these complex structures. Older, flat file implementations of systems led to higher overhead in maintenance and typically bad performance for the system. Some organizations also found that as they developed strategic applications, there was overlap in the use and collection of data elements and structures across their business.

From a logical perspective, data structures (collections of data elements) can be designed and implemented in a variety of physical structures. A set of data elements could be grouped together into a single record, which would require only a single input/output (I/O) to retrieve or update all the information. This record might also include many redundancies if groups of repeating data elements were included. Also, questions about how the data would be retrieved and updated could cause functional complexities in a system that accessed this information.

On the opposite end of the spectrum, each data element could be stored as a separate physical record which would eliminate redundancies but require multiple I/Os to retrieve information. The problem with this approach is representing logical relationships between the data elements. This could also cause increased complexity in the application and lead to poor system performance.

Early data structures were implemented using sequential files, with each record mapping to an occurrence of a record in the file. This led to sequential, transaction-based processing. Following this, indexed files were introduced that contained a sequential file along with an index file. The index file was sorted by key values and contained record numbers referencing the sequential file. In this fashion, keyed or indexed access was made available.

IBM and others developed hierarchical database management systems (DBMS) in the 1960s, which supported tree structures and database records that could be accessed using keyed fields, with relationships between records maintained by the DBMS. This was followed by the development of network DBMSs, which supported a network of records and relationships. In the 1970s, the relational data model was defined by E. F. Codd, and relational DBMSs soon gained widespread use.

Early DBMS vendors began pushing the concept of an integrated DBMS that contained all the information an organization used and eliminated any redundant data. Enterprise-wide DBMSs were designed with several goals in mind: to eliminate redundant data entry and collection, to reduce update anomalies that could occur, to reduce the cost of maintaining the data, to restrict access to the data, and to ensure the integrity and timeliness of the data.

Eliminating redundant data meant consolidating data elements and structures across the organization and defining which groups were responsible for data entry, etc. As part of the development process, the ownership of data began to be discussed along with synonyms for data elements.

Reducing the cost of maintaining the data led to the advent of data dictionaries and structured tools to access the data, most notably in the form of 4GLs. In the mid 1980s several data dictionaries appeared for specific DBMSs. Examples include

ADS/Online for IDMS, NOMAD, DataCom, and Total. 4GLs also made developers more productive, since they allowed procedural definitions of common functions to be defined and reused across applications. 4GLs are usually linked to a specific DBMS and may not support complex application functionality.

Restricting access to the data was also accomplished via the data dictionary, which prohibited access to the database. Data administration as a function within development led to centralized control over the data. Ensuring integrity and timeliness of data — referential integrity, etc. — became difficult when data began to be used widely across an organization. All of these factors contributed to the development of the enterprise-level data-oriented techniques and the success of 4GLs. The focus on sharing data and viewing data as a strategic asset led to the development of the IOTs described in Chapter 7.

5.2 Philosophy

The originators of data-oriented techniques noticed a recurring theme in software development:

The structure of the best programming solution mirrors the structure of the data being processed.

This statement means, for example, that if a program to produce a report is being developed, the structure of the most efficient program will be based on the structure, or layout, of the output report.

Warnier's team, doing the earliest research, concluded that data processing could be thought of as an extension of the branch of mathematics called set theory [HIG83]. This view of programs as representing a mapping of input data to output data is consistent across all the data-oriented techniques.

As a consequence, some of the data-oriented techniques emphasize the organization of data prior to defining application functionality. These techniques focus at the application level; they first define the data that the application will produce and then determine the inputs needed to produce the outputs. Finally, they delimit the processing, or application functionality, needed to transform the defined inputs into the defined outputs. The logic of the resulting application will have a structure identical to that of the processed data. For complex data structures, the use of a DBMS to store and retrieve the data facilitates the concept of an application built on the data.

Other originators of data-oriented techniques noticed another recurring theme in software development:

The structure of data is (generally) more stable than the structure of functions.

Most maintenance performed on an application occurs because of changes in required functionality rather than changes in data structure. As a simple example, consider an application that uses a data element called *Employee Name* that is defined as type *alphabetic* with a length of *30 characters*. How often will the type and length of the field change in comparison with how the field is used? Developers of data-structured techniques observed more change in how a field is used than in how the data is represented.

Based on this theme, these originators developed techniques that focus on data at the enterprise level. An *enterprise* can be defined as a range of activity broader than the scope of an application. An enterprise may be a department, a group of departments, an entire organization, etc. These techniques develop enterprise-wide data structures, or data models, upon which multiple applications operate. The idea is that once the relatively stable data structures are defined, we can place relatively unstable functionality, or applications, upon them. This leads us to the third theme in our view of data-oriented techniques:

Data should be viewed as an organizational resource independent of the systems that process the data.

Some have suggested that data-oriented and function-oriented techniques are two sides of the same coin. The two orientations, in fact, were developed (or "minted") over the same period of time and have the same objective: to provide an engineering-like approach to the analysis, design, and coding of software. Both attempt to deliver the same result: a working system, including a complete definition of its functions and data structures. Their primary difference is that they achieve that result in opposite ways. Data-oriented techniques are similar to function-oriented techniques in that they begin with a definition of the scope of the system to be worked on.

A data-oriented approach begins by defining the structure of data before any functions are defined. This means, for example, defining the outputs of a system and then defining the functions to produce those outputs. The idea is that the structure of data is most important in software design, and that it makes no sense to define functions when that structure is unknown. The approach starts at a system level and continues to refine the data structures, and consequently the functions, down to individual program modules.

The function-oriented techniques focus on the processing needed in a system and define the inputs and outputs required to support that processing. These approaches also start at a system level and continue to decompose functions, and data structure or flow, down to individual program modules.

An interesting contrast between the two approaches is pointed out by Orr [ORR81]. He indicates that top-down design, a feature of function-oriented techniques, produces systems that work but whose solutions seem "arbitrary." Orr believes that his output-oriented approach produces an application design that has just enough functionality to deliver the needed outputs. When using a function-oriented approach, however, which has no clear correspondence between needed outputs and functions, excessive functionality may be included in the application design. As discussed in Chapter 10, function-oriented techniques often generate arbitrary designs.

5.3 Characteristics

There are several variations on the data-oriented theme. One variation focuses on the solution to a specific data processing problem, and data structures are defined in terms of how they will be used in a particular program or system. DSSD and the techniques developed by Jackson, Orr, and Warnier all fall into this category. Another approach focuses on a solution to a set of data processing problems: creating data structures or databases that can be used by multiple systems. The entity-relationship approach, created by Peter Chen, is an example of this type of method.

The link between Orr's approach and Chen's approach is the fact that Warnier-Orr diagrams can be used to diagram the database for an organization, or something larger in scope than a system. All of the system-level data-oriented techniques support some form of data modeling notation and deal with physical data structure design prior to functional design.

In subsequent sections we will focus on two specific data-oriented techniques, using the Library problem to explain both methods. DSSD was selected as the system-level data-oriented technique because it best exemplifies the concepts of data-oriented techniques and is well-known outside the United States. The entity-relationship approach (ERA) is used to describe the enterprise-level data-oriented techniques, since it is also widely used and has been extended to support other methods, including object-oriented techniques.

Data-oriented techniques also tend to view a software product as a set of transactions (functions) applied against a set of data structures. This view is orthogonal to the function-oriented techniques, which perceive data structures as collections of data required by processes. These methods often require elaborate data models with data designs that are targeted towards specific relational database management systems (RDBMS). Selected CASE tools can generate the DBMS structures from the design specifications.

An interesting offshoot of the data-oriented techniques is the movement towards the object-oriented techniques described in Chapter 8. Many of the object-oriented methods are based on concepts and ideas defined by the architects of the data-oriented techniques, including Jackson, Orr, and Chen.

5.3.1 Notation

The primary notation for the system-level data-oriented techniques is a diagram which represents functions performed against data structures. Under the DSSD method, the notation used would be Warnier-Orr diagrams. Under the Jackson approach, Jackson structure diagrams are used to represent processing against data structures.

The Warnier-Orr diagram is very similar to other notations used, including the action diagram (described in Chapter 7), the flowform [SCA87], and the Nassi-Schneiderman diagram (discussed in the previous chapter).

One property of the Warnier-Orr diagram is its direct mapping to structured programming constructs. Some early CASE tools that supported the Warnier-Orr diagram allowed for the creation of COBOL code from the diagrams.

For data modeling, the DSSD method includes an entity diagram which represents the entities in a system and the relationships among the entities. This diagram is similar to the Chen entity-relationship diagram used in most of the enterprise-level data-oriented techniques.

Under the enterprise-level data-oriented techniques, the primary notation for data modeling is the entity-relationship diagram (ERD) created by Peter Chen [CHE76]. This diagram uses rectangles to represent entities and lines connecting the rectangles to represent relationships between the entities. The lines also specify the cardinalities of the relationships — one-to-one, one-to-many, or many-to-many. Figure 5.2 shows several variations on the symbols and notations used in ERDs. In the diagram shown, a customer can have many accounts, but an account must have one and only one customer.

Once the data model is complete, i.e., fully normalized and attributed, a physical database design is created along with the functions the application will perform against the data, often using a Create | Read | Update | Delete (CRUD) view. Under this view, all actions against the data structures are mapped into one of four possible functions, and these become the basis for the application design. The entity-relationship approach (ERA) uses the ERD and CRUD to develop applications based on a DBMS.

5.3.1.1 DSSD

There are several diagraming tools used in DSSD: the entity diagram, the assembly line diagram, the Warnier-Orr diagram, and the Warnier-Orr worksheet. The next four sections describe these tools and their associated notation.

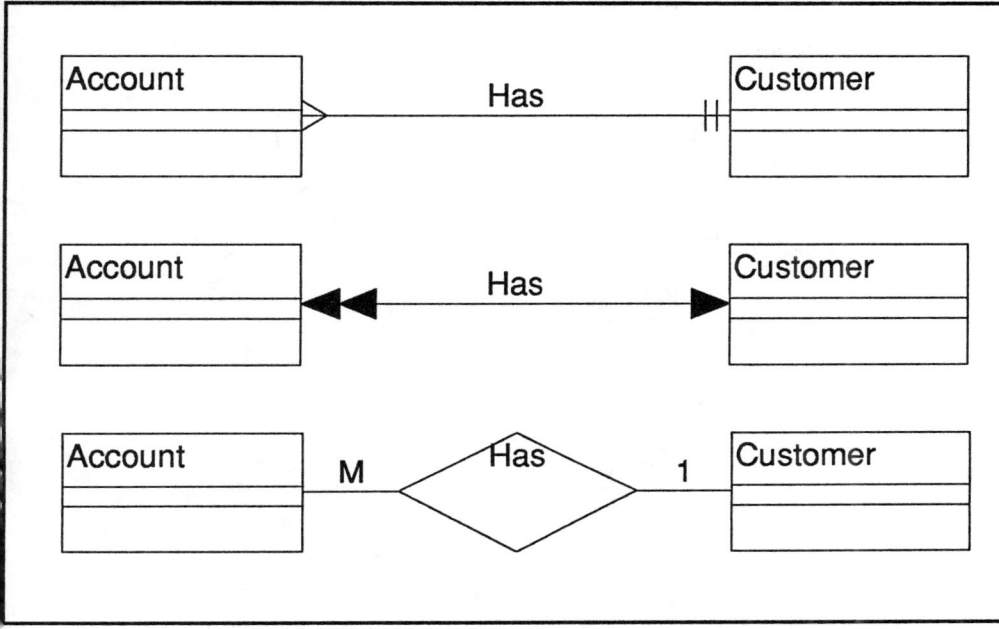

Figure 5.2
Variations on the entity-relationshp diagram.

Entity Diagram

Not only does the entity diagram (ED) look like a data flow diagram (DFD), but its purpose is similar as well. Like the context diagram (a high-level DFD), the ED is used to identify the scope of a system. The ED is the first diagram used in DSSD and shows who does what. DSSD identifies *entities* as components that provide or receive data. An entity may be a person, department, organization, system, etc. Once entities are determined, an ED is drawn for each one from the perspective of that entity. The ED has two symbols:

> *Circles* represent entities.
> *Arrows* depict transactions between entities which are caused by events.

The sample ED in Figure 5.3 shows entities that may be identified for an auto service center. The diagram is drawn from the perspective of the customer. The entity *Operations* issues a reminder to the entity *Customer* that service is required on a car. At the auto service center, the *Garage* provides the *Customer* with an estimate of work, and the *Customer* responds with an authorization. After the work has been completed, *Billing* issues a bill to the *Customer,* who responds with a payment.

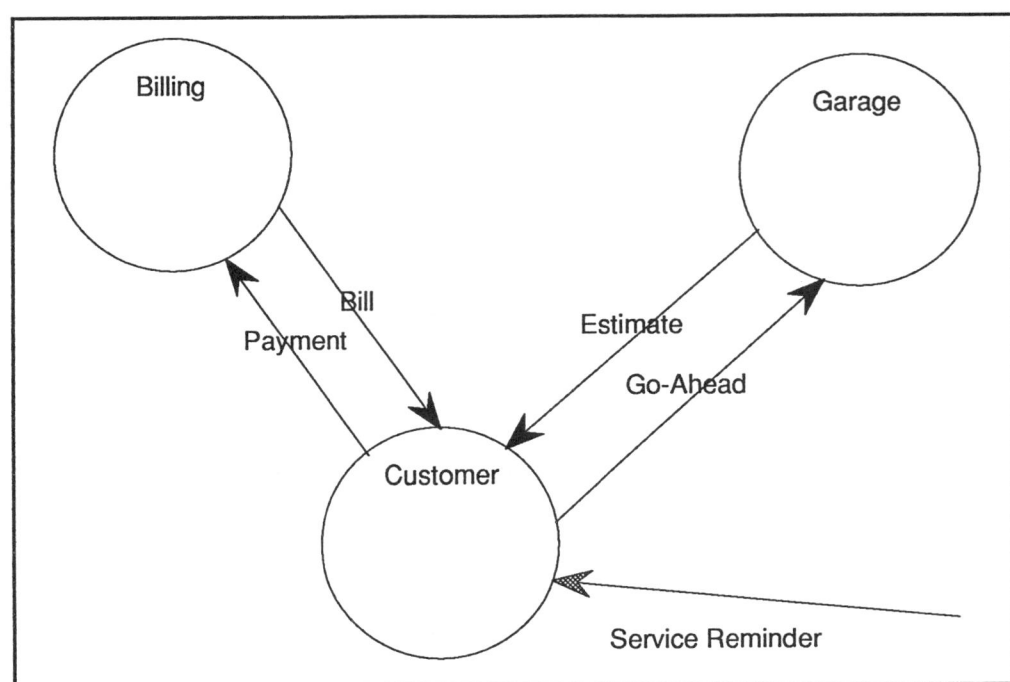

Figure 5.3
Entity diagram.

Assembly Line Diagram

The name of this diagram, borrowed from a manufacturing assembly line, implies that there is some sequence of operations that produces outputs from inputs. The assembly line diagram (ALD) shows such a sequence as a series of data structures and the functions that transform one data structure into another. Figure 5.4 shows an ALD that corresponds to the ED in Figure 5.3. It shows, for example,

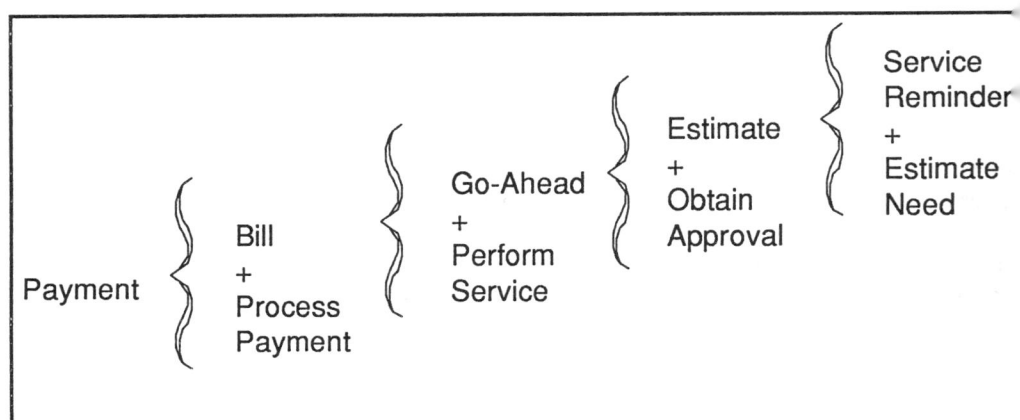

Figure 5.4
Assembly line diagram.

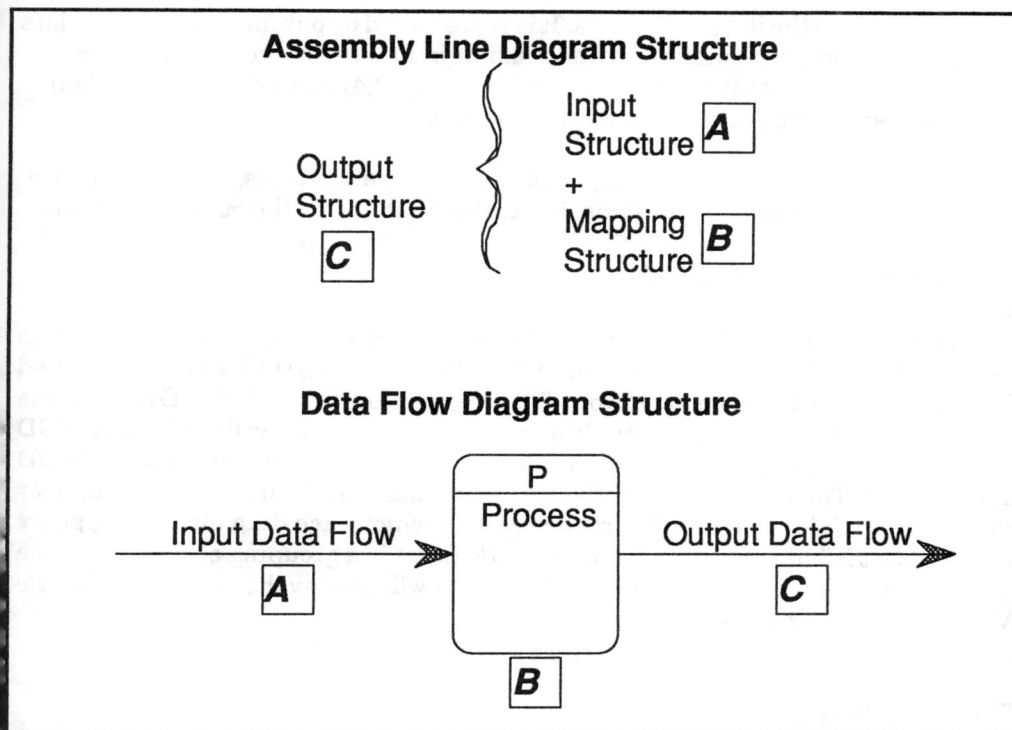

Figure 5.5
Connections
between the ALD
and the DFD.

that a Payment is produced by performing a Process Payment on a Bill. The ALD contains design information similar to that in the data flow diagram (DFD), and Figure 5.5 depicts the correspondence between the two diagram types. It indicates, for example, that an input structure on an ALD corresponds to an input data flow on a DFD.

Warnier-Orr Diagram

The Warnier-Orr Diagram (WOD) looks similar to the assembly line diagram (ALD). However, the WOD models data and processing structures, while the ALD shows the flow of information in an application [ORR81]. A sample WOD is shown in Figure 5.6. The WOD has four constructs to depict data and processing structure:

Hierarchy is the composition of data (or processing). The diagram shows greater detail as you read from left to right, with levels of detail separated by braces.

Sequence is the order in which data appears. The diagram shows sequence as you read from top to bottom.

Repetition is the iteration of data. It is represented by parentheses below a data item indicating its minimum and maximum number of occurrences. For example, $(1,n)$ means at least one occurrence, $(2,4)$ means from two to four occurrences, and (1) means exactly one occurrence.

Alternation is the partitioning of data into alternate forms. It is shown with a plus sign between data items, indicating that one or the other will occur.

Warnier-Orr Worksheet

The Warnier-Orr Worksheet (WOW) contains the information necessary to create a WOD. There is typically one WOW for every WOD (if you are a skilled developer, you probably get one "wow" for every deliverable, too). A WOW is a table of design information about an application's outputs, inputs, or functions. A WOD can be mapped from a WOW. Figure 5.7 displays a WOW corresponding to the WOD in Figure 5.6. The worksheet lists the data elements that the user wants to appear on a Monthly Sales Report. The frequency with which each data element appears on the report is indicated. For example, *Daily Sales* is a grouping of sales from one day, and for each *Daily Sales* grouping, the report will display the *Day*, multiple *Sale Numbers*, and a *Daily Sales Total*.

5.3.1.2 ERA

With any of the enterprise-level data-oriented techniques, some notation is required to represent the logical and physical data structures. The focus on these methods is in the creation of a data model and eventually a logical and physical database design. The most common data modeling notation is the entity-relationship diagram (ERD), which includes symbols for entities, connections between symbols as relationships between entities, super, and subtypes, and attributes.

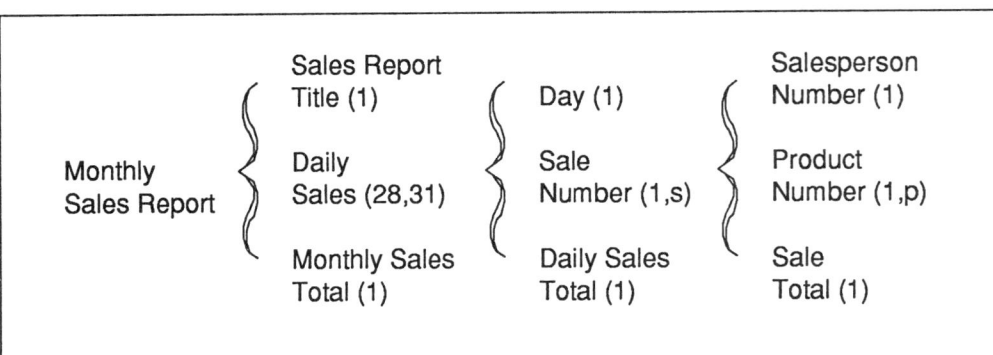

Figure 5.6
Warnier-Orr
diagram.

Underlying the ERD are textual descriptions in a data dictionary. Figure 5.2 describes common ERD notations.

In the design phase, the ERD is used to create a logical and physical database design specification, typically geared towards a relational database management system (RDBMS). Some enterprise-level data-oriented techniques, including the Bachman and CASE*Method methods, have extended the basic ERD to support additional constructs required to describe a complete database design.

The notation typically used for functionality under the enterprise-level data-oriented techniques is the CRUD view, with process specifications tied to data structures, or 4GL constructs associated with operations against the database. The latter are directly tied to the 4GL of choice and typically include various statements for traversing relationships and accessing database tables using primary or foreign keys.

Some of the object-oriented techniques use extensions to the entity-relationship model to support data abstractions including aggregation, sub/superclasses, and generalization. These areas are covered in more depth in Chapter 8.

5.3.2 Technique

The two groups of data-oriented techniques described in this chapter differ in the approach they take to building software applications and the steps they take in creating the resulting representations. We will attempt to describe each of the more popular techniques, both system-level and enterprise-level, and the representations used.

While there appears to be overlap in the use of various tools and representations, the two groups of techniques are also very different in the way software systems are described and designed.

Number	Data Element	Frequency
1	Sales Report Title	1/Report
2	Daily Sales	28-31/Report
3	Monthly Sales Total	1/Report
4	Day	1/Daily Sales
5	Sale Number	1-to-many/Daily Sales
6	Daily Sales Total	1/Daily Sales
7	Salesperson Number	1/Sale Number
8	Product Number	1-to-many/Sale Number
9	Sale Total	1/Sale Number

Figure 5.7
Warnier-Orr
worksheet.

5.3.2.1 System-Level Data-Oriented Techniques

There are three popular system-level data-structured techniques: logical construction of systems from Warnier, Jackson system development from Jackson, and data structured systems development from Orr. Features that are common to all three [ORR81] include:

They design programs using hierarchical structures.
They design systems from a small and simple set of building blocks.
They design systems based on "the aggregate structure of the outputs."

Logical Construction of Systems

In the mid-1970s, Warnier published his programming technique, logical construction of programs (LCP) [WAR74]. This evolved into the logical construction of systems (LCS), which was published in the early 1980s. LCS has the following steps [WAR81]:

Set step	Defines all the data necessary for outputs required by the organization
General study step	Defines the subset of organizational data required by the application
Data step	Defines files and record formats based on the required data

Jackson System Development

Jackson system development (JSD) is a data-structured approach popular outside the United States, particularly in Europe. It was developed in the United Kingdom by a team led by Michael Jackson (not the one of single-glove fame) in the mid-1970s. Like LCS, JSD determines the form of a program based on the composite structure of its inputs and outputs. There are four major steps in JSD [MCC89]:

Data step	Defines data structures for each program input and output
Program step	Merges the input and output data structures to form a program structure
Operations step	Identifies operations required to get the outputs from the inputs and indicate where they occur in the program structure
Text step	Transforms the program structure into processing logic, including conditions and iteration

Data and program structures are shown using *Jackson structure diagrams*. These hierarchical diagrams are similar to the structure charts used in the function-oriented techniques. The program structure diagram shows iterative and conditional module execution [GAN89]. The data structure diagram is a variation of the ERD but does not show relationships *between* entities [YOU89]. Processing logic is represented by *structure text*, JSD's version of pseudocode.

JSD is the only data-structured technique that is designed to be used to develop both business and real-time systems. Real-time systems are detailed in the chapter on control-oriented techniques, Chapter 6.

Data Structured Systems Development (DSSD)

Ken Orr, the architect of DSSD, calls the outputs of an application its *goals*. He believes that knowing the goals of a system at the outset is important in focusing the application development effort [ORR77]. DSSD is founded on three design principles [HIG83]:

Design should be output-oriented: The desired outputs from a program should be completely understood.

Design should be logical and then physical: Because of the rapid pace of hardware change, design should be hardware-independent first and hardware-dependent second.

Design should be data-structured: The structures of the best programs are the same as the structures of the data being processed.

The early steps of DSSD are designed to elicit from the user the outputs needed from the application. DSSD is composed of eight stages [HIG83]:

Planning	Evaluate data processing problems and select solutions.
Definition	Select and specify desired outputs.
Design	Develop logical designs of the outputs, and corresponding inputs and processes. Then develop physical implementations of the logical designs.
Construction	Translate the physical designs into an application and test it.
Installation	Place the application in the production environment.
Operation	Use the application to produce business results.
Use	Use the results to make decisions and take actions.
Evaluation	Judge the application on its performance.

The DSSD approach is featured later in this chapter and will be applied to our example system, the Library system.

5.3.2.2 Enterprise-Level Data-Oriented Techniques

The original enterprise-level data-oriented technique was developed by E. F. Codd [COD70] around the relational database and later refined by Chris Date [DAT74]. Peter Chen later defined notations and techniques for data modeling and application design in support of RDBMSs, and other methodologists took the entity-relationship diagram and modified it to suit their own needs in analysis and design. The following sections describe some of the more popular enterprise-level data-oriented methods and additional considerations in developing DBMS-based applications.

Interestingly, the enterprise-level data-oriented techniques place little emphasis on the functional view of an application and instead derive a database design from a logical data model. Programming under enterprise-level data-oriented techniques can occur using a 4GL or a SQL-based language incorporated into traditional 3GLs.

Normalization

Under the umbrella of data-oriented techniques is a concept called *normalization*. (Some of you may have experienced this concept first-hand in grade school as you responded to the pressure to behave like your peers.) *Normalization* was defined by E. F. Codd [COD70] as a mathematical basis for deriving tables (rows and columns of data) using relational calculus and a set of transformations that could be applied to data structures to ensure that they met the requirements for a relational DBMS.

Codd defined a relation as a two-dimensional table of columns and rows. The table has no repeating groups of data elements in a row, and each row contains an entity of the same type. Columns in a table are the attributes, or data elements, for an entity, and no two rows in a table can contain exactly the same values. The table rows represent occurrences of table entries of data in some physical database.

Under relational calculus, there are a number of possible table operations or functions that can be performed on the tables. For example, tables can be *joined* together to make other tables. In addition, selected attributes from an existing table can be *projected* onto a new table. Through these and other basic table operations, tables can be manipulated to support any functionality required.

Codd also defined a *primary key* as an attribute, or group of attributes, that uniquely identifies a row in a table. *Foreign keys* are primary keys from other entities that are required to uniquely identify a row in a joined table. Foreign keys also satisfy relationship requirements in a data model by allowing entities to be associated with other entities. In the bank example shown in Figure 5.8, we see the foreign key *Branch#* as an attribute of the *Bank Customer* entity. This was needed to maintain the association between *Bank Customer* and *Bank Branch*.

Functional dependencies exist within an entity if the value of an attribute always determines the value of another attribute. Looking at the bank example again, the *Branch Address* is functionally dependent on the *Branch#*.

Codd also defined a notation for representing relational tables using textual descriptions. He offered the following conventions:

List the name of the relation first.
List the names of the attributes in parentheses following the relation name.
Indicate which attributes compose the primary key.

Figure 5.8 depicts the three relations from the bank example using Codd's notation. Note that *Bank Account* contains a primary key, *Account#*, and foreign keys, *Branch#* and *Customer#*, which are required to satisfy the relationship among *Bank Account*, *Bank Branch*, and *Bank Customer*. In other words, a bank account is associated with a branch and a customer via the foreign keys in the *Bank Account* table.

Codd identified three primary levels or forms of normalization that could be applied to data structures to help eliminate possible anomalies when they are implemented as a physical database.

First Normal Form. A table is said to be in first normal form if it has no repeating groups of attributes. In other words, if there is a group of attributes that is repeated, remove it to a separate table.

Second Normal Form. A table is said to be in second normal form if it is in first normal form and every non-key attribute is fully dependent on the primary key. Each non-key attribute within a table with a multiple-attribute key is examined to transform a set of tables into second normal form.

Third Normal Form. A table is said to be in third normal form if it is in second normal form and every non-key attribute is dependent on the entire primary key.

Figure 5.9 depicts an example of transforming a single table of unnormalized attributes into third normal form. The unnormalized table shows a repeating group of attributes that is removed to a separate table to reach first normal form. The

---

Bank Branch (Branch# (K), Address)
Bank Account (Account# (K), Type, Branch#, Customer#)
Bank Customer (Customer# (K), Name, Address, Branch#)

(K) = key

Figure 5.8
Bank tables
with keys.

attribute *Course Name* is dependent only upon *Course Number* so a separate *Course* table is created to satisfy second normal form. The attribute *College Name* is dependent only upon *College Code,* so it is removed to a separate *College* table to reach third normal form.

With the success of the relational model and RDBMS throughout the 1980s, normalization became a critical aspect of any data modeling and database design effort.

The Entity-Relationship Approach

The entity-relationship approach (ERA) to software development, developed by Chen, favors the construction of a stable data structure upon which *multiple* applications can operate. The data structure is implemented on whichever database management system (DBMS) the organization requires. The primary tool of ERA is the entity-relationship diagram (ERD). The initial steps of ERA direct the developer to define the three components of an ERD:

Entities (rectangles) are things for which information is stored.

Relationships (diamonds) describe associations between entities and define the cardinality, or number of entities, that must be maintained within the relationship. There are several cardinalities, including one-to-one, one-to-many, many-to-many, etc.

Attributes (circles) are characteristics of both entities and relationships, and are the smallest units of data.

An example of a Chen ERD is shown in Figure 5.10 which models information used by a typical bank. Given the ERD in Figure 5.10, the following can be assumed

For each bank branch, its *Branch#* and *Address* are stored, and access to a bank branch is via its key, *Branch#*. The system supports multiple accounts and customers associated with a given branch.

For each bank account, its *Account#*, *Type*, *Branch#*, and *Customer#* are stored, and access to it is by *Account#*. The *Branch#* and *Customer#* are foreign keys to this entity, and this means that they are the primary key for another entity. In this case, they indicate which branch and customer are associated with an account.

For each bank customer, the *Customer#*, *Name*, *Address*, and *Branch#* are all stored, and the *Customer#* is the key. The *Branch#* indicates which branch is associated with a customer.

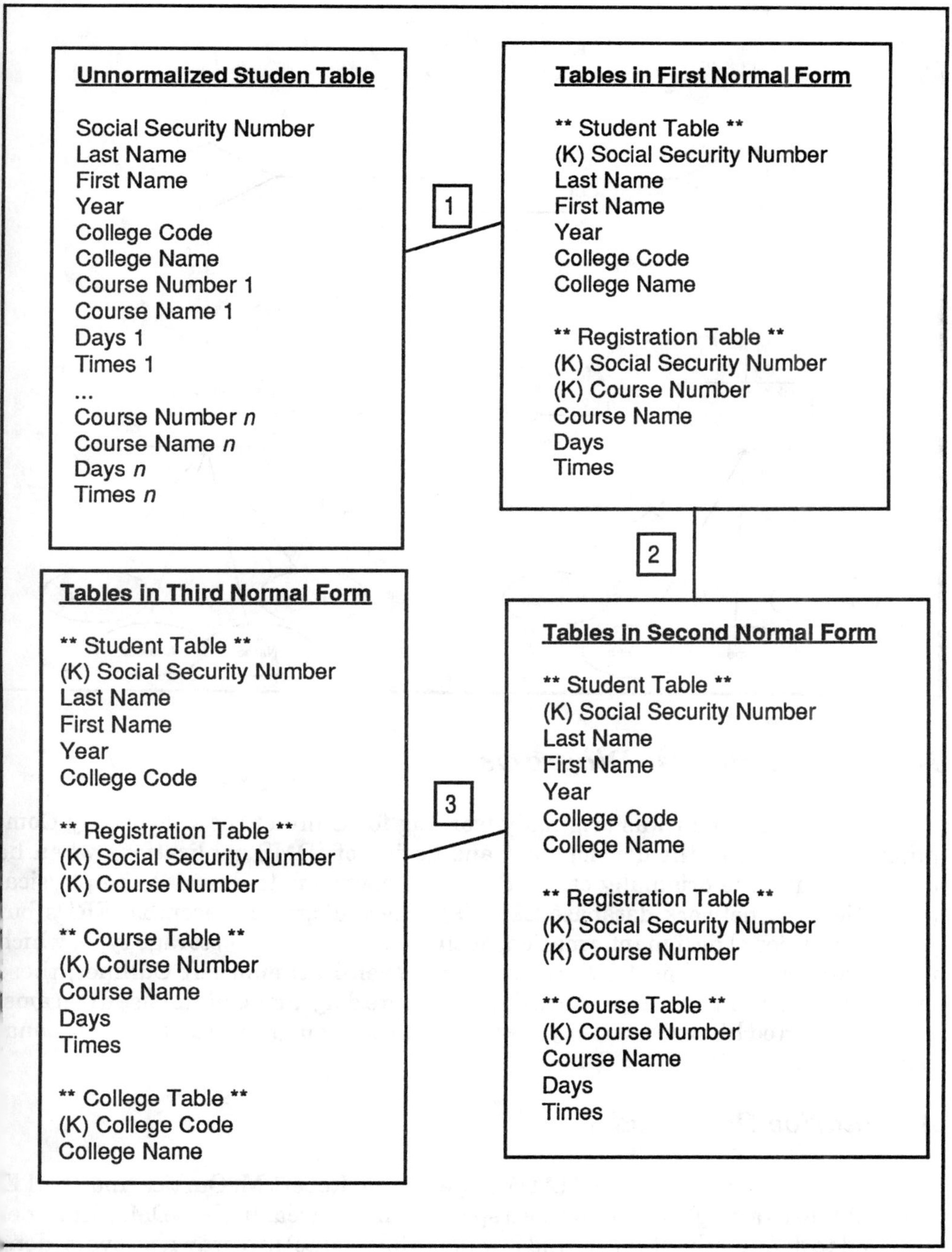

Unnormalized Studen Table

Social Security Number
Last Name
First Name
Year
College Code
College Name
Course Number 1
Course Name 1
Days 1
Times 1
...
Course Number n
Course Name n
Days n
Times n

1

Tables in First Normal Form

** Student Table **
(K) Social Security Number
Last Name
First Name
Year
College Code
College Name

** Registration Table **
(K) Social Security Number
(K) Course Number
Course Name
Days
Times

2

Tables in Third Normal Form

** Student Table **
(K) Social Security Number
Last Name
First Name
Year
College Code

** Registration Table **
(K) Social Security Number
(K) Course Number

** Course Table **
(K) Course Number
Course Name
Days
Times

** College Table **
(K) College Code
College Name

3

Tables in Second Normal Form

** Student Table **
(K) Social Security Number
Last Name
First Name
Year
College Code
College Name

** Registration Table **
(K) Social Security Number
(K) Course Number

** Course Table **
(K) Course Number
Course Name
Days
Times

Figure 5.9
Transforming tables into third normal form.

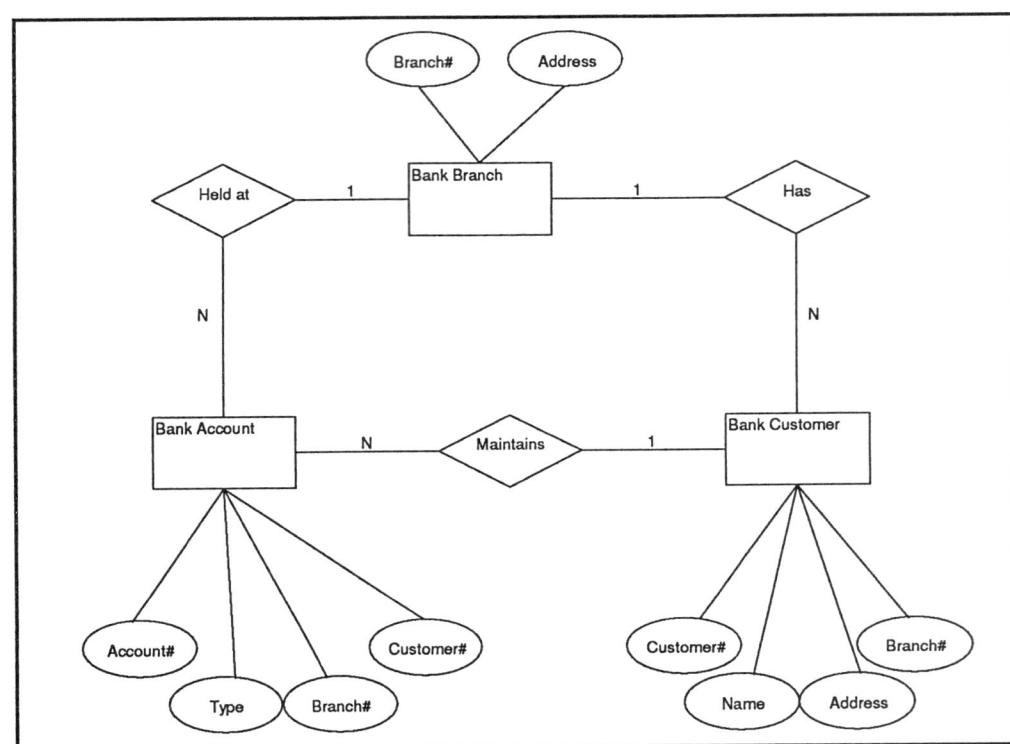

Figure 5.10
Chen entity-
relationship
diagram.

Bachman Database Diagrams

Charles Bachman was originally working for Cullinet (now owned by Computer Associates) in the development and design of IDMS applications when he created what were originally called Bachman diagrams to describe the physical properties of a network database [BAC69]. These diagrams resemble ERDs but provide additional design information, such as record size and storage type, which is relevant to the physical IDMS database. When Bachman left Cullinet, these diagrams became known as physical data structure diagrams or database diagrams. When he started his own company, he modified these diagrams to fit the relational requirements of DB2 and SQL.

Associative Data Model

The associative data model (ADM), created by Robert M. Curtice and Paul E. Jones, Jr., uses a diagram to describe a specific subject area. In the ADM, rectangles are used to define subject types, and key fields (elements) are drawn as ovals along with group attributes and relationships between entities. A data dictionary contains the definitions of the various entities and their elements.

IDEF1X

The U.S. Air Force uses the IDEF (ICAM DEFinition) technique, and this technique (IDEF0) has been modified by DACOM to model data instead of activities. The IDEF modeling technique was based on Structured Analysis Design Technique (SADT), and the data modeling notation, IDEF1X, uses rectangles to define dependent and independent entities, and identifies key elements as well as non-key attributes. Relationships are shown via lines connecting dependent entities (child entities) to their independent entities (parent entities).

*Oracle CASE*Method*

Another popular data-structured technique is CASE*Method from Oracle Corporation. Richard Barker of Oracle has published several books on CASE*Method, describing an approach for data modeling and application development. CASE*Method is based on database development for Oracle's relational DBMS. It is heavily dependent on database design and views an application as a set of transactions against the database [BAR90a] and [BAR90b].

CASE*Method is a top-down approach that focuses on shared databases and high-level strategic data modeling. Following creation of a data model, function models are defined for activities against the data. The database design is then optimized. Oracle's SQL*Forms is a fourth-generation language that is used to build functional programs that access and update the Oracle database. SQL*Report is used to create reports. For programming that is not conducive to SQL*Forms, Oracle offers a C programming interface and SQL*Plus.

Relational Database Design

Once a data model has been created in the analysis phase, it is used to perform the physical design for file and database structures. The programs that use the files and databases require definitions before they can be compiled. These definitions allow the programs to access data in the files and databases.

In most cases, the finished program will be running in a production environment and using a DBMS. The ability to populate the DBMS with information collected in the analysis and design phases is important. Information that should be available to the target DBMS dictionary includes definitions of fields or data elements, data structures, access requirements (keys), and relationships. This information is used by the run-time system when the application is in production.

Data definition language (DDL) statements are used to create file and database structures, while data manipulation language (DML) statements are used to access them. These statements must be processed before an application can access its files and databases. The statements are usually fed into a DBMS pre-processor along with DBMS utilities to allocate the required space, initialize tables, and update the DBMS dictionary. Typically, a database administrator (DBA) is assigned to perform this duty. The DBA continues to tailor and process DDL and DML statements to meet the changing needs of an application in production.

Denormalization

When migrating a normalized data model to a physical database structure, the DBA takes into account various design tradeoffs to support the functionality of the application in the most efficient manner possible. Implementation considerations lead to design tradeoffs that can help or hinder the performance of the application when it is finished.

Interestingly, once a set of database structures, or tables, has been normalized in analysis, a process of *denormalization* usually occurs in design. *Denormalization is the process of structuring the set of tables so that its performance is most efficient in the production environment.* A normalized set of tables is in the most efficient configuration *logically,* while a denormalized set of tables is in the most efficient form *physically.* There are several performance considerations that affect database design. These include table access or update frequency, table size, index requirements, and security requirements.

Application Design

Many organizations build their applications around their database structures by simply defining add, change, view, and delete functions for database tables. By also defining queries and reports against these tables, a complete application can be constructed.

Fourth-generation languages (4GLs) often provide support for a specific DBMS and when used with prototyping, can support a data-structured approach to software development. Vendors of 4GLs, including Computer Associates (CA-IDMS, CA-DatacomDB), Oracle (Oracle), Unisys (Linc), Ingres (Ingres), Informix, and Borland International (Paradox, dBaseIV), all provide development environments that revolve around their DBMSs.

Under this approach, once the database has been defined along with some basic transactions (add, change, delete, view), the remaining application is developed by defining the necessary underlying logic. Designing the application architecture under this approach can simply mean defining the menu structure for the on-line portion of the application and then creating any batch reports using the 4GL. As we have already indicated, 4GL functionality can be defined using the CRUD method.

5.3.3 Representation

As already mentioned in the "Notation" section, all of the system-level data-oriented techniques represent data structures and processes using different but similar notations. The Jackson approach extends the structure chart notation popularized by Constantine to support sequence, iteration, and selection.

Warnier took a very different approach in attempting to support all the constructs in a 3GL in his notation. The Warnier-Orr diagram represents the hierarchical structure of data as well as the structure of functions and procedures or programs.

Under the enterprise-level data-oriented techniques, the normalization approach calls for data structures to be defined as two-dimensional tables, which in turn become tables defined in third-normal form (3NF). As we have already seen, some form of data model is required within the enterprise-level data-oriented techniques to specify the logical structure and relationships among the entities and the attributes.

Peter Chen developed the ERD to represent data entities, relationships, and attributes in a single view. Charles Bachman extended the ERD to support database-specific information required to automatically generate databases from models and specifications. In the design phase, the data model is translated into a physical database design, based on the functional requirements (user views, access paths, etc.) and the target DBMS. Regardless of the DBMS uses, DDL commands are created to allocate the database structures, and DML commands are used in a 3GL or 4GL to access and update the actual database tables or files.

5.4 Stages and Tasks

For both techniques described, we chose the Library example, since it has a strong emphasis on data structures and transactions. We decided to show examples of both system-level and enterprise-level data-oriented techniques to clarify the differing views they both support.

For the system-level data-oriented technique we chose to use data structured systems development (DSSD) because it best displays the characteristics of a data-structured technique. In addition, it employs a widely known tool: the Warnier-Orr diagram. One drawback to using this technique is the limited CASE support provided in the industry for this method. We found that on many occasions we had to use paper and pencil to create and maintain the representations.

Of the enterprise-level data-oriented techniques, we chose the entity-relationship approach (ERA) for its simplicity and use of a fully attributed data model. One benefit to using the ERA approach is widespread support for the ERD and the generation of SQL-based DBMS structures in the available CASE tools.

5.4.1 DSSD

The essence of the DSSD approach is to (1) model the outputs required by an application, (2) identify the inputs and calculations needed to produce the outputs, and (3) define the processing required to take the inputs and produce the outputs. Providing a framework for these essential functions are the eight stages [HIG83] shown in Figure 5.11:

Planning   Evaluate problems and select possible solutions. Define application goals and draft a project plan to satisfy them.

Definition   Specify the desired outputs of an application. Create actual layouts of the outputs and then derive the logical layouts.

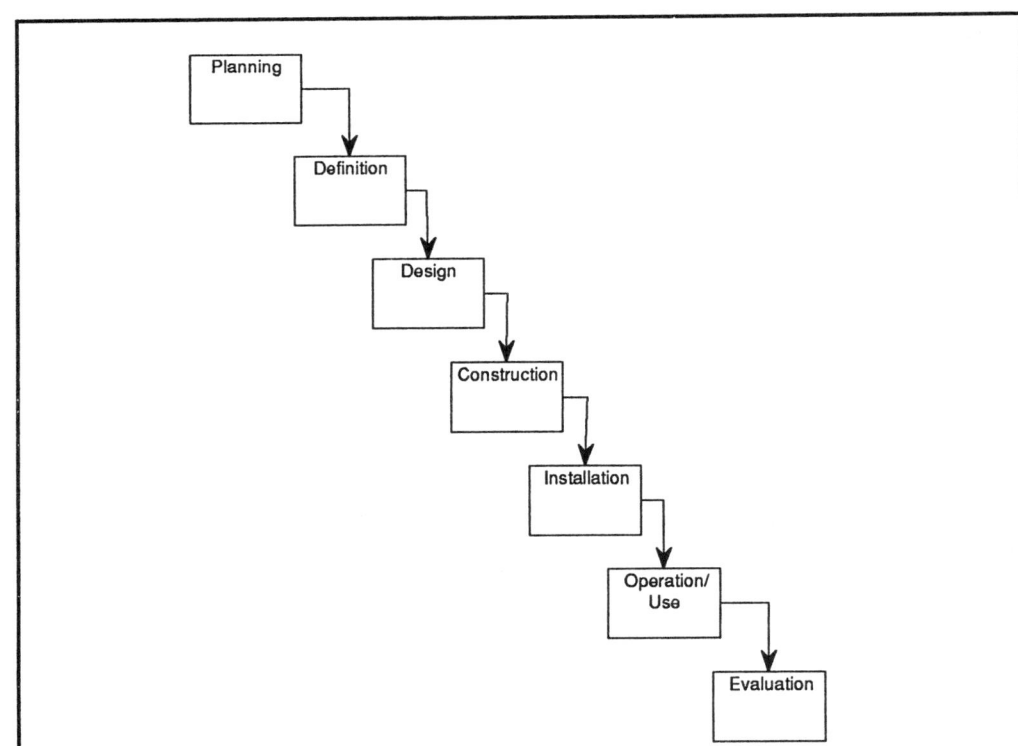

Figure 5.11
DSSD life cycle.

Design	Detail the logical and physical software architecture. Use the layouts to determine the application's output, input, and process structures.
Construction	Translate the software architecture into programs.
Installation	Place the software into a production environment.
Operation / Use	Use the software to produce results and make business decisions.
Evaluation	Judge the software on its performance.

5.4.2 ERA

The tasks of ERA are shown in Figure 5.12 and include [CHE89]:

Define entities and relationships in the problem domain.
Define the cardinalities for each relationship.
Identify entity and relationship *attributes*.
Transform the ERD into appropriate file or database structures.
Develop applications that access the file and database structures.

Defining the entities and attributes from the requirements for a system is fairly simple, since any nouns used to describe the system can become entities or attributes. Verbs used in the requirements specification map to functions against the data structures in the system.

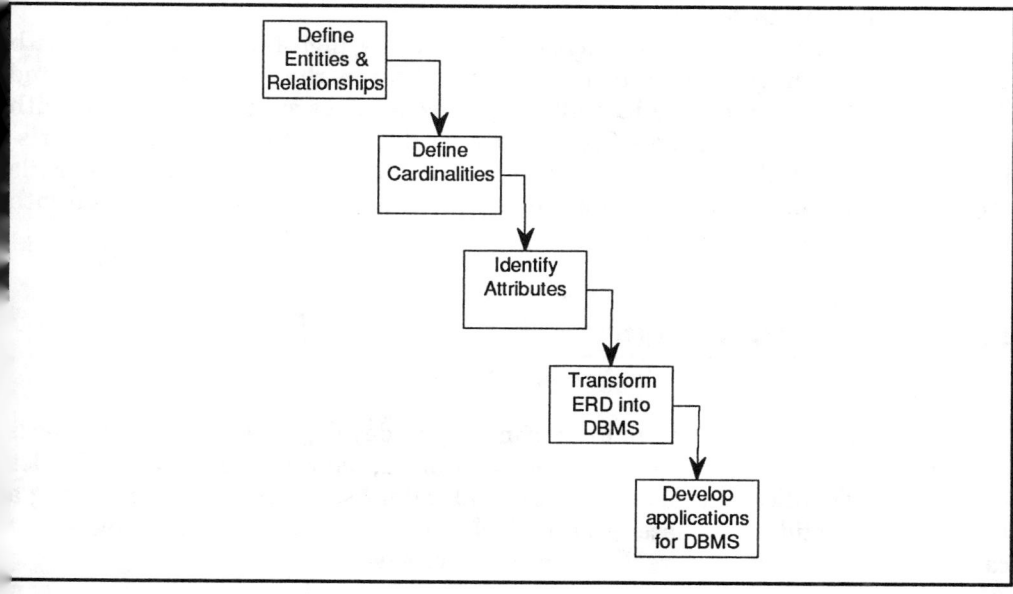

Figure 5.12
ERA life cycle.

Defining the relationships among the entities can follow directly from the requirements, but typically requires interaction with the end user to clarify the cardinalities. Some methods insist that all relationships be defined in sentences and then translated to cardinalities on the data model. Modeling the relationships among the entities involves understanding how the real-world entities relate and what constraints are placed on the entities.

Transforming the data model into an appropriate database design will vary depending on the file or database structure used. Most of the commercial CASE products now available support the generation of SQL DBMS structures from fully attributed data models. If a RDBMS is used, the data model must be normalized and then denormalized as described above.

The enterprise-level data-oriented techniques view functions as transactions against the database and use the CRUD view or a 4GL for designing and implementing the functionality. We chose to use this approach to simplify the process and describe how looking at functionality from the perspective of transactions compares with other methods.

5.5 Deliverables

The system-level data-oriented techniques provide deliverables which include models of data structures, application and program structures, and processing logic. These each take different forms depending on the notation used, but might include entity diagrams, assembly line diagrams, and Warnier-Orr diagrams. The Warnier-Orr diagrams can be used to represent data structures, program structures, and processing logic in the design phase.

For the enterprise-level data-oriented techniques, high-level data models with attributes and cardinalities are required, typically in the form of an ERD and dictionary. When moving to a RDBMS, normalized tables are required along with a database design specification. CRUD matrices define the functional characteristics for the system along with 3GL or 4GL commands to access the database or file structures. In some cases, the data-oriented techniques are used in conjunction with prototypes, which are described in Chapter 9.

5.6 Suitable Applications

Data-oriented methods are used primarily to develop and maintain business applications. Examples of these include accounting, payroll, personnel, and sales systems. Any application that requires complex data structures, typically using a DBMS, is a candidate for data-oriented techniques. Jackson system development can also be used to develop real-time or reactive systems.

If outputs for business applications are generally well-defined in an organization, system-level data-oriented techniques may be suitable for their development. Likewise, systems that have large volumes of inputs and outputs are good candidates for the data-oriented techniques.

System-level data-oriented methods focus on the design of screens, reports, database, and file structures. This makes them particularly useful for applications with complex input-output requirements, simple functionality, or a combination of the two.

Enterprise-level data-oriented techniques are excellent choices for applications targeting DBMSs, especially RDBMSs. These techniques require that an organization be committed to the use of a set of common data structures and use a data dictionary to maintain control over the database. This may mean that all applications for a department utilize the common structure or, more broadly, that all applications across multiple departments use the structure.

Whenever there is a need to share information across an organization, the enterprise-level data-oriented techniques or the information-oriented techniques described in Chapter 7 can provide support for applications built on top of an enterprise data model. If a strong database and/or data administration function exists within the development group, the use of data-oriented techniques or information-oriented techniques may be called for, and DA/DBA staff may already be using aspects of these methods.

5.7 Benefits and Drawbacks

"Output-oriented design is the only solid method for designing systems."
K. Orr [ORR81].

A distinct advantage of DSSD is its emphasis on the goals, or outputs, of an application. In most endeavors, it is important to know where you are heading before you invest any effort. DSSD ensures that goals are defined early and eventually satisfied. When the definition of outputs is the primary goal of design, we will know with certainty when design is over. That will occur when the outputs and all their supporting processes, databases, and inputs have been designed.

The system-level data-oriented techniques can produce excellent designs once the data structures needed by an application are defined. An additional benefit to using these methods is that they ensure that the outputs of an application are defined early on, and that the development and maintenance effort concentrates on designing the application to produce them. One of their weaknesses, however, is determining what data structures are required. DSSD has addressed this weakness by adding steps at the beginning of the technique to elicit and document user requirements.

The most critical drawback of the system-level data-oriented techniques is the dwindling support provided by CASE vendors. Today, there are fewer than five vendors offering a varying amount of automated support for the techniques. CASE support is an important factor in the use of a technique: Without adequate CASE support, techniques become burdensome. There are some CASE tools that can be customized to support any technique, and this may be the best way to address the current shortcomings in support for the system-level data-oriented techniques. The opposite situation holds for the enterprise-level data-oriented techniques: There are a variety of CASE tools available that support these methods. Organizations will need to evaluate the level of automated support needed versus the level that is available on the market.

Other criticisms of all the data-oriented techniques include how to address different views of data, typically in the form of synonyms, differences in the required lengths and types of data elements, and differences in defining ownership of data. Also, 4GLs tend to be limited to a single DBMS and don't support complex processing easily.

SQL standards may lead to better interoperability between different types of DBMSs, and the widespread use of these database systems will lead to more powerful development tools and languages. Several SQL-based 4GLs are now available for client/server development, including Uniface 4GL, Progress, PowerHouse 4GL, and Informix-SQL.

5.8 The Library Example

In this section, DSSD and ERA will be used to analyze and design our example, the Library system. Example representations will be used to explain these methods.

5.8.1 DSSD

Section 5.4.1 provided an overview of the DSSD technique and its eight stages. Within DSSD, there are several steps associated with each stage. To limit the size of this chapter, we will focus on the steps in the *definition* and *design* stages of DSSD only.

As in many other techniques, one of the initial steps in DSSD is to define the application context, or boundary, of the system. The boundary delineates what is inside and outside the system, and to determine the boundary, entities (producers and consumers of data) related to the system are listed and diagramed.

Step: Summarize System

A good approach to beginning the analysis of the Library system using DSSD is to describe how the system will operate. Based on conversations with library representatives, the following system summary document is drafted:

> Library staffers will survey lists of books from publishers and order those that are needed. When books are received from the publisher, book information (title, author, etc.) will be entered into a computer database. The staffer will assign a call number to each book and a copy number to each copy of the book ordered. Those numbers will also be entered into the computer database. The copies will then be shelved in the library.
>
> When checking out a book, a borrower will submit his or her name and address to a library staffer. The staffer will check the computer database to determine whether the borrow limit has been reached. If not, the staffer will assign the date checked out and the date due back to the book, and enter the dates into the computer database. The book will then be given to the borrower.
>
> The process when returning a book will be similar. The borrower will submit his or her name and address and the loaned book to the staffer. The staffer will check the computer database to determine whether the book is overdue or not. A fine will be assessed if necessary.
>
> Both staffers and borrowers will be able to request reports from the computer database. Staffer reports will list the status of all loaned books. Borrower reports will list all books loaned to this borrower.

Step: List Data Items

Surveying the system summary document, list all possible data items related to the Library system. These are the pieces of information necessary to running the library. The Library system has the following data items:

> Data Item List
> Order: title, author, date published, and number of copies ordered
> Book: title, publisher, author, date published, call number,
>   and copy number of book
> Borrower Info: name and password of borrower
> Loaned Book: title, publisher, author, call number, copy number,
>   borrower, date checked out, and date due back of book
> Borrower Report: list of all books loaned to a borrower
> Staffer Report: list of all books loaned

Step: List Entities

List all possible producers and consumers of data related to the Library system. These may be people, departments, organizations, machines, systems, databases, etc. Think of the major pieces that make up and interact with the system; these will be the entities. The Library system has the following entities:

    Entity List
    Borrower: borrows and returns library books
    Publisher: processes book orders from the library
    Staffer: maintains book and borrower data; requests staffer reports
    Reporting: produces library reports for borrowers and staffers

The tasks of listing data items and listing entities are complementary. As a data item is listed, a corresponding entity may emerge, and vice versa.

Step: Diagram Entities

An ED is drawn for each listed entity. Each ED is drawn from the perspective of how one entity relates to the others. As the diagrams are drawn, don't hesitate to make changes to the original lists of data items and entities. Figures 5.13a and 5.13b shows entity diagrams corresponding to the four listed entities.

Step: Merge Entity Diagrams

Draw a combined ED that shows the passing of data among all entities, and outline the boundary of the Library system. Then draw an application-level ED that shows the Library system as a single entity (see Figure 5.14). The boundary indicates what information the system will be processing. The flows crossing that boundary are the starting point for the next major DSSD step: defining application functions.

Now that the context of the Library system has been defined, the functions making up the application can be determined. This is accomplished by looking at the information flows moving across the system boundary, numbering them in the order that they cross the boundary, and defining the functions that affect each flow. Figure 5.15 shows the ordered flows across the system boundary.

Step: Number and Diagram Flows

Using the application-level ED, number the information flows in the order that they flow across the system boundary. The numbering indicates a dependency. For example, the Order flow should logically precede the Ordered Book flow as shown

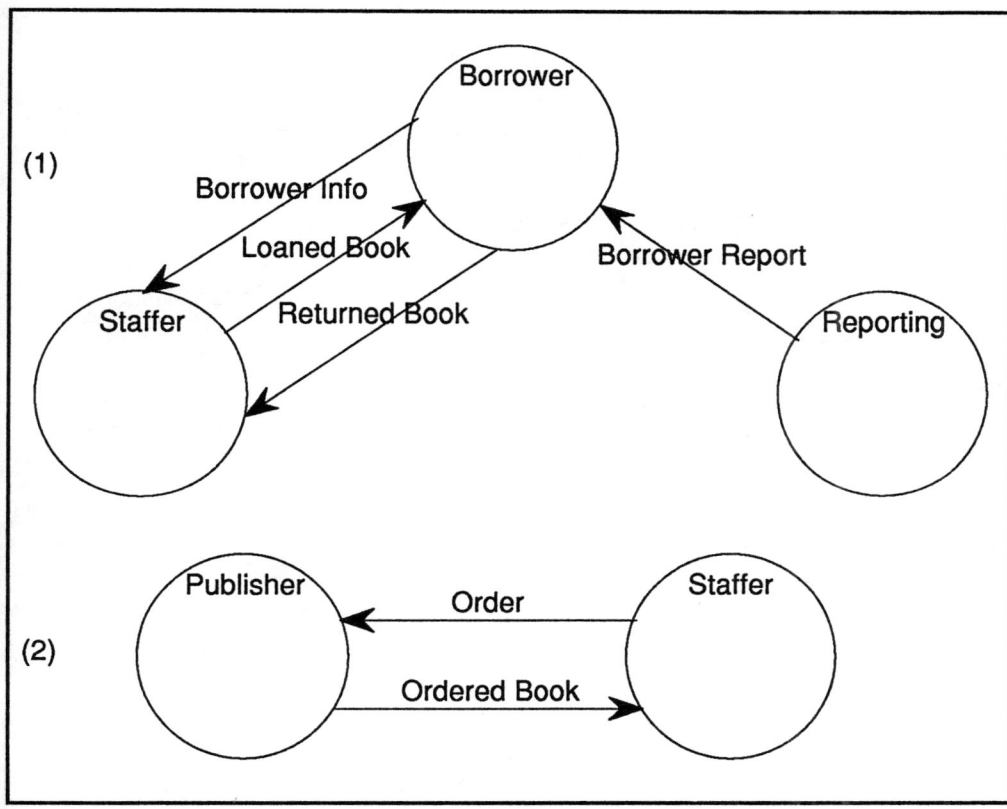

Figure 5.13a
Entity diagrams for entities (1) Borrower and (2) Publisher.

in Figure 5.15. Once numbering has been completed, an assembly line diagram can be created. Figure 5.16 shows what functions are needed to produce the flows across the system boundary.

The major functions for the Library system have been defined, and the next few steps determine the processing logic corresponding to each function. We will focus on the Borrower Report Generation function identified in the assembly line diagram in Figure 5.16.

Step: Prototype Outputs

For each screen or report output from the system, sketch its layout. Figure 5.17 shows an example of a possible layout for the Borrower Report produced by the Borrower Report Generation function.

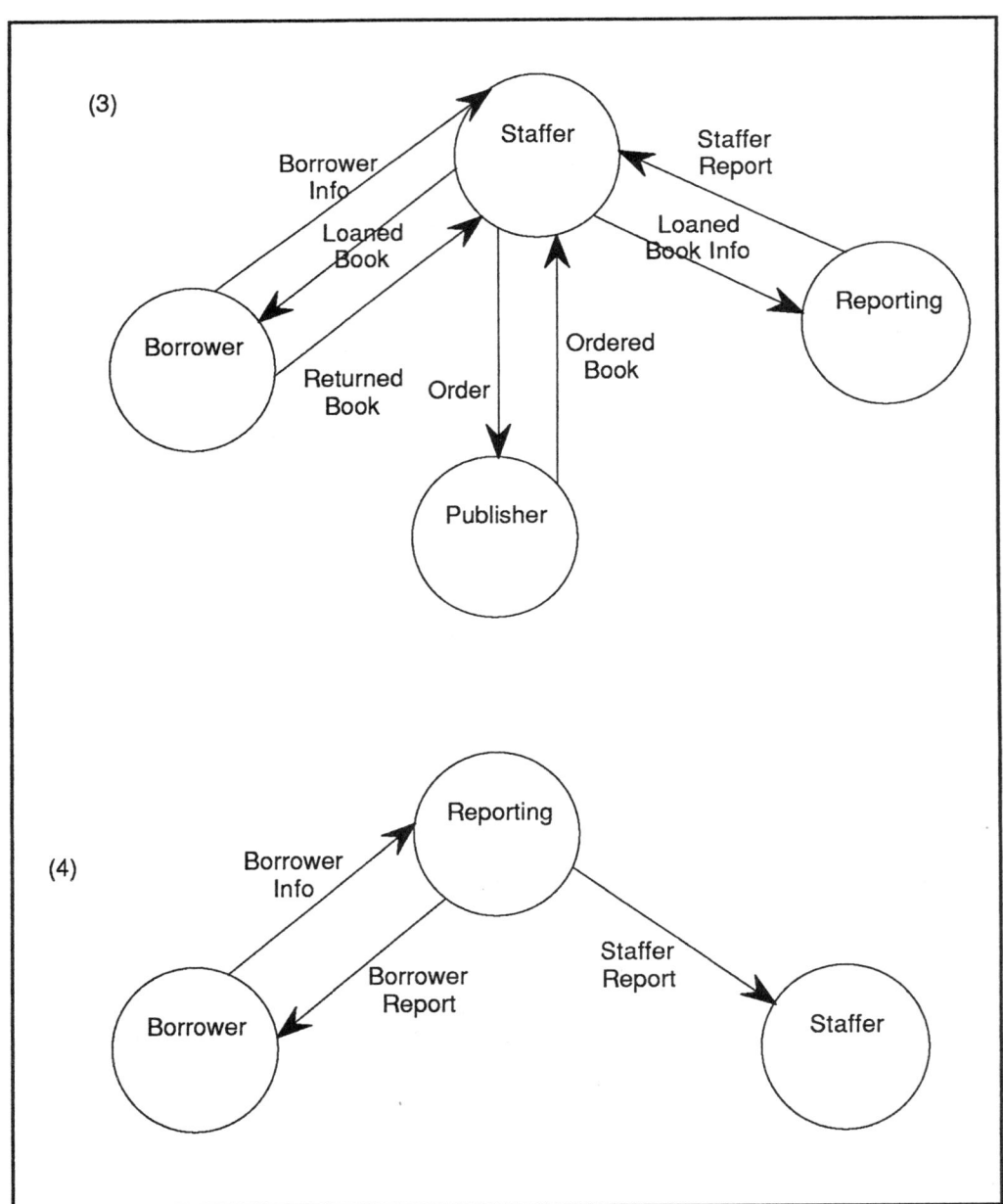

Figure 5.13*b*
Entity diagrams for
entities (3) Staffer
and (4) Reporting.

Step: Construct Output Worksheets and Structures

For each screen or report layout, derive its output worksheet and structure. The Borrower Report layout produces the output worksheet shown in Figure 5.18, which in turn yields the output Warnier-Orr diagram shown in Figure 5.19.

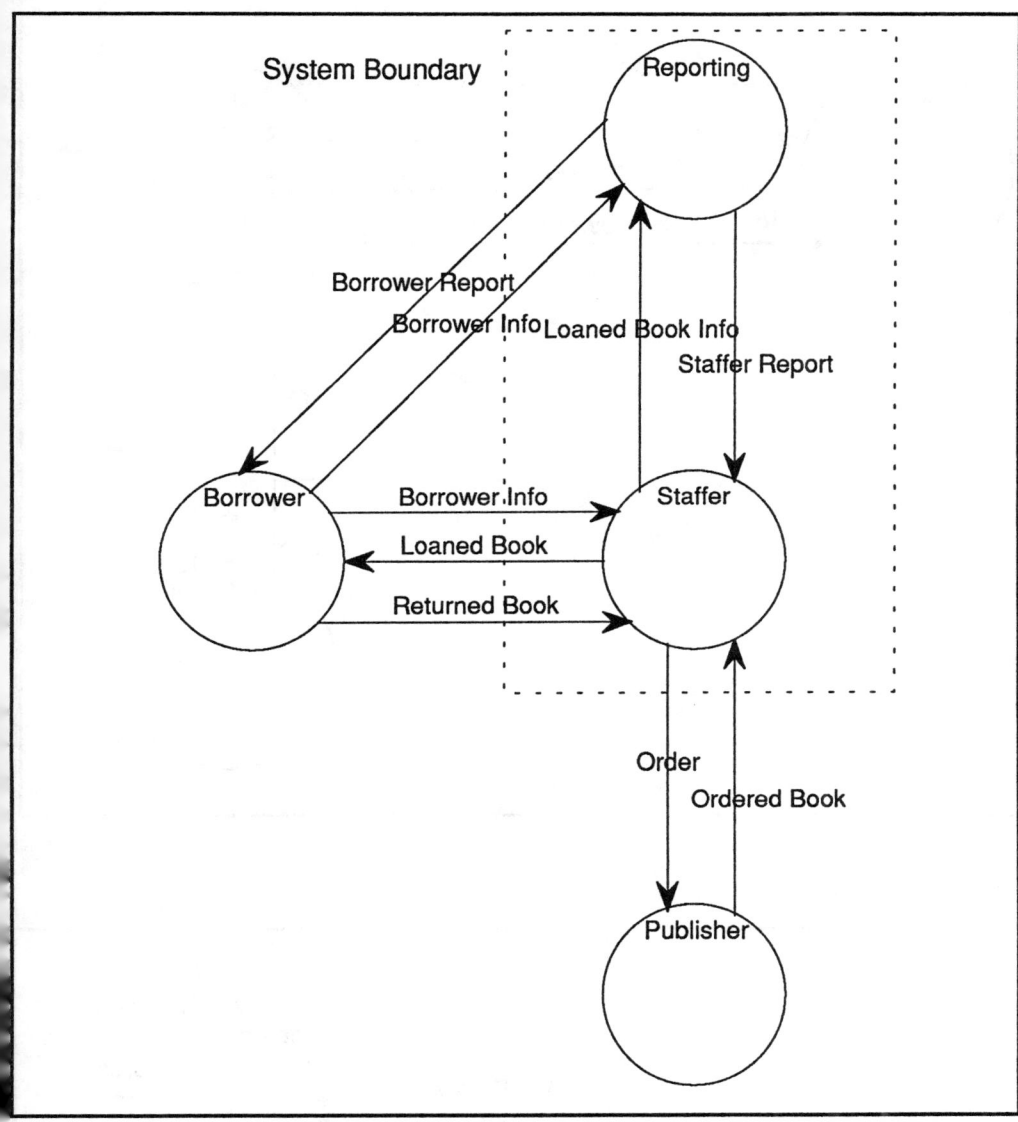

Figure 5.14
Combined entity
diagram.

Step: Construct Input Worksheets and Structures

Working backwards from the outputs, we determine each input structure for the output worksheet. Each data element in the output worksheet is labeled as computable (C), a label (L), or required as input (*). This results in the input worksheet shown in Figure 5.20, which produces the input Warnier-Orr diagram shown in Figure 5.21.

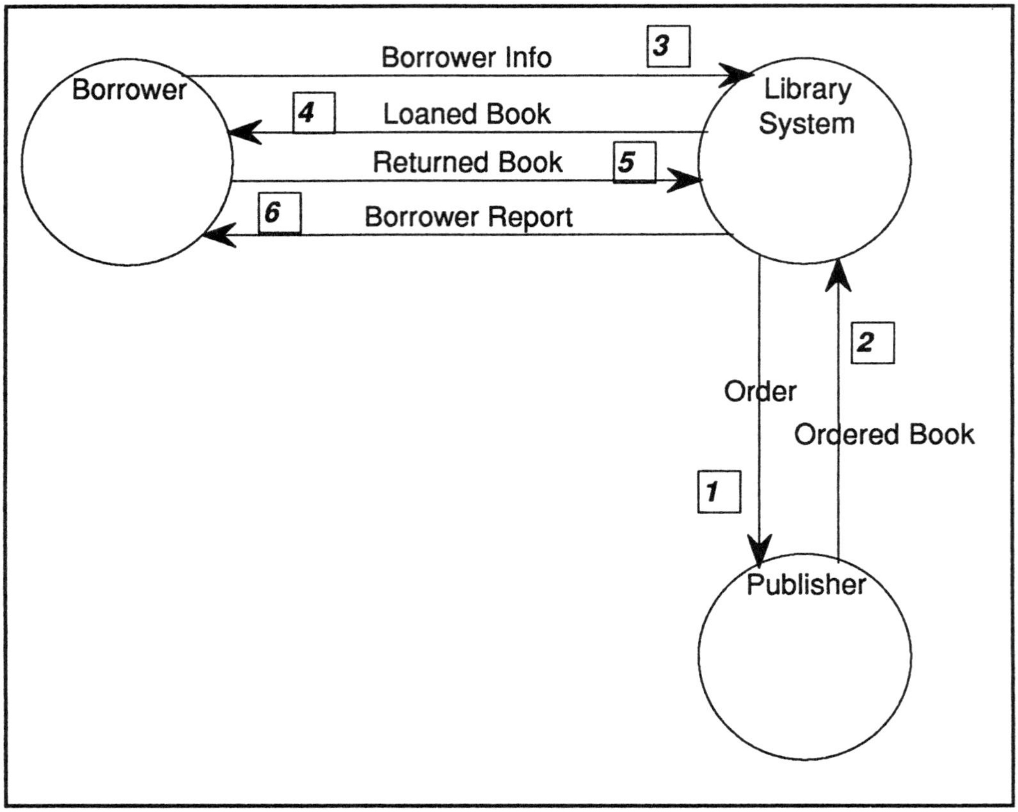

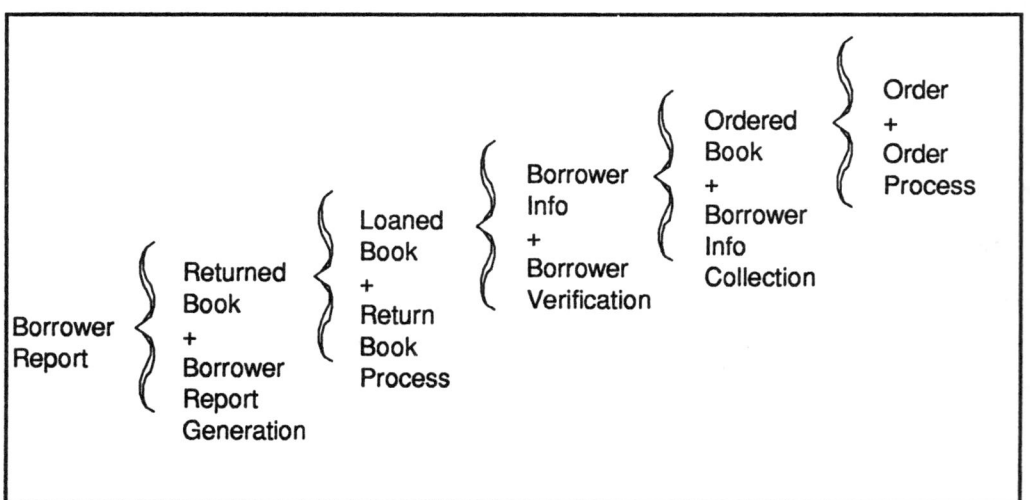

Figure 5.15
Application-level
entity diagram with
flows sequenced.

Figure 5.16
Assembly line
diagram of
application-level
functions.

```
+----------------------------------------------------------------+
|                      Borrower Report                           |
|                                                                |
|  Borrower: xxxxxxxxxxxxxxxxxxxx                                 |
|                                                                |
|  Book                Date Due      Date Returned    Overdue Fee|
|  xxxxxxxxxxxxxxxxx    mm/dd/yy      mm/dd/yy         $99.99     |
|                      mm/dd/yy      mm/dd/yy         $99.99     |
|                      mm/dd/yy      mm/dd/yy         $99.99     |
|                      Book Overdue                   $99.99     |
|                                                                |
|  xxxxxxxxxxxxxxxxx    mm/dd/yy      mm/dd/yy         $99.99     |
|                      mm/dd/yy      mm/dd/yy         $99.99     |
|                      mm/dd/yy      mm/dd/yy         $99.99     |
|                      Book Overdue                   $99.99     |
+----------------------------------------------------------------+
```

Figure 5.17
Borrower Report layout.

Step: Construct Process Worksheets and Structures

For each output-input worksheet pair, we next define the processing structure. We list in a worksheet the outputs from the output structure and the calculations and required inputs from the input structure, and then build a corresponding process structure.

Number	Data Element	Frequency
1	Report Heading	1/report
2	Borrower Heading	1/report
3	Borrower Name	1/report
4	Column Headings	1/report
5	Book Name	1/book
6	Date Due	1/borrow
7	Date Returned	1/borrow
8	Overdue Fee	1/borrow
9	Book Overdue Heading	1/book
10	Book Overdue Fee	1/book
11	Total Overdue Heading	1/report
12	Total Overdue Fee	1/report

Figure 5.18
Borrower Report output worksheet.

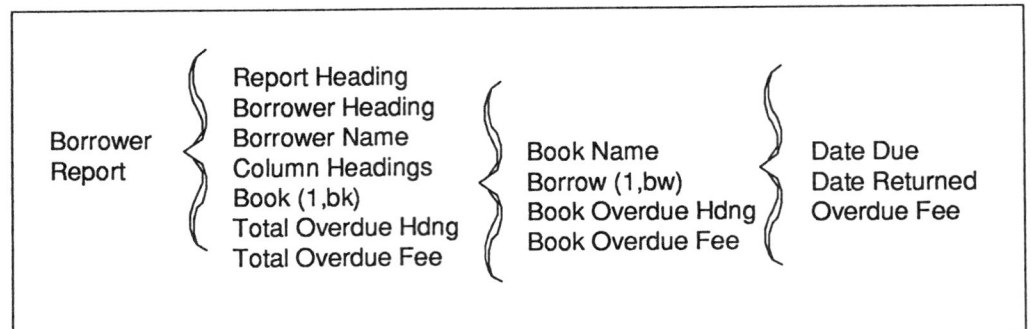

Figure 5.19
Borrower Report
Warnier-Orr
diagram.

The process structures may now be used to code the application in any 3GL or 4GL.

5.8.2 ERA

Step: Define Entities and Relationships

Defining the Library entities proved to be interesting given the textual description provided in Chapter 3. The entities that were obvious from the description included books, borrowers, and library staff. Other potential entities, given some thought, might include authors, list of books currently checked out by a user, list of users that recently checked out a book, and the archive structures for both of these lists. We chose to model each of these as entities in our Library system, which resulted in what we feel is a more interesting model.

Number	Data Element	Frequency	Type (C,L,*)	Calculations
1	Report Heading	1/report	L	
2	Borrower Heading	1/report	L	
3	Borrower Name	1/report	*	
4	Column Headings	1/report	L	
5	Book Name	1/book	*	
6	Date Due	1/borrow	*	
7	Date Returned	1/borrow	*	
8	Overdue Fee	1/borrow	C	(Date Returned-Date Due)*.05
9	Book Overdue Heading	1/book	L	
10	Book Overdue Fee	1/book	C	Sum of Overdue Fees
11	Total Overdue Heading	1/report	L	
12	Total Overdue Fee	1/report	C	Sum of Book Overdue Fees

C=calculation; L=label; *=needed as input

Figure 5.20
Borrower Report
input worksheet.

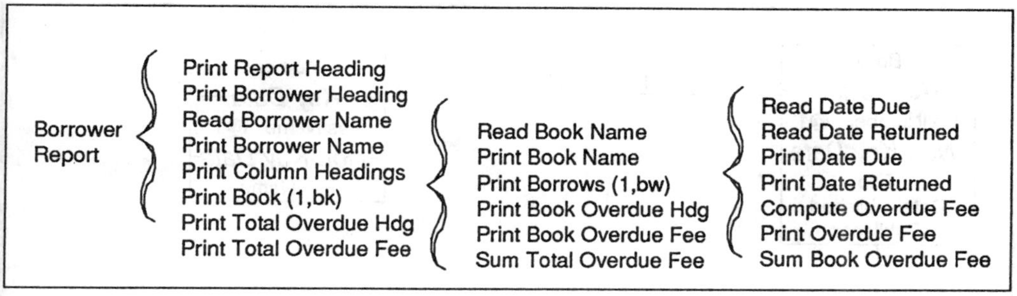

Figure 5.21
Borrower Report
Warnier-Orr diagram.

An interesting question concerns whether there might be more than one copy of a book available for checkout in the library. Mention is made in the problem statement of "a copy of a book," but this point is not completely clarified anywhere in the description. Another key question in modeling the library system is whether there should be an entity to specify that a copy of a book is checked out. We chose to use a relationship to model this instead of another entity because this allows the system to support multiple copies of a book in the library system.

Step: Define the Cardinalities for Each Relationship

When considering the cardinalities for the entities in the library system, some assumptions had to be made regarding constraints on the system. For example, we assumed that an author might write more than one book and that a book could be written by more than one author. We further assumed that a book is written by at least one author, not zero (0). All of these assumptions fit easily into our view of real-world libraries and books.

We also assumed that a book could be checked out to zero (0) users, thereby indicating that it was not currently checked out, and that when a book is not checked out, there is no relationship between the book and the previous user who had the book checked out. The list of users that have checked out a book contains this information in our model.

Step: Identify Entity and Relationship Attributes

Some entity attributes are described or inferred in the problem statement, including maximum borrowing limit, user name, book title, and author name. Obviously we could add any other attributes required to fully model and design a complete library system.

Concerning the question of differentiating between borrowers and library staff, an attribute in the user entity that specifies whether a user is staff or not easily addresses this problem. We also chose to specify attributes in the relationship Checked Out between book and user. These attributes include book status (available or checked out), date checked out, and date due back.

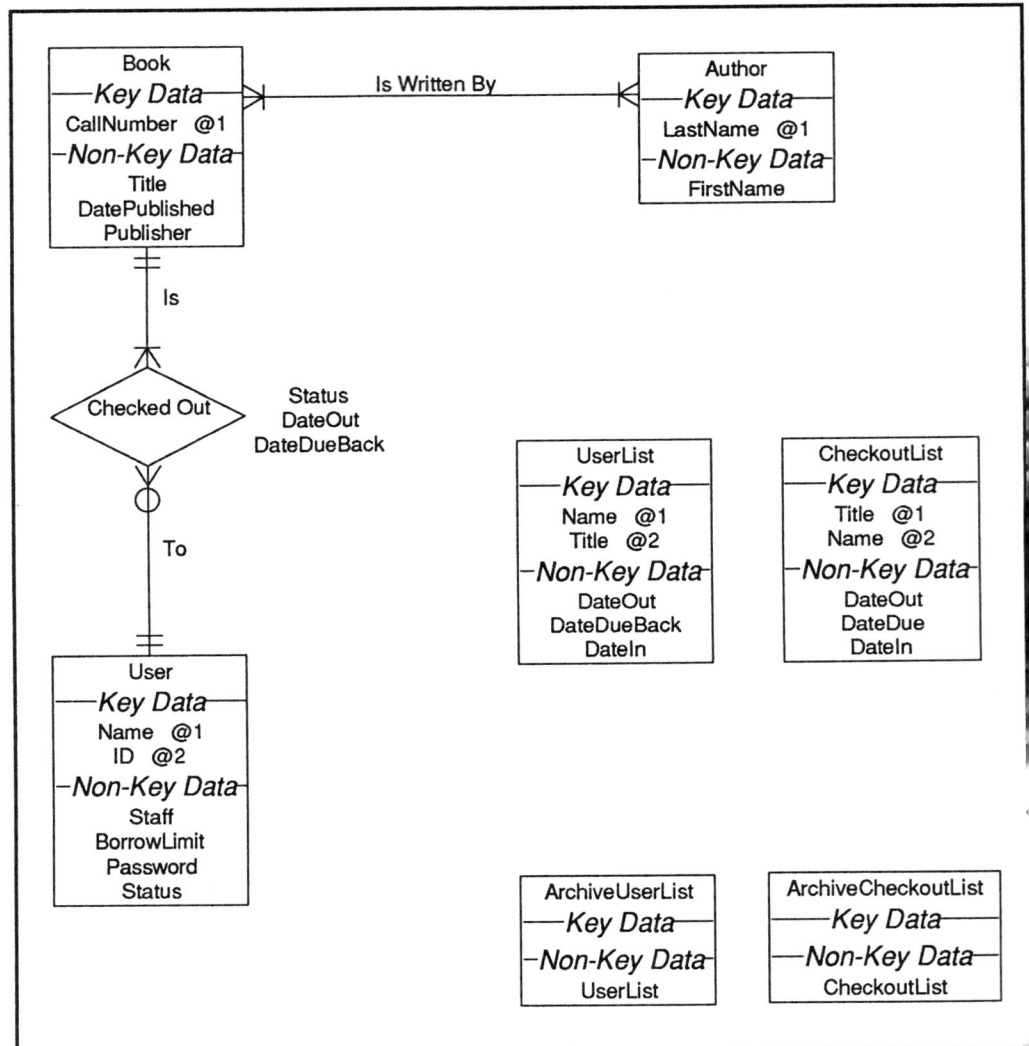

Figure 5.22
Library entity-relationship diagram.

The final ERD for the library system is shown in Figure 5.22. As shown, the relationships defined within the library system are as follows:

A copy of a book may be checked out to only one user.
A user may have zero or more books checked out at any time.
A book may be written by one or more authors.
An author may write one or more books.

Step: Transform the ERD into Appropriate File or Database Structures

We chose to transform our data model into a standard SQL-based database structure using a commercial CASE tool. The resulting SQL create statements are shown in Figure 5.23. The database could have been implemented on any of a variety of structures, and this obviously would have affected our specifications.

For example, if we had implemented our system using an indexed file system, we might have specified a unique key for Book, such as Call Number. We might also have assigned a unique ID for each user. Regardless of which structure we use, we may want to support the lists and archive lists as sequential structures and not as database tables. Given the size and requirements for updating and accessing these lists, we probably would choose to support these with sequential or indexed files outside the library database.

Step: Develop Applications that Access the File and Database Structures

When considering the functionality of the library system, it became obvious that the CRUD view might work well in representing the system. We mapped the transactions defined in the problem description to the entities they affect in the data model to come up with the CRUD view shown in Figure 5.24.

If we were using a 4GL to implement our system, we would further define processes for each of the entities and CRUD verbs — create, read, update and delete.

Creating and assessing the lists could be accomplished using batch programs in a 3GL or using a SQL-like language to extract and build the lists.

```
CREATE TABLE AUTHOR (
        NAME              CHAR (50)
)

CREATE TABLE BOOK (
        CALLNUMBER        CHAR (10) NOT NULL,
        TITLE             CHAR (75),
        PUBLISHER         CHAR (50) NOT NULL,
        DATEPUBLISHED     DATE NOT NULL WITH DEFAULT
)

CREATE TABLE USER (
        NAME              CHAR (50) NOT NULL,
        BORROWLIMIT       INT,
        STAFF             BIT,
        PASSWORD          CHAR (5) NOT NULL WITH DEFAULT
)
```

Figure 5.23
Sample SQL generated from library ERD.

CRUD Matrix	Book	Copy	Author	User	UserList	CheckoutList
1 Add book	C	C	CRU			
2 Remove book	D	RUD	RUD			
3 Checkout book	RU	RU		RU		
4 Return book	RU	RU		RU		
5 Books by author	R		R			
6 Books by user	R	R		R	CRU	
7 Users of book	R	R		R		CRU
8 Add users				C		
9 Remove users				D		
10 Set borrow limit				U		
11 Archive books						RUD
12 Archive users					RUD	

Figure 5.24
Library CRUD
matrix.

5.9 Resource List

Organizations that are planning to use data-oriented techniques should be aware that there is varying CASE support for the methods and notations. Several vendors now offer support for Jackson system development and the enterprise-level techniques. However, few vendors support logical construction of systems or data structured systems development. Publications are available, including the CASE Product Guide from *Software Magazine*, that contain detailed CASE product information.

For current information on data modeling and database design, see *DBMS magazine, Database Programming & Design*, and technical journals including *IEEE Transactions on Knowledge and Data Engineering, ACM Transactions on Database Systems*, and *ACM SIGMOD* (Management of Data).

Books on data modeling and database design include those from Barker [BAR90a][BAR90b], Batini [BAT92], and Date [DAT74] and the papers of Bachman [BAC69], Chen [CHE76][CHE89], and Codd [COD70][COD71]. For the Warner/ Orr and DSSD methods, see the books of Brown [BRO86], Hansen [HAN86], Higgins [HIG79][HIG83] [HIG86], Orr [ORR77],[ORR81], and of course Warnier [WAR74][WAR81]. See the books of Jackson [JAC75] [JAC82] and the paper by Cameron [CAM86] for more on the Jackson method.

5.10 References

[BAC69]   Bachman, C., "The data structure diagrams," Data Base (Bulletin of the *ACM SIGFIDET*, vol. 1, no. 2, Mar. 1969).

[BAR90a]   Barker, R., *Oracle CASE*Method: Tasks and Deliverables*, Addison-Wesley, 1990.

[BAR90b]   Barker, R., *Oracle CASE*Method: Entity-Relationship Diagramming*, Addison-Wesley, 1990.

[BAT92]   Batini, C., Ceri, S., and Navathe, S.B., *Conceptual Database Design: An Entity Relationship Approach*, Benjamin Cummings, 1992.

[BRO86]   Brown, K. and R. Whinery editors, *Data Structured Systems Development Methodology*, Ken Orr and Associates, 1986.

[CAM86]   Cameron, J., "An Overview of JSD," *IEEE Trans. on Soft. Eng.*, vol. SE-12, no. 2, February 1986, pp. 222-240.

[CHE76]   Chen, P. P., "The Entity-Relationship Model - Toward a Unifying View of Data," *ACM Trans. on Data Base Systems*, vol. 1, no. 1, March 1976, pp. 9-36.

[CHE89]   Chen, P. P., "The Entity-Relationship Approach," *Byte Magazine*, April 1989, pp. 230-232.

[COD70]   Codd, E.F., "A Relational Model of Data for Large Shared Data Banks," *CACM*, vol. 13, no. 6, June 1970.

[COD71]   Codd, E.F., "A Data Base Sublanguage Founded on the Relational Calculus," *Proceedings of the 1971 ACM-SIGFIDET Workshop on Data Base Systems*, ACM, 1971.

[DAT74]   Date, C. J., *An Introduction to Database Systems*, Addison-Wesley, 1974.

[GAN89]   Gane, C., *Rapid Systems Development: Using Structured Techniques and Relational Technology*, Prentice-Hall, 1989.

[HAN86]   Hansen, K., *Data Structured Program Design*, Prentice-Hall, 1986.

[HIG79]   Higgins, D., *Program Design and Construction*, Prentice-Hall, 1979.

[HIG83]   Higgins, D., *Designing Structured Programs*, Prentice-Hall, 1983.

[HIG86]   Higgins, D., *Data Structured Software Maintenance: The Warner-Orr Approach*, Dorset House, 1986.

[JAC75]   Jackson, M., *Principles of Program Design*, Academic, 1975.

[JAC82]   Jackson, M., *System Development*, Prentice-Hall, 1982.

[MCC89]   McClure, C., *CASE Is Software Automation*, Prentic-Hall, 1989.

[ORR77]   Orr, K., *Structured Systems Development*, Yourdon Press, 1977.

[ORR81]   Orr, K., *Structured Requirements Definition*, Ken Orr and Associates, 1981.

[ORR89]   Orr, K., "The Warnier/Orr Approach," *Byte Magazine*, pp. 221-224, April 1989.

[SCA87]   Scandura, J. M., "A Cognitive Approach to Software Development: The PRODOC Environment and Associated Methodology," *Journal of Pascal, Ada, & Modula-2*, vol. 6, no. 5, pp. 10-25 (1987).

[WAR74]   Warnier, J., *Logical Construction of Programs*, Van Nostrand Reinhold, 1974, translated by B. M. Flanagan.

[WAR81]   Warnier, J., *Logical Construction of Systems*, Van Nostrand Reinhold, 1981.

[YOU89]   Yourdon, E., *Modern Structured Analysis*, Yourdon Press, 1989.

Chapter 6
Control-Oriented Techniques

We turn now to the third axis of our model of the application domain — the control axis. As we saw in Chapters 4 and 5, the function and data axes emphasize the content and structure of an application. The focus of the control axis is behavior: Given all the possible things a system might do, when does it do them? How does a system respond to external stimuli? Can a stimulus ever be ignored? These and similar questions are (or should be!) resolved by descriptions of the application in the control dimension.

6.1 Introduction

Software developers typically conceive of a system in terms of its structure, whereas customers and testers typically comprehend a system in terms of its behavior. One of the advantages of the control dimension is that the information produced in this mode of thinking is very helpful both to the customer and to testers. In this chapter, we will first consider control drivers, followed by the three mainline notations for representing control: decision tables, finite state machines, and Petri nets. Each of these notations can be executed, thus providing a form of executable specification.

6.1.1 Threads

Another way to describe the contribution of the control axis is the is/does dichotomy. Data and processing models generally describe what a system is: its structure, its components, interfaces among the components, and so on. Control describes what a system does: what happens in response to inputs, sequential behavior, and so on. To help with this distinction, consider a term commonly used in real-time systems — a thread. A *thread* refers to one particular, execution-time behavior of a system. A thread is initiated by one or more stimuli, and culminates in possibly several responses. Some examples of threads are a "trace" of statements executed when a module is called, the sequence of actions that results from an input, and consequences of an interrupt. Clearly, systems support the execution of numerous distinct threads. The is/does dichotomy leads us to another useful distinction: Threads are orthogonal to structure. In simple applications, threads of behavior can usually be "derived" from the structural views by experienced analysts; in more complex applications, particularly real-time systems, the importance of behavior demands a strong control description.

What are the things that select a thread at execution time? The easy answer is "inputs"; it is instructive to consider types of inputs: events, signals, messages, and data. Figures 6.1 and 6.2 show the differences among these types of inputs, by their duration and by their location.

6.1.2 Events

Events occur at the port boundary of a system. If we represent the system with data flow diagrams, events are seen as information flows to/from the external entities in a context diagram. Some examples of events: arrival of a newly purchased book at the Library, a menu selection requesting the list of books by an author, pressing a digit key on an ATM terminal, sensing the last $10 bill in an ATM, and so on. We can speak about input and output events. Since these occur at external entities, we can therefore speak of input and output external entities, or, more simply, ports. A system has no control over its input events, but it must respond to them. Systems have complete control over their output events. Many times, event sequences are the only perception a customer/user has of a system.

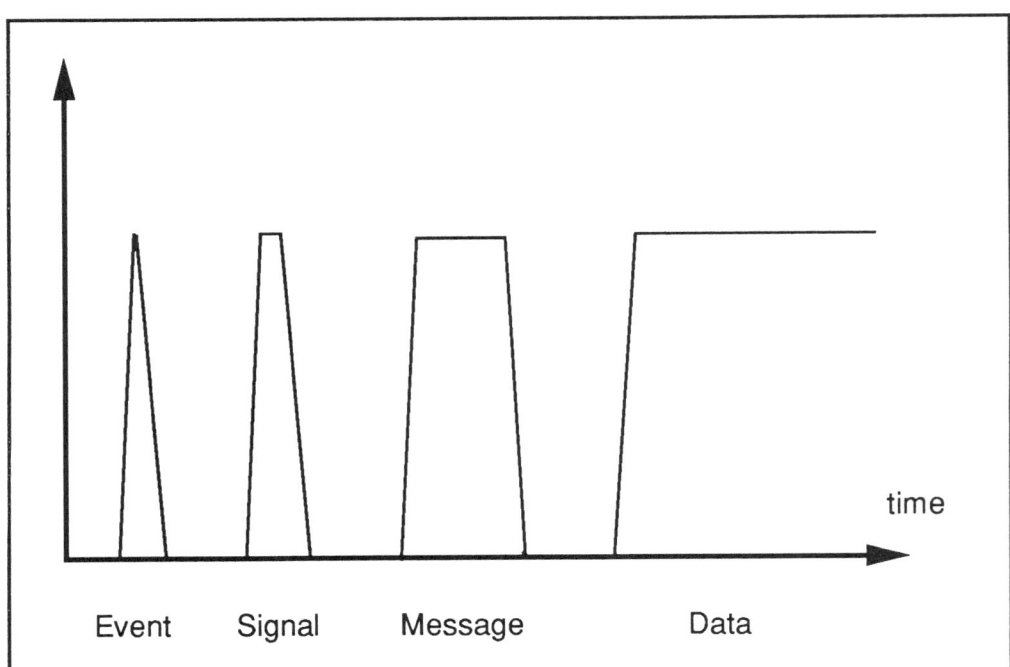

Figure 6.1
Duration of input types.

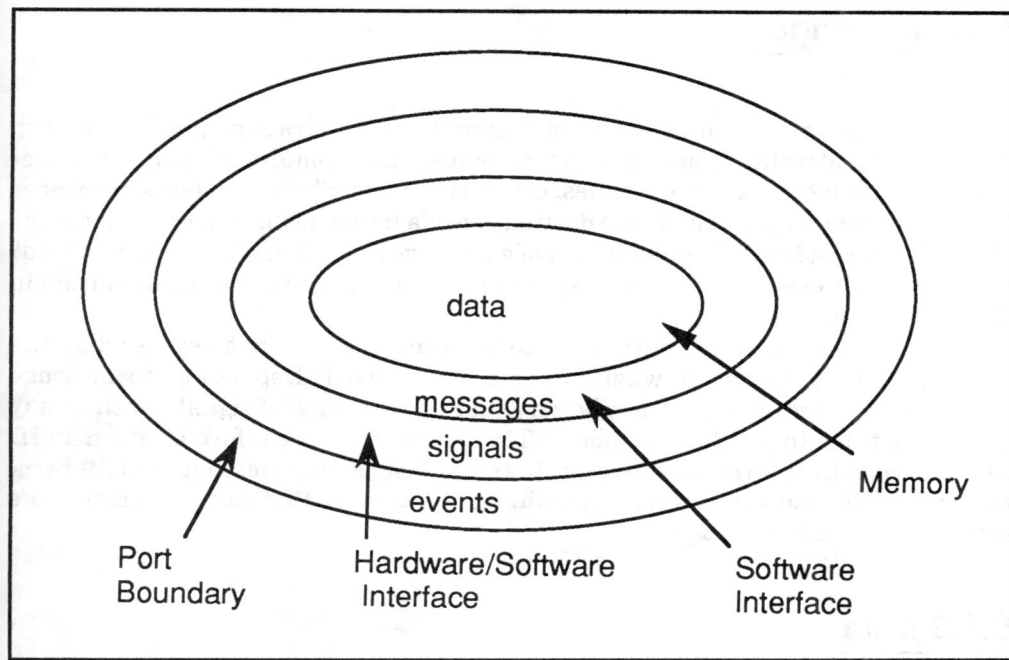

Figure 6.2
Location of
input types.

6.1.3 Signals

Signals typically occur at hardware/software interfaces; they can be either discrete or continuous. Many times, an input event "generates" a discrete signal which results in an internal record of the event having occurred. Systems often use signals to generate output events. Because of their location at the hardware/software interface, signals have a longer duration than events. Many times, signals are used to decentralize processing. In the Simple Simon ATM system, for example, consider the provision of the beeping tone that continues until the customer removes the ID card at the end of an ATM session. One way to implement this feature would be to have an ID card sensor that is observed by software. A tight control loop would check for the presence of the card and then emit another beep. Since such a loop precludes other processing, another implementation would be to have the ID card sensor attached to a signal, and have the signal continuously control the beeper.

Continuous signals are a lot like data in terms of duration — they are always present. One major difference is that we can picture continuous signals as being constantly rewritten. Continuous signals typically are associated with physical quantities, such as altitude, wind speed, temperature, fluid level, and time. The last major difference is that we usually think of discrete signals as binary — either present or absent; continuous signals assume a range of values.

6.1.4 Messages

Messages are a general form of internal communication, possibly among subsystems and certainly among software components. Modules call or invoke other modules with messages. Many times, especially in distributed systems, messages have an associated protocol. Is the destination of a message known, or is a message simply broadcast? How does the sender of a message know that it has been received? Can a message ever get lost? These questions need to be answered by definition in the control dimension.

The duration of a message refers to the time interval that begins when the message is sent, and ends when it has been received. Depending on message protocols, message durations may be very short, on the order of signals, or they may last a long time. In the Simple Simon ATM system, after the information on an ID card is decoded, the terminal sends it to the central bank via a message, and the bank responds with another message containing the correct PIN and the customer's present account balances.

6.1.5 Data

Data is (are is correct but awkward) the innermost level of the "system onion" shown in Figure 6.2. Data is written and read by software. We picture data as having a very long duration, from the time it is written to the time it is rewritten. Intermediate reads by software have no effect on the duration of data, hence there is a nice distinction between messages and data: Both begin with a write operation, but data ends with a rewrite, while messages end with a read. In this sense, data is more permanent than messages. In the Simple Simon ATM system, the following would be stored as data: customer ID, customer PIN, number of PIN attempts, deposit amount, withdrawal amount, number of ATM transactions in present month, and so on.

6.2 Philosophy

Recall that in Chapter 3, we made a refinement of the control axis with respect to applications that were either static or dynamic, and applications implemented with a single processor (sequential) or with several processors (concurrent). Taken together, these two distinctions add useful insight to our understanding of the role of control. Dynamism raises serious issues of control that simply do not occur on static applications. Similarly, concurrency raises still more complex control issues that simply are not present in sequential applications. The fundamental philosophy of the control axis is that behavior must be correctly represented; and more complex forms of behavior demand more sophisticated forms of representation. We can picture this control taxonomy as a two-dimensional plane, as shown in Figure 6.3.

This figure shows some examples of common applications within the control taxonomy, and it also shows appropriate choices of notation/technique: decision tables for static sequential applications, finite state machines for dynamic sequential applications, and Petri nets for dynamic concurrent applications. What about the static concurrent quadrant? Here, the issue is parallel computation, typically to improve real-time performance. None of the control notations are particularly helpful here; our best advice is to use mathematically expressive notations and PDLs with fork-join capabilities.

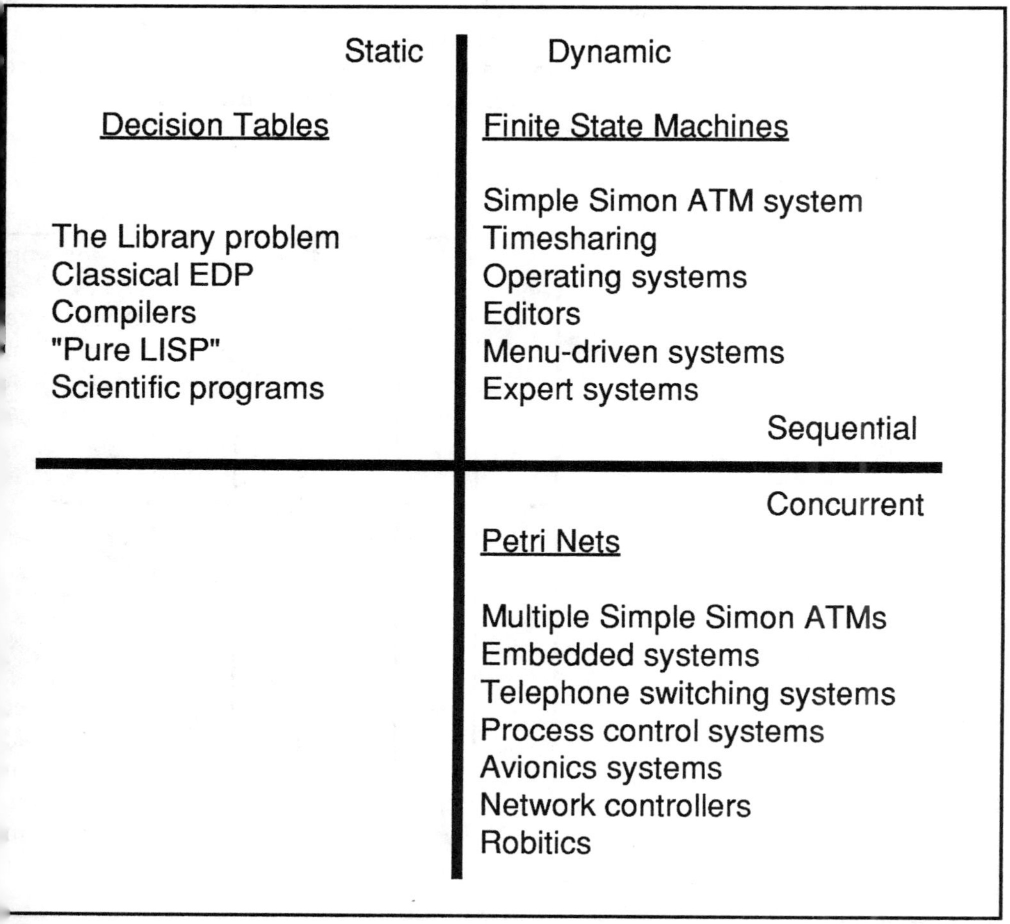

	Static	Dynamic
	Decision Tables	**Finite State Machines**
		Simple Simon ATM system
	The Library problem	Timesharing
	Classical EDP	Operating systems
	Compilers	Editors
	"Pure LISP"	Menu-driven systems
	Scientific programs	Expert systems

Sequential

Concurrent

Petri Nets

Multiple Simple Simon ATMs
Embedded systems
Telephone switching systems
Process control systems
Avionics systems
Network controllers
Robitics

Figure 6.3
Control taxonomy.

6.3 Decision Tables

Decision tables have been used for data processing purposes since the early 1960s; they are used much more frequently in Europe than in the United States. Decision tables are ideal for describing situations in which a number of combinations of actions are taken under varying sets of conditions. Some of the basic decision table terms are illustrated in Figure 6.4.

6.3.1 Notation

There are four portions of a decision table. The part to the left of the bold vertical line is the stub portion, and that to the right is the entry portion. The part above the bold line is the condition portion, and that below is the action portion. Thus we can refer to the condition stub, the condition entries, the action stub, and the action entries. A column in the entry portion is a rule. Rules indicate which actions are taken for the conditional circumstances indicated in the condition portion of the rule.

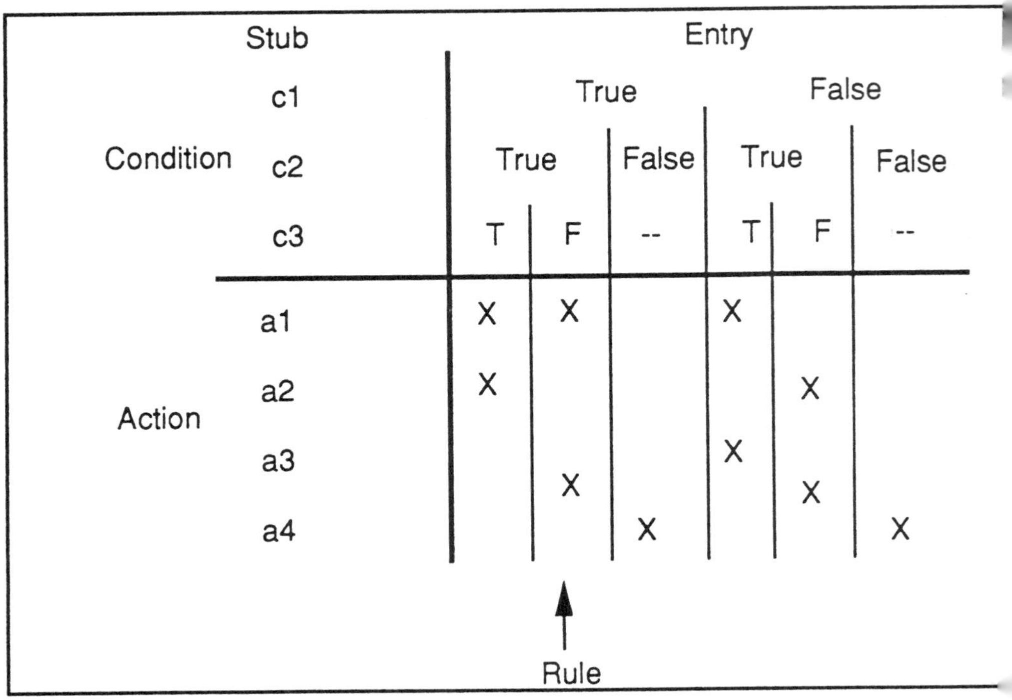

Stub		Entry					
	c1	True			False		
Condition	c2	True		False	True		False
	c3	T	F	--	T	F	--
	a1	X	X		X		
	a2	X				X	
Action	a3			X	X	X	
	a4			X			X

↑
Rule

Figure 6.4
Portions of a decision table.

Decision tables are somewhat declarative (as opposed to imperative): There is no particular order implied by the conditions, and selected actions do not occur in any particular order.

6.3.2 Technique

To apply decision tables to a problem, we first identify the important conditions and actions. Next, we complete the condition portion in the same manner as making a truth table. Note that two conditions yield four rules, three conditions yield eight rules, and so on. Now, for each rule, we select which actions are to be executed. In the process of doing this, we often identify additional actions, and occasionally we find additional conditions. If this happens, we simply iterate, knowing that we are gradually improving our representation of the reality of the application.

Figure 6.5 illustrates the results of this process on a portion of the Simple Simon ATM system. Recall that a customer has three tries to correctly enter his or her PIN. The relevant screens (see Chapter 3) are screens s2 (Enter PIN), s3 (Incorrect, try

c1: 1st Try	T	T	--	--	--	--
c2: 2nd Try	--	--	T	T	--	--
c3: 3rd Try	--	--	--	--	T	T
c4: PIN ok?	Y	N	Y	N	Y	N
a1: display Screen s2	--	X	--	X	--	X
a2: display Screen s3	--	X	--	X	--	X
a3: display Screen s4	--	--	--	--	--	--
a4: display Screen s5	X	--	X	--	X	--
a5: repeat table	--	X	--	X	--	X
a6: done	X	--	X	--	X	--

Figure 6.5
Decision table for PIN entry.

again), s4 (Card will be kept), and s5 (Select transaction). One helpful style is to add actions to show when a table is to be repeated and when it is done. Another handy action indicates when a rule is logically impossible.

In the PIN entry problem, we wish to capture what happens during up to three attempts to correctly enter a PIN. Conditions c1, c2, and c3 refer to which attempt we are on, and condition c4 refers to whether or not the entered PIN is correct. Rule 1 states that it is the first try and the PIN is correct. Under those circumstances, the screen s5 is displayed, and this portion of the problem is over. Rule 2 states that the customer failed to get the PIN correct on the first try, so screen s3 is displayed to announce that the entered PIN is incorrect, and then screen s2 1is displayed to afford a second attempt. Rules 3 and 4 repeat this logic for the second try. Rule 5 describes the situation where the customer gets the PIN correct on the third try, and rule 6 describes what actions occur on the third failed attempt.

Follow this logic carefully on the decision table in Figure 6.5. Notice that there are dashed entries, both for conditions and for actions. Dashes have at least three possible interpretations: does not apply, irrelevant (don't care), and "must be false."

Frequently, conditions are identified in such a way that they have an exclusive-or relationship, as do conditions c1, c2, and c3. Obviously, if it is someone's first attempt, it cannot be his or her second attempt, nor can it be the third attempt. Here, the meaning of the dashes is "must be false." Some notations will write F! to emphasize this.

The declarative aspect of a decision table can be seen in this example. Notice that we have no way to show that screen s3 should be displayed first, and then screen s2. We could put subscripts on the X's to show an action order.

The decision table in Figure 6.5 is a limited entry decision table, which means that all condition entries are binary (True/False, Yes/No, 1/0, Male/Female). Limited entry decision tables are often very large, and therefore hard to read. Many times, especially when conditions have an exclusive-or relationship, several conditions can be collapsed into one condition with "extended" entries. The Extended Entry Decision Table in Figure 6.6 is derived from the limited entry table in Figure 6.5. Notice that conditions c1, c2, and c3 are collapsed into the new condition c1 (Try =). The condition entry completes the conditional clause, and is assumed to be true. In general, extended-entry decision tables are easier to read because they are more compact.

Because of their structure, decision tables can be analyzed for completeness and consistency. They can also be manipulated algebraically. Figures 6.7 and 6.8 show the results of two such manipulations. In Figure 6.7, we note that there are three rules with identical action entries (rules 1, 3, and 5). We combine these, noting that, as long as the PIN is correct, the attempt number is irrelevant (here the dash means irrelevant). Now the same stub portion has four rules instead of six. In the second simplification, we note that the logic for the first and second tries is identical, thus the only relevant condition is whether or not this is the third try. In Figure 6.8 condition c1 is changed slightly, and we have a limited-entry decision table with only four rules.

c1: Try =		1		2		3	
c2: PIN ok?	Y	N	Y	N	Y	N
a1: display Screen s2	--	X	--	X	--	--
a2: display Screen s3	--	X	--	X	--	--
a3: display Screen s4	--	--	--	--	--	X
a4: display Screen s5	X	--	X	--	X	--
a5: repeat table	--	X	--	X	--	--
a6: done	X	--	X	--	X	X

Figure 6.6
Extended-entry decision table for PIN entry.

c1: Try =	--	1	2	3
c2: PIN ok?	Y	N	N	N
a1: display Screen s2	--	X	X	--
a2: display Screen s3	--	X	X	--
a3: display Screen s4	--	--	--	X
a4: display Screen s5	X	--	--	--
a5: repeat table	--	X	X	--
a6: done	X	--	--	X

Figure 6.7
First simplification of PIN entry table.

In practice, decision tables can be quite provocative. Consider an analyst trying to capture the domain knowledge of an expert in an application area. If the analyst uses a decision table as the "skeleton" of an interview, together they will consider situations which might otherwise be overlooked by the expert. This concept extends directly to artificial intelligence with rule-based and knowledge-based systems. One final comment: The first set of conditions and actions may not be the "right" set. It is frequently necessary to iterate to find better condition and action sets.

6.3.3 Representation

Decision tables are an oddity in our notation-technique-representation scheme: The notation is the representation. Recall that for the function- and data-oriented discussions, the techniques used the basic notations, possibly in slightly varying ways. The end result, however, was always expressed in a desired target representation. Although decision tables are widely used in Europe, they are not common in the United States. The only standard we know of was developed by CODASYL nearly a decade ago [COD82]. The Gane and Sarson version of Structured Analysis recommends decision tables [GAN79]. Some CASE products support decision tables (Excelerator RTS, TurboCASE), but this is not common. Also, the Hatley/Pirbhai real-time extension (see Section 6.6.2) uses a form of decision tables; in that representation they are known as process activation tables.

	N		Y	
c1: 3rd Try				
c2: PIN ok?	Y	N	Y	N
a1: display Screen s2	--	X	X	--
a2: display Screen s3	--	X	X	--
a3: display Screen s4	--	--	--	X
a4: display Screen s5	X	--	--	--
a5: repeat table	--	X	X	--
a6: done	X	--	--	X

Figure 6.8
Second simplification of PIN entry table.

6.4 Finite State Machines

Finite state machines are composed of states and transitions. As a mathematical structure, additional information is provided that relates to the events that cause transitions. Formally speaking, there are notions of independence and no memory. We shall see that these have significant implications later on. In use, finite state machines (FSMs) describe situations in which there are distinct steps, stages, or phases to a process. States are used to represent these steps; they are also used to represent data, or even complex combinations of conditions. If we wished, we could use a state to represent the condition entry portion of a rule in a decision table. Transitions are used to represent actions; transitions are caused by events, and when a transition occurs, an output may be generated. All of this (and more) can be expressed both textually and in drawings, such as those shown in Figure 6.9.

6.4.1 Notation

Look closely at Figure 6.9: There are four states, s1, s2, s3, and s4; there are also four transitions: from s1 to s2, from s1 to s3, from s2 to s3, and from s3 to s4. The style on the left is more commonly used by electrical engineers. The labels on the edges describe events that cause the transition and outputs or actions that are generated as the transition occurs. The event/output labels are usually written as fractions, where the event(s) that cause the transition are the "numerator" and the output(s) or action(s) are the "denominator." The rectangular style is more often used by computer scientists; our guess is that variable-sized "states" make it easier to draw

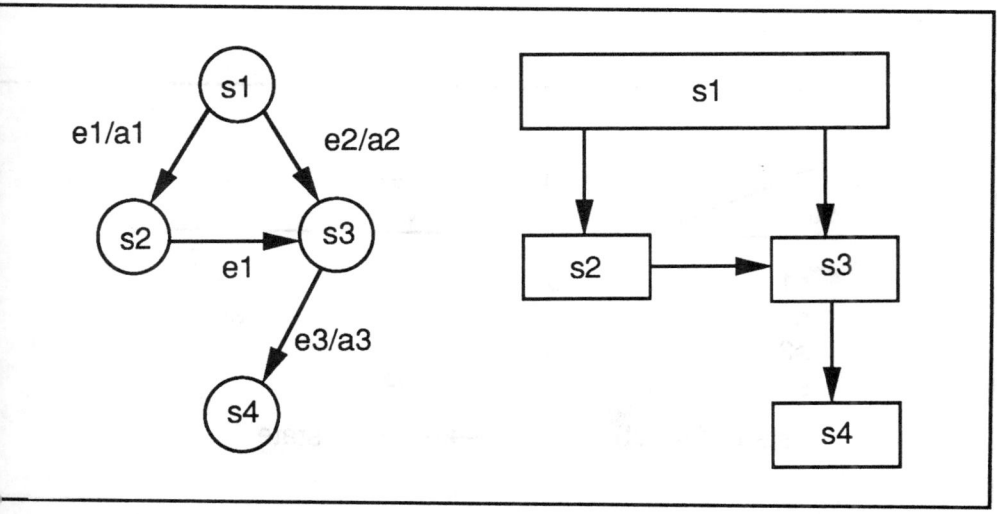

Figure 6.9
Drawing notations for state-transition diagrams.

diagrams with few crossing lines. Most CASE products that support state transition diagrams use the rectangular notation.

Finite state machines are inherently dynamic. They have an associated semantics that must be understood: The system is in exactly one state at any point in time (we speak of "being in state s1"), and there are never two exactly simultaneous events. In the pure mathematics view of an FSM, transitions occur in infinitely small times; most practitioners like to think of transitions, especially those that have attendant actions or outputs, as having some finite execution time.

We could give a completely textual description of a finite state machine. To do so, we would simply list the states (a finite set), the transitions (a finite set of ordered pairs of states), and what the mathematicians call the input alphabet (a list of events that cause transitions) and the output alphabet (a list of output events and actions associated with transitions). All of this information is contained in two frequently used tables, shown in Figures 6.10 and 6.11.

The transition table relates states to input events. Given a state and an event, the next state is shown; hence a transition is identified. The event table relates states and events to outputs and actions. Given a state and an event (which we already know define a transition), this table shows what outputs (if any) are generated when the transition occurs. Notice that the transition table and the event table are complementary.

Once a finite state machine is defined, we think of it as a dynamic entity that can execute. A few more definitions will help with this. We can speak of source and sink states. Source states have no incoming transitions (some graphical styles show an incoming transition that does not originate in any state); sink states have no outgoing transitions. We can trace a path from source states to sink states. Such paths can be viewed in two ways: as a sequence of transitions or as a sequence of states. Either way, a path represents an execution of the finite state machine which corresponds to a thread of system behavior.

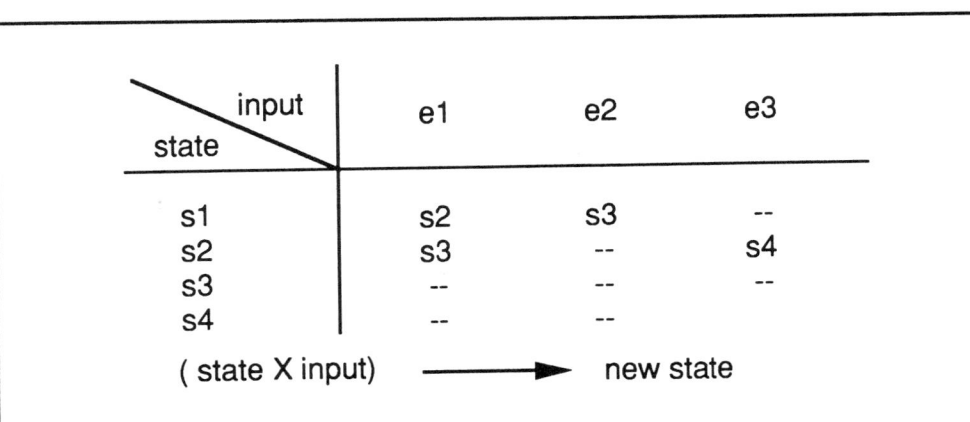

Figure 6.10
State transition table.

input state	e1	e2	e3
s1	s2	s3	--
s2	s3	--	s4
s3	--	--	--
s4	--	--	

(state X input) ──────▶ new state

state \ input	e1	e2	e3
s1	a1	a2	--
s2	--	--	--
s3	--	--	a3
s4	--	--	--

(state X input) ⟶ action

Figure 6.11
State event table.

6.4.2 Technique

To use finite state machines to describe an application, we generally start by identifying states. States can represent any of the following:

1. Stages of processing
2. Status (active, enabled, ...)
3. Logical conditions
4. Data values.

Once we have identified a candidate set of states, we postulate transitions among the states and the circumstances that cause these transitions. We usually identify outputs or actions last. As with decision tables, our first cut at states and transitions might not be our final version. Figure 6.12 shows the result of doing this to the PIN entry problem that we modeled with decision tables.

One style that is handy is to have an Initial or Idle state that is the source state for an FSM. A question we need to resolve right away is how to treat the screens in the Simple Simon ATM system. Are screens states? Are they outputs that occur with transitions? We did the example both ways; it turned out better when we viewed screens as outputs rather than as states. Thus when we are "in" the Idle state, the Welcome screen (s1) is being displayed. When an ID card is entered in the card slot, we transit to the Await PIN Entry state. Screen s2 is displayed, and the terminal will remain in this state until a PIN is entered.

At this point, the FSM "assumes" a lot of processing. After the ID card was entered, it was decoded, and a message was sent to the central bank to get the correct PIN and the customer's account balances. The digit keystrokes (and cancels) are monitored until a four-digit PIN has been entered. Finally, a process (in a data flow diagram somewhere) compares the entered PIN with the correct PIN, and produces one of two results: PIN ok or wrong PIN. We view these results as events that cause

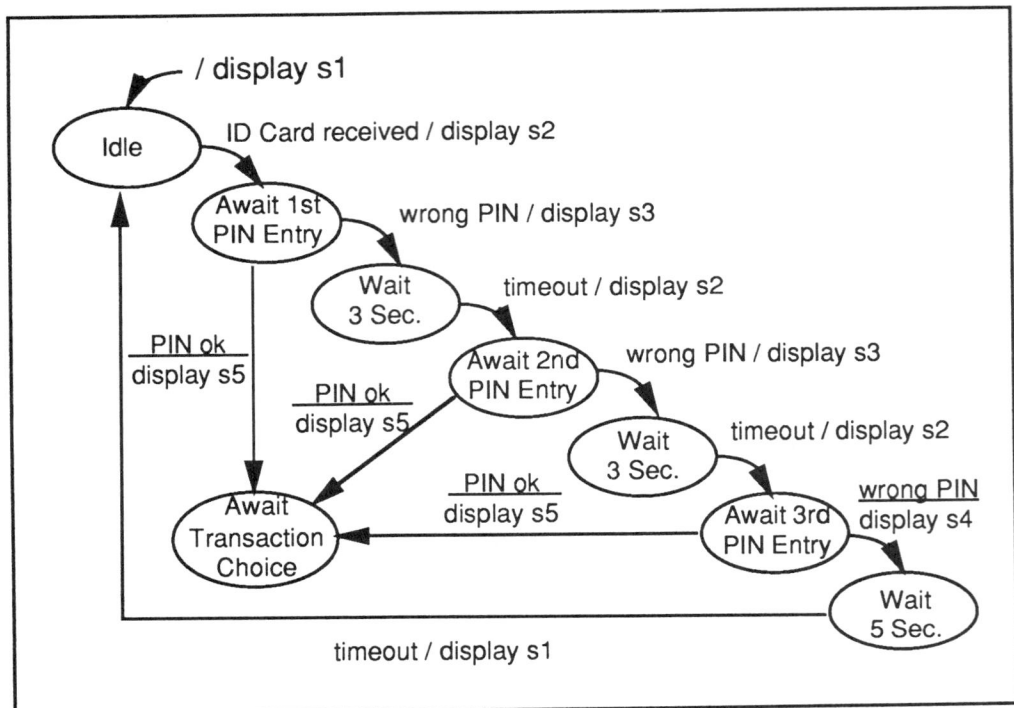

Figure 6.12
PIN entry state machine.

transitions either to the Await Transaction Selection state or to the Wait 3 Seconds state. (If we wished, we could decompose the Await PIN Entry state into a lower-level FSM that deals more explicitly with the processing we just described.)

Let's follow the wrong PIN path. Notice that, after screen s3 is displayed, we wait for 3 seconds in the wait state. During this interval, screen s3 instructs the customer to try again. After a 3 second timeout (an event!), we transit to the Await 2nd Try state. As with the Await PIN Entry state, there are two possible exits. Notice that the same processing of PIN input will occur in this state. Suppose the wrong PIN is entered a second time. We will go to the next state, Wait 3 Seconds, and then transmit to the Await 3rd Try state, where the PIN entry processing will be as before. The only difference is that this time, if an incorrent PIN is entered, we will display screen s4 informing the customer that the card will be retained, wait 5 seconds, and return to the Idle state.

At this point, we can make several observations. One is that if we had made a Final State (after the Wait 5 Seconds state), there would be one source state and two sink states. There would be three paths from the source (Idle) state to the Await Transaction Selection state, and one path to the Final state. These four paths correspond to the four rules in the final specification of the PIN entry decision table. We can consider each path as a scenario of system execution (thread). We can also consider these paths as the subjects of system test cases. In fact, we can derive a system test case from a path by capturing the inputs that cause the state transitions and the sequence of observable outputs.

A second, slightly more obscure observation is that the system exhibits what we might call "context-dependent" behavior. Consider the Wrong PIN event (it's probably a message). When this event occurs in the Await PIN Entry and Await 2nd Try states, we display screen s3, but when it occurs in the Await 3rd Try state, we cause a different output (screen s4). Notice that the same physical input causes two distinct outputs depending on the context in which it occurs. This is a highly expressive capability of finite state machines. (We could express a context as a combination of condition values in a decision table, but this leads to very large decision tables.)

When we first introduced finite state machines, we said they were memoryless. This means that the FSM has no recollection of how it got to a particular state. In this example, once we reach the Await Transaction Selection state, we could have been in any of three states, but there is no recollection of which one we were in. As a state definition style, we can "fudge" memory by the way we name states. Here, we named the states Await PIN Entry, Await 2nd Try, and Await 3rd Try. These states serve as "memory" in the sense that we can reconstruct the past. The other esoteric aspect of finite state machines, independence, is related to memorylessness. Whatever happens in a particular state is completely independent (no memory) of what may have happened in previous states. These features of FSMs are violated in the "simplification" shown in Figure 6.13.

In this figure, we try to simplify the FSM of Figure 6.12 by noting that the activities of the three PIN entry states are almost identical. Also, there are two Wait 3 Second states. Is this really one state, or are they really two different states? One way to clarify this is to rename the states: 1st 3 Second Wait, 2nd 3 Second Wait. The real problem is that we have no way of knowing how many times we traverse the loop between the PIN entry and the Wait states. Look carefully at the events that cause transitions, and notice that the same event, Wrong PIN, can cause a transition to the Wait 3 Seconds state and to the Idle state. How does the machine know which transition to take? We know which one, because we know about the three-try limit. For a finite state machine, this is essentially (and irreparably) ambiguous. The choice depends on memory, and the FSM has no memory.

6.4.3 Representation

Finite state machines can be represented either graphically, usually called state transition diagrams or STDs, or textually. Several examples of state transition diagrams are given in this chapter. It is useful to note that nearly all of the information in a diagram can be captured in a strictly textual representation.

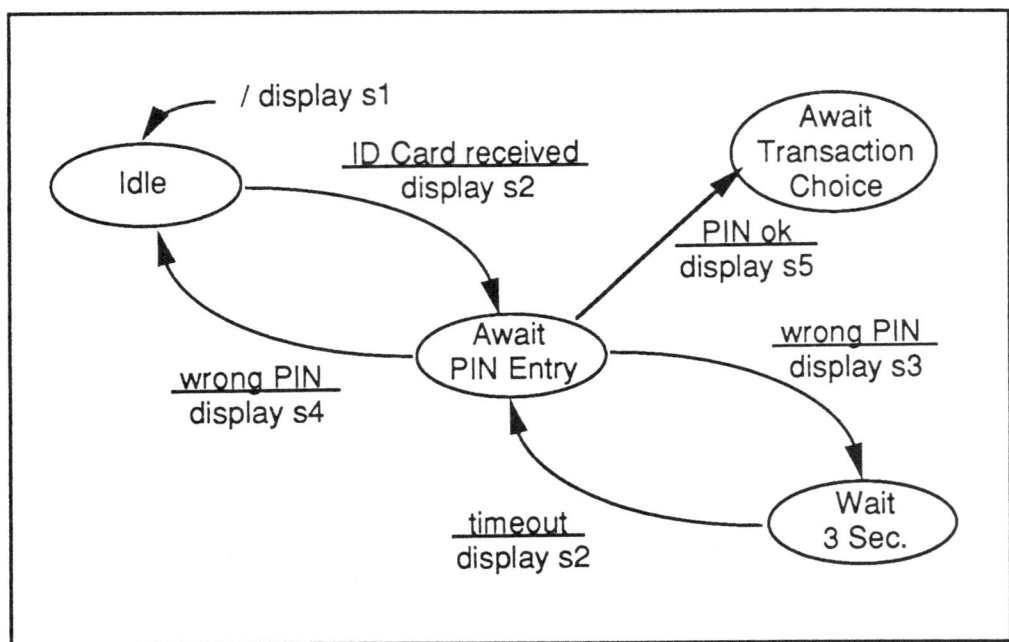

Figure 6.13
Incorrectly simplified
PIN entry state
machine.

Typically, textual representations of finite state machines use a template such as the one below:

        <state> <state name>
        <state narrative>
        <activities in state>

        <transition list>, where each transition is described as follows:

        <successor state>
        <inputs causing transition>
        <outputs generated by transition>

Such textual descriptions capture all of the essential information, and can support FSM execution engines. The only edge that state transition diagrams have is that they are inherently two-dimensional, and thus parallelism, connectivity, and lengths of paths can be seen instantly, whereas in a textual representation, these would be products of analytic tools.

6.4.4 Benefits and Drawbacks

As we have seen, paths in an FSM correspond to threads of system behavior. The mathematical basis of FSMs supports several types of analysis; one of these is reachability. If there is a path from state A to state B, we say that state B is reachable from state A. Here are some common questions about system behavior:

1. Can _____ ever happen?
2. Once we are at _____, can we ever get to _____?
3. Once we are at _____, what are all the things that could happen?
4. What are all the circumstances that could have left me at _____?
5. Is there any state that can never be reached?

These questions can all be answered by analyzing the reachability in a finite state machine. They become even more important if we identify states as being either safe or hazardous. Then we would like to know if there is always an escape from a hazardous state (never a sink state).

Clearly, finite state machines are more expressive than decision tables. They graphically display threads of behavior, and can be extensively analyzed. They do have their limitations, however. They do a fine job at describing prescribed behavior (things that should happen), but it is difficult to describe proscribed behavior (things that shouldn't happen). One possibility is to identify proscribed states. Another limitation, this time from the "one state and one event at a time" constraint, is that finite state machines can never represent concurrency. Communicating finite state machines can, but representing the communication is complex. Finally, finite state machines are vulnerable to the "state explosion" syndrome. It is easy to start adding states that relate to independent situations (communicating FSMs, for example). If an N-state machine communicates with an M-state machine, there will be $N \times M$ states. This is very similar to adding conditions to a decision table. As an example of how quickly the state explosion can occur, we calculated the number of states needed to describe an elevator system in a nine-floor building with three elevators — 110,596 states. Needless to say, we didn't draw the diagram.

6.5 Petri Nets

Petri nets were the subject of the Ph.D. dissertation of Carl Adam Petri in 1963. Since that time, they have become the notation of choice for concurrent systems. They are far more expressive than finite state machines; in fact, finite state machines are a very restricted, special case of a Petri net. Concurrency raises a variety of issues relating to "tasks," where a task is an atomic unit of processing in a distributed system. One issue is communication among tasks, as governed by a protocol. The second set of issues involves coordination among tasks: sequencing, synchronizing, resolving conflicts, and exclusion. All of these, and many more system properties, such as fair scheduling, deadlock, and liveness, can be represented and analyzed with Petri nets.

Petri nets have been extended in scores of ways; here we will only touch on the basics to suggest the potential richness of their expressive power.

6.5.1 Notation

A Petri net consists of a finite set of places and a finite set of transitions. Places can be inputs to transitions, and they can be outputs of transitions; thus, defining a Petri net entails defining the input and output relationships among the places and transitions. Figure 6.14 shows a graph of a common Petri net. Places are represented by circles, and transitions by bars. The input and output relationships are shown by flow arrows from places to transitions (inputs), and by arrows from transitions to places (outputs). In Figure 6.14, place p1 is an input to transition t1 and an output of transition t2. Place p3 is an output of t2 and an input to both t3 and t5.

Perhaps the most important concept about Petri nets is that of Petri net markings. A marked Petri net has an integer associated with each place; the integer signifies the number of tokens said to be "in" that place. Tokens are drawn as black dots, as seen in Figure 6.15, where places p2, p4, and p7 are marked.

Markings permit the definitions of transition enabling and transition firing. A transition is enabled if each of its input places is marked (contains a token). A transition can fire only if it is enabled. When a transition fires, a token is removed from each of its input places, and a token is deposited in each of its output places. Tokens may be created and destroyed as needed. Conservation of tokens is not necessary; however, nets which do conserve their tokens have a significance to operating systems. Figure 6.16 shows an enabled transition before and after firing. One whole branch of Petri net theory deals with various extensions of the basic definitions of enabling and firing. For example, there is the notion of an inhibitor arc. When a place is connected to a transition by an inhibitor arc, the place must be empty to contribute to enabling.

6.5.2 Technique

Developing a Petri net representation of an application is very similar to the process used for finite state machines (not surprisingly, since FSMs are a special case of Petri nets). We start by identifying places, only now places can be used for

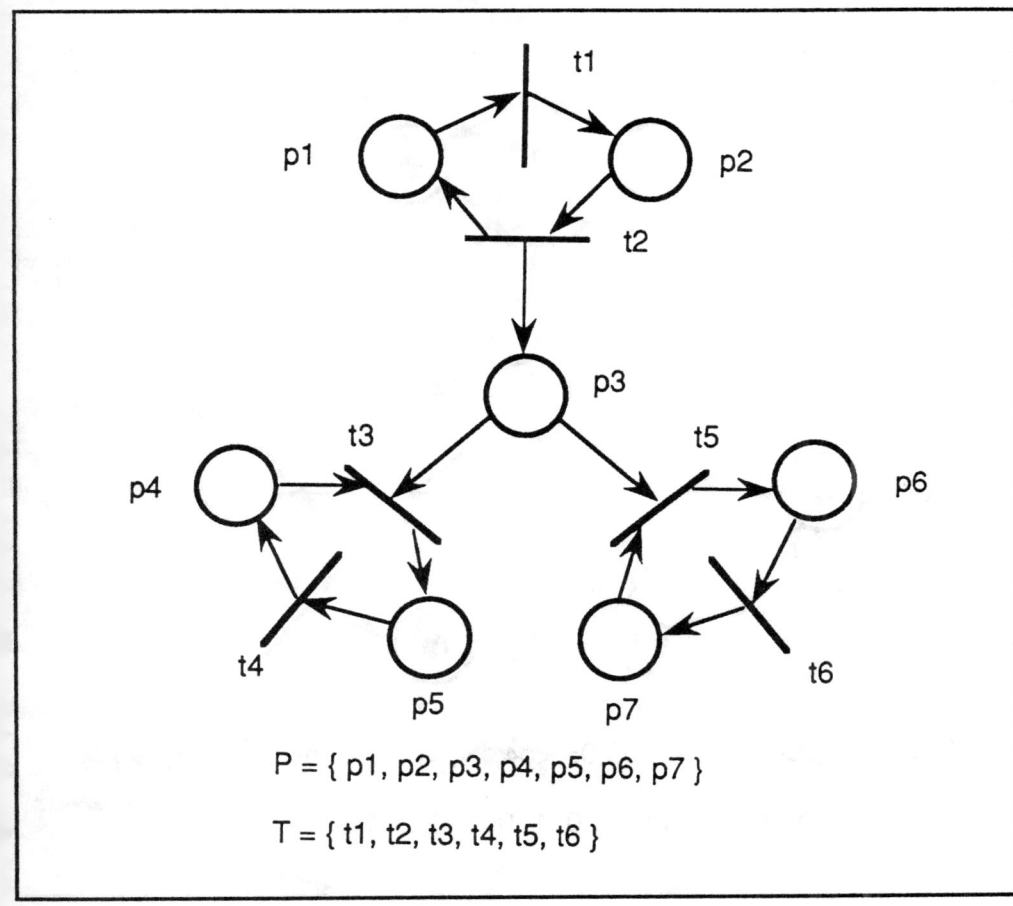

P = { p1, p2, p3, p4, p5, p6, p7 }

T = { t1, t2, t3, t4, t5, t6 }

Figure 6.14
Petri net graph.

any of the types of inputs we described at the beginning of this chapter. We also identify tasks, which will be represented either as individual transitions or as subnets. Petri net transitions are always action-oriented. We then proceed by composition. That is, we develop nets of places and transitions for threads of system behavior, and compose these into larger nets.

In the net in Figure 6.14, transitions t1 and t2 and places p1 and p2 constitute a "producer" task. Places p4 and p5 and transitions t3 and t4 constitute one "consumer" task, and places p6 and p7 and transitions t5 and t6 constitute the second consumer task. The three tasks are related by a buffer place, p3. We could picture the producer as baking chocolate chip cookies, where t1 signifies baking and t2 is removing cookies from the cookie sheet and placing them on a plate for the consumers. Cookies appear as tokens in place p3. Consumers eat cookies (transitions t3 and t5) and request more cookies (transitions t4 and t6). What happens if the consumers eat cookies faster than the producer can bake them? This situation

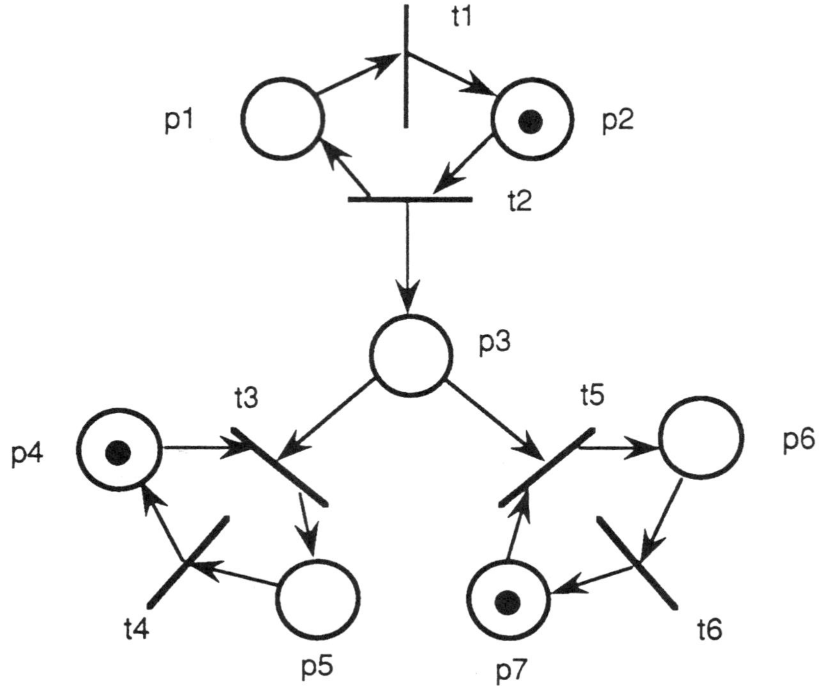

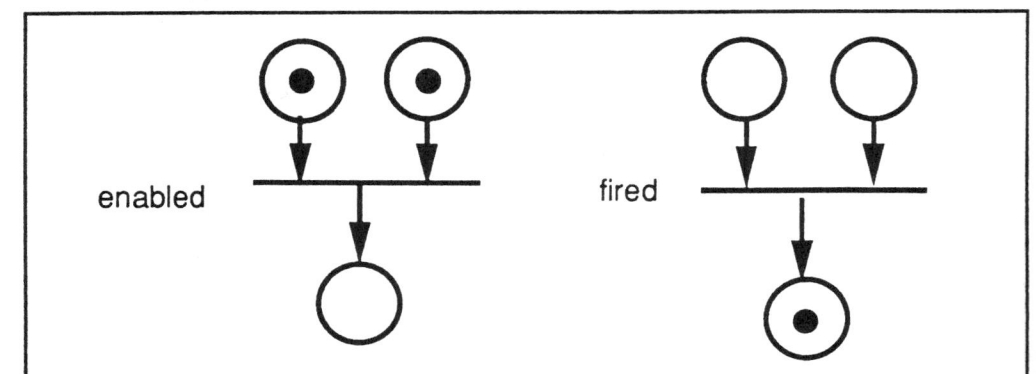

$$M = \{ <p1,0>,<p2,1>, <p3,0>,<p4,1>, <p5,0>,<p6,0>, <p7,1> \}$$

alternative notation: $m = < 0, 1, 0, 1, 0, 0, 1 >$

Figure 6.15
Marked Petri
net graph.

Figure 6.16
Transition enabling
and firing.

is a form of contention for limited resources, which is common in concurrent applications. It is known as Petri net conflict, and is shown in Figure 6.17.

The basic pattern of Petri net conflict is that a place is an input to two (or more) transitions. The conflict arises when both transitions are enabled. Firing one transition consumes the token from the conflict place, thereby disabling the other transition. If we extended the Simple Simon ATM system to include several ATM terminals, we would like to represent the situation where two customers try to make a withdrawal from the same account. The interaction between their respective ATM sessions should be one of Petri net conflict. This form of indirect interaction among separate tasks is typical of the situations in which Petri nets are the representation of choice. (Incidentally, this form of conflict cannot be represented with a finite state machine.)

Another common Petri net situation is mutual exclusion between two tasks. This would be another way to handle two customers who try to withdraw from the same account. With mutual exclusion, the tasks start out in conflict. When one task executes, the other is "locked out." When the first task is complete, the lock is removed, and the two tasks are in conflict once again. This time, the other task may execute, excluding the first task. This situation is shown in Figure 6.18.

6.5.3 Representation

As was the case with finite state machines and decision tables, the notation for Petri nets is the representation. We can also repeat the discussion of textual representations. These can certainly be developed and also analyzed. There are a few CASE tools that support Petri nets, most notably Design/CPN from Meta Systems.

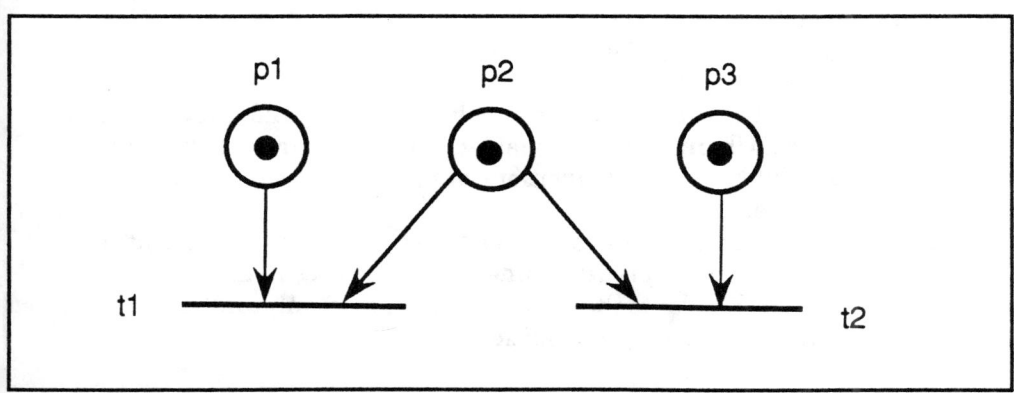

Figure 6.17
Petri net conflict.

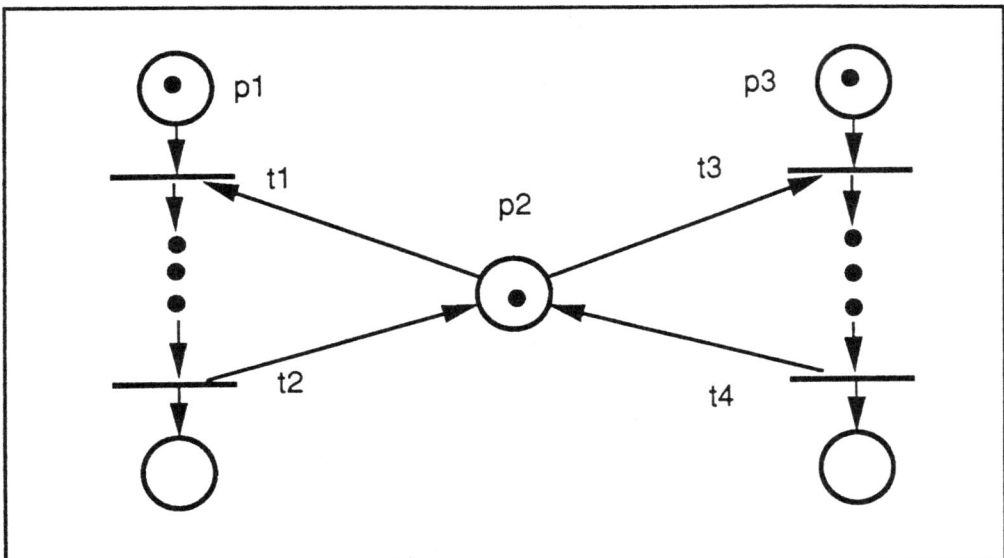

Figure 6.18
Mutual exclusion.

6.5.4 Benefits and Drawbacks

Petri nets have a very sophisticated set of execution possibilities. The simplest form is to start with an initial marking and determine which transitions are enabled. Select one of these and fire it, thereby changing the marking. Then determine which transitions are enabled, choose one, and fire it. We might call this "user directed net execution," since someone must choose which transition to fire when two or more are enabled. Figure 6.19 shows an execution sequence of our producer/consumer net.

In steps 1 and 2, the producer produces a token in place p3. At step 3, the second consumer (on the right) consumes the token, disabling the first consumer. In steps 4 and 5, the producer produces another token, which is consumed by the first consumer in step 6.

We have identified seven levels of Petri net execution:

1. Interactive: User marks places, resolves conflicts, and directs execution.
2. Burst mode: Chains of singly enabled transitions are automatically executed. When several transitions are enabled, the user selects one to be executed.
3. Predetermined: An input script marks places and directs execution.
4. Batch mode: A set of predetermined scripts is executed.
5. Probabilistic: Similar to the predetermined mode, only conflicts are resolved using transition firing probabilities.

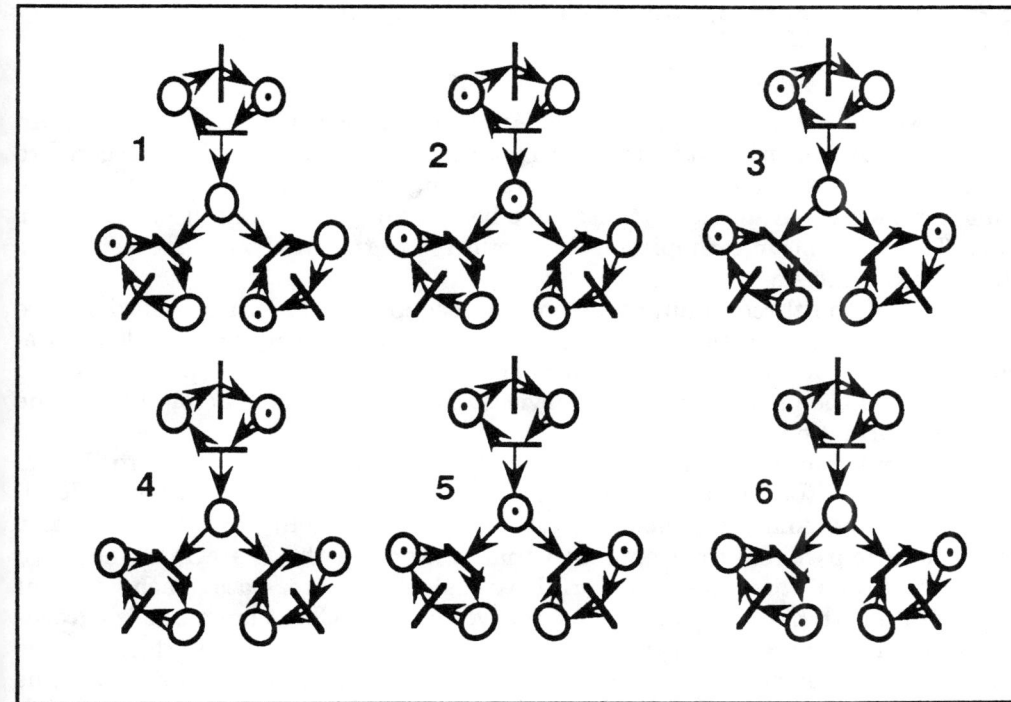

Figure 6.19
Executing a
Petri net.

6. Traffic mix: A demographic set of batch scripts are executed in random order.
7. Exhaustive (maybe exhausting is better): For a system with no loops, execute all possible threads. Exhaustive execution is more sensibly done with respect to the reachability tree of a Petri net.

Clearly, Petri nets represent the issues raised by both dynamism and concurrency. The main drawbacks of Petri nets are that they are not widely understood (and hence not widely used) and that they do not scale up very well. We have student projects that give Petri net representations of the Simple Simon ATM system. These usually take a dozen pages of drawings which must be placed together on a large table to see the entire net. The end result is a sophisticated equivalent of the "spaghetti code" horror of the pre-structured programming days.

The best response to this is that graphical representations for Petri nets (and for finite state machines) should be replaced by engines that execute the notations. Such executable specifications then serve as rigorous rapid prototypes (see Chapter 9).

6.6 Real-Time Extensions to Structured Analysis

As we saw in Chapter 4, Structured Analysis deals with the function axis of an application. At this point it is useful to recall that the control axis is orthogonal to (and independent of) the function axis. Even though most practitioners now realize that these are separate views, there have been attempts to integrate them in the past. The best known examples of these efforts are the "real-time extensions" to Structured Analysis.

Each of the three mainline extensions began with practitioners who were confronted with applications in which the control considerations demanded representation. In each case, the practitioners started with traditional Structured Analysis and then added notational devices and conventions to accommodate the control information.

The three mainline real-time extensions are briefly presented here: the Ward/Mellor method (the Transformation Schema), the Hatley/Pirbhai method (Real-Time Structured Analysis), and the Extended Systems Modeling Language (ESML). There is a fourth real-time approach that centers on the StateChart notation [HAR90]. StateCharts are a powerful extension of finite state machines that incorporate both hierarchy and concurrency. The StateChart language is exceedingly rich and complex, giving it the expressive power of Petri nets. We feel that the StateChart approach is far more comprehensive than the real-time extensions, thus it is excluded from consideration here. We also feel it is very appropriate for real-time practitioners, so the fact that it is not covered here should not be construed as a devaluation. Quite the contrary, a good discussion of the StateChart approach would require half this book.

6.6.1 The Transformation Schema

The Transformation Schema [WAR86a] incorporates control considerations directly into traditional data flow diagrams. The notational symbols are shown in Figure 6.20. There are control and data variations of transforms, stores, and flows. The Transformation Schema further elaborates flows by separate notations for discrete and continuous data flows and for converging and diverging flows.

The Transformation Schema retains the notions of hierarchy and balancing from traditional Structured Analysis; thus the final representation will be a leveled set of transformation schema drawings in which control is somewhat integrated with data processing. The one significant addition is that every control transform is given a supplemental definition on a separate page. This supplemental definition is usually a finite state machine, although provision is made for decision table descriptions.

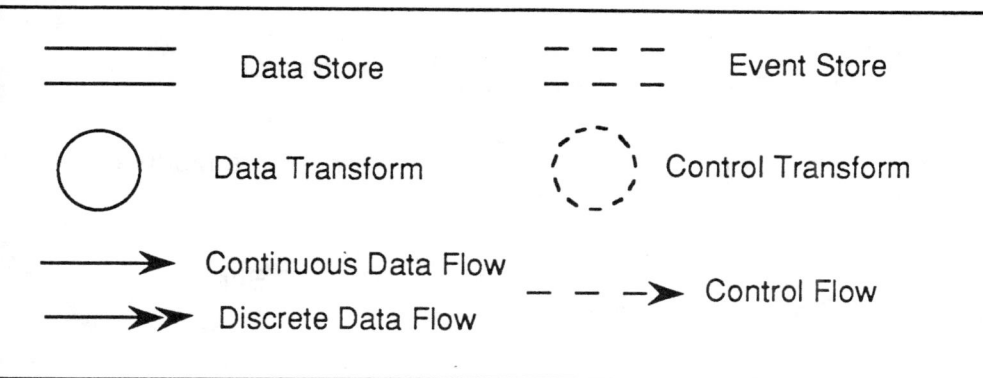

Figure 6.20
Transformation
schema symbols.

6.6.2 Real-Time Structured Analysis

Real-Time Structured Analysis [HAT87] features nearly the same symbol set as the transformation schema (the CSPEC Bar is added and the control transform is deleted), with different conventions, however (see Figure 6.21). One distinction is that in Real-Time Structured Analysis, the control dimension is separated from the processing dimension. Data flow diagrams are created in much the same way as in traditional Structured Analysis, resulting in a leveled set of Pspec (for process specification) diagrams. A parallel set of control flow diagrams CFDs is created. The same transforms appear in both the DFDs and the CFDs. The difference is that in the DFDs, data processing is shown, while in CFDs, control considerations are given. Also in the CFDs, the new symbol, the "CSPEC Bar" is used to indicate that some off-page supplemental information is given. This may be in the form of a finite state machine (as in the Transformation Schema), or it may be expressed as a process activation table, which is basically a horizontal decision table.

The major contribution of Real-Time Structured Analysis is its emphasis on implementation architectural considerations. These are expressed in the Architecture Model, which can be viewed as an envelope to the processing and control hierarchies. The Architecture Model forces the consideration of the user interface, input and output processing, and maintenance processing. These are not considered often until after what we usually think of as requirements specification activities. The net effect, however, is that these considerations become sources of "new requirements." By forcing attention to the architecture model, Real-Time Structured Analysis helps the developer uncover requirements which might otherwise go unrecognized.

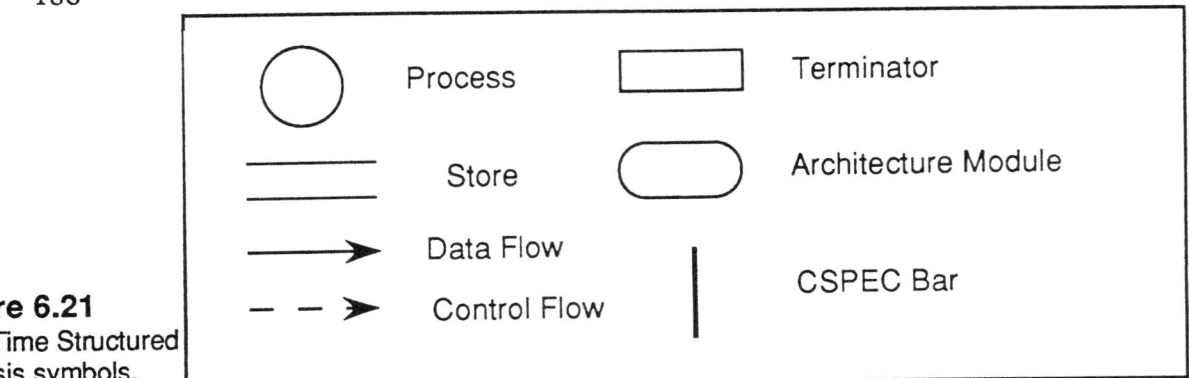

Figure 6.21
Real-Time Structured
Analysis symbols.

6.6.3 Extended Systems Modeling Language

The Extended Systems Modeling Language (ESML) is the product of an industrial committee composed of avionics companies, CASE vendors, and other interested parties [BRU88]. The original intent of the ESML working group was to merge the ideas found in the Transformation Schema and in Real-Time Structured Analysis into a cohesive, standard notation for real-time systems. Figures 6.22 and 6.23 present the ESML objects and connections.

The main contribution of ESML is its emphasis on "prompts." ESML prompts emanate from control transforms, and are used to describe the interaction of flow transforms. There are seven ESML prompts: Trigger, Enable, Disable, Activate, Suspend, Resume, and Pause. Two of these are composed of others: Activate is an Enable followed by a Disable, and Pause is a Suspend followed by a Resume. Taken together, the ESML prompts are a useful way to describe the way control transforms interact with processing transforms. In our experience, these prompts are also good interpretations for the messages in an object-oriented approach described in Chapter 8. Because of the important of ESML prompts, we will clarify the meanings of some of them with Petri nets.

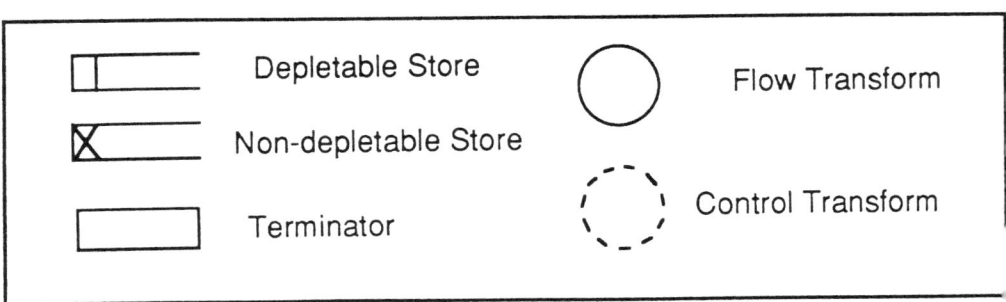

Figure 6.22
ESML objects.

6.6.3.1 Trigger

The Trigger prompt causes the recipient transform to execute immediately. Let S be the transform to be triggered. We interpret S as a Petri net transition (also labeled S) and consider its input places. Suppose there are just two input places, as shown in Figure 6.24, and that one of these is already marked. The only thing that prevents S from firing is that the other input place is not marked. Since this place can be marked only by firing the trigger transition T, we see how firing T triggers S.

6.6.3.2 Enable

The Enable prompt is slightly different from the Trigger prompt. When a transform is enabled, it may execute, but it won't necessarily execute (its other

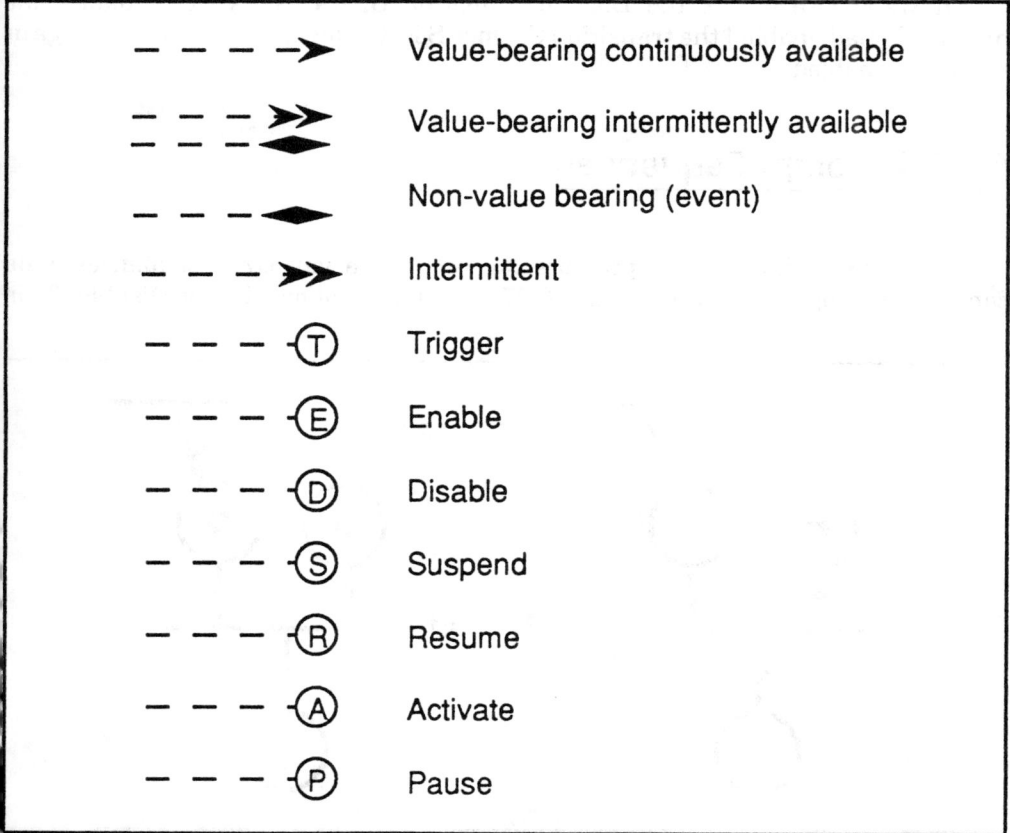

Figure 6.23
ESML connections.

inputs may not yet be available). Referring to Figure 6.25, we see that the transform (and Petri net transition) S has two input places, and neither is marked. When the Enable transition E is fired, a token is placed in one of the input places of S. In this way, S is (partially) enabled to fire. Notice that the Petri net definition of "enable" and the ESML Enable prompt are subtly different. Once a transform is enabled, it remains enabled until something else disables it. We show this in the Petri net by having the enabling place be both an input to and an output of the transform (transition) S.

6.6.3.3 Disable

The Disable prompt is closely associated with the Enable prompt. When a transform is enabled, it can execute (fire) continuously (or discretely) until it is disabled. In Figure 6.26, the Disable transition D shares an input place with the transition S. This is an instance of the pattern of Petri net conflict we discussed in Section 6.5.

If we choose to fire the Disable transition D, we remove the token that previously had enabled the transition S. Once S is disabled, it can never fire again until it is enabled.

6.6.3.4 Prompt Sequences

In an executing system, prompts can occur in a variety of sequences. One common pairing is shown in Figure 6.27: an Enable followed by a Disable. This

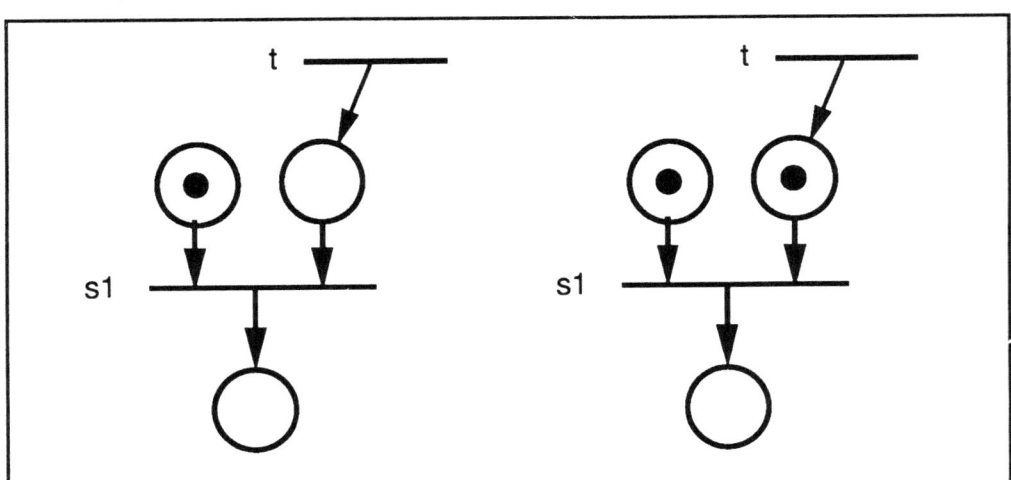

Figure 6.24
Petri net for the ESML Trigger prompt.

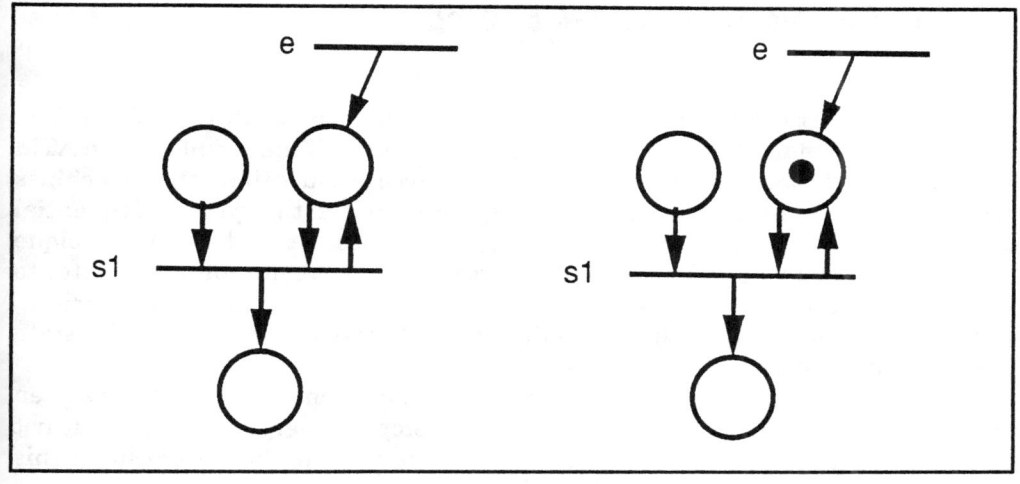

Figure 6.25
Petri net for the
ESML Enable
prompt.

sequence is also known as the ESML Activate prompt. When we activate a transform, it is enabled, it executes for a while, and then it becomes disabled.

The Suspend and Resume prompts are analogous to Disable and Enable. The main difference is that when a transform resumes after being suspended, we picture it as starting where it left off; that is, any intermediate results that had been created before suspension are still available at resumption. An ESML Pause is simply the Suspend prompt followed by a Resume prompt.

Of the three real-time extensions to Structured Analysis, ESML has the most explicitly defined syntax of prompts and permitted flows. Figure 6.28 shows the end result of all possible pairs of ESML prompts [RIT91]. The complete syntax of permitted ESML flows is given in Figures 6.29 through 6.32.

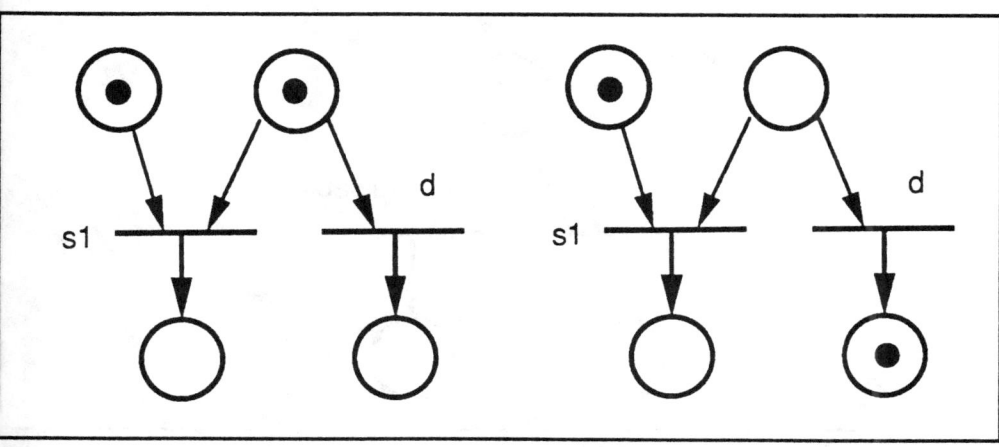

Figure 6.26
Petri net for the
ESML Disable
prompt.

6.7 The Simple Simon ATM Example

We included the Simple Simon ATM example to help illustrate the issues raised in the control domain. Here we present a full description of the Simple Simon ATM system as a finite state machine. We made this choice because finite state machines are the most appropriate model, since the application is in the dynamic sequential quadrant of our control taxonomy. Earlier, we discussed two distinct technique choices: using states to reflect what the customer sees (screens), or using states to reflect what the system does (stages of processing). To provide a direct comparison, Figure 6.33 describes the full Simple Simon ATM system as a single finite state machine with states that are screens.

We did not include the steps that cause transitions from state to state (or screen to screen). Part of the reason for this is that these steps are very complex, and do not display well in a figure. The better reason is that, after having done the example this way, we decided that the "internal view" is more expressive.

In the "internal view," we view the Simple Simon ATM system in terms of processing stages. We could choose three very simple stages: opening, performing and closing an ATM session. Instead, we elaborate slightly on these, with the result shown in Figure 6.34. Here we show some of the mainline events that cause state transitions. Notice that the Await Transaction Selection state in Figure 6.34 corresponds exactly with the screen 5 state in Figure 6.33.

One advantage of choosing states as processing stages is that we can decompose a state into more specific stages of processing, very much like functional decomposition. Think about the PIN entry portion of an ATM session. The customer has three tries to correctly enter his or her PIN. We could decompose this into a more specific finite state machine — in fact, we did in the discussion on FSM technique (see

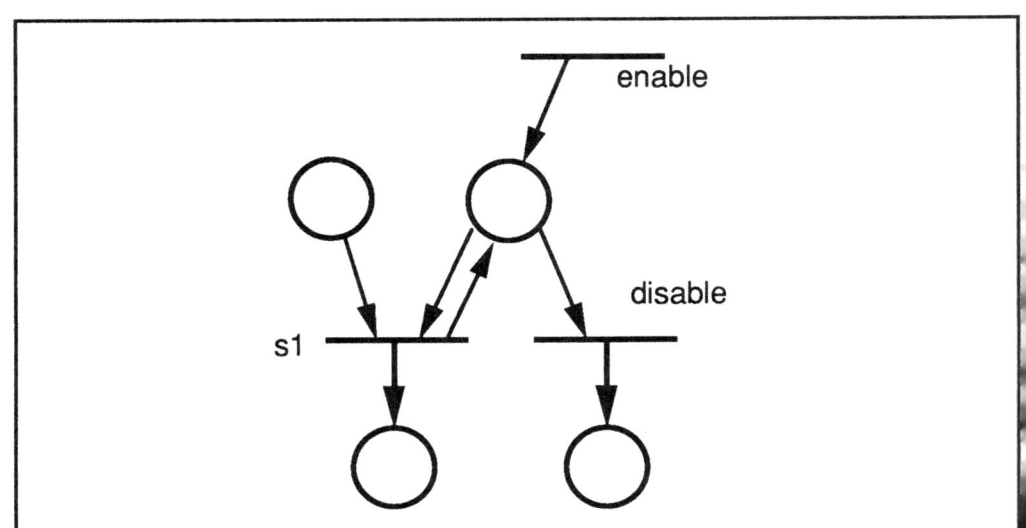

Figure 6.27
Petri net for the ESML Enable and Disable prompts.

Next Prompt					
Current Prompt	Trigger	Enable	Disable	Suspend	Resume
Trigger	Trigger	illegal	Disable	Suspend	ambiguous
Enable	illegal	Enable	Disable	Suspend	Resume
Disable	Trigger	Enable	Disable	ambiguous	Resume
Suspend	illegal	ambiguous	Disable	Suspend	Resume
Resume	ambiguous	ambiguous	Disable	Suspend	Resume

Figure 6.28
Effect of sequence pairs on ESML prompts.

Section 6.4.2 and Figure 6.12). Here we further decompose the PIN entry stage to reflect the actual digits in a PIN. What happens (or should happen) if the customer enters only part of a PIN? In a real ATM system, there is an elaborate structure of timers for such cases. The timers allow the system to maintain control of the session when confronted by a wide variety of user behaviors.

This decomposition suggests that there might be some notion of balancing, similar to that for data flow diagram decomposition. Look closely at the Await PIN state in Figure 6.34. There are two transitions back to the Idle state; one happens when a bad ID card is inserted, and the other occurs for two reasons: either the PIN failed or the Cancel key was pressed. There is one other transition, to the Await Transaction Selection state, which occurs when the PIN ok message is received. Now, if you look closely at Figure 6.12, the Idle and Select Transaction states are shown (note a name change which would be detected by a good tool), and the ID card received and PIN ok and Wrong PIN messages. These last two messages occur three times, so balancing is more complex. What we really have is a case of dynamic balancing, where we had static balancing in data flow diagram decomposition. Even though there are three static occurrences of the PIN ok message, at execution time only one can occur; similarly for the Wrong PIN message. The second decomposition is also balanced. The Verify PIN state in Figure 6.35 has two messages on its transitions: PIN ok and Wrong PIN. In the earlier states, the machine attempts to collect each of the four digits. If a time-out occurs, the machine allows a second chance. (How many time-outs are allowed? Our source tells us they quit after three.) If the Cancel key is pressed, digit acquisition terminates. Note that the Cancel balances with the uppermost level, but is not shown in the intermediate level.

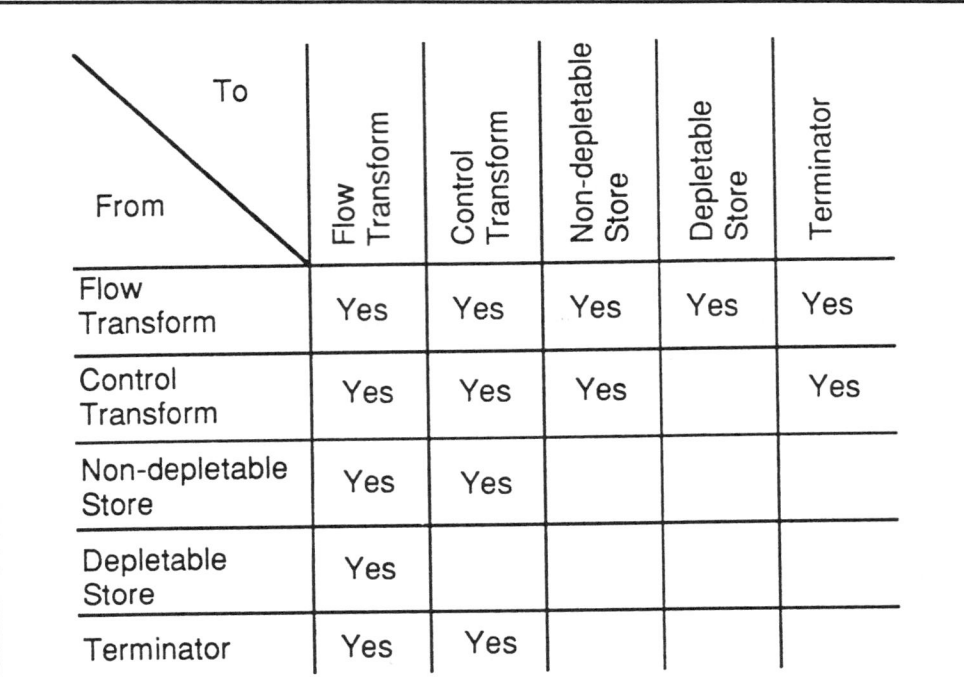

From \ To	Flow Transform	Control Transform	Non-depletable Store	Depletable Store	Terminator
Flow Transform	Yes	Yes	Yes	Yes	Yes
Control Transform	Yes	Yes	Yes		Yes
Non-depletable Store	Yes	Yes			
Depletable Store	Yes				
Terminator	Yes	Yes			

Figure 6.29
Permitted continuously available flows.

From \ To	Flow Transform	Control Transform	Non-depletable Store	Depletable Store	Terminator
Flow Transform	Yes		Yes	Yes	Yes
Control Transform	Yes		Yes		Yes
Non-depletable Store					
Depletable Store	Yes	Yes			
Terminator	Yes				

Figure 6.30
Permitted intermittently available flows.

From \ To	Flow Transform	Control Transform	Non-depletable Store	Depletable Store	Terminator
Flow Transform	Yes	Yes		Yes	Yes
Control Transform	Yes	Yes			Yes
Non-depletable Store					
Depletable Store					
Terminator	Yes	Yes			

Figure 6.31
Permitted signals.

From \ To	Flow Transform	Control Transform	Non-depletable Store	Depletable Store	Terminator
Flow Transform					
Control Transform	Yes	Yes			
Non-depletable Store					
Depletable Store					
Terminator					

Figure 6.32
Permitted prompts.

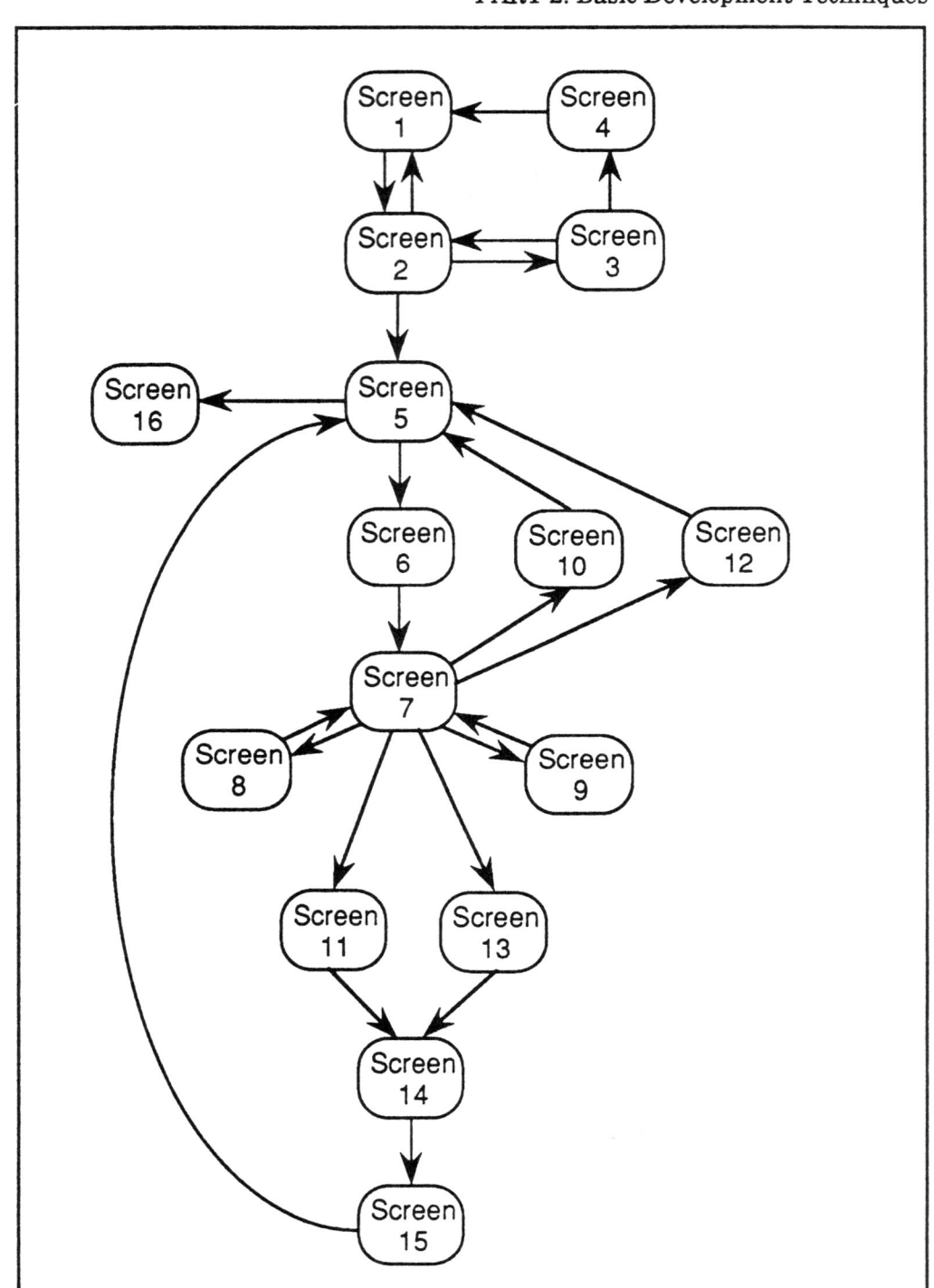

Figure 6.33
ATM with states
as screens.

6.8 Resource List

For a discussion of the control-oriented techniques, see [BOE85], [BRU88], [HAT84], [MCM84], and [WAR86b]. For more on decision tables, see [COD82]. For discussions on Petri nets, see [JOR87], [JOR89], [PET81], and [RIT91]. For general information on real-time systems development, see [GLA83] and [GOM86].

6.9 References

[BOE85] Structured Methods Standard, Boeing Commercial Aircraft Co., Document Number D6-53036, Seattle, 1985.

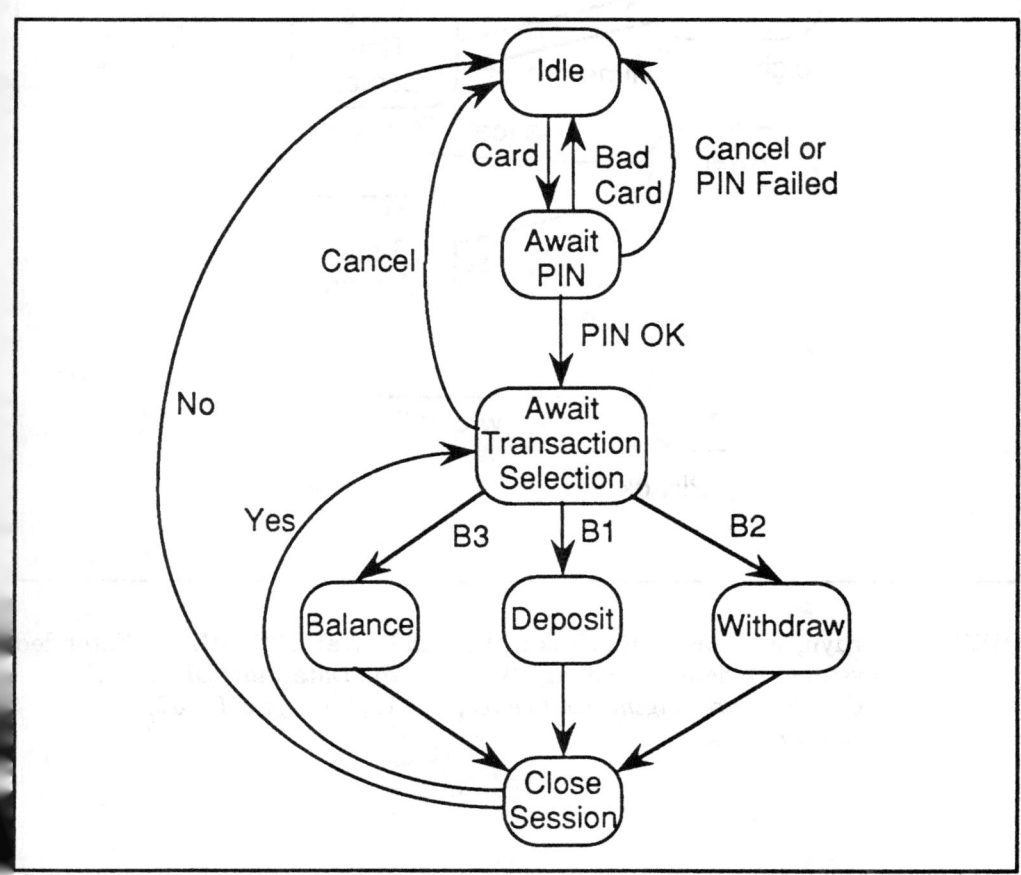

Figure 6.34
ATM with states as processing stages.

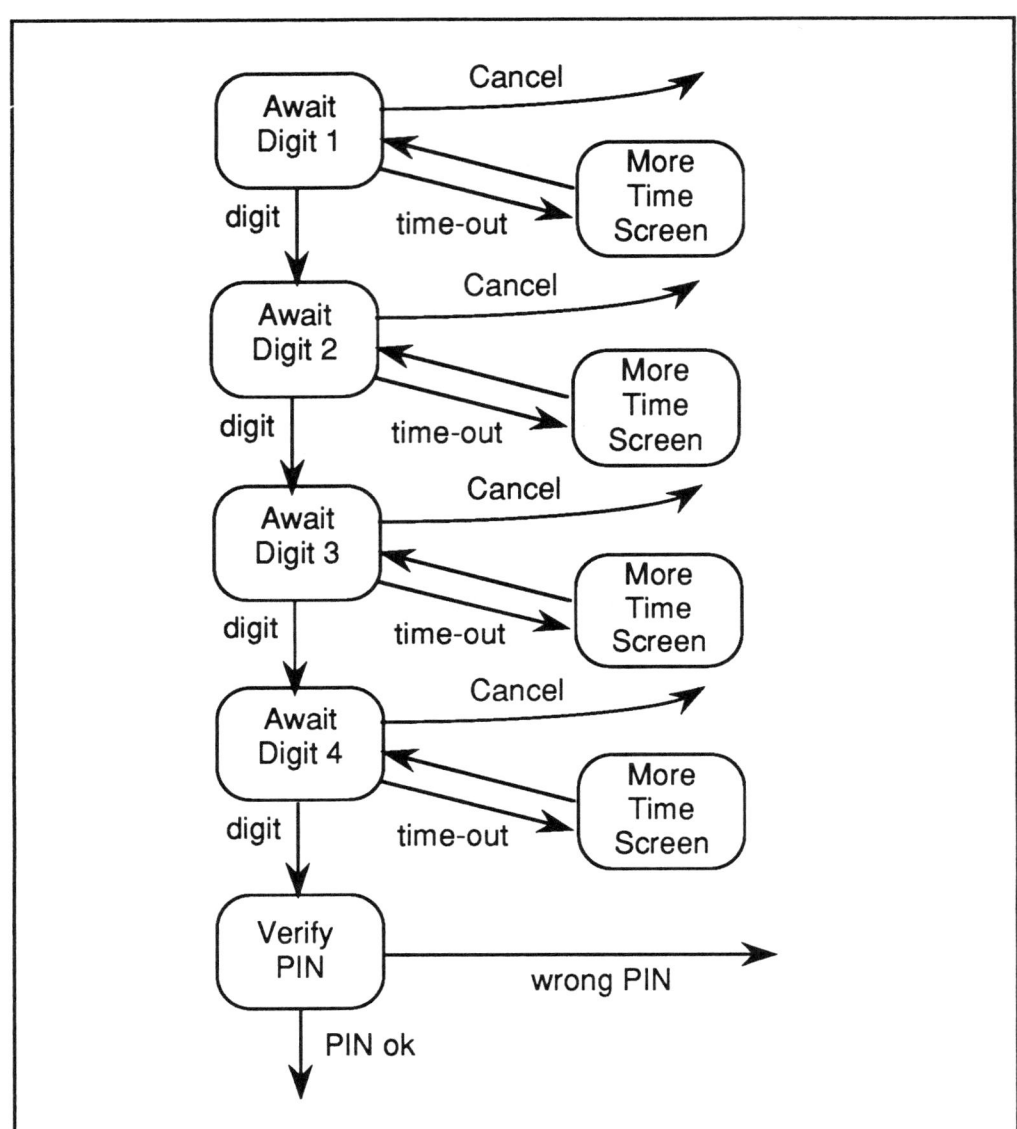

Figure 6.35
Expansion of the
Await PIN Entry
state.

[BRU88]   Bruyn, W., Jensen, R., Keskar, D., and P, Ward, "ESML: An Extended
Systems Modeling Language Based on the Data Flow Diagram,"
ACM Software Engineering Notes, vol. 13, no. 1., pp. 58-67,
January 1988.

[COD82]   *CODASYL Decision Table Task Group,* "A Modern Appraisal of Decision
           Tables," Association for Computing Machinery, 1982.
[GAN79]   Gane, C., and T. Sarson, *Structured Systems Analysis: Tools and
           Techniques*, Prentice-Hall, 1979.
[GLA83]   Glass, R. L., *Real-Time Software*, Prentice-Hall, 1983.
[GOM84]   Gomaa, H., "A Software Design Method for Real-Time Systems," *CACM*,
           vol. 27, no. 9, September 1984, pp. 938-949.
[GOM86]   Gomaa, H., "Software Development of Real-Time Systems," *CACM*, vol.
           29, no. 7, July 1986, pp. 657-668.
[HAR90]   Harel, D., et al, "Statemate: A Working Environment for the
           Development of Complex Reactive Systems," *IEEE Trans. on Soft. Eng.*,
           vol. 15, no. 4, April, 1990, pp. 403-414.
[HAT84]   Hatley, D., "The Use of Structured Methods in the Development of Large
           Software-Based Avionics Systems," *AIAA/IEEE 6th Digital Avionics
           Conference*, Baltimore, 1984.
[HAT87]   Hatley, D. J. and I. A. Pirbhai, *Strategies for Real-Time System
           Specification*, Dorset House, 1987
[JOR87]   Jorgensen, P. C., "Petri F.Y.I.—An Intelligent, User-Extensible System
           Specification Tool," *Proceedings of the Structured Methods Conference
           XII*, Chicago, August 1987.
[JOR89]   Jorgensen, P. C. and W. Smith, "Using Petri Net Theory to Analyze
           Software Safety Case Studies," *Proceedings of the Fourth Annual
           Computer Assurance Conference* (COMPASS'89), Gaithersburg,
           June 1989.
[MCC85]   McCabe, T. J., "Structured Real-Time Analysis and Design," *COMPSAC
           85*, IEEE, October 1985, pp. 40-51.
[MCM84]   McMenamin, S., and J. Palmer, *Essential Systems Analysis*, Yourdon
           Press, 1984.
[PET81]   Peterson, J. L., *Petri Net Theory and the Modeling of Systems*, Prentice-
           Hall, 1981.
[REI87]   Reilly, E., and J. Brackett, "An Experimental System for Executing
           Real-Time Structured Analysis Models," *Proceedings of the 12th
           Structured Methods Conference*, Chicago, August 1987.
[RIT91]   Ritzema, E. L., "Petri Net Resolution of ESML Prompts," Master's thesis,
           Grand Valley State University, 1991.
[WAR86a]   Ward, P., "The Transformation Schema: An Extension of the Dataflow
           Diagram to Represent Control and Timing," *IEEE Trans. on Soft. Eng.*,
           February 1986, pp. 198-210.
[WAR86b]   Ward, P., and S. Mellor, *Structured Development of Real-Time Systems*,
           Volumes 1-3, Yourdon Press, 1986.
[YOU78]   Yourdon, E. and L. Constantine, *Structured Design*, Yourdon Press,
           1978.

PART 3

Advanced Development Techniques

Chapter 7
Information-Oriented Techniques

The information-oriented techniques, often referred to generically as information-engineering (IE) methods, approach software development from a very different perspective than the other techniques described in this book. IE methods take a strong business orientation, include strategic business planning (SBP) as a critical first step in the process of developing software, and focus on defining an overall enterprise model (including a data or information architecture) prior to beginning software development.

IE methods often are marketed by big consulting firms, and are sold hand in hand with SBP services for the organization as well as the information system (IS) function. Proponents of IE methods contend that IS can begin to build quality software only after helping an organization define its critical goals and success factors, functional organization, and data architecture.

Like other techniques, IE methods use decomposition from the higher levels of a business, the enterprise level, through discrete business areas (some might call these application domains), into software products developed and designed to solve specific business problems.

Interestingly, the enterprise-level data-oriented techniques described in Chapter 5 share many characteristics with the techniques described in this chapter. Both the enterprise-level data-oriented and the information-oriented techniques focus on the definition of data, concentrate on the shared use of data across an organization, target relational database management systems (RDBMS), and include a high-level assessment in the planning stage of software development. However, while the enterprise-level data-oriented techniques view software functions as transactions against a database (i.e., CRUD), the information-oriented techniques provide complete and parallel support for functional views in analysis and design. In fact, the information-oriented techniques include a specific notation, the action diagram, to represent process and procedural specifications.

IE methods are based on data modeling, RDBMS design, strategic planning, and decomposition techniques, but also include new notations for software development. Another influence on the creation of IE methods was the work of John Zachman [ZAC87]. Zachman defined a framework for information systems architectures which strongly parallels the IE methods in their focus and approach. Also interesting is the fact that both Zachman and James Martin worked for IBM at one time.

IE methods also rely on the use of integrated CASE (ICASE) tools that support the generation of systems from design specifications.

7.1 Introduction

"Information Engineering is an interlocking set of formal techniques in which [models] are built up in a comprehensive knowledge base and are used to create and maintain information systems."
    J. Martin [MAR90].

In this chapter, we will evaluate a set of techniques that attempts to capture the best of the function- and data-oriented methods. These newer techniques are known collectively as the information-oriented techniques, and they offer comprehensive coverage of software development with an emphasis on the planning phase. They also begin at the highest level of detail in an organization and work progressively down to a specific software application's code.

While there are many variations on the original theme of IE, the differences tend to be more cosmetic than substantial, and the underlying philosophy of all these methods is the same. In this chapter, we will evaluate all of the major variations of IE, and, using the Library example, describe in depth the results of applying IE.

7.1.1 Definitions

It is useful to define the following terms when discussing information engineering. Quoted definitions are from *Information Engineering: Book II, Planning and Analysis* by James Martin [MAR90].

Information is "any formal, structured data that is required to support a business and can be stored in or retrieved from a computer." Information is modeled at various levels in IE, starting at the organization or enterprise level and ending at the application or implementation level.

Enterprise model is "a description of the [data and activities] that define an enterprise and the interrelationships." The enterprise model is the highest-level view of the data used and activities performed by the enterprise and also includes critical success factors, goals and objectives, functional organization and high-level business areas.

Data model is "a logical map of data which represents the inherent properties of the data independently of software, hardware, or machine performance considerations."

Function model is "a representation of one or more activities that a system performs."

Business area is an application domain which includes a cohesive group of business functions and data.

7.1.2 History

Information engineering evolved from the "data analysis" work of Ian Palmer and others in England in the early 1970s [WIL89]. Palmer, Ian Macdonald, and Clive Finkelstein continued development of IE in the late 1970s and early 1980s. In 1981, Finkelstein and James Martin produced a report on IE for the Savant Institute which became the basis for all IE methods [MAR81]. Martin later wrote a book on IE which was originally published in 1983 [MAR90].

Another book that serves as a detailed description of automated support for IE was written by Martin and Carma McClure in 1985 [MAR85b]. This book led to the development of the Information Engineering Workbench (IEW) from Knowledgeware, which was developed with help from Martin and Arthur Young. This was followed by the development within Texas Instruments of the Information Engineering Facility (IEF). Other IE-based CASE tools came onto the market in the late 1980s, and with the advent of automated support for IE came wider acceptance of the information-oriented techniques.

IE, perhaps more than other development techniques, is dependent on the use of automated tools throughout the development life cycle. IE was created with the assumption of automated tools supporting the method, the incorporation of an encyclopedia to capture the development information, and the generation of systems from a design specification, the action diagram [MAR85a]. IE has as its goals the creation and maintenance of software via code generation and the sharing of information systems across an organization.

Zachman also proposed viewing the process of developing software along similar lines but espoused an architectural view of development. Zachman compared the development of software with the creation of a building and proposed a framework for representing the different levels of detail. The Zachman approach, when combined with other techniques, begins to look a lot like the IE methods described in this chapter.

7.2 Philosophy

The most distinguishing feature about IE when contrasted with the other techniques is its comprehensive approach to software development. With IE, before any application development occurs, a strategic business plan is created for the organization, the organization is partitioned into business areas, and data models and process models are developed for each business area.

IE seeks to align the direction of IS with the direction of the organization or business, since this ensures that IS resources, which are often significant, remain focused on serving the specific needs of the organization.

The first phase of IE, Information Strategy Planning (ISP), is devoted to determining the goals and objectives of the organization, critical success factors, organization and major functions, and information needs. Consideration of the organization first enables IS to define its specific role and priorities.

IE is also the first automation-dependent approach. Earlier techniques, including function- and data-oriented methods, were originally carried out using pencil and paper. Because IE attempts to maintain and coordinate an organization-wide collection of data on information systems, and because of the reliance within IE on the generation of code from specifications, it requires automated support.

In a previous chapter, enterprise-level data-oriented techniques were described, and IE is similar to these approaches in that it also attempts to build a common data model upon which applications can operate. Under IE, each functional area of the organization has a data model supporting its applications, and these models are synthesized from an enterprise-level model of the data in the organization. As we have already discussed, the enterprise-level data-oriented techniques view functionality as transactions against the database, while the IE methods view functions in parallel with data structures and include steps to identify the dependencies between the data and the functions.

In much the same way that function-oriented techniques center development around the data flow diagram (DFD), IE bases development on the entity-relationship diagram (ERD). While some function-oriented techniques have evolved to include the expanded use of data models, IE has always had the data model as its focus [GAN90].

IE is a sound approach to software development, but there are some IE proponents who would like you to believe that it is much more. Some advocates believe that IE is a framework for techniques, rather than a technique itself, and that this framework enables the latest development techniques to be plugged into IE. In the late 1980s, the emergence of Rapid Application Development (RAD) techniques caused IE to include these methods. With the growing appeal of object-oriented techniques, there appears to be a nervous movement among these advocates to claim that "ours is object-oriented, too." For more on this issue, see Chapter 8.

7.3 Characteristics

Just as there are variations in the way the English language is spoken, there are several versions of IE. However, because there are only a few originators of the approach, the versions have a high degree of similarity. These variations have evolved over time as the techniques have been used.

With its focus on the enterprise, IE is the only technique that attempts to define an information architecture for the organization prior to developing systems. The fact that the first step in IE is the creation of a strategic plan further separates it from other development techniques. As already discussed, IE methods attempt to link the business functions and organization to the IS organization and its goals and objectives.

IE methods introduced new terminology and notations that also are unique as compared with those of other techniques. Action diagrams, one of the critical notations within IE, were created to address problems with existing architectural notations (structure charts, etc.) and PDL. In other techniques, different notations are required to specify the overall flow of control for a program or module and the lower-level logic of the program or module. Within IE, action diagrams support both capabilities. Action diagrams include procedural block structures and a standard PDL-like set of commands which include references to data structures and can be nested in a hierarchy. Action diagrams also translate easily into many third- and fourth-generation programming languages [MAR85a] and are used in CASE tools to generate functional systems.

7.3.1 Comparison of Methods

Arthur Young/Ernst & Young

In the mid-1980s, the Arthur Young Information Technology Group developed a version of IE through an association with James Martin and Knowledgeware [ART87]. Arthur Young has since merged with Ernst & Whinney to form Ernst & Young, which recently introduced its incarnation of the IE method called Navigator. The Navigator product is both paper- and CD-ROM-based and is supported by automated tools — most notably those sold by Knowledgeware. Navigator is a four-stage version nearly identical to the James Martin IE method.

Information Engineering Systems Corporation

Clive Finkelstein, one of the developers of IE, founded this organization (IESC) in the 1980s, and its IE version, perhaps more than any other, stresses data over process. Once the initial enterprise planning has been completed, work focuses on the strategic and tactical modeling of data. This is followed by process modeling, and then the integration of data and process modeling into a system design. Like Ernst & Young, IESC provides automated support for its method with USER:Expert Systems [FIN89].

James Martin

This is a four-stage approach that is one of the earliest versions of IE. It is described in a three-volume series by James Martin and is supported by the Knowledgeware tools, IEW and ADW [MAR90].

James Martin & Co. / Texas Instruments

This version of IE is used in partnership with the Information Engineering Facility, a CASE tool from Texas Instruments (TI). Management at TI saw the need for a better software development approach and contracted for the services of James Martin, who convinced them that IE was the approach they were seeking. TI subsequently developed a product set around an expanded version of James Martin Information Engineering (see above) [TEX90].

Pacific Information Management (PIM)

PIM has developed its own version which incorporates the concepts of IDEF modeling (see Chapter 5) with the IE method. IE/IMPACT is the implementation of the IE method sold by PIM and includes an Information Resource Management (IRM) perspective coupled with the traditional IE method. IE/IMPACT includes the four-stage IE method described by Martin with an IRM prior to ISP and the use of IDEF notations in analysis and design.

7.3.2 Notation

IE methods include a variety of notations that are related and used to specify computer systems. Figure 7.1 identifies common IE diagrams and their relationships. Two symbols are used consistently throughout IE notations (see Figure 7.2) the rounded rectangle, which represents an *activity*, such as a function, process, procedure, or program module; and the squared rectangle, which is used to represent *data*, including entity types, records, or data sets. The squared rectangle can also be used to depict organizational units in an organization chart. The table in Figure 7.3 compares notation usage of popular IE methods. An activity is defined as the processing performed on data.

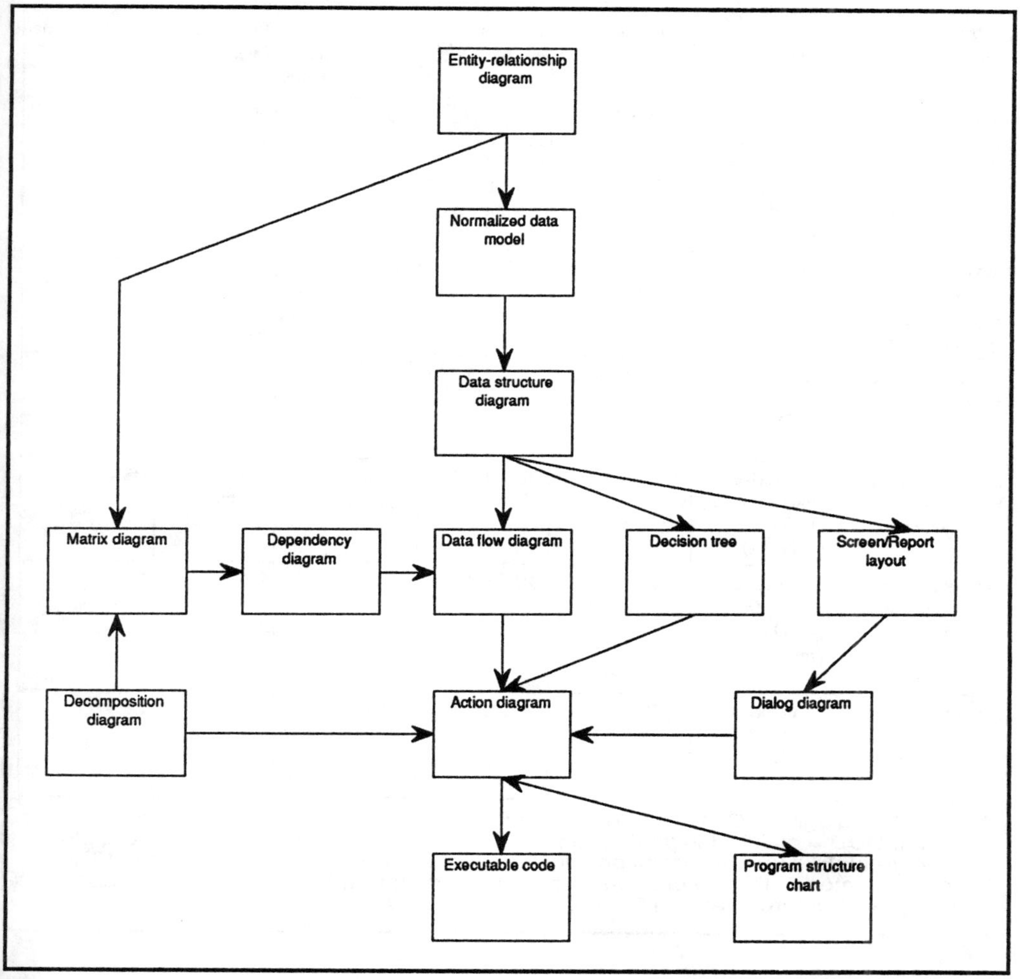

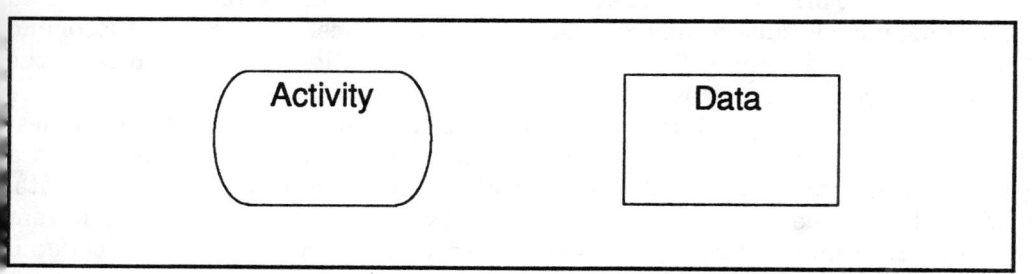

Figure 7.1
IE diagrams and
their relationships.

Figure 7.2
IE symbols for
activities and data.

Notation Technique	Planning Notations	Data Model	Process Model	Procedure Architecture	Procedure Logic	Database/File Design
IEM from James Martin and Company	Data architecture (ERD) and Enterprise model (DCD and matrices)	ERD and ESD	DCD, AD, PDD, STD and DFD - current systems only	AD	PDD, AD and DDD	DSD
IEM from Information Engineering Systems Corp.	Enterprise model (DCD, ERD and matrices)	ERD	DCD and PSpecs	CRUD		DSD
Navigator System Series from Ernst and Young	Enterprise model (DCD, ERD and matrices)	ERD and DSD	DCD, PDD and DFD	AD	AD	DSD
IE/Impact from Pacific Information Management	Enterprise models (ERD, DCD & matrices)	ERD and LDM	DCD, IDEF0, DFD and PDD	SC and AD	AD and Module specs	DSD
ForeSight from Computer and Engineering Consultants/ Knowledgeware	Enterprise model (ERD, DCD and matrices)	ERD	DCD and AD	AD	AD	DSD
Aim from Axiom	Enterprise model (ERD, DCD and matrices)	ERD	DCD and AD	AD	AD	DSD

AD = action diagram, CRUD = create, read, update and delete, DCD = decomposition diagram, DDD = dialog design diagram, DFD = data flow diagram, DSD = data structure diagram, ERD = entity-relationship diagram, ESD = entity-state diagram, LDM = logical data model, PDD = process dependency diagram, PSpecs = process specifications, SC = structure chart, STD = state-transition diagram.

Figure 7.3
Comparison of IE notations.

Data Modeling Notation

The three primary notations used in information-oriented techniques for data modeling include subject area diagrams, entity-relationship diagrams (ERD), and data structure diagrams. The IE data modeling notations are derived from the techniques and representations described in Chapter 5.

Subject area diagrams represent data in its most general form and at its highest level of detail, ERDs show more detailed entity types and relationships, and data structure diagrams represent the physical or implementation view of the data. While these three separate diagrams are used within IE, they represent different views of the same constructs, data structures, at various stages and levels of detail in the IE method.

Data Types

There are three terms used to define data in IE, depending on the level of detail. The highest category of data is the *subject area* which is composed of *entity types,* which, in turn, are made up of *attributes.*

Entity-Relationship Diagram

The entity-relationship diagram (ERD) did not originate with information-oriented techniques, but it certainly plays a key role in them. One of the foundations of information-oriented techniques is the modeling and use of data across an enterprise, and the primary tool used is the ERD. The ERD is used to model high-level data and, as its name implies, depicts entities (the things we wish to store data about) and the relationships among them. Each entity in an ERD may or may not have a relationship with other entities. If it does, a line connects them and indicates a *cardinality* at either end. Chapter 5 includes a more detailed discussion of ERDs.

Subject Area Diagram

The subject area diagram (SAD) is used to model the highest levels of data in an enterprise. The SAD is useful for managing a large number of entities and provides the developer with a tool for classifying data above the level of an entity. An early step in information-oriented techniques is to identify subject areas and refine them into more detailed subject areas and entities. A SAD is created for each level of detail needed, and the result is a leveled set of SADs. (Developers struggling with this step have known to become so SAD.)

SAD notation includes two symbols: A *square-cornered box* represents a subject area or entity; a *connecting line* indicates a relationship between two entities.

Data Structure Diagram

The data structure diagram (DSD) is used to model the lowest levels of data in an enterprise. It is used to model data in a physical database or file system including:

Hierarchical (IMS, e.g.) database structures
Network (IDMS, e.g.) database structures
Relational (DB2, e.g.) database structures
Sequential and indexed file structures

The DSD depicts an arrangement of records and fields which are constructed from corresponding entities and attributes. It contains enough detail to automatically generate statements to define and access databases and files. In the design phase, automated tools generate code from a combination of DSDs and action diagrams.

Process Modeling Notation

There are several deliverables used in information-oriented techniques to model processes or activities at various levels of detail. In this section, we will examine five diagram types that provide distinct views of the information processing hierarchy. As with the data modeling notations described in the previous section, the process modeling notations support decomposition of detail in a hierarchy.

Activity Types

Depending on the level of detail, information-oriented techniques assign different terms to processes or activities. The most general processes in an organization are called *functions*, which are decomposed into *subfunctions*, which in turn are decomposed into simple *processes*. Processes represent the basic functional units of work performed by the organization. In the design phase, *procedures* are decomposed into *modules*, which collectively are grouped into *programs*. Figure 7.4 depicts the various activity types and their relationships.

Decomposition Diagram

The decomposition diagram (DCD) represents a simple hierarchical structure showing a set of parent-child relationships. A parent is defined by the children it is composed of. DCDs resemble the structure charts described in Chapter 4, but have two specific differences:

> In a decomposition diagram, children fully describe their parents, while in a structure chart, a parent may perform or call functions not represented among its children.
> A decomposition diagram doesn't show data or control couples passing between activities.

The decomposition diagram is used extensively in the first two stages of Information Engineering: Information Strategy Planning (ISP) and Business Area Analysis (BAA). In ISP, it is used to model subject areas, organizational units, and organizational functions. In BAA, it is used to model processes carried out within a business area. Figure 7.5 shows an example DCDs.

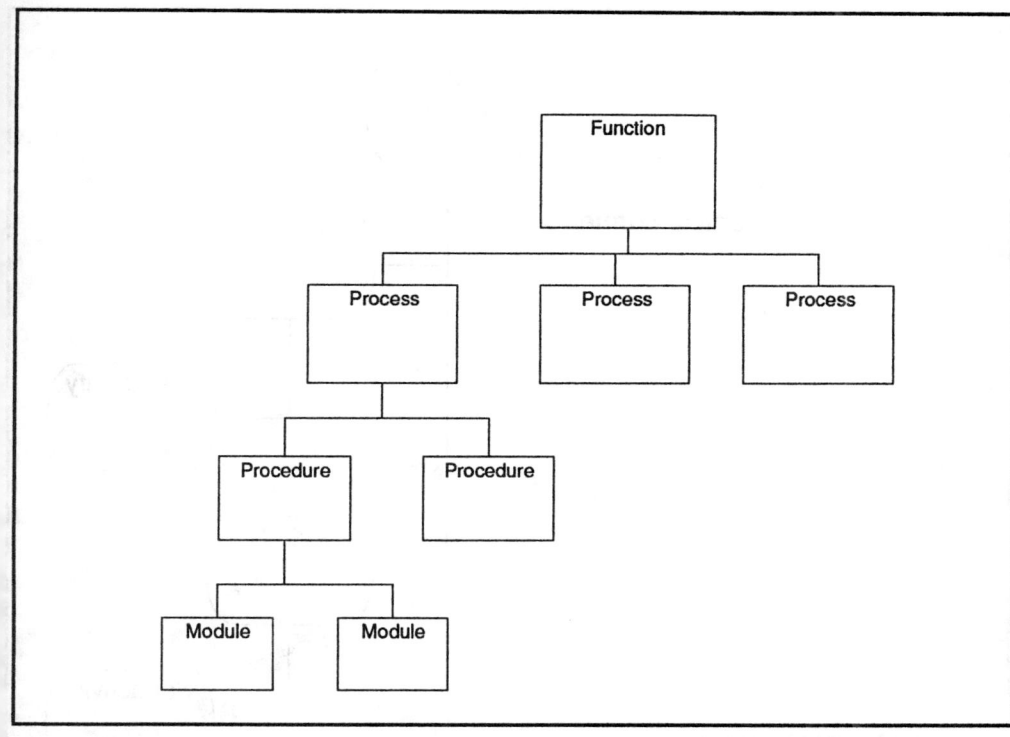

Figure 7.4
Activity types
in IE.

Dependency Diagram

The dependency diagram (Figure 7.6) is identical to the decomposition diagram with the inclusion of a logical sequence of processing. The rounded rectangles represent functions, and the arrows connecting them indicate a prescribed order of processing. The dependency diagram is also similar to data flow diagrams, but does not show data flows, data stores, or external entities.

Action Diagram

Action diagrams (ADs) are actually a combination of text and pictures — with more emphasis on the text than the picture. Although ADs can be used to represent various levels of functional detail, they usually represent the logic of a program or a module in a program. ADs are similar to mini-specifications used in function-oriented techniques, but include a syntax with a standard set of keywords and serve as a basis for code generation.

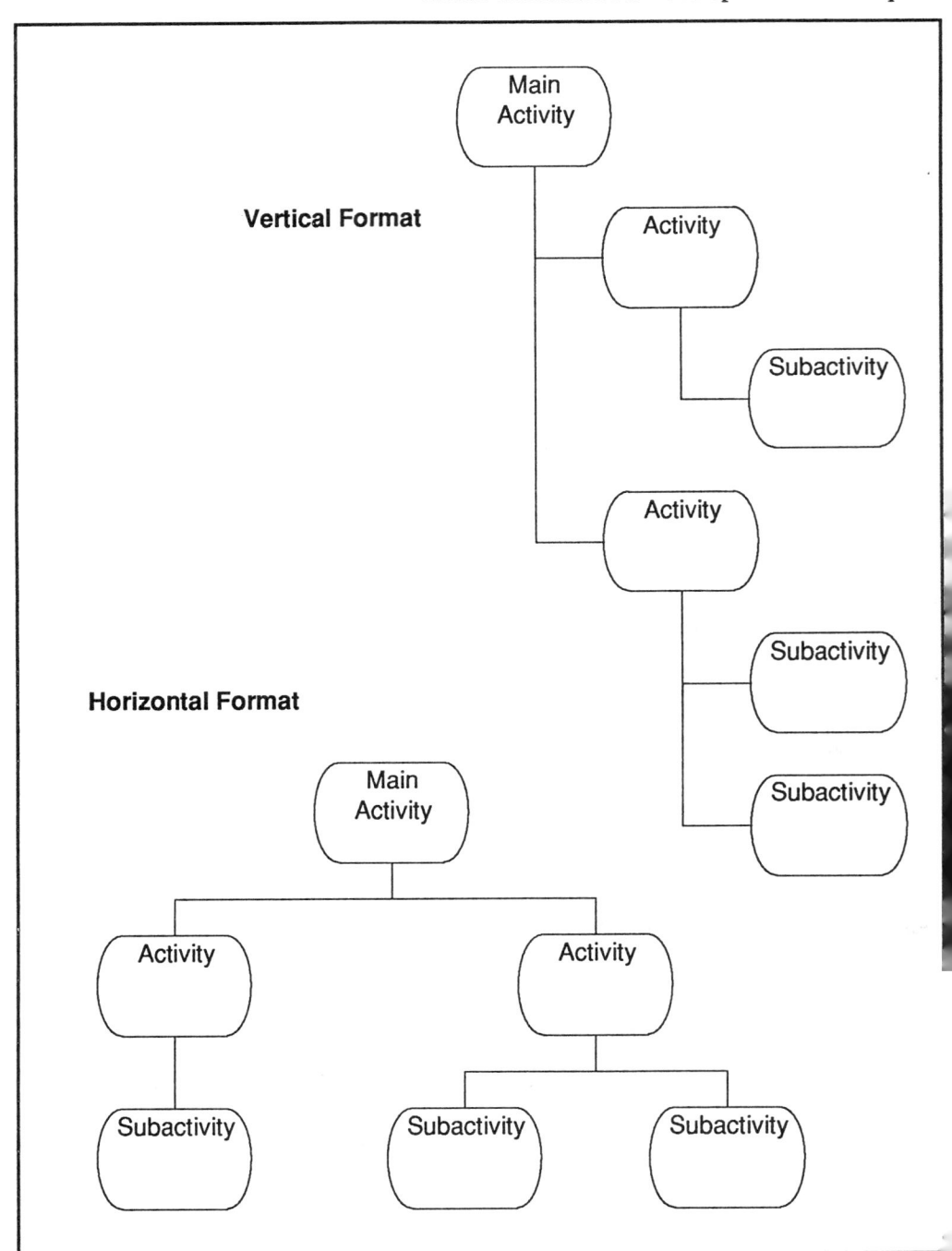

Figure 7.5
Decomposition
diagrams.

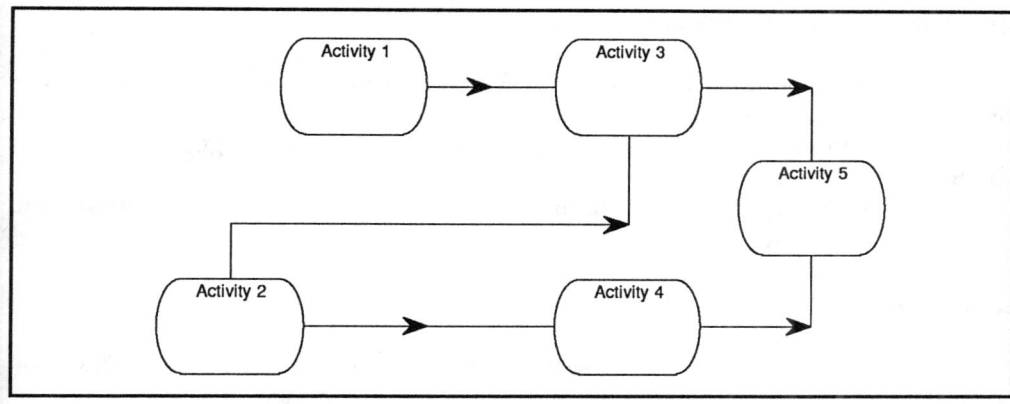

Figure 7.6
Dependency
diagram.

Depending on the context, these keywords may be generic or may be specific to a third- or fourth-generation language. The action diagram can be used in all stages of Information Engineering, but it is most often used in the analysis, design and construction phases. The action diagram can also be used to automatically generate other diagram types, including decomposition, dependency, data flow, data navigation, and dialog diagrams.

7.3.3 Technique

Several IE variations and their notation have been introduced. In this section, the technique of each variant will be presented along with how the notation is used. There is much similarity among the approaches. Figure 7.9 describes the popular IE methods and their techniques.

Arthur Young/Ernst & Young

This four-stage approach is probably the best-known version of IE and is the direct result of early research by James Martin and others into Information Engineering. In the mid-1980s, Martin worked in partnership with Arthur Young to develop a working version of IE for Arthur Young Consulting. Arthur Young published a practical guide to IE that served as the basis for the Navigator Systems Series (NSS), an IE methodology product now marketed by Arthur Young's successor, Ernst & Young. The James Martin and Ernst & Young versions of IE are very similar, but one difference is that NSS accommodates purchased software packages. The stages and major activities are shown in Figure 7.7 and include [ERN90]:

<u>Stage 1</u>: Information Strategy Planning

Assess the organization in terms of the efficacy of its applications and its use of technology.

Model the organization, including its hierarchy, data usage, and business functions performed.

Identify the organization's application, data, and technology directions and plans for implementing them.

<u>Stage 2</u>: Business Area Analysis

Model a subset of the organization, including its hierarchy, data usage, and processing performed.

Identify and prioritize additional data needs.

Issue and process Request for Proposals (RFPs).

<u>Stage 3</u>: Business System Design

Define a system in terms of its screens, reports, procedures for using, and database design.

Outline the data conversion software needed to transform data from the old system to the new system.

Describe the approach for testing the system.

<u>Stage 4</u>: Construction and Implementation

Build or generate code for the system.
Develop procedures for using the system.
Conduct system and acceptance testing.
Train users in use of the system.
Convert data to required format.
Move the system into production.

James Martin & Co. / Texas Instruments

This version of IE consists of seven stages, with the first three stages focusing on three system components: data, activities, and the interaction between the two. Models are created for each component in the three stages, and each stage begins with task planning for that stage and ends with groundwork prepared for the next stage. This version of IE is the one used to describe IE methods in general using the Library example (See Section 7.7.1 below) and is shown in Figure 7.8.

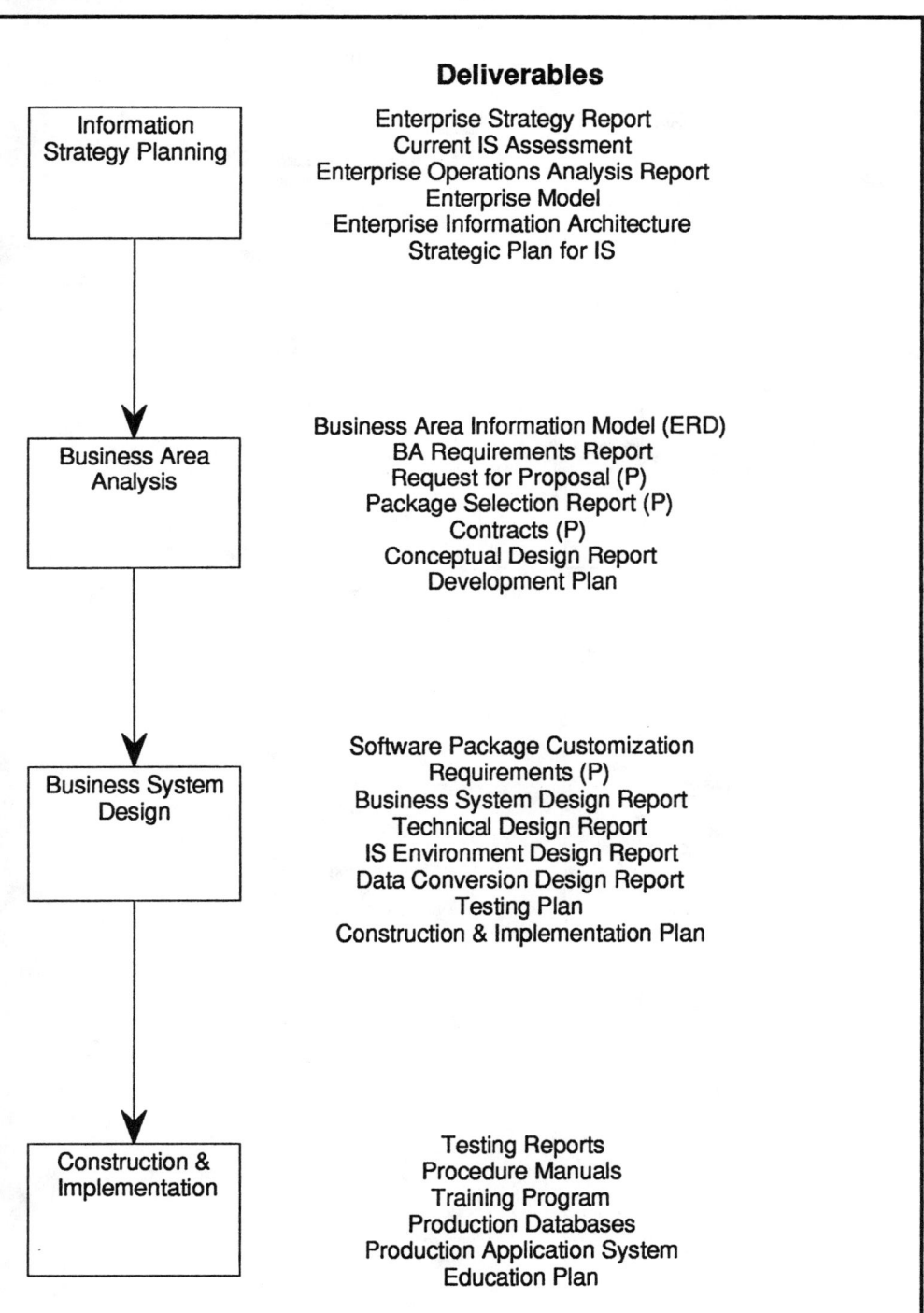

Deliverables

Information Strategy Planning

Enterprise Strategy Report
Current IS Assessment
Enterprise Operations Analysis Report
Enterprise Model
Enterprise Information Architecture
Strategic Plan for IS

Business Area Analysis

Business Area Information Model (ERD)
BA Requirements Report
Request for Proposal (P)
Package Selection Report (P)
Contracts (P)
Conceptual Design Report
Development Plan

Business System Design

Software Package Customization
Requirements (P)
Business System Design Report
Technical Design Report
IS Environment Design Report
Data Conversion Design Report
Testing Plan
Construction & Implementation Plan

Construction & Implementation

Testing Reports
Procedure Manuals
Training Program
Production Databases
Production Application System
Education Plan

Figure 7.7
Ernst & Young's
Navigator life cycle.

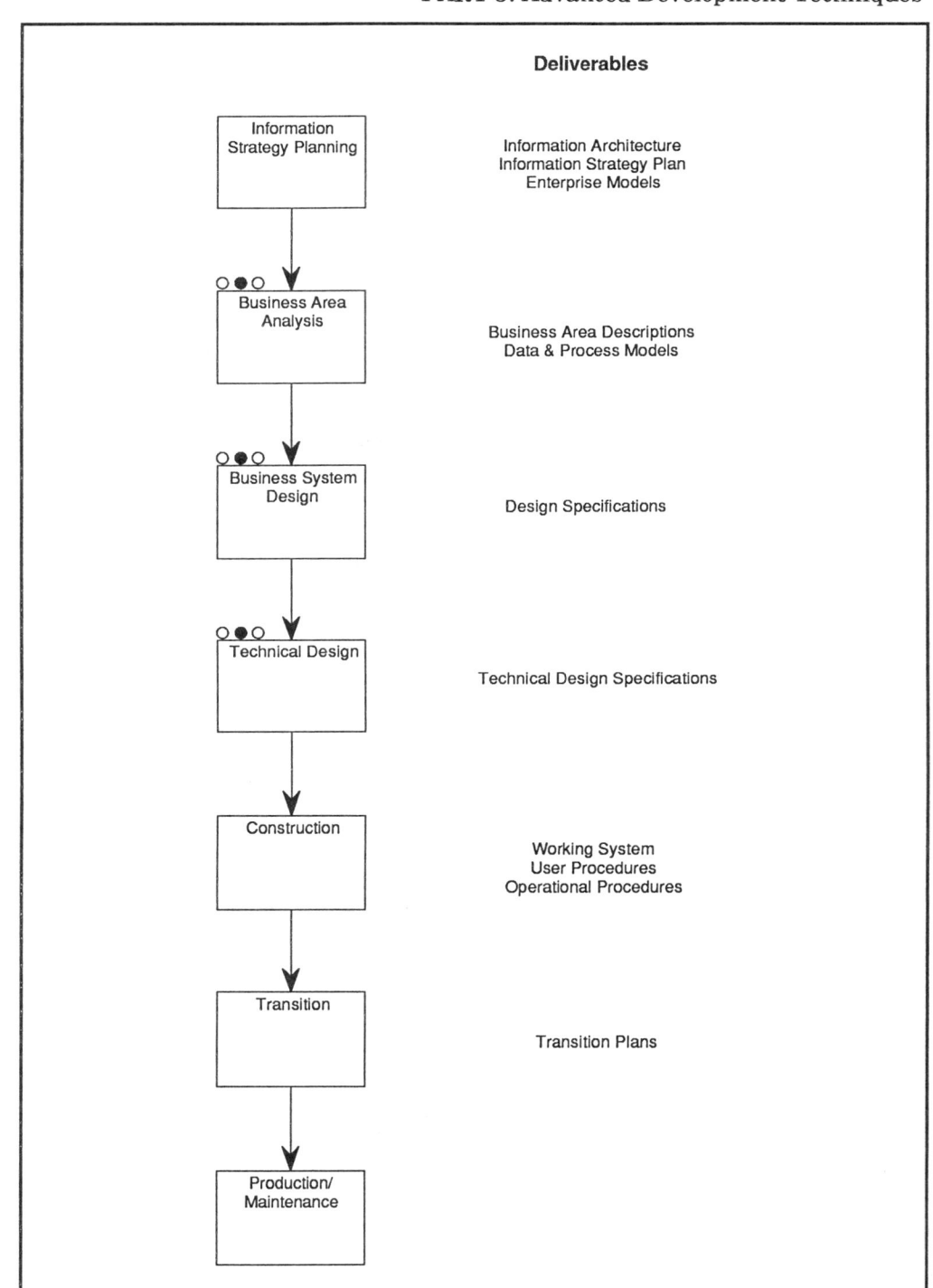

Figure 7.8
James Martin &
Company IEM
life cycle.

Stage 1: Information Strategy Planning (ISP)

This initial stage looks at everything within the scope of the ISP effort (sometimes the entire organization) and develops high-level models, or architectures. The *Information Architecture* consists of the most general definitions of the data and activities needed by the organization. The *Business System Architecture* defines how the business is partitioned into business areas. The *Technical Architecture* describes the hardware and software needed to support the planned business systems.

Stage 2: Business Area Analysis (BAA)

BAA completes the definition of the Information Architecture initially defined in ISP. BAA is further divided into two substages: outline and detail. The outline BAA stage defines the data and processes used within the business area, while the detail BAA stage provides more detail on these models and their interaction (dependencies).

Stage 3: Business System Design (BSD)

BSD defines the screens, menus, and reports for the system and the interactions between the data and procedures for the system. Prototypes are created to give users the "look and feel" of the system.

Stage 4: Technical Design (TD)

TD is concerned with how a system will operate under a particular database management system (DB2, IMS, etc.) and teleprocessing monitor (CICS, IMS/DC, etc.). TD takes the outputs from BSD and maps them to the implementation environment to ensure late binding with the details of implementation.

Stage 5: Construction

This stage builds the system specified in previous deliverables. Code is generated for the system based on the models developed in previous stages, along with any required database structures.

Stage 6: Transition

Transition involves making the new or updated system operational. This includes having the user perform an acceptance test, receive training in use of the system, etc.

Stage 7: Production

The system is run in a production status and is monitored for performance.

Information Engineering Systems Corporation

This variant is similar to the other versions of IE in that it begins the software development process at the highest level of the organization [HUG91]. IESC's method is broken into three distinct phases: strategic modeling, which is based on a strategic business plan; tactical modeling, which is based on tactical plans for a specific business area; and operations modeling, which is based on business rules and operational requirements.

Stage 1: Strategic Business Planning (SBP)

The direction of the enterprise is determined and documented in this stage. Deliverables from this stage include the corporate mission, purpose, goals, objectives, strategies, policies, and business rules.

Stage 2: Strategic Data Modeling

This stage identifies the key elements of the business plan and translates them into a data model which will serve as the basis for further work. Tactical business areas are prioritized, and an initial tactical data modeling plan is drawn up.

Stage 3: Tactical Data Modeling

In this stage, the business area and data model created in the prior stage is expanded and further defined to support management statements.

Stage 4: Operations Modeling

This stage further refines the data model defined in stages 2 and 3 and includes normalization of the model. Some process modeling is performed in this stage, and application areas are defined and prioritized for further development.

Stage 5: Process Modeling

This stage continues the process modeling begun in the previous stage and defines the functional requirements for the business area down to the level of simple or primitive processes.

Stage 6: System Design

This stage translates the business models into technology-dependent database and application designs based on the implementation environment. Interfaces are designed, along with programs and migration and test plans.

Stage 7: System Implementation

This stage delivers the finished system to clients and includes creation of documentation, populating the database for production, generating appropriate code, and integrating the system components with external systems.

IE/IMPACT from Pacific Information Management (PIM)

IE/IMPACT is a combination of traditional, James Martin IE with Information Resource Management (IRM) and IDEF modeling notations. IE/IMPACT is a result of the work of D. S. Coleman [COL81] and others at PIM who collectively combined IRM concepts with IE techniques and IDEF notations [PAC89]. Within IE/IMPACT, a traditional seven-stage IE method is preceded by an assessment of the IRM and followed by a step that includes system tuning and maintenance.

Stage 1: Information Resource Management Situation Assessment

Prior to the beginning of a traditional ISP phase, IE/IMPACT includes this step to define the current and future positioning of the organization relative to IRM and how IRM affects the organization.

Stage 2: Information Strategy Planning

ISP focuses on projects defined in the previous step and includes partitioning the organization into business areas, etc.

Stage 3: Business Area Analysis

BAA focuses on developing data and process models using the business areas defined in the ISP phase. Unlike other IE methods, IE/IMPACT uses different notations, specifically activity models which are based on the IDEF0 diagraming standard used in the defense industry.

Stage 4: Business System Design

BSD defines a plan for implementing systems based on the models built in the previous step. Includes the creation of a prototype for development.

Stage 5: Technical Design

In this stage, system components are designed based on the implementation requirements for the organization.

Stage 6: Construction and Test

The automated system is generated from the specifications defined in the previous steps and tested.

Stage 7: Implementation and Assimilation

The systems created in the previous step are implemented.

Stage 8: Tuning and Operational Enhancement

The system is tuned and maintained through its useful life.

7.3.4 Representation

Information-oriented techniques have essentially four stages, or major divisions of work, which progress in a top-down fashion beginning with organization-wide planning (ISP). Representations are defined and viewed within these major stages as described below.

Planning

The entire enterprise is studied in terms of its objectives, goals, critical success factors, organization, business functions, and high-level data needs. In addition, the organization is partitioned into business areas for further work in the analysis phase.

Information planning matrices show the relationship between the business goals, objectives, and functions, and the data used. In addition, the critical success factors and goals/objectives are defined for each business area. Entity-relationship diagrams describe the high-level data structures and relationships within the business areas, and decomposition diagrams represent the functional hierarchy and organization within those areas.

Analysis

For each business area, the entities and relationships identified in the previous step are analyzed, and the business area is partitioned into business systems, which are prioritized for future development/maintenance projects.

Data models (ERDs, etc.) describe the data used by each subject area in more detail, data flow diagrams can be used to model existing business processes (process models) and the data produced and consumed, decomposition diagrams represent the functional view of the business area and its processes, and entity/process matrices describe the relationship between the processes and the data structures. In some cases, dependency diagrams are used to show the flow of processing that occurs within specific business functions.

Design

Data structure diagrams represent the physical database and/or file structures to be used in the system, prototypes are defined for the screens and reports, decomposition diagrams are used to describe the hierarchy or architecture of procedures and modules in a system, and action diagrams describe the logic within each procedure or module. Action diagrams can also represent the architecture of an individual program and are used to generate code in the construction phase.

Dialog flow diagrams can be used to represent the flow of control in an on-line program, with function key assignments and processing requirements for the screen or menu. Screens, menus, and reports are designed along with maps of data elements and structures to the input/output forms used.

Construction

In construction, CASE tools are used to generate the system from the design specifications. Action diagrams are used to generate the source code in a third- or fourth-generation language. The database or file design diagrams are used to generate the data structures in their physical form.

7.4 Stages and Tasks

The two common versions of the IE method include four and seven stages, respectively. The four-stage version includes Information Strategy Planning, Business Area Analysis, Business System Design, and Construction. The seven-phase version separates the BSD phase from Technical Design, and includes phases for Transition and Production. Other versions of IE, including the one offered by Information Engineering Systems Corp. and Pacific Information Management, are described in Section 7.3.3.

Figures 7.7 and 7.8 represent the two most popular versions of IE and show the deliverables from each phase.

7.5 Deliverables

IE methods introduce several new deliverables and notations, including decomposition diagrams, matrices, and action diagrams. The deliverables produced are as follows:

Information Strategy Planning - Enterprise models, including goals, objectives, critical success factors, organizational and functional hierarchies, and a data architecture.

Business Area Analysis - Models of the data and functions, and interactions between the two. In most versions of IE, this phase includes prototypes of screens, menus, and reports, and may include data flow diagrams representing the current system functionality.

Business System Design - Application specification, including database/file structures; procedure and module definitions (action diagrams) and screen, menu, and report descriptions.

Construction - A working system and documentation are delivered from construction, including the source and executable code, user and operation manuals, and any DBMS or file-specific information required to place the system into production.

7.6 Suitable Applications

There are a wide variety of organizations that would benefit from the use of information-oriented techniques. Essentially, any organization in which there is a reasonable degree of data overlap between applications would benefit. Organizations that have not defined their business goals, objectives, and critical success factors are ideal candidates for IE methods, along with organizations that view information as a strategic asset.

Those organizations that are not interested in or have already defined business plans and strategic models may find the ISP work unnecessary or too expensive and may not be suitable for IE methods. Those organizations that do not require integrated database applications will find it hard to justify the expense of an ISP as a precursor to ongoing software development.

7.7 Benefits and Drawbacks

As already described, the chief benefit of using IE methods is the ability to develop and deploy shared, integrated information systems across an organization. Additionally, the focus on strategic planning forces an organization to identify the factors that are important to it and automate these initially. This brings a strong business orientation to IS development, and when business functions are closely tied to IS, the systems developed are more closely aligned with business needs.

For IE to be successful, there must be agreement among users and developers as to which data is to be shared and what common definitions will be used. Getting this agreement may take a long time, especially if users are accustomed to exclusive ownership of data and its definition. A strong data administration (DA) function within the organization will help here. To make IE work, the visibility and importance of the DA function must be elevated.

A drawback of the IE methods is their lack of appreciation for exising systems and their focus on ISP as the first step in the development of information systems. Some IE CASE tool vendors have begun providing re/reverse engineering services for their clients to help them create data and process models for their existing systems. Some organizations have adopted IE methods without bothering to develop strategic plans and have backed upward into an ISP phase from BAA work.

Another drawback is the relatively limited number of CASE vendors supporting IE. Because of the required integration of and consistency among IE models, use of a CASE tool is imperative.

Perhaps the most serious limitation of IE methods is their requirement for automated support of the development process and the need for a centralized repository or encyclopedia across an organization. Current integrated-CASE (ICASE) tools provide limited support for IE methods and support only IBM mainframe-based applications (CICS, COBOL, DB2, etc.).

A final criticism of IE techniques is how prototypes are integrated with action diagrams in the Construction stage to generate code. Some have suggested that prototypes be used to define screen, menu, and report layouts, and then the action diagrams mapped from the function descriptions created in analysis, while others suggest that the prototype be further defined using action diagrams until all the functionality is in place. Regardless of the approach used, the issue of how action diagrams map to a functional prototype of the system should be addressed in any IE methodology selection decision.

Another question is how action diagrams, which are by their nature procedural, are able to support event-driven GUI prototypes and applications. GUI-based systems are not procedural in the traditional sense, and whichever specification tool is used for designing a solution under these circumstances must incorporate and support event-driven behavior.

7.8 The Library Example

In this section, James Martin's four-stage version of Information Engineering will be used to analyze and design our common example, the Library system. Since IE begins at the organizational level, our example is expanded and places the library in the middle of a university. Early steps, like those in Information Strategy Planning and Business Area Analysis, focus at the university level, while later ones in System Design and Construction focus on the Library system.

7.8.1 Information Strategy Planning

In this stage, we handle university-wide concerns. The goals and critical success factors of the university are defined. High-level groupings of functions and data are identified and diagramed, and matrices are developed to show relationships between the two and guide a partitioning of the university into business areas.

Step: Draw an Organization Chart

Draw an organization chart showing the hierarchy of personnel making up the organization. Since IE involves users throughout the enterprise, the organization chart serves as a guide for identifying them. The organization chart looks just like a decomposition diagram except that the boxes have square corners. Each box represents an organizational unit within the university led by an individual. This may not necessarily reflect the functional organization of the university, but reflects the current organizational structure.

Step: Diagram Major University Functions

Draw a decomposition diagram showing the major functions of the university. The diagram in Figure 7.9 shows the major functions of the university down two levels. Notice the Libraries function, which will eventually decompose down to our example Library system.

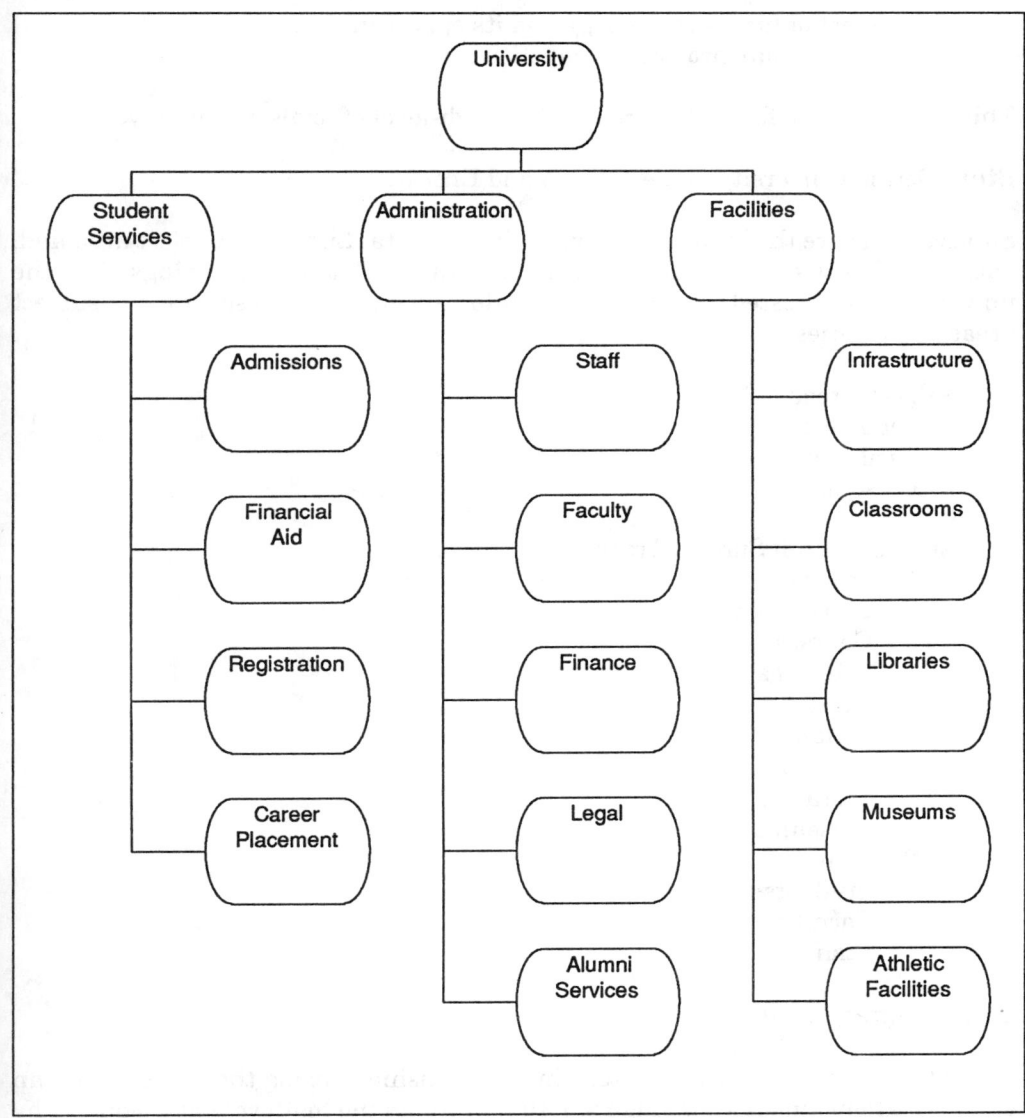

Figure 7.9
Function
decomposition
diagram.

Step: Study the University

Analyze the university and define one or more of the following:

   Goals and problems - These are used to guide all system development
      and maintenance efforts.
   Critical success factors - These are the most important goals of the
      university; they must be attained for the university to succeed.

The impact of future technology and its opportunities.
Systems that may provide a competitive edge.

This step is most effectively performed by high-level officials of the university.

Step: Define University Subject Areas and Entities

Subject areas are the highest-level groupings of data. List every subject area and, within each subject area, list associated entities. Entities are things that the university is interested in storing information about. Here is a short list of subject areas and entities:

    Subject Areas
        Academics
        Facilities
        Personnel

    Entities within Subject Areas
        Academics
            Departments
            Courses
            Offerings
        Facilities
            Offices
            Classrooms
            Libraries
            Museums
        Personnel
            Students
            Faculty
            Staff

Step: Diagram Entities

Using the list of entity types, determine relationships among them and create an entity-relationship diagram. Figure 7.10 represents the hig-level data required by the university.

Step: Map Functions to Entities

Determine which entities are used by which functions, and draft a matrix showing the information. Each cell of the matrix indicates whether a function creates (C), reads (R), updates (U), and/or deletes (D) an entity.

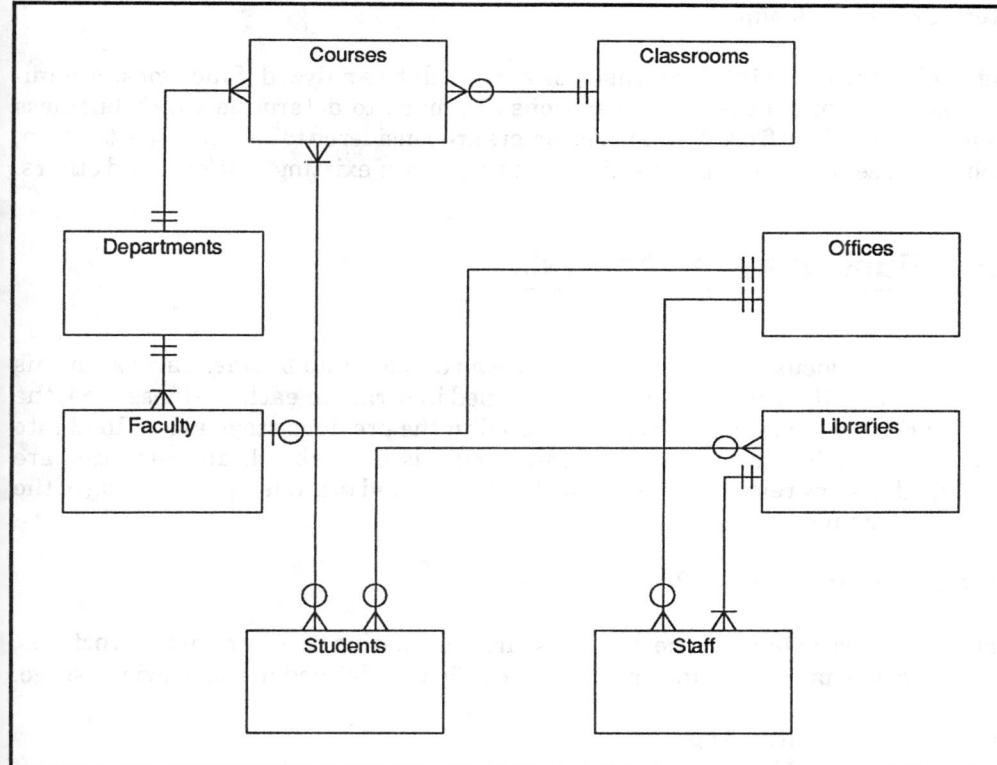

Figure 7.10
Entity-relationship diagram of selected entities within the university.

Step: Determine Business Areas

Cluster the function-entity matrix to determine how the organization is decomposed into business areas. Clustering is accomplished by first listing the functions in the order that they naturally occur and then arranging the entities such that:

The entity created or updated by the first function appears first.
The entity created or updated by the second function appears next.
    ...
The entity created or updated by the last function appears last.

The clusters of creates and updates indicate probable business areas. Figure 7.11 shows the clustered matrix with business areas personnel, facility management, administration, and academic affairs (corresponding to admissions, financial aid, and registration).

Step: Prioritize Business Areas

Determine the order in which business areas will be analyzed. Since most organizations have limited resources, decisions are made to determine which business areas will be tackled first. A number of factors are considered to aid this prioritization, including user demands, potential benefits, values of existing systems, and others.

7.8.2 Business Area Analysis

In the previous stage, the university was divided into business areas. In this stage, the identified business areas are studied in turn. For each business area, the high-level function and data models created in the previous stage are refined into models for the business area. The data model is normalized, and matrices are developed to show relationships among the models and to guide a partitioning of the business area into systems.

Step: Determine Scope of Business Area

Determine the extent of the business area by listing the pertinent functions, entities, goals, problems, and critical success factors defined in the previous stage.

Step: Diagram Entity Types

Create an entity-relationship diagram for this business area. Draw from the entities defined in Information Strategy Planning.

Step: Diagram Functions

Draw a decomposition diagram for this business area as shown in Figure 7.12.

Step: Refine Data Model

Using the entity-relationship diagram for this business area as a starting point, completely define and normalize the attributes for each entity.

Figure 7.11
Function-entity
matrix.

CRUD Matrix	Faculty	Staff	Classrooms	Libraries	Museums	Departments	Courses	Students	Offerings
Personnel	CRUD	CRUD				R			
Facility Management			CRUD	CRUD	CRUD	R	R		RU
Administration	R	R				CRUD	CRUD		
Admissions						R		CRUD	
Financial Aid								RU	
Registration	RU		RU			R	R	RU	CRUD

Step: Refine Process Model

Using the decomposition diagram for this business area as a starting point, refine the functions down to elementary processes.

Step: Diagram Process Dependencies

Create dependency diagrams relating all the elementary processes. An example of a dependency diagram is shown in Figure 7.13.

Step: Map Processes to Entities

Determine which entities are used by which processes, and draft a matrix showing the information.

Step: Determine Systems

Cluster the process-entity matrix to determine how the business area is decomposed into systems.

Step: Prioritize Systems

Determine the order in which systems will be tackled. Use system importance and resource availability.

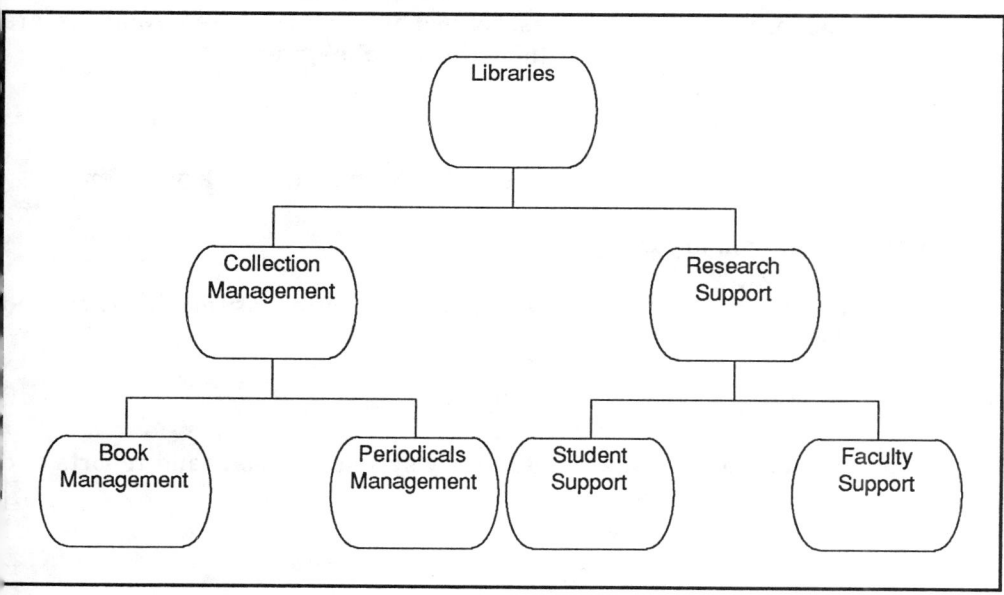

Figure 7.12
Decomposition diagram for Libraries business area.

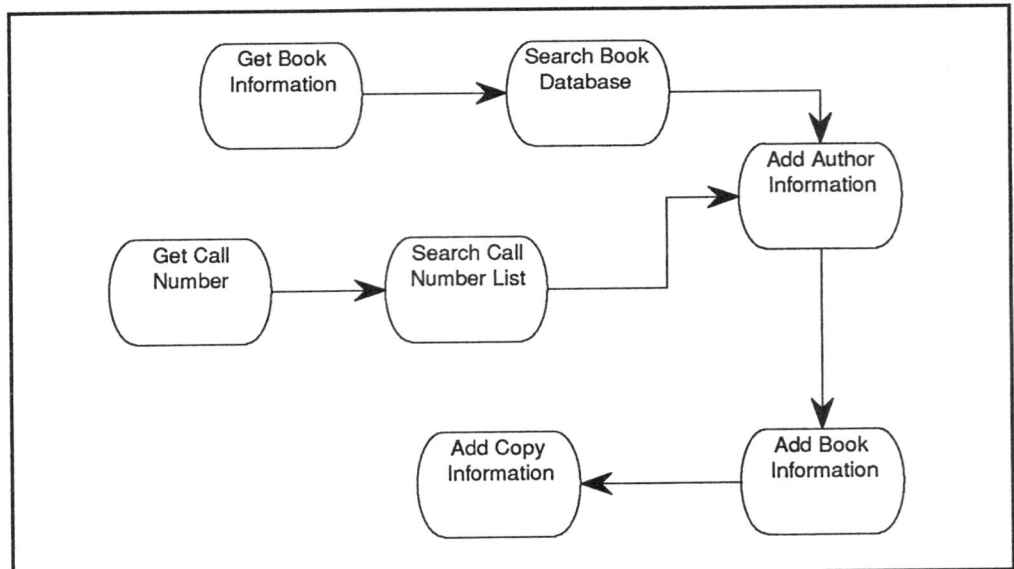

Figure 7.13
Dependency
diagram for Add
Book process.

7.8.3 System Design

In the previous stage, we determined which systems compose the business area. In this stage, the design of a system is conducted. This is the point where most other techniques begin. For each system to be designed, the user requirements are determined and prototyped. Processes defined in Business Area Analysis are refined into procedures, which are detailed in action diagrams.

Step: Determine User Requirements

Document the general and specific needs of the user for the Library system.

Step: Conduct Preliminary Design

Perform a cursory design of the Library system using decomposition diagrams and dependency diagrams.

Step: Prototype Design

Using a prototyping tool, simulate the Library system's screens and reports and gradually refine the prototype with input from user representatives until it represents their view of the system. Chapter 9 describes prototype-oriented techniques and includes a prototype of the Library example.

Step: Diagram Procedures

Draft a set of action diagrams that represent the processing logic of the system. Figure 7.14 shows an example action diagram for the Add Book process.

Step: Diagram Dialogs

Use dialog flow diagrams to show the movement among screens in the system.

7.8.4 Construction

In construction, the system is produced from the set of specifications and designs created thus far. Depending on the capability of the CASE tool used, code can be automatically generated. Transition and production prepare the system and move it to a production status.

7.9 Resource List

There are a small number of companies marketing CASE tools that support IE methods. These include Cortex Corp. (CorVision), Knowledgeware, Inc. (Application Development Workstation and Information Engineering Workbench), Synon, Inc. (Synon), System Software Associates, Inc. (AS/SET), and Texas Instruments Inc. (Information Engineering Facility).

Companies that market IE methods include Computer and Engineering Consultants, Ltd. (ForeSight), Ernst and Young (Navigator Systems Series), Information Engineering Systems Corp. (IEM and IE:Expert), James Martin & Co. (IEM and IE-Expert), and Pacific Information Management, Inc. (IE/Impact).

A wealth of books and reports is available on IE methodologies, including those of Martin [MAR90] [MAR87a] [MAR86] [MAR85a] [MAR81] and Finkelstein [FIN89], and those from IE methodology vendors including Axiom [AXI90], Ernst & Young [ART87] [ERN90], James Martin & Company [JAM91], Pacific Information Management [PAC89], and Texas Instruments [TEX90].

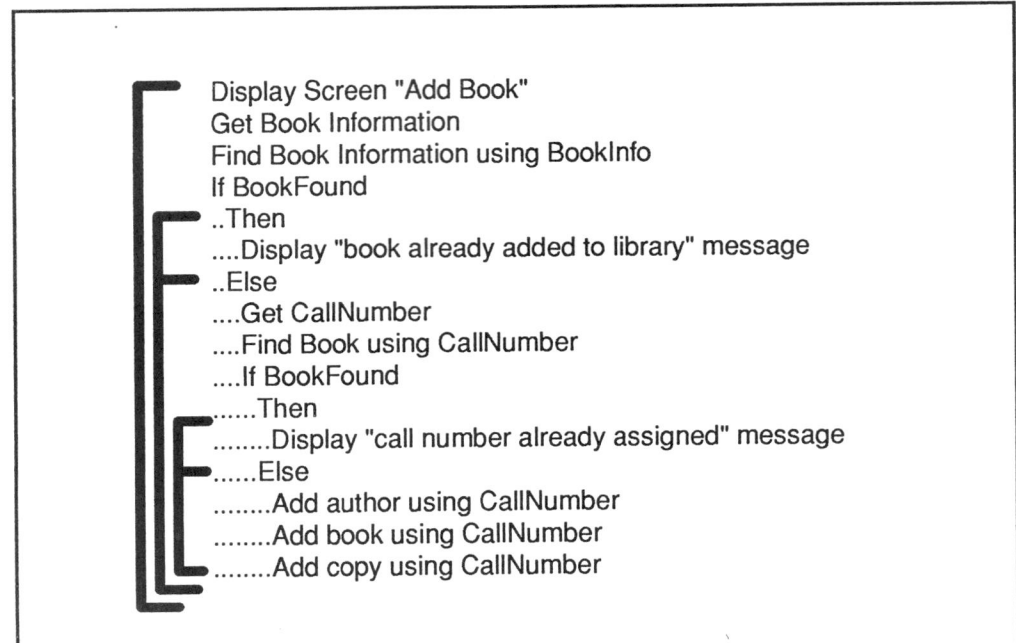

Figure 7.14
Action diagram for
Add Book process.

7.10 References

[AXI90]   Axiom Information Consulting, *AIM Overview*, 1990.

[ART87]   Arthur Young, *Practical Guide to Information Engineering*,
           Wiley, 1987.

[COL81]   Coleman, D. S., "The Use of IDEF-1 Information Models for Database
           Design," U. S. Air Force, Wright-Patterson Aeronautical Laboratory
           (AFWAL), Dayton, OH, 1981.

[ERN90]   *Ernst & Young Navigator Systems Series: Life Cycle
           Charts*, Ernst & Young, 1990.

[FIN89]   Finkelstein, C., *An Introduction to Information Engineering, From
           Strategic Planning to Information Systems*, Addison-Wesley, 1989.

[GAN90]   Gane, C., *Computer-Aided Software Engineering: The Methodologies,
           the Products, and the Future*, Prentice-Hall, 1990.

[HUG91]   Hughlette, G., "Information Engineering: From Strategic Planning to
           Information Systems," *Executive Briefing:CASE*, January/February
           1991, pp. 3-5.

[INN88]   Inmon, W. H., *Information Engineering for the Practitioner: Putting
           Theory Into Practice*, Yourdon Press, 1988.

[JAM91]   James Martin & Company, *The Information Engineering Methodology*, 1991.

[MAR90]   Martin, J., *Information Engineering*, Books I, II, and III, Prentice-Hall, 1990.

[MAR87a] Martin, J., "Information Engineering," *Savant Technical Report*, Savant Institute, 1987.

[MAR87b] Martin, J., *Recommended Diagramming Standards for Analysts and Programmers*, Prentice-Hall, 1987.

[MAR86]   Martin, J., and E. Hershey, "Information Engineering Whitepaper," *Technical Report*, Knowledgeware, 1986.

[MAR85a] Martin, J., and C. McClure, *Action Diagrams: Clearly Structured System Design*, Prentice-Hall, 1985.

[MAR85b] Martin, J., and C. McClure, *Diagramming Techniques for Analysts and Programmers*, Prentice-Hall, 1985.

[MAR81]   Martin, J., and C. Finkenstein, "Information Engineering," 2 Vols, Savant Institute, 1981.

[PAC89]   *Information Engineering Management Guide*, Pacific Information Management, 1989.

[TEX90]   Texas Instruments, "Information Engineering Facility: Technology Overview," Texas Instruments, 1990.

[WIL89]   Williamson, M., "Focus on Methodology: Information Engineering," *CASE Strategies*, volume I, number 2, July 1989, p. 1-2.

[ZAC87]   Zachman, J., "A Framework for Information Systems Architecture," *IBM Systems Journal*, vol. 26, no.3, 1987.

Chapter 8
Object-Oriented Techniques

Perhaps the newest, most visible, but least understood software development techniques are the object-oriented methods. "Object-oriented" seems to have quickly become the hot term or buzzword of the 1990s, and some experts are predicting that this technology will revolutionize the entire computer industry.

When investigating object-oriented technology, it is essential to differentiate between the different types of products and techniques that are available. There are, for example, object-oriented databases, object-oriented environments, and object-oriented operating systems. But in this chapter we will focus on object-oriented techniques for analysis and design. In doing so, we will also discuss object-oriented programming languages and the issues related to creating object-oriented software.

One inherent difficulty in describing object-oriented "stuff" is the ambiguity over the definition of terms. Everyone seems to agree on the benefits of developing software based on an object perspective, but few seem able to adequately define exactly what an object is. There are a number of object-oriented theorists who have slightly different definitions for some critical object-oriented concepts, and this further confuses the object-oriented landscape.

Before proceeding, we need to define what we mean by *object* and how this definition relates to the techniques we will be discussing.

Object: Something that is or is capable of being seen, touched, or otherwise sensed; something physical or mental of which a subject is cognitively aware; a thing that forms an element of or constitutes the subject matter of an investigation or science; a noun or noun equivalent denoting in verb constructions that on or toward which the action of a verb is directed.

Class: An order or grouping of persons or things possessing the same characteristics or status; a group of students taught together; a grouping of plants or animals; rank or standing in society; v.t. to rank together; v.i. to rank.

From Webster's New Collegiate Dictionary.

Very simply, objects are things that we see all around us in our everyday lives. Objects include automobiles, telephones, houses, chairs, etc. In an object-oriented approach, objects (not unlike the physical objects we interact with daily) have attributes or characteristics, communicate with one another using messages, and have predictable behaviors.

Most children are taught very early how to categorize things into groups. They are taught how to identify things that are alike and things that are different. They learn how to group things that are similar and to identify any differences between things.

This process of organization, often called "classification," is a basic premise of the object-oriented paradigm. Grouping objects together by attributes or characteristics and identifying how objects are different are essential tasks in object-oriented software development.

8.1 Introduction

"...object technology's many other boosters predict that it will do for software what the microchip has done for hardware. Instead of microchips, the software revolution will be built on so-called objects - simple, self contained, reliable software components. Like the microprocessor, object technology has the potential to radically change the economics of the business - and not just the $30 billion packaged-software industry."

From "Software Made Simple," *Business Week,* September 30, 1991.

How do the concepts of an object and classification relate to analysis, design, and programming? What deliverables are required from object-oriented analysis and design to successfully implement a solution using an object-oriented programming language? How are object-oriented techniques different from traditional structured techniques?

Object-Oriented Analysis (OOA) is a process of analyzing or modeling the requirements for a system using objects, attributes, and relationships. Traditional OOA techniques identify system components (objects) and their relationships and behaviors in an object model.

Object-Oriented Design (OOD) is a process of translating or specifying a physical software structure that is composed of reusable components (objects) built from the object model defined in Analysis. OOD delivers an object specification to programming and must consider existing objects for reuse in the completed software product.

Object-Oriented Programming (OOP) is a process of creating programs using collections of self-sufficient objects with encapsulated data and behavior that interact with one another via messages. A critical aspect of OOP is inheritance, which allows objects to share constructs with other objects. Class libraries make object-oriented programming a building-block process.

Object-Oriented Programming Languages (OOPLs) support the concept of classes, objects, methods, inheritance, encapsulation, and message passing. Optional features that OOPLs may support include multiple inheritance, dynamic binding, and polymorphism. While true OOPLs exist, some traditional languages have been extended to support some concepts of object-orientation.

In the programming phase, objects act differently from procedural programs in that they are event- or message-driven and autonomous. A collection of objects is assembled to carry out the required functionality for a system, with an application or operating system object often serving as the starting point. But unlike procedural systems, there is no inherent hierarchy of control in an object-based application. Also, systems built with objects pass control back and forth based only on messages sent, not any defined control flow or sequence. Procedural programs, on the other hand, are composed of subroutines or functions which can only receive control from higher up in the hierarchy (often from a main routine). Objects, from a conceptual perspective, work in parallel; they receive control from some other object, perform the operations requested, and then pass control (via another message) to some other object.

Building object-based applications becomes a process of assembling the required objects and establishing message passing to elicit the required operations. Objects may also execute and behave differently based on the context in which they receive messages. For instance, the ATM example in this chapter describes a keyboard object that collects keystrokes and passes the appropriate information back to the ATM controller. This keyboard object can collect the ID number for a bank customer, a transaction type, or an amount and will send back an appropriate message that depends on the context in which it is called. The ATM controller, in this case, simply sends the appropriate message to the keyboard controller to elicit the appropriate response.

Object-oriented applications exhibit behavior common in declarative languages rather than procedural languages. Under object-oriented development, we declare the classes and objects, their attributes and methods, how they interact, and their interfaces. But existing OOPLs are more procedural than declarative, because their implementation of objects and methods is similar to traditional subroutines (e.g.., C++).

8.1.1 Definitions

According to Grady Booch [BOO91], an object is an entity that:

* Has state
* Is characterized by the actions that it suffers and that it requires of other objects
* Is a unique instance of some (possibly anonymous) class
* Is denoted by a name
* Has restricted visibility of and by other objects
* Can be viewed either by its specification or by its implementation

A *class* is a group or category of objects that all share the same functions and data. A *class library* is a collection of generic classes that can be adapted (inherited) and tailored for a new application. Through the use of class libraries, common abstractions and code can be reused across many applications.

Inheritance is a property that allows child objects to reuse data and functions from parent objects. As a son or daughter might inherit eye or hair color from his or her mother or father, objects inherit characteristics and operations from their parent objects. *Multiple inheritance* is the process of inheriting from more than one parent. Currently, not all OOPLs support multiple inheritance.

Object *methods* are simply procedures or operations that reside in an object and determine how the object will act when it receives messages. Methods are similar to program subroutines but are implemented differently from subroutines or functions in a traditional procedural programming language. Figure 8.1 compares object methods with traditional subroutines. Unlike subroutines, objects include or encapsulate the data as well as the operations on the data. In structured programs, the data and operations are always kept separate.

In object-oriented approaches, objects communicate via *messages*. These messages are the only acceptable means of objects interacting. An example of a message might be a user object requesting that a specific book be checked out to him or her in the Library system. Messages cause objects to change states or instance values.

Information hiding refers to operations (methods) that are carried out by objects but are hidden from other objects. Because of information hiding, objects can be modified or enhanced without changing the way they are used by other objects. Objects can be thought of as black boxes that can send and receive messages without any knowledge of other objects, underlying data structures or mechanics.

Polymorphism results when a single message causes different actions when received by different objects. For example, a circle object and a square object might both receive a "draw" message, but each will perform a separate and different function upon receiving this message. In a similar fashion, one object may respond to a message in a different manner depending on the context in which the object is acting at the time. In this way, messages and object behavior can be context dependent.

Persistence is the permanence of an object or the period of time that space is allocated and available for the object in memory. *Binding* refers to the mechanism for associating the address of a called procedure with a caller; *static binding* occurs at compile and link time, while *dynamic binding* occurs at run time.

8.1.2 History

Object-oriented development has its roots in the development of Simula in the late 1960s and in the work of Alan Kay and his team at the Xerox PARC in the 1970s. Simula 67 included most of the fundamental concepts that are now common in

Objects reflect a deeper level of detail than subroutines.

Objects respond only to certain strictly defined messages that are passed to them.

Objects receive messages and take full control of their environment until they pass control to another object via another message.

Objects communicate with other objects in a clearly defined manner that cannot be subverted.

Figure 8.1
Comparing objects with traditional subroutines.

OOPLs and affected the development of many object-oriented technologies. Bertrand Meyer, the architect of Eiffel, was once the chairman of the Association of Simula Users. Alan Kay, an originator of GUIs and Smalltalk, first developed his Sketchpad in Simula. Smalltalk combined the objects and classes in Simula with the incremental development environment of LISP. Bjarne Stroustrup also originally used Simula, as did Jean Ichbiah, one of the designers of Ada.

Smalltalk 80 was the first OOPL that was based on objects and classes in a GUI and led to the general acceptance of object-oriented development. Apple Computer was one of the first major users of Smalltalk and offered a version for the Lisa computer in 1981. LISP was extended to support object-based concepts in 1977 by MIT. C++ was developed by Stroustrup in 1985, and Eiffel was introduced by Interactive Software Engineering in 1986.

On the methods front, the object-oriented design method for Ada was described in a book published by Grady Booch in 1983, and in 1988, Shlaer and Mellor published their book on OOA. The Coad/Yourdon method was introduced in 1990 and 1991, and the object-oriented modeling technique (OOMT) was defined in a book published in 1991. Recently, much has been written on the subject of object-oriented analysis/design (OOA/D) techniques, and many CASE tools now support OOA/D methods and notations.

8.2 Philosophy

"Object-Oriented Software Development seeks to identify the objects in a problem, to understand the structural and behavioral modularity and properties of each object, and to recognize objects which are members of a common class and so share modularity and properties, so as to create a single consistent abstract model based on the elements of the problem. In OOA, a requirements model identifies 'what' the required objects, classes, functions, behavior and attributes of the problem are. OOD models the 'how' and is refined into an architecture for software components with a smooth transition to code."

E. Colbert [COL89].

Proponents of object-oriented technology claim that an object perspective facilitates modification and enhancement of a software product. Since data structures tend to be more stable than processes that act on the data (see Chapter 5), it follows that software oriented around data structures will be more stable than software oriented around the processes themselves. Software that is built around data structures will also limit the impact of changes to a software system. Maintenance of software oriented around functions can be drastically affected by changes to those functions, while modification to software that has as its focus the data structures will be less affected by functional changes. But in the same sense, modifications to the data used in an object-oriented software product will require significant changes where only minor changes would be needed in a functional product. Larry Constantine's article [CON90] is an excellent treatment of the differences in modifications to software products developed using either approach.

Object-oriented techniques differ from data-oriented techniques in that they encapsulate data structures and the procedures or operations that act on the data together. Whereas data-oriented techniques allow data to be accessed and updated in a central location (usually a database), object-oriented techniques require that data be local to the object that accesses it. To access or update data, object-oriented techniques require messages to be passed between objects. Data-oriented techniques also tend to group data structures together based on access requirements for the software system and are typically converted to a database management system (DBMS). Object-oriented programs can use object-oriented database management systems to store objects, but can also use traditional file structures or databases.

The underlying principle of all object-oriented techniques is focusing on identifying objects, encapsulating data and process within the objects, and defining interactions between objects, using a messaging perspective.

8.3 Characteristics

"Object-oriented design is the construction of software systems as structured collections of abstract data type implementations. The emphasis is on structuring a system around the classes of objects it manipulates rather than the functions it performs on them, and on reusing whole data structures, together with the associated operations, rather than isolated routines."
B. Meyer [MEY89].

All of the object-oriented techniques have as their basic unit an object. As we have already seen, an object is an entity which includes the attributes and operations that can be performed by the object.

Regardless of the object-oriented technique chosen, an object model will be developed in the analysis phase, an object specification will be created in the design phase, and the finished system will be written in an object-oriented programming language. But unlike traditional programming, object-oriented programming considers existing class libraries and a defined set of objects, attributes, and messages that become the starting point for any new program. Therefore, when creating an object specification, the contents of existing class libraries must be considered and included. When creating an object model, however, we need not be concerned with the physical characteristics of objects and classes. We need only model the objects within the domain of our application.

Different OOA/D techniques might model different aspects of a system or use different notations for designing object-oriented software, but most of the popular OOA techniques model the classes and objects in the problem space along with relationships between them. Many OOA techniques also model the dynamic aspects of objects or classes using finite state machines, typically in the form of state-transition diagrams and/or timing diagrams. Likewise, most OOA/D techniques use some diagraming notation to define interactions between objects, and class hierarchies showing inheritance relationships. In the detailed design phase, few existing OOD techniques provide notations that can support the generation of object-oriented code from specifications. Until existing class libraries are documented using standard notations, such as object and/or class hierarchy diagrams, the promise of reusability will not be realized. Understanding and effectively using existing class structures is a key to reusing objects in the object-oriented paradigm.

Another aspect of object-oriented techniques is their use with existing development methods. Some OOA/D techniques combine object-oriented and structured concepts and allow a developer to mix objects with traditional subroutines. In making the transition to object-oriented techniques, this ability to mix and match different aspects of the object and procedural perspectives can help organizations effectively adopt an object-oriented approach. Those organizations that already have an investment in resources using traditional structured techniques can adapt their approach to include object-oriented concepts, while those that are not using software engineering techniques may be better able to adopt the object-oriented methods.

8.3.1 Comparison of Methods

When comparing object-oriented techniques, it is helpful to look carefully at the objectives of analysis and design in the object-oriented paradigm. Object-oriented analysis (OOA) techniques share as their goals identifying a correct set of objects, their attributes and operations, and any relationships among objects (object model).

Likewise, object-oriented design (OOD) techniques refine candidate objects into classes, define message protocols for all objects, define data structures and procedures, and map these to an object-oriented programming language (object specifications).

Several techniques for OOA/D have been proposed and are being used to some degree within the industry. We will briefly examine each of the popular techniques before attempting to develop an example using one of these techniques. Prior to discussing methods, we need to consider how OOA/D methods might be compared and evaluated for selection. Figure 8.2 identifies several popular OOA/D techniques and their notations and representations.

In the past year, several technical journals have included articles that compare OOA/D methods, including [BUL92],[FIC92],[MON92],[PAG92], and [SON92]. Some of these papers compare only OOA/D methods, while others compare traditional development methods with object-oriented techniques. [MON92] is an excellent paper on comparing object-oriented techniques and includes a typology for methods based on OOA processes, OOD processes, representation, and complexity management. Another good examination of popular OOA/D methods can be found in [FIC92], which also compares object-oriented techniques with traditional methods and notations. See Chapter 10 for more information on comparing and selecting methods.

The Booch technique for object-oriented design supports class and object structures and relationships along with dynamic behavior using traditional finite state machine representations. Booch provides notations for object and class behavior, and in his book describes techniques for creating effective class hierarchies. Booch also provides support for a design notation oriented around the Ada language. While the Booch approach is more focused on design, it has been used effectively with traditional structured analysis techniques, object-oriented analysis techniques, data modeling, and informal requirements specification techniques. Some have criticized the Booch approach as ignoring requirements definition and lacking non-Ada design specifications.

The Shlaer/Mellor approach includes traditional structured techniques and notations in analysis and an object-oriented design language (OODL). Some critics of the Shlaer/Mellor approach argue that it is really just a rehashed use of the Ward/Mellor technique (see Chapter 6) for analysis with a focus on information modeling instead of control modeling. This technique also does not support many object-oriented concepts, including message passing, inheritance, and encapsulation in the analysis phase. The Shlaer/Mellor specifications reflect a functional modularity rather than a structural and behavioral modularity of objects. In this respect, the Shlaer/Mellor approach is very similar to structured analysis/design, and using their approach can result in the same problems often observed when using the structured (function-oriented) techniques.

Under the Shlaer/Mellor approach, an information model is built that identifies the objects, relationships, and attributes, along with the multiplicity and conditionality specifications. Then, for each active object in the information model, a state model is created that contains all the potential states in the object's life cycle and the events that cause transitions from one state to another. Actions in the state models will also become processes in function models. This process is followed by creating an object communication diagram that illustrates all the object state models and communication among objects.

For each state transition, a data flow diagram is created, and process specifications are used to describe the processing that causes the state to change. At this point, the boundaries of the system are defined, and an imaginary line can be drawn between the abstract system and the portions outside the system. Next, an external event list is created along with a functional requirements document.

The Shlaer/Mellor approach uses recursive design and an object-oriented design language (OODL). There are four separate but related views within the Shlaer/Mellor OOD technique:

A class view is drawn for each external view of a class and illustrates the details of the interface for the class.
A class structure view shows the internal structure of the code.
A dependency view shows invocation and friend relationships between classes.
An inheritance view shows inheritance relationships between classes.

The Coad/Yourdon approach focuses on building data models at a number of different levels and uses an extension of the traditional entity-relationship diagram (ERD) from data modeling (see Chapter 5). Their OOD technique maps directly to the analysis models and involves four components: problem domain, human interaction, task management, and data management. The Coad/Yourdon approach focuses more on the user interface component of a system and tends to be geared towards graphical user interfaces (GUIs) in design. Like the Booch technique, Coad/Yourdon recommends an iterative method that constructs a prototype to help learn more about the system and look at cohesion and coupling in design.

Coad/Yourdon also supports five views of an object model: class/object, structure, subject, attribute, and service. Subjects are mechanisms for controlling which portions of a model are considered or viewed by the developer at any given time. Classes and objects are abstractions of data and exclusive processing on the data, while structures allow the problem domain to be classified by complexity and inheritance to show how classes and objects are organized and assembled. Attributes or data elements (instance variables) are the characteristics of objects that are acted upon by the object itself, and services are the operations performed by objects.

Representation Technique	Class relationship	Object relationship	Class/Object Attributes	Class/Object Methods
Booch	Class diagram	Object diagram	Template	Template
Coad/Yourdon	ERD (Class/Object & Structure layer)	ERD (Class/Object & Structure layer)	ERD (Attribute layer)	ERD (Service layer)
OOMT	Object Model (ERD)	Object Model (ERD)	Template	Template
Shlaer/Mellor	Information structure diagram (ERD) & Class diagram	Information structure diagram (ERD)	Template	Template
Synthesis	Class definition diagram & Class hierarchy diagram	Object communication diagram & Object module	Class definition diagram	Object module diagram and dictionary

Figure 8.2
Comparison of OOA/D techniques with notations and representations.

Each view of the model is shown in an ERD, with connections indicating relationships — instance and message connections — between classes and objects. *Kind of* and *part of* structures are defined with special nodes and connections. For example, an apple and an orange are kinds of fruits, while seeds and a skin are parts of an apple. In addition, Coad/Yourdon also uses state-transition diagrams to model dynamic object behavior, and service charts or PDL to describe threads of control within a system.

Coad/Yourdon supplements the OOA model with additional implementation details when moving into OOD, and this approach seems more oriented towards Smalltalk and OODBMSs than other object-oriented software products.

Class/Object Behavior	Object Interaction/ Communication	Class/Object Structure (internal)	Object Packaging (external)	Class hierarchy (inheritance)
State-transition diagram & timing diagram	Object diagram		Module diagram	Class diagram
State-transition diagram	ERD (Service layer)			ERD (Structure layer)
State-transition diagram	Function model (DFD)			
Entity life history diagram (State-transition diagram)	Object communication diagram (DFD)	Class structure chart		Inheritance diagram
Event list	Object communication diagram	Object module diagram	Package communication diagram	Class hierarchy diagram

The Object-Oriented Modeling Technique (OOMT) from Rumbaugh et al. is very much like the Shlaer/Mellor and Coad/Yourdon approaches and also uses traditional structured techniques and notations. OOMT uses an enhanced entity-relationship diagram for object modeling, along with data flow diagrams for object interaction and an event-response diagram (which is similar to a state transition diagram) for dynamic modeling. The Rumbaugh, Coad/Yourdon, and Shlaer/Mellor techniques are very similar in concept, all focusing on using data or information models in analysis and providing limited support for design. Shlaer/Mellor and Rumbaugh both use traditional DFDs to show messages passed between objects.

The Rumbaugh object modeling notation and Coad/Yourdon class/object level views are almost identical. Both allow objects and classes to be shown and support generalization/specialization connections and part of/aggregation connections between classes and objects. Both also support instantiation connections—Rumbaugh with an instantiation relationship, Coad/Yourdon with an instance connection — and messages — Rumbaugh with propagation of operations, Coad/Yourdon with a message connection. Rumbaugh prefers Statecharts to STDs for the dynamic object behavior and also proposes building a prototype of a system early in the development life cycle.

Synthesis, created by Meilir Page-Jones and Steven Weiss, is a combination of object-oriented and structured techniques but was still being defined when this book was written. The Synthesis technique is largely based on extensions to the traditional structure chart notation and the uniform object notation (UOM). The UOM is composed of six basic diagrams or views: external views of object modules, interface views of object modules, class definition (or object interface) diagrams, class hierarchy (or inheritance) diagrams, object communication (or neighborhood) diagrams, and object internal (or method structure) diagrams.

The object module external view is used to show objects without their internal or interface information. The object module interface view shows an object with its supported methods and distinguishes between class and instance methods. Class definition diagrams provide the external interface or abstract definition of the features of a class that are available in a normal way to external clients. These diagrams show messages (and their elements) being passed between classes and defined as a list of formal object names with the object couple.

Class hierarchy diagrams depict sub-class/parent directed relationships, highlighting tightly coupled relationships and single or multiple inheritance. Object communication diagrams show the interaction of selected objects through message passing. These diagrams show only the methods of each object that are called into play by the messages shown, and events are drawn and labeled.

Object internal diagrams show the internal or detailed design of an object module. These diagrams are derived from structure charts but have been extended to handle object-oriented concepts, including message passing, hierarchy of components, class and instance variables, etc.

OOD methods can be compared on the basis of the process used to design data structures, the level of detail provided in their notations, and the level of detail describing the design process. Some OOD methods include traditional function-oriented concepts such as cohesion and coupling, while others deal more exclusively with class design or object interactions.

Some object-oriented techniques, including Object-Oriented Structured Design (OOSD) from Interactive Development Environments and Synthesis, are modifications of traditional functional techniques with some object-oriented concepts added. One benefit to using these techniques is that they support both a functional and an object-oriented perspective. While these techniques may serve to help organizations move toward OOA/D methods in an evolutionary fashion, they also retain some of the problems and drawbacks associated with the functional techniques.

Many object-oriented techniques are geared toward DOD and Ada development, including HOOD, MOOD, and Ray Buhr's approach. Buhr has developed an OOD technique that is similar to the Booch technique and is also aimed at Ada development, with inspiration from Structured Design techniques and an orientation towards objects, graphical notation and a conceptual model. The Buhr technique combines some aspects of Structured Analysis and Structured Design techniques and uses structure charts along with Ada structure graphs (ASGs). One drawback to using the Buhr (as well as the Booch) approach is that it is very closely tied to the Ada language.

Still other object-oriented methods, including Responsibility-Driven Design [WIR90], Object Behavior Analysis [RUB92] and Object-Oriented Analysis and Specification [KUR91], focus most of their efforts on object interactions and behavior, and provide few details on identifying and classifying objects, attributes, and methods. While these methods provide good techniques for specifying the behavior of objects in the solution domain, they assume an intuitive understanding of the problem domain that rarely exists in real-world development.

Monarchi and Puhr [MON92] have identified several areas for improvement in the existing OOA/D methods. These include:

1. Models that synthesize static and dynamic aspects of an object-oriented system at different levels of abstraction
2. A clear definition of what layers and views are important for representing and designing an object-oriented system and a means of integrating and balancing these views
3. Evaluation models for OOA/D methods that can measure the quality of the analysis and design process

8.3.2 Notation

The Booch OOD technique provides support for designing object-oriented software, but does not directly address the specification of requirements (analysis) or provide a notation for capturing and tracking requirements.

The Booch OOD notation consists of several diagrams and modeling notations that are used together to represent the system through analysis and design. These include: (1) _class (structure) diagrams_ which express the relationships between classes and provide a representation of the key abstractions; (2) _object (structure) diagrams_ that express the relationships among objects and represent the key mechanisms in the object; (3) _dynamic class and object diagrams,_ including state-transition or timing diagrams, which describe the time ordering of external events and the changes in state of each object; (4) *a context (or process) diagram* showing the scope of the system and interaction between hardware and software components; and (5) *architecture (or module) diagrams* which describe how the modules in the system interact and the visibility of each object within the resulting system.

The class diagrams represent inheritance, uses, instantiates, and metaclass relationships between classes. Under the Booch method, objects in object diagrams map to instances of classes defined in a class diagram. Class, object, and message templates describe textual aspects in a dictionary or repository and include persistence, concurrency, and visibility. The Booch approach also supports decomposition of higher-level objects into child objects and dynamic models for classes and objects. The Booch module diagram is geared towards Ada and has limited use outside the Ada language other than showing clusters of logically related modules in subsystems.

8.3.3 Technique

At the time we wrote this book, there was no established or standard object-oriented analysis and design technique, so we were faced with a decision: Which OOA/D technique should we describe in the book, and how do we acknowledge the alternatives that were not chosen?

The major OOA/D techniques that are currently available include techniques from Sally Shlaer and Stephen Mellor, Peter Coad and Ed Yourdon, Grady Booch, Ray Buhr, the Object-Oriented Modeling Technique (OOMT), Synthesis (from Steven Weiss & Mielir Page-Jones), and several techniques that combine aspects of structured techniques with object-oriented concepts.

For this book, we decided we would use the Booch technique and describe it using the Simple Simon Automated Teller Machine (ATM) example. While we might have chosen any of the other popular object-oriented techniques, we felt the Booch approach presented the purest form of OOA/D. In this book, we are interested in presenting the concepts of object-oriented techniques and how they differ from other approaches, and the Booch technique was the best choice given these criteria. This is not to say we were completely happy with all the notations and representations in the current Booch technique, and, as we will see later, we had some problems using the Booch technique to create the example system.

But for purposes of exploring how object-oriented techniques work, we will use the Booch technique because (1) at the time we wrote this book, there were several automated tools available that supported the Booch approach, (2) training and consulting services were readily available for the technique, (3) much had been written on the Booch approach, and (4) we felt it best defined the critical aspects of OOA/D at the time. Figure 8.3 describes the tasks in the Booch object-oriented development approach.

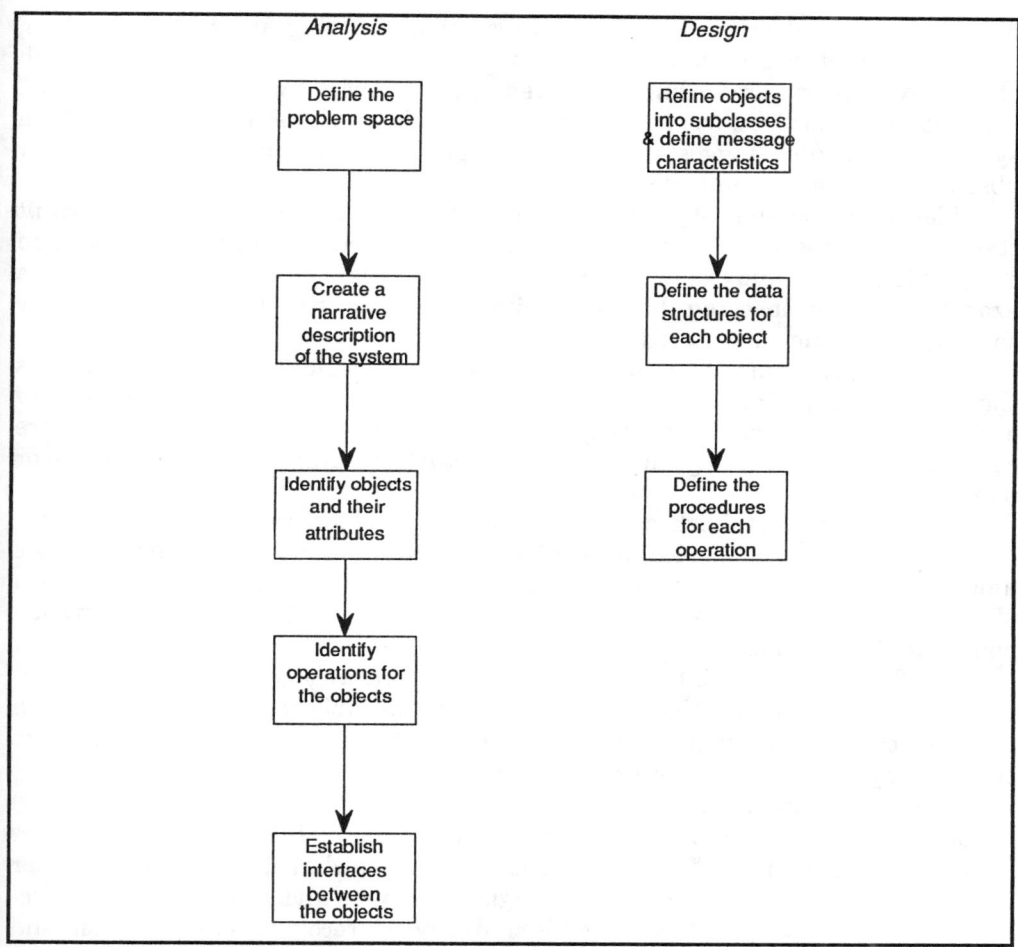

Analysis

- Define the problem space
- Create a narrative description of the system
- Identify objects and their attributes
- Identify operations for the objects
- Establish interfaces between the objects

Design

- Refine objects into subclasses & define message characteristics
- Define the data structures for each object
- Define the procedures for each operation

Figure 8.3
Booch analysis and design tasks.

The first step in the Booch technique is to define the scope of the problem space. This typically involves writing down the scope of the development effort and defining some type of context for the system under study. In many cases, drawing a context diagram (using a data flow or control flow diagram) for the system in question can help to answer some basic questions about what is inside and outside the system under review.

The second step is to state the problem requirements in textual form. Once the requirements are defined, candidate objects and classes can be extracted in the third step. Interestingly, the Booch approach does not focus on defining requirements for a system. In his book, Booch suggests that developers use OOA techniques from Shlaer/Mellor or Coad/Yourdon, traditional data modeling techniques, domain analysis (Bailin, etc.), or informal English descriptions of a system to help identify potential classes, objects, attributes, and operations. In doing our example problem, we chose the latter and found it raised many interesting questions about which objects and classes were within the problem space and which were outside. Usually, the objects are derived from the nouns used to describe the requirements for a system. Booch also suggests using prototyping to better understand the key abstractions from the problem space.

Identifying possible objects and their attributes, which is the most important step in the process, involves recognition of the major actors, agents, and servers in the problem space, plus their role in our model of reality. As we found with the example problem, choosing objects is an iterative, subjective, and acquired ability that may not come easily to all developers.

The fourth step in the Booch technique is to identify and describe the operations that each object performs. This serves to define and characterize the behavior of each object and class of objects. At this point, the static semantics of each object are established by determining which operations can be meaningfully performed on or by the object.

The next step establishes the visibility of each object in relation to all other objects in the system. We accomplish this by identifying the static dependencies among objects and classes of objects. Once these are defined, the interface for each object (or class) must be described along with a description of the outside view of each object (or class), using the Booch notation.

The final Booch step is to implement each object in an object-oriented programming language (OOPL). This involves choosing a suitable representation for each object or class of objects and implementing the objects and interfaces using the constructs provided by the programming language.

In practice, the Booch technique is not a sequential process, but rather an iterative, evolutionary approach to software development. Booch describes OOD as "round-trip gestalt design" which is iterative and somewhat obscure. As with other iterative processes, deciding when a design is complete and supports the requirements for the system is difficult. To his credit, Booch recognizes this problem and suggests that developers design the key abstractions and mechanisms in the problem domain and leave other design details to the programming staff.

Choosing an appropriate OOPL in which to implement the solution can be a difficult step, since at this time there are some limitations in availability of language compilers and class libraries for hardware and software platforms. Additional considerations for the programming tasks include compiler support, cross platform support, and whether a full, object-oriented environment is available (class browsers, inspectors, profilers, incremental compilers, debuggers, etc.).

The Booch method defines two major views of a system: a logical view, which focuses on the abstractions and mechanisms in a system, and a physical view, which focuses on issues related to the physical constraints on the system — contractor/subcontractor relationships, client/server relationships, etc.

Every object identified has two perspectives: an outside view and an inside view. The outside view of an object captures the abstract behavior of the object, while the inside view describes how that behavior is implemented. Objects can interact with one another using only the outside view, without knowing how the object is implemented internally (information hiding). When designing a system using the Booch method, we are initially concerned with the outside view.

The outside view of an object or class of objects can also be considered as its specification. As such, the specification captures all of the static and (as much as possible) dynamic semantics of each object.

8.3.4 Representation

While the OOA/D representations may vary from method to method, there are some common components of each technique. Figure 8.2 compares the major OOA/D methods and identifies their specific representations and notations.

Under the Booch method, class relationships are defined in the class diagram, and object relationships are defined in the object diagram. Attributes under the Booch method are defined using templates for objects and classes, often in a data dictionary. Booch suggests specific templates for each which are supported by many of the OOA/D CASE tools [TOP92].

Booch does not specifically include an object interaction or communication diagram, but his object diagram can be used to show messages and interactions among objects. Likewise, Booch does not include an internal class or object view, but the object and class diagrams and templates can represent the same information. Class hierarchy is shown using the Booch class diagram.

Booch provides specific support for object packaging or an external view using module diagrams, but these are oriented towards the Ada language and may provide little benefit in terms of representing non-Ada systems. Booch does include sub-systems and visibility in the module diagram.

8.4 Stages and Tasks

"Object-oriented development is based on identifying objects with their informational and functional features and grouping them into classes, which in turn are integrated into a system of the world in which those objects 'live'."
D. Rine [RIN92].

At a very basic level, object-oriented software development involves three tasks or activities: identifying classes, objects, attributes, and operations; defining structure and behavior for objects and messages; and implementing these structures in a chosen OOPL. As already mentioned, the OOA phase delivers an object model, the OOD phase an object specification, and the OOP phase a system built using self-contained objects and structures.

Regardless of the OOA/D technique chosen, an object model is required in analysis which should show the classes, objects, attributes, and their relationships. In design, an object specification should further specify the behavior of the objects and the interactions among objects in the problem domain. The resulting object specification would then be used to drive the object-oriented programming step. Figure 8.4 describes the Booch approach to object-oriented development.

One obvious characteristic of most object-oriented development techniques is their reliance on prototyping and an evolutionary life cycle with repetition and iteration. Object models and specifications must evolve to reflect the nature of the real-world problem domain. Booch and others describe a series of steps that is undertaken in sequence, but with much rework of the details as new information is gathered. Prototype-oriented techniques are described in the next chapter.

8.5 Deliverables

As we have already seen, different object-oriented techniques may create different representations (deliverables) throughout the development life cycle. But we can identify some generic representations that most (if not all) OOA/D techniques capture.

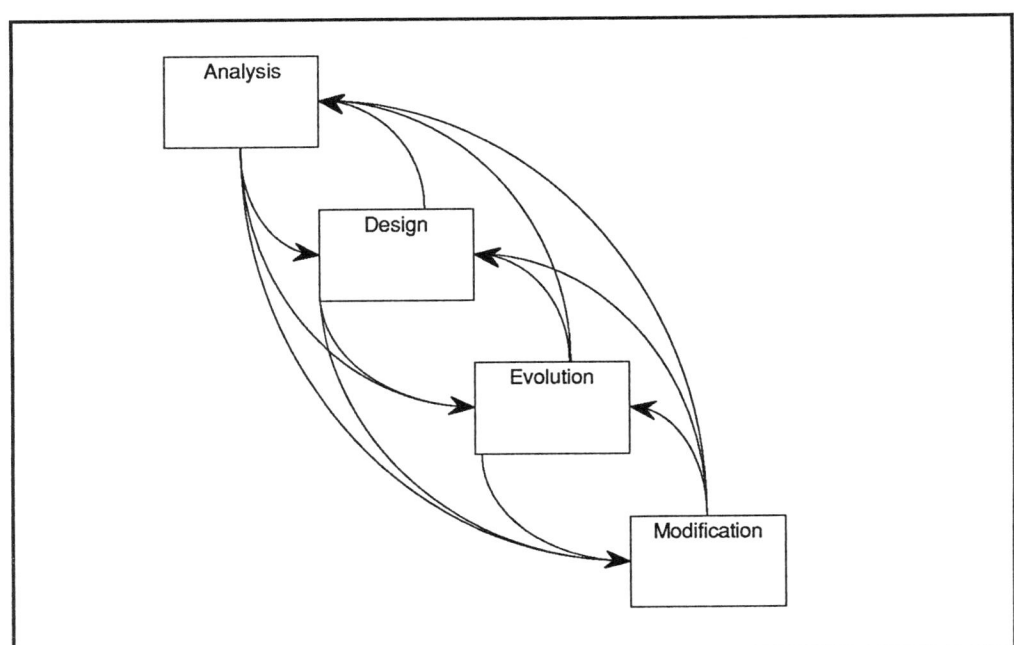

Figure 8.4
Booch object-
oriented life
cycle.

The OOA process delivers an object model that defines the objects, classes, relationships, attributes, and operations abstracted from the problem space. This model should be complete and consistent across objects and classes and should define the instance variables used by objects. While some OOA techniques often use traditional data models to specify objects and classes, others use informal techniques for object identification. As we have seen, a list of objects, attributes, and operations can also be extracted from a textual description of a system by identifying the nouns and verbs in the text.

The OOD process delivers an object specification that defines how the objects will be constructed, which classes will be defined, how the objects will communicate and interact, and the dynamic behavior of the objects throughout their life. OOD must consider the role of existing classes and objects in the design of a new system and must also consider the limitations of the chosen OOPL in implementing the solution. Dynamic and static aspects of objects and classes should be specified in OOD, and the design process is typically iterative and evolutionary in nature.

When moving to programming, object-oriented techniques should strive to reuse existing objects and classes. As we have already seen, object-oriented programming is more a matter of identifying and extending existing objects than of creating programs from scratch.

8.6 Suitable Applications

While organizations have had success using object-oriented techniques on a wide variety of applications, some general guidelines can help developers select possible projects for using these techniques. Software that executes in a graphical user interface (GUI) lends itself very nicely to object-oriented programming and thus OOA/D. The Macintosh, Microsoft Windows, IBM OS/2 Presentation Manager, and OSF/Motif environments can provide a wealth of existing classes and objects that can be reused on new applications. Often, identifying and documenting the class organization is required before these objects can be effectively used.

Some developers of real-time systems have claimed that the performance of object-oriented programming languages (OOPLs) is lacking, but studies suggest that a mixed OOPL and traditional programming language environment can produce adequate embedded systems (see [BAR91]). Much progress has been made in integrating OOPLs with traditional programming languages. As we have already seen, object-oriented software is ideal for event-driven environments, and many embedded class libraries are beginning to become available.

Similarly, developers of MIS have complained about lack of support for traditional business software under the object-oriented umbrella. While more development has occurred in C++ and Smalltalk, there are standards groups which are working on an object-oriented version of COBOL. In addition, many vendors now offer object-oriented database management systems (OODBMS) that can be used in conjunction with or in place of traditional relational databases.

Also, one CASE tool vendor (Netron) supports the Bassett Frame Technology (BFT), which is an object-oriented approach to developing COBOL applications. BFT defines code frames as mutually adaptive models, and Netron offers a product, Netron/CAP, which includes a standard set of frames in a hierarchy that can be assembled to form a finished product. Basset has even suggested that OOD techniques (such as the Booch approach used in this chapter) can be adapted to designing frames [BAS91]. In a sense, the BFT frame hierarchy is similar to a class hierarchy in a traditional OOPL.

From a practical standpoint, most organizations will want to consider moving incrementally toward an object-oriented approach, and for this reason, those techniques that combine structured and object-oriented concepts will hold great appeal. Other considerations or suggestions for applications that might be suitable for the object-oriented techniques include client/server software, which is usually touted as part of a cooperative or distributed processing environment, and vertical packaged software.

One key question to consider when evaluating object-oriented techniques is whether to adopt them and replace whatever is currently in use or to adapt the existing development methods to include aspects of object-orientation. Any organization that has a significant investment in function- or data-oriented techniques will think twice before scrapping its existing approaches and beginning with object-oriented techniques. For more on how object-oriented techniques compare to other techniques, see Chapter 10.

Object-oriented software fits very easily into a client/server model, and the model can be considered as a description of the interaction between two objects: a client and a server. A client makes requests of the server to perform services, and the server provides a set of services upon request.

The Object Management Group has defined a standard communication vehicle for clients and servers called the Object Requestor Broker specification. This standard defines how objects interact remotely and defines procedures for locating, invoking, and communicating between objects.

8.7 Benefits and Drawbacks

While many people have written extensively on the potential benefits of object-oriented technology, it is difficult to find documented studies that support the promises of increased productivity, reuse, and ease of maintenance most often cited by object enthusiasts. Perhaps one reason for this is that few organizations have begun experimenting with object-oriented technology, and those that have are reluctant to call their efforts totally successful.

Published experiences with object-oriented technology have found that software built using these methods was delivered with fewer requirements changes, fewer bugs in the completed software, required an incremental or phased delivery of the software, and the software was completed on schedule (see [LEV91]). Other studies have reported that the development of reusable, shared objects and code has resulted and software size was reduced from 25,000 to 67,000 of C code to 3,000 to 10,000 of C++ code [WYB90].

One problem in reviewing the potential benefits of object-oriented development is separating the myths of object-orientation from the practical realities of using the existing technology. For example, the benefit most often touted when discussing object-oriented development is reusability, but there are few (if any) studies that back up a promise of increased reusability for medium- to large-scale software products. Another benefit typically mentioned is ease of maintenance because of limited impact of changes on the resulting object-oriented software product. But other papers have disputed the realities of this benefit based on the type of software product created and the design used [CON90]. Many users of object-oriented technology are still looking for real benefits from using the products and techniques, and while some isolated examples have been described, many of these provide no hard data on the actual amount of code that was reused or the benefit in reduced time or costs in maintenance.

Figures 8.5 and 8.6 describe some potential benefits and drawbacks to using object-oriented techniques.

8.8 The Simple Simon ATM Example

Before reviewing our example using the Booch object-oriented technique, we need to discuss some preliminary items. First, as we have already seen, the Booch technique is iterative, and benefits from a prototype-oriented development approach so that the object model can be refined until it supports the functionality of the system. Booch calls this "Gestalt round-trip design" and this is common to other object-oriented techniques, including Synthesis and Shlaer/Mellor's recursive design. One problem with these approaches is knowing when to stop doing the design, and there are few practical suggestions offered that address this issue.

In creating the SSATM, we found prototyping the user interface under a GUI (in this case, Microsoft's Windows 3.0) to be very helpful. As Booch suggests, prototyping can help to clarify, and address earlier, questions about how the finished product will look and act, and this leads to further questions about the functionality of the product (see also Chapter 9, "Prototype-Oriented Techniques").

One inherent drawback to using the Booch technique is that it begins after requirements for a system have been clearly defined. As we have already seen, Booch recommends using domain analysis or some form of object-oriented analysis (such as Shlaer/Mellor or Coad/Yourdon) as a prerequisite to his OOD technique.

Less arbitrary partitioning, since the consistency and coupling between
the data, behavior, and process models limit the number of decompositions.

Stability of the specification, since even if requirements change
(as they always do), the impact of these changes is minimized because
of the nature of the models.

Applicability of OOA to different life cycle models because of the stability
of the models described above.

Direct mapping to OOD, since the object classes defined in OOA can
provide a first approximation of the objects of the OOD phase and
a suitable architecture.

Applicability to non-object-oriented design and programming, since
the results of OOA can be translated easily into standard,
hierarchical structured design, temporally partitioned or other
design approaches.

Simplified expression of concurrency is provided, since each object
operates asynchronously in the system and can communicate only
with well-defined events and data flows. This can lead to a very
simple expression of concurrency in the specification.

Improved implementation because of encapsulating pieces of the
program into components that can be implemented without considering
the interactions with the rest of the system.

Improved testing because classes can be isolated and tested once and
because an error can be easily traced to a specific class.

A rigorous specification of the interfaces between classes allows testers
to more easily spot discrepancies between the output of one component
and the input required to another.

Easier maintenance, since encapsulation and information hiding rigidly
constrain the patters of communication within the application so that they
can be more easily understood (it is easier to find a problem and limit the
impact on other components).

Easier refinement and enhancement because new components can
be added with the same interfaces which can perform different functions
- thus functionality can be enhanced at a lower cost.

Figure 8.5
Potential
benefits of
using object-
oriented
techniques.

Without some formal definition of requirements, the Booch technique (or any other design technique, for that matter) cannot fully support the development process.

The approach we chose to take was to use an informal English description of the SSATM system and then examine the resulting text for candidate objects, classes, attributes, and operations. In this approach, the text is scanned and all nouns are highlighted (or underlined), and these become possible objects, classes, or attributes. This is followed by another scan that identifies all verbs and noun sets (of the form noun verb noun), and these are used as a first cut for operations by objects.

It is not always easy to see what happens when the system is presented with an external event, and this tends to make debugging and testing object-oriented software more difficult.

Skepticism can arise when the models are introduced and it isn't intuitively obvious that the method will work.

Moving to OO techniques can be difficult, since the technology may be the limiting factor.

Existing tools and techniques may not address all of the needs of developers, specific weaknesses include incomplete compiler support across platforms, lack of measurements related to objects, and lack of support for multiple inheritance in all OOPLs.

Existing class libraries must be expanded to cover more specialized objects before the promise of reuse can be fully realized.

Figure 8.6
Potential drawbacks to using object-oriented techniques.

The Simple Simon ATM example has a fairly complete, detailed description (see Chapter 3) which was used to extract candidate objects. An initial examination of the text identified about thirty candidate objects (nouns), along with an equivalent number of operations (verbs), shown in Figure 8.7. From the initial list of candidate objects, a smaller list was created that eliminated synonyms and attributes. This list produced some interesting discussions that resulted in the finished group of objects and classes shown in Figure 8.8. In addition, we created a data model to further facilitate discussion of the objects and attributes in the example.

When investigating the SSATM example, we came up with some interesting questions. First, what are the major classes and objects in the problem space? For example, are ATM users objects or classes within the system? Which aspects of the SSATM system are outside the system and which are inside? If, for example, the hardware interface (keyboard, CRT, slots, etc.) is external to the SSATM, the modeling and design process gets much more interesting than if we include these elements within the SSATM system. We chose to make the hardware components external to the SSATM system because we felt it led us to better insight into how the objects interact.

When considering possible classes for the SSATM, there appeared to be some intuitive classes of objects (for example, transactions: deposit, withdrawal and balance inquiry) and some subjective groupings of similar but subtly different objects (card slot, deposit slot, withdrawal chute, and receipt tape). Deciding which classes would be defined and which attributes and methods would be inherited was a difficult process and required an iterative approach. One is never really sure if the correct objects and classes were chosen until one tries to reuse them on subsequent projects.

Example Booch diagrams created for the SSATM include the process diagram (Figure 8.9), the class diagram for the SSATM system (Figure 8.10), the object diagram for the user interface (Figure 8.11), and the module diagram (Figure 8.12).

Simple Simon ATM system
Bank customers
Checking account
Savings account
(Plastic) Card
Transaction
Deposits
Withdrawals
Balance inquiries
Personal Account Number (PAN)
Customer account file: name and account information
Personal Identification Number (PIN)
Current date
Number of ATM sessions
Beginning balance (unposted balance, customer balance, account balance)
Local ATM file
Unposted transactions
Sensor
Transaction receipt (tape)
Terminal Control file
Deposit Envelope slot
Transaction amount (deposit amount, unposted amount,
   withdrawal amount)
Deposits per month
Withdrawal chute
Terminal Status File
Card slot
Money (cash)
Withdrawals per month
Master ATM system

Figure 8.7
Initial candidate
objects/classes
in the SSATM.

By far the most expressive diagram in the Booch technique is the object diagram, which specifies the objects in a system and the interaction between objects via messages. The SSATM example resulted in several different objects, some of which were decomposed from higher level objects. In addition, state-transition diagrams could be created for objects and classes in the system, and timing diagrams could be used as well. We chose not to exhibit these here because they are covered in more depth in Chapter 7.

Another consideration when using the Booch technique is which programming language will be used to implement the solution and what existing class libraries will be available for reuse. For example, if we choose to develop the system in Turbo Pascal for Windows, we will have available the entire ObjectWindows library of

Objects	Attributes	Operations
Checking account	Account number, Name, PIN,	Open account
Savings account	Balance, Open	Close account
		Check balance
		Make deposit
		Withdraw funds
?Card	Name, PIN	Activate card
		Deactivate card
?Transaction	Amount, Date, Type	Apply against account
Deposit slot	Status	Open & Close
Withdrawal chute		Open, Dispense, & Close
Card slot		Accept & Eject
Receipt tape		Print receipt
Local ATM file	Collection of transactions	
Master ATM file	Amount, Date, Type	Apply transactions
Terminal Controller	Terminal ID, Status of [deposit slot, withdrawal chute, receipt tape, card slot], cash available	Get TCF info
		Update TCF info
		Get cash available
		Update cash available
		Get status
User Interface	Buffer, Status	Accept card
		Eject card
		Display screen
		Accept PIN
		Accept tran. type
		Accept amount
		Open/Close slot
		Dispense cash
		Update cash available

? = Not represented as objects or classes in the object model (may be outside the problem domain, etc.).

Figure 8.8
Final objects, classes, and attributes in the SSATM.

objects to reuse. Likewise, choosing a character-based operating environment over a windowed environment would lead to a different design and implementation. We chose to implement the SSATM system under Windows, and Figure 8.13 shows one possible set of Windows objects that could be used for the SSATM example and serves as a prototype of the SSATM system.

Another potential concern in using the Booch technique is the apparent lack of design notation (diagrams) for component and architectural specification beyond the module diagrams, which are very much oriented towards Ada. While the module diagrams can be used for languages other than Ada, they seem to provide little benefit except when used with the Ada language. As is evidenced by the module diagram in Figure 8.12, the design notation provides little in the way of practical design specification details other than subsystem hierarchy and must be supplemented with PDL or actual programming language statements.

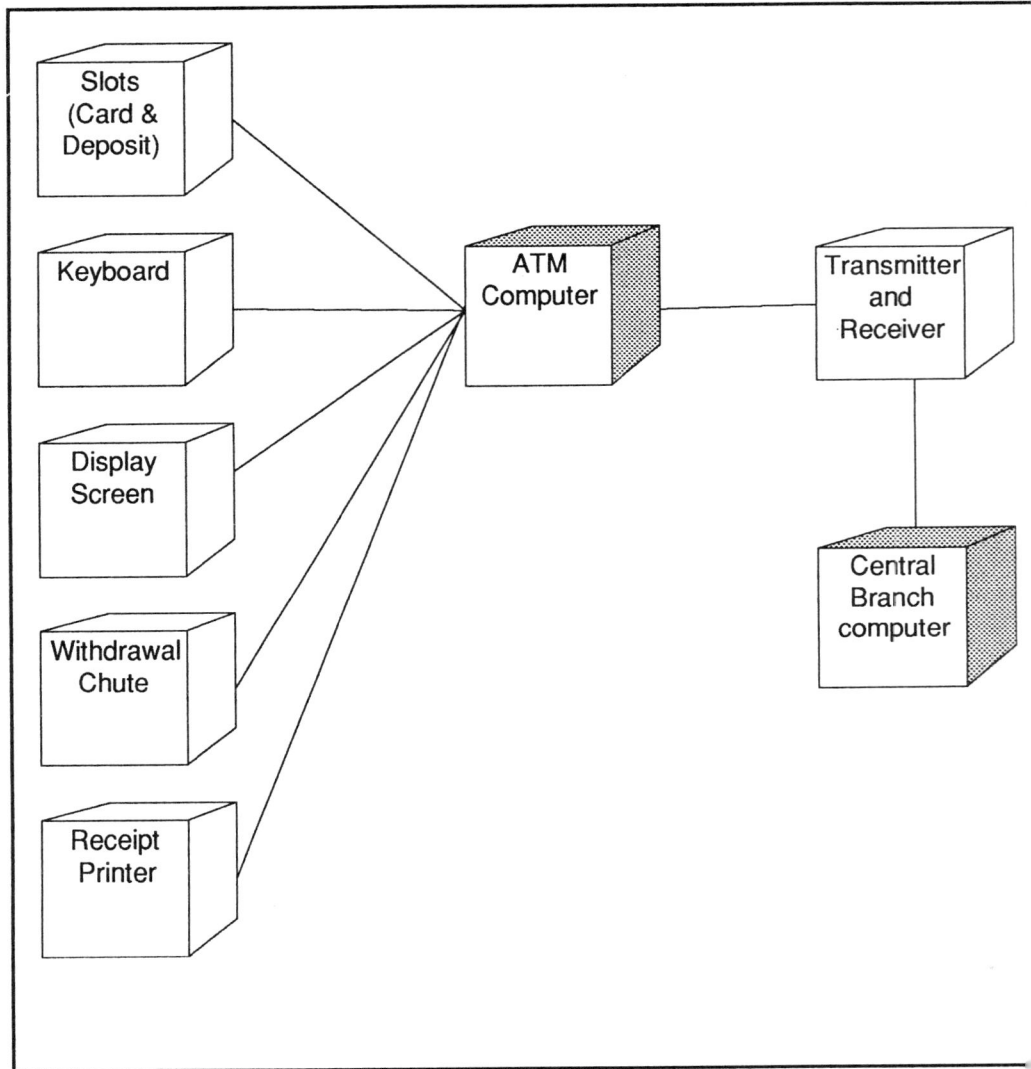

Figure 8.9
SSATM process
diagram.

8.9 Resource List

Recently, several technical journals have covered aspects of object-oriented development. The September 1990 issue of the *Communications of the ACM (CACM)* is an excellent overview of major OOD techniques and the object-oriented community in general. Within this issue, [KOR90], [GIB90], and [HEN90] are three excellent treatments of issues for OOD, class design, and an object-oriented life cycle.

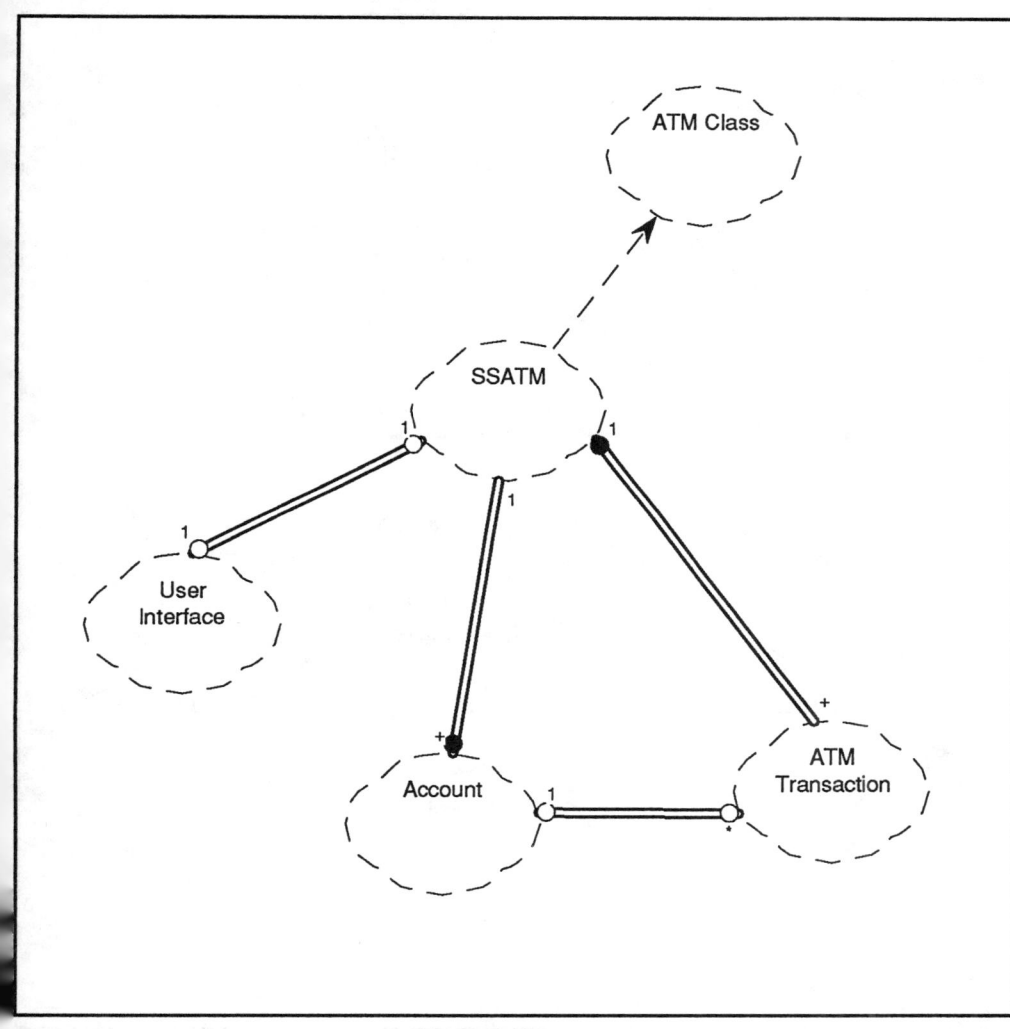

Figure 8.10
SSATM class
diagram.

The September 1992 issue of *CACM* also includes several good references for OOA/D methods, including the article by Monarchi [MON92], which provides a comparison of popular methods. The October 1992 issue of *IEEE Computer* is on object-oriented computing and has several good articles on various topics. The January 1993 issue of *IEEE Software* is also dedicated to object-oriented development and has some very good papers in it.

An excellent reference for class and object design is the Booch book [BOO91], which along with previous Booch books [BOO83] and papers [BOO89] serves as a good introduction to OOD concepts. Other OOD techniques are covered in [BUH86], [COA91], [MEY88], [MEY92], [NER92], [RUB92], and [WIR90].

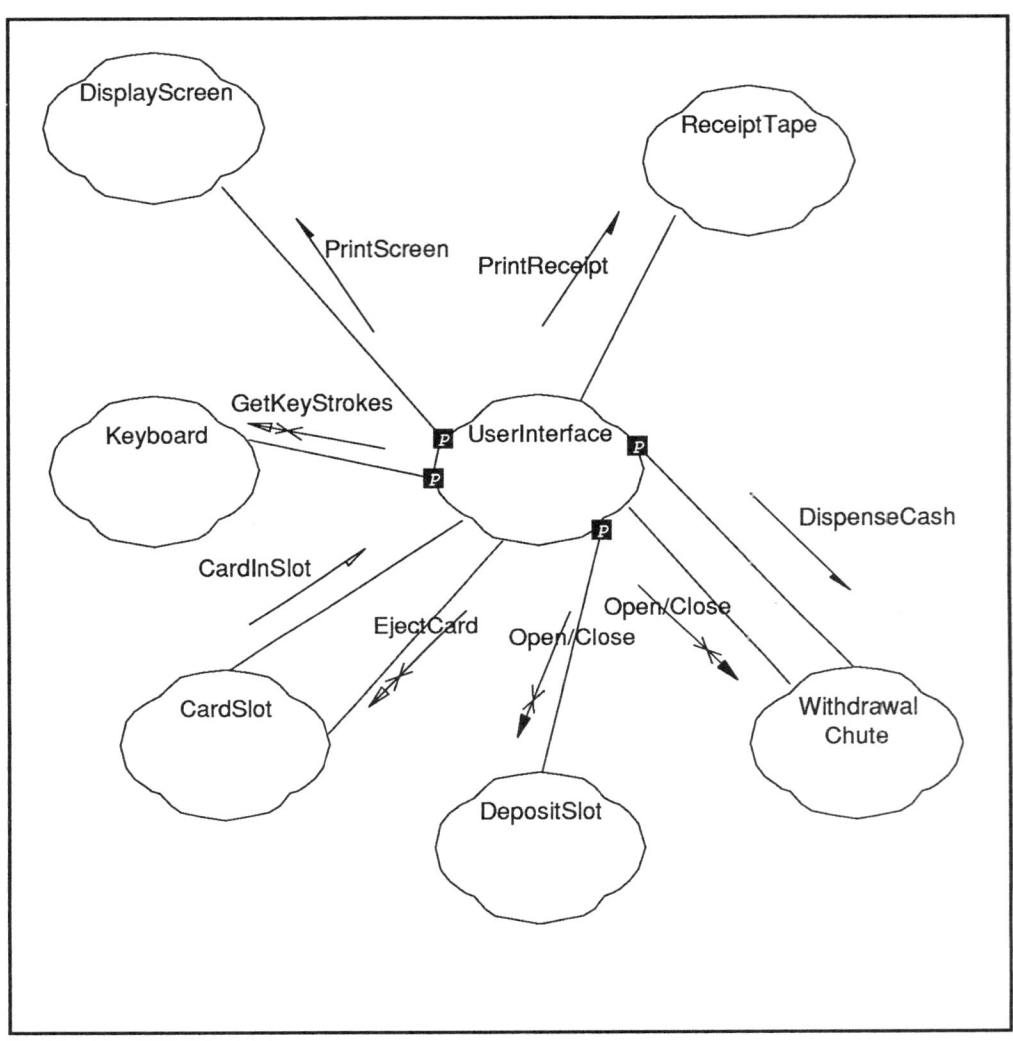

Figure 8.11
SSATM user
interface object
diagram.

The Shlaer/Mellor books [SHL88][SHL92] deal exclusively with OOA and offer very little in the area of OOD. Coad/Yourdon [COA90], and Rumbaugh et al. [RUM91] also deal with OOA and only slightly with OOD concerns. Bailin [BAI88] and Gibson [GIB90] both deal with defining requirements for OOA toward an Ada perspective.

For discussions on combining object-oriented techniques with structured techniques, see papers by Wasserman [WAS89], Ward [WAR89], Page-Jones/Weiss [PAG89], Constantine [CON89] [CON90], and Tockey et al. [TOC90]. Works covering data modeling include [ROS88] and [DAT86], domain analysis [ISC88] and specification using informal English text can be found in [ABB83] and [FRE90].

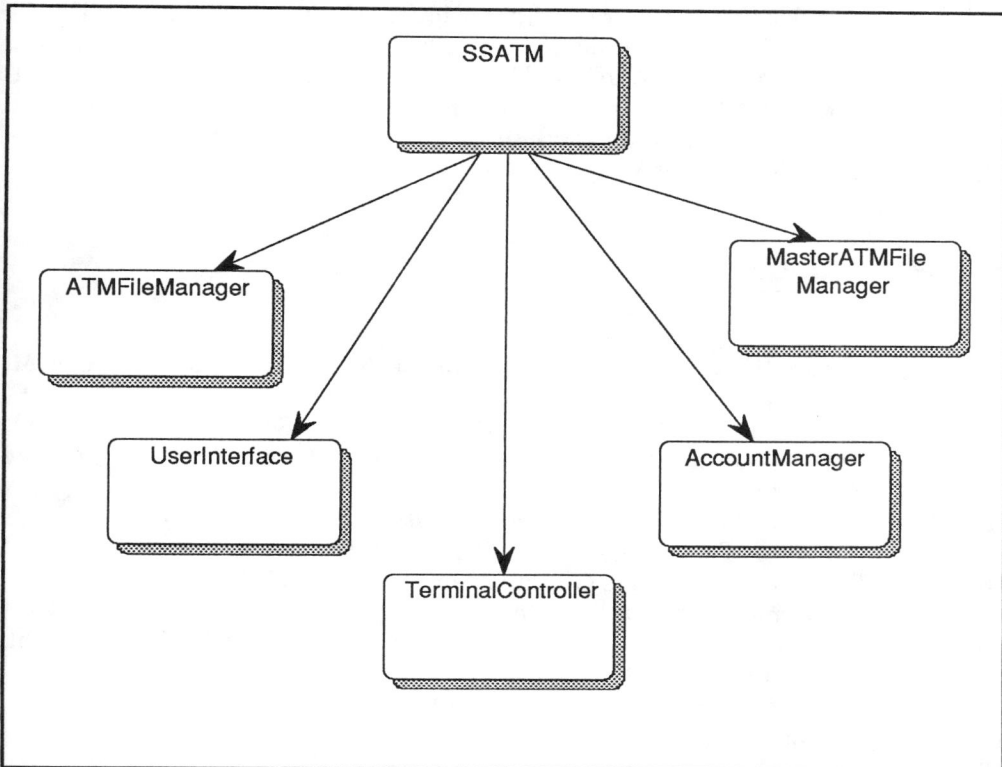

Figure 8.12
SSATM module
diagram.

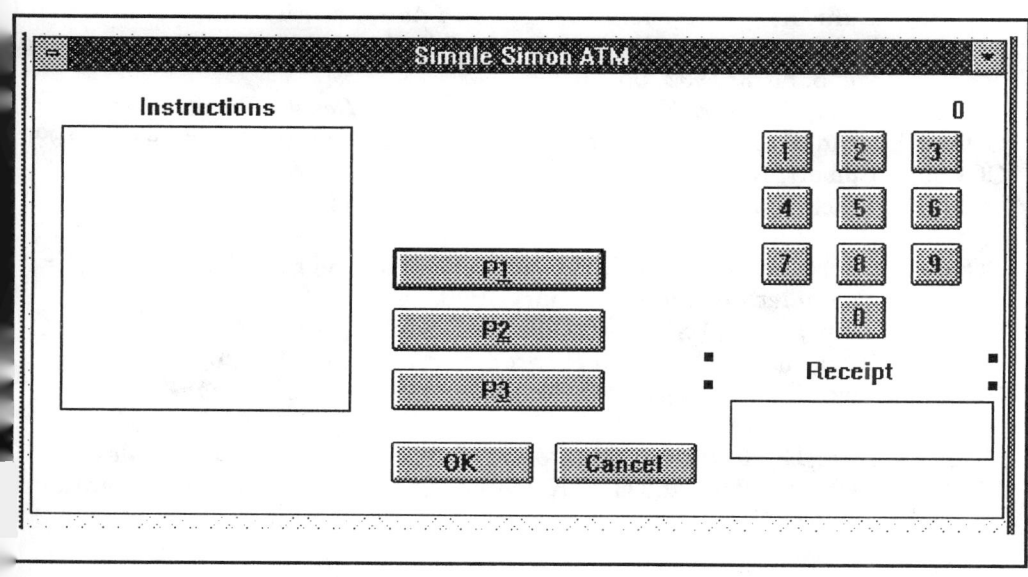

Figure 8.13
Windows GUI
SSATM objects.

Excellent sources on object-oriented programming include the Meyers [MEY91], Stroustrup [STR86] and Cox books [COX86]. For an overview of object-oriented technology, see [KIM89] and [WIN90]. For more information on embedded and real-time object-oriented software, see [BAR91]. For experiences with object-oriented development, see [LEV91] and [WYB90]. Also, see [TOC89] and [TOP92] for a discussion on CASE requirements in support of object-oriented techniques.

8.10 References

[ABB83]   Abbott, R., "Program Design by Informal English Descriptions," *CACM*, vol. 26, no. 11, November 1983, pp. 882-894.

[AND89]   Anderson, J., J. McDonald, L. Holland, and E. Scranage, "Automated Object-Oriented Requirements Analysis and Design," *Proceedings of the Sixth Washington Ada Symposium*, June 26-29, 1989, pp. 265-272.

[BAI88]   Bailin, S., "Remarks on Object-Oriented Requirements Specification," Computer Technology Associates, Inc., 1988.

[BAR91]   Barry, B., "Real-Time Object-Oriented Programming Systems," *American Programmer*, October, 1991, pp. 11 - 20.

[BAS91]   Bassett, P., "Frame-Based Software Engineering," *IEEE Software*, vol. 4, no. 4 (July 1987), pp. 9-16.

[BOO91]   Booch, G., *Object-Oriented Design with Applications*, Benjamin/ Cummings, 1991.

[BOO89]   Booch, G., "Object-oriented development," *IEEE Trans. on Soft. Eng.*, SE-12(12) pp. 211-221, 1986.

[BOO83]   Booch, G., *Software Engineering with Ada*, Benjamin/Cummings,1983.

[BUH86]   Buhr, R. J. A., *Systems Design with Ada*, Prentice-Hall, 1986.

[BUL92]   Bulman, D., "An Objective Survey," *Embedded Systems Programming*, vol. 5, no. 3, 1992, pp. 20-31.

[COA91]   Coad, P. and E. Yourdon, *Object-Oriented Design*, Prentice Hall,1991.

[COA90]   Coad, P. and E. Yourdon, *Object-Oriented Analysis*, Prentice Hall,1990.

[COL89]   Colbert, E., "The Object-Oriented Software Development Method: A Practical Approach to Object-Oriented Development," Absolute Software Co., Inc., 1989.

[CON90]   Constantine, L., "Objects, Functions, and Program Extensibility," *Computer Language*, January 1990, pp. 34 - 56.

[CON89]   Constantine, L., "Object-Oriented and Structured Methods: Toward Integration," *American Programmer*, Summer 1989, pp. 34 - 41.

[COX86]   Cox, B., *Object-Oriented Programming - An Evolutionary Approach*, Addison-Wesley, 1986.

[DAT86]   Date, C., *An Introduction to Database Systems*, Addison-Wesley, 1986.

[FIC92]   Fichman, R. G. and C. F. Kemerer, "Object-Oriented and Conventional Analysis and Design Methodologies," *IEEE Computer*, October 1992, pp. 22-39.

[FRE90]   Freitas, M., A. Moreira, and P. Guerreiro, "Object Oriented
           Requirements Analysis in an Ada Project," *Ada Letters*, vol. X,
           no. 6, July/Aug. 1990, pp. 97-109.

[GIB90]   Gibson, E., "Objects - Born and Bred," *Byte*, October 1990, pp. 245-254.

[HEN90]   Henderson-Sellers, B., and J. M. Edwards, "The Object-Oriented
           Systems Life Cycle," *CACM*, vol. 33, no. 9, pp. 142-159.

[ISC88]   Iscoe, N., *Domain Models for Program Specification and Generation*,
           University of Texas, Austin, Texas, 1988.

[KIM89]   Kim, W., and F. Lochovsky, *Object-Oriented Concepts, Databases,and
           Applications*, ACM Press/Addison-Wesley, 1989.

[KOR90]   Korson, T., and J. D. McGregor, "Understanding Object-Oriented:
           A Unifying Paradigm, " *CACM*, vol. 33, no. 9, pp. 40-60.

[KUR91]   Kurt, B., S. Woodfield, and D. Embley, *Object-Oriented Systems
           Analysis and Specification: A Model Driven Approach*, Prentice-Hall,
           1991.

[LEV91]   Levin, M., "OOA - Ways and Means," *Structured Development Forum
           12*, August, 1991, Portland, Oregon.

[MAS88]   Masiero, P., and F. Germano, "JSD as an Object-Oriented Design
           Method," *Software Engineering Notes*, vol. 13, no. 3, July 1988,
           pp. 22-23.

[MEY92]   Meyer, B., "Applying 'Design by Contract'," *IEEE Computer*, October
           1992, pp. 40-52.

[MEY91]   Meyer, B., *Eiffel: The Language*, Prentice-Hall, 1991.

[MEY89]   Meyer, B., "Eiffel: An Introduction," TR-EI-3/GI, Version 2.2,
           Interactive Software Engineering, Inc., 1989.

[MEY88]   Meyer, B., *Object-Oriented Software Construction*, Prentice-Hall, 1988.

[MON92]   Monarchi, D. E., and G. I. Puhr, "A Research Typology for Object-
           Oriented Analysis and Design," *CACM*, vol. 35, no. 9, pp. 35-47.

[NEL92]   Nelson, J., "Applying Object-Oriented Analysis and Design," *CACM*,
           vol. 35, no. 9, pp. 63-74.

[NER92]   Nerson, J., "Applying Object-Oriented Analysis and Design," *CACM*,
           vol. 35, no. 9, pp. 63-74.

[PAG92]   Page-Jones, M., "Comparing Techniques by Means of Encapsulation and
           Connascence," *CACM*, vol. 35, no. 9, pp. 147-151.

[PAG89]   Page-Jones, M., and S. Weiss, "Synthesis: An Object-Oriented Analysis
           and Design Method," *American Programmer*, Summer, 1989, pp. 64 - 67.

[RIN92]   Rine, D. D., and B. Bhargava, "Object-Oriented Computing," *IEEE
           Computer*, October 1992, pp. 6-10.

[ROS88]   Ross, R., *Entity Modeling: Techniques and Application*, Data Research
           Group, 1988.

[RUB92]   Rubin, K. S., and A. Goldberg, "Object Behavior Analysis," *CACM*, vol.
           35, no. 9, pp. 48-62.

[RUM91]   Rumbaugh, J., M. Blaha, W. Premerlani, F. Eddy, and W. Lorensen,
           Object-Oriented Modeling and Design, Prentice-Hall, 1991.

[SCH92]   Schaschinger, H., "ESA - An Expert Supported OOA Method and Tool," *ACM SIGSOFT*, vol. 17, no. 2, pp. 50-56.

[SEI88]   Seidewitz, E., "General Object-Oriented Software Development: Background and Experience", Goddard Space Flight Center, January 1988.

[SHL92]   Shlaer, S., and S. Mellor, *Object Life Cycles: Modeling the World in States*, Prentice-Hall, 1992.

[SHL88]   Shlaer, S., and S. Mellor, *Object-Oriented Systems Analysis: Modeling the World in Data*, Prentice-Hall, 1988.

[SON92]   Song, X., and L. J. Osterweil, "Toward Objective, Systematic Design-Method Comparisons," *IEEE Software*, May 1992, pp. 43-53.

[STR86]   Stroustrup, B., *The C++ Programming Language*, Addison-Wesley, 1986.

[TOC90]   Tockey, S., B. Hoza, and S. Cohen, "Object Oriented Analysis: Building on the Structured Techniques," Boeing Computer Services, Seattle, WA.

[TOC89]   Tockey, S., "Using Off-the-Shelf CASE Tools to Build Object-Oriented Analysis Specifications," Boeing Computer Services, Seattle, Washington.

[TOP92]   Topper, A., "Building a CASE for Object-Oriented Development," *American Programmer*, October 1992, pp. 36-47.

[WAR89]   Ward, P., "How to Integrate Object-Orientation with Structured Analysis and Design," *IEEE Software*, vol. 6, no. 2, pp. 74-82, March 1989.

[WAS89]   Wasserman, A. I., P. A. Pircher, and R. J. Muller, "Concepts of Object-Oriented Structured Design," Interactive Development Environments, 1989.

[WEG92]   Wegner, P., "Dimensions of Object-Oriented Modeling," *IEEE Computer*, October 1992, pp. 12-20.

[WEG90]   Wegner, P., "Concepts and Paradigms of Object-Oriented Programming," Expansion of October 4 OOPSLA-89 Keynote Address, *OOPS Messenger*, vol. 1, pp. 7-87, August 1990.

[WIN90]   Winblad, A., S. Edwards, and D. King, *Object-Oriented Software*, Addison-Wesley, 1990.

[WIR90]   Wirfs-Brock, R., Wilkerson, B. and Wiener, L., *Designing Object-Oriented Software*, Prentice-Hall, 1990.

[WYB91]   Wybolt, N., "Experiences with C++ and Object-Oriented Software Development," *ACM SIGSOFT*, vol. 15, no. 2, April 1990, pp. 31-39.

Can Information Engineering be Object-Oriented?

With the hype concerning object-oriented technology, many vendors and methodologists are clamoring to jump on the object-oriented bandwagon. Companies are quickly changing their marketing and sales literature to incorporate "object-oriented" into their products and services. The bandwagon effect has been used extensively in the past in the software industry to prop up sales of products or services that have reached their peak and are sliding backward.

Such is the case with the recent touting of Information Engineering (IE), an information-oriented technique, as being included with the object-oriented methods and techniques discussed in Chapter 8. James Martin, a chief architect of IE, has recently written a book (with James Odell) on combining object-oriented concepts with IE. Given Martin's previous success with published works, this book will eventually sell many copies and become very popular.

It is the opinion of the authors that this discussion of whether or how IE could be object-oriented is little more than the bandwagon effect waged wholeheartedly by the IE vendors and service providers. IE and object-oriented techniques are diametrically different. One only needs to trace back to the roots of IE and object-oriented techniques, and study the philosophy of each approach along with the notations used, for the differences to become very clear.

History

"Information Engineering was developed because it is necessary to apply top-down planning, data modeling and process modeling to an enterprise as a whole. IE applies structured techniques to the enterprise as a whole, or to a major segment of the enterprise.

IE helps to integrate the separate data processing and decision-support systems built by different teams at different times in different places. It focuses on the top-management goals and critical success factors of the enterprise."

James Martin, *Information Engineering*, Books I, II, and III, Prentice-Hall, 1990 .

IE evolved from the enterprise-level data-oriented techniques described in Chapter 5 and was created to bridge the gap between the technical development of information systems (IS) and the strategic goals and objectives of the organization IS serves. To this end, the architects of IE focused on the creation of an information architecture for an organization and the separation of business areas for analysis and design of software systems.

IE methods were developed with an orientation towards data structures — not the localized data structures typically used in object-oriented development — but corporate or enterprise-wide databases. These databases are typically integrated, and the processing defined for these databases is oriented towards transactions that modify the value of the data. IE is often beneficial to large organizations that must share data in an integrated DBMS.

Object-oriented techniques also evolved from data-oriented methods but took a significantly different route in their evolution. While some object-oriented techniques incorporate data modeling as a first step to identifying potential objects and classes, the history of object-oriented technology actually began with a focus on programming with objects. These objects encapsulated local data structures and the functions performed on those structures.

OOPLs provide constructs for creating and using objects that support the inheritance of attributes and methods down a library of classes of objects. Methods deliver the services within the object and are not visible to outside objects. Messages serve as actions to stimulate other objects. Object-oriented techniques followed from the evolution of OOPLs and model and specify the classes and objects used in an OOPL.

Philosophy

The basic philosophies behind IE and object-oriented methods further indicate the differences between the two approaches. Object-oriented methods were created to help developers model and create applications with localized data, while IE methods were created to help organizations model and build integrated systems with shared data across the enterprise.

Key to the concept of any object-oriented method is the localization of data within the objects and the exclusion of any modification of these data structures by outside sources. Object-oriented methods for analysis and design were developed to address issues in designing software based on components, with information hiding as the overriding concern, and modeling the abstractions in the problem space using objects that are easily understood by the users. This has led to the view that object-oriented development is the composition of software systems from logical objects already observable within the business.

IE, on the other hand, was developed with the intent of satisfying the need large organization have to share data structures across their areas of business. IE seeks to define an overall information architecture upon which software products can be built that share common data structures.

This point is the primary focus of all IE methods and is critical to the success of IE in an organization. IE methods are based on decomposition of high-level models (enterprise models) into business area (problem domains) models, which are further decomposed into applications in design and construction.

IE has as its goal the development of strategic information systems. Object-oriented techniques take a completely different approach, focusing on the development of tactical software systems. Also key to the concepts within IE are the notions of normalized data models and a RDBMS. Object-oriented techniques, on the other hand, seek to define applications that might have complex data structures and might use OODBMSs for permanent storage of these objects.

"One side effect of functional decomposition is that all interesting data end up being global to the entire system, so that any change in representation tends to affect all subordinate modules. Alternately, in the object-oriented approach, the effect of changing the representation of an object tends to be much more localized."

From "On the Concepts of Object-Oriented Design," by Grady Booch.

Another major philosophical difference between IE and object-oriented techniques is in their focus on analyzing and designing software products. IE incorporates top-down functional decomposition techniques for modeling and design and focuses on the generation of code from procedure-oriented representations of modules and programs (action diagrams). IE methods were developed to support mainframe-based batch and on-line systems in COBOL. Object-oriented techniques, on the other hand, use object decomposition in analysis and object composition in design. Object-oriented design incorporates existing classes of objects into any solution, while IE focuses on the generation of source code directly from specifications. In programming, object-oriented development maps to abstract data types and class-based constructs supported by a variety of languages, including Smalltalk, C++, and Eiffel.

IE was developed with the intent of using code generation in the construction phase of software development, while the object-oriented techniques were developed to assemble software systems from existing libraries of objects and classes.

Notation

"An object model has four major elements: abstraction, encapsulation, modularity and hierarchy. Three minor elements of the object model: typing, concurrency, and persistence."

From "What Is and What Isn't Object-Oriented Design," Grady Booch, *American Programmer*, vol. 2, Nos.7-8, Summer 1989.

Object models, the outcome of object-oriented analysis, model the key classes and objects in the problem domain, the relationships between the objects and classes, and their attributes and operations. Some object model notations use extensions to entity-relationship diagrams (ERDs), a standard data modeling notation. Some often include a functional and dynamic views of objects and classes, but the basis for these methods is always the object view.

Data models are also used in IE to define the data structures and their relationships, while process models describe the functions that are performed on the data. In this sense, data models are similar to object models, and several IE experts have pointed to these similarities in describing IE as object-oriented. But most other techniques, including function- and control-oriented methods, also incorporate data models, and so any argument for IE being object-oriented based solely on the use of data models is equally viable for these techniques as well.

Some in the industry have attempted to imply that objects are really only entities and that data models can adequately model the relationships in an object model. But this is simply not true, since the types of relationships object models describe are different from those described by data models. For example, data models describe binary relationships between entities, while object models may contain several different types of relationships, including kind of, type of, uses, inherits, etc.

Function models are a primary focus of IE, and the notation used in analysis and design is the decomposition diagram. Functional decomposition is the technique used in IE, and the notation directly supports this approach. IE analysis (called Business Area Analysis) looks at decomposing functions into processes in a top-down fashion. In design, IE methods map the processes to modules, which are grouped into programs based on the functions required. IE methods do not support dynamic system behavior.

While the notations often used in object-oriented design vary from method to method, most of these techniques incorporate an internal class or object view (sometimes called object structure), an external class or object view, and some form of object interaction notation. Most object-oriented design methods incorporate dynamic models of classes and objects to describe the time-dependent behavior of the objects and classes. Finite state machines are often used to represent this dynamic behavior.

The primary design notation used in IE is the action diagram, which maps directly to third- and fourth-generation language procedural programming constructs. The action diagram is a procedural notation for describing the flow of control in a program or module along with the logic performed. Action diagrams can refer to data structures and database tables, but the focus within all IE methods is on the actions performed (thus the name) and not on the data structures used. Also, in object-oriented design notations, data structures are internal and apply only to the object itself, whereas in the action diagram, data structures are external and can apply to any number of diagrams.

Reuse: The Basis for Object-Oriented Development

"The structured paradigm focuses on algorithmic decomposition of an application, with emphasis on the transformation of data. Although the paradigm supports the concepts of abstraction and algorithmic hierarchy, no support exists for the notation of multiple hierarchies of abstractions. This lack of support for multiple forms of hierarchy limits the extent to which the structured paradigm can support large scale reuse."

From "The Object Paradigm Requires Object-Oriented Methods and Tools," Jon Williams, *Object Magazine*, November/December 1991, pp.51-58.

One area where object-oriented techniques and IE have possible similarities is in supporting the reuse of software components. But prior to discussing how each approach can facilitate this process, we need to examine where opportunities for reuse exist in the software development process. Reuse can occur at different levels of scale within the development process, including:

Code-level: The reuse of existing executable code or program
  algorithms is fairly common and typically occurs within the
  programming environment.
Specification-level: The reuse of existing design components
  or specifications in building new applications.
Model-level: The reuse of existing models of system components.

While the majority of the reuse that occurs in object-oriented development to date has been at the code-level, there are opportunities for future reuse at the following levels as well:

Class-level: The reuse of whole specialized classes through
  inheritance.
Collection-level: The reuse of collaborating collections of objects.
Frameworks: The reuse of very large class libraries that support
  a specific behavior or functionality.

IE, when supported by an automated tool, can facilitate the reuse of models, specifications, and design constructs. Many development environments can also incorporate reuse, but reuse within IE methods is at the design- or model-level, not at the code-level. Object-oriented techniques, on the other hand, must incorporate and reuse code level objects into any new system. Object-oriented techniques often must incorporate design objects and classes into their specifications, but the actual reuse occurs in the construction phase of the development life cycle. Future object-oriented development will incorporate collections of objects and frameworks that provide selected functionality.

IE, or for that matter any other development technique, could promote the reuse of constructs defined in analysis, design, or construction, and in fact, many organizations have derived benefits from reusing models and specifications. The question that should be asked is: How do the different techniques support the concept of reuse, and at what levels in the development process are components reused?

While IE was developed with the goals of reusing data structures, design constructs, and code, these goals are addressed at the business area or preliminary design-level. The object-oriented techniques also strive to reuse components, but at the code or component level.

There is no doubt that with some effort, lower-level tasks within IE could be modified to support some of the constructs of object-oriented methods, but not without significantly affecting and perhaps nullifying the basic premises and goals of the method.

This brings to mind one final question: Could IE be modified or extended to support object-oriented concepts? The answer to this question is obviously, yes. But one has to wonder under what conditions such a mutated form of IE would be beneficial to organizations, and this begs still another, perhaps more important question: Why would anyone want to make IE object-oriented?

Chapter 9
Prototype-Oriented Techniques

Prior to introducing or manufacturing a new car, auto makers will build a model and eventually a working prototype of the car. Likewise, before a new airplane is ordered by the Air Force, a prototype airplane will be built and tested to ensure that it meets the requirements and can actually fly.

The auto maker and the Air Force can learn a lot from their prototypes and don't mind spending money to develop them. From the prototypes, they can learn how the products will function, what their limitations will be, how much it will cost to produce them, how they will perform under specific circumstances, and whether they can be manufactured in a cost-efficient manner.

Software prototypes can provide similar benefits to software developers. Very simply, a prototype is a working model of something. A prototype provides customers or users and developers with the appearance of a finished system before all the details for it have been defined. It gives users the illusion of a finished product but is missing some (or many) of the attributes of a production system.

There is currently some difference of opinion regarding when a prototype should be created (in analysis for requirements or in design for a specification) and what should happen to the prototype when it is complete. There is almost universal agreement, however, that with the right tools, building a prototype can be accomplished quickly and helps developers and users learn much about a proposed system prior to the creation of the actual system.

Several development techniques that focus on the creation and evolution of prototypes and rapid development have gained widespread use and have generated much interest lately. Some of these techniques develop a simulation of a software system as part of the development process. Examples of these prototype-oriented techniques include Rapid Application Development (RAD), Operational Prototyping, and TimeBox, along with many others. These approaches create a functional prototype of a system early in the development life cycle, and this prototype evolves throughout the life cycle until the finished system becomes operational.

9.1 Introduction

Before discussing prototype-oriented development techniques, we need to define exactly what a prototype or simulation is.

Prototype (noun): An original model on which something is patterned; an individual that exhibits the essential features of a later type; a standard or typical example; a first full-scale and usu. functional form of a new type or design of a construction (as an airplane).

Simulation (noun): The act or process of simulating; a sham object; the imitative representation of the functioning of one system or process by means of functioning of another; examination of a problem often not subject to direct experimentation by means of simulating device.

Simulate (verb t): To assume the outward qualities or appearance of usu. with the intent to deceive; to make a simulation of (as a physical system); syn see ASSUME.

From Webster's New Collegiate Dictionary.

Along with being a working model of a software system, a prototype is also a definition of requirements. But unlike a traditional paper requirements document, it is executable and in the hands of users can provide the developer with valuable feedback concerning the system under consideration. For real-time or embedded systems, a prototype is a simulation of the finished system that mimics the behavior of the actual system. To be effective, a prototype must evolve and change based on new requirements or insights into how the system should respond to external and internal events.

In many cases, a prototype is similar to an operational specification. Both are models of a software product that can be executed to show behavior, and both help users and developers better understand the software and clarify user needs.

Because of the nature of the user-developer loop with regard to an evolving prototype, it is essential in all these techniques that feedback from users focuses on improving the prototype. In this sense, the development process must take on an evolutionary or iterative nature. Life cycles that include support for this evolutionary view are described in Chapter 2.

Since all the techniques in this chapter focus on the creation and evolution of a prototype, it is important that the prototype be created quickly and modified easily. Another premise with all of these techniques is that once the prototype is complete and satisfies all the requirements for the system, it is used to generate the actual production system. Later in the chapter we will look at some constraints and considerations in making this jump from functional prototype to finished system and the role of automated tools in this process.

Before continuing, we should discuss why using a prototype can help developers and users better understand a system prior to creating the source and executable code on the target environment.

9.2 Philosophy

As Bernard Boar so appropriately said [BOA84]:

"If a picture is worth a thousand words, an animated model [prototype] is worth a thousand pictures."

Problems with traditional requirements specification techniques often cause errors or bugs in the finished system after it is delivered. In many cases, the cause of these errors can be directly related to errors in the specification of requirements for the system. Prototypes can provide a more visceral form of requirements specification to users than traditional, paper-based models and specifications created with structured techniques.

A communication gap between the system developer and the user can often prevent both groups from fully understanding the requirements and behavior of the system before it is delivered. This gap may be generally caused by a number of factors, including failure of communication between users and developers, different ideas about roles in the development process, lack of technical understanding of specification and modeling tools on the part of users, and failure by both parties to fully describe and document the details of complex system behavior.

Under the right conditions, this gap in understanding can be eliminated or reduced by developing a prototype of the proposed system. With a prototype, the user can exercise the system just as though it were already operating in his or her own environment, and thereby provide vital feedback to the developer on the suitability of the specification. Also, a prototype is a model of a system represented in a form already familiar to users.

Some developers are reluctant to allow changes to paper specifications and put off making these changes until the finished system is delivered. This can add to the level of dissatisfaction for users. Prototypes, unlike traditional paper-based models, are easier to modify and enhance, and this encourages changes in the requirements and specifications throughout the development process.

A prototype can also help to clarify the impact of design decisions prior to generating a large amount of rework. In addition, a prototype can be easily understood by users and developers alike, can describe in detail the functionality of a system, and can encourage refinement of functionality down to a very low level earlier in the development process.

Software specifications can often be ambiguous, incomplete and inconsistent, and a prototype can help identify these limitations prior to proceeding into programming and testing. Also, prototypes can help users determine if the information they require is provided by a system, if that information has value, and which components of the system will be more difficult to use or confusing for them. For developers, a prototype gives them insight into how the system should be designed and structured.

Traditional software specifications often fail to exhibit the operational characteristics of a finished system. Research indicates that the reasons for this failure are typically behavioral as well as technological [BOE84]. Users often have a preconceived notion of what they want and assume that developers innately understand this. Unfortunately, users are often unable to adequately specify in a clear manner exactly what they want. The paper models serve to limit the communication between developers and users and can become a major problem in software specification.

Likewise, developers often speak a different language from users, talking about models, flow of control, and specifications. Even when users think they understand the terminology, they often fail to provide enough detail about the behavior of the system to adequately define the system.

Studies with prototyping techniques have found that for users, exercising a prototype was easier than using paper models, and systems created from a prototype were more likely to meet user requirements [GOM81]. Feedback from building the prototype has also proved to be extremely valuable in developing the finished system.

Studies have also shown that prototyping tends to produce a smaller software product with roughly the same functionality, requiring less effort. Prototyping can produce higher productivity as measured by user satisfaction per person-hour and also an improved human-machine interface, delivering something that works, and a reduced deadline effect at the end of the project.

Experimental results suggest that prototyping increases the actual utilization of an information system by the users. Furthermore, user satisfaction with the information systems delivered is higher for prototyped systems than for systems developed using traditional techniques [ALA91]. Field and laboratory observations suggest that prototyping makes communication between users and designers relatively easy and conflict-free. Given the expressive nature of the prototype, it is not hard to understand how it can be effective in bridging the communication gap between developers and users.

Before committing to using a prototype as part of a development process, it is important to decide what the objective of the prototype will be. A basic question that should be answered by both developers and users is, What do we expect to learn from developing a prototype, and how will this help us create better software? There are different types of prototypes and, likewise, many different reasons for building a prototype.

The two basic types of prototype are a *throw-away prototype*, which is used to validate the user requirements by modeling the behavior of the system, and an *evolutionary prototype*, which is repeatedly refined until it becomes the final product. These two types, while similar, have very different purposes. A throw-away prototype is built to help define the requirements for the system prior to a traditional development process, while an evolutionary prototype is part of a traditional development effort and must include practical design considerations. When finished, a throw-away prototype is discarded, while an evolutionary prototype becomes the finished system. The implication in creating an evolutionary prototype is that design decisions must be made with an awareness of a real-world system and all the restraints imposed on the implementation environment.

Davis [DAV92] suggests that these prototypes be used for very different types of problems and help to define different types of requirements. While we don't necessarily agree that throw-away and evolutionary prototypes are orthogonal, we do see benefit from both under the right circumstances. Davis also suggests combining the two types of prototypes into what he calls "operational prototyping," which we discuss further under the topic of operational specifications in this chapter and in Chapter 6.

Prior to building a prototype, the objectives for it should be clearly defined. As Roger Pressman has said [PRE92]:

"The objective of prototyping is to clarify the characteristics and operation of a product or system by constructing a version that can be exercised. A software prototype is an executable object for which the users and developers have different expectations than they have for the corresponding delivered software product."

Different software applications may require different types of prototypes. For example, a traditional MIS application may require a prototype of the screens, menus, and reports. For enhanced functionality, the prototype might also support editing of data values, links between different programs, database lookups, or even report generation. A fully functional prototype for an MIS application could take on all the characteristics of the production system without all the underlying structural attributes.

For software targeted to a graphical user interface (GUI) environment, a prototype might be the objects within the GUI itself. These might include windows, menus, icons, dialog boxes, and other graphical constructs. A prototype in a GUI environment would thus be all the "things" that a user interacts with in the GUI. But the GUI prototype has nothing underneath to support the functionality; it simply models the "look and feel" of the actual system. Studies suggest that a prototype can help better define the human-machine interface for computerized systems.

In an embedded or real-time environment, a prototype might be a simulation of the system [COO90] or an executable specification [HAR88]. These prototypes can be very sophisticated and can provide a wealth of information to developers prior to the creation of any code. A good example of a real-time prototype is a radar jamming system in a helicopter which gives developers information about how the system will function based on a series of events and conditions. This type of prototype could be very helpful in determining if the finished system can respond to and begin jamming a radar signal before the helicopter is shot out of the air by the enemy. Chapter 6 describes in more depth some executable specification tools for real-time systems.

Prototyping uses the power of demonstration to enable the user and developer to literally see their specifications and models in action. One basic goal of prototyping is to put a working model of the system into the hands of the user as quickly as possible. When this is accomplished, users can provide invaluable feedback about the system.

With rapid prototyping techniques, a quick executable specification can be created and can clarify the requirements for the system before a large development effort is undertaken. Rapid prototyping also provides a tool for analyzing the behavior of a system prior to creating the system itself.

Rapid prototyping can be very helpful for systems that have time constraints where critical properties with respect to time must be understood and stated right from the initial phases of development. Prototypes can also verify the technical or functional concepts in a proposed solution without spending the time or resources on building a full-scale system. In those cases where system functionality can be isolated, a reduced-size or reduced-scope prototype can deliver a simplified system to users in a short period of time.

Many powerful executable specification languages exist, including StateMate [HAR88], Requirements Specification Language [DEG90], Communicating Sequential Processes (CSP) [HOA85], Petri nets [JOR88], and operational specification techniques [ZAV82].

Powerful prototyping tools and languages are only part of the prototype solution, or as Bernard Boar said [BOA84], prototyping works best in a quick turnaround environment:

"Application prototyping refers to a strategy for performing requirements determination wherein user needs are extracted, presented, and developed by building a working model of the ultimate system - quickly and in context."

One area that has been largely unresolved is how prototyping can be integrated with reusable components. It is possible to reuse screens, reports, menus, logic, and DBMS I/O logic in multiple prototypes and projects, but how can a prototype incorporate these components? Research indicates that the most difficult part of reusing components is identifying and finding them when they are needed. Some of the object-oriented techniques described in the previous chapter include prototyping (see Chapter 8).

Not all requirements can be specified adequately.
Tools for quick creation of a prototype are readily available.
Inherent gaps in communication exist between developers and users.
Once requirements are known, building a system becomes much easier.
Iteration and evolution are necessary and desirable.

Figure 9.1
Underlying
assumptions of
prototyping
techniques.

9.3 Characteristics

All of the prototype-oriented techniques share common characteristics and attributes. First and foremost, all these techniques focus on building a prototype of a system in the early stages of the development process. The goal of building a prototype is to help developers and users better understand the system. Harel [HAR92] has found that developers using his StateMate product have found conceptual errors in a specification, unknown patterns of behavior, and insight into the problem not often found with other development tools and techniques. All these techniques can be helpful if other specification techniques have failed in the past or if other assumptions are valid for a project. These assumptions are shown in Figure 9.1.

The major difference between prototype-oriented techniques and other techniques is in the focus on creating the prototype. The prototype becomes the specification for the system and replaces or supplements the traditional "paper" models created when using other techniques. In some cases, the models are created in a CASE tool and executed by the tool to perform the prototyping function. Statecharts, for example, created by David Harel, illustrate an executable model for control-oriented or reactive systems [HAR88].

Some organizations have used prototypes in their development life cycles along with traditional techniques and have had much success. Others have used CASE tools to execute their specifications and this has performed a prototype-like function. But prototyping is not simply another tool to be inserted somewhere in the development process. A working prototype must satisfy some need, should have a purpose unto itself, and must be integrated into the development environment with whatever tools and techniques are used.

Paper models do not often adequately explain to users what a software product will be. Even when users think they understand modeling terms, it is often difficult for them to anticipate all the issues that relate to the functional system without some form of working model. In this sense, prototyping techniques help to guarantee better understanding between developers and users throughout the life cycle.

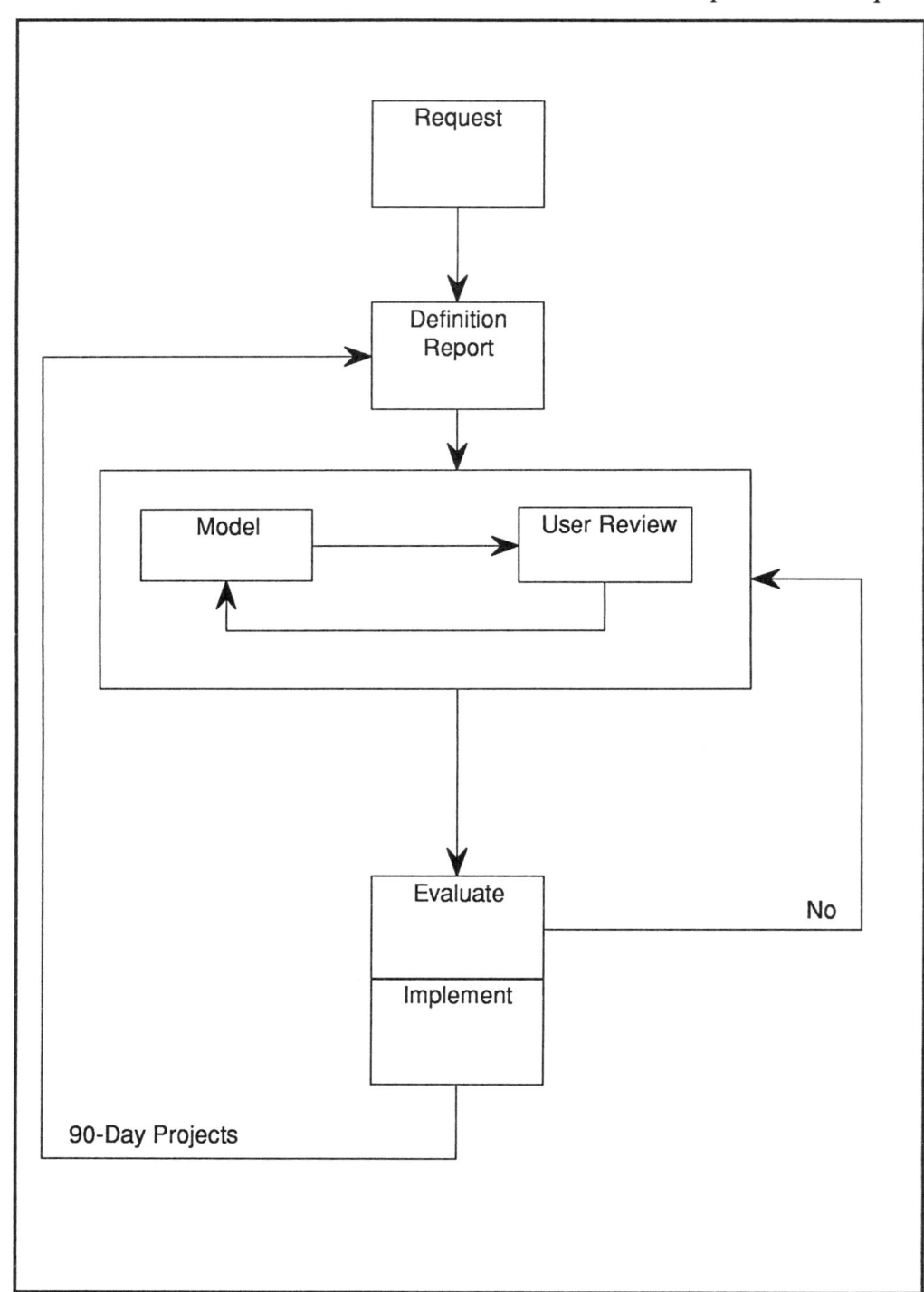

Figure 9.2
Rapid Iterative
Production
Prototyping
(RIPP) life cycle.

Prototype-oriented techniques also require sophisticated tools, in the form of code generators, computer-aided prototyping tools, 4GLs, etc., that allow developers to create working software quickly. Without adequate prototyping tools, rapid development techniques cannot be successful. Many powerful tools are now available from IBM, DEC, HP, Unisys, and Amdahl, along with others.

Rapid Iterative Production Prototyping (RIPP) is a technique developed at the DuPont Textile Fibers Plant. RIPP limits all development projects to 90 days or less, and 60 of those 90 days are spent prototyping. The RIPP life cycle is shown in Figure 9.2.

DuPont found that RIPP helped its developers and users define better requirements for a system and encouraged its developers to change the system in response to user needs. The users were willing to give up full functionality and customized reports in return for a working system delivered much quicker.

Rapid Application Development (RAD) and TimeBox were created by James Martin, architect of the Information Engineering technique described in Chapter 7. RAD and TimeBox combine aspects of joint application design (JAD), CASE, prototyping and design automation tools. By placing a rigid limit on the time allowed for producing a working system, RAD and TimeBox help to eliminate ever-expanding system functionality.

The general rationale for using TimeBox is that it is better to have a working system of limited functionality developed quickly than to wait two years (or more) for a more comprehensive system. By creating the prototype, much experience is gained, and developers have specific, short deadlines for delivering functional software to the user community.

Martin has advocated incorporating prototyping into all software development projects [MAR91]:

"Prototyping ought to be used in the development of all interactive systems without exception. It should be made an integral part of the development life cycle. A software prototype is a simplified version of a system that has most of the functions but not the scale or performance of a production system."

For RAD/TimeBox to be successful, Martin suggests that an executive sponsor must be committed to the effort and must participate in the project initiation. A typical TimeBox team is composed of a user coordinator, lead IS developer, and other developers as needed.

9.3.1 Notation

The working prototype can be viewed as the primary notation and represents a working model of a software product in all of the prototype-oriented techniques. The prototype serves as a simulation of the finished system and as such represents

282

the functionality of the system. Obviously, the prototype can be as expressive as the tool used to create the working model.

Indeed, some executable specifications are based on formal representations that provide support for analysis and inspection of the models. StateMate [HAR88] is a very powerful executable specification for reactive systems that includes three basic views:

Behavioral - Statecharts, which are extended finite state machines
Functional - Activity charts, which are extended data flow diagrams
Structural - Module charts, which are modified structure charts

But a prototype alone may not adequately describe all aspects of a software product and may need to be supplemented with other descriptive components. When specifications are executed, those specifications define the notation for the technique, and the benefits provided are directly related to the limits of the specification tool. In other cases, the prototype may be in the form of a 4GL, and some form of data modeling and database design notation will be used in conjunction with the prototype itself. For example, a system developed in a 4GL will also have database and functional information in a data dictionary or production repository. Together, these components may form the complete system representation.

Documentation will probably need to be added to any prototype to describe it fully, along with other notations commonly used in other development techniques. Along the same lines, when a prototype is created, does the prototype eliminate the need for other representations? If not, then those other representations will still need to be created in support of the prototype. A data model, function model, control model, and procedural design specifications may be created as part of a prototype-oriented technique.

When prototyping is added to other development methods, whatever notations are used in that technique would also be used with the prototype.

9.3.2 Technique

When a prototype drives the analysis and design of a software system, the initial functional requirements for the system should be documented. Other development techniques can provide notations for representing and tracking these functional requirements in any number of different forms. Tracking requirements, change requests, and sign-off on prototype versions are all tasks that must be managed and scheduled when a prototype is used in the development process. In addition, prototypes can help define and may even generate test cases for the system.

Whether building a prototype is beneficial will depend to a great degree on the development environment and the tools available. When a 4GL is used, the 4GL will serve as the prototyping language, and the prototype will evolve over time to include full system functionality. 4GLs can be very effective in allowing developers to quickly create functional systems but may also have limitations in handling complex functionality and performance constraints. Since many 4GLs are interpreted and not compiled, this can lead to less responsive systems that may be unacceptable for certain applications.

When an automated prototyping tool is used, the tool will serve to drive and constrain the development process. For instance, a prototyping technique that uses a product that generates code will restrict the types of specification collected and the approach used to specify the system. C code generators typically specify the system functionality by creating screens, menus, or reports, and may be of little help in designing other types of applications.

When an evolutionary prototype becomes the operational system, it is essential that the same technique and tools be used for maintaining the system throughout its useful life. Many of the tools used to generate software systems contain sophisticated requirements tracking and impact analysis capabilities that can make maintenance much easier.

As we have already seen, the type of prototype used will determine the process used in developing a system. If a throw-away prototype is used, the prototype may be designed and built quickly to help learn how the system will function or whether specific technology can support the system requirements. Once this prototype has served its purpose, a traditional development process will begin, using the prototype as a starting point for system requirements and functionality. If an evolutionary prototype is created, the process will be slower and will require design decisions based on the finished system and the environment it will operate in. The prototype will evolve and must be included as part of the eventual system.

9.3.3 Representation

As previously stated, the prototype-oriented techniques all deliver a working prototype as their principal representation of the software product, beginning in the requirements definition and design phase. Representations beyond the design phase will vary depending on the type of prototype used. If the prototype is evolutionary, the prototype will continue to serve as the representation throughout the useful life of the system. In this case, the specification used to generate the operational system must be used whenever the system is modified or enhanced. This brings up additional questions about how the prototype will be maintained once the system becomes operational.

An important factor to remember when a working system is generated from a specification in a CASE tool is that any modifications to the system must be made within the tool, not to the external source code generated by the tool. Changes made to the code that are not reflected in the specifications will be erased the next time the system is generated from the specifications.

If the prototype is disposed of following design, some form of representation will need to be created in the phases following design. If traditional software engineering techniques are used along with a disposable prototype, these will serve as the representations for the system after the prototype is discarded. There are obvious drawbacks to these representations in terms of both user understanding and maintaining connections between the representations and the prototype.

Regardless of which type of prototype is created, the prototype must be incorporated into the development process. Specifically, in the design phase, the prototype can help specify the behavior and structure of the system.

David Harel has identified different levels of executable specification for reactive systems [HAR92] and how these prototypes can help developers better understand or think about a system. Harel suggests that prototypes can help developers uncover unknown patterns of behavior, correct subtle conceptual errors before they are coded, and minimize the unpredictable aspects of analyzing and designing complex systems.

9.4 Stages and Tasks

While prototype-oriented techniques can vary widely, Figure 9.3 shows a generic prototype-oriented development process. This development process begins with a request from the user community for a new system. In this phase, the user identifies some basic requirements for the system. The needs of the user are defined, along with the scope of the system and an estimate of costs and benefits. These requirements should be documented and hopefully placed into a CASE repository so they can be tracked and verified throughout the remainder of the development process.

In a prototype-oriented approach, some quick design decisions are made, and an initial prototype is created and given to the user community. The users exercise the prototype and give feedback on its functionality to the developers. With all of these techniques, an essential ingredient is quick turnaround on requests for change from users and modifications to the working prototype by the development staff.

The developers modify the prototype based on the suggestions from the users, and the users in turn continue to exercise the prototype once changes are implemented. As the prototype evolves, design issues are reviewed and modified to fit

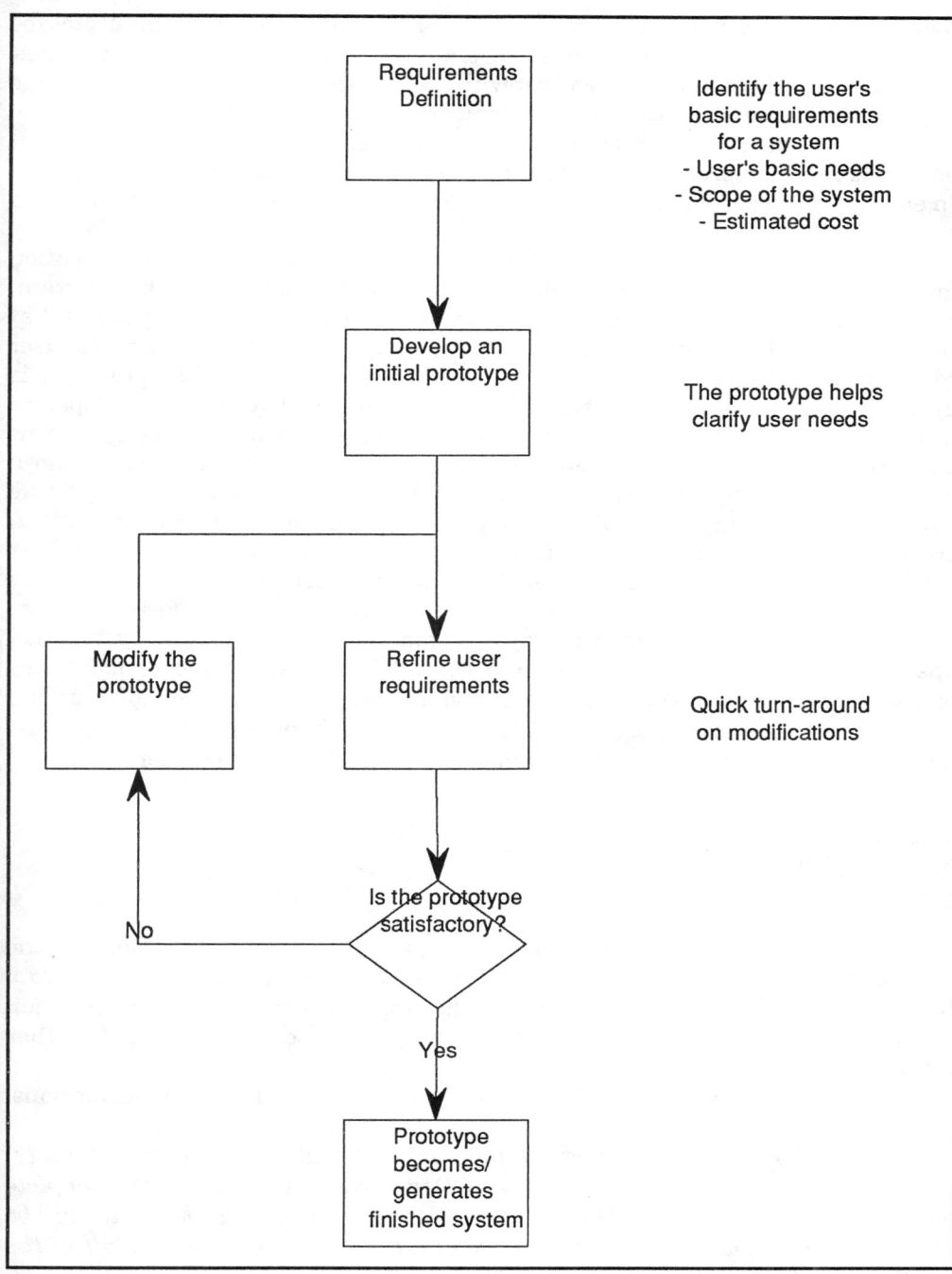

Requirements Definition

Identify the user's basic requirements for a system
- User's basic needs
- Scope of the system
- Estimated cost

Develop an initial prototype

The prototype helps clarify user needs

Modify the prototype

Refine user requirements

Quick turn-around on modifications

Is the prototype satisfactory?

No

Yes

Prototype becomes/ generates finished system

Figure 9.3
A generic prototyping life cycle.

more closely the functionality of the system. Regardless of how the prototype evolves, there must be some formal review process whereby users can submit requests for modification and, together with the developers, a decision can be made regarding how the modification will be accomplished.

Once the prototype supports all the requirements identified by the users, it either becomes the production system or is used to develop the production system. In either case, the prototype serves as the "model" of the finished system for future steps.

If the prototype does not become the finished system, it is used as a specification for developers, who will proceed with a traditional design, followed by programming, testing, and then implementation. In this case, it is extremely important that the finished system maintain the same functionality as the prototype or the user community will consider prototyping as irrelevant. For instance, if a prototype is developed under a workstation-based GUI but the finished system is developed as a character-based mainframe application, users may not accept the system as delivered. Developers can gather a better understanding of the system from a prototype, including the flow of control of programs, data structures, reporting needs, menu structures, security considerations, and general logic for functions. A critical factor in the success of this type of prototype is the time required to deliver the finished system to the users after the prototype is completed.

If the prototype evolves to become the finished system, some underlying design decisions must be made along the way regarding how the production system will operate. For example, the database may need to be modified to support high levels of transactions, or the low-level logic of individual programs may need to be further specified, etc. The system can be scaled up to a full implementation only if the prototype was designed from the beginning to support the environment.

9.5 Deliverables

The primary deliverable from all of these prototype-oriented techniques is the functional prototype itself. In addition, models for data, processes, and control behavior can be developed in parallel with the prototype itself. In some cases, when an executable specification is used, the prototype will encompass all the other models.

As Ed Yourdon has said [YOU89], prototyping is based on specific assumptions:

"The major difference between prototyping and traditional structured analysis / structured design (SA / SD) is that SA / SD requires that at some point a complete paper model of the system will be built. Prototyping assumes that the model will be a working model, a collection of programs that will simulate some or all of the functions that the users want. The assumption is that when the model is finished, it will be replaced with a real system."

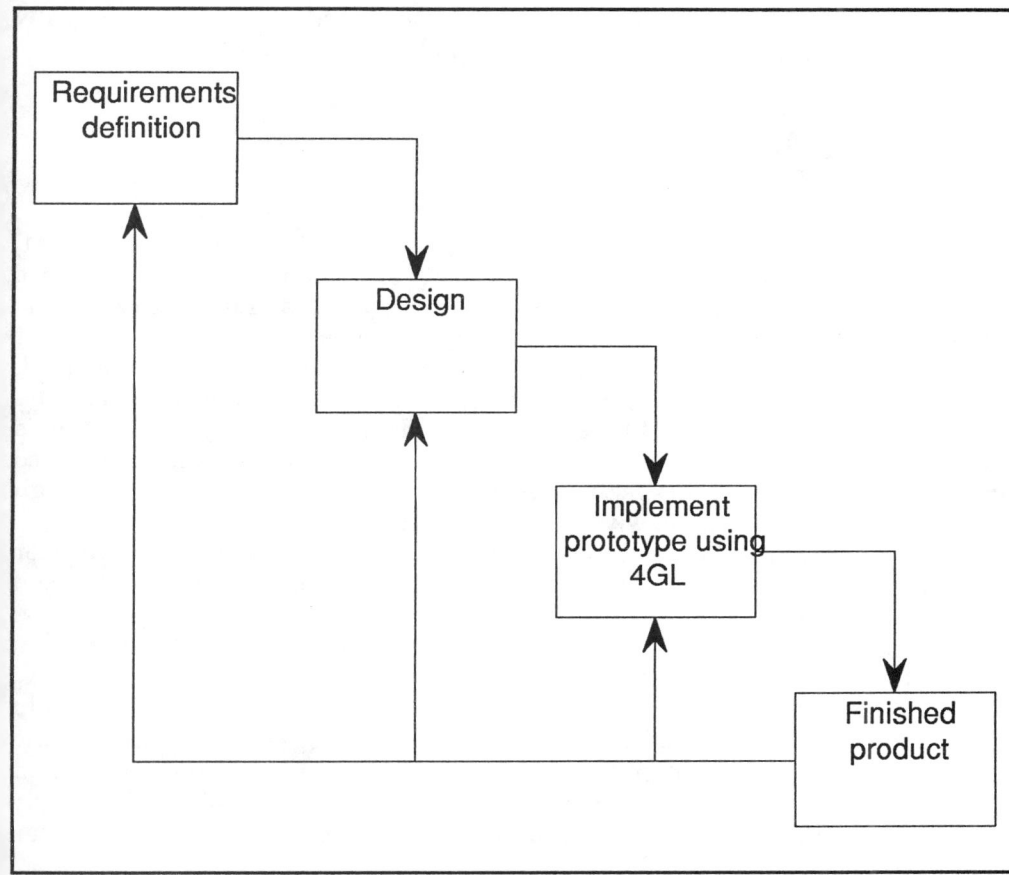

Figure 9.4
4GL prototyping
life cycle.

In addition to the prototype, a fully attributed data model may be created and used to generate the database structures. These models help to define the requirements for the data that the functional prototype will be accessing. In many cases, 4GLs are used to prototype a system, since they are integrated with DBMSs. Figure 9.4 describes an example 4GL prototyping life cycle. Problems of performance and complexity can limit the effectiveness of 4GLs in certain types of applications.

If a throw-away prototype is used, additional deliverables will need to be created following delivery of the prototype. These include architectural design documents, detailed design documents, database design documents, etc.

With an evolutionary prototype, the prototype becomes the production system, so source and executable code must be generated from the prototype in the language of choice. In addition, once the prototype becomes the production system, maintenance, documentation, and configuration management issues must be resolved by the development staff. In most cases, documentation for the system can be created directly from the prototype. Some code generation products can automatically generate documents from the specifications used to create the system.

9.6 Suitable Applications

Prototypes have been successfully used in all types of software development, from decision support systems to embedded software for communication and control systems. As previously stated, several powerful prototyping languages are available for reactive systems and for traditional MIS applications.

A recent experiment created a prototype for a generic command, control, communications, and intelligence station and generated Ada code from the prototype's specifications automatically [LUQ91]. These and other results prove that it is feasible to use prototyping for MIS and real-time applications. Experience also suggests that prototyping allows the developers to experiment with various design variations in a timely fashion without having to cut corners.

The type of application and the organization will largely determine whether prototyping can be of value or not. 4GL and DBMS environments are good candidates for prototyping, since a prototype can be created quickly and easily. Developers using a 4GL or report writer can generate functional subsystems in a matter of days instead of weeks or months.

Using a prototype when user requirements are unclear or ambiguous can help clarify them for both users and developers. A prototype often helps to better define "fuzzy" requirements. Prototyping can also be helpful when experimentation and learning are required before a commitment of resources for a full-scale system is practical. Figure 9.5 describes some conditions when prototype-oriented techniques might prove useful.

Figure 9.5
Candidate projects for prototype-oriented techniques.

When a user is unable or unwilling to review paper models that are produced by traditional techniques
When a user is unable or unwilling to spell out, in detail, what requirements a system has without using the system
["I'll know what I want (and don't want) when you deliver it to me"]
When a user has had a negative experience with traditional specification techniques
An on-line, interactive system using a DBMS
A system that doesn't require detailed specification
A system with a small number of functions
A system that can stand-alone and has few interactions with other systems
A system that may not be feasible for a large-scale application
A partial or incomplete system
A system using an unproven approach or technology

Other considerations include the application area, complexity of the application, and customer (user) and project characteristics. Good candidates for prototyping include systems that use dynamic visual displays, interact heavily with the user, or demand algorithms or logical processing that must be developed in an evolutionary fashion. In addition, if functionality can be isolated, a evolutionary prototype can be used to implement pieces of the system slowly over time. The only danger in this approach is that if these discrete pieces of the system must eventually be integrated, design decisions must be made as part of the prototyping process.

Many of the hardware vendors have announced development approaches that embrace prototyping. IBM, Unisys, and Amdahl include prototyping as a critical component of their development strategies. Under AD/Cycle, IBM has defined prototyping as a stage in the analysis phase of the development life cycle. Likewise, Unisys relies on LINC, its prototype/4GL product, as the basis for its development approach, the Integrated Information Environment (IIE) [DEN88]. Amdahl also promotes a prototype-oriented approach to software development in its Huron development system.

Applications that may not be suitable for prototyping include complex batch applications, complex functional and procedural software, and systems that require small, optimized software or are constrained by factors including the operating environment or platform. Also, systems that may require mega-programming or that span several years and involve hundreds of developers may not be suitable for prototyping techniques, simply by virtue of their size and scope.

In some cases, the availability and capabilities of automated tools to support the prototyping process will dictate which types of applications can be developed using a prototype-oriented technique. For example, a 4GL prototyping approach may incur performance problems and may require a mixed development of third- and fourth-generation language code. Mixing 4GL and other programming languages offers its own set of problems in maintenance, etc. Also, when an evolutionary prototype is used, the tools used to generate the final system may have limitations, and these will dictate how much of the final product can be generated and how much must be manually created.

An additional consideration when using a prototype-oriented technique is how costs and resources will be estimated for the project. Studies suggest that estimation for prototype-oriented techniques differs significantly from that for traditional approaches [BAL90]. Powerful executable specification languages can provide a wealth of information in the analysis, design and testing phases of software development. Some of the specification languages can also generate software and hardware components.

A prototype-oriented technique should be undertaken by developers and users who are well informed and who clearly understand the prototyping approach. Whenever a prototype is used, its purpose must be defined prior to its creation, and both developers and users must agree on what will happen to it when the prototyping is finished. If there is disagreement about the purpose of the prototype or its role in the development process, this can lead to failure to benefit from the creation of the prototype.

Prerequisites for a successful prototype include technological tools that facilitate quick response to user requests and motivated and knowledgeable users and developers. As we have already indicated, sophisticated tools can make or break a prototype approach. With inadequate tools, developers cannot respond quickly enough to user requests, users may find the prototype to be different from the finished (delivered) system, or the prototype may prove to be unusable.

Often cited in the literature is the need for a high-level corporate sponsor for prototyping to be successful. This sponsor must take an active role in the creation and evolution of the prototype and must ensure that whatever resources are needed, from both users and developers, they are provided. This sponsor must also make a commitment to what will happen to the prototype when it is complete and stick with this commitment.

Perhaps more than other techniques, prototype-oriented approaches require active user involvement throughout the life cycle. The iterative nature of prototyping requires quick response to user requests for modification, and users must take the time to use the prototype as they would the finished system.

Developers must work harder with prototype-oriented techniques to allow the prototype to evolve naturally to fit the needs of the users. They (developers) must force themselves to allow changes and even encourage further refinement of the prototype. A functional prototype can deliver benefits to the developers only if it accurately represents the behavior of the finished system.

9.8 Benefits and Drawbacks

"When the prototype becomes the production system, it is a method of system construction as well as a technique for system definition. Prototyping forces the analyst to widen his iterative circle, because by definition he must perform some detail design and program generation as he builds and modifies a system model."
L. Scharer [SCH83].

As already discussed, prototypes can be very helpful in getting end-users more involved in the software development process, since the prototype is a deliverable from the process early in the life cycle. Users who are normally given only a finished computer system will be more excited about helping to define and then using a functional prototype of their system weeks or months into the development process.

Prototypes can also help developers better define the requirements for a system by getting more input from the users earlier in the life cycle. When users actually work with a functional prototype, they typically define more requirements, and these requirements are defined in more depth than without the use of the prototype.

In the design phase, a prototype can give developers a wealth of information about editing criteria, screen and report formats, menu structures, security consid-

End users get more involved and stay involved longer.
Helps users define requirements earlier and in more detail.
Can establish flow of control and time-dependent behavior in great detail.
Can help to eliminate errors from invalid, incomplete, or inconsistent
   requirements specification.
Can help to improve the human-machine interface.
Can prove "unproven" technology or development approach.
When using "evolutionary prototyping," can reduce errors from
   specification to programs.

Figure 9.6
Potential benefits of using a prototype-oriented technique.

erations, database requirements, and even the flow of control within a system. Prototypes help developers to focus on human-machine interface issues and may result in systems that are easier to use and better support the needs of the users.

If a prototype can be used to directly generate source and executable code for the production system, then this should help eliminate any errors in moving from specification to programming. In addition, this can provide a vehicle for modifying the system via the specification. Figure 9.6 describes some of the potential benefits of using prototype-oriented techniques.

One danger with prototyping in some organizations is that developers may feel that creating a prototype eliminates the need to do any detailed analysis or design. As we have already indicated, a prototype is a model of a finished system. A model airplane may represent the behavior of an actual 747 but cannot carry over 300 people. Users must understand the limitations of the prototype before it is created.

Another danger is getting the users to release or give up the prototype after it is completed so that a traditional design, code, and implement process can begin. To the end users, the prototype represents the functional system, and they may not understand (or want to understand) why the prototype is not the finished system. Attempting to explain that not all the design decisions for a production system have been made with a prototype may not satisfy users.

Still other problems can occur if the finished system does not exactly match the prototype, as is often the case when a mainframe application is developed on a PC, or when a throw-away prototype is developed and users want it to become part of the finished system.

"Creeping functionality" is a condition that occurs when users fail to decide on the functions they require in the system, but continue to ask for modifications to the prototype. While modifying a prototype is helpful, there must eventually be a "final" prototype that everyone agrees is satisfactory or development will go on forever without a finished system being created. Figure 9.7 lists some potential dangers or pitfalls of using prototype-oriented techniques.

Getting the users to give up the prototype; i.e., they think they have the
actual system, not just a prototype of it, and there are many dangers in
using a prototype in a production environment.

Users keep changing their minds and never really come up with a
"functional" prototype.

Finished systems do not exactly match with the working prototype;
i.e., PCs and GUIs used in prototype vs. CICS and terminals.

Quick design decisions have adverse effects on the final system; i.e.,
failure to scale up to the production environment (number of
transactions, levels of activity, etc.).

The prototype might indicate that the system should not or cannot
be created (i.e., in a cost-efficient manner).

Figure 9.7
Possible drawbacks
of prototype-oriented
techniques.

9.9 The Library Example

Using rapid development techniques with the Library problem produced a
functional system in about one day of development. It should be noted, however, that
prior to beginning the prototype, the requirements for the Library system were fully
defined and an initial data model for the library was created. The data model used
is described in more detail in Chapter 5. In addition, the development team was
already experienced with the 4GL used and required no learning curve for the
language.

From these items, functional screen, menu, and report programs were created
using a 4GL (Dataflex from Data Access). The 4GL provided a very flexible, fast
development environment for creating the Library system. In the case of the Library
example, the prototype was an evolutionary prototype and became the finished
system. The completed system supports all the functionality of the library, runs
single-user on a PC or multi-user on a LAN, supports ad hoc reporting, and has no
performance limitation for large library systems. As already discussed, the performance of some 4GLs may prohibit specific applications from being developed with
4GLs. Using the Library example, if the number of books in the library could exceed
100,000, the size of the database and the access of individual books may prove too
slow on some systems.

Examples of the menus and screens created in the prototype are shown in
Figures 9.8 and 9.9. Figure 9.8 shows the staff menu, while Figure 9.9 shows the
Checkout Book screen. Also, sample 4GL code from the Checkout Book program is
depicted in Figure 9.10. Like other 4GLs, the language provides a wealth of DBMS,
logic, screen, and report handling and editing constructs which made it easy to
create and modify the system.

```
                    Library System
                      Main Menu

              1 Add/Update Books
              2 Add/Update Authors
              3 Add/Update Users
              4 Checkout books
              5 Return books
              6 View copies of a book

              8 Reports Menu
              9 Update Control record

            Please enter your choice: 1_
Use Up Arrow or Down Arrow to select option, then Return
```

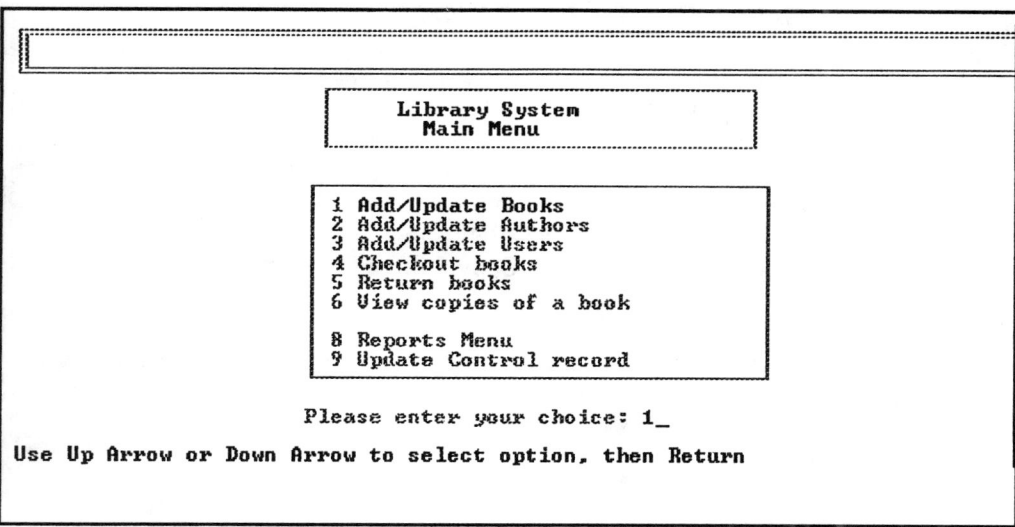

Figure 9.8
Prototype of Library staff menu.

One issue that came up early in the creation of the prototype was what the underlying database structure for the Library system would be. To a large extent, this determined how the prototype was created. In this case, as in Chapter 5, the decision was made to use a relational database management system (RDBMS) for the Library system. This led to a question about how to handle the Author to Book relationship, since a book can be written by more than one author and an author might write more than one book (many-to-many).

In a traditional RDBMS, a joined table would be created with only the keys from the Author and Book tables to satisfy this requirement. In the prototype system, the decision was made to store the key of the authors for a book physically in the Book

```
CHECKOUT.FRM                                         Date : 11/12/92
                      User Checkout Books Program

 *Call Number : 3
  Title : MODERN STRUCTURED ANALYSIS

  User : USR2            Name : BARNY RUBBLE

  Copy checked out :    1         Date Checked Out : 11/12/92

  Number of books this user has checked out :    3


  F1 = Help, F2 = Prev. Field,  F6 = Delete Record, F9 = Clear Screen
  F10 = Save, Tab = Find by Key (* fields only), Esc = Exit
```

Figure 9.9
Prototype of Checkout Book screen.

```
Get_Copy:
    Accept CheckOut.6    to CopyNumber  { Required }
    [Key.Clear] Goto Be_Gin
    [Key.Field] Goto Get_User
    Display "                    " to CheckOut.9
    Clear Copies
    Move CallNumber     to Copies.CallNumber
    Move CopyNumber     to Copies.CopyNumber
    Find EQ Copies by Index.1
    [Not Found] Begin
     Display "No copy found with that number - try another" to CheckOut.9
     Goto Get_Copy
    End
    [Found] Begin
     If Copies.CheckedOut NE "Y" Begin
       Display Sdate      to CheckOut.7
       Accept CheckOut.7 to Copies.DateOut { Required }
       [Key.Clear] Goto Be_Gin
       [Key.Field] Goto Get_Copy
       Display "                     " to CheckOut.9
       Move Users.UserID  to Copies.CheckedOutTo
       Move "Y"           to Copies.CheckedOut
       Saverecord Copies
       Calc (Users.NumberOut + 1) to Users.NumberOut
       Saverecord Users
     End  // Copy is not checked out
```

Figure 9.10
Example 4GL
code, Enter Copy.

record itself. This made it easier to access the authors, reduced the amount of space required for the finished system, and simplified the Author and Book reports in the Library system. This decision had a definite impact on the prototype, since any screens or reports that accessed the authors of a book had to use the key provided in the Book table to locate the information, but this decision was not made without compromises, since it forced checking for a fixed number of authors for any book and an error condition when the number entered is greater than the limit.

Documentation for the Library system was created externally to the 4GL and development environment. Also, the 4GL used provided little help in managing and maintaining the Library system once it was made operational. Some CASE tools and 4GLs provide extensive repositories and support environments that include capabilities that make maintenance much easier.

Documenting and tracking the functional requirements for the Library system was accomplished using System Architect from Popkin Software and Systems (see preface).

9.10 Resource List

There are several excellent books on rapid application development and prototyping. Books by Martin [MAR90] [MAR91], Boar [BOA84], and Hekmatpour [HEK88] cover prototyping and rapid application development in some depth. For real-time or embedded systems, Harel [HAR84], Hoar [HOA85], Luqi [LUQ88] [LUQ90], and Zave [ZAV82] are all excellent resources.

For information on combining traditional software engineering techniques with prototypes, see books and papers by Connel [CON89], Gane [GAN88], Mason [MAS83], McClure [MCC89], and Yourdon [YOU89].

For prototyping with 4GLs, the book by Denton [DEN88] and the paper by Scharer [SCH83] are good sources.

General software engineering works often include a brief discussion or chapter on prototyping, including Pressman [PRE88] [PRE92] and McClure [MCC89].

For technical papers covering prototyping, refer to the special issues of *ACM SIGSOFT* [ACM82] and *IEEE Computer* [TAN89], along with the IEEE Computer Society work edited by Agresti [AGR86]. These papers all cover prototype-oriented techniques and issues related to using prototypes in software development.

9.11 References

[ACM82]   *ACM SIGSOFT* (Special Issue on Rapid Prototyping), vol. 7, no. 5, 1982.

[AGR86]   Agresti, W., *New Paradigms for Software Development*, IEEE Computer Society Order Number 707.

[ALA91]   Alavi, M., "An Assessment of the Prototyping Approach to Information System Development," *Software Engineering Benchmark Handbook*, Applied Computer Research, Phoenix, 1991, pp. 91-100.

[BAL82]   Balzer, R., et al., "Operational Specifications as a Basis for Rapid Prototyping," *ACM SIGSOFT*, vol. 7, no. 5, 1982, pp. 3-16.

[BAL90]   Balda, D., and D. Gustafson, "Cost Estimation Models for the Reuse and Prototype Software Development Life-cycles," *ACM SIGSOFT*, vol. 15, no. 3, pp. 42 - 50.

[BER91]   Bersoff, E., and A. Davis, "Impacts of Life Cycle Models on Software Configuration Management," *CACM*, August 1991, pp. 104-118.

[BOA84]   Boar, B., *Application Prototyping: A Requirements Definition Strategy for the 80's*, Addison-Wesley, 1984.

[BOE84]   Boehm, B., T. Gray, and T. Seewaldt, "Prototyping vs. Specifying: A Multiproject Experiment," *IEEE Trans. on Soft. Eng.*, vol. 10, no. 3, 1984, pp. 39-44.

[BRU86]   Bruno, G., and M. Marchetto, "Process-Translatable Petri Nets for the Rapid Prototyping of Process Control Systems," *IEEE Trans. on Soft. Eng.*, vol. SE-12, pp. 346-357, Feb. 1986.

[CON89]   Connel, J., and L. Shafer, *Structured Rapid Prototyping*, Yourdon Press, 1988.

[COO90]   Coomer, C. J., and R. E. Childs, "A Graphical Tool for the Prototyping of Real-Time Systems," *ACM SIGSOFT*, vol. 15, no. 2, 1990, pp. 70-82.

[DAV92]   Davis, A. M., "Operational Prototyping: A New Development Approach," *IEEE Software*, September 1992, pp. 70-77.

[DAV88]   Davis., A. M., et al., "A Strategy for Comparing Alternative Development Life Cycle Models," *IEEE Trans. on Soft. Eng.*, October 1988, pp. 1453-1461.

[DAV82]   Davis, A. M., "Rapid Prototyping Using Executable Requirements Specifications," *ACM SIGSOFT*, vol. 7, no. 5, 1982, pp. 39-44.

[DEN88]   Denton, J., *Information Systems Using LINC*, UNISYS New Zealand Ltd., 1988.

[DEG90]   Degl'Innocenti, M., G. Luigi Ferrari, G. Pacini, and G. Turini, "RSF: A Formalism for Executable Requirement Specifications," *IEEE Trans. on Soft. Eng.*, vol. 16, no. 11, November 1990, pp. 1235-1246.

[DOK90]   Doke, E., "An Industry Survey of Emerging Prototyping Methodologies," *Information and Management*, 18, 169-176.

[GAN88]   Gane, C., *Rapid Systems Development: Using Structured Techniques and Relational Technology*, Rapid Systems Development Inc., 1988.

[GOM81]   Gomaa, H. and D. Scott, "Prototyping as a Tool in the Specification of User Requirements," *Proceedings of the Fifth International Conference on Software Engineering*, IEEE Computer Society, pp. 333-342, 1981.

[GOM83]   Gomaa, H., "The Impact of Rapid Prototyping on Specifying User Requirements," *ACM SIGSOFT*, vol. 8, no. 2, pp. 17-28.

[GOM86]   Gomaa, H., "Software Prototypes: Keep Them or Throw Them Away?," in *InfoTech State of the Art Report on Prototyping*, M. Lipp, ed., Pergamon Press, Oxford, 1986.

[GRA89]   Graham, D., "Incremental Development: Review of Nonmonolithic Life-Cycle Development Models," *Information and Software Technology*, 31, 7-20.

[HAR92]   Harel, D., "Biting the Silver Bullet: Toward a Future for Software Development," *IEEE Computer*, January 1992, pp. 8-20.

[HAR88]   Harel, D., "On Visual Formalisms," *CACM*, vol. 31, no. 5, 1988, pp. 514-530.

[HEK87]   Hekmatpour, S., "Experience with Evolutionary Prototyping in a Large Software Project," *ACM SIGSOFT*, 12:1, 1987, pp. 38-41.

[HEK88]   Hekmatpour, S., and D. Ince, *Software Prototyping Formal Methods and VDM*, Addison-Wesley, 1988.

[HOA85]   Hoare, C. A. R., *Communicating Sequential Processes*, Prentice-Hall Intl., 1985.

[JOR88]   Jorgensen, P., "Early Detection of Requirements Specification Errors," *Proceedings of the Third Annual Computer Assurance Conference* (COMPASS'88), Gaithersburg, June 1988.

[JOR87]   Jorgensen, P., "Petri F.Y.I. — An Intelligent, User-Extensible System Specification Tool," *Proceedings of the Structured Methods Conference XII*, Chicago, August 1987, and *Proceedings of the International Phoenix Conference on Computers and Communications*, Phoenix, March 1988.

[LUQ91]   Luqi, "Computer-Aided Prototyping For a Command-and-Control System Using CAPS," *IEEE Software*, January 1991, pp. 56-67.

[LUQ90]   Luqi, and M. Ketabchi, "A Computer-Aided Prototyping System," *IEEE Software*, March 1988, pp. 66-72.

[LUQ88]   Luqi, V. Berzins, and R. Yeh, "A Prototyping Language for Real-Time Software," *IEEE Trans. on Soft. Eng.*, October 1988, pp. 1409-1423.

[MAR90]   Martin, J., *Rapid Application Development*, Macmillan, 1990.

[MAR91]   Martin, J., *Information Engineering: Book III, Design and Construction*, Macmillan, 1991.

[MAS83]   Mason, R., and T. Carey, "Prototyping Interactive Information Systms," *CACM*, vol. 26, no. 5, pp. 347-354.

[MCC89]   McClure, C., *CASE Is Software Automation*, Prentice-Hall, 1988.

[PRE88]   Pressman, R., *Software Engineering: A Beginner's Guide*, McGraw-Hill, 1988.

[PRE88]   Pressman, R., *Making Software Engineering Happen*, Prentice-Hall, 1988.

[PRE92]   Pressman, R., *Software Engineering: A Practitioner's Approach*, McGraw-Hill, 1992.

[SCH83]   Scharer, L., "The Prototype Alternative," *ITT Programming*, 1:1, 1983, pp. 34-43.

[TAN89]   Tanik, M. M., and R. T. Yeh, eds., "Rapid Prototyping in Software Development," *IEEE Computer* (Special Issue), vol. 27, no. 5, May 1989.

[YOU89]   Yourdon, E., *Modern Structured Analysis*, Prentice-Hall, 1989.

[ZAV82]   Zave, P., "An Operational Approach to Requirements Specifications for Embedded Systems," *IEEE Trans. on Soft. Eng.*, vol. SE-8, no. 3, pp. 250-269, May 1982.

[ZEL80]   Zelkowitz, M., "A Case Study in Rapid Prototyping," *Software Practice and Experience*, 10:12, Dec 80, pp. 1037-1042.

PART 4

Implementation Issues and Strategies

Chapter 10
Comparing Software Development Techniques

When an organization is looking to adopt a new approach to software development, which of the techniques described in Chapters 4 through 9 should it select and use? Which criteria should it use to evaluate the various techniques? Which types of applications are best suited for the different techniques? Which types of applications are not fully supported by them?

While there is general agreement that there is no single development technique that best supports all types of software, there is also agreement that comparisons can be made among the techniques described in Chapters 4 through 9. In this chapter we will attempt to describe alternative approaches to comparing these techniques using some form of objective criteria and process. Obviously, the developers of these techniques envisioned specific criteria when they created the techniques, and this should not be overlooked when evaluating them.

As you read this chapter, recall where development techniques fit into the software production framework defined in Chapter 1, and the organizational level the techniques most directly affect. Techniques define the "how" and "why" of a software process, and deal with project team level issues, including communication and representations.

We can characterize the differences among the techniques in a number of ways; by philosophy; by orientation; by the notations and representations used, by the inclusion/exclusion of business strategy, prototyping, and long-range planning; by technique; as well as by the support for evolution or iteration. It should be pointed out that with adequate training and support, all of these approaches can work in an organization. The degree to which the techniques will support the tasks and representations required for each type of application will vary, thus making some methods more beneficial than others for certain application domains.

We chose to separate the techniques in this book by the areas of focus or orientation they cover for a number of reasons, not the least of which was our plan to compare them along these lines. We will use these areas of focus later in the chapter to discuss how these development techniques are alike and different.

10.1 Introduction

"Formal methods are not a panacea but a step that must be taken to put software engineering on solid footing."
S. Gerhart [GER90].

Each of the software development techniques described in this book has different orientations or points of focus in its approach to understanding and building software systems. But before to discussing how software development techniques are different, it is helpful to consider how they are similar.

All software development techniques share common characteristics, including their dependence on a disciplined engineering development process that includes tools for representing software products at various points in the process. Perhaps most important, all of these techniques define a standard approach to modeling and designing software based on methods that have been proven to help address complexity and problems in communication throughout the development process. This standard approach helps organizations to embrace a shared view of software development and representations throughout the life cycle.

Whether they use data flow diagrams or action diagrams, all of these techniques include notations and representations that are standardized and help facilitate better communication and understanding. While the individual diagrams, representations, or approaches to describing the software at these various points will vary among the techniques, they all require that some form of representation be created as part of the development process. Whether we represent functional requirements using data flow diagrams, action diagrams, object diagrams, CRUD matrices, or a prototype, the underlying goal is that the representation help to communicate and explain how a system should function. Sometimes we get so caught up in the specifics of the techniques that we forget the purpose of the technique is to help understand and develop solutions to real problems.

Each of these techniques also includes defined practices (the "how") that help deal with abstraction and complexity. Whether they employ decomposition or composition, the techniques provide a process for helping people deal with the inherent complexity in software. As software matures, its overall complexity continues to grow, and therefore the need to control this complexity must be addressed.

Each of the techniques also focuses strongly on the analysis and design of software systems, in opposition to the traditional focus most organizations have on programming and testing. This change in focus is important when we consider that most of the errors in software don't result from programming or testing errors, but from errors in requirements specification or design.

The process of comparing and selecting a software development technique has far-reaching implications and should not be undertaken lightly. Chapter 12 describes the process of selecting and implementing development techniques in more detail and serves as a supplement to the process described in this chapter.

10.2 Comparison of Development Techniques

While there are many different approaches to developing software and we have described six general orientations in this book, organizations often need to compare these techniques to decide which will best fit their environment. This process of comparison is somewhat imperfect, however, since there have been no studies that have qualitatively compared these techniques on the same set of people and projects.

While various papers have studied the results of some of these techniques [WIN88] and have suggested a metric for comparing methods based on stability of models [CLA90], most have focused on the notations or representations of the technique [LIS86] [PLA90] [WOO89]. Very few papers or books have compared available development techniques in any detail. Some of the previous works in this area can offer insight into the process of comparing development techniques with an eye toward selecting appropriate methods for development.

Roger Pressman [PRE87] suggests a common set of characteristics that all development techniques share, including:

1. Mechanisms for information domain analysis (data modeling support)
2. Approach or technique for functional representation (process modeling)
3. Definition of interfaces (data flow between processes and external entities)
4. Mechanisms for problem partitioning (complexity management)
5. Support for abstraction
6. Representation of physical and logical views

Pressman further defines three basic types of analysis techniques: (1) data flow oriented, (2) data structure-oriented, and (3) language-based formal specifications; he later added an object-oriented view in [PRE92].

In design, Pressman compares notations and characteristics of these notations, including support for modularity, support for machine readability, support for structured programming constructs, support for data structure representations, automatic verification of design logic, and links with code generation capabilities. Pressman also defines three major orientations for design techniques: data flow, data structure, and object-oriented design.

Larry Constantine, the architect of structured design, provides a comparison of object-oriented design and function-oriented design in [CON90]. While this paper deals with only two of the six orientations in this book, it brings out the similarities and differences between two of the more popular design techniques in use.

Constantine offers his view on the inherent complexity of functional modules vs. object methods, cohesion between modules in both orientations, benefits and drawbacks in a software product structured around functions vs. objects, and practical considerations in selecting an appropriate approach.

The Software Engineering Institute (SEI) has published various reports on assessing and classifying formal development methods, including [FIR87] and [WOO88]. Most of the SEI work has focused on control-oriented methods and the representations of reactive systems, but SEI suggests that all methods can be evaluated using three views: function, behavior (control), and structure (system architecture, data modeling, and language platforms).

The SEI work characterizes methods based on the life cycle, waterfall vs. spiral, and development approach used, bottom-up vs. top-down vs. middle-out vs. rapid prototype.

Another relevant paper on this topic was written by Tamer Uluakar [ULU91] and compares function-oriented methods (specifically, the Yourdon Structured Method) with the information-oriented technique supported by the IEF CASE tool. While the paper focuses on only the analysis portion of each technique, it does compare the principles and philosophies of the methods in some depth.

Uluakar points out differences between IE and YSM in the use of data modeling, the movement from analysis to design, and the impact of the specification tools used (data flow diagrams vs. process dependency diagrams). He also discusses the benefit of using events in YSM and the lack of support for dynamic or event-driven behavior in the IE method.

One recent paper that does compare methods in some detail is from Fichman and Kemerer of MIT [FIC92]. Fichman and Kemerer studied and compared function-oriented, information-oriented, and object-oriented methods with a focus on how the other two techniques are similar and different from object-oriented techniques. While their paper didn't cover all of the object-oriented techniques, or include data-oriented methods, it did offer some interesting thoughts on how structured methods compare with object-oriented methods.

Fichman and Kemerer point out that object-oriented analysis methods are radically different from function-oriented techniques, but only incrementally different from data- or information-oriented analysis methods. They suggest that the difference between data and object models is in the support required in the latter for encapsulation and in the representation of dynamic behavior at different levels in the methods. In traditional methods, dynamic behavior is defined for system components, while in object-oriented methods, dynamic behavior is required for individual objects. Figure 10.1 is an excerpt from the Fichman and Kemerer article that compares analysis techniques.

Except from Table 1 Comparison of analysis methods	Yourdon MSA	Information Engineering	Coad/Yourdon OOA	
Identification/ classification of entities	Entity-relationship diagram (ERD)	ERD/Data Structure diagram (DSD)	Class/Object diagram level 1	
General-to-specific and whole-to-part relationships	ERD	ERD/DSD	Class/Object diagram level 2	
Other Entity Relationships	ERD	ERD/DSD	Class/Object diagram level 4	
Attributes	Data dictionary	Bubble charts & encyclopedia	Class/Object diagram level 4	
Large-scale model partitioning	Event-partitioned Data flow diagram (DFD)	Subject databases	Class/Object diagram level 3	
States and transitions	State-transition diagram (STD)	Not Supported	Service chart	
Detailed logic for functions/ services	Mini-specification	Action diagram (process)	Service chart	
Top-down decomposition of functions	DFD	Decomposition diagram	Not Supported	
End-to-end processing sequences	DFD	Process dependency diagram	Not Supported	

Figure 10.1
Comparison of analysis techniques.

Except from Table 2 Comparison of design methods	Yourdon/ Constantine Structured Design	Information Engineering	Booch Object Oriented Design	
Hierarchy of modules (physical design)	Structure chart	Decompositon diagram (DCD)	Module diagram	
Data definitions	Hierarchy diagram	Data Structure diagram (DSD)	Class diagram	
Procedural logic	Process Description Language (PDL)	Action diagram	Operation template	
End-to-end processing sequence	Data flow diagram (DFD)	DFD/Process Dependency diagram	Timing diagram	
Object states and transitions	Not Supported	Not Supported	State-Transition diagram (STD)	
Message connections	Not Supported	Not Supported	Object diagram and template	

Figure 10.2
Comparison of design techniques.

When comparing object-oriented design techniques with other methods, Fichman and Kemerer found the other methods to be radically different from the object-oriented design techniques. They also suggest that the design methods are different because of the implementation-specific issues addressed in design and the differences in units of modularity. Under traditional methods, modules are used for modularity, while under the object-oriented design methods, objects are used for modularity. Figure 10.2 is an excerpt from the same article that compares design methods.

Function-oriented techniques, data-oriented techniques, and information-oriented techniques each include decomposition in analysis, which follows a top-down analysis approach, while object-oriented techniques provide a mechanism for aggregating system functionality using objects and classes, which suggests a bottom-up approach. Fichman and Kemerer claim that objects and classes are defined too late in the development process to provide a valid basis for partitioning large development projects.

"A functional decomposition of systems violates encapsulation because operations can directly access a multitude of different entities and are not subordinated to any one entity; this view is the antithesis of the object-oriented technique view."
R. Fichman [FIC92].

Other papers that compare development techniques and offer insight into the process include [BUL92], [MON92], [PAG92], and [SON92]. Bullman [BUL92] compares only object-oriented analysis methods, while Page-Jones suggests a comparison vehicle for object-oriented methods.

Song and Osterweil [SON92] compare a variety of method components using a framework based on method concepts, artifacts, representations, and actions. Included in the comparison are three data-oriented techniques (Jackson system design, data structured system development, and logical construction of programs), a function-oriented technique (structured design), and an object-oriented technique (Booch object-oriented design).

10.3 Our Method of Comparing Development Techniques

Recently, David Monarchi and Gretchen Puhr have proposed a typology for comparison of object-oriented analysis/design methods [MON92]. Their approach compares techniques based on four criteria:

1. Problem domain analysis technique
2. Solution domain design technique
3. Representation
4. Complexity management

Technique Comparisons	Analysis technique	Analysis representation	Design technique	Design representation	Complexity management	Programming languages
Function-oriented techniques	Functional decomposition or event partitioning	Function model	Module partitioning	Procedural design	Decomposing and partitioning	3GL
Data-oriented techniques	Normalization and CRUD	Data model	Database/Data structure design (denormaliz-ation)	Database design	Normalization	4GL
Control-oriented techniques	Control decomposition	Control model and threads	Module partitioning	Procedural design (interfaces)	Decomposing or partitioning	3GL
Information-oriented techniques	Functional decomposition and normalization	Function & data model	Database design (CRUD)	Database and Procedural design	Decomposition and normalization	4GL and 3GL code generation
Object-oriented techniques	Classification	Object model	Composition and reuse	Class libraries, object interaction and communication	Composition and classification	OOPL
Prototye-oriented techniques	Prototyping	Prototype or executable specification	Prototyping	Prototype or executable specification		4GL or code generation (executable specification)

Figure 10.3
Comparison of techniques - representations.

This approach, which is applied selectively to object-oriented methods in the article, could be applied equally well to all software development techniques with some minor modifications.

A more generic typology for development techniques would include the following characteristics:

1. Analysis technique
2. Design technique
3. Representation
4. Notation
5. Complexity management
6. Implementation issues

By further refining aspects of analysis and design representations and notations into support for data, process, and control modeling, for data structure, for procedure design, for architecture, and for low-level logic design, we were able to apply this approach to all the methods and clarify the differences among the various techniques. We have used this extension to the Monarchi and Puhr typology as the basis for our comparison of the methods presented in this book.

Technique Representations	Data Model	Function Model	Control Model	Definitions	Procedural Architecture	Procedural logic
Function-oriented techniques	Entity-relationship diagram (ERD) [optional]	Data flow diagram (DFD)	State-transition diagram [optional]	Data Dictionary	Structure chart	Program Description Language (PDL)
Data-oriented techniques	Entity diagram or ERD	Warnier/Orr diagram or CRUD matrix	Structure diagram [optional] or Not Supported	Descriptions or Data Dictionary	Warnier/Orr diagram, Structure diagram or Not Supported	Warnier/Orr diagram or Not Supported
Control-oriented techniques	ERD [optional]	DFD	Control flow diagram or Finite State Machine (STD)	Data Dictionary	Not Supported	PDL, Decision table, etc.
Information-oriented techniques	ERD, subject area diagram and Data Structure diagram (DSD)	Decomposition diagrams, DFD [optional]	Not Supported	Encyclopedia	Decomposition diagrams & Action diagrams	Action diagrams
Object-oriented techniques	Object and Classes	Object operations and messages	Object behavior (State-transition diagram)	Dictionary templates	Object interaction/ communication	Object methods and operations
Prototype-oriented techniques	ERD (optional)	Prototype or executable specification	Prototype or executable specification	Prototype	Prototype or executable specification	Not Supported

Figure 10.4
Comparison of technique notations.

It was not by accident that we decided to describe each development technique in this book in terms of how it supports notation, technique, and representation. We did this to help you, the reader, gain a better understanding of how the techniques are different, from a representation point of view as well as from a methodological view. Along the way, we found that in some sense these techniques have much in common, with some sharing a common history. Figures 10.3 and 10.4 compare the six development techniques described in Chapters 4 through 9 using the extended typology. Figure 10.3 compares the techniques for analysis and design, along with their representations, support for complexity management, and implementation language guidelines. Figure 10.4 compares the notations used in each of the techniques based on the representations that are common to all or most of the methods. When comparing the methods from this vantage point, some relevant observations come to mind. These observations are described and discussed in the sections that follow.

10.3.1 Comparison of Analysis Techniques, Representations, and Notations

1. With the exception of the object-oriented and prototype-oriented techniques, the methods use functional decomposition or event partitioning as their major analytical technique. Both the function-oriented and the control-oriented techniques use decomposition or partitioning exclusively, while the information-oriented techniques use functional decomposition together with data modeling methods. Data-oriented methods use data modeling techniques, including normalization and function/data dependency analysis, often with CRUD analysis (described in Chapter 5). The object-oriented techniques analyze the problem domain in terms of identification and classification of objects, while the prototype-oriented techniques use an executable specification or a working model as the primary method of analysis. All of the techniques can include a prototype as part of their analysis process, and the prototype can add to the analysis techniques if it is integrated as described in Chapter 9.

2. Except in the information-oriented and data-oriented techniques, support for data modeling is optional or data modeling is not supported. While the function-oriented, control-oriented, and prototype-oriented techniques can optionally support data modeling, the question of how the data view can be integrated with the function and control views, is largely unresolved. This raises the question of how complex data structures can be represented if methods do not specifically support them. The information-oriented and data-oriented techniques both focus on data modeling and provide basic support for a strong data view, with the information-oriented methods also supporting a functional view. The object-oriented techniques support data structures, but from a local perspective, not a shared, enterprise-wide view. (See the sidebar beginning on page 267.) Object models also require substantially different types of relationships from entities in a data model, including inheritance, sub/supertypes, and generalization/specialization.

3. Control modeling is supported only by two of the method types: control-oriented and object-oriented techniques. The prototype-oriented techniques may provide support based on the type of tool used for prototyping, i.e., executable specification. Dynamic behavior is unsupported with data-oriented techniques and information-oriented techniques, and is optionally supported in the function-oriented techniques (this again raises the question of integration of views). Interestingly, the object-oriented techniques support a dynamic view at the object level, while the control-oriented techniques support dynamic behavior at the subsystem level.

4. There is much similarity in how the function-oriented, data-oriented, and information-oriented techniques approach analysis and the notations they employ to communicate and represent the problem domain. In other words, these techniques are more alike than different, at least in their approach to understanding the problem domain. The functional view seems to dominate these methods, with decomposition or event partitioning providing the basis for most of the other methods.

5. All the methods use some form of data dictionary to collect and manage the underlying textual descriptions of the symbols used in the notations. The prototype-oriented and information-oriented techniques require automated support for the data dictionary function, along with code generation from design specifications or an executable specification facility.

10.3.2 Comparison of Design Techniques, Representations, and Notations

6. Data structure design support is provided only by data-oriented, information-oriented, and object-oriented techniques. Both the data-oriented and information-oriented methods support enterprise-wide database design with support for shared data at the organizational-level, while the object-oriented techniques support localized control of data structures. When complex data structures are required, the function-oriented and control-oriented techniques lack sufficient notations, representations, and methods for designing adequate solutions. While both of these types of techniques can be extended to support data structure design, the issue of how these representations are integrated with the functional design components must be resolved for practical use. The prototype-oriented techniques may include data structure design facilities depending on the tools used.

7. The function-oriented, control-oriented, and information-oriented techniques support architectural design and provide notations to represent this view. Structure charts and action diagrams, respectively, represent the structure of an application for these methods. Data-oriented, prototype-oriented, and object-oriented techniques provide little, if any, support for architectural design. Some object-oriented techniques provide limited support for object packaging, but these methods are dependent on the language used in implementation.

8. Function-oriented, control-oriented, and information-oriented techniques provide detailed design notations and methods for logical representations that are procedure-oriented. These methods map directly to the procedural languages often used in third- and fourth-generation language environments, but fall short when describing dynamic, event-driven environments. Object-oriented techniques provide methods or operations encapsulated within objects that can map to specific, OOPL constructs. Data-oriented techniques view procedural design as transactions applied against data structures, with the exception of the system-level methods described in Chapter 5. Prototype- and information-oriented techniques rely on automated tools to generate systems from specifications and are thus limited by the capabilities of these tools.

9. Function-oriented, control-oriented, and information-oriented techniques partition systems based on structural aspects of a system, whereas object-oriented and data-oriented techniques use a data structure view. In those systems where data structures are more stable than system functions, these techniques provide methods for building applications that are more resistant to structural change.

10.3.3 Comparison of Implementation Issues

10. The function-oriented and control-oriented techniques map specifically to the procedural languages common in most organizations. The data-oriented, information-oriented, and prototype-oriented techniques are more oriented towards the 4GL environment, with the information-oriented and prototype-oriented techniques requiring support for code generation based on design specifications.

11. The control-oriented and object-oriented techniques support event-driven behavior in the implementation phase, which is not supported by the other methods. Object-oriented methods support design constructs that map to objects or OOPLs and support event-driven environments.

10.4 Orientation and Focus

Beyond the specific comparisons among their representations, notations, and methods, these techniques can also be compared based on their philosophical views. The three primary orientations of the development techniques described in this book differentiate the techniques. (See Chapter 3 for more discussion on this.)

Function-oriented techniques focus on functions, and while they may include representations for data structures and control flow or time-dependent behavior, their overall philosophical emphasis is on processes or transformations of data. Structure charts, the primary design notation in the function-oriented techniques, represent a hierarchy of structure and do not support data structures. Functionally complex applications are adequately supported with any of the function-oriented techniques.

Likewise, data-oriented techniques concentrate on the data structures and focus less on the functional and dynamic behavior of systems. Many of the data-oriented techniques consider the functional behavior of a system to be transactions (i.e., CRUD) applied against the data structures themselves. Some data-oriented techniques do not provide representations for functional architecture or logic in their design approach. Complex data structures in applications may require data-oriented methods for development.

Control-oriented techniques are most concerned with the time- or context-dependent behavior of systems and usually downplay the functional and data perspectives. Like the function-oriented techniques, the control-oriented techniques may include support for data structure, but typically this information is collected as an afterthought and weakly linked with the dynamic behavior of the system. Systems with a strong control view should use the control-oriented methods, alone or in combination with the data-oriented or function-oriented techniques.

Information-oriented techniques, even though they are based on data-oriented concepts, integrate a process view with the data perspective, but the overriding focus in the information-oriented techniques, as in the data-oriented techniques, is on the data structures and more specifically on a defined data architecture for an enterprise. Information-oriented techniques provide more complete support for function and data in combination via the action diagram, the primary design notation used. Missing from the information-oriented techniques are any sufficient representations for dynamic or control behavior in a system.

Object-oriented techniques combine data structures with processes that act on those structures and so perhaps represent the best of both worlds, but unlike the other techniques, object-oriented methods combine a decomposition of entities or objects in analysis with a synthesis of objects and classes in design. While some object-oriented methods include traditional data and function modeling notations, their role in the overall development process is significantly different from that in the data-oriented and function-oriented methods from which they originate.

Prototype-oriented techniques are dependent on the tools used to build and modify the working model of the system. In the case of evolutionary prototypes, the model of the system evolves to become the system, and must support all the characteristics of the production system. When a throw-away prototype is used, it must be integrated with other, traditional techniques and representations as the software product moves from requirements to design to implementation.

When considering developing complex software products, we often find all three basic perspectives in a system, and developers may not be able to disregard or ignore one or two of these views. Given the presence of all three of these viewpoints in a software project, how would an organization choose an appropriate technique? In these cases, what is called for is a combination of the techniques that supports all three views. The function-oriented methods, when extended to support data structure and control-dependent behavior, and might adequately support three-dimensional applications.

Combining views, while beneficial, offers its own series of challenges and problems. In this case, the functional, data, and control views must be integrated, coordinated, and balanced, something many of the CASE tools fail to support. This can mean that complex manual processes will be required to fully support a three-dimensional application, along with customization of the functional methods to adequately model and design these types of systems.

Suffice it to say that while the major orientations are different, they also are similar in a number of ways. Function-oriented techniques evolved through the 1980s to include a stronger data perspective and incorporate data modeling concepts. Likewise, several function-oriented methodologists, including Ward/ Mellor and Hatley, extended the notations to support control behavior. These extensions, when used appropriately, can support all three views of a system.

Beyond the basic viewpoints of these techniques, the three other orientations, information, object, and prototype, also differ from one another and from the first three methods.

10.4.1 Comparing Function-Oriented Techniques with Other Techniques

The function-oriented techniques were developed first, historically, and are perhaps most studied of all the methods. The techniques within the function-oriented methods have percolated throughout the other methods, and there are strong similarities between the function-oriented techniques and the other methods because of this. The function-oriented techniques have also been modified to support both a data and a control view in analysis, and when combined with a strategic planning phase, strong data modeling, and prototyping can support most of the processes used in the information-oriented techniques.

10.4.2 Comparing Data-Oriented Techniques with Other Techniques

The data-oriented techniques, when compared to the other methods, are most similar to the information-oriented techniques and the object-oriented techniques. The enterprise-level data-oriented techniques are almost identical to the information-oriented techniques, and historically the information-oriented techniques drew from the methods used in them. The system-level data-oriented techniques are substantially different from the other methods, except the object-oriented techniques with their focus on defining entities (objects) and attributes. As discussed in Chapter 5, the system-level data-oriented techniques are not widely supported with automated tools, and this makes their practical use on large-scale projects questionable.

10.4.3 Comparing Control-Oriented Techniques with Other Techniques

The control-oriented techniques include support for dynamic or time-dependent behavior and focus on the control perspective in specification and modeling. Unlike the other methods, the control-oriented techniques support time- and context-dependent views. The control-oriented methods employ the same design techniques and notations as the function-oriented methods. The object-oriented techniques also support dynamic behavior, but at a different level of abstraction for objects, not subsystems. The function-oriented methods can be extended to support control modeling, and the object-oriented techniques also provide support for the dynamic behavior of systems.

10.4.4 Comparing Information-Oriented Techniques with Other Techniques

When comparing information-oriented techniques with other methods, the most striking difference is in their focus on high-level, strategic information planning and the creation of an information architecture as a precursor to software development. By their very nature, information-oriented techniques begin the software development process by defining overall business goals, objectives, and success factors. Enterprise models, which include data and function models, are created in the information-oriented techniques prior to beginning any development projects, and bring home the high-level view that the information-oriented techniques bring to software development.

The information-oriented techniques, like the data-oriented methods, focus on the data an organization uses, and this orientation leads to the view of data over function. While the information-oriented techniques evolved from the enterprise-level data-oriented techniques, they include an integrated functional and data view, with the action diagram acting as the primary point of focus in design and the generation of source code.

Information-oriented methods lack control modeling support, require close integration with 4GLs and code generators, require an integrated computer-based repository, and use data modeling techniques, including normalization and database design.

10.4.5 Comparing Object-Oriented Techniques with Other Techniques

"Using an object-oriented approach, we proceed in an entirely different manner; indeed, we suggest that structured design and object-oriented design are orthogonal views. Rather than factoring our system into modules that denote operations, we instead structure it around the objects that exist in our model of reality."
G. Booch [BOO88].

Comparing object-oriented with function-oriented techniques is easy in one sense, but difficult in another. At a very basic level, function-oriented techniques separate the function from the data structures, while object-oriented techniques encapsulate the two views. Also, the function-oriented techniques use functional decomposition to address complexity in analysis and design, while object-oriented techniques employ composition throughout the life cycle. In this sense, object-oriented techniques are the opposite of function-oriented techniques in their approach to designing and building software products.

Structured design focuses on the architecture or structure of the system and tends to place less emphasis on module or component design. Structured design partitions a system into modules and identifies their hierarchy, organization, and communication. Coupling and cohesion are critical factors in structured design, and the primary deliverable is the structure chart which was created to drive structured programming.

Object-oriented design focuses on component design and places much less emphasis on the architecture of the resulting system. In object-oriented design, the architecture of the system may be literally irrelevant, since the components (i.e., objects) define the system. In fact, many object-oriented design techniques describe a process of simply packaging the objects together and delivering them to the programming phase.

"Comparing structured development with OO development — structured development addresses intra-procedure and intra-data structure organization while object-oriented development addresses inter-procedure and data structure organization."
S. Tockey [TOC90].

Comparing object-oriented techniques with data-oriented techniques reveals many similarities. Some object-oriented techniques use data models along with process and control models to identify and define the objects in the problem domain. Where the methods differ significantly is in the design and implementation phases, where the object-oriented methods require substantially different specifications.

Like the function-oriented and information-oriented techniques, the data-oriented techniques do not tightly couple a data structure with its associated functions. This means that a function can be defined and shared among multiple data structures if needed. For instance, a library module shared among several programs is a typical implementation of this idea.

In addition, the data-structured approach disperses the structure of the data throughout a program [CON90]. Conversely, the object-oriented approach integrates data structures with the functions that operate on them into objects.

Comparing object-oriented techniques with control-oriented techniques indicates some similarities. Some object-oriented techniques, most specifically the Shlaer/Mellor method, are derived from control-oriented techniques, in this case the Ward/Mellor technique. But while some of the notations and representations may be the same — for example, the use of data, function, and control models in both approaches — they are also significantly different. Object models contain a dynamic view of classes and objects, but these models are defined to represent the interaction between objects.

10.5 Strengths and Weaknesses of the Techniques

While organizations have had success using all of these techniques on a wide variety of applications, some general guidelines can help developers select possible applications for these techniques.

10.5.1 Strengths

Software that executes in a graphical user interface (GUI) lends itself very nicely to object-oriented programming and thus object-oriented analysis and design. The Macintosh, Windows, OS/2 Presentation Manager, and OSF/Motif environments can provide a wealth of existing classes and objects that can be reused on new applications. Often, identifying and documenting the class organization is required before these objects can be effectively used.

Some developers of real-time systems have claimed that the performance of object-oriented programming languages (OOPLs) is lacking, but studies suggest that a mixed OOPL and traditional programming language environment can produce adequate embedded systems [see BAR91]. Much progress has been made in integrating OOPLs with traditional programming languages. As we have already seen, object-oriented software is ideal for event-driven environments, and many embedded class libraries are beginning to become available.

Similarly, developers of MIS have complained about lack of support for traditional business software under the object-oriented umbrella. While more development has occurred in C++ and Smalltalk, there are standards groups which are working on an object-oriented version of COBOL. In addition, many vendors now offer object-oriented database management systems (OODBMS) that can be used in conjunction with or in place of traditional relational databases.

Also, one CASE tool vendor, Netron, supports the Bassett Frame Technology (BFT), which is an object-oriented approach to developing COBOL applications. BFT defines code frames as mutually adaptive models, and Netron offers a product, Netron/CAP, which includes a standard set of frames in a hierarchy that can be assembled to form a finished product. Bassett has even suggested that object-oriented design techniques (such as the Booch approach used in this chapter) can be adapted to designing frames [BAS91]. In a sense, the BFT frame hierarchy is similar to a class hierarchy in a traditional OOPL, and other organizations are moving towards developing object-oriented extensions to the COBOL programming language.

From a practical standpoint, most organizations will want to consider moving incrementally toward an object-oriented approach, and for this reason, those techniques that combine structured and object-oriented concepts will hold great appeal. Other considerations or suggestions for applications that might be suitable for the object-oriented techniques include client/server software, which is usually touted as part of a cooperative or distributed processing environment, and vertical packaged software.

Object-oriented software fits very easily into a client/server model, and the model can be considered as a description of the interaction between two objects, a client and a server. A client makes requests of the server to perform services, and the server provides a set of services upon request. In an object-oriented environment, both the client and the server are objects.

The Object Management Group has defined a standard communication vehicle for clients and servers called the Object Requestor Broker specification. This standard defines how objects interact remotely and defines procedures for locating, invoking, and communicating between objects.

For embedded and real-time systems, the control-oriented methods offer the best support for dynamic behavior. The control-oriented techniques are supported by some very powerful automated tools, some of which are described in Chapter 11. Support for an executable specification represents a valuable tool to organizations that have large, complex, reactive systems that incorporate software and hardware constraints.

The function-oriented and information-oriented methods support complex functionality, with the information-oriented techniques providing an integrated data view alongside the functional view. When an enterprise-level view of software development is required, the information-oriented methods offer the best option, with support for strategic business planning and enterprise modeling.

Along with the information-oriented methods, the data-oriented techniques support complex data structures and a simplified view of functionality. When a relational DBMS is required, both the data-oriented and the information-oriented methods will support the required techniques and representations for these applications.

In those applications where the requirements are poorly understood or undefined, the prototype-oriented methods offer the best alternative, but will be limited by the automated support provided by the prototyping tool. Object-oriented methods also incorporate prototyping and evolution in their approach to software development.

10.5.2 Weaknesses

As the individual methods have strengths, they also have limitations or weaknesses for certain types of applications. For example, information-oriented and data-oriented techniques would be a bad choice for designing reactive or real-time systems, since they don't support the dynamic or control view, probably the most important view in these types of systems.

Lack of integrated support for control behavior in function-oriented methods may also prove to be a major weakness for those applications that have a dominant control view.

The control-oriented methods, along with the function-oriented techniques, might be a poor choice for complex data structured applications.

In those cases where strategic business planning is required, the control-oriented and object-oriented methods would prove to be unsupportive. While these inherent weaknesses are fairly obvious, with the inclusion of extensions to some of the methods, these limitations can be overcome.

10.6 Prototyping, Evolution, and Reuse in Development

Using a prototype in the software development process can enhance and improve the finished product (Chapter 9 describes the prototype-oriented techniques in detail), but a prototype also calls for a completely different approach to developing software than the other techniques. The prototype can be successful only when its purpose is clearly defined and understood, and when the prototype can be quickly built and modified. While some of the methods have attempted to incorporate prototypes into their approach, they have failed to consider the impact and role of the prototype in the development process. Key issues to consider when using a prototype with the other methods in this text include: How will the prototype be integrated with the other methods and representations? What will happen to the prototype once it has served its purpose? What limitations will the prototyping tools used have on the application?

Evolution is the operative word when a prototype is used in software development, and if a prototype is to be used with other techniques and notations, the prototype must be integrated into the development environment. Evolution also has an impact on management of software development, and when a prototype is used, management must understand and accept this change to the management process.

While object-oriented development has promised increase reuse, other, traditional techniques can support reuse at different levels as well. Early development methods, including structured design, were created to improve reuse of development components, and the object-oriented methods are not without their own limitations in these areas. Reuse must be made cost-effective before it will provide benefit to an organization [BAR91].

Most studies on reuse suggest that the primary inhibitor to component reuse is locating an available reuse "unit." Some organizations have had much success in formally defining procedures that encourage reuse and developing repository storage schemes that allow quick access to reusable components. Along with the technical challenge of reuse come the organizational and cultural issues. For reuse to be widespread, developers must be rewarded for reusing components. Tracking reuse represents a significantly different perspective and must be considered regardless of the methods used.

While the object-oriented methods provide support for reuse at the code-level, they fall short in facilitating reuse at the specification or model level. Also, class libraries, the chief tool used today for reuse, often have incompatibilities among themselves and may not be represented adequately in design notations.

10.7 Using the Three-Dimensional Taxonomy to Select Techniques

The three-dimensional taxonomy described in Chapter 3 helped to introduce the sample problems and explain different aspects of software systems. Organizations that need help can also use the taxonomy defined in Chapter 3, alone, or in conjunction with other characteristics, to select appropriate methods.

For those organizations that already have systems that represent the types of applications they develop, any of the metrics described in Chapter 3 could be used to analyze the existing suite of applications and provide a basis for future development technique selection. The drawbacks of using either function points or Halstead or McCabe's metrics can be eliminated when these are applied to existing systems that are available in source code. One method that could be beneficial would be to examine the existing legacy systems and apply one or all of these metrics to determine which of the three dimensions in our taxonomy are dominant. This could provide great insight into appropriate methods. We have already discussed possible methods for three-dimensional applications, and suggested possible combinations for two-dimensional systems. For more on this, see Chapter 3.

The process of selecting appropriate methods is non-trivial, and while we cannot offer specific recommendations for each organization, we can offer suggestions and guidelines for considering possible techniques. Chapter 12 covers technical issues related to process improvement, Chapter 13 describes processes for selecting and implementing techniques and tools, and Chapter 14 discusses issues related to developing or purchasing a methodology.

10.8 Resource List

While there are many papers on comparisons among development techniques, most only compare two types of methods or focus on specific types of software applications. For comparisons among popular object-oriented techniques, see [BUL92] and [MON92]. For comparisons among other methods, see [ULU91] (information-oriented vs. function-oriented techniques), [CLA90] (function-oriented vs. data-oriented techniques), [CON90] and [LOY90] (function-oriented vs. object-oriented techniques).

For reactive development techniques, see [PLA90] and [WOO89]; for comparisons among function-oriented, information-oriented, and object-oriented techniques, see [FIC92]. For comparisons of requirements specification techniques and tools, see [COL84], [LIS86] and [WIN88].

10.9 References

[ALB83]   Albrecht, A. J., and J. E. Gaffney, "Software Function, Source Lines of Code and Development Effort Prediction: A Software Science Validation," *IEEE Trans. on Soft. Eng.*, vol. SE-9, no. 6, November 1983, pp. 639-648.

[BAR91]   Barnes, B. H., and T. B. Bollinger, "Making Reuse Cost-Effective," *IEEE Software*, Jaunuary 1991, pp. 13-24.

[BAS91]   Bassett, P., "Engineering Software for Softness," *American Programmer*, February 1991, pp. 1- 15.

[BOO88]   Booch, G., *On the Concepts of Object-Oriented Design*, 1988

[BUL92]   Bullman, D., "An Objective Survey," *Embedded Systems Programming*, vol. 5, no. 3, 1992, pp. 20-31.

[CLA90] Clark, J., "Function vs. Data-Driven Methodologies: A Prescriptive Metric," *ACM SIGSOFT*, vol. 15, no. 2, April 1990, page 26.

[COL84] Colter, M. A., "A Comparative Examination of Systems Analysis Techniques," *MIS Quarterly* (March 1984), pp. 51-66.

[CON92] Connors, D. T., "Software Development Methodologies and Traditional and Modern Information Systems," *ACM SIGSOFT*, vol. 17, no. 2, pp. 43-49.

[CON90] Constantine, L., "Objects, Functions, and Program Extensibility," *Computer Language*, January 1990, pp. 34-56.

[FIC92] Fichman, R. G. and C. F. Kemerer, "Object-Oriented and Conventional Analysis and Design Methodologies," *IEEE Computer*, October 1992, pp. 22-39.

[FIR87] Firth, Wood, Pethia, Roberts, Mosley, and Dolce, "A Classification Scheme for Software Development Methods," *Tech. Rept. CMU/SEI-87-TR-41*, SEI, Carnegie Mellon University, November 1987.

[GER90] Gerhart, S., "Applications of Formal Methods: Developing Virtuoso Software," *IEEE Software*, September 1990, pp. 7-10.

[HAL77] Halstead, M., *Elements of Software Science*, North Holland, 1977.

[LIS86] Liskov, B. H., and V. Berzins, "An Appraisal of Program Specifications," in *Software Specification Techniques*, N. Gehani and A. T. McGettrick, eds., Addison-Wesley, 1986, p. 3.

[LOY90] Loy, P., "A Comparison of Object-Oriented and Structured Development Methods," *ACM SIGSOFT*, vol. 15, no. 1, January 1990, pp. 44-49.

[MCC76] McCabe, Tom, "A Complexity Measure," *IEEE Trans. on Soft. Eng.*, December 1976, pp. 308-320.

[MON92] Monarchi, D. E., and G. I. Puhr, "A Research Typology for Object-Oriented Analysis and Design," *CACM*, vol. 25, no. 9, pp. 35-47.

[PAG92] Page-Jones, M., "Comparing Techniques by Means of Encapsultation and Connascence," *CACM*, vol. 35, no. 9, pp. 147-152.

[PLA90] Place, P. R. H., Wood, W. G., and M. Tudball, "Survey of Formal Specification Techniques for Reactive Systems," *Tech. Rept. CMU/SEI-90-TR-5*, SEI, Carnegie Mellon University, May 1990.

[PRE87] Pressman, R. S., *Software Engineering: A Practitioner's Approach*, Second ed., McGraw-Hall, 1987.

[PRE88] Pressman, R. S., *Software Engineering: A Beginner's Guide*, McGraw-Hill, 1988.

[PRE92] Pressman, R. S., *Software Engineering: A Practitioner's Approach*, Third ed., McGraw-Hill, 1992.

[SAN88] Sannella, D., "A Survey of Formal Software Development Methods," *Tech. Rept. ECS-LFCS-88-56*, Edinburgh University, 1988.

[SON92] Song, X., and L. J. Osterweil, "Toward Objective, Systematic Design-Method Comparisons," *IEEE Software*, May 1992, pp. 43-53.

[TOC90] Tockery, S., B. Hoza, and S. Cohen, *Object-Oriented Analysis: Building on the Structured Techniques*, Boeing Compuer Services, Seattle, Washington, 1990.

[TOP90]   Topper, A., "CASE Meets Real-Time," *Embedded Systems Programming*, July 1990, pp. 39-60.

[ULU91]   Uluakar, T., "From Structure Methods to Information Engineering: A Comparison," Texas Instruments, 1991.

[WIN88]   Wing, J., "A Study of 12 Specifications of the Library Problem," *IEEE Software*, July, 1988, pp. 66 - 76.

[WOO88]   Wood, W., R. Pethia, L. Gold, and R. Firth, "A Guide to the Assessment of Software Development Methods," *Tech. Rept. CMU/SEI-88-TR-8*, SEI, Carnegie Mellon University, April 1988.

[WOO89]   Wood, D., and W. Wood, "Comparative Evaluations of Four Specification Methods for Real-Time Systems," *Tech. Rept. CMU/SEI-89-TR-36*, SEI, Carnegie Mellon University, December 1989.

[YOU89]   Yourdon, E., *Modern Structured Analysis*, Yourdon Press, 1989.

Chapter 11
Computer-Aided Software Engineering

It is hard to imagine using software engineering techniques on any scale without the support of automated tools. Originally, computer-aided software engineering (CASE) products were simple, crude diagraming tools that didn't include a dictionary or repository for textual descriptions or verification checking of models or diagrams. Over the years, CASE tools have evolved to provide sophisticated support for verification checking, requirements collection and tracking, prototyping, and the generation of source and executable code from specifications. Some CASE tools also claim to support the generation of specifications from existing source code.

While CASE tools promise to provide benefits in the areas of increased software quality, reduced costs and resources for software development, increased documentation, reduced costs and resources for maintenance, and increased productivity, many organizations have failed to successfully implement CASE or realize these benefits. Also, CASE tools are not without their faults, the most serious of which is lack of integration among different tools, different tasks in the development life cycle, and among different hardware and software platforms.

In this chapter we will review the current state of the CASE tool industry, discuss the practical benefits of CASE and the actual drawbacks, introduce the concept of CASE and a software development environment, and cover the problems inherent in providing automated support for the entire development life cycle. Along the way we will also discuss some interesting findings related to how automation affects software development, strategies for tool integration, and the future of CASE tools.

11.1 Introduction

While software engineering techniques have been around for over 25 years, CASE tools didn't really appear on the market until the early 1980s. The sidebar beginning on page 354 describes the genesis of the early CASE tools and the CASE industry. Future CASE products will probably incorporate emerging technologies, including expert systems, hypertext, groupware, and multimedia.

The driving factor for the boom in the CASE industry was undoubtedly the introduction of the personal computer (PC), which IBM delivered in 1981. While

CASE tools had been developed before the introduction of the PC, the ability to deliver a workstation-based CASE product quickly spawned an industry and the early tools that appeared took advantage of the PC environment.

The first PC-based CASE products were not much more than crude diagraming tools that provided little or no support for the collection of textual specifications and no verification checking of the models or diagrams created. Slowly, the tools evolved to include support for rule checking, the collection of requirements, the development of prototypes, and eventually, some vendors used expert systems in their products to enforce constraints in software engineering techniques.

With the evolution of PC-based CASE tools, the CASE industry blossomed. Anyone who ever tries using software engineering techniques such as the ones described in Chapters 4 through 9 of this book on a medium- to large-scale project without the aid of automated tools quickly learns how futile this process is. Without the help of automation, creating and maintaining the diagrams, specifications, and documentation for any non trivial system is cumbersome and requires a substantial manual effort to keep things current and error-free.

Some things, including making a change to a symbol or connection on a lower-level diagram in a set of related diagrams, can cause hundreds of changes to specifications or models that refer to that symbol or connection. Likewise, trying to verify every element or flow in a series of decomposed specifications is complete, consistent and balanced can take hours or even days. Clearly, these types of tasks cry out for support in the form of automated tools.

In 1986, the CASE market had grown to $50 million, and by 1988 it had tripled in size to over $150 million. By the early 1990s, CASE had become a $1 billion market and had changed dramatically from a cottage industry to a major market for IBM, DEC, and others.

While the CASE marketplace grew quickly, however, the use of the tools in everyday software development did not. By the end of 1990, it was estimated that only 10 to 17 percent of software developers were using CASE tools, so it was apparent that CASE was not catching on as many had predicted. The reasons for this were varied and led to a somewhat stagnant market for tools in the late 1980s.

Around this time, code generation products, which were originally mainframe-based, had begun to be used in conjunction with analysis and design tools. But code generators had limited acceptance in the late 1980s, around 2 to 5 percent, and represented a small portion of the overall CASE market. Also, organizations that attempted to use analysis and design tools with code generators found that significant manual effort was required to coordinate the links between the products.

By the late 1980s, the CASE marketplace had begun to experience growth problems based on the limits of individual tools and issues related to moving information from one CASE product to another.

In September of 1989, IBM announced its CASE strategy, AD/Cycle, and shortly afterward DEC announced its, Cohesion. With these announcements, IBM and DEC established business partnerships with many of the leading CASE vendors and began to push their own standards in CASE integration, primarily in the form of proprietary repositories.

11.2 The State of Existing CASE Tools

As of the middle of 1992, the CASE industry has evolved to represent a dichotomy of products in the marketplace. There are sophisticated, expensive CASE products from a handful of vendors that some have called integrated-CASE (ICASE), and then there are several hundred other products that are typically inexpensive or serve a market niche. Some have labeled these latter products component CASE (CCASE) tools. While a few CASE products have added expert systems to perform verification checking, many tools provide only reports that can be run against the data dictionary and provide no guidance in the use of the tool or technique.

Some in the industry have criticized CCASE tools for lack of support of the entire software development process, while others have trumpeted the capabilities of ICASE products. Existing CASE tools generally support requirements definition and design, code generation for simple, on-line systems and some limited real-time systems, and testing and maintenance of MIS and real-time systems.

Much work is underway in the CASE industry to better support maintenance through reverse engineering capabilities. These products promise to take existing source and executable code and generate design specifications and, eventually, models of the functions and data in an existing system. Unfortunately, at the time this book was written, these products had not yet appeared.

CASE tools now support all types of software development, from MIS to embedded systems, and there is a movement towards integrating software engineering and hardware engineering. Computer-aided systems engineering tools bridge the gap between software development and hardware development and provide systems management and tracking capabilities.

But the problems of tool integration have not vanished with the announcements by IBM and DEC, and many organizations have remained skeptical of the true value of CASE. Some in the industry have decided that the market has again stagnated, and few significant product deliveries have been made since the announcements of 1989. IBM has yet to deliver on the promise of AD/Cycle, and DEC has also had trouble delivering its Cohesion products on its mainframe and Ultrix platforms. There is a general pessimism in the industry, and many organizations have put their plans for automation on hold until the industry delivers on the promise of integration.

In addition, while there are a number of different CASE products to choose from, many organizations have found selecting appropriate CASE technology to be a daunting task. We suggest a process for selecting and implementing CASE based on a practical, objective evaluation of the needs of an organization [TOP91b] which is described in more detail in Chapter 13. (A partial list of CASE tools is included at the end of this chapter.)

11.3 Potential Benefits of CASE Tools

With or without the benefit of an integrated set of automated tools, the products currently available can deliver benefits to organizations if used wisely and appropriately. Some of these benefits are more directly related to the software engineering techniques described in Chapters 4 through 9, but without automated support, organizations would be unwilling and unable to derive these benefits because of the overhead involved in maintaining the representations manually.

More complete requirements and design specification

"Ok, guys, we just found out we're starting a big project for Purchasing, so Bob, you go talk with the V.P. of Purchasing, and the rest of you get busy coding."
Process often found in real-world development shops.

This humorous story, though perhaps overstated, effectively brings out the view of many software development organizations. While requirements definition has been proven to be the cause of most of the errors in a finished software product, most organizations instead have as their focus programming, testing, and maintenance. This usually leads to very little requirements analysis and design, and this often contributes to the delivery of inadequate software.

All of the development techniques described in Chapters 4 through 9 force an extensive effort in the requirements specification and design of software and less effort on the programming and testing of the finished product. The benefit here is obvious to anyone who has ever seen a graph that indicates the cost of a change or fix to software throughout the life cycle. Reducing changes in the latter stages of software development, especially major changes in functionality or structure, greatly reduces the overall cost of the system.

The collection of this information and dissemination of it to users also leads to a better understanding of their part in the development process, and this in turn leads to higher levels of satisfaction with the finished product. Often, users of software are given few (if any) deliverables in the long development process until the system is finally delivered. Timely interaction between developers and users can often lead to more requirements defined earlier and in more detail. When using development techniques and CASE, users can become more involved in the process and review deliverables, in the form of models, prototypes, specifications, etc., throughout the process.

More accurate requirements and design specification

Along with the effort required to define requirements and a design specification, the development techniques described in Chapters 4 through 9 also recommend techniques for verifying the accuracy and content of software representations. CASE tools help to make this verification process manageable for medium- to large-scale projects.

Examples of error checking typically included in a CASE tool include syntax checking diagrams and textual specifications, cross-diagraming checking, consistency checking, completeness checking, and requirements tracking. Some or all of these can be implemented using expert systems for rule checking within the CASE tool. Of these, perhaps the most beneficial is requirements tracking.

Simply defined, requirements tracking allows requirements, in the form of user, engineering, or change requests, to be entered into a CASE repository and associated with models and specifications throughout the development process to indicate the requirements have been satisfied. This leads to better tracking and management of requirements and helps to ensure that major requirements are not left out of the finished product.

Configuration management of the representations created by these development techniques often involves tracking and controlling the deliverables throughout the development process. Often, objects defined are components of other objects or structures. In some cases, the models and specifications are executed within the CASE environment, which further adds to the understanding of the behavior of the system.

Standardized tools and techniques lead to a well-defined, repeatable software development process and to increased communication among the development group

By using a software engineering technique, and a CASE tool that supports that technique, an organization will establish a de facto software development process. The process of migrating to a new development technique, however beneficial in the long run, often leads to discontent in the staff during the transition. Cultural change, the largest inhibitor to this migration, must be addressed and dealt with on all levels for an organization to be successful in this process.

Establishing a standard development process will in turn lead to a more repeatable process. In addition, when migrating towards a software engineering technique and CASE tool, organizations may also perform an assessment of their existing development environment, which can also lead to a more defined process.

When developers and clients share a common set of representations and techniques for the collection and dissemination of development information, the level of communication in the organization typically improves. As we have shown in previous chapters, developers need a shared view of the product, process, and tools that is as unambiguous as possible if they hope to understand the requirements for a complex software product. Towards this end, development techniques and standard deliverables (representations) help to focus the groups' understanding and to facilitate the free exchange of ideas in the development process.

As discussed in Chapter 9, the use of a prototype can help facilitate further communication between developers and clients. When models, especially executable models, can be exercised by users, the resulting increase in information and understanding by both parties leads to a higher level of satisfaction with the finished product.

Higher-quality software results from the three previous benefits

As a result of the previous benefits, more complete and accurate requirements and design specifications and better communication, the quality of the software delivered usually improves. This can be measured in hard metrics, in the form of defects/1000 lines of code (KLOC), or in soft metrics, such as in the level of user satisfaction with the final product.

Regardless of how it is measured, more information earlier in the development process leads to fewer major modifications later in the development process. More accurate information throughout the process leads to less rework, and improved communication leads directly to an improvement in overall software quality.

Standard tools and techniques serve to establish communication within the development environment and lead to better understanding of the problem domain and the specifications for design. When technical and nontechnical staff share a common understanding or view of the development process, and thus their role in that process, the process can be improved.

Better measurement and estimation

"When integrated with metrics and a suitable software process model, CASE can form the core of a testbed for modeling, measurement and management of the software process."
G. Tate [TAT92].

Software engineering techniques, including all the ones described in this book, represent a defined approach to developing software. As we have already seen, a defined software development process is, by definition, a repeatable process. A repeatable process is one which can be estimated, while estimating a nonrepeatable process is often like shooting in the dark: You don't know how much you will hit or how far off you might be.

In addition, standard deliverables, tasks, roles, and responsibilities which are defined as part of software engineering techniques can be tracked and managed within a CASE tool. Once collected, past project size and effort data can be used in estimating new projects. In this fashion, CASE and software engineering techniques can greatly facilitate the collection and management of software process information, which can be used for modeling and improving the process.

The relationship between CASE, software development techniques, and an improved software process has been covered by many authors, including [TAT92]. These studies have shown that:

1. CASE tools can support empirical model verification
2. CASE tools can be embedded within a metrics envelope which can collect data automatically and, in conjunction with a process model, provide traceability for measurements
3. CASE tools can help provide progress reporting and data to which earlier and later activities and products can be related for purposes of estimation, planning, and monitoring.

Some in the industry have suggested wrapping a software process model and metric collection environment around a CASE tool so that metric information can be collected automatically and software process models can be defined in the notations and representations of development techniques. Others have used the notations common in development techniques to model the software process. Modeling the software process with these notations has proved to be beneficial and can help identify areas for improvement of the development process. Chapter 12 covers software process models and process improvement in more detail.

Better documentation

Textual specifications, including requirements, can be collected within the CASE tool and tracked throughout the development process. A report which identifies the requirements that have yet to be satisfied can be helpful to both developers and clients. Higher-level requirements, or user requirements, can be decomposed into lower-level requirements, or engineering requirements. Since all forms of models and specifications can be tracked within a CASE repository, better management and control of these requirements occurs.

Requirements, once entered into the CASE tool, can also be associated with the representations (deliverables) that satisfy those requirements as the development process proceeds. Using the library system as an example, a CASE tool could allow the functional requirement "Check out a book from the library" to be associated with the data structures, processes, and procedures that satisfy this requirement. This association serves to indicate that the functional requirement has been satisfied at a specific point in the development process.

Assuming that models and specifications are placed into a CASE repository, there is also an ability to produce a wealth of documentation to support the maintenance of the software through its useful life. This information can take the form of printed reports, diagrams, and specifications, or can be given to the maintenance staff in the CASE tool itself, which helps to support impact analysis and change control on the product as it is maintained.

All forms of documentation, including user documentation and design documents, along with design decisions and can be produced, in printed and on-line format, for maintenance. In addition, all models and specifications entered within a CASE tool can be printed or plotted. Plotting large, complex diagrams can be made much easier using a Postscript printer under MS Windows, OS/2, or Motif. This in turn can lead to better understanding on the part of developers and users of the representations (models and design specifications) for a system.

Lower cost of maintenance (see above)

Given that the information described above is available to maintenance staff, the cost of changing a system can be greatly reduced when a CASE tool is used in development. All of the models, design specifications, and requirements can be delivered to the maintenance staff, in the form of the CASE repository, and they too can follow the development technique.

In addition, CASE repositories can provide impact analysis of potential changes to data structures or processes. Since all types of information collected by the CASE tool and the associations between data can be managed by the CASE repository, there is an ability to determine which objects will be affected by a planned change to a lower-level component.

Also, the collection, tracking, and management of change requests, test plans, and other technical documentation can be facilitated within the CASE tool. Functional requirements can be tracked, along with test plans and change requests, within the CASE repository.

For maintenance of software that was developed without the benefit of CASE tools, reverse engineering tools promise the ability to examine existing source and executable code for systems and derive representations (design specifications and models) which can be used by maintenance staff.

Long-term reduced development time and costs (reuse, etc.)

Given the benefits listed above in combination with the ability of a development organization to improve its software development process, in the long term the cost of developing software can be reduced. This benefit occurs because of a number of factors, including reuse of models and specifications, improved quality and delivery of software that better satisfies the functional requirements, better knowledge of the business on the part of development staff, and increased user involvement in software development.

While many object-oriented enthusiasts have touted the possible benefits of reuse, software engineering has provided this benefit as well. Reuse of specifications and models has been widely documented, including [MAI92], which describes an intelligent reuse advisor. Models, including data, process, control, and prototypes, often contain components that are similar to other aspects of systems across an organization or development area. A CASE repository makes identification of these components easier, and this in turn can lead to increased reuse.

Improved software quality and user satisfaction often lead to higher morale on the part of developers and users and less of an "us vs. them" perspective in communications between the two groups. This improvement in communication can lead to a reduction in major problems or missing functions later in the development life cycle.

Developers using models and specifications also experience better understanding of the business functions, and this in turn leads to an improvement in communication with users. This heightened awareness of the business also leads to more intelligent discussions and can ultimately lead to a view of IS and clients as business partners.

Increased user involvement throughout the development process often results from better communication and team building [BOE84]. This in turn can lead to a more efficient requirements definition and specification process, which can also reduce the overall costs of systems development.

11.4 Drawbacks to Existing CASE Tools

While the current CASE tools are not without their benefits, they are also not without their drawbacks, some of which have already been briefly discussed. In this section we will discuss some of the more serious drawbacks to using the existing CASE tools.

Integration among phases, tools, and platforms

"A CASE environment must maintain a consistent view of the system under development, despite demands placed on it by varied users, data representations and formalisms."
C. Fernstrom [FER92].

As already discussed, the most pressing issue facing the CASE industry is that of tool integration. Integration includes the use of CASE objects among different phases of the SDLC, including among design, programming, and maintenance, among tools sold by different vendors, and among different hardware and software platforms.

Integration among phases must move beyond the current levels of support to include complete support for changes reflected forward and backward through the process. For example, changes to design specifications should cause changes to code; likewise, changes to code should produce changes to design specifications. Without these changes managed and instigated by the CASE tool, its true benefits in generating working systems from specifications will be limited.

Integration among different tools from different vendors is difficult because each CASE vendor has a vested interest in the technology developed, and there are conflicting architectures and design goals in the tools. Also, different CASE vendors have taken different approaches to generating code: some generate code from diagrams, some from prototypes. Other factors that will affect the integration issue include: How will the widespread use of OOP affect this issue? Will there need to be a refocusing of effort away from generating code from specifications to assembling code (objects)?

One major problem with integration is sharing development information across different hardware and software platforms. For example, an organization that includes computers from IBM and DEC as well as Unix workstations and PCs cannot currently share development information among these platforms. The increased use of LANs will undoubtedly help in this area, but the industry has tended to move towards proprietary standards and has moved only slowly towards open standards.

Numerous authors ([CHE92], [THO92], [WAS90]) have identified several different levels of CASE integration. These include the following:

> _Data_ - to ensure that tools share common definitions of information in the repository
> _Control_ - to ensure that tools follow the processes of the integration platform and access/update objects accordingly
> _Presentation_ - to ensure that tools share a common user interface or appearance
> _Process_ - to ensure that tools use a defined process for interacting

These views of integration are described in more detail in Figure 11.1 from [THO92]. Thomas and Nejmeh have further refined these four types of integration into more detail as follows:

> _Data integration_: Interoperability, or the ability of a tool to operate on data produced by other tools
> > Nonredundancy, the ability of different tools to share single occurrences of data instead of maintaining multiple copies of the data
> > Data consistency, the ability of tools to cooperate on the maintenance and use of the data they manipulate
> > Data exchange, the ability of a tool to reuse data created by another tool
> > Synchronization, the ability of a tool to communicate changes it makes to the values of data to other tools

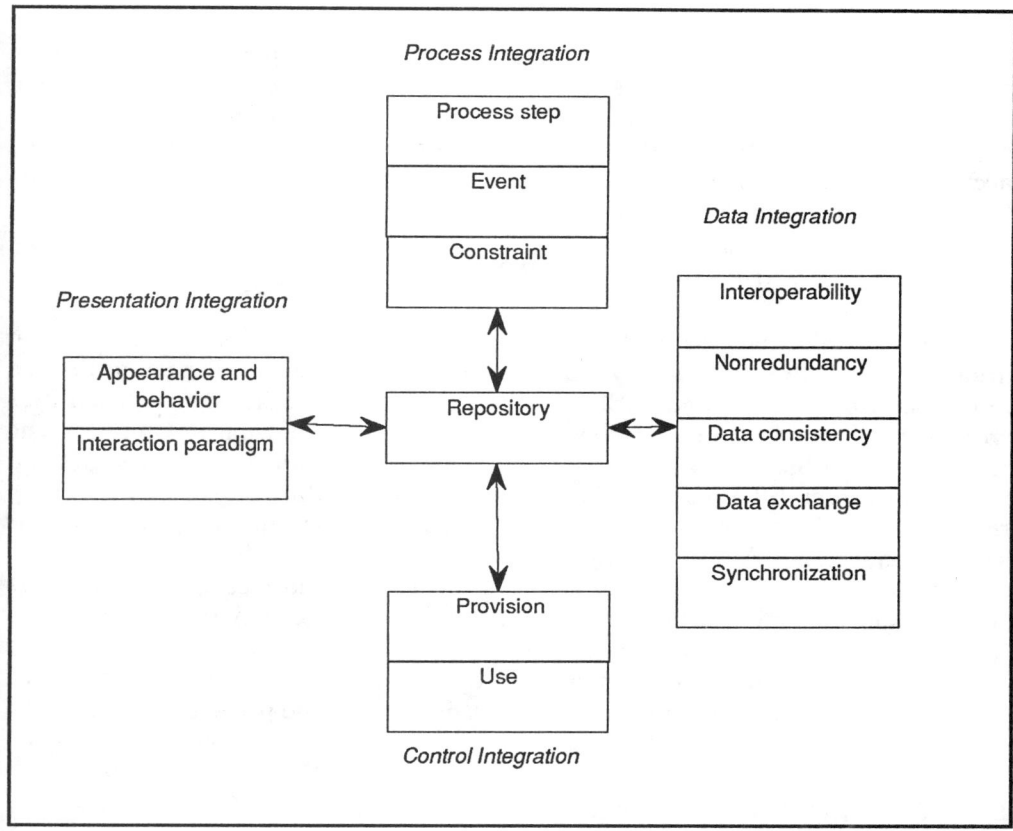

Figure 11.1
Views and relationships of integrated CASE.

Control integration: <u>Provision</u>, the extent to which a tool's services or operations are used by other tools in the environment
   <u>Use</u>, the extent to which tools use the services provided by other tools in the environment

Presentation integration: <u>Appearance and behavior</u>, the common screen appearance and interaction behavior of different tools in the environment
   <u>Interaction paradigm</u>, the extent to which tools use similar metaphors and mental models

Process integration: <u>Process</u>, how well the tools combine to support the development process
   <u>Event</u>, the degree to which the tools share a common definition of the events that take place in the development process
   <u>Constraint</u>, the degree of cooperation in enforcing constraints in the development process

Any software engineering environment that plans to support and automate the entire software development life cycle (SDLC) must contend with the passage of development objects from one phase to another. Such an environment must also support concurrent access to the objects and must ensure that the objects are used according to specified rules. We will discuss the issue of integration and standards for tool interaction in Section 11.5.

Multiuser repository support on PCs and LANs

While CASE repository support has been provided by a few vendors on a local area network (LAN), the majority of products that are PC-based still provide limited multiuser capabilities. Some CASE vendors provide simple lock and unlock facilities without an intelligent check-in/check-out capability for information stored in the repository. This has led many organizations to assign technical staff to extract and merge data from different repositories. This process is difficult, consumes many resources, and is error-prone. Automated support for this capability is a must for second generation CASE products.

In addition, only a few of the vendors include adequate security and access controls for the information stored in the repository. Given the value of the information in the repository, the tool should support limiting access to select objects or groups of objects in a fashion similar to traditional computer security systems. Ideally, a CASE tool should include user IDs, passwords and project- or group-level IDs, and should support security restrictions down to the object or diagram level.

Long learning curve for techniques, and the potential for failure is quite high

Learning a new development technique like the ones described in Chapters 4 through 9 typically takes 18 months and may take upwards of two years. At a basic level, successfully introducing software development techniques into an organization requires cultural change in that organization. Adding to cultural change the other factors that can inhibit successful migration to CASE and software development techniques, it is not difficult to see why many organizations fail.

Developers must learn a "new" way of developing software, and this process takes time and must be nurtured. While developers are learning the "new" way, their productivity will fall off, and management is often reluctant to stay committed to a migration effort in the face of higher short-term costs and longer development times. The education process developers must go through is described succinctly using the J curve and the seven levels of expertise described by Wayland Systems (see Chapter 13).

Cultural change is by far the most serious, but not the only, impediment to realizing the benefits described in the previous section. The costs for training, new technology, tools, and support required in the environment typically can lead to failure if underestimated.

The case studies in Chapter 15 describe some common reasons for failure. The reasons for failure vary by organization, but some general inhibitors to success include a lack of understanding of the "real" benefits of development techniques, the lack of a long-term view by organizations, the lack of realization of the cultural change implied in the migration to new technology, the focus on productivity over quality improvements, a lack of measurements and thus proof of value, and a focus on the technology (i.e., CASE) and not the process and development technique.

Limited code generation capability - specifically, GUI, client / server, real-time / embedded systems, etc.

While many CASE products generate COBOL code for standard on-line transaction processing systems (DB2, CICS, etc.), and some even support the generation of batch programs, there are many types of software applications these products still cannot generate code adequately for. These include real-time and embedded systems, client/server or distributed processing systems, and systems that execute under the control of a graphical user interface (GUI).

The CASE industry is still waiting for code generation technology to mature to support complex operating environments, specifically event-driven systems. While some CASE products can generate C or Ada code from design specifications, these often do not scale up sufficiently for large systems and typically rely on code templates to satisfy requirements for complex logic.

Inherent limits on the specification tools and languages used to generate and prototype systems will always prevent some types of systems from being generated completely. Other types of systems may be targeted at less popular or unique operating environments that major CASE vendors will not support. CASE vendors will support the more popular environments and implementation platforms, and this in turn will limit the eventual success of code generation.

Graphical User Interface applications, which are event-driven, present problems for code generator products. Client/server applications also present problems for code generation, if only from the perspective of where specific functionality should reside in the application, at the client or the server. OMG efforts may resolve this for object-oriented methods and tools, but what about non-object-oriented products?

Evolving techniques — movement towards OOA/OOD

As software development techniques have evolved, the CASE industry has been presented with a moving target, which has made it harder to deliver full support for methods. The use and support of both structured and object-oriented techniques represents a distinct challenge to CASE vendors who must provide automated support for either or both.

Some CASE vendors have opted to design their products around meta-methods with rule-based verification checking and object definition. Supporting meta-methods allows the user of the tool to tailor the CASE environment to fit specific needs.

Future methods, notations, and representations may require CASE vendors to adopt the meta-method approach to stay competitive with the changing face of the methods used.

11.5 A Repository for Development Information

While the topic of CASE integration has garnered much interest lately, there are a number of difficult questions that must be answered before a repository can be defined for the development process. Some of these questions include:

Is there a definite need for a CASE repository, or should vendors simply use defined standards for communicating in a software development environment?

What types of information should reside in a CASE repository?

Who should control the CASE repository?

How should tools access/update the information in the CASE repository?

Who should define these services?

Where should the repository reside?

Should there be more than one copy of a repository in an organization? If so, how will an organization manage its repositories (i.e., move information between repositories)?

Should the repository include intelligence or knowledge about the software development process used?

Recall our initial discussion on repository centered development in Chapter 1. Hardware vendors, including IBM, DEC, and HP, have announced and begun delivering proprietary CASE integration products that support integration of different automated tools and development platforms. Other standard efforts, most notably IEEE-CS, IRDS, and PCTE, have been proposed but have received limited support throughout the industry.

The Information Resource Dictionary Standard (IRDS) has been defined and accepted by the ANSI committee (X3H4) and by some vendors in the CASE community. The IRDS defines a shareable repository with an application system that manages the information in the repository and access to it by automated tools. Underlying the IRDS is a database which can be implemented using a relational, hierarchical, network, flat-file, or object-oriented structure.

The IRDS defines, stores, manipulates, and controls the information in the repository in support of software development. The ANSI committee has defined a description of the IRDS which includes a data architecture and tool functionality. The standard also defines a modular structure which includes a core model that manages access to the IRDS data. The IRDS tool set is described in Figure 11.2.

The Portable Common Tool Environment (PCTE) has been accepted by the European community as a CASE tool integration standard. Future direction for the PCTE is controlled by the PCTE Interface Management Board, which currently contains 26 member organizations. A PCTE newsletter is published regularly, and a promotional group is actively promoting the use of PCTE throughout the world. The PCTE standard is rapidly becoming accepted in the Unix community but has seen less acceptance in other areas.

The PCTE effort was begun in 1983 and has attempted to define a fully integrated CASE framework which will support multiple languages, a migration path for existing tools, and a distributed development environment.

IEEE-CS P1175 is a reference model for interconnections between development tools defined by the IEEE computer society. While the IEEE committee has discussed issues related to a repository, it has primarily focused on the services and semantic connections between tools.

The CASE Integration Services (CIS) Standards Committee is an ad hoc group of vendors attempting to define a standard for CASE tool integration. CIS has adopted a subset of the IRDS-A Tool Integration Standards (ATIS) proposal submitted by DEC and Atherton Technology. The ATIS proposal has also been submitted to the ANSI committee as an extension to the IRDS. Atherton Technology and DEC have announced strategies to support the integration of PCTE with ATIS and the IRDS.

IBM has defined its Repository Manager/MVS which will integrate software development information under the AD/Cycle platform. Currently, IBM is working with its AD/Cycle business partners to define an information model for the RM/MVS. IBM's repository will be available on its mainframe, minicomputer, PC, and LAN environments with a RDBMS underneath [SAG90].

DEC has announced its CDD/Repository which will eventually support a distributed repository. The initial CDD/Repository product is based on DEC's RDBMS, Rdb. DEC has also include the A Tool Integration Standard (ATIS) as an object-oriented interface to its repository [DIG91].

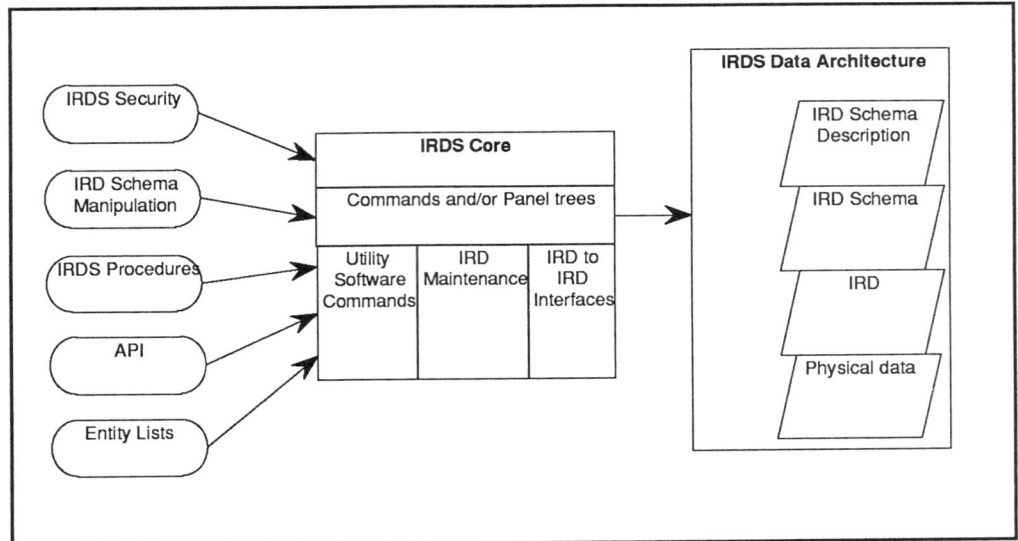

Figure 11.2
IRDS tool set.

HP now offers its SoftBench which is a Unix-based integration platform that supports tool management, text editors, builders, configuration management, static analyzer, C, C++, and Ada development tools and a GUI. SoftBench is more of a tool-to-tool communications standard than a true repository standard.

11.6 CASE and the Software Development Process

"Technical frameworks exist but they do not put tools in the context of the development organization. Therefore, any comprehensive integrated CASE development and implementation strategy must have an organizational framework as well."
M. Chen [CHE92].

Eventually, when considering CASE and automation, some additional questions should be asked: What is or should be the role of automation (i.e., CASE) in the software development process? Should the entire development process eventually be automated? What are the long-term effects of automation on software development? How will CASE tools integrate with other tools (project and process management, metrics, estimation, etc.)?

One only has to look at other industries to gain some insight into the possible limits that might be placed on the eventual automation of software development. For example, the hardware development industry has evolved to include automation for the design, manufacturing, and testing of computer hardware. But the design of integrated chips (ICs) is not fully automated, and probably never will be. People have the skills, expertise, and creativity to place circuits on a board or chip, and machines help people do this more quickly and control some of the inherent complexity in the process.

Likewise, the architectural field now supports the design of structures, and machines help deliver more force and lift, but people must eventually build these structures. Machines do not build complex structures, people do. Others, most notably Watts Humphrey [HUM89], see parallels between the software development process and the manufacturing process.

Software development is inherently a complex and difficult process. A humorous story often told in the industry goes something like this: If bridge builders built bridges like software developers build software, none of the bridges would still be standing. Some would argue that the reason for this is that each software system is unique or has unique attributes that must be addressed, while most bridges share common characteristics. Others might suggest that software requires creativity and therefore cannot be truly automated. Regardless of how we perceive the software development process, an important question is how much automated support will ever be possible.

The Eureka software factory (ESF) concept was created in 1986 as a consortium of 13 tool providers with the goal of defining an architecture for a supporting framework and factory concepts in software development within 10 years [FER92] [ROC92]. The ESF project, and others like it, is defining software as a product and software development as a manufacturing or product process. Specifically, the ESF is defining an architecture for coordinating development information at three levels: the organizational, team, and individual software engineer level. Key issues that are being addressed in the ESF project are how information should be provided to developers in a timely and consistent manner, as well as what validation procedures should be applied to this information to ensure that it is correct. The current state of the ESF project evolution is shown in Figure 11.3.

11.7 The Future of CASE

While it is helpful to consider the eventual role CASE will play in the software development process, this should be tempered with the realities of where the CASE industry is headed in the short and long term. Obviously, any predictions about the future of the CASE industry must be made with a large grain of salt. What follows are some of the characteristics the authors envision for the short- and long-term CASE industry.

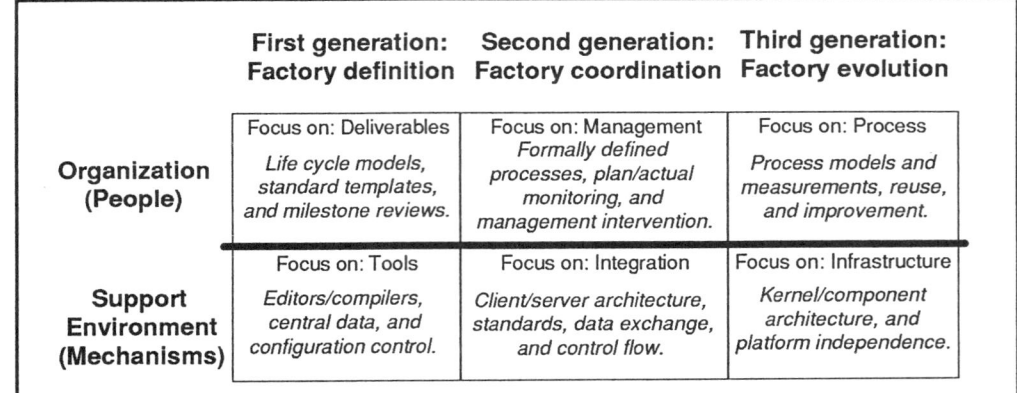

Figure 11.3
Eureka Software
Factory evolution
to date.

	First generation: Factory definition	Second generation: Factory coordination	Third generation: Factory evolution
Organization (People)	Focus on: Deliverables *Life cycle models, standard templates, and milestone reviews.*	Focus on: Management *Formally defined processes, plan/actual monitoring, and management intervention.*	Focus on: Process *Process models and measurements, reuse, and improvement.*
Support Environment (Mechanisms)	Focus on: Tools *Editors/compilers, central data, and configuration control.*	Focus on: Integration *Client/server architecture, standards, data exchange, and control flow.*	Focus on: Infrastructure *Kernel/component architecture, and platform independence.*

11.7.1 CASE as a Methods Advisor

Recent studies have shown that for CASE tools to be more effective, they need to move from a passive role in the development process to more of a guided or advisory role [VES92]. These and other findings suggest that CASE tools should enforce or guide developers in the selected method or technique to ensure that developers follow the proper intent of a technique. This leads to the concept of a CASE environment as an advisor to software developers. In the study cited, the authors identified three basic types of CASE tools:

Restrictive tools which are designed to encourage the developer to use them in a normative manner. For example, a restrictive tool that supports functional decomposition would require a developer to start a system at the top with a context diagram and then decompose the system into lower-level detail.

Guided tools which are designed to encourage, but not rigidly force, the developer to use them in a normative manner. Using the same example above, a guided tool would suggest, but not require, that developers use a top-down partitioning process.

Flexible tools which are designed to allow developers complete freedom in using them. Following collection of specifications, the developer could verify that the specifications are consistent and complete, but would not be required to begin at the top when using the tool.

"...this research suggests that tools providing support should not force the systems developer to follow a top-down process in designing a system. Rather, CASE tools should provide support primarily for the specifications produced. . . . Hence, restrictive and guided CASE tools, which directly support the disciplined approach and indirectly the untrained personnel, might be the most likely to result in increases in software productivity, as well as quality."

I. Vessey [VES92].

Already, some of the CASE tool vendors have incorporated expert systems into their products, but for verification checking only. There is much research underway on the role of CASE tools as software process advisors or guides for the development process [KAI88] [PUN88]. Some of these efforts include matching an expert system or knowledge-based support tool with a CASE repository. The Knowledge-Based Requirements System (KBRS) under development at George Mason University provides computer support for collection and analysis of system and software-level requirements and coordinates all aspects of requirements definition and tracking [PAL92]. Others incorporate knowledge-based systems with software process models. Softman is a process-driven CASE environment developed at the University of Southern California with a system for process guidance for developers that navigates through a software process model and integrates a CASE environment for forward and reverse engineering [MI92].

In the future, CASE tools will act more as advisors for the software development process, and will include knowledge bases of technique and tool expertise that will be drawn upon and applied to new development projects. There will also be a merging of development techniques (methodologies) and CASE environments, together with process and project management facilities, reuse, and measurements and estimation.

11.7.2 Multiple Technique Support in CASE Tools

Multimethod support or support for metamethods, including structured, real-time, and object-oriented techniques, will be required of future CASE products. Some CASE vendors have recognized this and already offer support for many techniques and notations. New products, including ProtoGen, ObjectMaker, Ipsys, Envison, and the Visual Software Factory, already provide support for many of the popular notations. But future CASE products must move beyond simple notational support and provide technique and method support in the form of tailorable rule checking for whichever method is used in an organization.

In addition, future products will have to integrate all of the life cycle tasks and deliverables within a common repository. Probably these products will also include metrics and project and process management facilities. Sophisticated configuration management facilities will be required that can track requirements, change requests, test plans, goals, and objectives, and provide browsing for reusable components.

Underlying support for multiple methods will be a repository that can manage metadata about the development process. Examples of this data might include traditional deliverables, i.e., diagrams, textual specifications, etc., but will also include video, sound, and animation.

11.7.3 Reverse Engineering

Future CASE tools will also provide facilities for extracting design information from existing, legacy systems. This design recovery will allow organizations that have significant investments in 3GL systems without adequate documentation to capture the architecture, logic, and, ultimately, business rules and models that are buried within the older systems that are outdated and must be replaced.

Some existing CASE products, including Bachman's Reengineering Product Set, can reverse engineer database and file structures to data models, but so far there are no products available that can perform the same function for functional code. Some products can deliver portions of the design recovery, typically in the form of control flow or module hierarchy, but the difficult part will be to decipher the logic within the modules and to map this logic to design specifications.

Undoubtedly, expert systems will be required to analyze the program code to make inferences about the underlying business rules, but people will be required to make decisions regarding how the code should be represented and when code is redundant. But the promise of reverse engineering is perceived as the silver bullet for the maintenance nightmare most development organizations face.

11.7.4 Future Software Development Environments

Future software development environments will embody the facilities of many diverse technologies, including hypertext, groupware, artificial intelligence, and process management.

We see a definite marriage between CASE tools, hypertext, groupware, and multimedia capabilities to create a complete team-oriented software development environment. Others have discussed the benefits of combining CASE and hypertext, most notably [AIK89] [BIG88]. We expect to see these technologies combined in the future to help provide more of the advisor role in CASE discussed above. Many of the commercially available methodologies are now being offered in hypertext format, with some plans for multimedia formats in the near future.

We see a time when CASE environments will eventually include an expert advisor to software engineers and provide specific recommendations as well as suggestions for standards for software development. With the use of hypertext, the areas of training and supporting software development techniques can be greatly improved. Also, verification and rule checking provided by a CASE tool can be based on the software process used and tailored to the software development process within the organization.

Existing research with CASE and hypertext has been undertaken at the Amdahl Australian Intelligent Tools Program and provides an architectural framework for integrating CASE tools [CYB92]. HyperCASE combines a hypertext-based interface with a knowledge-based document repository. Future work in this area will incorporate groupware, configuration management, planning and tracking, and multimedia document presentation.

Other research is underway on merging CASE with multimedia to produce interactive, flexible documentation to developers and users of software. Ed Yourdon, the father of structured development, argues that inexpensive CASE tools will become commonplace in the years to come, and will be extended to include multimedia capabilities, groupware functions, and support of pen-based development [YOU92].

Many in the industry have given us creative insight into the possible future of software development environments. Interesting components of this future environment include groupware, multimedia, software factories with product and process integration, and hypertext. Some of these were covered in previous sections so we will only introduce the additional topics here.

The movement towards groupware support in software development tools will facilitate better communication among developers. Such a combination might eventually include electronic mail, calendars, facilities scheduling, document preparation, project and process planning, shared database access, and automatic message notification.

Ed Yourdon, an architect of many software development techniques, describes this possible combination as a "great leap forward" with CASE [YOU91]. Others, including [KAS91], see the eventual merging of CASE environments with distributed computing environments. The Xerox PARC and MIT Athena projects are examples of studies in these areas.

The incorporation of multimedia, including sound, video, animation, and hypertext, inside a CASE tool should further enhance the development process. Recent papers have described the benefit of delivering documents and deliverables using multimedia [RAD92]. In addition, the concept of multimedia as a methodology training and support tool in combination with CASE capabilities can go a long way toward reducing the costs of implementing and supporting software engineering.

11.7.5 DesignWare

Texas Instruments, Anderson Consulting, and other packaged software vendors are beginning to market DesignWare, using CASE templates or repositories. With DesignWare, a software package is developed using a CASE tool, and the contents of the CASE repository are delivered to the client along with or instead of the source code for the system. This allows the client to enhance or modify the models and specifications for the package directly in the CASE tool, and then generate the resulting source and executable code for their specific environment.

The benefit to the vendor of providing DesignWare to its clients is in the flexibility the vendor can offer in its product. Clients can modify the package as needed without having to acquire technical support for its run-time environment. Also, vendors can offer wider support for operating environments, including PC, LAN, minicomputer (Unix), and mainframe packages from the same models and specifications without having to customize their packages for each environment. In the future, GUI, client/server, and cooperative processing capabilities may be incorporated into these packages from within the CASE environment.

The benefit to clients in purchasing DesignWare include ownership of the models and design specifications for the package vs. the source code, less of a need for technical maintenance of the package (i.e., business models vs. source code perspective), an ability to target different operating environments with different DBMS, TP, GUI, etc., and better documentation for the package (in the CASE repository).

As more packaged software vendors recognize the benefits of placing their products in a CASE repository, more of the packaged products will be available as DesignWare.

11.8 Resource List

Excellent resources exist in both technical and non-technical journals on CASE and software automation. For an excellent reference on CASE integration and the issues involved, see the March 1992 issue of *IEEE Software*. For papers on CASE, see the March 1988 issue of *IEEE Software* and *Computer Aided Software Engineering*, edited by Elliot Chikofsky (IEEE Computer Society Press, 1988). An excellent reference for CASE integration standards is the article by Sharon and Radding [SHA90].

For discussions on CASE and automation, see [BRA90], [CAS86], [DAV83], [FIS88], [GAN90], [LEW90], [MCC88], and [TOW89]. For specific papers on CASE tool integration, see [WAS90] and product-specific information for IBM's Repository Manager [SAG90] and DEC's CDD/Repository [DIG91]. For more on comparing CASE tools, see [TOP91b] and [VES92].

Various newsletters, journals, and conferences are available on many topics related to CASE. Some of these include *CASE Strategies* (Cutter Information Corp.), *CASE Outlook* (CASE Research Corp.), and *CASE Trends* (Software Productivity Group). Perhaps the best coverage of the CASE industry with honest opinions is *American Programmer*, written by Ed Yourdon and published every month by Cutter Information Corp. Each year, Yourdon publishes an issue on CASE, and each year the issue itself is worth the subscription price.

Many major cities now have local CASE user groups that meet regularly to discuss current topics. Also, there is an international CASE users group that can be reached at (206) 453-5853.

11.9 References

[AIK89]   Aiken, P. H., "A Hypermedia Workstation for Requirements Engineering," doctoral dissertation, George Mason University, Fairfax, Va., 1989.

[BIG88]   Bigelow, J., "Hypertext and CASE," *IEEE Software*, March 1988, pp. 23-27.

[BLA83]   Blank, J., and M. J. Krijger, *Software Engineering: Methods and Techniques*, Wiley-Interscience, 1983.

[BOE84]   Boehm, B., T. Gray, and T. Seewaldt, "Prototyping vs. Specifying: A Multiproject Experiment," *IEEE Trans. Soft. Eng.*, vol. 10, no. 3, 1984, pp. 39-44.

[BRA90]   Braithwaite, K. S., *Application Development Using CASE Tools*, Academic Press, 1990.

[BRO92]   Brown, A. W., and J. A. McDermid, "Learning from IPSE's Mistakes," *IEEE Software*, March 1992, pp. 23-28.

[CAS86]   Case, A. F., *Information Systems Development: Principles of Software Engineering and CASE*, Prentice-Hall, 1986.

[CHE92]   Chen, M., and R. Norman, "A Framework for Integrated CASE," *IEEE Software*, March 1992, pp. 18-22.

[CYB92]   Cybulski, J., and K. Reed, "A Hypertext-Based Software-Engineering Environment," *IEEE Software*, March 1992, pp. 62-68.

[DAV83]   Davis, W., *Tools and Techniques for Structured Systems Analysis and Design*, Addison-Wesley, 1983.

[DIG91]   Digital Equipment Corp., "Digital's Distributed Repository: Blueprint for Managing Enterprise-Wide Information," 1991.

[FER92]   Fernstrom, C., K. Narfelt, and L. Ohlsson, "Software Factory Principles, Architectures, Experiments," *IEEE Software*, March 1992, pp. 36-44.

[FIS88]   Fisher, A. S., *CASE : Using Software Development Tools*, Wiley, 1988.

[GAN90] Gane, C., *Computer-Aided Software Engineering: The Methodologies, the Products, the Future*, Prentice-Hall, 1990.

[HUM89] Humphrey, W., *Managing the Software Process*, Addison-Wesley, 1989.

[JAR92] Jarke, M., "Strategies for Integrating CASE Environments," *IEEE Software*, March 1992, pp. 54-61.

[KAI88] Kaiser, G. E., "Intelligent Assistance for Software Development and Maintenance," *IEEE Software*, Vol. 5, pp. 40-49, May 1988.

[KAS91] Kashdan, N., "CASE and Distributed Computing Environments," *American Programmer*, July 1991, pp. 30-35.

[LEW90] Lewis, T. G., *Computer-Aided Software Engineering*, Van Nostrand Reinhold, 1990.

[MAI92] Maiden, N., and A. Sutcliffe, "Exploiting Reusable Specifications through Analogy," *CACM*, vol. 35, no. 4, pp. 55-64.

[MCC88] McClure, C., "The CASE for Structured Development," *PC Tech Journal*, vol. 6, no. 8, pp. 51-67.

[MCC88] McClure, C., *CASE Is Software Automation*, Prentice Hall, 1988.

[MI92] Mi, P., and W. Scacchi, "Process Integration in CASE Environments," *IEEE Software*, March 1992, pp. 45-53.

[NOR92] Norman, R. J., and M. Chen, "Working Together to Integrate CASE," *IEEE Software*, March 1992, pp. 13-16.

[NOR92] Norman, R. J., and M. Chen, "A Framework for Integrated CASE," *IEEE Software*, March 1992, pp. 18-22.

[PAL92] Palmer, J. D., and N. A. Fields, "An Integrated Environment for Requirements Engineering," *IEEE Software*, May 1992, pp. 80-86.

[PRE88] Pressman, R. S., *Making Software Engineering Happen: A guide for instituting the technology*, Prentice Hall, 1988.

[PRE91] Pressman, R. S., *Software Engineering: A practitioner's approach*, McGraw-Hill, 1991.

[PUN88] Puncello, P., "ASPIS: A Knowledge-based CASE Environment," *IEEE Software*, pp. 53-65, March 1988.

[RAD92] Radding, P., and M. Farrell, "Multimedia Documents," *American Programmer*, vol. 5, no. 5, pp. 44-49.

[ROC92] Rockwell, B., "The Comming of EuroCASE," *American Programmer*, November 1992, pp. 2-13.

[SAG90] Sagawa, J. M., "Repository Manager Technology," *IBM Systems Journal*, vol. 29, no. 2, 1990, pp. 209-227.

[SHA90] Sharon, D., and P. Radding, "The CASE of the Missing Links: Standards Efforts," *American Programmer*, September 1990, pp. 16-28.

[TAT92] Tate, G., J. Verner, and R. Jeffery, "CASE: A Testbed for Modeling, Measurement and Management," *CACM*, vol. 35, no. 4, pp. 65-72.

[THO92] Thomas, I., and B. Nejmeh, "Definitions of Tool Integration for Environments," *IEEE Software*, March 1992, pp. 29-35.

[TOP91a] Topper, A., "Automating Software Development," *IEEE Spectrum*, vol. 28, no. 11, pp. 56-62.

[TOP91b] Topper, A., "Evaluating CASE Tools: Guidelines for Comparison," *American Programmer*, vol. 4, no. 7, pp. 12-20.

[TOP88] Topper, A., "Excelling in CASE," *PC Tech Journal*, vol. 6, no. 8, pp. 71-79.

[TOW89] Towner, L. E., *CASE: Concepts and Implementation*, McGraw-Hill, 1989.

[VES92] Vessey, I., S. Javenpaa, and N. Tractinsky, "Evaluation of Vendor Products: CASE Tools as Methodology Companions," *CACM*, vol. 35, no. 4, pp. 90-105.

[WAS90] Wasserman, A. I., "Tool Integration in Software Engineering Environments," in *Software Engineering Environments: Proc. Int'l Workshop on Environments*, F. Long, ed., Springer-Verlag, Berlin, 1990, pp. 137-149.

[WEA87] Weaver, A. M., *Using the Structured Techniques - A Case Study*, Prentice-Hall, 1987.

[YOU92] Yourdon, E., "CASE: Whither or Wither?," *American Programmer*, November 1992, pp. 16-27.

[YOU91] Yourdon, E., "A CASE of the Blahs," *American Programmer*, July 1991, pp. 37-45.

[YOU88] Yourdon, E., *Managing the Structured Techniques: Strategies for Software Development the 1990s*, Yourdon Press, 1988.

11.10 CASE Tools List

Analysis & Design CASE Tools

Product	Company	Platforms
Anatool/Blues	Advanced Logical Software	Apple Macintosh
Auto-Mate Plus	LBMS	IBM PS/2
Bachman Analyst	Bachman Information Systems	IBM PS/2
CA-DB:Architect	Computer Associates Intl.	IBM System/370 & PS/2
Canonizer	Six Sigma Case, Inc.	Sun, DEC, AT&T, & NCR
CASE*Designer	Oracle Corporation	DEC VAX, Sun, Apollo, & IBM PS/2
DEFT	Deft Inc.	Apple Macintosh
DesignAid	CGI	IBM PS/2
DevelopMate	IBM Corporation	IBM System/370 & PS/2
EasyCASE	Evergreen CASE Tools	IBM PS/2
Envison	Future Tech Systems	IBM PS/2
EPOS	Software Products & Services	IBM PS/2
E-R Modeler	Chen & Associates Inc.	IBM PS/2
ERwin	Logic Works, Inc.	IBM PC
Excelerator	Intersolv	IBM PS/2
Foundation	Menlo Business Systems	Apple Macintosh & Tandem
IDEF/Leverage	D. Appleton Company, Inc.	IBM PS/2
IEF	Texas Instruments	IBM PS/2
IEW/ADW	Knowledgeware, Inc.	IBM PS/2
MacAnalyst and MacDesigner	Excel Software	Apple Macintosh
MacBubbles	StarSys Inc.	Apple Macintosh
MetaDesign	Meta Software Corporation	IBM PS/2
NSChart	Siltronix	IBM PC & Apple Macintosh
POSE	Computer Systems Advisers, Inc.	IBM PS/2
PowerTools	ICONIX Software Engineering	Apple Macintosh
Software through Pictures	Interactive Development Environments	HP/Apollo, DEC VAX, Sun, & IBM RISC System/6000
System Architect	Popkin Software & Systems	IBM PS/2
Systems Engineer	LBMS	IBM PS/2
Teamwork	Cadre Technologies	DEC VAX, Sun, HP/Apollo, IBM PS/2, & RISC System/6000
TurboCASE	StructSoft, Inc.	Apple Macintosh
Yourdon Toolkit	CGI	IBM PS/2

Real-Time CASE Tools

Product	Company	Platforms
ACPVision	Andyne Computing Ltd.	Apple Macintosh
ObjctMaker, Cgen & Adagen	Mark V Systems	IBM PC, Apple Macintosh, Sun, HP/Apollo & DEC VAX
A.S.A. & Geode	Verilog USA	HP/Apollo, Sun & DEC VAX
CARDtools	Ready Systems	Sun & DEC VAX
CASEStation	Mentor Graphics Corp.	Apollo & DEC VAX
Cradle	CGI	All Unix BSD 4.2 or later
DECdesign	Digital Equipment Corp.	DEC VAX
Developer	ASYST Technologies Inc.	IBM PS/2
Foresight	Nuthena Systems Inc.	HP & Sun
RDD	Ascent Logic Corporation	Apollo, Apple Macintosh, & Sun
SES/Workbench	Scientific & Engineering Software	DEC VAX, Sun, & HP/Apollo
Statemate	i-Logix, Inc.	Sun, DEC VAX, & Apollo

Code Generation Tools

Product	Company	Platforms
APS	Intersolv	IBM System/370 & PS/2
CASE:W & :PM	CaseWorks, Inc.	IBM PS/2
Cross System Product	IBM Corp.	IBM System/370, AS/400 & PS/2
Easel	Easel Corp.	IBM System/370 & PS/2
ezX	Sunrise Software Systems	DEC and Unix
IEW & Construction & GAMMA	Knowledgeware, Inc.	IBM System/370 & PS/2
Genesis V	Softbro Midwest	System/38 & AS/400
IEF	Texas Instruments	IBM System/370 & PS/2
Infront/DS	Multi Soft	IBM System/370 & PS/2
JAM	JYACC Inc.	IBM PS/2 and Unix
MAGEC	Al Lee & Associates, Inc.	IBM System/370 & PS/2
METAgen	Trimarand	IBM System/370 & PS/2
Micro-CAPS	Software Research, Inc.	BTOS/CTOS systems
MicroSTEP	SysCorp International, Inc.	IBM PS/2

Product	Company	Platforms
Mozart	Mozart Systems Corp.	DEC VAX, HP, IBM System/370, AS/400, System/36, and /38, & PS/2
mrc-Productivity Series	Michaels, Ross & Cole, Ltd.	IBM AS/400
Netron/CAP	Netron Inc.	DEC VAX, Wang, IBM System/370, & PS/2
ORIN	Objective Solutions	DEC VAX
PACBASE	CGI Systems, Inc.	IBM System/370 & PS/2, Unisys, Honeywell, & Unix
Pro-C	C Solutions Inc.	IBM PS/2, DEC VAX, & Unix
ProDoc	Scandura	IBM PS/2
ShowCase	Rochester Software	IBM PS/2 & AS/400
Syntek CASE/Ap	Synthesis Computer Tech.	DEC VAX
System 1032	CompuServe Data Tech.	DEC VAX
Teamwork	Cadre Technologies In	DEC VAX, Sun, HP/Apollo, IBM PS/2, & RISC System/6000
Tele-Use	Telesoft	DEC, DG Aviion, & Sun
TELON	Computer Associates	IBM System/370 & PS/2
Transform Family	Transform Logic Corp.	IBM System/370 & PS/2
WinPro/W	Xiam Corp.	IBM PS/2

Maintenance Tools

Product	Company	Platforms
Application Browser	Hypersoft Corp.	IBM PS/2 & DEC VAX
AutoFlow	AutoCASE Technology	IBM PS/2
Reengineering Product Set	Bachman Information Systems	IBM PS/2
Clear+	Clear Software, Inc.	IBM PS/2
COBOL/Structuring Facility	IBM Corp.	IBM System/370
InterCASE Reverse Engineering Workbench	InterPort Software Corp.	IBM System/370 & PS/2, DEC VAX & Unix
Pathvu & Retrofit	CGI	IBM System/370 & PS/2, Unisys, Bull & Wang
PM/SS	Adpac Corp.	IBM System/370
ProDoc Reverse Engineer	Scandura Intelligent Systems	IBM PS/2
Q/Auditor	Eden Systems Corporation	IBM System/370 & PS/2
Recoder & Inspector	Knowledgeware	IBM System/370

Product	*Company*	*Platforms*
RE-SPEC	Software Products & Services	IBM System/370 & PS/2, DEC VAX, Apollo, Sun, & HP
RevEnge	Alben Software	IBM PC/AT & PS/2
Reverse DBMS	Chen & Associates Inc.	IBM PS/2
SuperCASE SCI	Advanced Technology Intl.	DEC VAX
SuperStructure	Computer Data Systems, Inc.	IBM System/370 & Unisys
SMARTsystem	Procase Corporation	Apollo, HP, DEC, Sun, & IBM RISC System/6000

Integrated CASE Tools

Product	*Company*	*Platforms*
AS/SET	System Software Associates	IBM AS/400
CorVision	Cortex Corporation	DEC VAX, NCR & IBM PS/2
EPOS	Software Products & Services	DEC VAX, IBM System /370, PS/2, HP/Apollo, & Sun
Foundation	Andersen Consulting	IBM System/370 & PS/2
IEF	Texas Instruments	IBM System/370 & PS/2
IEW/ADW	Knowledgeware, Inc.	IBM System/370 PS/2
Maestro	Softlab, Inc.	Unix & IBM PS/2
The Manager Family	Manager Software Products	IBM System/370 & PS/2
PABASE family	CGI Systems, Inc.	IBM System/370 & PS/2, Unisys, Unix & Honeywell
ProDoc	Scandura Intelligent Systems	IBM PS/2
Software through Pictures	Interactive Development Environments	HP/Apollo, Sun, DEC VAX, & IBM RISC System/6000
Synon/2	Synon, Inc.	IBM AS/400, System/38, & PS/2
Teamwork	Cadre Technologies Inc.	DEC VAX, Sun, HP/Apollo, IBM RISC System/6000, & PS/2

Genesis of the CASE Industry

James Martin is considered by many to be the "father of CASE," and he was involved, personally and financially, in the genesis of major CASE products, including those of Knowledgeware, Intersolv (formally, Index Technology), and Texas Instruments. Martin is one of several individuals whose contribution to modern CASE should be remembered as establishing the capabilities and direction for the early CASE products.

Daniel Teichroew, an early proponent of CASE, formed the Information Systems Design and Optimization Systems (ISDOS) project at the University of Michigan in Ann Arbor, Michigan in the late 1960s. The ISDOS project originally focused on industrial engineering, but eventually produced several products supporting software engineering. The project developed one of the first repository products, Problem Statement Language/Problem Statement Analyzer (PSL/PSA), a mainframe-based tool that allowed systems to be specified in a non-procedural language (PSL), stored in a database, and verified for completeness and correctness (PSA). In the late 1970s, the project began experimenting with graphics to support system development, and in the mid-1980s, the project split into two commercial ventures: ISDOS, Inc., and Meta Systems Ltd. Meta Systems was later purchased by Learmonth & Burchett Management Systems (LBMS) Inc., which continues to offer PSL/PSA to their clients.

Knowledgeware, Inc. was founded in 1979 under the name Database Design, Inc. (DDI) (also in Ann Arbor) by James Martin, Dixon Doll, and Robert Holland. (Holland went on to found Holland Data Systems, a firm providing data modeling and planning services.) DDI provided consulting services for logical data modeling and created two mainframe-based tools for internal use to support the work of its consultants: Information Planner and Data Designer; these products were the forerunners of products now sold by Knowledgeware. By 1982, enough interest was generated for the tools that DDI began to market them to their clients. With the burgeoning market of personal computing, Martin decided to take the paper-based structured techniques popularized in the 1970s, modify them, and automate them on desktop computers. In 1984, he joined with Arthur Young (now Ernst & Young) to fund development of one of the earliest CASE tools, the Information Engineering Workbench (IEW). IEW was ready for release in 1985, and, in the same year, DDI changed its name to Knowledgeware.

Excelerator, a CASE tool marketed by Index Technology (now Intersolv). proved strong competition for IEW, and Knowledgeware sought a back-end (coding and testing) component to complement the IEW front-end (planning, analysis, and design) product. Knowledgeware management met with Fran Tarkenton, head of Tarkenton Software and the greatest scrambling quarterback in the history of professional football. Tarkenton's company marketed a mainframe-based code generator called GAMMA, and in 1986, Tarkenton Software merged with Knowledgeware. Two years later, Knowledgeware release a desktop-based code generator, and in 1989, Knowledgeware became a publicly owned company and joined IBM's AD/Cycle effort. It released the OS/2-based Application Development Workbench (ADW) in the following year, and today Knowledgeware earns over 90 percent of its tool revenues from its OS/2-based product line.

One graduate student who originally worked with Teichroew on the ISDOS project was Elliot Chikofsky, who later joined with Richard Carpenter at Index Technology. Carpenter planned to produce and market a desktop-based CASE tool and originally held discussions with Martin of DDI, but they could not reach an agreement. So Carpenter went on to found Index Technology and developed and marketed Excelerator, a highly successful CASE tool that supported analysis and design. Excelerator garnered a significant share of the CASE market through the late 1980s, when Index Technology merged with Sage Software in 1991 to form Intersolv. Today, Intersolv markets Windows- and OS/2-based versions of Excelerator and is a business partner with IBM under AD/Cycle.

In the early 1980s, Texas Instruments (TI) also held discussions with Martin and decided his information engineering (IE) approach supported its philosophy for software development. TI began internally developing, with the assistance of Martin, an integrated set of CASE tools called the Information Engineering Facility (IEF). TI initially wanted to use a code generator from Sage Software to support the construction phase of IE, but later decided to develop its own product. The product was used extensively within TI and eventually reached the market in the mid-1980s. Martin later went on to form James Martin & Associates (JMA), a venture that provided IE consulting and marketed the IEF in Europe. JMA later become James Martin & Company (JMC) and still provides consulting and training in Information Engineering in the United States. James Martin is still actively involved with JMC and has recently begun working with Intersolv on development of an IE-based version of Excelerator.

Chapter 12
Software Process Improvement

Recalling our definition of the software engineering triad and the software production framework from Chapter 1, we now can examine more closely the software process and models that help analyze and improve software development.

In this chapter, we will introduce the concept of software process models, discuss various popular modeling approaches, and provide a generic software process improvement plan.

Software processes fit into our holistic view of a software production framework in level 2, generally at the development group or organization level. Recall that software processes focus on the roles, responsibilities, and generic deliverables within the software life cycle, and that they must address the dynamics and interaction between individuals and groups within the organization.

Software processes are less concerned with the specific artifacts, which are defined by the development techniques, and are more concerned with the "who," "what," and "when" of software production. Within some of the software process models, the focus is on quality improvement, and this often relates to Total Quality Management (TQM) initiatives inside and outside the development group.

12.1 Introduction

Software process improvement is a special case of the general notion of process improvement pioneered by W. E. Demming [DEM82]. In Demming's view, process improvement involves four steps: (1) understand the existing process, (2) identify parts of the process that can be improved, (3) select an improvement and implement it, and (4) continue to iterate this process. We follow the first two steps of Demming's prescription in this chapter; Chapter 13 is devoted to the third step, with specific reference to the techniques and tools used within the software process.

To arrive at an understanding of the software process, we survey a variety of ways in which the software process can be modeled. The second part of this chapter presents a generic software process improvement plan which is a more detailed expansion of Demming's basic process improvement steps.

Before beginning, we need to clarify why an organization might want to improve its software process. There are two fundamental reasons: to improve productivity, or to improve quality. The choice between these two motivations is critical, and must be a conscious, "up front" choice. All participants in a process improvement effort must know the real reason, for this determines how eventual success will be judged. Each choice has passionate adherents; in our opinion, the productivity rationale is a near-term choice, while the quality rationale is a longer-term choice. Crosby argues that, eventually, productivity becomes a by-product of quality [CRO79]. In the past few years, the U.S. Department of Defense has endorsed this view in its TQM program.

Regardless of which aspect of the development process is to be improved, it is impossible to show actual improvement unless measurements have been taken prior to attempting any change in the process. If, for instance, we expect productivity will be improved by using some new development technique or tool, in order to show improvement in this area, prior productivity measures must be available to be compared with. Likewise, if quality improvement is the goal, previous quality measurements must be made to justify an improvement in the product or process.

12.2 Software Process Models

The goal of any model is to improve our understanding of the thing being modeled. Typically, modeling accomplishes this by emphasizing parts of reality and suppressing other parts. The result is that any model presents a limited, distorted view of reality. Intelligent use of models is therefore increased when the goals and limitations of the models are clearly understood.

Within the software development industry, many organizations have found it useful to apply the notations and techniques used to develop software (described in Chapters 4 through 9) to model the software development process itself. Perhaps the most interesting application of this is with the statechart described briefly in Chapter 6.

A software process model must, at a minimum, answer the following questions:

What tasks make up the process?
Who performs these tasks and what artifacts are created or used?
How are these tasks actually performed (i.e., development techniques)?
What relationships exist among the stakeholders involved in the process?

Process definitions must capture three views: functional, or what tasks are performed; organizational, or who performs each task; and behavioral, when and how tasks are performed. A common approach, such as the SEI method, might stress modeling software processes over functionality.

12.2.1 Reasons for Software Process Modeling

Much of the recent work on software process modeling has been done at the Software Engineering Institute (SEI) in Pittsburgh. One of the SEI researchers has identified four reasons to develop software process models [KEL89]:

1. To foster effective communication of the software process
2. To facilitate reuse of the software process
3. To support evolution of the software process
4. To facilitate management of the software process

Kellner goes on to list a baker's dozen requirements and attributes of a representation for the software process:

1. Highly visual notation
2. Scales up well (comprehensive yet concise)
3. Supports multiple views
4. Supports levels of abstraction
5. Formal syntax and semantics
6. Supports extensive analysis
7. Supports process simulation
8. Helps identify and manage reusable process components
9. Supports analysis of the effects of constraints on the process
10. Enables presentation of purposes and goals
11. Integrates easily with other modeling techniques (e.g., PERT)
12. Has an active role in the execution of the modelled process
13. Offers automated tools to support the approach

The Software Engineering Institute (SEI) is using the statechart notation [ILO87] to model software processes. This notation provides three views: activity charts, statecharts, and module charts. These are used to describe, respectively, the processing, control, and architectural views. Figures 12.1 and 12.2 (not from the SEI) show how two of these views would be used to describe the activities related to the review of a detailed design representation of a module.

A review process is a good candidate for a statechart-based model, because three disciplines (development, management, and configuration management) all come together in this one process. Figure 12.1 shows the "states" that a detailed design object passes through as it migrates from being a "design object" to a "software configuration item." Design objects are not final, and they are subject to change, while software configuration items have been reviewed and approved, and hence can only be changed by first being demoted to design object status. The corresponding activities are shown in Figure 12.2.

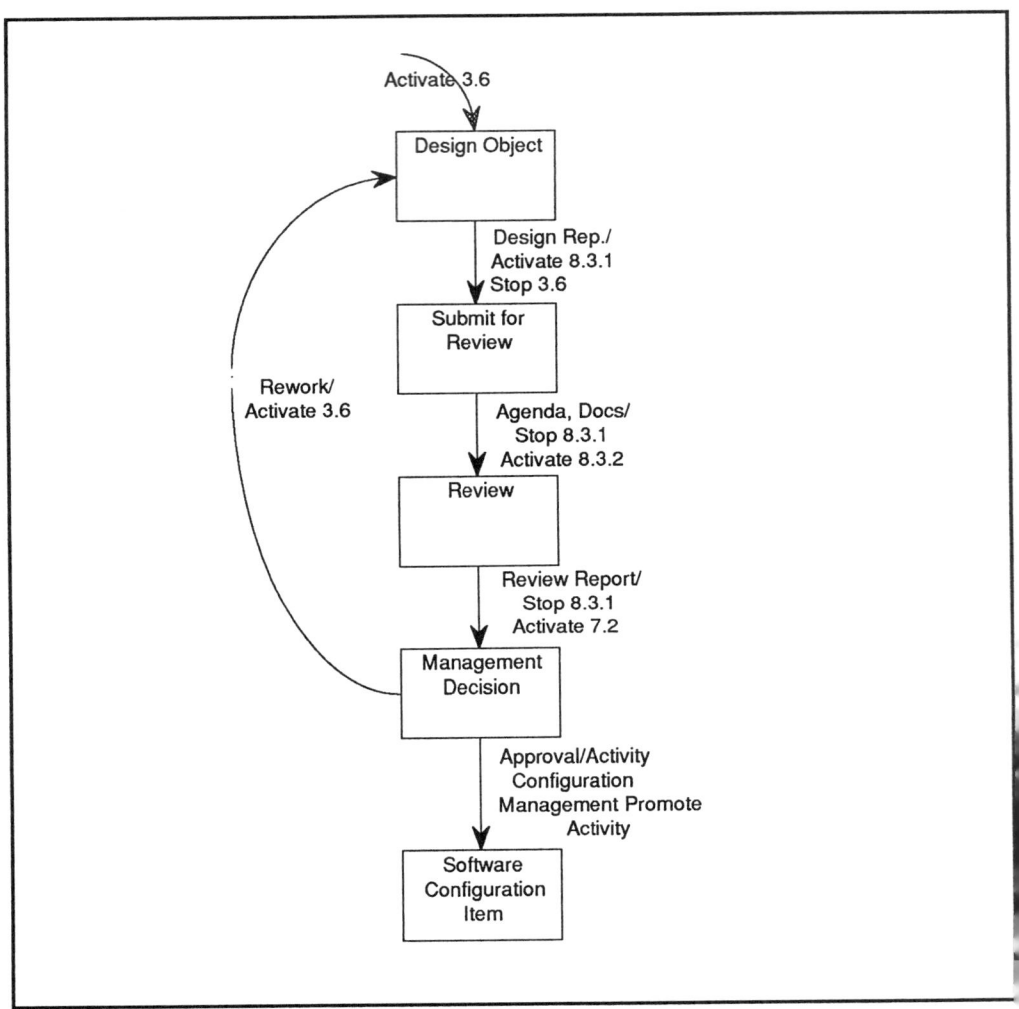

Figure 12.1
Statechart for
review process.

Notice that transitions in the statechart control the activation and termination of activities in the activity chart. The statechart notation permits definitions of time intervals, so we could postulate, for example, that the "prepare for review" activity must not take place within five working days, thereby giving all review participants sufficient preparation time. Similarly, "execution times" (or estimates) can be associated with each activity. Since the statechart notation can be executed, this model can be run to see the effects of various process choices. The net schedule impact of a review, for example, can be simulated, and then later compared with the error correction activity loops to see if reviews really decrease the overall development interval (they do).

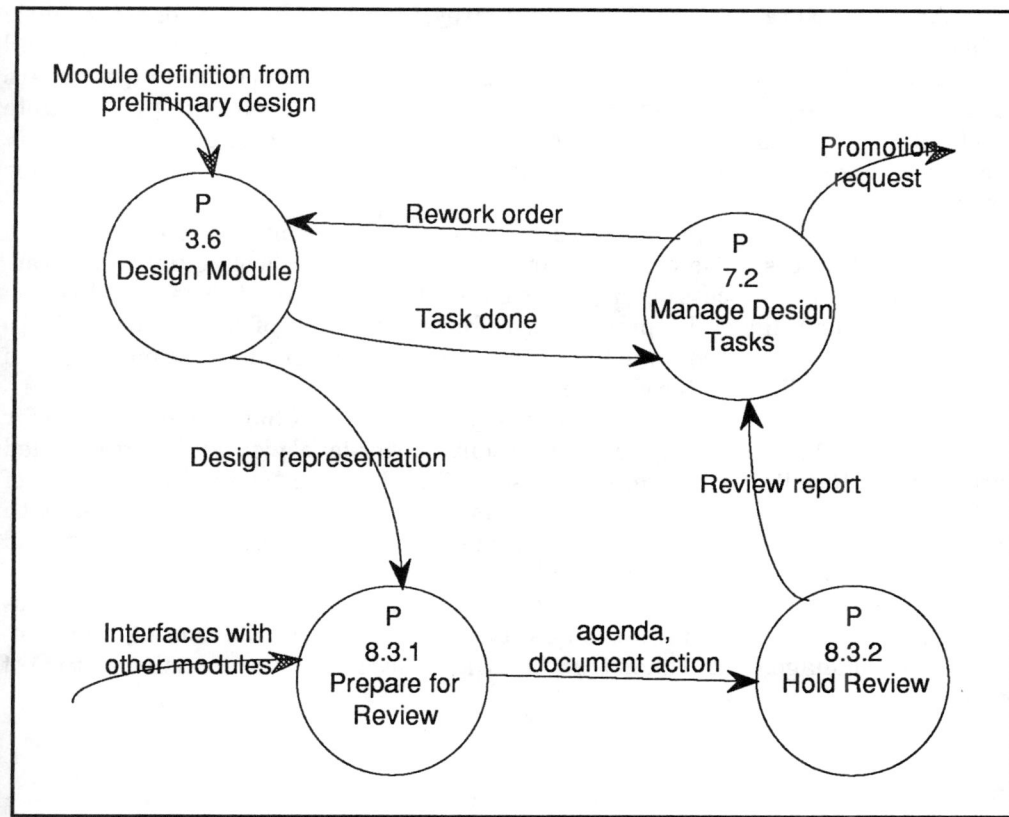

Figure 12.2
Activity chart for design, review, and management tasks.

The SEI's conclusion from all of this is to use statecharts to model the software process. The statechart notation satisfies all thirteen requirements postulated by Kellner. If we were to add criteria such as ease of learning and use, however, the notation suffers; and if we require understanding by untrained people, the notation fails.

12.2.2 Types of Software Process Models

One useful result of the SEI software process modeling effort is that the software process has many points of analogy with a real-time system: There are tasks, which are typically concurrent; tasks are performed by people; people are assigned to several tasks, so conflicts often occur; and timeliness of work products is frequently an issue.

Another SEI researcher, Watts Humphrey, identifies the need for three levels of software process models [HUM89]. He refers to them as universal, worldly, and atomic models. Life cycle models, such as the ones we discussed in Chapter 2, are universal models; they provide the broadest overview of a software process. Life cycle models are usually stage- or phase-based, where a phase refers to many activities conducted by several participants. As such, they provide a framework for more specific models.

By themselves, life cycle models are an oversimplification of the entire software development process. Their large granularity ignores details of actual work practices, resulting in a process description that is often too abstract to be useful. As we saw in Chapter 1, life cycles provide focus for higher-levels of an organization. To be effective, life cycle models must be supplemented with more detailed models, such as the ones described in this chapter.

In the next sections, we review a variety of models that have been proposed for modeling software processes, which represent a lower-level view and more detailed granularity. Recall that software processes define the "who," "what," and "when" of software development. As such, the models of software processes must deal with issues such as roles and responsibilities, communication among stakeholders, and management of the artifacts produced.

The software process models described in this chapter include process maturity, system dynamics, continuous quality improvement, goal-oriented, and common-sense management. Taken together, they provide a comprehensive picture of the software process.

12.2.2.1 Process Maturity Models

We first described the SEI Software Process Maturity Model (SPMM) in Chapter 1, and we revisit it in this chapter. Here we use the model as a yardstick for software process improvement. Recall the five levels of maturity in the SPMM, initial, repeatable, defined, managed, and optimizing. Our focus here is the practical meaning of "Defined Process." What does it mean for an organization to have a defined process? How does an organization go about defining a process?

From our brief look at process modeling techniques, we note quite a variety. Clearly a life cycle model, by itself, is simply not enough. We must know more about the participants in the software process, the roles we expect them to perform, and the tasks which they must execute. We should also identify primary communication links and expected sequences of tasks. We also need to identify the actual work products and when they must be available. Finally, we need to describe the interactions among roles, people, and tasks. Quite an order. The end result of all of this is what a good journalist already knows; provide answers to four basic questions: Who? What? When? Where?

One advantage of having a clearly defined software process is that all participants know what is expected of them, and what they can expect of their colleagues. A second advantage is that, given a detailed process definition, estimates of effort and schedule are improved. A longer-term advantage is that with a defined process, we can begin to measure and evaluate process steps, and we have an orderly way in which to identify and implement improvements to the software process. A less tangible advantage is that a defined process increases the esprit de corps in an organization. When the Software Engineering Division of Hughes Aircraft attained the defined level, they reported a noticeable improvement in "the quality of work life" [HUM91]. They noted "a more stable work environment with fewer overtime hours and fewer gut-wrenching problems." SEI suggests that only by having a defined process can that process be improved.

12.2.2.2 Models of Roles and Activities

Modeling the various roles and responsibilities of the stakeholders in the software development process also brings insight into the software process. The mainline roles for software production are software development, testing, project management, and maintenance. Secondary roles include software quality assurance, configuration management, auditing, and possibly process and reuse management. These roles are conducted by people, and this is a point where a data modeling technique is applicable.

If we consider Roles and People as entities in a data model of a software process, we can describe the relationship between people and their roles. In a small organization this might be a one-to-many relationship (i.e., one person wears many hats). In a large organization, this might be a one-to-one relationship (each person has only one role). Most organizations are somewhere in the middle, so we typically see a many-to-many relationship, that is, one person may have several roles, and several people may have the same role. Think of the implications this has for project management.

Activities or tasks typically culminate in the creation of a work product, artifact, or deliverable, such as a piece of code, a test procedure, or a review report. Going back to the data model representation, roles have a one-to-many relationship with activities. The role of testing, for example, involves such activities as creating an overall testing plan, developing test procedures at various levels, reviewing portions of software for testing implications, executing test procedures, reporting discovered errors, and so on. Activities also mark a point where process models can cross over to project control models. If activities are defined to represent small units of effort, say 4 to 40 hours of designer effort [ZEL90], then activities are the units of scheduling in a Work Breakdown Structure and in a PERT chart.

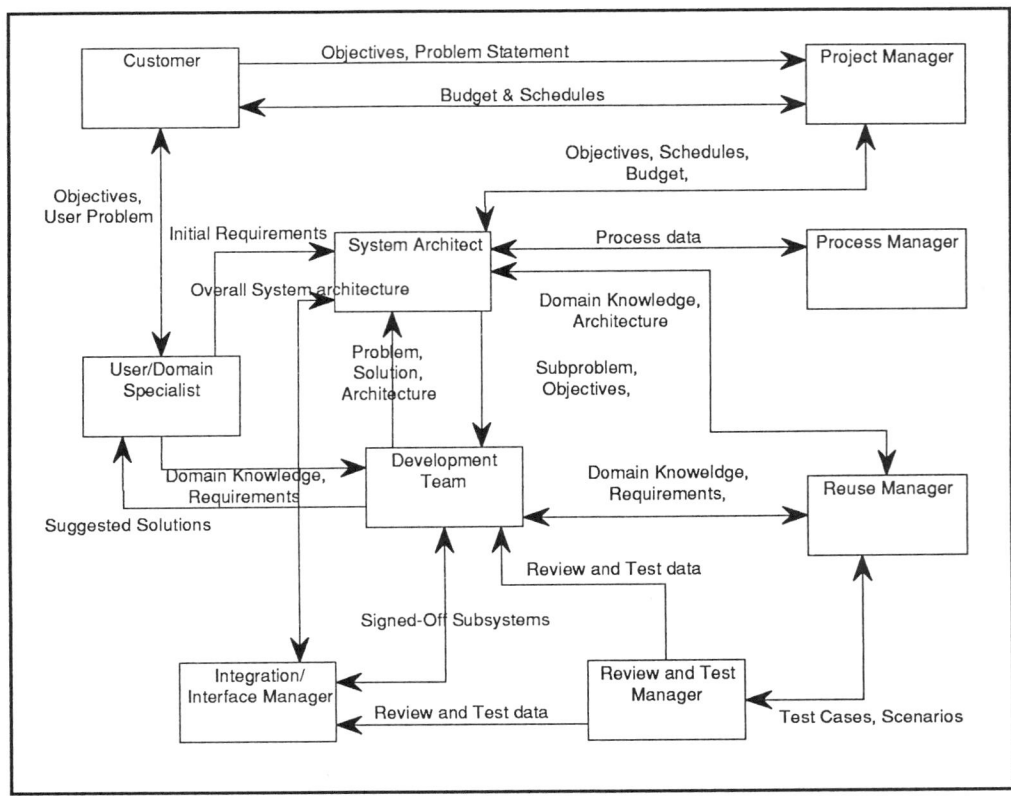

Figure 12.3
Possible roles and
interactions.

An example of possible roles and relationships represented as a data model is shown in Figure 12.3. In this model, the relationships represent the passage of end products or artifacts amongst stakeholders.

Aoyama [AOY87] offers an object-oriented view that is dualistic to Humphrey's action-oriented hierarchy. In Aoyama's model, work products are objects, and the methods associated with an object correspond to Humphrey's activities. In the object-oriented view, a review object, for example, would have scheduling, preparing, conducting, and reporting as associated methods or services. Aoyama emphasizes that his object-oriented view is explicitly static; he prefers a Petri net model to describe process dynamics.

12.2.2.3 Models of Interactions/Communication

When we consider the dynamics of the software process, the real-time metaphor becomes very useful. Consider the myriad of interactions and communications among roles and activities on a software development project. We can easily imagine long feedback loops, situations where deadlock may occur, and so on. How do/should we represent such interactions? In her book on project management, Zells maintains that much of the reason project estimates are so unreliable is that so many activities are never identified, and hence never scheduled in the first place [ZEL90]. To more fully appreciate this, we give a Petri net model of a well-defined software review process (see Figure 12.4).

An orderly software review process might entail four distinct roles/participants: the review leader, the responsible designer, the review secretary, and the reviewer(s). Using this as an example of a software review task, these steps could be followed:

1. The responsible designer delivers all base materials to the review leader.
2. The responsible designer and the review leader identify a list of (other) reviewers.
3. The review leader gives the review materials and list of reviewers to the review secretary.
4. The review secretary schedules the review meeting, obtains commitments from all participants, and distributes the materials at least five working days in advance.
5. The reviewers examine the review materials and prepare a list of Action Items.
6. The reviewers give copies of the Action Item list to the review leader by the day before the review meeting.
7. The review leader consolidates the Action Item lists, prioritizes them, and prepares a review agenda.
8. During the review meeting, the prioritized action items are discussed (not resolved!), and additional action items may be identified.
9. The review meeting concludes with a recommendation: accept as is, accept pending action items, or reject.
10. The review secretary prepares a review report, and distributes copies to all review participants.
11. The responsible designer's supervisor makes a management decision on the review disposition.

We chose this example for the high degree of interaction and communication among the individuals in the process. The places in Figure 12.4 correspond either to tangible items (documents, review participant list, review report) or to stages in the process (work complete, reviewer commitment), and the transitions correspond to actions (deliver documents, prepare agenda, hold review). Notice the parallel activities between transitions t4 and t8. In terms of Petri net representations, transitions t4 and t6 indicate synchronized starts of parallel activities, and transitions t6 and t8 indicate synchronized terminations of parallel activities.

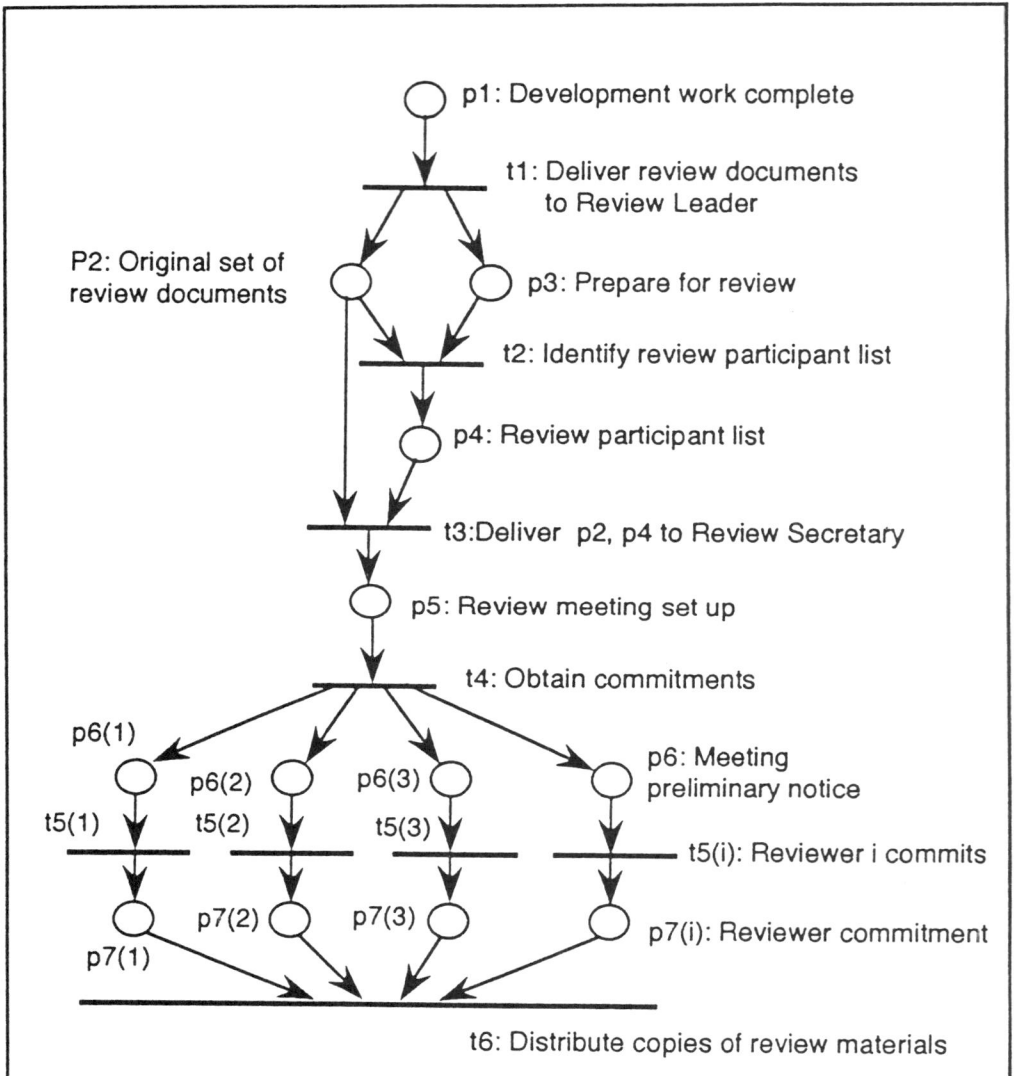

Figure 12.4
Petri net of the
review process.

Petri nets translate easily into PERT charts (transitions become activities, and input and output relations are reflected in activity fan-in and fan-out). When viewed as a PERT chart, we can (must) attach duration times to the activities. This, in conjunction with a Gantt chart showing assignments of tasks to people, provides a still clearer picture of the review process.

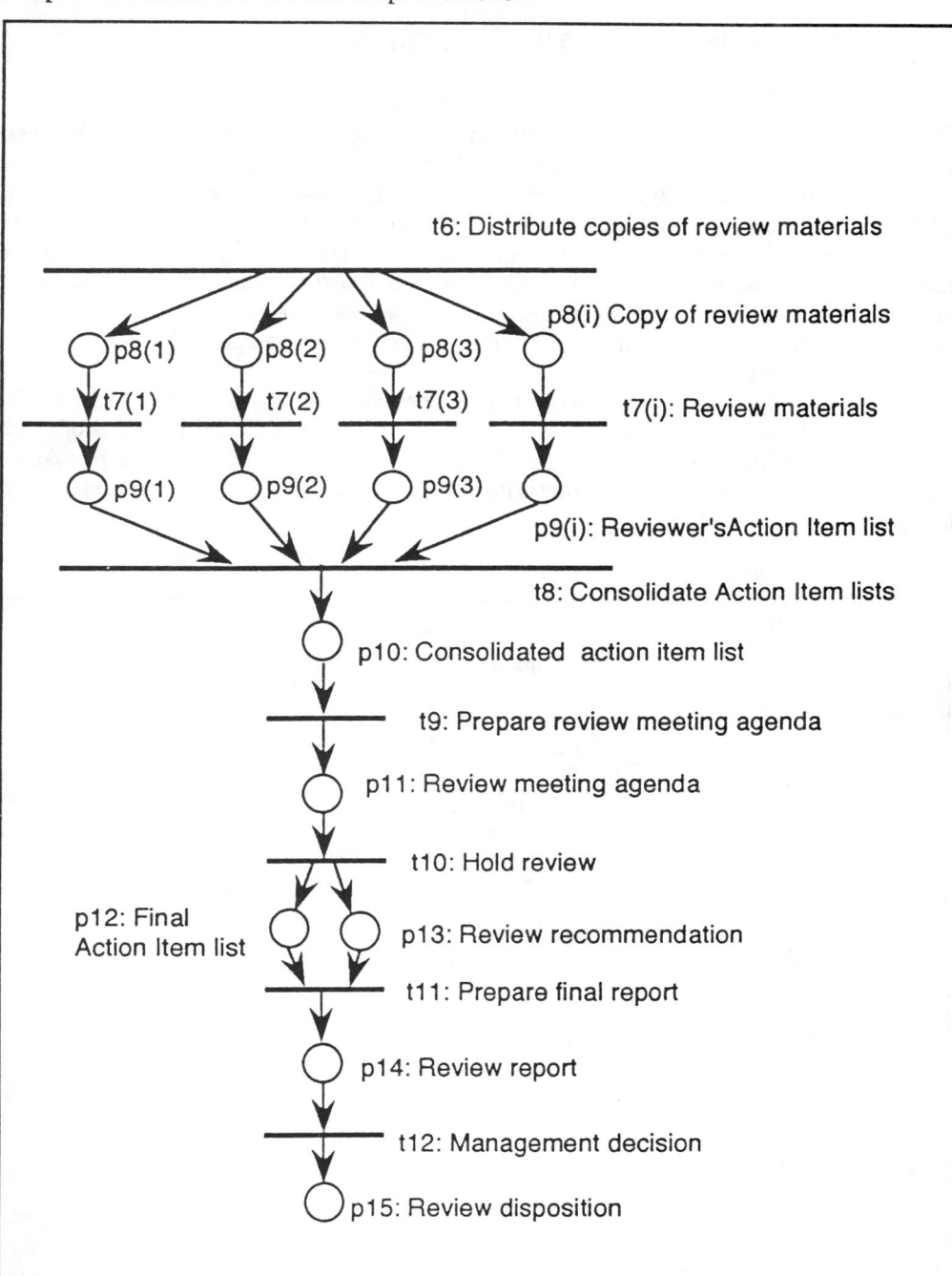

t6: Distribute copies of review materials

p8(i) Copy of review materials

p8(1)   p8(2)   p8(3)

t7(1)   t7(2)   t7(3)   t7(i): Review materials

p9(1)   p9(2)   p9(3)

p9(i): Reviewer'sAction Item list

t8: Consolidate Action Item lists

p10: Consolidated action item list

t9: Prepare review meeting agenda

p11: Review meeting agenda

t10: Hold review

p12: Final
Action Item list

p13: Review recommendation

t11: Prepare final report

p14: Review report

t12: Management decision

p15: Review disposition

**Figure 12.4 -
continued**
Petri net of the
review process.

12.2.2.4 Models of System Dynamics

System dynamics is an industrial engineering term that has recently been applied to the software process [ABD91]. System dynamics uses feedback loops to model control systems, especially where the item being controlled is a social activity. Abdel-Hamid's main contribution is to highlight the fact that software project management, like software process, is a nonlinear activity. Figure 12.5 shows the four main components of the System Dynamics Software Process Model. When the output of a subsystem changes (increases or decreases), the successor subsystems are affected. Trace through a couple of paths to convince yourself that the various subcycles make sense.

Figure 12.6 takes a closer look at the Resource Management subsystem. The simplistic view of resource management shown in Figure 12.6 is the basis of most project management models. Figure 12.7 shows the effects of schedule pressure: how it affects staff turnover, productivity, and rework, and how these in turn, affect the project work rate.

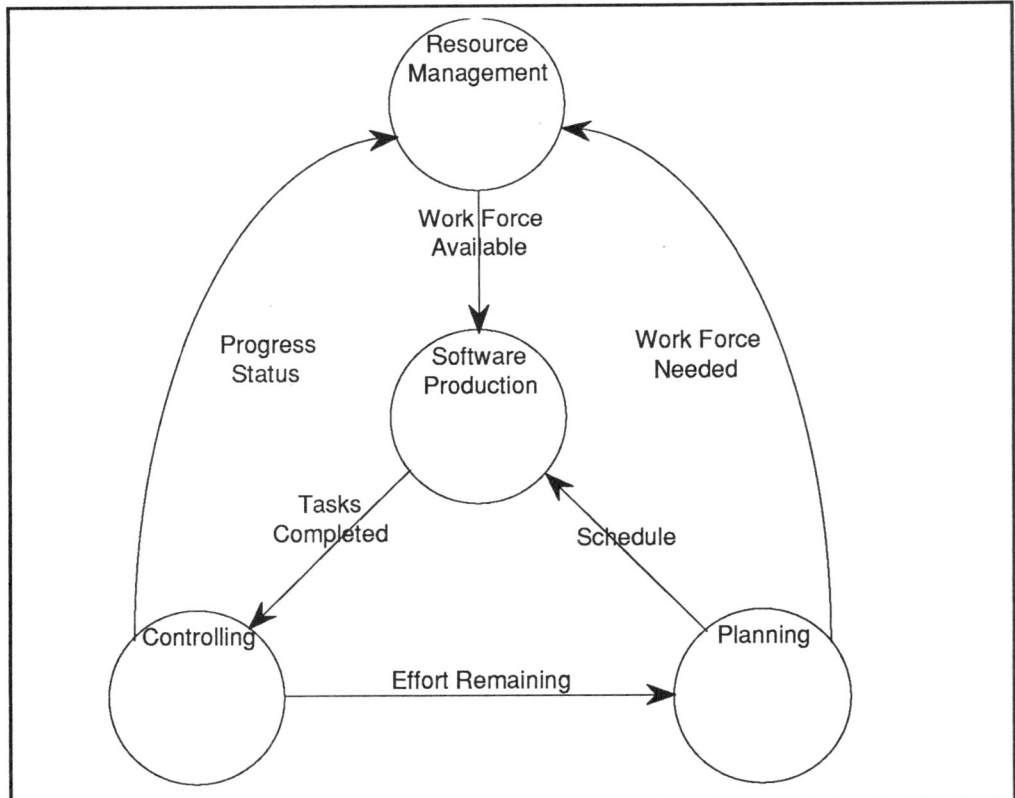

Figure 12.5
Subsystems in the System Dynamics Software Process Model.

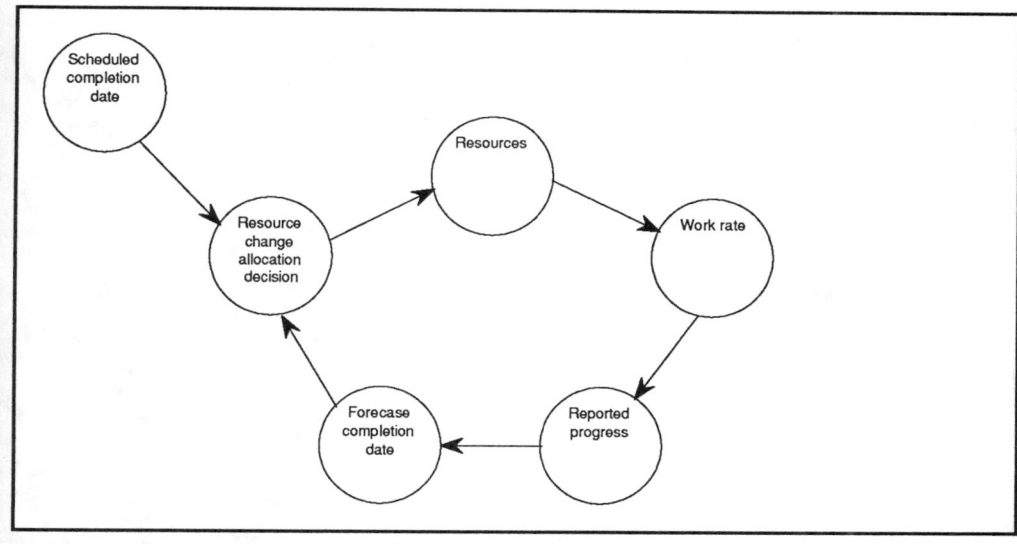

Figure 12.6
Simplistic view of
resource
management.

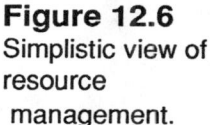

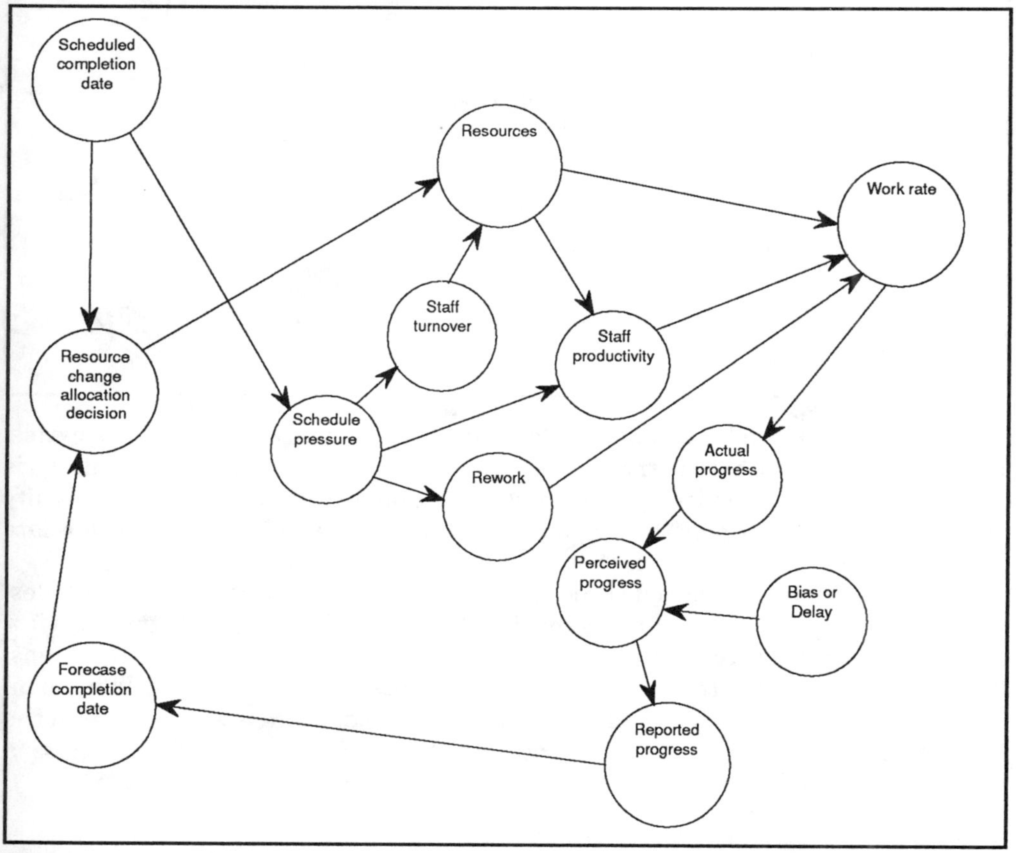

Figure 12.7
Refined view of
project work rate.

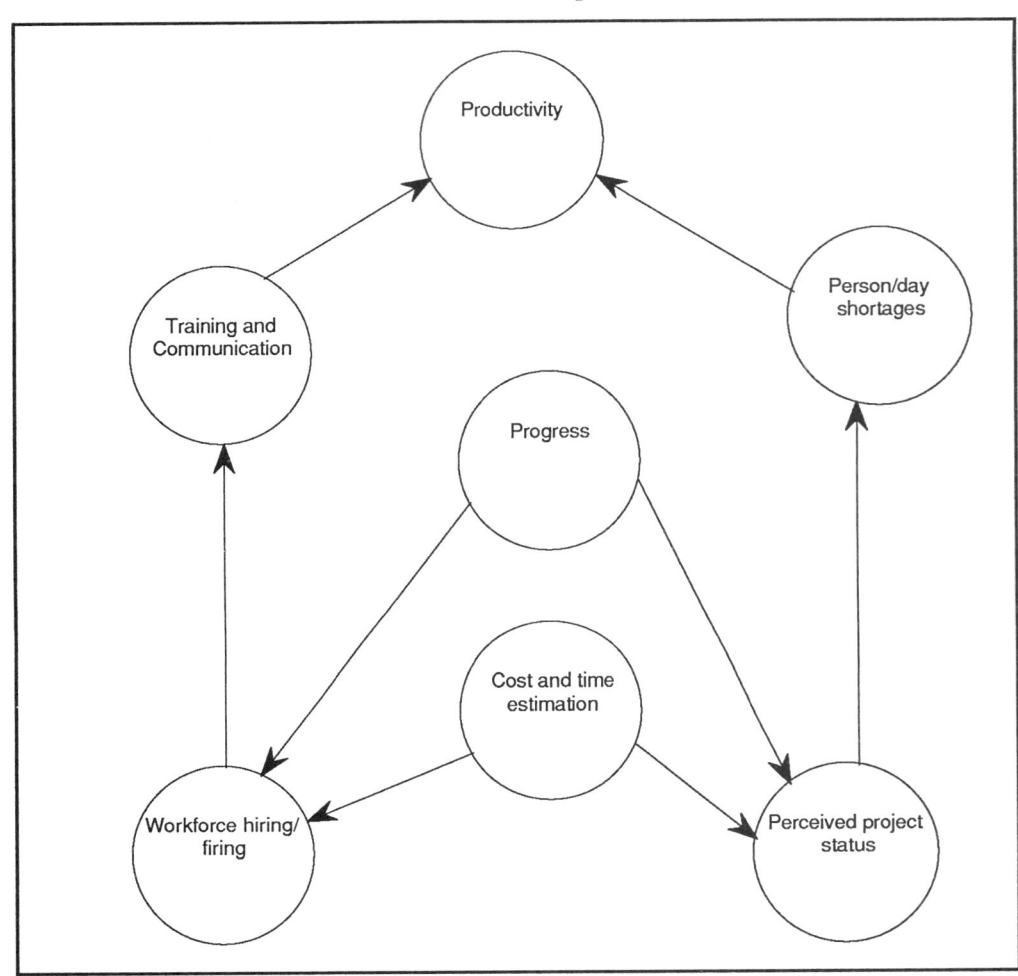

Figure 12.8
Primary factors
that affect project
schedules.

In their book, Abdel-Hamid and Madnick explore many such feedback cycles, quantifying them with industry studies where they can. One of the contributions is that they "test" their model against widely held beliefs (we should probably dignify them by calling them hypotheses), such as Brooke's law (adding people to a late project makes it later). Their model supports many of these scenarios.

Figure 12.8 is their model of the primary factors that affect project schedules, and the causal relationships among these factors. As with Figure 12.5, tracing a few subcycles is a good exercise. For instance, if productivity drops, progress also drops. This adds to the estimated project development interval, which puts a demand on the workforce hiring activity. As new people are hired, there is an increase in the communication and training overhead, which decreases productivity. Quite a vicious circle, and their model bears it out.

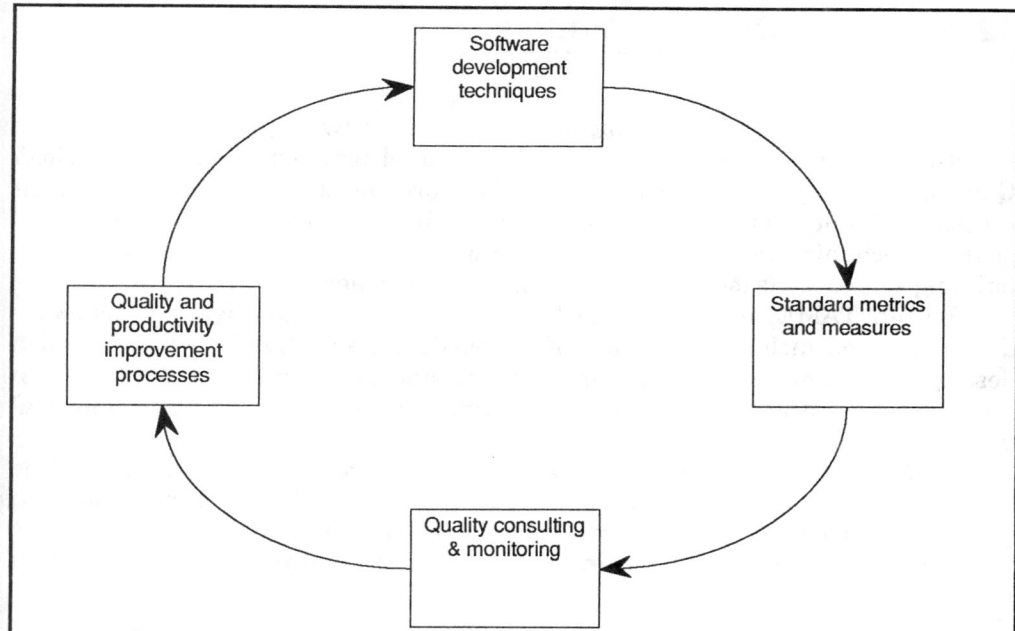

Figure 12.9
Quality management process model.

12.2.2.5 Models of Continuous Quality Improvement

Other organizations, including AG Communication Systems (AGCS), a joint venture between GTE and AT&T, have found a quality management perspective and an orientation towards continuous process improvement to be effective in process modeling [CLA91]. AGCS has developed the quality management process model shown in Figure 12.9 and uses it to drive a continuous improvement of their development process.

AGCS has used software metrics extensively to affect change in its software process, and has instituted quality consultants to help improve the quality of the process and the product. Within AGCS, these quality consultants develop and monitor quality plans, monitor and consult on metrics used, conduct post-mortems on projects completed, lead regular quality council meetings, and focus on continuous process improvement.

AGCS has found that establishing a software engineering process improvement group and a quality council helps it keep focused on the concept of continuous improvement. AGCS also reports that a critical aspect of its success in improving quality is the use of metrics within the larger scope of continuous improvement.

372
12.2.2.6 Goal-Oriented Models

The TAME project [OIV92] includes a model of software processes that has an object-oriented meta-model and uses a goal-oriented approach. TAME uses a Goal/Question/Metric paradigm, geared towards improving the software development process. A Quality Improvement paradigm establishes project and organizational goals, a mechanism for measuring progress against these goals, and an approach to building software measurements and applying them against these goals.

Within TAME, an experience factory collects the experience of software developers and includes two types of knowledge: descriptive knowledge, which describes the "how" of software development, and procedural knowledge, which includes experience in setting goals, answering questions, and collecting empirical data.

Under the TAME approach, a Goal Question Metric Program is used to define and interpret software goals, which include a purpose and a perspective for each goal. The purpose of a goal represents the process or product used, and the perspective represents the measurable aspects of the end result and the point of view of the stakeholders involved.

12.2.2.7 A Common-Sense Management Model

Another model of software processes that has been proposed is the Common-sense Management model (CMM) [YEH91]. CMM proposes a model that can guide management in process modeling away from parts of the process to a three-dimensional view of software development.

The CMM includes activities, which define the phases of development and are sequential, communication structures, which define explicit communication channels for all stakeholders involved, and an infrastructure, which supports long-range goals of continuous quality improvement. The resulting model, called Cosmos, supports separation of concerns, coevolution of artifacts, evolutionary prototyping, tangible definitions of artifacts, and continual improvement.

Within Cosmos, there is a two-level process hierarchy that includes control, to allow coordination and management of process and project functions, and execution, which supports specific tasks or activities. Key to the Cosmos view is the support for explicit communications between stakeholders and an infrastructure to support the creation and evolution of software development artifacts.

12.3 Generic Software Process Improvement Plan

There are two "old saws" about software process improvement: One is that if you don't know where you are going, any road will take you there; the other is that if you don't know where you are, you can't even find a road. Taken together, they are a fair summary of a workable software process improvement plan. In this section we present a common-sense, twelve-step plan for software process improvement. (We didn't intend a pun with twelve-step programs for substance abuse, but there are some useful comparisons with behavior modification.)

The process works. Hughes Aircraft reports [HUM91] that, in two years, spending $445,000, the resulting software process improvement saved about $2 million per year. Hewlett-Packard reports that, on the first project with new techniques, that it experienced an 18 percent increase in requirements specification time and a 19 percent increase in design time, offset by a 71 percent decrease in testing time [GRA92]. Hewlett-Packard's objective was quality improvement, yet it still experienced a modest productivity increase (about 5 percent due to the use of structured analysis and structured design on a project that consumed 22,857 engineering hours) on the first project using new technology.

12.3.1 Model Existing Process

Before any form of process improvement can begin, the status quo must be understood. As we noted in Chapter 1, every organization has some software process, no matter how ill-defined. Whatever the existing process is, it must be documented so that it can be used as a point of reference for process improvements.

What modeling form is appropriate for describing an existing process depends on how well the existing process is defined. If the process is at the initial or repeatable maturity level, as defined by the SEI SPMM, it is probably sufficient to record the life cycle model in use and then do one's best to make a PERT chart of the typical activities. This will be very rough, because there are probably many interactions and communication paths that are simply not remembered.

12.3.2 Assess Existing Process

Once the status quo process is recorded, it must be assessed. There are several sources for software process assessments. Defense contractors can avail themselves of the Software Engineering Institute's process assessment service [HUM91]. Such assessments generally cost about $50,000 and can consume ten person-months of effort.

Do-it-yourself process assessments are the other extreme. We received notice of a process assessment package from a consultant that includes an assessment guide, videotapes, and a complete set of instructions for under $1,000. Self-assessments can work, but an organization must be very disciplined and very honest as they can easily degenerate into self-deception.

As a middle ground, we recommend using a consultant who specializes in software assessments. Consultants know the questions to ask, they are independent (both of vendors and organizational tendencies to be overoptimistic), and they can usually focus in on weak portions of a software process from past experience.

However it is done, the assessment should identify the strong and weak points of the existing software process, as a basis for the next step.

12.3.3 Identify Objectives

Any software process improvement program must have a goal; the main choices are productivity and quality. It is essential that the organization clearly identify the real goal, so that actual progress can be observed. (Here is where the "any road will take you there" fits in.) Either of these goals is preferable to more abstract goals like "attain SEI maturity level 3 by 1995." An organization must determine its own goals; consultants can help, and academics can preach, but in the end, the people in an organization must pull together toward an accepted goal.

What happens when there are mixed goals? One common pattern is that practitioners are more inclined toward quality, while management is more inclined toward productivity. Who prevails in such a conflict? The organization must decide.

12.3.4 Develop a Strategic Plan

Once an assessment is made and goals are agreed upon, the organization can begin to develop a strategic software process improvement plan. The strategic alternatives are determined mostly by the choice between quality and productivity. There are three fundamental strategies: build on present strengths, focus on present weaknesses, or try to maximize payoff.

When productivity is the goal, the first and last strategies make the most sense. Making changes to the strongest parts of an existing process is a low-risk move. When an organization is already good at something, it can more easily recognize and appreciate improvements in that area. Success builds success, so making improvements to the strong points of a process is effective, especially if management "buy-in" is an issue. With this strategy, an organization can gradually move toward the weak points of its process, and it can stop at any point having realized tangible benefits.

The payoff maximization strategy presumes that the existing process is fairly well quantified. If not, how might the high-payoff areas be identified? The introduction of software reviews is a classic example of a high-payoff process improvement. Another maximization strategy might be to see where most of the effort budget is consumed (typically maintenance) and focus process improvements there. If an organization spends three-fourths of its budget on maintenance, and only 10 percent of its effort on coding, how much impact can the organization expect from an automatic code generator?

For organizations motivated by quality, the most sensible strategy is to focus on the weakest parts of the existing process. Hewlett-Packard, for example, identified the points at which errors are most frequently introduced (specification and design in their case), and addressed these areas first. Many organizations find that they are best at coding, then testing, followed by design, and they are weakest at requirements specification. The focus on weaknesses is a longer-term commitment, but the eventual rewards are greater.

12.3.5 Define Success Criteria

Success criteria are a refinement of the overall goal of software process improvement. Without specific success criteria, an organization can never know when a process improvement initiative has been successful. Success criteria are definitely strategy dependent. Suppose an organization has identified testing as a process weakness. The corresponding success criterion might well be "90 percent of testers are using X," where X is a testing process technology identified in the next step.

12.3.6 Investigate Technology

In a sense, much of this book is directed at helping the reader investigate both software engineering techniques and software development tools. This step is more important to organizations that focus on improving weaknesses in their process. An organization that determines that its weakest point is requirements specification might examine its application mix in terms of the taxonomy described in Chapter 3 and then look at the corresponding techniques in Parts 2 and 3. The next step might be to use Chapters 11 and 13 to identify appropriate tools and techniques.

There are three other possibilities that are often overlooked: attending technology-centered conferences and expositions, working with users groups and professional groups, and software engineering courses at local universities. In all of these situations, it is easy to meet people from other organizations who are faced with problems similar to those in your situation.

12.3.7 Acquire and Introduce Technology

Technology acquisition has two parts: methodology and tools. After appropriate software engineering technologies have been selected in terms of the organization's needs, the organization will need appropriate tools to support the techniques. The techniques should come first. Find a good source of technology training and use it. Repeated studies show that companies simply do not spend enough time and effort on technology training. Once an organization has become knowledgeable in the selected techniques, it is time to look for supporting tools.

We have one observation to contribute about technology training: CASE tool vendors offer excellent training on their products, but they are probably the worst source of straight methodology training. For obvious reasons, vendor instructors will never teach you about techniques that are not supported by the vendor's product.

Chapter 13 is devoted to strategies for introducing technology into an organization. Participants in the process must understand how the selected technology fits in with the strategic plan and goals.

12.3.8 Change Corporate Culture

Changing corporate culture is highly analogous to changing individual behavior. Earlier, when we referred to twelve-step programs for substance abuse, we mentioned that there are some real implications for this chapter. The key to success in these programs is that the substance abuser must want to change his or her behavior. The implications for corporate culture change are direct.

AG Communication Systems has a remarkable success story in changing its corporate culture [WEB90]. The key element is to focus on people realizing the consequences of the choices they make. That organization structured its policies in terms of kinds of consequences: positive or negative, immediate or future, and certain or uncertain. They use the PICNIC acronym to remind their staff that consequences of choices should be Positive, Immediate, and Certain. They have found that this approach to corporate behavior modification is extremely effective.

12.3.9 Implement Process Management

Once new tools and techniques have been successfully introduced, by definition the process has been changed. The measured and optimizing levels of SEI process maturity require a process group to continuously monitor the process and to recommend changes. Process groups identify process metrics tailored to an organization's process and goals, and then they gather data for these metrics. Process metrics are more difficult to identify than product metrics. We relate one such process metric here.

AG Communication Systems examined the characteristics of an effective review process [CLA91]. Reviewers had checklists of errors appropriate to the kind of review being conducted (design, test plan, etc.), and these checklists were organized by severity of errors. Reviewers were required to keep track of their review preparation time. After several months and scores of reviews, the process group demonstrated what may seem obvious: Reviewers need more preparation time to discover the difficult errors. If a reviewer only spent an hour or two, he or she typically only found the trivial errors (spelling, conformance to standards, etc.). Reviewers who spent four to eight hours of preparation found the significant errors (missing or incorrect functionality, unexpected side effects). The significance of this is that, prior to the study, supervisors were reluctant to let their talented designers "waste" time on review preparation. Once the process group had demonstrated that review preparation was highly productive time, the corporate (management) culture was easily changed.

Product and process metrics tend to be self-fulfilling prophesies. If people know how they will be judged, they will conform to those expectations. Suppose, for example, that your employer announces that your salary increment is directly tied to how frequently you wear a blue shirt to work. Buy blue shirts and wear them every day! The key to effective process metrics is that they must encourage desired behavior. For a more useful example, suppose we posit a metric that reflects reviewer effectiveness: number of discovered errors (by severity) per hour of preparation time.

12.3.10 Evaluate Intermediate Results

In a comprehensive software process improvement program, the process group should monitor and evaluate the results of all process changes. This is like applying the spiral life cycle model to process improvement. Each cycle represents a process change that is examined and acted upon.

12.3.11 Repeat/Refine/Redefine

We agree with Watts Humphrey that process improvement is a continuing process. It takes time to change a corporate culture. The Software Engineering Institute estimates a decade to go from the initial to the optimized level of process maturity. GTE Communication Systems worked on its software process for fifteen years. In 1990, one industry observer claimed that organization was the closest thing to a level 5 organization he had ever seen [YOU91].

12.4 Summary

Software processes can be modeled using a variety of methods and notations as described in this chapter. To be effective, software processes must be viewed in terms of the entire software development environment. As we defined the software production framework in Chapter 1, software processes encompass the roles, responsibilities, artifacts, and interchange of the work products among stakeholders. Only when viewed within the framework of the entire software production environment can software process improvement be realized.

12.5 Resource List

For information on the SEI software models, see [BOL91], [FIN92], [HUM88], [HUM89], [HUM91], [HUM92], [KEL90], and [SCO92]. See the book by Abdel-Hamid and Madnick [ABD91] for dynamic systems models. For a quality focus, see [CRO79] and [DEM82]. For metrics and process improvement, see [CLA91] and [GRA92].

12.6 References

[ABD91]   Abdel-Hamid, T. and S. E. Madnick, *Software Project Dynamics - An Integrated Approach*, Prentice Hall, 1991

[AOY87]   "Concurrent Development of Software Systems: A New Development Paradigm," *Soft. Eng. Notes*, vol. 13 no. 3, July 1987, ACM SIGSOFT, pp. 20-23.

[BOL91]   Bollinger, T. B., and C. McGowan, "A Critical Look at Software Capability Evaluations," *IEEE Software*, July, 1991, pp. 25-41.

[CLA91]   Clay, A. W., G. Grzybowski, S. Webber, and E. Yourdon, "Quality Metrics at AG Communication Systems," *American Programmer*, vol. 4, no. 9, September 1991.

[CRO79]   Crosby, P., *Quality Is Free*, McGraw-Hill, 1979.

[DEM82]   Demming. W. E., *Out of the Crisis*, MIT Center for Advanced Engineering Study, 1982.

[FIN92]   Finkelstein, A., "A Software Process Immaturity Model," *Soft. Eng. Notes*, vol. 17, no. 4, October 1992, ACM SIGSOFT, pp. 22-23.

[GRA92]   Grady, R., *Practical Metrics for Project Management and Process Improvement*, Prentice-Hall, 1992.

[HUM88]   Humphrey, W. S., "Characterizing the Software Process: A Maturity Framework," Technical Report CMU/SEI-87-TR-11 (also in *IEEE Software*, March 1988, pp. 73 - 79).

[HUM89]   Humphrey, W.S., *Managing the Software Process*, Addison Wesley, 1989.

[HUM91]   Humphrey, W. S., T. R. Snyder, and R. R. Willis, "Software Process Improvement at Hughes Aircraft," *IEEE Software*, vol. 8, no. 4, July 1991, pp. 11 - 23.

[HUM92]   Humphrey W. S., and P. H. Feiler, "Software Process Development and Enactment: Concepts and Definitions," Technical Report SEI-92-TR-4, Software Engineering Institute, Carnegie Mellon University, Pittsburgh.

[ILO87]   *The Languages of StateMate*, i-Logix, Inc. 1987.

[JOR90]   Jorgensen, P.C., "Accelerating Process Maturity with CASE," *American Programmer*, vol. 3, no. 9, September 1990.

[KEL89]   Kellner, M. I., "Representation Formalisms for Software Process Modeling," Proceedings of the 4th International Software Process Workshop: Representing and Enacting the Software Process, also in *Soft. Eng. Notes*, vol. 14, no. 4, June 1989, ACM SIGSOFT.

[KEL90]   Kellner, M.I., "Software Process Modeling: Value and Experience," private copy.

[OIV92]   Oivo, M., and V. R. Basili, "Representing Software Engineering Models: The TAME Goal Oriented Approach," *IEEE Trans. on Soft. Eng.*, vol. 18., no. 10, pp. 886-898.

[SCO92]   Scott, G. J., "Can Software Engineering Afford to Improve the Process," *Soft. Eng. Notes*, vol. 17, no. 2, April 1992, ACM SIGSOFT, pp. 39-42.

[WEB90]   Webber, S., "Performance Management: A New Approach to Software Engineering Management," *American Programmer*, vol. 3, nos. 7-8, July-August 1990.

[YEH91]   Yeh, R. T., D. A. Naumann, R. T. Mittermeir, R.A. Schlemmer, W. S. Gilmore, G. E. Sumrall, and J.T. Lebaron, "A Commonsense Management Model," *IEEE Software*, November 1991, pp. 23-33.

[YOU91]   Yourdon, E., Preface, *American Programmer*, vol. 4, no. 9, September 1991.

[ZEL90]   Zells, L., *Managing Software Projects*, QED Information Sciences, Inc., 1990.

Chapter 13
Transition to CASE and Software Development Techniques

Moving from an ad hoc development environment with no formal software development technique in place to an engineering, CASE-oriented development environment involves much time and energy on the part of everyone involved in the process of developing software. Having a planned approach to this process can help reduce the risk of failure and can help to ensure a leveled commitment to the transition process itself. Many organizations fail to define objectives and goals or to formalize a plan for this transition, and this often results in failure.

The process of technology transfer has been studied from technical as well as psychological perspectives, and the results often point to general guidelines for improving the transfer process. The introduction of any new technology into an organization involves cultural change in that organization. Those organizations that fail to deal with the issue of cultural change often fail in their transition efforts.

In this chapter we will investigate the process of technology transition, suggest an approach to this transition, discuss the issues involved in selecting and implementing software development techniques and CASE tools, and review the costs for this transition. Development techniques specify the tasks, methods, and representations for the software production framework, and CASE tools support the notations and diagrams within the techniques. Adopting techniques and CASE tools directly affects development teams and individual staff, and represents a significant change for practitioners.

Luckily, organizations that are planning to migrate to software development techniques and CASE can benefit from the experiences of other organizations that have been successful or failed in this migration process. Chapter 15 further investigates the technology transfer process at organizations, includes case studies, and serves as a companion to this chapter. Chapter 15 also investigates how organizations deal with cultural change, what strategies have been used for technology transition, and processes for selecting and implementing development techniques and CASE tools.

13.1 Introduction

Undertaking to select and implement CASE and software development techniques affects everyone in the software development organization as well as the users of the software product. Moving towards development techniques and CASE is a risky, long-term endeavor that cannot succeed without adequate management, development staff, and client commitment. Some studies suggest that primary reasons for failure include lack of management commitment, inadequate organizational resources, lack of integration with existing tools, no proof of value of CASE, inexperience with CASE, and fear of change. Other studies estimate the rate of failure with adopting CASE and software development techniques at 50 percent.

Technology transition is a topic that has received much focus in the industry in the past, and there is a wealth of relevant information on the process and the costs associated with this transition. Several studies suggest that the transition to CASE and software development techniques parallels other types of transition, including innovation and adaptation. Others have shown how a movement towards Total Quality Management (TQM) is linked with a transition to development techniques and CASE.

Studies of organizations that have failed to successfully make the transition to new technologies would suggest that these organizations focused more on the tools than on the development techniques that are the basis for CASE, planned for improvements in productivity in the short term, and failed to deal with the cultural change issue in the transition process.

13.2 Technology Transition Strategies

Along with the experiences of those organizations cited in the case studies, others in the industry have written on the subject of technology transfer as it relates to CASE and software development techniques. When reviewing the results of these efforts, there are some common findings that surface and point to several viable strategies for the technology transfer process.

Five major models for technology transition have been identified, including breadth of impact of change, organizational maturity, levels of learning a new technology, diffusion of innovation, and mutual adaptation. Each of these views will be discussed in more depth in the following sections.

13.2.1 Barb Bouldin

Barbara Bouldin has written on managing the cultural change required to make the transition to software development techniques and CASE [BOU89]. Bouldin's view is that the breadth of impact of change must drive the technology transition process. Bouldin spent several years at AT&T as a change agent for CASE and structured methods and has identified a life cycle for implementing change along with several key factors to successfully managing this change. These factors include:

Providing information in familiar terms to everyone
Listening effectively, brainstorm and developing a basic game plan
Planning intermediate deliverables
Not using edicts - involving users and staff
Building on what is already effective
Avoiding excessive ambition
Managing the expectations
Implementing without disruption
Keeping everyone involved
Performing periodic review and sign-off

13.2.2 Roger Pressman: Software Engineering Life Cycle

Roger Pressman has also written on the process of making the transition to software development techniques and CASE [PRE88] and introduced a Software Engineering Life Cycle (SELC) for this transition. Pressman's approach (see Figure 13.1) involves five basic steps:

Assessment - Assess where the organization is in its software development environment and identify strong and weak points in the process. Pressman recommends that organizations perform a software engineering audit or detailed assessment of their current development environment prior to moving forward with CASE and development techniques.

Education - Educate everyone involved in the methods, techniques, and tools to be used or already available.

Selection - Select any new techniques and/or tools that can help improve the software development process.

Installation - Install selected techniques and tools.

Evaluation - Evaluate whether the software process has been improved by the tools and techniques installed and how the process can be further improved with other tools and techniques.

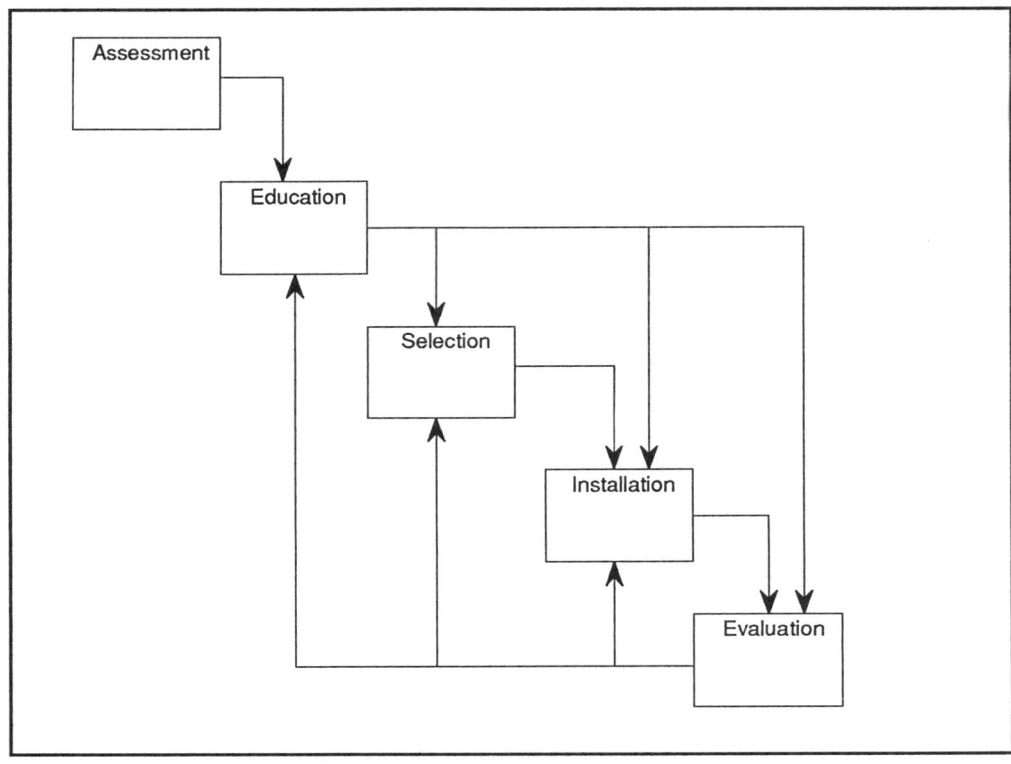

Figure 13.1
Pressman's Software Engineering Life Cycle.

Pressman strongly suggests, as others do, that a SELC is a repetitive process that doesn't stop once techniques and tools have been successfully implemented. This view is shared by the TQM initiatives and the focus on continuous process improvement which is described in Chapter 12.

13.2.3 Watts Humphrey: Software Process Control

Watts Humphrey, while at the Software Engineering Institute (SEI) at Carnegie Mellon University, pioneered the Software Process Maturity Model (SPMM) and has written about it in [HUM89a]. This model has generated much discussion in the industry and is evolving within the SEI.

The SPMM has been widely used by organizations to determine whether they are ready for CASE and software development techniques. Humphrey has also identified a life cycle for improving and controlling the software process itself which is shown in Figure 13.2. Humphrey pioneered the concept of a defined software process, considering the product or outcome of the process (the software itself) the same way one would that of a manufacturing process. Quality standards should be

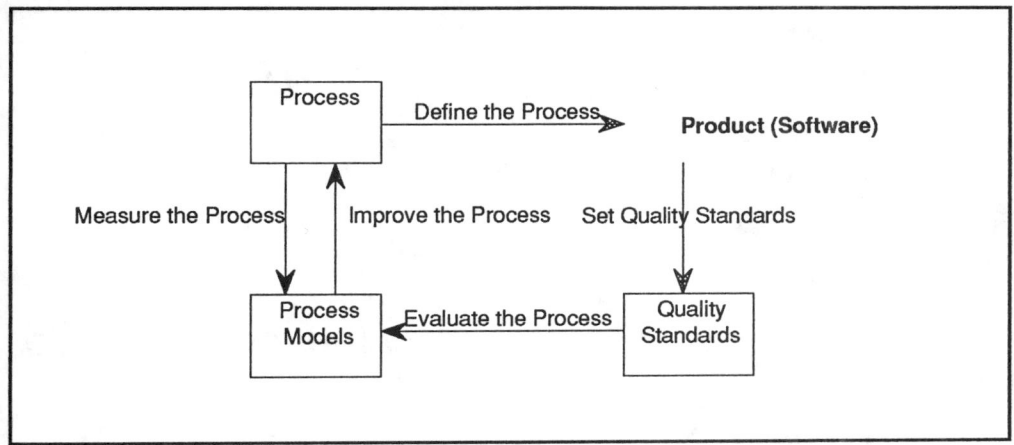

Figure 13.2
Watts Humphrey's
Software Process
Control loop.

established to define the product, software. Evaluating the process for quality improvement can be done with software process models like the SPMM. Measuring the process can help identify ways of improving the process.

Phil Crosby has identified stages of quality management maturity that are shown in Figure 13.3 [CRO79]. These stages of maturity represent the views of management in an organization related to the concepts of quality and the process of improving quality of a product or service. Taken together, Crosby's levels of quality awareness present a goal-directed view of software process improvement.

Humphrey and the Software Engineering Institute (SEI) recommend that a software process assessment be the first step in defining a software process. SEI provides training and consulting for five-day assessment sessions to their clients.

1. Uncertainty	"We don't know why we have problems with quality."
2. Awakening	"Is it absolutely necessary to always have problems with quality?"
3. Enlightenment	"Through management commitment and quality improvement, we are identifying and resolving our problems."
4. Wisdom	"Defect prevention is a routine part of our operation."
5. Certainty	"We know why we don't have problems with quality."

Figure 13.3
Phil Crosby's
Stages of Quality
Management
Maturity.

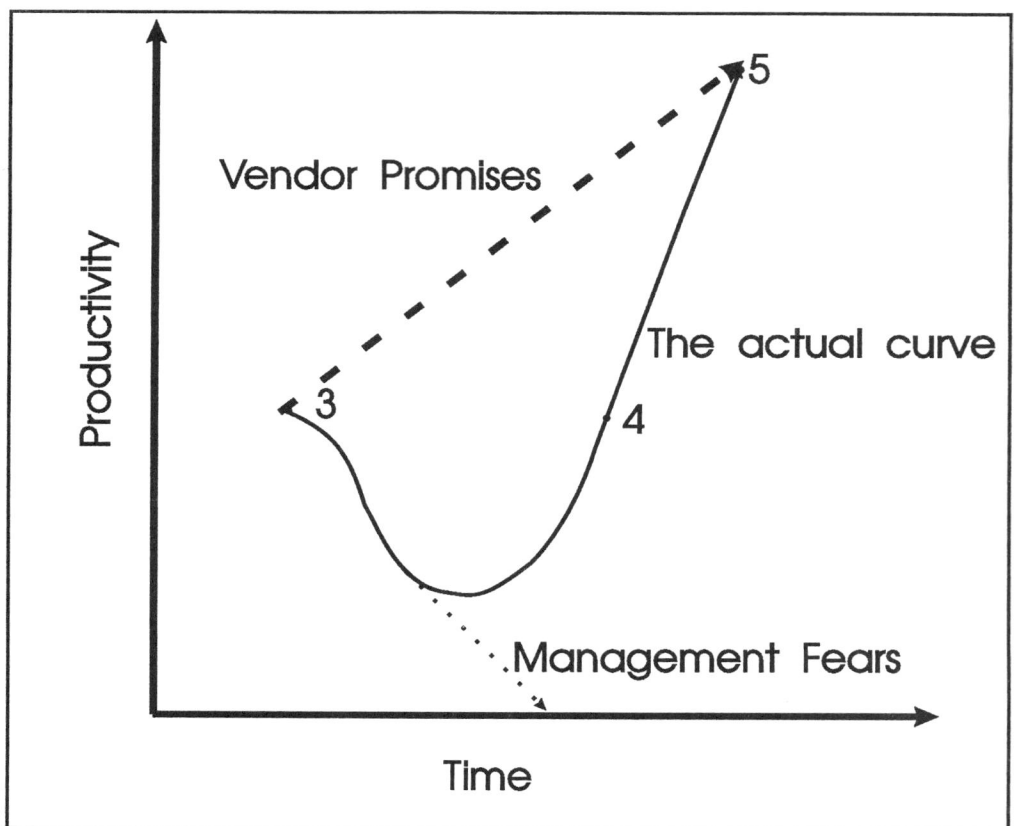

Figure 13.4
The J curve.

13.2.4 Wayland Systems: The J Curve

Steven Weiss and Meilir Page-Jones of Wayland Systems suggest viewing technology transition as a process of knowledge acquisition. They use a curve that they feel describes the process of acquiring knowledge with software development techniques. The J curve and the seven stages of software engineering expertise help to explain the changes that occur when developers are introduced to development techniques and as they acquire expertise with these techniques (see Figure 13.4).

Stage 1: Innocent people have never heard of software engineering methods and have no knowledge of their applicability. Stage 1 people may be blissfully unaware of any problems or a perceived "software crisis."

Stage 2: Exposed people have heard of software engineering methods through colleagues, magazine articles, or whatever, and believe that these methods have some relevance to them and their jobs.

Stage 3: Apprentice people have been through a seminar or tutorial on software engineering methods and have a broad, superficial understanding of the methods themselves. But stage 3s have no practical experience applying the methods on real-world problems.

Stage 4: Practitioners have actually used software engineering methods seriously at least once. They know about the tough parts and how to make the methods work, but at this stage, the methods are not always second nature. Additional guidance is often required with stage 4s to ensure productivity.

Stage 5: Journeymen (or Journeywomen) use software engineering methods regularly and naturally in their day-to-day work. Once at this stage, staff are typically more productive and rarely need any advice or guidance on using the methods.

Stage 6: Experts are thoroughly conversant with software engineering and know the rules so well, they even know when to break them in order to achieve better results. They are often found training others in software engineering methods.

Stage 7: Researchers are at the leading edge of software engineering practices and are often called upon to write books, give papers, and speak on software engineering methods. They discover new ideas and advance the state of the art in software engineering.

The J curve focuses on the transition from learning about development techniques to using them regularly and effectively.

13.2.5 Alternative Views on Technology Transition

The J curve is similar to other observations that have been made about the process of learning new concepts. Bloom's taxonomy, shown in Figure 13.5, is often used by educators to describe levels of mastery of forms of knowledge or experience. These levels of knowledge, to a certain extent, parallel the levels of expertise described by the J curve. The process of acquiring knowledge is directly applicable to any technology transition process, since staff must accept knowledge or expertise to begin effectively using new tools or techniques.

1. Knowledge:	Recalling information
2. Comprehension:	Understanding information
3. Application:	Using information in a new situation
4. Analysis:	Breaking down information
5. Synthesis:	Creating new information
6. Evaluation:	Making a judgment based on established criteria

Figure 13.5
Bloom's taxonomy.

One way of viewing the acquisition of knowledge regarding software development techniques and tools is presented by David Harel [HAR92]. Harel identifies the critical separation between the accidental and essential aspects of a system. Accidental aspects of a system are the properties that may not reflect its nature or structure, but that are generally easy for inexperienced developers to identify. Essential properties are the underlying conceptual aspects of the problem domain that determine the basis for the system.

If we apply the concept of accidental and essential aspects to software development techniques, the parallel is that inexperienced developers focus on the notations used in the method, whereas experienced developers focus on the technique (process) used and the representations. Beginning developers tend to view the problem domain in terms of the symbols and terminology of the notation, whereas experienced developers view a system and its essential nature as represented by the notations within the method. The process of learning how to see the "forest for the trees" when using a formal method is a critical stumbling block to effectively using these methods. Experienced developers often use the representation and technique to help them ask questions about the system and think about the problem, whereas beginning developers tend to spend their time defining terms and drawing diagrams, forgetting that the diagrams are simply a means of better understanding the problem and not an end in themselves.

This view of focusing on different aspects of the methods described in this text can help organizations prepare for and deal with the cultural change required to learn new ways of developing software. Technology transition is often the problem that organizations that fail to implement tools and techniques successfully do not address adequately.

The SEI has undertaken the Transition Models Project, which is demonstrating and studying the process of adopting software engineering technologies. SEI advocates the development of capability for planning and implementing technology transition within its customer base through a technology receptor function (TRF). TRF includes management oversight, work groups tracking and evaluating technology, pilot projects for new technologies, and a core group of planners who coordinate and report on implementation projects.

Staff at the Consortium for the Management of Emerging Software Technologies (COMSOFT) have defined a framework for technology transfer that includes a search of all relevant literature, knowledge engineering to validate the knowledge in the literature, basic research to address gaps in existing knowledge, and an advanced knowledge delivery vehicle based on hypertext and expert systems technology [KOR92]. COMSOFT has developed a pilot of the delivery vehicle called the Management Support System (MSS), which includes levels of knowledge and was developed to support the AT&T Object Modeling Resource Base. Figure 13.6 describes the MSS framework for knowledge on development techniques. The staff at COMSOFT envisions a framework for technology transfer that includes some entity to synthesize and integrate research and make this knowledge available to

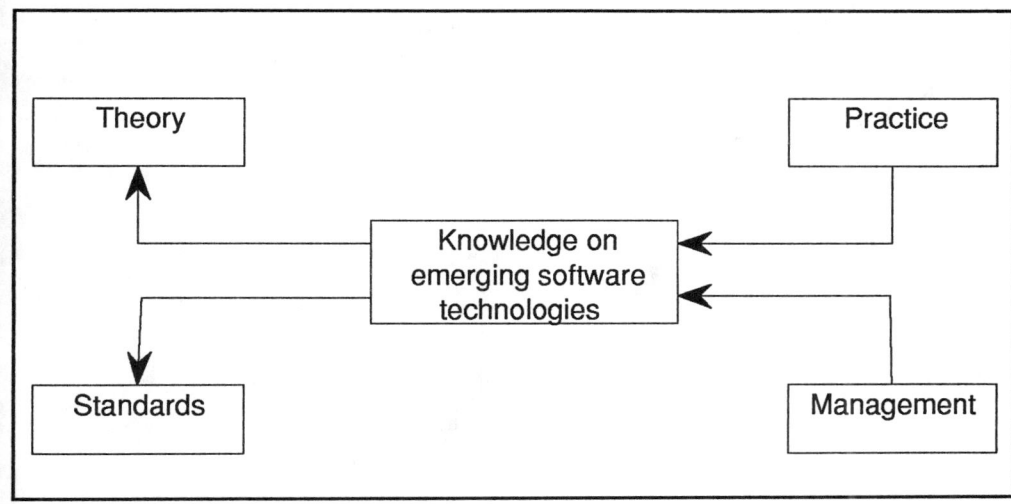

Figure 13.6
Management
Support
System framework.

organizations. The COMSOFT effort suggests a partnership between universities and private organizations to synthesize and address these gaps in knowledge.

Others in the industry [FOW92] have identified three views of technology transition: (1) a research and development (R&D) life cycle view, (2) an innovative organization view, and (3) a technology-driven change view. Of these, the R&D view relates technology transition to a specific technical or organizational community and focuses on the technology as it matures. The innovative organization view concentrates on the development of a sound climate for change which enables technology to be immersed easily. This view is often shared by TQM initiatives and a quality improvement perspective. The final view, where technology drives change, focuses on the change process itself and provides management and direction for this change.

But as has been said so well in [FOW92], "Yet sets of transition mechanisms do not necessarily lead us to more effective transition planning or, even more important, to a strategic basis for that planning."

Others, including Dan Mosley, have expressed the process of technology transition in innovation life cycles. Mosley [MOS92] concludes that Bright's innovation chain equation, shown in Figure 13.7 represents a model which can be adapted to fit the technology transition process. This life cycle includes stages for technological discovery and perception of a need for new technology, synthesis of existing knowledge as a basis for the new technology, verification of the conceptual basis for adoption, demonstration of the viability of the new technology, development of alternative versions and selection of prototypes to demonstrate the value of new technology, commercial introduction with limited use, widespread adoption of the technology, and proliferation of generic technology into new areas.

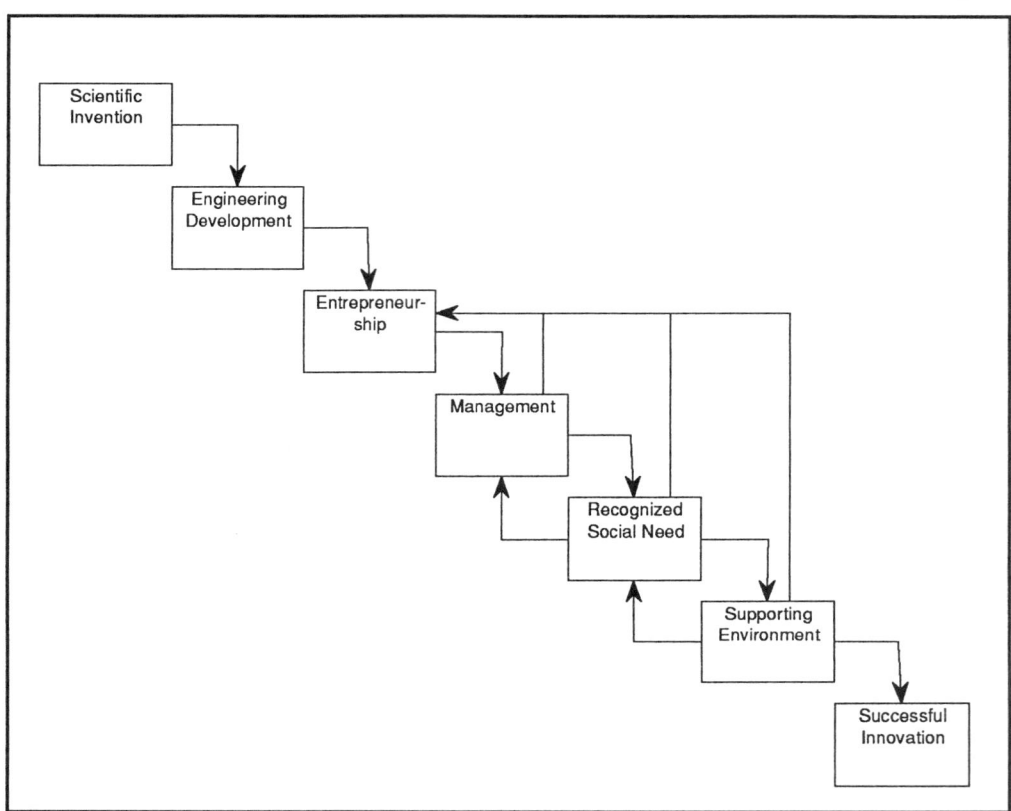

Figure 13.7
Bright's innovation
chain with feed-
back loops.

13.3 Steps in Transition

An approach we have found helps organizations manage the transition from an ad hoc to an engineered development process is based on an initial assessment and evaluation process, followed by a gradual transition to development techniques and automated tools. This process is described in Figure 13.8 and is composed of four basic steps:

Assessment of the current development environment, a definition of a future, engineered development environment, and a strategic plan to migrate from the current to the future environment.

Evaluation and selection of appropriate tools and methods/techniques along with training of staff in the use of these products and methods.

Implementation of selected tools and techniques with further training and support to diffuse the use of these methods across the organization.

Follow-up evaluation to determine if further steps are needed and if the transition was successful.

Recognizing that not all organizations can benefit from CASE or software development techniques goes a long way toward an objective view on the issue of technology transfer. Some organizations fail in attempting to implement CASE, and if an organization will not substantially benefit from the transition, one possible outcome from the assessment process should be a recommendation that it not implement CASE. Some organizations, for example, are small, develop relatively simple systems, or may have no need to improve their software development process or the quality of their product. As we have already examined in Chapter 11, organizational readiness is a major factor that leads to successful implementation of CASE technology, and some organizations may not be ready for a successful transition.

13.3.1 Assessment

At the beginning of the assessment phase, the scope of the assessment should be clearly defined, along with the goals and objectives and the tasks and deliverables for the assessment process. The process of developing software should be viewed in detail, with a focus on the roles and responsibilities of staff and the creation and management of the representations or deliverables throughout the development life cycle.

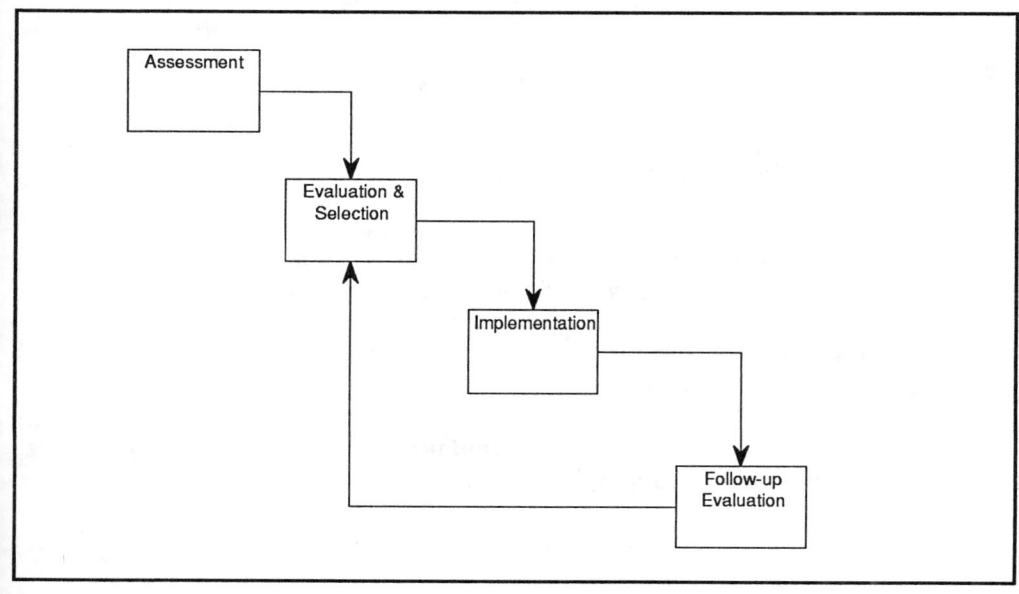

Figure 13.8
Steps in transition.

Any assessment process must consider the practical issues related to making the transition to development techniques and CASE, and we strongly recommend the creation of an evaluation team that consists of development staff and represents everyone involved in the development process. From our experience, failure to involve or represent everyone in the development process can quickly lead to failure of the transition.

Before moving to a future software development environment that includes CASE and software development techniques, it is critical that the current state of software development be defined. Once the current environment is defined, this information should be distributed to all development staff for comment. This first step should define the current state of software development in the organization such that someone outside the organization can understand the development environment. This current environment document should describe the use of existing development techniques and tools, project management, measurements, and staff skills.

Following this, a future environment that strives to improve the development process and the quality of the software delivered can be defined. This future environment may or may not include new software development techniques and CASE tools. Finally, a strategic plan for migration towards the future environment should be defined along with short- and long-term objectives in the transition to this future environment. This plan should include any appropriate training in development techniques and tools, along with recommendations for the purchase of additional equipment, software, and consulting or support help to facilitate this transition.

One important factor in this initial step is to keep management expectations realistic and to clearly define any potential benefits for the organization in the short and long term. If an organization expects to show substantial improvement in software quality or productivity, it must measure before and after making the transition.

13.3.2 Evaluation and Selection

Once the current and future development environments have been defined, and a plan has been drawn up to move from the current to the future environment, specific software development techniques and tools can be evaluated and selected. The process of selecting and evaluating CASE tools and techniques will be discussed in more depth later in this chapter. Some issues that should be considered in this phase include whether an in-house evaluation of products should be undertaken, whether a pilot project should be used to evaluate selected products and methods, and what criteria will be used to judge the success of these efforts.

Our experience suggests that until an organization uses a development technique and CASE tools on real projects, it will not fully understand the strengths and weaknesses of the products. We also recommend that organizations evaluating and selecting development techniques and tools realize they will not have perfect foresight and will probably need to make modifications to these methods and tools to fit the needs of their environment.

13.3.3 Implementation

Once tools and techniques have been selected, the process of spreading their use throughout the organization can begin. This process may take several years, and management in the organization must be committed to a long-term transition to these new technologies. Successfully implementing CASE and software development techniques implies that all development staff will eventually change the way they develop software. This transition cannot happen without adequate training and support for the staff and a strategic plan to implement CASE and development techniques. Dealing with the cultural change implied in this transition is often the most important but most often overlooked aspect of the process. Until the use of CASE and software engineering techniques has been established as the status quo, the benefits of using these tools and techniques will be only partially realized.

One important factor in successfully spreading the use of these tools and techniques is the creation of support groups and an environment where development staff can feel comfortable in learning these new methods. Of primary importance in acquiring new skills is the need for an environment that recognizes that mistakes will be made and does not penalize people for making these mistakes.

Some organizations have had success establishing software process improvement and/or quality assurance groups that are responsible for identifying, measuring, and facilitating change to the development process.

13.3.4 Follow-up Evaluation

An important step in the transition process is a follow-up evaluation to determine if the tools and techniques selected have been beneficial to the organization. It should not be assumed that simply bringing in expensive CASE tools and having developers learn a new way of developing software will prove to be inherently helpful or improve overall software quality. Some tools and techniques may not fit in the existing development environment and may have to be modified or replaced before any substantial benefit can be accomplished.

Without adequate measurements, an organization cannot truthfully report that the development process or the software developed has improved. If measurements have been taken prior to the transition process, it is a fairly straightforward process to show increases in overall quality or productivity. If no measurements have been taken before the process has begun, it is impossible to show any quantifiable improvement.

Regardless of how success is measured, organizations should assess their development environments following acquisition of new technologies to determine how these tools and techniques have affected the environment. If a cost/benefit analysis is to be performed, the costs will be measured against the realized benefits from using the tools and techniques, and some savings or improvement will be calculated. Section 13.9 discusses some factors to consider in estimating the cost of the transition to development techniques and CASE.

13.4 Transition Team Characteristics

For an organization to successfully implement CASE and software development techniques, commitment and direct involvement in the process is required of all stakeholders in the software process. This effort should be generally directed at three different organizational levels:

1. *Management* - both upper and middle managers
2. *Users* - direct users of software
3. *Software development staff* - i.e., everyone involved in the process of developing software

Additionally, an outside consultant may be brought in to help facilitate the assessment and evaluation process. Outside consultants also can bring in experience with an assessment process, make recommendations without regard to political issues, and evaluate an organization from an objective perspective that may not be possible from within.

Who within the organization should be involved in the assessment process? Ideally, anyone involved in the software development process should be represented on an assessment team. This helps to ensure that each development group is committed to successfully selecting and implementing the technique and CASE. Without adequate representation on the assessment team, there is a higher probability that those groups not represented will work to derail the implementation effort.

While it may not be practical or politically viable to include representatives from each development group, at a minimum the assessment team should contain staff from the following areas:

1. Management, from IS and other areas, to help identify business plans, goals, and success factors; also, to determine the role of software in the business
2. Development staff, including:
   A. Project leaders/managers
   B. DA/DBA staff
   C. Development center staff (business analysts, systems analysts, programmers, etc.)
   D. Maintenance staff
   E. Quality assurance staff (if available)
3. Operations/production control staff for data collection, etc.
4. Training and education staff
5. People from the user or client community

While all of the people described above may be involved in the assessment and evaluation process, they may all have slightly different roles. For example, a core group of staff may perform the data collection, while others may meet formally on a regular basis to review and analyze the data collected and make recommendations, etc.

13.5 Transition to Development Techniques

Different organizations may choose different strategies or plans for implementing development techniques and CASE. There are a number of considerations that organizations making this transition should evaluate before they choose an appropriate method for selecting and implementing CASE and software engineering techniques. There is no guarantee that an approach will work for all organizations. Several popular approaches that have been successful in the past are described below.

13.5.1 Pilot Project vs. Across-the-Board Implementation

When choosing to select and implement CASE and development techniques, an organization can approach the transition from one of several possible angles: by choosing to evaluate the tool and technique using a pilot project, by attempting to apply them across the entire organization, or by some combination of these approaches.

Using a pilot project can be helpful in proving to the development staff the value of the technique and tool before requiring that they be used within the organization. This can help to show developers that there is a "better way" to develop software and can lead to a path of least resistance within the development organization. One possible outcome from a pilot approach is that using a tool and technique may not prove to be beneficial.

Attempting to make an across-the-board transition to CASE and development techniques requires the total commitment of everyone in the development group to the technique and tool. Many organizations that have attempted to implement CASE by management edict have failed miserably. When making an across-the-board transition, formal procedures should be established to deal with the cultural and technical changes in the organization.

13.5.2 Management-Led vs. Implementation Team-Led

Two different approaches to leading a transition are management- or development staff-led projects. Both have positive and negative aspects. A management-led approach can focus on the issues relevant to managing software development, but development staff must be convinced that new methods and tools will work, and every attempt must be made to avoid management edict in these situations.

A development team-led or grass-roots transition must get management to understand the resources required and the commitment needed to succeed. Developers cannot successfully implement CASE and development techniques without management approval and adequate resources. While developers must deal with the cultural change, they cannot write the checks or solicit user support during the transition process.

13.5.3 New Systems vs. Existing Systems

A basic consideration when approaching a transition to software engineering and CASE is which aspect of the development life cycle will be addressed. Most of the development techniques described and used in this book focus on development of new systems. While it is often easier to implement a new approach or tool on a system under development, most organizations spend the majority of the resources maintaining existing systems.

When development techniques and CASE tools are used to develop systems, the benefit to the maintenance of these systems is substantial. But what about all the systems developed prior to the introduction of CASE and development techniques? How are these systems affected by the introduction of new technologies?

Existing or legacy systems are often large and complex and rarely include current documentation and specifications. Changes to systems often result in bugs or problems cropping up which result in more resources to fix these problems. This ripple effect typically causes the cost of maintaining these systems to increase.

Some automated tools, include re- and reverse engineering products, can help to development documentation, specifications, and cross-reference information for existing systems, which can help reduce the cost of maintaining these systems.

13.6 Technique Evaluation and Selection

Most organizations today take a haphazard approach to software development and have not adopted the techniques described in this book. Nor have they standardized their approach across software development projects. The result is marginal software that is difficult to maintain.

The "techniques" actually used in these organizations can be characterized in two ways. First, project teams invent them over and over again. Development steps taken and deliverables produced invariably differ from project to project. Second, the "techniques" are informal, undocumented, and usually focused on coding and testing. There are a number of factors explaining why this situation exists. Unfortunately, none of them promote the quality of the software produced. Common reasons are project resource constraints and development experience of the project team.

An example of a resource constraint is the time allocated to complete a software development project. When time becomes short, a project leader will often direct her team to "get coding while I figure out what the user wants." This is a common, but informal, software development approach.

Some organizations are beginning to understand the benefits of employing a formal, documented approach to software development. They are realizing that an approach based upon a technique and applied across projects will eventually yield higher-quality software and more productive developers. Once they reach this understanding, they can move from an ad hoc software development environment to an engineered one. Part of that process includes selecting and implementing a formal technique.

13.6.1 Definitions

Earlier in the chapter, we discussed an assessment step in which the current and future development environments are documented along with a plan for getting from one environment to the other. With that in mind, let's define what is meant by technique selection and technique implementation.

Technique selection is the task of choosing a formal technique that is compatible with the defined future environment. The selected technique will come from one of the six categories detailed in this text. More than one technique may be selected to support different phases of the SDLC and/or to support development of different types of software.

Technique implementation is the task of making a selected technique operable in an organization. This includes defining, and then buying or building, a framework around the selected technique. This framework is commonly known as a *methodology*. At a minimum, a methodology describes where the technique is used, what roles developers play, and what deliverables are produced.

13.6.2 Tasks

Once the assessment step has been completed, technique selection and implementation can begin. The following technique-related tasks need to be performed:

Select a technique. The future environment document produced in the assessment step may indicate a specific technique that will be used. If not, select a technique using the documents produced in the assessment step. Several factors affecting technique selection will be addressed shortly.

Define the technique framework. Invariably, the selected technique will have to be tailored to fit the organization. Define requirements for a framework around the technique that will enable it to be used by the organization.

Assess the methodology market. Examine the array of methodology vendors offering products that satisfy your framework requirements.

Build or buy a methodology. Develop or purchase a methodology that best provides a framework for your technique. This step "procedurizes" your technique, enhancing it with steps, roles, and deliverables. (See Chapter 14.)

Conduct technique training. Train developers in use of the technique.

Conduct follow-up training. Ensure that developers are properly using the technique by observing and assisting their use of it in their project work.

Evaluate technique usefulness. Appraise the fit and effectiveness of the selected technique.

13.6.3 Technique Team

The same group of people conducting other transition tasks — the transition team — should be involved in selecting and implementing a technique. The team, as described earlier, should have representation from three groups: managers, developers, and users. Failure to do so may generate additional resistance to use of the technique. Depending on the pace of the transition effort, significant time may be required of transition team members.

13.6.4 Technique Selection

There are several factors that can be considered when selecting a technique. Some of these are related to the organization, while others are related to the technique. Let us look at some of them.

Organization Factors

These are some of the factors that should be addressed in either the current or the future environment document.

Current Practices

An important consideration in selecting a technique is the current practices of the software developers. Those practices that are yielding higher-quality software should be highlighted. Conversely, those that are producing lesser-quality software should be discarded. The selected technique should best approximate these practices.

Current Skills

Another factor is the skills of the development staff that are not currently being utilized. These should be considered and tapped by the selected technique.

User Involvement

The amount of user involvement in the software development process slightly affects the kind of technique selected. All of the techniques described in this text require some user involvement; however, some require relatively more. The information- and prototype-oriented techniques emphasize user participation at all levels of software development.

Application Integration

The degree of integration desired between systems affects the type of technique selected. Two systems are integrated if they are built upon common data and process models. This means they share definitions of data and function, and those definitions are maintained in one place. If a high degree of integration is needed, then the data-structured and information-oriented techniques should be considered.

Technique Factors

These are characteristics of techniques that affect the technique selection process. These factors should be addressed in the future environment document.

SDLC Support

In Chapter 2, the traditional software development life cycle (SDLC) was described as composed of phases: planning, analysis, design, coding, testing, and maintenance. One consideration when selecting a technique is the degree to which it supports these phases. All of the techniques support the analysis and design phases. Some of the techniques offer specific support for the other SDLC phases. For example, the information-oriented techniques are explicit about how planning is conducted. That a technique does not support all SDLC phases is not necessarily a drawback for two reasons:

Phase Needs. Unsupported phases may not be needed in an organization's life cycle. The organization may simply wish to focus on the phases supported by a particular technique. This is especially true of an organization just beginning to use a technique.

Phase Development. Unsupported phases may be filled in by an organization. If the organization wishes to perform a phase in a specific fashion, it can author the phase.

Tool Support

A significant factor when selecting a technique is the extent to which it is supported by CASE tools. Using a technique today without CASE support is senseless. The CASE industry has matured to the degree that there is support for all types of techniques. There is a wide variance in the degree of support, however.

The function-oriented techniques currently enjoy the greatest support. A majority of CASE vendors support these methods. There is also adequate assistance for the control-, information-, and prototype-oriented techniques. The techniques with the least support are the data- and object-oriented techniques. Support for these two techniques is heading in opposite directions, however. There is dwindling help for some of the data-oriented techniques but growing support for the object-oriented ones.

Technique Maturity

Some of the techniques have been around for two decades and are well established. Other techniques, like the object-oriented ones, are still evolving. Established techniques have a wealth of experience on their use, while newer ones offer fresh approaches to software development.

13.6.5 Technique Implementation

Once a development technique has been selected, the process of adopting the technique within the organization can begin. This process involves providing developers with support and timely training in use of the technique and use of the CASE tool. This process of technology transfer is described in more detail in Section 13.2, but cannot occur without an environment that encourages effort and allows for mistakes without punishing those responsible. During this transition period, development staff, management, and users must be allowed to learn a different method of development.

13.7 Transition to CASE

As we have already seen, selecting and implementing CASE and software development techniques implies a cultural change in a software development organization, and this change can be very painful. The risk of failure is high, with some estimates as high as 50 percent. Given these factors, a measured commitment of resources and time is required from upper management, the user community, and the development staff.

While it is helpful to know what CASE tools are, sometimes it is helpful to look at what CASE tools are not. CASE tools are not silver bullets or solutions unto themselves, but require training and support as well as the commitment of the company using them.

It is very important to remember that CASE tools are simply tools — not unlike a hammer or a saw — and as such can be misused or abused like any other tool. Without adequate training, CASE tools can hinder, not improve, the process of developing software. In most cases, a CASE tool simply automates a software engineering approach, and the method or technique is the disciplined approach to developing software — like a blueprint for building a house — that most people find actually helps improve quality and productivity. Together the CASE tool and the method or technique - like the hammer, saw, and blueprint - help organizations build better, higher-quality software.

CASE tools, like any other tool, can be very beneficial or only marginally beneficial depending on how they are used. When CASE tools are used in conjunction with a software engineering approach, they can reduce development time and effort considerably. When CASE tools are implemented without a supporting method, they can provide minimal benefit and may even impede the software development process.

In some organizations, using a CASE tool may prove very costly and may take many months and even years before providing any visible benefit to development. This is based on a learning curve for development team members and resistance to cultural change. Companies that are planning to implement CASE tools and engineering methods should plan to invest significant resources prior to realizing any substantial improvement in the development of software.

13.7.1 Selecting CASE Tools

With over 300 CASE tools on the market, organizations that are evaluating tools for adoption have a daunting task just deciding which products might meet their needs. The process is made harder by the CASE vendors making claims about their products that are partially truthful and often misleading. How can an organization select tools that are appropriate for its development organization without spending months or even years studying the marketplace and the claims of the tool vendors?

One approach we have found helps organizations to select appropriate tools is to use a four-step process that includes:

1. Develop some high-level requirements for tools and review the available products to select candidates for further study. There are many resources available for lists of CASE tools that include their cost, the platforms they run on, and the methods and techniques they support. High-level evaluation criteria might include operating platforms, support for specific methods and techniques, requirements tracking support, prototyping support, links with project management systems, multiuser repository support, and code generation capabilities.

2. Bring a small group of products in-house and perform an analysis of the products on a pilot project or in a detailed evaluation. Only by studying CASE tools in depth can the actual limitations of the products be understood. Many organizations have selected tools based solely on a demonstration given by a marketing person and found out later that the products have serious drawbacks that make them unusable in specific environments. Ideally, a specific set of detailed evaluation

criteria should be developed and each product tested against these criteria. Some organizations have found that having more than one staff person evaluate each product helps to find problems more quickly.

3. Score the products and select the product or products that score the highest. Each organization must establish its own weighting factors for the tool based on its environment, the methods and techniques it plans to support, the language used, the operating environment, the training required, etc. Products should be scored by internal staff or with the help of outside consultants, and the resulting scores should be used to select appropriate tools for adoption.

4. Use the products on actual projects and then follow up the use with an evaluation of the actual benefits and costs associated with adopting the tools throughout the organization. Once CASE tools have been evaluated in a pilot project environment, the real challenge is spreading their use throughout the organization. This process requires a long-term commitment by all involved and requires substantial training and support. Some organizations will establish a group or staff position to support the CASE tools and the methodologies used. Some formal follow-up evaluation should be performed after a period of time to assess whether the organization has realized any substantial benefit from the adoption of tools and techniques.

13.7.2 Development Technique and CASE Selection

Regardless of how slick or powerful CASE tools appear, the development technique and life cycle used will determine which products can provide benefit to the development staff. Tools that fail to support the creation and maintenance of critical development deliverables or representations will often be disposed of by developers. Tools that do not support and integrate with the development environment will be left unused. Ideally, selecting CASE tools follows selection and adoption of development techniques, but many organizations attempt to select both at the same time. The risk in attempting this is that once the tools are selected, if a decision on methodology changes, the tools may prove to be unacceptable. When a method has been chosen, the process of selecting appropriate tools becomes much easier.

Some organizations have found that selecting less sophisticated and powerful CASE tools while selecting methods and techniques helps them acquire expertise in the method without spending large amounts of money on tools they may eventually throw away. Most studies suggest that the largest costs associated with methodology adoption are in the training and consulting areas, with the tools often representing only 25 to 30 percent of the overall costs. Selecting interim tools that are not expensive also allows an organization to learn a method and later reevaluate its tool options with a much clearer picture of the support it requires. This often leads to a more educated choice of tools.

Those organizations that already have formal methods in place and are simply looking for automated support for those methods face a much easier selection process. With a set of defined notations and deliverables, choosing a CASE tool that supports the creation and maintenance of those objects becomes fairly easy. In some cases, organizations may have to modify their development methods to the limits of whatever CASE tools they select.

13.7.3 Full Life Cycle CASE vs. Component CASE

One initial consideration when evaluating CASE products is which phases or stages of the development life cycle will be supported in the short term and which will be supported in the long term. While many organizations like the appeal of integrated CASE (ICASE) tools, or tools that support most of the entire life cycle, upon acquiring these tools, many organizations find they do not require or cannot benefit from full life cycle support.

Component CASE (CCASE) tools support specific tasks within the development life cycle and must be integrated with other tools. These products were not developed to work together and often require significant manual effort to bridge the products. While the vendors of these products tout them as integrated, the levels of integration are often low. For example, most of the so-called ICASE products allow only a few of the design deliverables to be passed to the code generation component. Often, the only information passed is the data structures and screen/report layouts, not the architectural design, the underlying logic and flow of control, or any of the prototype information. Organizations must consider the type of integration offered and how that level of integration will benefit them before selecting an ICASE tool.

Experience suggests that organizations that selected CCASE tools initially have had better success in adopting these tools and their underlying methods than those groups that have gone directly to an ICASE solution. The adage that you must crawl before you can walk seems an appropriate metaphor in this situation.

13.7.4 Maintenance Tools

While most of the CASE products currently available support new development, most of the organizations supporting software spend the majority of their resources maintaining existing systems. How can CASE tools that support new development help with the maintenance of existing systems which were not developed with tools or formal methods? Also, can organizations that perform little new development benefit from CASE tools and methodologies that are focused on analysis, design and construction tasks?

The answer to some of these issues is maintenance tools, which come in a variety of flavors and can perform a variety of tasks. Some maintenance tools support the creation of documentation for existing, legacy systems, while others can identify unreachable code. Still other maintenance tools can help define the complexity of programs or modules that may be causing the majority of the problems in maintenance. Tom McCabe has written extensively on determining the complexity of code, and his company offers sophisticated maintenance tools in this area.

Other maintenance products can reengineer existing systems to a new deployment environment, without losing any inherent functionality. Still other products can reverse-engineer existing file and database structures into data models that can be modified in a CASE repository.

Those organizations that are expending the majority of their resources on maintenance have a variety of tool options available and should identify the types of problems they are having and tools that might address those problems.

13.7.5 Repository Issues

Eventually, organizations that hope to support the entire development life cycle must address a basic issue: Will a central repository be required for all software development information?

In many cases, the answer to this question will be yes. IBM, DEC, HP, and other computer vendors have seen the handwriting on the wall concerning this issue and have announced and are beginning to deliver repositories for their platforms. IBM, for example, introduced its Repository Manager/MVS in 1990 and is now planning on offering an OS/2-based version of this product. DEC has been selling its CDD/Repository product to its customers for several years, and HP offers its own Unix-based repository, SoftBench.

Some in the industry have suggested that any repository must be workstation-based and that vendors that require a mainframe- or minicomputer-only product will be forced out of the market. Others argue that centralized control is required for a repository based on the breadth of the information collected. Still others suggest that only a distributed repository can support large organizations' needs for development information. Some repository vendors have even begun to experiment with object-oriented DBMS (OODBMS) as the implementation platform for their repository.

In the future, the question of purchasing CCASE or ICASE tools may be moot if the repository products evolve to support bidirectional representation transfer between tools. The challenge for the repository vendors is to offer a product that can be used by any software development organization, whatever its different tasks, methods, and deliverables.

13.7.6 Other Issues

In addition to the issues described above, there are other, less obvious risk factors that should be considered when evaluating CASE tools. Some of these are technical; others are more cultural in nature.

13.7.6.1 Client/Server Development

Client/server, distributed, or cooperative applications are another hot topic in the software development industry, and while there are few standard definitions of what these terms mean, there is a high level of interest in developing applications within this framework. We define client/server applications as software that operates across a variety of computing environments with functionality distributed among the different environments. Often, a client/server environment consists of a workstation-based component (client) that performs user-interface functions and intelligent editing, and a server-based component that handles data access and update functionality. Key to the client/server environment is a standard protocol that both the client and the server share.

While many of the current CASE tool vendors claim they already support client/server applications, what this translates to is wrapping a COBOL, character-based 3270 screen with a GUI window. The resulting application, while satisfying some primitive aspect of the workstation portion of client/server, provides little benefit over 3270-emulation products that already support mainframe sessions within an OS/2 or Windows environment.

One question that should be addressed when considering CASE tools and client/server development is, Should client/server code be generated by the tool, and if so, for which environments (languages and DBMS) and from which specifications? Some in the industry have suggested that code generation will never support true client/server development, and that instead, intelligent, GUI 4GLs should be used to develop client/server applications. Examples of 4GLs that support client/server development include Uniface 4GL, Progress, and PowerBuilder.

In the object-oriented world, the CORBA standard defined by the Object Management Group (OMG) establishes a protocol for objects to communicate over a distributed environment. Any product that supports the CORBA standard will be addressing the client/server issue, and this may eliminate the need for 4GLs or code generators to develop their own proprietary client/server functions.

13.7.6.2 Object-Oriented Development

Object-oriented development, in its many forms, is already affecting the CASE industry. Some CASE vendors have already begun to support OOA/D methods, and others have plans to use OODBMS for their repositories. Still other vendors have begun to support the generation of OOPL code from design specifications.

On the negative side, the object-oriented marketplace is still too dynamic to make any educated guess as to which technologies will succeed and which will fall by the wayside. Certainly, as evidenced by the methods described in Chapter 8, OOA/D methods offer benefits to those organizations that are willing to adopt them. Future CASE tools will have to support these methods to be competitive in the industry.

Support for other object-oriented technologies, including OOPLs, OODBMS, object-oriented environments, and class libraries, offers more of a challenge to the industry. One question regarding supporting OOPL in CASE tools is, Should object-oriented code be generated from design specifications? The most often touted benefit of OOP is reuse, and this implies that any code generated must consider and include existing objects and classes. Another questions is, Which representation should be used to represent objects and classes available for reuse? Since there are currently no standard modeling and design notations in OOA/D, selecting a notation might be a mistake if the industry subsequently chooses a different representation as the standard for class libraries.

Some OOPL vendors have begun to link their products to CASE products, including ObjectCenter from CenterLine and InteliCorp. In the future, some standards will be required for the representation of classes and objects in a repository, along with guidelines for their reuse.

13.7.6.3 Software Metrics

One topic that often comes up when considering adopting CASE tools is showing some measurable benefit. While many organizations that adopt CASE are not required to show benefits associated with the costs of adoption, in some cases management needs to see some quantifiable improvement in the development process or in the software product itself.

Measuring software development can take one of two forms: product or process. Measuring the software product often takes the form of the costs associated with the development of the product. In some cases, the costs of supporting the product through its useful lifetime are also measured, but this occurs less often than one might guess. Interestingly, many organizations don't even measure the costs of developing systems, beyond the number of staff on the project and the elapsed time to deliver the product.

Another measurement of a software product is the quality of the product, which is often measured in relation to the cost of maintaining it or in terms of how much value the users of the product derive from it. Some hard metrics can be collected on the number of defects per 1000 lines of code (KLOC) or the number of functional changes required of a system once it is operational, but many organizations do not quantify these costs. Softer metrics can be collected that measure the level of satisfaction users rate the system once it is delivered, and this view is often used in organizations that are adopting quality improvement processes.

Measuring the process often proves to be more beneficial, but is also more difficult, especially when there is no standard, repeatable formal process within the organization. SEI and Watts Humphrey have done significant work in this area [HUM91]. Hopefully, adopting one of the techniques described in this book will help an organization develop a repeatable process that can subsequently be measured and improved. For more on this, see Chapter 11.

13.7.6.4 Project/Process Management

While many organizations focus on the technical issues related to adopting CASE, the majority of the failures stem from a failure to address the cultural issues in the transition. Management issues are often cited as the biggest problem associated with CASE failures, and process and project management, two critical aspects of this view, represent additional areas of concern for organizations migrating to formal methods and tools.

Project management and the tools and techniques that support this function should be part of any CASE adoption process, and ideally, CASE tools selected should be integrated with whichever project management software is used. Some of the project management tools currently available allow organizations to specify the tasks, roles and responsibilities, and deliverables into their software and drive the planning process directly from these items. In this case, the plan for a development project can be tailored to the process in use at the organization.

Process management, less understood than project management, involves planning and tracking the development process without the focus on staff and deliverables. Unlike project management, process management seeks to define and track the development process, including the methods, techniques, and tools used, and measure the quality of the deliverables created. Once quality measures have been defined for each task in the software development process, these deliverables can be tracked, and the process used to create them can be improved. This approach is similar to those used in the manufacturing industry.

13.8 Duration of Transition

The assessment, evaluation, and implementation process can vary in length from a few months to several years. Ideally, the assessment process will take three to four months, most of which will be spent researching the current development environment. The evaluation process might take from four to six months, depending on the evaluation criteria, the number of tools and techniques to be evaluated, and the staff available. One question that must be answered early in the evaluation process is whether a pilot project will be used to evaluate the technique and tool. If a pilot project is to be used, the length of the evaluation process will be directly tied to the pilot project. The scope of the assessment process must define whether an individual development group will be targeted or the entire development organization.

Estimates of how long the implementation process will take vary widely and are dependent on the organizational structure, the staff characteristics, the number of project groups and whether a single technique and or tool will be used by all groups or if each group will select and use its own tool and technique.

The implementation portion of the technique selection and implementation effort will take most of the time. If a decision is made to develop an in-house methodology, allocate at least six months to a year to accomplish this task. Add another year or two to introduce the staff to the methodology and begin activating it among project teams. Plan on at least two more years before all projects begin using the tools and techniques. This leads to a rough estimate of three to five years to successfully make the transition to the widespread use of CASE tools and development techniques. Areas where this time frame may be reduced include when staff already have experience using specific tools and techniques or when small groups of staff are allowed to spread the use of tools and techniques into the larger group (seeding). Obviously, some staff will learn to use new methods and tools more quickly than others, and each staff person should have a curriculum defined for him or her as part of any adoption process. This will ensure that all staff are included in the change process and are given the time and training required to learn to use the new development methods.

13.9 Cost of Transition

The cost of the transition to successfully using CASE and software development techniques depends largely on the scope of the transition and the number of staff involved. Scope is determined by a number of factors, including the number of software developers targeted by the effort, the number of additional staff involved, and the degree of difference between the current and future environments.

The most expensive component of the selection and implementation effort is typically the time required to conduct it. This is especially true if a decision was made to develop an in-house methodology. While it is often difficult to estimate the total cost of selecting and implementing CASE tools and development techniques, the following factors should be considered.

The cost of upgrading hardware to support the CASE tool

Since most of the CASE tools available require a Unix workstation or a fast PC (80386/80486 or 68040-based CPU) with much RAM (8 to 16 MB) and disk space (100+ MB) and high-resolution monitors and display cards (VGA or better), existing PC/XTs or even PC/ATs are not adequate platforms for CASE. An additional factor to consider is how information will be shared across the workstations, via a LAN or Unix computer.

The cost of the CASE tools and techniques themselves

While most organizations assume this to be the highest cost, most studies suggest that these costs are not necessarily the highest. These costs include the costs of the tools themselves multiplied by the number of copies to be purchased and any costs to purchase or acquire the methodology used.

The cost of consulting and support services

Many organizations will bring in outside consultants to facilitate the assessment, selection, and implementation process, and these costs must be factored into the equation. These costs often include on-site sessions, recommendations, and follow-up support for implementation.

The cost of training staff in the tools and techniques

Training costs are typically the highest of all the other costs, and most estimate 10 days of training in the tool and the technique each year. Studies suggest that learning a tool takes six to nine months, while learning to effectively use a development technique takes over eighteen months. Some staff will obviously learn to use tools and techniques more quickly than others, and these estimates should be used only for guidelines.

The cost of lost productivity of staff during the process

The lost staff time while they assess, evaluate, and implement a CASE tool and development techniques, since their productivity will be lower as they learn a new technique and/or CASE tool. Often, this lost productivity is perceived as unacceptable, and an organization must recognize and plan for this drop in staff productivity during the transition period.

When considering the transition process, organizations should also keep in mind the short- and long-term costs of implementing CASE. These costs can total from $500,000 to several million dollars depending on the organization, the number of development staff, and the approach. Estimating the cost of implementing CASE and engineering techniques requires a thorough understanding of the tasks and risks involved.

Papers from the SEI CASE Technology Project-sponsored CASE Adoption Workshop [HUF92b] provide organizations with insight into the costs of selecting and implementing CASE and associated technologies. These efforts reflect the costs, per development life cycle phase, based on the Industrial Technology Institute's HiTOP categories [MOR90] and include categories for technology, organization, people, and management. The SEI research has identified several cost drivers, including CASE scope, environmental complexity, target organization size, change culture, current technology and practices, skill levels, speed of technological advance, and assessment factors.

Included in the studies are estimates for training costs for developers, CASE tool costs, consulting and support costs, etc. Findings from the study suggest that a team of six to nine staff will take one to two years of preparation to reach the pilot stage for CASE, that the total acquisition cost for CASE might approach $18,000 per developer per year with a five-year cost of $40,000 per developer. For a staff of 75 developers, SEI estimates that the one-year costs might be $1.3 million and the five-year costs might approach $2.7 million [HUF92].

Others, including Howard Rubin [RUB91], have also defined some estimates for the cost of CASE. Rubin has developed an organizational readiness perspective which includes motivation, investment, skills, education, innovation, diffusion, technology, and applicability. Rubin also calculates the cost of CASE implementation as the cost of acquisition plus the cost of technology transfer. Rubin maps the characteristics for organizational readiness against specific CASE tool attributes using Kiviat charts and has postulated that if a specific tool's attributes exceed the readiness of the organization there is a low probability, that the organization will use that tool.

13.10 Resource List

The March 1992 issue of *American Programmer* is dedicated to Technology Transfer and includes several excellent articles on the subject; see also [BRI69], [CUT89], [HAV85], [KOR92], and [RON92]. References for articles on the cost of adopting CASE include [HUF92a] and [RUB91]. For articles on the SEI SPMM, see [BOL91], [HUM91], [HUM90], [JOR90], and [SCO92].

For experiences with adopting CASE see [MOR90], [HUF92b], and Chapter 15.

Books by Bouldin [BOU89], Case [CAS86], Fisher [FIS88], Gane [GAN90], Humphrey [HUM89a], Pressman [PRE88], and Yourdon [YOU88] all include discussions of the process of making the transition to software development techniques and CASE.

13.11 References

[BAR92]　　Barton, R., "Educating the Luddites: Technology Transfer is More than Training," *American Programmer*, vol. 5, no. 3, pp. 32-37.

[BLA83]　　Blank, J. and M. J. Krijger, *Software Engineering: Methods and techniques*, Wiley-Interscience, 1983.

[BOL91]　　Bollinger, T., and C. McGowan, "A Critical Look at Software Capability Evaluations," *IEEE Software*, July 1991, pp. 25-41.

[BOU89]　　Bouldin, B., *Agents of Change: Managing the Introduction of Automated Tools*, Prentice-Hall, 1989.

[BRA90]　　Braithwaite, K. S., *Application Development Using CASE Tools*, Academic Press, 1990.

[BRI69]　　Bright, J. R., "Some Management Lessions from Technical Innovation Research," *Harvard Business Review* (January/February 1969), pp. 36-41.

[CAS86]　　Case, A. F., *Information Systems Development: Principles of Software Engineering and CASE*, Prentice-Hall, 1986.

[COM90]　　Computer Science and Technology Board, "Scaling up: A research agenda for software engineering," *CACM*, vol. 33, no. 3 (Mar. 1990), pp. 281-293.

[CRO79]　　Crosby, P. B., *Quality is Free*, Mentor, 1979.

[CUT89]　　Cutler, R. A., "A Comparison of Japanese and U.S. High-Technology Transfer Practices," *IEEE Trans. Eng. Manage.*, vol. 36, no. 1 (Feb. 1989), pp. 17-24.

[DAV83]　　Davis, W., *Tools and Techniques for Structured Systems Analysis and Design*, Addison-Wesley, 1983.

[FIS88]　　Fisher, A. S., *CASE : Using Software Development Tools*, Wiley, 1988.

[FOW92]   Fowler, P., and L. Levine, "Toward a Defined Process of Software Technology Transfer," *American Programmer*, vol. 5, no. 3, pp. 2-10.

[GAN90]   Gane, C., *Computer-Aided Software Engineering: The Methodologies, the Products, the Future*, Prentice-Hall, 1990.

[HAR92]   Harel, D., "Biting the Silver Bullet," *IEEE Computer*, January 1992, pp. 8-20.

[HAV85]   Havelock, R. G., and D. S. Bushnell, "Technology Transfer at DARPA: A Diagnostic Analysis," *DTIC AD-A164 457*, Technology Transfer Study Center, George Mason University, December 1985.

[HUF92a] Huff, C. C., "Elements of a Realistic CASE Tool Adoption Budget," *CACM*, vol. 35, no. 4, pp. 45-54.

[HUF92b] Huff, C. C., D. Smith, K. Stepien, E. Morris, and P. Zarrella, CASE Adoption Workshop, *Tech. Rep. CMU/SEI-91-TR-14*.

[HUM91]   Humphrey, W., T. Snyder, and R. Willis, "Software Process Improvement and Hughes Aircraft," *IEEE Software*, July 1991, pp. 11-24.

[HUM90]   Humphrey, W., "Introducing Process Models into Software Organizations," *American Programmer*, September 1990, pp. 1-7.

[HUM89a] Humphrey, W., *Managing the Software Process*, Addison-Wesley, 1989.

[HUM89b] Humphrey, W., "CASE Planning and the Software Process," *Tech. Rept. CMU/SEI-89-TR-26*, SEI, Carnegie Mellon University, May 1989.

[JOR90]   Jorgensen, P. C., "Accelerating Process Maturity with CASE," *American Programmer*, September 1990, pp. 10-15.

[KOR92]   Korson, T. D., and V. K. Vaishnavi, "Managing Emerging Software Techhnologies: A Technology Transfer Framework," *CACM*, vol. 35, no. 9, pp. 101-111.

[LEW90]   Lewis, T. G., *Computer-Aided Software Engineering*, Van Nostrand Reinhold, 1990.

[MCC88]   McClure, C., *CASE Is Software Automation*, Prentice Hall, 1988.

[MOR90]   Morell, J., L. Tornatzky, and J. Behm, "CASE Implementation: Dynamics through the Technology Life Cycle," Industrial Technology Institute, 1990.

[MOS92]   Mosley, D. J., "A Framework for Technology Innovation," *American Programmer*, vol. 5, no. 3, pp. 20-26.

[PRE88]   Pressman, R. S., *Making Software Engineering Happen: A Guide for Instituting the Technology*, Prentice Hall, 1988.

[PRE91]   Pressman, R. S., *Software Engineering: A Practitioner's Approach*, McGraw-Hill, 1991.

[RED92]   Redwine, S. T., C. DelFosse, and W. Spencer, "1991 Technology Transfer at the Software Productivity Consortium," *American Programmer*, vol. 5, no. 3, pp.11-19.

[RON92]   Rone, K. E., R.B. MacDonald, and A.G. Houston, "Technology Development: A Partnership that Makes Sense," *Comput. Res. News,* 4, 3 (May 1992).

[RUB91]   Rubin, H., "In Search of the True Cost of CASE," *CASE Outlook*, 2 (1991).

[SCO92]   Scott, G. J., "Can Software Engineering Afford to Improve the Process," *ACM SIGSOFT*, vol. 17, no. 2, pp. 39-42.

[TOW89]   Towner, L. E., *CASE: Concepts and Implementation,* McGraw-Hill, 1989.

[WEA87]   Weaver, A. M., *Using the Structured Techniques - A Case Study,* Prentice-Hall, 1987.

[YOU88]   Yourdon, E., *Managing the Structured Techniques: Strategies for Software Development the 1990s*, Yourdon Press, 1988.

Chapter 14
Methodology Issues

The absence of a formal software engineering technique leads to an ad hoc, undefined, and often nonrepeatable development process that is difficult to manage, estimate, and improve. The hope is that by following a software engineering technique, an organization can improve the quality and productivity of its development efforts.

But organizations that hope to adopt software development techniques face serious issues and challenges along the way. Previous chapters have discussed comparing and selecting methods (Chapter 10), automated tools for development techniques (Chapter 11), using a formal software process (Chapter 12), and adopting techniques and tools (Chapter 13). A software development methodology, equally defined as a formal development process, represents a development life cycle and the three components of the software engineering triad. Methodologies can be created within an organization or acquired from a methodology vendor.

In this chapter, we will introduce the concept of a formal development methodology, which represents all of the components of the software production framework we described in Chapter 1. We will also review and compare commercially available methodologies, introduce a process of selecting or building a methodology, and discuss the issues involved in adopting a methodology.

14.1 Introduction

As with other concepts discussed in this book, we begin by providing a working definition of methodology:

A documented, step-by-step strategy for completing one or more phases of a software development life cycle. A methodology offers its own standards and techniques for the development process, includes specific roles and responsibilities, deliverables, tasks and activities, and automated tools that support the methodology.

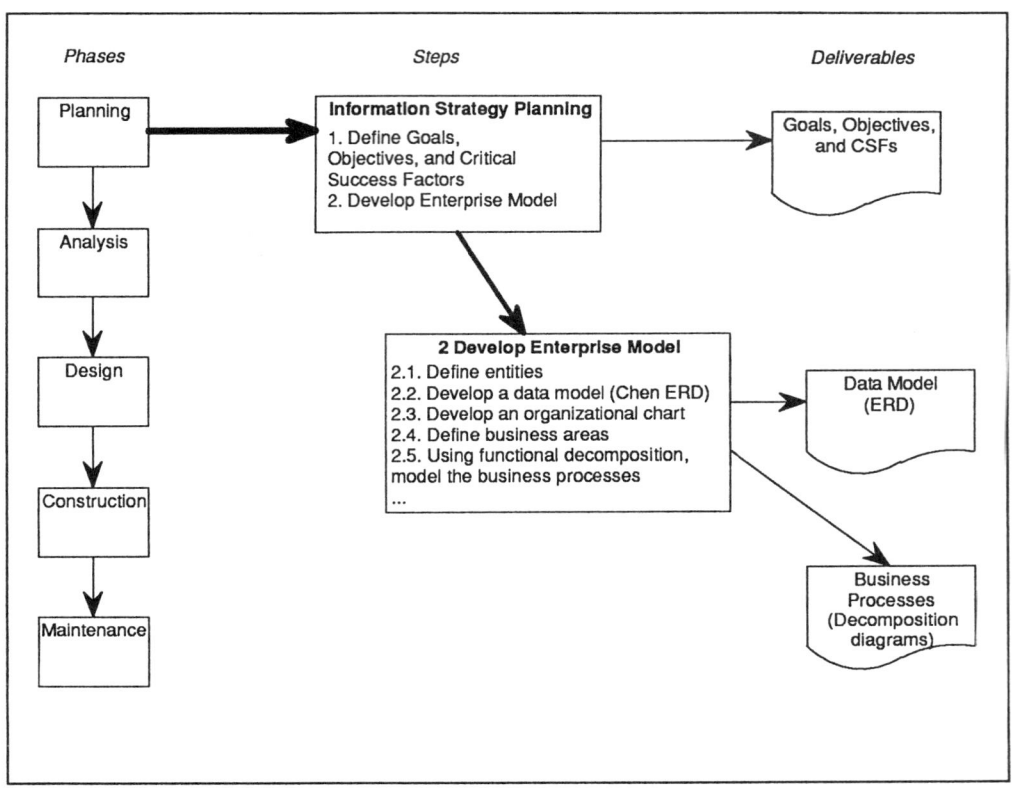

Figure 14.1
Components of a
methodology.

Any methodology provides a generic SDLC with specific phases or stages of work, which are further subdivided into steps and substeps until individual activities are defined. The example methodology shown in Figure 14.1 includes planning, analysis, design, construction, and maintenance phases. While these may be the generic paths for traditional development, the methodology might also provide alternative paths for specialized projects, for instance projects of small size or scope, rapid development projects, or redevelopment projects.

An organization that uses the methodology described in Figure 14.1 considers the planning phase as Information Strategy Planning, and this phase would includes two steps:

1. Define goals, objectives, and critical success factors
2. Develop an enterprise model

Again using Figure 14.1, step 2 would be further divided into the following tasks:

2.1. Define entities about which relevant information is collected in the enterprise.

2.2. Develop a data model which shows these entities and their relationships using an entity-relationship diagram.

2.3. Develop an organization chart for the enterprise.

2.4. Define business areas for each major organizational unit.

2.5. Using functional decomposition, model the high-level business processing for each business area.

etc.

Methodologies include specific software development techniques which we describe in Chapters 4 through 9. Some methodologies are considered to be development techniques, but not all techniques are sold as stand-alone methodologies. For instance, information engineering is a commercially available methodology but is also considered a development technique (see Chapter 7).

As we have already seen, development techniques call for the creation of representations or deliverables from the software development process. Example deliverables shown in Figure 14.1 include textual descriptions of goals, objectives, and critical success factors, a data model, and a matrix mapping the critical success factors to the high-level business functions.

Techniques call for the use of specific diagraming and textual notations with a common set of symbols and connections. Underlying any notation are the definitions of the symbols and connections in a CASE dictionary or repository. Example notations shown in Figure 14.1 include a Chen entity-relationship diagrams (see Chapter 5), decomposition diagrams (see Chapter 7) and textual descriptions of goals, objectives, etc.

Computer-aided software engineering (CASE) tools help manage and control the representations and deliverables created throughout the development life cycle. For example, the methodology shown in Figure 14.1 might require use of the IEF CASE tool from Texas Instruments. CASE tools also provide rule checking against the technique and notations and between the deliverables collected to ensure consistency and completeness of the software product.

An entire industry exists for methodologies, as complete frameworks for software development techniques that specify the tasks, roles, and deliverables for software development. Some of these methodologies are not inexpensive, costing upwards of $75,000 for a site license. Organizations can acquire a methodology from a vendor who will help train, tailor, and introduce a formal development process, or they can build their own methodology to suit their specific needs.

The commercial methodology industry is quickly merging with the CASE industry, and many CASE vendors now offer specific methodologies in their own tool with its representations or in an external, disk-based document. Some of the methodologies are now available in hypertext to better facilitate on-line references and control complexity.

14.2 Rationale

Why would an organization adopt a methodology? For several reasons, including all of the potential benefits we have already covered in previous chapters - higher-quality software, increased client participation, earlier error detection, more efficient maintenance, a standardized process and potential component reuse, etc. By adopting a methodology, an organization can implement a formal process with standard representations or deliverables, standard project measurement and management tools and techniques, development methods, notations, automated tool support, training and education, and process improvement.

If a commercial methodology is purchased and implemented, the organization can acquire training and support from an external source, the methodology vendor, and not have to develop or hire specific expertise. Commercially available methodologies also have automated support in CASE tools and come delivered with predefined stages in a SDLC, roles and responsibilities, and guidelines for development and management staff. In short, purchasing a methodology is a quick way of formalizing a software development process. On the downside, a methodology delivered by a vendor may not match the skills and cultural mindset of development staff, which may lead to rejection of the methodology or, worse, the methodology becoming shelfware.

An organization might choose instead to develop its own methodology, and tailor it to the skills, experiences, and requirements of the organization and its staff. While this process can take several months or even years and require extensive resources, it might ultimately lead to a methodology that is adopted and used instead of being discarded.

Another alternative approach would be to select a commercial methodology, begin using it on projects, and then tailor it to fit the specific needs of the organization. This approach offers the best of both worlds, allowing an organization the opportunity to quickly select and use a methodology without having to develop it from scratch, and to tailor or fit the methodology into their development environment in the long run to better fit the needs of the development group.

One caution when considering adopting a methodology: regardless of the approach used, methodologies by themselves cannot solve cultural, organizational or business problems related to software production. As Ed Yourdon, one of the architects of the function-oriented techniques, says:

"... the best methodologies don't guarantee the technical success of most systems development projects, and technical success can't save a project from the larger issues of corporate politics in these whirligig days of mergers and downsizings."
E. Yourdon [YOU91].

14.3 Selecting and Adopting a Methodology

Several steps are involved in selecting and adopting a methodology within an organization. These include performing an assessment of the organization, defining requirements for a methodology, building or buying a methodology, and adopting the methodology. If a methodology is purchased, this process includes an assessment of the commercially available methodologies, selection of an appropriate methodology, and adoption of that methodology. This process is described in Figure 14.2.

Whether building or buying a methodology, the potential impact of a methodology on an organization should be considered prior to spending time and money. Since a methodology includes all the components of the software production framework, it affects all organizational levels, from high-level management to individual developers. A methodology defines roles and responsibilities, tasks, deliverables, techniques, and notations, and thus has long-term implications for everyone involved in software development.

14.3.1 Readiness Assessment

Before attempting to build or purchase a methodology, an organization should define its current development environment, assess its readiness for a methodology, and develop a plan to adopt a methodology if appropriate. Not every organization can benefit from adopting a methodology, and many organizations have failed in attempting this transition.

All of the cultural and organizational issues covered in previous chapters apply equally well to adopting a methodology. Organizations that attempt to purchase or develop a methodology without bothering to assess their current environment greatly increases their chances of failure. Examples of organizations that followed similar paths are described in Chapter 15.

An initial step in the process is to define the current development environment, including development skills, organizational profile and structure, MIS strategy, software procurement policies, development platforms and life cycles, use of methods, techniques, and automated tools, project management and planning tools, training and education, and example project case histories.

Once this is completed, a definition of the future development environment can be created, along with a strategic plan to move towards that environment. The plan may include upgrade of staff skills, acquisition of tools and methodologies, etc.

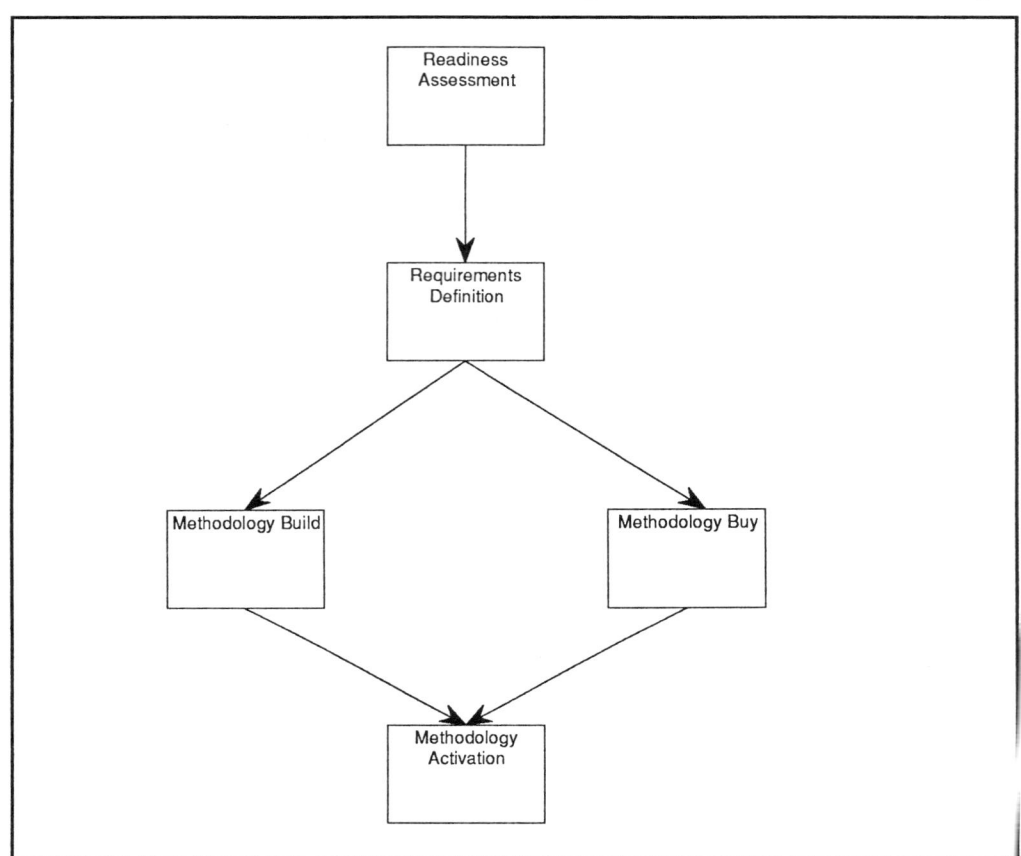

Figure 14.2
Methodology
adoption
process.

14.3.2 Methodology Requirements Definition

Once a strategic plan has been defined for moving an organization towards a methodology, specific requirements can be identified for the methodology. Some of these requirements will be defined at a high level, perhaps identifying the orientation of the methodology, while others will be more detailed, for instance support for specific types of development and prototyping. We include some generic methodology requirements in Section 14.3.4.3 that can be used as guidelines for comparing methodologies.

An organization considering a methodology should evaluate, at a minimum, the following items:

SDLC: The high-level phases or steps in the methodology
Tasks or activities: The lower-level tasks that deliver the representations
    and artifacts

Development techniques: The specific techniques used within the
methodology

Notations and diagrams: Any methodology-specific notations

Deliverables: The set of artifacts produced by the task

Roles: The people involved, both the individuals and the groups, in
software development and maintenance

Responsibilities: The tasks and deliverables each person or group is
responsible for in the software process

Decision points: Specific points in the methodology where someone,
management, users, or developers, is required to review, evaluate, and
sign off on work products

Measurement and estimation: Metrics and predicted outcomes within
the methodology

Project management: Support in the methodology for the creation of project
work schedules, assigning staff, tracking deliverables, etc.

14.3.3 Methodology Building

One option for an organization would be to develop its own methodology. Following this approach, an organization might use this book to help identify and select appropriate tools and techniques for software production. An organization could, for instance, use Chapter 10 to help select appropriate development methods and techniques. Once development techniques were selected, Chapter 13 could be used to develop a plan for adoption of these techniques, and Chapter 11 could be used to make sound automation choices. Chapter 12 would provide information on implementing a software process and defining the necessary roles and responsibilities within software development.

While the process described is feasible, many organizations don't have the time, resources, available expertise, or inclination to follow a process like this. This approach requires active involvement of all the stakeholders in the software process, and may take several years to complete.

14.3.4 Methodology Purchase

Another option would be to purchase a methodology from a vendor and adopt that methodology in the organization. Commercially available methodologies are described in Section 14.5, but we will briefly describe some generic methodology characteristics in this section.

Most commercial methodologies can be licensed from a vendor and generally are delivered in printed or disk-readable media. Some methodologies are cumbersome and overly complex, and may include many thick manuals, with dry, boring descriptions of tasks, activities, deliverables, and notations. Methodologies are, by their nature, complex, but what is required from a workable methodology is a delicate balance between an overwhelming amount of text and enough descriptive information to describe a process that involves people and complex abstractions.

Some methodologies include different perspectives for different roles in an organization, from high-level management to development staff and users. Most methodologies include descriptions of tasks and activities, along with guidelines or experiential reports that contain important suggestions and advice on the practical aspects of applying the technique to different sets of problems.

14.3.4.1 Methodology Market Assessment

The first step in acquiring a methodology is to determine which products are available and which vendors offer these products. While there are a variety of commercially available methodologies, there are few current references that provide contact information, along with enough information to make a meaningful comparison. DataPro offers selected reports on some commercially available methodologies in its Application Development Software reports, which include pricing, a short analysis of the products, company profiles, and financial information.

We provide a list of available methodologies in Section 14.5 which can be used as a starting point for identifying potential methodology products.

14.3.4.2 Methodology Selection Criteria

After a list of candidate methodologies has been defined, the process of defining evaluation criteria for the products can begin. This process involves all or most of the stakeholders in the development process, and should at a minimum include representatives of developers, management, and clients.

Specific methodology selection criteria will vary by organization, but we can suggest some generic evaluation criteria as a guideline for the process. These criteria also provide a basis for the comparison of methodologies in Section 14.5.

Orientation or focus of the methodology

All of the commercial methodologies include development techniques and include orientations or points of focus as described in Chapters 4 through 9 of this book. Most of the current methodologies claim to be information-oriented, with a few offering function or data orientations as well. One reason for this is the popularity of the information engineering (IE) method and the perceived need for strategic business planning, which is directly supported within the IE method.

Support for alternative paths

Most development organizations support a variety of development and maintenance projects, from large, multiyear new development efforts involving numerous staff to smaller, rapid development projects with a few developers. As commercial methodologies are evaluated, they should be graded based on the support they provide for the types of projects most often found in the organization. For instance, if an organization spends most of its development resources on maintenance of existing applications, it should look for a methodology that includes a strong maintenance or redevelopment perspective with appropriate tasks, deliverables, etc., to support a maintenance effort.

CASE tool support provided for the methodology

Some methodologies are supported by a wide variety of commercial CASE tools, while others are supported only by proprietary tools provided by the methodology vendor. Special consideration should be given to the environments the CASE tools operate on, if there are existing workstations in an organization that will be used to support the methodology, and tools.

Cost of the methodology

Any methodology will have associated costs that will be incurred by the organization that adopts it. These costs include the original license fees, yearly maintenance costs, and initial and ongoing training costs. Methodology license costs range from $25,000 per copy to $200,000 for a site license. Training costs vary from $1,800/day for offsite to $3,500/day for onsite sessions plus expenses.

Methodology complexity

The format a methodology is available in will determine how usable it is in practice. Most methodologies are available in printed form, and while this format is helpful to some, it is often overwhelming to most developers. Some methodologies offer practical guidelines that include suggestions and hands-on examples, while others offer CD-ROM or hypertext-based versions of their products that can be called up alongside CASE tools on a workstation.

General measures of methodology complexity include the number of stages, tasks, deliverables, activities, pages in the manuals, and required disk space for on-line versions.

Extensibility of the methodology

If there is a possibility that a methodology will have to be tailored to fit an organization, the product should be extendable by the organization. Generally, most methodologies can be tailored or modified as required, but there are costs associated with this process, including vendor consultants and additional support and training for staff.

Project and process management support provided

Many commercial methodologies incorporate project and process management within their products, and other products have links with popular project management products. When a methodology is used, it can provide work breakdown structures, Gantt charts, staff and deliverable schedules, timelines, etc., for any applicable project. A methodology includes all the components required for effective project management and should be integrated with project management facilities to be most effective.

Some methodologies incorporate process management components, including software metrics and estimation based on previous projects. Other methodologies can track staff work, report the status of tasks and deliverables, and provide data for further analysis during a project and after it is completed.

Vendor viability

Given the cost and scope of methodology adoption, the overall viability of the vendor should be considered in any methodology acquisition process. While many methodology vendors have been in business for several years, others have been offering services for only a few years, and some may have small support and training staffs. Assuming a methodology adoption process that takes three to five years, questions about the long-term viability of a methodology vendor should not be overlooked.

Support for specific techniques

Perhaps the most important criterion for any methodology is the set of development techniques, notations, and methods used. The development techniques that will define the "how" and "why" of the methodology are discussed in other chapters of this book. An organization that already has expertise using a specific technique should look for inclusion of this technique in their methodology.

Following the readiness assessment step, any preexisting experience or skills that an organization has should be considered in a methodology decision. Experienced developers can act as mentors to other staff members, and this can reduce the cultural impact and the costs of adopting the methodology.

One approach that should be considered when purchasing a methodology is to visit existing users of the methodology and inquire about their experiences. Site visits and interviews can provide a wealth of helpful information on the practical side of using a methodology, and users will be much more likely to provide honest, direct answers to specific questions than the vendor representatives. A methodology vendor should provide a list of users that can be interviewed with or without the vendor attending.

14.3.4.3 Methodology Selection

The process of evaluating and selecting a methodology parallels any serious acquisition process, and should include an objective comparison of products, information, and experiences collected from current users of a methodology, background checks on vendors, and selection of a primary and a secondary choice in light of any procurement problems that might arise.

The process of selecting a methodology should consider all of the practical issues related to adopting the methodology, and should include representatives of all the roles within the organization. A consensus should be reached, and after the methodology is purchased, training and support should be defined and scheduled.

14.3.5 Methodology Adoption

Once the methodology is acquired, the development staff must gradually gain exposure to it and the selected technique. One approach is to offer the methodology training on an as-needed or team-by-team basis, and apply the methodology to selected projects so as to gain experience and confidence with it. Both internal and external consultants can help here, and should be considered when building or buying a commercial methodology.

Methodology training and support will be required, and can be provided internally or from outside sources, and some methodology vendors provide training as part of the initial purchase cost of the product. Some companies also offer specific methodology or technique training that can be used for this purpose.

Availability and costs of training should be estimated as part of the initial purchase price, and should include sites (onsite and offsite), scheduled dates, price, number of staff that can attend, etc. In some cases, methodology user groups are available and can serve as additional support for the methodology adoption process.

If there is a need to tailor the methodology at some point, the question of who will be responsible for this should be considered. While the vendor may have the expertise to extend the methodology, this will add significantly to the overall cost of acquiring the methodology.

14.4 Methodology Considerations

Roles and responsibilities are an important part of any methodology, and should map directly to specific job descriptions or staff positions in the organization adopting the methodology. An excellent place to start the process of identifying roles and responsibilities is the company organization chart, and any personnel job descriptions that are available.

Possible roles described in a methodology might include any or all of the following:

User analyst: Determines and documents user requirements
Data administrator: Maintains organizational data model
Database administrator: Maintains production and test databases
System designer: Creates system design from requirements specification
Programmer: Translates system design into new or modified code
Project leader: Oversees MIS project involvement
Project manager: Oversees multiple projects
Security administrator: Maintains data security
User: Participates in user interviews; conducts system testing
User manager: Oversees user project involvement

Organizational business plans should be aligned with software development and procurement plans, and many organizations will perform strategic business planning for the organization and for the software development group. Any MIS plans must be integrated with organization plans for acquisition of technology, training, and support — staff and organizational changes, costs, and impact on the organization.

Strategic business planning is the long-term setting of a mission or charter for the MIS organization within the framework of the overall success of the business. This definition implies that with strategic business planning (SBP), we are not necessarily concerned with managing specific MIS development efforts (single projects), but more with the overall goals and business needs of the company as they relate to information systems. Strategic business planning usually involves deciding which information systems should be implemented in which order based on the overall goals of the company.

Studies suggest that for a methodology to be successfully used, an executive sponsor must be identified and actively involved in the process. As we have seen in other chapters, including Chapters 2, 11, 12, and 13, cultural change cannot occur without adequate management backing.

Prior to undertaking a methodology implementation project, issues including where funding for the methodology will come from and long-term funding requirements must be defined. Factors that affect the costs of methodology adoption include purchase costs for the methodology, staff costs, including support, training, etc., and maintenance costs.

14.5 Commercially Available Methodologies

Typically, when selecting a methodology, an organization undergoes an objective assessment by outside consultants. In most cases, recommendations are based on the existing skills of development staff, the current development environment, any existing use of development techniques and tools, the application portfolio (real-time, DBMS, etc.) for the organization, the maturity of the development group, any perceived needs for integration of data, for strategic business planning, etc.

A partial list of the commercially available methodologies includes the following products:

AD/Method and STRADIS from Structured Solutions, Inc.
Aim from Axiom
firstCASE from AGS Management Systems
CASE*Method from Oracle
ForeSight from Computer & Engineering Consultants/Knowledgeware Inc.
4Front from Deloite & Touche
HyperAnalyst from Rapid Systems Development
IE/IMPACT from Pacific Information Management
IEM from James Martin & Company
IEM from Information Engineering Systems Corp.
LBIM from LBMS
MATE from Advanced Development Methods
Method/1 from Anderson Consulting
Navigator from Ernst & Young
The Pride Information Factory from M. Bryce & Associates
Synergy from CASE Methods Development Group
Yourdon Structured Method from CGI

Most of the commercially available methodologies are geared towards organizations that require strategic business planning, along with development management and support. Most of these methodologies are information-oriented or include an information perspective. Some offer alternative paths through the life cycle and support purchased packages, rapid application development, and small projects.

Some methodology vendors claim their products are independent of development technique and CASE tool. These methodologies provide a blueprint for formal methods and tools, but do not require the use of specific development techniques, notations, or automated tools. Typically, these products are delivered as project management tasks or on-line references for software development, with specific activities defined for each phase. Any organization that implements these methodologies must ultimately choose, however, specific techniques, notations, and tools to use within the framework or the methodology has no value. A methodology is like the table of contents of a book, and without the accompanying chapters and pages (like tasks and methods), the book is incomplete.

Software development methodologies are, by their nature, complex and cumbersome. Many organizations, in attempting to implement a formal methodology, have realized that the method they selected has turned into "shelfware" and is never used. To be effective, a methodology must offer a balance between the inherent complexity of software development tasks and what can be reasonably accomplished in the available period of time by development staff.

Often, methodologies get in the way of software developers and provide no actual benefit in helping those developers perform the tasks associated with software development. To be useful, a methodology must provide a framework of tasks, deliverables, roles, and responsibilities. Ideally, the methodology should act as a guide for developers, and should be scaleable downward as required by the development group.

Some methodology vendors have begun to offer their methodologies in hypertext format, and this has helped address the complexity issue. Others have implemented their methodologies in a CASE tool and have used the tool to help reduce the complexity of the methodology. As commercial methodologies are evaluated, the complexity of these methods, especially as it relates to smaller projects, should be considered in any final recommendations.

Few (if any) detailed comparisons of available methodologies exist, and those that have been done typically compare a few selected products on a limited basis. For this book, we classified the major methodologies on the basis of their point of focus or orientation (philosophy) and have defined specific characteristics for further comparison and evaluation. These characteristics are subjective but are based on research in the area of the comparison of development techniques. See Chapter 10 for more on comparing development techniques.

A formal software development methodology will provide a common vision and also management and control facilities for the project, and standard notations, representations, and deliverables which can be more easily tracked and understood by everyone involved. A common CASE repository can provide enormous benefits in the tracking of functional requirements, evolution of prototypes, models, and specifications and design decisions made throughout the development process.

The likelihood that any methodology or tool will adequately address all types of software development is slim. Most methodologies were developed for a specific type or kind of software development, whether it be for strategic management information systems (MIS), on-line transaction processing systems, or real-time systems. For purposes of these recommendations, the overall philosophy of the methodology and the available tools dictates in a practical sense the types of development environments supported. Without automated support, any methodology is of little use on a medium- to large-sized project.

14.5.1 Orientation

The orientation of a methodology dictates, to a large degree, the approach and philosophy that will be used by the development techniques. Most of the commercially available methodologies are information-oriented. With the popularity of information engineering (IE), most of the methodologies now claim they are IE-based or can support IE methods. In some cases, the methodologies are actually function- or data-oriented, and simply provide support for strategic business planning and data modeling.

None of the commercial methodologies provide specific support for control-oriented systems or object-oriented development. James Martin and Company has specific plans to incorporate object-oriented models in a future version of its IEM, and undoubtedly other vendors will include these methods as they gain in popularity.

Most of the commercial methodologies also support prototyping, and many support rapid application development and facilitated meeting techniques (i.e., JAD sessions).

14.5.2 Evaluation Criteria

We provide a subjective comparison of some commercial methodologies for explanation purposes only. The following evaluation criteria were used in our example comparison because they are general enough to be applicable to a variety of organizations, yet specific enough to help organizations compare the methodologies.

1. Orientation or focus (F=Function, D=Data, I=Information)
2. Support for strategic business planning (Y or N)
3. Alternative paths for:
   3.1 Small projects
   3.2 Rapid application development
   3.3 Packaged procurements
   3.4 Maintenance/redevelopment projects
4. CASE tool support — i.e., CASE tools that support the methodology
5. Cost of onsite training, in $/day (if available)
6. Overall methodology complexity, as measured in:
   6.1 Number of methodology components (manual pages, number of phases, tasks, deliverables, etc.)
   6.2 On-line help available (Y or N)
   6.3 Methodology includes guidelines for developers (Y or N)
   6.4 Hypertext support included

7. Extensible methodology (Y on N)
8. Integrated project management (Y or N)
9. Vendor viability in the marketplace, as expressed by:
    9.1 Size of the company — i.e., total number of employees
    9.2 Support for the product — number of support staff
    9.3 Training staff — number of training staff
10. Support for specific techniques, including:
    10.1 Facilitated sessions (JADs, etc.)
    10.2 Prototyping

14.5.3 Comparison

Figure 14.3 compares some commercially available methodologies based on the evaluation criteria described above. Recall that this information is provided for explanation purposes only, and we make no guarantee as to the accuracy of the information provided. Also, the information was supplied by the vendors and is undoubtedly out of date, and our evaluation should imply no endorsement of any methodology, included in or excluded from those in Figure 14.3.

14.6 Sample Methodology

To help describe methodologies, we provide some samples of a fictitious methodology that includes generic techniques, roles, and responsibilities, etc. The methodology is fictional, but represents most of the components commonly found in a commercial methodology. We provide these examples to give you the reader a flavor of a methodology.

14.6.1 Sample Life Cycle

Figure 14.4 shows an example software development life cycle that covers planning a project through evolution of the system. The specific phases or stages of the SDLC include many of those one would expect to find, and we can see from the figure that there are inherent relationships between the phases. For instance, we can infer from the figure that planning occurs prior to analysis, that programming occurs prior to testing, etc. We can also see from the figure that a design specification document is created in design and used in coding as well as in testing.

14.6.2 Sample Stages and Tasks

Again referring to Figure 14.4, the stages in the methodology can be further decomposed into the following tasks:

Planning - Plan the project, estimates the resources required, identify high-level requirements, perform a cost/benefit analysis, and present the findings to a steering committee for approval; if approved, develop a project plan with staff assigned to specific tasks.

Analysis - Define functional requirements, model the data, processes, and dynamic behavior (control) for the system; create a functional prototype of the screens, menus, and reports; identify the dependencies between the models; and deliver the requirements document to the next phase.

Design - Design an application structure from the models created in analysis, refine the structure down to the module level, define the logic in each module, define a database or file structure to support the system, create test cases for each functional unit, and deliver the design document to the programming phase.

Coding - Develop source code for the modules and programs identified in the design document, compile the programs, create the appropriate DBMS structures, and provide the results to the next phase.

Testing - Clients and developers perform functional testing on the modules, programs, and the system, using the test cases defined in design; as problems are identified, resolve them and retest affected programs; clients sign off on the system when it meets their needs.

Operation - Documentation (models, specifications, test cases, etc) is given to production control, along with JCL, run books, etc.; any database initialization or migration is scheduled and performed, and the system is placed into a "production" status and turned over to the next phase.

Evolution - As requests for changes are collected, they are analyzed in terms of cost/benefit, and an impact analysis is performed to determine the true cost of each change. Changes that are approved are made following the analysis, design, code, test, and implement phases described above.

While following this process of decomposition down through all the stages might prove helpful, it is beyond the scope of this book to do so, so we will describe how each task would be defined within the methodology. Each task within the methodology has a standard format, and includes the following information:

Purpose: The reason the task is followed, and the benefit
Activities: Any underlying subtasks that must be followed or references to
    other tasks in the methodology

Methodology Evaluation Criteria	AIM	firstCASE	ForeSight	Hyper Analyst	IE/Impact	IEM (JMC)
1. Orientation	I	F	I	F	I	I
2. SBP support?	Y	Y	Y	Y	Y	Y
3.1 Alternative paths - Small projects	Y	Y	N		Y	Y
3.2 RAD	N	Y	Y	Y	Y	Y
3.3 Packaged purchase	N	Y	Y	N	Y	Y
3.4 Maintenance	N	Y	Y		Y	Y
4. CASE tool support	2	M	1	1	2	1
5. Cost of onsite training	$1,800	$3,000	$4,000	$3,000	$2,500	$1,500
6.1 Complexity - number of manuals, pages, stages, tasks, etc.	4 manuals, 1,600 pages, 4 phases	6 manuals, 3,000 pages 18 phases	3 manuals, 1,770 pages 12 phases, 190 tasks	500 pages 8 phases, 130 tasks	6 manuals, 1,500 pages, 9 phases	20 manuals, 7 phases, (40 MB of text)
6.2 Online help?	Y	Y	Y	Y	Y	Y
6.3 Guidelines for staff?	Y	N	Y(1993)	Y	Y	Y
6.4 Hypertext support?	OS/2 & DOS	DOS	OS/2	OS/2	OS/2 & Windows	OS/2
7. Extensible methodology?	Y	Y	Y	Y	Y	Y
8. Integrated PM?	Y	Y	Y	Y	Y	Y
9.1 Vendor viability - Total number of employees	100	>100	60	12	30	300
9.2 Number of support staff	3	15	6	6	15	>50
9.3 Number of training staff	70	9	20	6	15	>50
10.1 Special support - facilitated sessions	Y	Y	Y	Y	Y	Y
10.2 Prototyping	Y	Y	Y	Y	Y	Y
11.1. Costs - (s) = site, (i) = individual, (#) = # of copies	$75,000 (s)	$29,000 (i)	$37,500* (i) $70,000* (s)	$30,000 (10) $200,000 (s)	$47,500 (s)	$30,000 (10)
11.2 1 year maintance	$11,250 (s)	$4,350 (i)	$12,000* (s)	$4,500 (10)	$20,000	$4,500 (10)

Figure 14.3
Comparison of methodologies.

Methodology Evaluation Criteria	IEM (IESC)	METHOD/1	Navigator System Series	PRIDE Information Factory	Synergy
1. Orientation	I	D	I	I	I
2. SBP support?	Y	Y	Y	Y	Y
3.1 Alternative paths - Small projects	Y	N	Y	Y	Y
3.2 RAD	N	N	Y	N	Y
3.3 Packaged purchase	Y	Y	Y	Y	N
3.4 Maintenance	N	Y	Y	Y	Y
4. CASE tool support	2	1	2	P	2
5. Cost of onsite training	$3,000	$3,000	$3,500	$2,000	$2,500
6.1 Complexity - number of manuals, pages, stages, tasks, etc.	4 manuals, 1,200 pages, 7 phases	10 manuals, 9 phases	16 manuals, 3,200 pages, 9 phases	3 manuals, 20 phases, 93 tasks	10 manuals, 2,000 pages, 7 phases
6.2 Online help?	Y	Y	Y	Y	Y
6.3 Guidelines for staff?	Y (1993)	N	Y(1993)	N	Y
6.4 Hypertext support?	OS/2	N	OS/2	N	OS/2 & Windows
7. Extensible methodology?	Y	Y	Y	Y	Y
8. Integrated PM?	Y	Y	Y	Y	Y*
9.1 Vendor viability - Total number of employees	50	>150	65,000	10	10
9.2 Number of support staff	25	21,000	1,000	6	4
9.3 Number of training staff	20	1,000	20	3	4
10.1 Special support - facilitated sessions	Y	N	Y	N	
10.2 Prototyping	N	Y	Y	Y	Y
11.1. Costs - (s) = site, (i) = individual, (#) = # of copies	$50,000 (s)	$50,000 (s)	$55,000 (s)	$40,000 (i)	$25,000 (i)
11.2 1 year maintance	$7,500 (s)	$7,500 (s)	$8,250 (s)	$4,000 (i)	$3,750 (i)

Figure 14.3 (continued)
Comparison of methodologies.

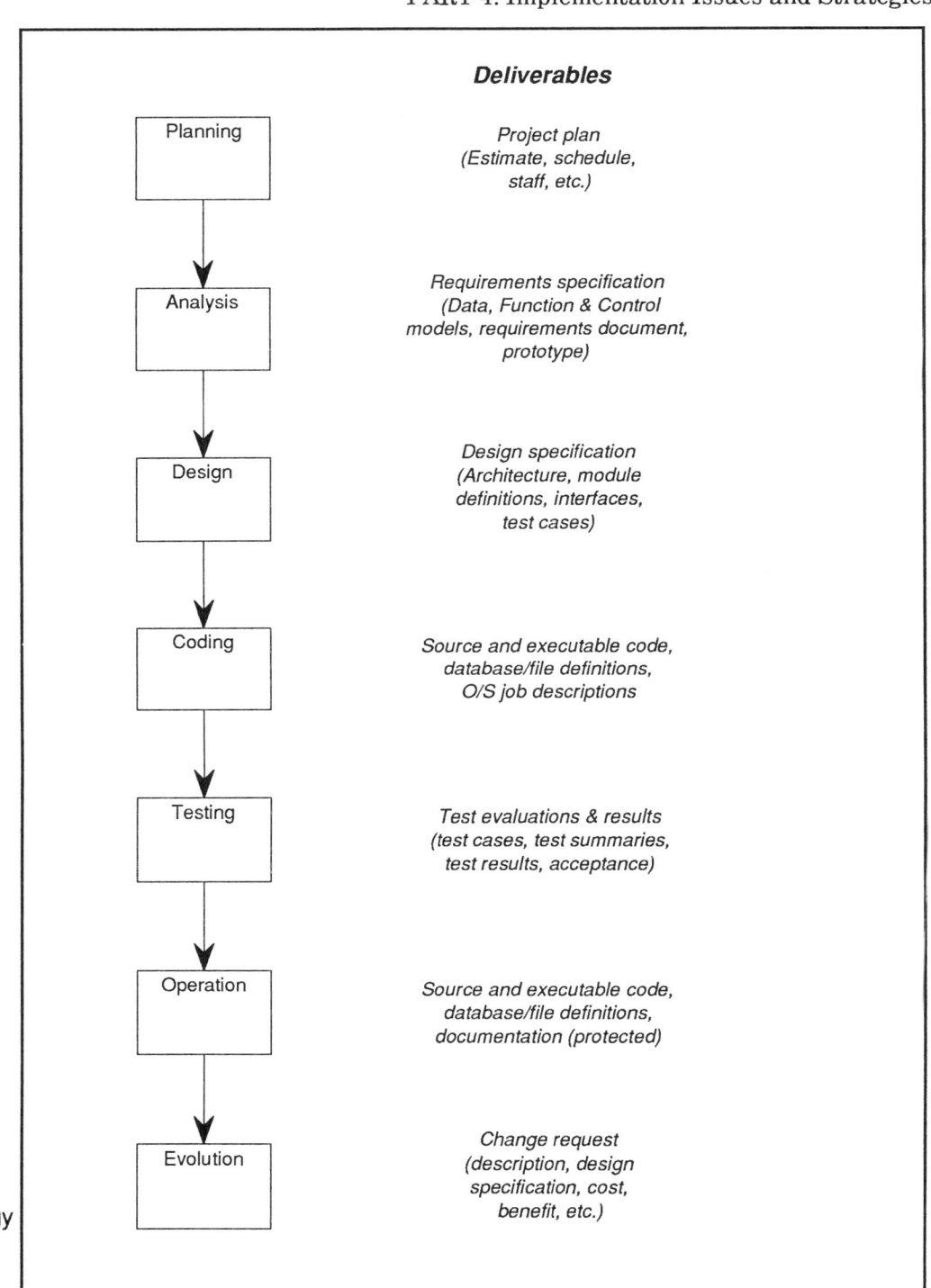

Figure 14.4
Sample methodology
life cycle and
deliverables.

Personnel: A list of the different organizational roles involved in the task, with a brief description of their responsibility for task completion

Techniques: A description of the specific development technique or method, or a reference to a method or technique used to perform the task

CASE notations: Specific CASE supported notations or diagrams that are used within the task

Time estimates: Rough estimates of the time required, often in a low and high range of days; used to schedule the task

Underlying each technique in the methodology would be guidelines for performing the task and using the notation, which might include examples from previous projects, experiences of other staff that have performed the task, and any relevant information related to the specific task that might help someone understand how to perform the task and why the task is required.

14.6.3 Sample Deliverables

Again using Figure 14.4, we can see that the following deliverables are created as part of the methodology:

Planning - Project plan (estimates, schedule, staff assignments, etc.)

Analysis - Requirements specification document (data, function, and control models, requirements document, prototype, etc.)

Design - Design specification document (system architecture, module definitions, interfaces, and test cases)

Coding - Source and executable code for the system, along with database or file definitions, and any required JCL

Testing - Test results (test cases used, results, summary of results, and acceptance of the results by clients)

Operation - Source and executable code, DBMS and/or file definitions and documentation

Evolution - Change requests (description of the change, design specifications, cost/benefit, etc.)

14.6.4 Sample Roles and Responsibilities

Sample role descriptions and responsibilities for the methodology might include the following:

Problem domain expert: A user or client who has knowledge of the
problem area

Project team leader: A technical staff person who oversees individual
software projects and manages staff, resources, and deliverables

Project manager: A management person who oversees several Project Team
leaders and reports to the MIS director

Data analyst: A staff person responsible for maintaining and monitoring
naming standards, ownership of data, and data models for the organization

Systems analyst: A technical person who acts as a liaison between the client
and the technical staff, and helps define requirements for systems
using models

Systems designer: A technical person who takes requirements for a system
and available implementation information and creates a working design of
a software product

Programmer: A technical person who translates design specifications into
programming language constructs

Quality assurance consultant: A nontechnical staff person responsible
for measuring and reporting on the quality of the deliverables created in
the development process.

14.7 Resource List

All of the methodology vendors provides sales and marketing materials on its
products, but few objective descriptions of these methodologies are available. We
recommend the DataPro Application Development Software report on CASE, since
it includes information on some of the methodologies.

In addition, the methodology materials provide helpful, albeit one-sided
information, including [ART87], [AXI90], [CEC91], [CGI92], [ERN90], [JAM92],
[MBR92], [PAC89], and [TEX90]. For resources on methodologies, see [CON89],
[FIN89], [GAN90], and [MCC89].

14.8 References

[AGS91]   firstCASE Methodology Overview, AGS Management Systems, 1991.
[AND92]   METHOD/1 Methodology Version 9.0 Overview, Andersen Consulting,
           1992.
[ART87]   Arthur Young, *Practical Guide to Information Engineering*, Wiley,
           1987.
[AXI90]   Aim Overview, Axiom Information Consulting, Inc., 1990.
[BOU89]   Bouldin, B., *Agents of Change*, Prentice-Hall, 1989.

[CEC91]   IE/Systems Life Cycle, Computer & Engineering Consultants/ Knowledgeware, 1991.

[CGI92]   Yourdon Structured Method Overview, CGI, 1992.

[CON89]   Constantine, L., "Any Which Way Will Do," *CASE Directions*, vol. 2, no. 1, 1989.

[DAT91]   DataPro Application Development Software Report: CASE, DataPro Information Services Group, McGraw-Hill, 1991.

[EDS92]   STRADIS Reference Release 92.1, Electronic Data Systems, 1992.

[ERN90]   Ernst and Young Navigator Systems Series: Life Cycle Charts, Ernst & Young, 1990.

[FIN89]   Finkelstein, C., *An Introduction to Information Engineering, From Strategic Planning to Information Systems*, Addison-Wesley, 1989.

[GAN90]   Gane, C., *Computer-Aided Software Engineering: The Methodologies, the Products, and the Future*, Prentice-Hall, 1990.

[JAM92]   The Information Engineering Methodology, James Martin and Company, 1992.

[MBR92]   PRIDE Information Factory, M. Bryce and Associates, 1992.

[MCC89]   McClure, C., *CASE Is Software Automation*, Prentice-Hall, 1989.

[PAC89]   Information Engineering Management Guide, Pacific Information Management, 1989.

[TEX90]   Texas Instruments, Information Engineering Facility: Technology Overview, Texas Instruments, 1990.

[WHI89]   Whitten, J., L. Bentley, and V. Barlow, *Systems Analysis and Design Methods*, 2nd Ed., Irwin, 1989.

[YOU91]   Yourdon, E., "Sayonara, Once Again, Structured Stuff," *American Programmer*, November 1991, pp. 40-49.

Chapter 15
Case Studies

To better understand the transition to CASE and software development techniques, it is useful to consider the experiences of organizations that have attempted to make this transition. We collected information from several such organizations and summarized their experiences in this chapter. There are a variety of experiences ranging from those who benefited from the transition to those who decided that CASE and software development techniques provided no advantage.

We have tried to remain objective about whether an organization achieved some level of success or not. We judged a transition effort to be successful if there was a measurable benefit to the organization. It is interesting to note that only one of the organizations we studied actually measured its software development effort. Without measurement, an organization cannot show any quantifiable success. We also judged a transition effort to be somewhat successful if the organization felt that there was some improvement in its software development process, or if the tools and techniques were in continued use. It is likely that if a technology remains in use, there is some benefit derived from it.

In the following case studies, the names of the organizations and the CASE tools used are omitted to protect the innocent — as well as the guilty. For each case study, background information about the organization is provided, followed by a description of its transition effort. Recall the transition steps described in Chapter 13: assessment, evaluation and selection, implementation, and follow-up evaluation. These steps are used as a framework for describing each transition effort. One note: The follow-up evaluation step is ignored in the case studies because none of the organizations performed this step. Following each case study is our analysis of the transition effort, and the chapter ends with a discussion of some general comments about the case studies.

15.1 Case Study Categories

The case studies are divided into five categories:

Quantified successes include organizations that showed a *measurable* benefit from adoption of the tools and techniques. These organizations took measurements of their software development environment before and after the transition effort, and compared them to confirm the benefits. A number of measurements may be taken to quantify success, including quality metrics (for example, defects per 1000 lines of code) and productivity metrics (like function points per month).

Unquantified successes comprise organizations that did not measure their software development efforts, but "feel" that they have benefited from the tools and techniques, and continue to use them. These organizations have a level of tool or technique usage that is proportional to the financial investment they made. For instance, if an organization invests in tools and techniques for a project team, and that team consistently uses those tools and techniques on its projects, we consider this to be a success. On the other hand, if an organization invests in tools and techniques for its entire staff, and only a handful of developers consistently use these products, we consider this effort a failure.

Failures represent organizations that experienced no benefit implementing techniques and tools and, consequently, halted the transition effort and shelved its products.

Continuations describe organizations that have not yet realized a substantive benefit adopting techniques and tools, but continue the transition efforts.

Evaluations encompass those organizations that have evaluated techniques and tools, but decided there was no benefit in implementing them at the time.

15.2 Quantified Successes

The following organizations evaluated the CASE market, purchased and implemented tools, and adopted software development techniques. Only one of these organizations showed measurable improvements; others either felt that there were improvements (but were unable to quantify them) or continue to use the tools and techniques.

Organization A

Location	Southeast U.S.A.
Product/Service	Chemicals
Number Employed	Not available
Annual Sales	Not available
Year Founded	Not available

Assessment. The organization reviewed its development environment and defined three goals at the start of the transition effort: implement a methodology, acquire a tool to support analysis and design, and obtain a code generator.

Evaluation and Selection. The organization conducted its evaluation in the mid-1980s, so the available tools supporting analysis and design at the time were limited. It purchased a tool and a methodology, and a three-month comparison was made between two code generators, with one selected and purchased.

Implementation. Several developers were given two weeks of training by the CASE vendor in use of the analysis and design tool and the related methodology. The organization then purchased the training materials and continued the training program internally. An internal group was established to support use of the tools and the methodology. Some deficiencies in the analysis and design tool have limited its use, but the code generator has been well received.

Analysis of the Transition Effort. Given that the organization is using CASE tools selected in the mid-1980s, it would probably benefit from an updated appraisal of the CASE market.

Organization B

Location	Southeast U.S.A.
Product/Service	Business-related software
Number Employed	748
Annual Sales	$91 Million
Year Founded	1971

Assessment. About half of the employees at this organization are software developers who develop software products for several hardware platforms. An internally developed set of coding and testing tools and a well-defined methodology are used for software development. There is a strong measurement program in place to monitor the software development process, but the organization sought to enhance and automate the front-end activities of its methodology.

Evaluation and Selection. No wide-ranging evaluation of the CASE market was conducted, since the organization had an existing relationship with a CASE vendor and decided to swap its business-related software for copies of the vendor's tool.

Implementation. An internal group, responsible for training and support, handled the integration of the new tools and upgraded methodology into the organization. Classes were created for and attended by developers.

Analysis of the Transition Effort. This organization is led by management with a strong appreciation for control of the software development process through use of a methodology and measurements. This is the only organization described in this chapter with measurements comparing development performance before and after the transition effort. After the tools were installed, it found project times to be 48 to 55 percent faster, and the software it developed had 60 to 65 percent fewer bugs than before the transition.

15.3 Unquantified Successes

The following organizations evaluated the CASE market, purchased and implemented tools and techniques, and "felt" they were somehow better off than before they used these products. In all cases, these organizations continue to use these tools and techniques in their development efforts.

Organization C

Location	South Central U.S.A.
Product/Service	Gas dispensing and card payment systems
Number Employed	300
Annual Sales	$150 Million
Year Founded	1970s

Assessment. The software developers at this organization produce real-time systems (Chapter 6), and use networked Intel 80386-based machines with software written in C. Prior to the transition effort, they used no techniques or CASE tools, and measured only overall project costs. They wanted to improve software quality and take advantage of the skills of newer developers. Management planned to implement a comprehensive improvement program that included a review of coding standards, software reviews, CASE tools, and configuration management. Task groups, composed of developers, were formed to address each issue.

Evaluation and Selection. The CASE team surveyed the market and selected seven tools for in-house demonstrations. One of these tools was selected because it was one of the least expensive.

Implementation. Throughout the improvement program, developers were provided training in structured techniques. The training was conducted by an outside consultant over a period of two years. Tool training was also provided.

Analysis of the Transition Effort. There are several positive characteristics about this transition effort. First, management believed from the start that CASE was only part of the improvement program. It addressed multiple aspects of the development environment. Perhaps the most common mistake made with CASE technology is believing that it is a complete solution — designed to solve all your development problems. Second, it directly involved many of the developers in the transition effort. Participation in an effort generally means commitment to it. Third, it provided a significant amount of technique training. Technique training tends to be more critical and complex than tool training.

Organization D

Location	Southeast U.S.A.
Product/Service	Billing and bookkeeping services
Number Employed	600
Annual Sales	$28 Million
Year Founded	1961

Assessment. The goal of this transition effort was to reduce maintenance costs over a two-year period. The company decided to develop an in-house methodology.

Evaluation and Selection. The tool evaluation was conducted in 1988 and resulted in the selection of an analysis and design product. A code generator was evaluated by testing the efficiency of the code produced. It proved more efficient than the existing approach, and so the tool was selected.

Implementation. New systems are developed using the two purchased tools. Maintenance activities are supported by the code generator only. The organization decided that corporate data modeling is needed and will review mainframe-based dictionaries.

Analysis of the Transition Effort. The organization appears to be benefiting from the tools and methodology, although there are no measurements proving that the original maintenance goal was achieved. It would benefit from an updated assessment and evaluation of the CASE market.

Organization E

Location	Southeast U.S.A.
Product/Service	General warehousing and storage
Number Employed	64,000
Annual Sales	$5.33 Billion
Year Founded	1921

Assessment. The 100 software developers at this organization support the business systems required to provide storage services. They decided to take a new technique direction and sought CASE tools to support it. Their mission was to have all development occur under the new technique.

Evaluation and Selection. The CASE market was surveyed, and three tools were brought in-house for closer inspection. Initially, the organization wanted only front-end (planning, analysis, and design) capabilities but decided, after seeing the tools, to evaluate their back-end features as well. A benchmark system was designed to be able to compare the tools, and one of the tools won.

Implementation. A pilot project lasting seven months was used to begin integrating the tool and technique into the organization. Training was provided by the tool vendor and was found to be expensive but effective. It was found that the average time required for a developer to gain familiarity with the tool and technique ranges from six months to one year. It was also found that additional vendor assistance was needed in applying the tool to existing systems.

Analysis of the Transition Effort. This organization made the important realization from the start that technique is as important as tool. It also conducted a deliberate evaluation and pilot project. It is benefiting from the investment and is planning to increase the number of CASE workstations available to developers.

Organization F

Location	Southeast U.S.A.
Product/Service	Life Insurance
Number Employed	2,300
Annual Sales	Not Available
Year Founded	1987

Assessment. The goal of this transition effort was to bring in CASE technology supporting an adjustable set of development techniques.

Evaluation and Selection. Information was collected on five major CASE products and used to narrow the list down to two. An evaluation team attended overview courses presented by two vendors, and then recommended one of the products based on those presentations. The transition plan called for a benchmark system to be developed using the recommended tool, but management decided that enough data had been collected, and the benchmark step was skipped.

Implementation. A short pilot project was conducted to begin introducing the development staff to the CASE tool, and the team discovered that higher productivity was attained when techniques supported by the tool were properly used. Training provided by the tool vendor was not well received, but it did help the organization to focus on the techniques supported by the tool.

Analysis of the Transition Effort. The organization reported improvements in productivity and software quality, but since no measurements were made before the transition effort, it could not justify these improvements. A decision was made to investigate only the major CASE products, and the organization made a greater financial commitment to the technology than was needed.

15.4 Failures

The following organizations evaluated the CASE market, purchased and implemented tools, but did not realize any benefits from the investment. It has since discontinued use of the tools.

Organization G

Location	Northeast U.S.A.
Product/Service	Group hospitalization plans
Number Employed	2,500
Annual Sales	Large
Year Founded	1934

Assessment. Some 350 software developers support the business systems required to provide health insurance services. They develop COBOL applications on IBM mainframes. Prior to the transition effort, a few of the developers used an internally developed methodology. Many of them used word processors to support system analysis and design. Some were using function point analysis for measurement. They began the transition effort to improve communication between users and developers, and had the ambitious goal of reducing development time by 75 percent.

Evaluation and Selection. Since the organization was interested only in IBM AD/Cycle business partners, the tool search was narrowed considerably. The selection process consisted of a visit to an IBM decision-support center by a large group of managers and developers. Each of the business partners provided a demonstration of its tool. That proved to be enough information for management. It selected one of the vendors and purchased fifteen copies of their tool.

Implementation. Training consisted of one week of data modeling and one week of tool usage for the entire development staff. To date, one or two of the copies are used. Developers said that the tool "takes too much time" to learn and use, and that the tool was conflicting with corporate priorities.

Analysis of the Transition Effort. Purchasing a CASE tool in this fashion is akin to buying a car at an automobile show. To determine the fitness and suitability of a tool to an organization, it must be "test-driven." A CASE tool must be brought in-house and used on "real" projects before it will be used by developers.

15.5 Ongoing Implementations

The following organization evaluated the CASE market, purchased and implemented some tools, but has yet to realize benefits.

Organization H

Location	Northeast U.S.A.
Product/Service	Paper products
Number Employed	Not available
Annual Sales	Not available
Year Founded	Not available

Assessment. This organization has a staff of over 200 developing and maintaining COBOL/DB2 applications. Before the transition effort, no techniques and few tools were in use. The organization heard that the "outside world" was using CASE and wanted to do the same. It also wanted to bring in a methodology to support the entire software development life cycle.

Evaluation and Selection. This evaluation progressed fine until management got too indecisive. An evaluation team was formed, and tool and methodology criteria were established. Several tool vendors were brought in, data was collected, and a tool (let us call it Tool A) was selected. Without seeing Tool A, management then decided that only IBM AD/Cycle business partners be considered in the evaluation. This excluded Tool A. The tool criteria were modified at management's direction to favor the vendor of Tool B, and copies of the product were purchased. Frustration was encountered as developers tried to use Tool B. Management later saw a public demonstration of Tool A, liked it, and mandated its use throughout the organization. A methodology was selected to match the tool.

Implementation. The tools and methodology were applied to a pilot project, and the pilot team received training in their use. Although current tool usage is low, the organization will not give up on the technology. It predicts that productivity will eventually improve as a result of the investments.

Analysis of the Transition Effort. Management took a risky approach by determining, without developer input, what tool would be used. In addition, management lacked an appreciation for what seemed to be a judicious evaluation effort.

15.6 Evaluations

The following organizations studied the CASE market and decided not to implement the technology at this time.

Organization I

Location	South Central U.S.A.
Product/Service	Petroleum and chemical bulk stations
Number Employed	1,100
Annual Sales	$120 Million
Year Founded	1985

Assessment. The 58 software developers at this location support the business systems required to manage a petroleum reserve. They develop software in the DOS and OS/2 environments on PCs. Prior to the transition effort, they used no techniques or CASE tools, and measured only lines of code. They sought higher productivity and a more consistent approach to software development.

Evaluation and Selection. A team of three was formed and a brief evaluation of the CASE industry was performed. The team focused on analysis and design tools. It was decided that because of the high ratio of maintenance work done by the organization, the benefit of CASE technology was questionable at this time.

Implementation. None performed.

Analysis of the Transition Effort. This organization held the common misconception that CASE tools are only applicable to the creation of new systems. Let the record show that tools and techniques are applicable in any software development effort — whether development or maintenance. CASE tools that might benefit this organization include the reengineering or reverse engineering tools (Chapter 13).

Organization J

Location	Northeast U.S.A.
Product/Service	Industrial instruments; precision measuring tools
Number Employed	1,260
Annual Sales	$100 M
Year Founded	1940

Assessment. These software developers produce real-time systems (Chapter 6). They develop software in two environments: DOS and Windows on PCs, and Ultrix and Motif on DecStations. Prior to the transition effort, they used no techniques or CASE tools, and took no measurements. They sought to provide more complete analysis and better design documentation via tools and techniques.

Evaluation and Selection. An evaluation of the CASE market was conducted, and a CASE tool was recommended to management. Interestingly, the recommendation was overridden by management, who decided to invest in another tool. A copy of the tool was purchased and introduced to developers. Most of them found the tool to be powerful but the interface awkward. Training on use of the tool was inadequate, and eventually the tool became shelfware. The organization decided not to invest in additional copies of the tool, but to wait for the CASE industry to provide a more complete solution. Specifically, it wants an automated link between the design of a system and its code so that when a change is made to either, the other will be automatically updated. It is also waiting for better support for its primary development language, C++. In the interim, it will continue to use word processors as its primary development tools.

Implementation. None performed.

Analysis of the Transition Effort. This is another one of those curious situations where management empowers a team to evaluate the CASE market, the team recommends a tool, and then management ignores the recommendation. In some cases, management may be justified in ignoring an evaluation team recommendation. However, in most cases like these, management simply decides that the recommendation is inadequate and wastes the evaluation team's effort. A way to avoid this is to specifically identify, with management's involvement, the criteria and methodology that will be used during the evaluation. This makes it more difficult for management to act against the evaluation's advice.

15.7 Conclusions and Opinions

Now we summarize the findings of the case studies and offer our own opinions based on the results.

Focus on tool rather than technique

You may have asked yourself as you read through the case studies, What about techniques? In nearly all of the studies, there is far more attention given to tools than to techniques. Since one functions best in the presence of the other, they should receive equal treatment in the evaluation and implementation. Emphasizing tools is probably the most common mistake made by organizations looking to improve their software development environments. Why does this occur?

One reason is that tools are more tangible than techniques — they can be seen and they can be used. (Many tools also have glitzy packaging and colorful interfaces, but we would insult you if we believed that that had an effect on you!) Techniques are less glamorous. They are procedural and visible only when they have produced something.

Another reason for tool emphasis is that it is much more effective to change the way a developer develops through a tool than a technique. Generally, a tool is less flexible than a technique. There is usually a specific way a tool operates, and there are few or no alternatives. Here, the tool is the enforcer. On the other hand, since a technique is often paper-based, tasks can be changed or ignored at will. To prevent this, some person or group (quality assurance) must act as the enforcer, and that usually proves to be a more difficult job.

Focus on productivity rather than quality

Some of the organizations established "higher productivity" as a goal of the transition effort. In most cases, higher productivity is not attained in the first several months or years of the transition effort, depending on its scope. Generally, there are near-immediate improvements in quality where the tools and techniques are applied in the software development process. Some researchers maintain that the result of higher quality is higher productivity.

Management Meddling

Management commitment is extremely important to a transition effort. At the same time, mismanagement often means wasted resources. Some of the case studies described efforts where management either decided, with little information, which tool should be purchased or ignored the work of an evaluation team. Management

must recognize and give responsibility to the best internal or external resources available to perform the evaluation, but then get out of the way and let the development staff adjust to the use of the new technology.

Transition Focus

In many of the case studies, there is a lack of focus on the transition effort. This usually results because the effort has no goal or plan. At the start of the effort, it is important that this information be documented. The organization should know why the transition is being conducted and what it hopes to accomplish. Most of these efforts are expensive endeavors, and this will help to justify and focus them.

Unquantified Success

One interesting observation of the case studies is that most of the organizations involved fell into the "unquantified successes" categories. Based on industry experience, this is not necessarily a reflection of reality, since at least one estimate indicates that about half the organizations that attempt to adopt CASE and formal development techniques fail. We found it particularly difficult to collect case studies on those organizations that failed, because for most of these organizations, to admit failure would be difficult if not impossible.

Appendix

Glossary

Glossary of Acronyms

AD	Action Diagram
ANSI	American National Standards Institute
BFT	Basset Frame Technology
CASE	Computer-Aided Software Engineering
CCASE	Component Computer-Aided Software Engineering
CD-ROM	Compact Disk Read Only Memory
CMM	Commonsense Management Model
COBOL	COmmon Business Oriented Language
CODASYL	COnference on DAta SYstems Languages
CRUD	Create, Retrieve, Update, Delete
DBMS	Data Base Management System
DFD	Data Flow Diagram
DoD2167A	Department of Defense development standard 2167A
DP	Data Processing
DSSD	Data Structured Systems Development
DT	Decision Table
EDP	Electronic Data Processing
ER	Entity-relationship
ERD	Entity-relationship diagram
ESF	Eureka Software Factory
ESML	Extended Systems Modeling Language
FSM	Finite State Machine
FORTRAN	FORmula TRANslator
FP	Function Point
GUI	Graphical User Interface
HIPO	Hierarchy plus Input, Process, Output
ICASE	Integrated Computer-Aided Software Engineering
IDB	Integrated Database
IE	Information Engineering
IEEE	Institute of Electronics and Electrical Engineers
IEEE-CS	Institute of Electronics and Electrical Engineers Computer Society

IEEE-CS P1175	IEEE-CS Provisional Standard 1175
IRDS	Information Resource Dictionary Standard
JCL	Job Control Language
JSD	Jackson Systems Development
KLOC	Thousand(s) of Lines of Code
LCP	Logical Construction of Programs
LCS	Logical Construction of Systems
LOC	Lines of Code
MIS	Management Information Systems
MSA	Modern Structured Analysis
OOA	Object-Oriented Analysis
OOA/D	Object-Oriented Analysis/Design
OOD	Object-Oriented Design
OODBMS	Object-Oriented Database Management System
OOPL	Object-Oriented Programming Language
PCTE	Portable Common Tools Environment
PDL	Program Description Language
RAD	Rapid Application Development
RDBMS	Relational Database Management System
RIPP	Rapid Iterative Production Prototyping
SA/SD	Structured Analysis and Structured Design
SDLC	Software Development Life Cycle
SEI	Software Engineering Institute
SPD	Structured Program Development
SPF	Software Production Framework
SPMM	Software Process Maturity Model
SQL	Structured Query Language
STD	State Transition Diagram
TQM	Total Quality Management
YSM	Yourdon Structured Method
3GL	Third Generation Language
4GL	Fourth Generation Language

Glossary of Terms

action diagram A process modeling and procedure design notation used in Information Engineering.

analysis A technique that breaks a problem down into simpler parts — the opposite of synthesis.

balanced DFDs A leveled set of DFDs in which the decomposition of each transform preserves the incoming and outgoing data flows.

Basset Frame Technology An object-oriented technique directed at COBOL applications that features a strong notion of selective inheritance.

build (a noun) A subset of a system developed with incremental development.

build sequence The order in which builds are developed.

class A group of objects that share common characteristics.

coding or **programming** The fourth phase of the waterfall model of software development that creates source and executable code for a system.

cohesion The degree of singularity of purpose of a module.

Commonsense Management Model A software process model that emphasizes an infrastructure of artifacts and communication among project participants.

Component Computer-Aided Software Engineering A CASE product that supports a particular SDLC phase and automates the use of a development method or techniques.

composition A strategy that employs synthesis to create a whole from smaller component parts.

Computer-Aided Software Engineering (CASE) The automation of engineering principles and methods in the development of software.

context-dependent behavior The behavior exhibited by some systems where specific actions must occur in sequence without interruption.

context diagram The highest level diagram in Structured Analysis, showing all external entities to the system.

control behavior One of three basic views of all systems, the others being function and data.

control model A model of the dynamic behavior of a system, which often includes time and context-dependent behavior. Control models are often represented as finite state machines (state-transition diagrams), petri nets, decision tables, or control flow diagrams.

Control-oriented techniques Methods that view systems in terms of the dynamic behavior or context/time-dependent perspective.

coupling The degree of dependence between two modules.

Create, Read, Update, Delete A functional view of software based on the four generic operations performed on any database application.

cyclomatic complexity An indicator of software complexity based on the number of decisions in a structured program.

data The information used by a program; also one of three basic views, the others being function and control.

database A collection of related logical data accessed through a DBMS.

Database Management System (DBMS) A set of runtime routines that performs access to data stored in a hierarchical, network, relational, or object-oriented format.

data dictionary (also called **encyclopedia** or **repository**) A central collection point for software development information.

data element The smallest addressable unit of information normally stored and accessed by a computer system.

data flow diagram The central notation to structured analysis that portrays the flow of data in a system, and the way data is transformed by functional components.

data model A model of the data elements and structures of a system, that includes entities, attributes, and relationships. Common data modeling tools include entity-relationship diagrams, data structure diagrams, and physical database design diagrams.

Data-oriented techniques Methods that organize information systems around the data structures and the inputs and outputs to the system.

data store An element in a data flow diagram that represents permanent, passive data.

data structure A collection of data elements that form a logical entity and can take many different physical forms, including files, tables, records, arrays, linked lists, etc.

Data Structured Systems Development A technique for developing software based on the structure of data.

decision table A notation that relates actions that are taken under a wide variety of conditions.

decomposition A strategy that employs analysis by dividing a whole into smaller parts.

Detailed Design The third phase of the waterfall model of software development.

dynamic balancing An extension of static balancing that deals with execution time transitions in finite state machines.

dynamic thread A thread in which determining inputs first occur after the onset of the thread; the essence of reactive systems.

Enterprise-level data-oriented techniques Methods that support a data perspective with an emphasis on multiple systems using a common set of data structures.

Enterprise model A collection of planning models that include data architecture, business goals, objectives, organization, functions, and critical success factors.

entity-relationship diagram Representing data models using symbols for entities, relationships, and attributes.

entity-relationship model A model that portrays characteristics of data in an application.

Essential Model An idealized model in Structured Analysis in which all implementation constraints are repressed.

estimation Used to determine what resources will be required for a new development effort and how long the effort will take.

executable specification A model of the behavior of a system that can be executed to study the system in detail.

Eureka Software Factory A consortium of software providers trying to view software development as a manufacturing process.

event A type of input that occurs at the port boundary of a system.

event partitioning An extension to Structured Analysis in which threads initiated by events at the port boundary of a system are composed into a data flow diagram.

Evolutionary Development An alternative software life cycle, similar to incremental development, in which a system is developed as a series of builds or increments. Build contents are identified as the system evolves.

extended entry decision table A decision table in which condition entries assume values in a discrete range.

Extended Systems Modeling Language An extension to Structured Analysis that helps express the control properties of real-time applications.

finite state machine A control notation that features states and transitions among states.

fully flattened DFDs The result of replacing each transform in a leveled set of DFDs by its decomposition, such that only the lowest layer remains.

function Business activities or procedures that are performed within a specific area of an organization; also, one of three basic views of a system, the others being control and data.

functional decomposition The process of decomposing a system into its component parts based on the procedures performed.

function model (also called **process model**) A model of the tasks or activities performed within a business.

Function-oriented techniques Methods that view software in terms of the functions performed.

Halstead Metrics Indicators of software complexity based on the number of operators and operands.

IEEE-CS P1175 A CASE tool interface standard developed by an international committee of IEEE members.

Incremental Development An alternative software life cycle in which a system is developed as a series of builds or increments.

Information Engineering A development technique that concentrates on identifying and modeling, at a very high level, the data or information architecture of an organization prior to deciding which systems should be developed. This approach is often associated with James Martin and Clive Finkelstein, and requires the use of an I-CASE tool with a repository which incorporates rule checking for the methods and techniques used.

information hiding A functional decomposition strategy that defines modules that reveal only their interfaces, not the implementation details underneath.

Information-oriented techniques Methods that view software development using a data-orientation, but focus on the entire organization and balance the data and the function view (also see Information Engineering).

Information Resource Dictionary Standard A repository standard approved by the American National Standards Institute (ANSI).

information system The collection of data, programs, and procedures that support business actions using computers.

inheritance The mechanism by which an object acquires attributes from another object (see multiple and single inheritance).

Integrated Computer-Aided Software Engineering A CASE product that supports all SDLC phases.

Integration Testing The sixth phase of the waterfall model of software development.

Jackson Systems Development A technique to develop software based on the structure of data.

KLOC A unit of measure that describes the size of a program in terms of thousands of lines of code.

leveled set of DFDs The end product or representation of a system as a set of data flow diagrams that are numbered to reflect the functional decomposition.

limited entry decision table A decision table in which condition entries are binary (true/false, 1/0 ...).

LISP A functional, applicative programming language used in Artificial Intelligence applications.

Logical Construction of Programs A technique to develop programs based on the structure of data.

Logical Construction of Systems An extension of the Logical Construction of Programs technique to support entire systems.

marking A function defined on places of a Petri net that describes the number of tokens in a place. Markings are used to execute a Petri net.

measurement The collection of data for the purpose of monitoring, estimating, and improving the process of developing software. Measurements can be of two forms, productivity or quality metrics.

message The means by which software components, especially objects, transfer control.

method An action associated with an object.

methodology The study of methods; commonly (and incorrectly) used as a synonym for technique or method.

Modern Structured Analysis An extension to Structured Analysis that begins with development of an essential model.

module The smallest compilable unit of code in a system; the stopping point of functional decomposition.

multiple inheritance The mechanism by which an object acquires attributes from two (or more) objects.

normalization A formal process to eliminate potential access and update anomalies in relational database systems.

notation The expression or representation of a work product or deliverable of a software process using a defined set of symbols, connections, and textual descriptions. Example notations include Gane/Sarson data flow diagrams, Chen entity-relationship diagrams, structure charts, etc.

object A thing that includes data and operations; the central concept in object-oriented techniques.

object model A model of the objects, attributes, relationships, and messages in a system.

Object-Oriented Analysis An object-oriented approach to requirements specification.

Object-Oriented Analysis/Design An object-oriented approach to requirements specification and software design.

Object-Oriented Database Management System An implementation of data structures for persistent objects that include the data and the operations on the data.

Object-Oriented Design An object-oriented approach to software design.

Object-Oriented Programming Language A language that supports the essential concepts of object orientation.

Object-oriented techniques Methods that view software in terms of objects that encapsulate data and procedures and communicate using messages.

Operational Specification A form of requirements specification that results in an executable specification. Also, an alternative software life cycle model in which the requirements are developed using an operational specification technique.

Petri Net A control notation that features places, transitions, and markings.

place An element of a Petri net that is either an input to, or an output of, a transition.

polymorphism The property (in an object-oriented setting) in which the behavior of a method depends on the context of the method.

port boundary The interface of a system with its environment. The external entities in a context diagram constitute the port boundary of the system being described.

Portable Common Tools Environment A CASE tool integration standard widely accepted in Europe.

Preliminary Design The second phase of the waterfall model of software development.

process Business tasks or activities that are performed within an organization (see function).

process management The management and control of the software development and maintenance process itself. Specifically, the modeling and monitoring of the process (tasks), improvement of the process, etc.

process specification A supplemental textual description of a process defined in a data flow diagram; also known as a primitive or mini-specification.

Program Description Language A combination of structured programming constructs and natural language used to rigorously describe the function of a program or module.

Progression Testing A form of testing used in incremental development and maintenance to test new software after regression testing has occurred.

project management The management and control of the tasks, roles and responsibilities, and deliverables of software development and maintenance. Specially, the assignment of tasks, the monitoring of deliverables, task completions, etc.

prompt A control flow in Extended Systems Modeling Language by which control tasks communicate.

prototype A working model of a system used to elicit an improved system definition from clients.

Prototype-oriented techniques Methods that use a working model of a system (i.e., a prototype) to facilitate the definition and development of a finished system.

Rapid Application Development A form of rapid prototyping that involves both the customer and the developer.

Rapid Iterative Production Prototyping A form of rapid prototyping restricted to 90 days.

rapid prototyping An alternative software life cycle model in which a prototype of the eventual system is developed quickly and delivered to clients for their evaluation.

reactive or **real-time system** A dynamic system that reacts to stimuli at its port boundary.

Regression Testing A form of testing used in incremental development and maintenance to assure that new software has not corrupted existing software.

Relational DBMS A DBMS that supports the relational model using tables as elemental data structures.

repository A database where information supplemental to diagrams is kept. An extension of traditional data dictionaries, typically implemented in CASE products.

representation The expression of the results of applying a software development method to an application; the method is based on a notation, and the technique refers to how the notation is used to describe the system.

Requirements Specification The first phase of the waterfall model of software development.

roles and **responsibilities** The tasks and deliverables that staff undertake in the development and maintenance of software.

signal An input at a hardware/software interface.

single inheritance The mechanism by which an object acquires attributes from its parent object.

sink state A state in a finite state machine that is never the origination of a transition.

Software Development Life Cycle A macro model of a software process that defines phases and deliverables.

software development method (SDM) A formal process of developing and maintaining computer software. Synonyms for SDM might include software development life cycle, software development process, methodology, or formal software development method.

software engineering The use of formal methods for analysis, design, programming, testing, etc. for the creation and maintenance of software (see also software development method and technique).

software engineering triad A three-component view of software development that includes software development processes, methods, and automated tools.

software process Procedures by which an organization develops software.

Software Process Maturity Model A model of software process sophistication developed at the Software Engineering Institute.

software process model A model used to describe some aspect(s) of a software process.

software production framework A holistic view of the organizational, technical, and social aspects of software development.

software productivity measurements Data collected to monitor the rate at which the development process can be completed and the time required. Example productivity metrics include function points, lines of code, etc;

software quality measurements Data collected to monitor the quality of the deliverables in the development process or the process itself.

software synthesis Production of working systems from high-level conceptual models.

source state A state in a finite state machine that is never the destination of a transition.

spiral model An alternative software life cycle, similar to incremental development, in which a system is developed as a series of builds or increments. Build contents are identified as the system evolves and the primary objective is the reduction of risk throughout the process.

state transition diagram A graphical notation to depict a finite state machine.

statechart A complex extension of finite state machines that permits hierarchical states and a notion of concurrency.

static balancing The form of balancing used on data flow diagrams.

static thread A thread in which determining inputs are available before the onset of the thread; the essence of transformational systems.

Strategic Business Planning The use of high-level data and function models to ensure that the information systems an organization builds supports their business goals and objectives.

structure chart A notation used in Structured Design that describes modules and their major interfaces in a system.

Structured Analysis A function-oriented technique that defines system requirements using data flows. It was developed by Ed Yourdon, Larry Constantine, Tom DeMarco, Chris Gane, and Trish Sarson.

Structured Design A function-oriented technique that describes a system design based on decomposition and partitioning. It was developed by Ed Yourdon and Larry Constantine.

structured program development A development technique later expanded into Data Structured Software Development.

structured programming A programming discipline that employs a top-down strategy, single-entry and single-exit modules, and the exclusive use of three basic constructs: sequence, selection, and repetition.

Structured Query Language A language to express database queries that is independent of the underlying data model.

synthesis Combining parts into a larger whole; also the opposite of analysis.

system dynamics An industrial engineering model that stresses control and feedback loops.

System-level data oriented techniques Methods that view software development based on the data structures used and focus on individual applications.

System Testing The seventh phase of the waterfall model of software development.

terminator An element in a data flow diagram at the port boundary of a system; source of system inputs, destination of system outputs. Also known as an external entity.

thread A particular execution time behavior of a system.

time-dependent behavior The behavior exhibited by some systems where specific actions must occur within a specified period of time without interruption.

tools Including CASE products that help automate the procedures and methods/techniques used in software development that ensure that the methods are followed rigorously.

transaction-centered design A Structured Design technique to derive a structure chart from a data flow diagram with significant decisional processing.

transform-centered design A Structured Design technique to derive a structure chart from a data flow diagram with little decisional logic.

transformation A functional component in a data flow diagram; also known as a process, an activity, a transform, or an action.

transformation schema A extension to Structured Analysis that helps express the control properties of real-time applications.

transformational implementation An alternative software life cycle in which the requirements are specified in a formal language which is transformed into working code.

transition An element of a Petri net that corresponds to an action. Petri net transitions have places as inputs or outputs.

Unit Testing The fifth phase of the waterfall model of software development.

waterfall model A fundamental software development life cycle model that flows downward (see also SDLC).

Yourdon Structured Method A function-oriented method of analysis and design developed by Ed Yourdon and his associates (see Structured Analysis and Structured Design).

Index

About the authors

Andrew G. Topper is president of Foresite Systems and consults on CASE tool evaluation, selection, implementation, and development methods for organizations around the world. Mr. Topper teaches workshops and seminars on CASE tools and formal development techniques, and has written on the subject of CASE and software development for major computer periodicals, including American Programmer, ComputerWorld, Embedded Systems Programming, IEEE Spectrum, and PC Magazine. He is a member of the Association for Computing Machinery and the IEEE Computer Society, and has been listed in Who's Who of the Computer Industry and Who's Who of the Midwest. He regularly speaks at software development conferences worldwide on the topics of CASE, development techniques, and object-oriented technology. Mr. Topper received his Bachelor of Science in Computer Science from Grand Valley State University.

Paul C. Jorgensen is Associate Professor of Computer Science at Grand Valley State University, and president of Software Paradigms, a Michigan-based consulting firm offering structured methodology, CASE, and software testing services to organizations worldwide. Dr. Jorgensen has held the positions of Assistant Professor at Arizona State University and Visiting Scientist at the Software Engineering Institute, and was a member of the Adjunct Faculty at Triton College. Dr. Jorgensen also has over 20 years of industrial experience in the software engineering field and has consulted extensively on CASE and software development. He has developed corporate methodologies for four major U.S. corporations. Dr. Jorgensen has written for a number of publications as well as writing books, including *A Modern Appraisal of Decision Tables* (ACM Press, 1982) and *Mathematics for Data Processing,* with S. M. DeAngelo (McGraw-Hill, 1970). Dr. Jorgensen has a Ph.D. in Computer Science from Arizona State University, an M.A. in Mathematics from the University of Illinois, and a B.A. in Mathematics from North Central College. Dr. Jorgensen is also a senior member of the ACM and IEEE, and a member of Sigma Xi, Upsilon Pi Epsilon, and Pi Mu Epsilon.

Daniel J. Ouellette has been active in the implementation of software development techniques and CASE. He has been involved in writing, reviewing, and implementing methodologies and has developed and presented seminars on methodologies and their underlying techniques. He has spoken on the topic of methodologies in various forums, including the Software World conference, the Information Systems Executive Forum, the CASE World conference, and the Government Technology conference. Mr. Ouellette was listed in <u>Who's Who in the Computer Industry</u> and is a charter member of the Michigan CASE Users Group. He received his Bachelor of Science in Computer Science from the University of Michigan, and while attending college, worked at the ISDOS project, originator of the PSL/PSA repository product.